HOLY TERROR

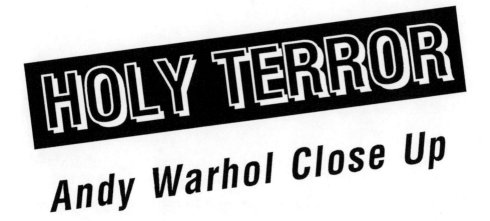

HOLY TERROR

Andy Warhol Close Up

BOB COLACELLO

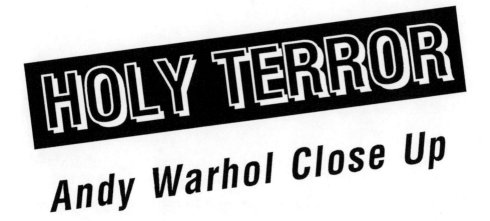 HarperCollins*Publishers*

FIRST EDITION

Designed by C. Linda Dingler

Library of Congress Cataloging-in-Publication Data

Colacello, Bob.
   Holy terror: Andy Warhol close up/Bob Colacello.—1st ed.
     p. cm.
   ISBN 0-06-016419-0
   1. Warhol, Andy, 1928–1987. 2. Artists—United States—Biography.
I. Title.
N6537.W28C55 1990   89-46226
700′.92—dc20
[B]

90 91 92 93 94 CG/RRD 10 9 8 7 6 5 4 3 2 1

To my mother and father

Contents

Illustrations follow pages 212 and 372.

Acknowledgments

Above all, there are three people whom I cannot thank enough: Chris Schillig, my brilliant editor at HarperCollins, for her clear vision and unwavering commitment; Miles Chapman, who helped edit this book with exceptional intelligence and finesse, and who got me to write when I felt like giving up; and Barbara Colaciello Williams, my extraordinarily dedicated researcher, sounding-board, and friend.

I am also deeply grateful to: Tina Brown, editor-in-chief of *Vanity Fair*, for her patience and support; my agent, Morton Janklow, for his faith and guidance; São Schlumberger, for a month in Tangier, where I wrote my prologue and first chapter; and Kevin Farley, for a summer in Rhode Island, where I wrote the next eleven chapters.

The following people were kind enough to give me interviews: Glenn Albin, Lady McCrady Axom, Brigid Berlin, Bruno Bischofberger, Susan Blond, Sam Bolton, Douglas Cramer, Ronnie Cutrone, Katy Dobbs, Robert du Grenier, Rose Erde, Mica Ertegun, Cornelia Guest, Halston, Victor Hugo, Barry Kieselstein-Cord, Fran Lebowitz, Sarah Lee, Benjamin Liu, Daniela Morera, Paul Morrissey, Glenn O'Brien, John O'Connor, Philip and Dorothy Pearlstein, Keith Peterson, Stuart Pivar, Paige Powell, Joan Quinn, John Reinhold, Rupert Smith, Jessica Strand, Geraldine Stutz, and Gregor von Rezzori; in Pittsburgh, Mary Bradenton, Tilly Cohen, John and Helen Elachko, Joseph Fitzpatrick, Lillian Gracik, Stanley Greenfield, Mrs. Thomas Kunsak, Robert Lepper, Ann Elachko Madden, Mary McKibbon, Catherine Metz, Dean Akram Midani, Don Miller, Dorothy Pauley, Michael Roman, Sr., Michael Roman, Jr., Chester Stanek, Tinka Swindel, Donald Warhola, John Warhola, Michael and Kay Warhola, Paul and Ann Warhola, John Zavacky, Anna Zeedick, and Albert Zionts; in Lyndora, Pennsylvania, the Reverend Ronald Borsak, Julia Gavula, Eugenia King, Amy Passarelli, Noel Passarelli, Alan Soley, Andy and Christine Soley, Tina Soley, Matthew and Paula Vavro, Emil Zavacky, Mark Zavacky, Olga Zavacky, and Sally Zymboly.

I am appreciative to the following for everything from fact checking to moral support: Walter Anderson, Thomas Ammann, Lily Auchincloss, Irving Blum, Georgina Brandolini, Marie Brenner, Mathias Brunner, Pat Buckley, Margaret Campbell, Virginia Cannon, Peter Castro, Marina Cicogna, Gustavo and Patty Cisneros, Scott Cohen, Dagny Corcoran, Charles Cowles, Dr. Denton Cox, Consuelo Crespi, Barbara de Kwiatkowski, Barry Diller, Sean Driscoll, Frederick and Isabel Eberstadt, Fernanda Eberstadt, Harold Evans, Vincent Fremont, John Fries, Ina Ginsburg, Eric Goode, Florence Grinda, Pat Hackett, Prentis and Denise Hale, Ed Hayes, Holly Hayes, Joy Henderiks, Reinaldo and Carolina Herrera, Brooks Jackson, Bianca Jagger, Angela Janklow, Linda Janklow, Hugo Jereisati, Jed Johnson, Lana Jokel, Howard and Susan Kaminsky, Nan Kempner, Calvin and Kelly Klein, Jesse Kornbluth, Kenny Jay Lane, Wayne Lawson, Leo Lerman, JoAnn Lewis, Iris Love, Bill and Wendy Luers, Christopher Makos, Pam McCarthy, Patrick McCarthy, Patrick McMullan, Liza Minnelli, Chris Murray, Jeremiah Newton, William Norwich, Judy Orbach, Walter Owen, Ronald and Claudia Perelman, Laughlin and Jennifer Phillips, Paloma Picasso and Rafael Lopez Cambil, George Plimpton, Lee Radziwill, John Richardson, D.D. Ryan, Julio and Vera Santo Domingo, Jane Sarkin, Marina Schiano, E.B. and Maureen Smith, Liz Smith, Ray Stark, Wendy Stark, Jean Stein, Diane von Furstenberg, George Wayne, Jann Wenner, Mark Williams, Paul Wilmot, Lynn Wyatt, Louis Zeffran, and Jerry Zipkin. Unfortunately, some of the people who encouraged me most are no longer with us: Paulette Goddard, Elizinha Gonçalves, Adriana Jackson, Jonathan Lieberson, Steve Rubell, and Diana Vreeland.

At HarperCollins, I am grateful to Matthew Martin, for his savvy legal reading; Karen Mender and Steven Sorrentino for their inspired promotion; Joseph Montebello, for his stylish design; Nancy Peske, for always pitching in; and Rena Kornbluh for her diligence and care.

At Janklow & Nesbit Associates, I am indebted to Anne Sibbald, for her good cheer under pressure; Bennett Ashley, for his sage counsel; Cynthia Cannell, for her overseas diplomacy; and Michael Kunkel, for xeroxing above and beyond the call of duty.

Special thanks to Denise Auclair, typist extraordinaire.

Thanks also to Ann Schneider, a great photo researcher, and to all the photographers whose work appears on these pages. We have made every attempt to locate each photographer and give proper credit; I apologize to any photographer whose name does not appear on this list: Peter Beard, Mark Cafferty, Otto Fenn, Mel Finkelstein, Betty Burke Galella, Ron Galella, Burt Glinn, Tony Guzewicz, Robert Hayes, Ken Heyman, Frank Kolleogy, Christopher Makos, Philip Pearlstein, Paige Powell, Brian Quigley.

And many thanks to Sam Bolton, for his cover photograph of Andy with that holy terror smile; and Annie Leibovitz, for taking the best photograph of me since Andy snapped that Polaroid in 1970.

Prologue:

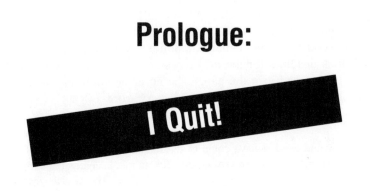

I knew I was going to do it, but I didn't know how. Then everything just happened as if according to a long-laid plan.

> Thursday, January 6, 1983: Got up. Wrote my resignation letter. Went to the office. Typed my resignation letter. Xeroxed my resignation letter. Put my resignation letter in two envelopes, the original for Andy, a Xerox for Fred [Hughes]. Handed the two envelopes to [my secretary] Doria [Reagan] with instructions to give them to Andy and Fred five minutes after I left.

Looking back at my diary entry, I can smile at my obsession with the letter. Then, though, it was all high drama, the most crucial decision of my career, the most important moment of my life. On my way out of the office (which is what we who worked there actually called the Warhol Factory), I stopped at my sister Barbara's desk in the advertising department and told her I had to talk to her outside "about something personal." The elevator was broken as usual so, clutching a shopping bag containing my Rolodexes, one for America, one for Europe, as if they were the family jewels, I ran down the two flights of stairs, ran up Broadway, ran down 18th Street. I was thirty-five years old, and I felt like a teenager running away from home.

I didn't stop running until the corner of Park Avenue South—far enough from the Factory, my raging ego calculated, so that no one could come and drag me back. I finally turned to Barbara, who had been panting behind me, wondering what the hell was going on, and told her, "I just quit."

"That's great," she said, hugging me.

Then I taxied home and called Liz Smith. I wanted to reach her before the one o'clock deadline for the next day's column. I knew Andy wouldn't believe it until he read it in the paper—he never believed anything until he read it in the paper, and then he believed every word.

Adrenalized, I read her the earth-shattering letter:

> Dear Andy and Fred: I have come to the realization that it is time for me to move on. Therefore, I am resigning, effective immediately, as Executive Editor of *Interview* and as an employee of Andy Warhol. The twelve years I have spent working . . .

The nation's most widely syndicated gossip columnist oozed boredom, not that I let it stop me. I was eager to tell people what I had done, perhaps to believe it more myself. I began calling the people who had helped *Interview* most through the seventies and early eighties.

First, Diana Vreeland. Fired by *Vogue* in 1970, at about the same time I joined *Interview,* she had offered us a guiding hand, a critical eye, plus the wisdom and wit of the ages.

Next, Steve Rubell. Studio 54 had been the setting for so many *Interview* columns, and of so many of my own Stolichnaya-and-cocaine excesses in the late seventies. It was the only time in all our conversations that Steve had to catch his breath before replying.

I found Jerry Zipkin, who had helped get Nancy Reagan for the cover of *Interview,* at Betsy Bloomingdale's house in Los Angeles. To my amazement, he offered me a loan. "If I find out you've asked someone else for money," he said, "I'll break your leg."

I wanted to call Zipkin's arch-enemy, Truman Capote, whom I had edited when he did the pieces for *Interview* that became *Music for Chameleons.* I didn't because we had recently fought about the Reagan crowd and because he still hadn't delivered the chapter of *Answered Prayers* he had promised us.

By then, Steve Rubell had caught his breath and made some calls himself. Calvin Klein, *Interview*'s largest advertiser, called me to say he'd advertise wherever I went.

The truth is, though I didn't need a loan, I didn't know where I was going, and the realization of what I had done was beginning to sink in. The teenager who had run away from home may have been exhilarated, but the father who had abandoned his child—which is what *Interview* was for me—was feeling lonely and afraid. I called the friend who had taken me to lunch a year earlier and had berated me, "You're much too *normal* to continue working with those sickos down at that Factory one minute longer!" Pat

Buckley answered with a bellowing "Congratulations! I've heard all about it from Doria." The President's daughter-in-law had been working with me for the past two years. "And, I might add, it's about time."

I read her my resignation letter. I didn't have a magazine, I didn't have an office, I didn't have a job, but I had that letter. "It would do Bill proud," pronounced Mrs. William F. Buckley, Jr.

Revived by praise, I started dialing again and didn't stop until six: São Schlumberger, the wife of the oil-equipment magnate, who had led me through the incestuous salons of *le tout Paris*. Mort Janklow, the lawyer-agent I had turned to months earlier to help me get a better deal from Andy (to no avail). My mother in her colonial on Long Island. My father in his office on Wall Street. California. Washington, D.C. Switzerland. Rome. Rio. I dialed and dialed and dialed.

"I quit."

"I quit."

"I quit."

Somehow one caller got through to me. Brigid Berlin, who had been with Andy since the early sixties, and had worked her way down from Superstar to receptionist, was calling from the front desk at the Factory.

"Andy told Fred to tell everyone you're taking a leave of absence," she whispered.

"Wait until he sees Liz Smith tomorrow," I said, gleefully.

Hurrying, and very low, Brigid added, "I love you, Bob. I always knew you weren't a lifer."

1

The Beginning

When I first met Andy Warhol, the only thing I wanted to be was a Factory lifer.

It all started with a phone call, one cold day in April 1970. I still have a mental Polaroid of that moment—the fruit bowl on the kitchen table filled with a mix of real *and* plastic apples, oranges, bananas, and grapes. After graduating from Georgetown University School of Foreign Service, I was back living with my parents in Rockville Centre, Long Island, and commuting to the city, where I was getting a master's degree in film criticism at Columbia under Andrew Sarris of the *Village Voice*.

We were just finishing dinner when the phone rang. A strange voice introduced himself as Soren Agenoux, the editor of Andy Warhol's new film magazine. He had seen a review I had written for an alternative paper—remember alternative papers?—called *New Times*. Would I be willing to write reviews, he asked, for *inter/VIEW* (which is how it was originally spelled).

Would I be willing? Would Lana Turner wear a sweater?

My father, who had been through World War II instead of college and had worked his way up from clerk to executive at a Wall Street commodities firm, was less enthusiastic. "I worked so hard all these years to get you kids out of Brooklyn and put you through Georgetown and now Columbia, so you could end up working for that *creep* Andy Warhol?" he shouted. My mother, who sold evening dresses at Saks Fifth Avenue's Garden City branch, tried to calm him down. "Didn't I read somewhere," she said, "that Andy Warhol painted Governor Rockefeller's portrait?"

"Are you kidding?" I exulted. "Andy Warhol is the most important artist and filmmaker in the world today!" Like much of my generation I idolized Mick Jagger, Timothy Leary, Marshall McLuhan and Jean-Luc Godard. I was also wild about William *(Naked Lunch)* Burroughs, Jean *(Our Lady of the Flowers)* Genet, and Susan *(Notes on Camp)* Sontag. But above them all there was Andy Warhol, the soulless soul of cool, the heartless heart of hip.

The thing is, I grew up Pop. Plainview, Long Island, where I lived from eight to sixteen, was Pop Art come to life: a potato field covered with split-levels and the occasional shopping strip, two new cars in every garage, two new mortgages on every house—all the seductive banalities of the postwar American dream. The highlight of Plainview social life was the fiercely fought annual neighborhood Christmas and Chanukah lights competition, which my parents once won.

As a teenager, I had come across Warhol's Marilyns and Elvises in *Time* and *Life* and decided, If this is Art, I like Art. Later, when *The Chelsea Girls,* Warhol's three-hour, split-screen psychedelic movie extravaganza, came to Washington, D.C., I sat through it three times—the last high on acid—with some Georgetown buddies from a band called The Brave Maggots. One afternoon in Madrid, during my junior year abroad, I lit up a joint and penned a poem entitled, "One Nite in Madrid Remembering the U.S. of Andy." I'd even written in Andy Warhol for President in 1968, the first year I was old enough to vote.

In September 1969, I went to the New York Film Festival opening of *Lion's Love,* a French film made in Hollywood, starring Viva, the best-known of Warhol's Superstars. I was overwhelmed by Viva's public appearance that night. The audience gave her a standing ovation and she thanked them, as I wrote in my report for Sarris's class, "by throwing grandiose kisses from her box in Alice Tully Hall . . . and then doubling over in laughter at her own stardom." How cool, I thought; she not only loves being a star, she's also hip enough to know it's all a joke. She was having her cake and eating it too.

That same fall, at the end of the decade when he had conquered the worlds of Pop Art and Underground film, Andy Warhol decided to start a magazine. His initial impulse was jealousy. The overnight success—Andy's favorite kind—of *Rolling Stone* and *Screw* drove him crazy.

"Jann Wenner is so powerful. Al Goldstein is so rich," he moaned to his three right-hand men: Paul Morrissey, who directed Andy's movies; Fred Hughes, who sold Andy's paintings; and Gerard Malanga, who needed something to do. "And both *Rolling Stone* and *Screw* use such cheap paper. Let's just combine the two ideas—kids and sex—and we'll make a fortune." By "we'll" he meant "I'll."

Andy later liked to say in interviews that he'd started a magazine "to give Brigid something to do"—her father, Richard E. Berlin, the retired chairman of the Hearst Corporation, had started out as a magazine ad salesman, and he hoped that she'd inherited his talent. Gerard says the immediate reason was to get press passes for the New York Film Festival.

When volume one, number one appeared in November 1969, *inter/VIEW* was a youth-oriented magazine on newsprint like *Rolling Stone,* full of nudity like *Screw.* Resemblances stopped there. *inter/VIEW*'s beat was film, not rock, and the sexy movie stills came from Fellini's *Satyricon,* not *Deep Throat.* That avant-garde quality, as well as a kind of striving for elegance and seriousness, was implied in its tag line, "A Monthly Film Journal." It was an obvious choice since the Factory's principal business by the late sixties was making movies. It was also a clever and timely choice. Film directors were replacing rock stars as role models for American college students.

Reclining naked on the first cover was Viva, flanked by her *Lion's Love* co-stars, James Rado and Jerome Ragni, of *Hair* fame, also naked. The cover tells a lot about the Factory's—and Andy's, always Andy's—hopes and ambitions for the new magazine in the new decade. *Lion's Love,* directed by Agnes Varda, was an intellectual film trying to be commercial, an indication of where the avant-garde was heading. It was supposed to carry Viva up from the Underground into the big time, just as the cover nudity was supposed to make *inter/VIEW* an instant newsstand hit. It didn't, *inter/VIEW* wasn't, and Warhol went on being jealous of Wenner and Goldstein. One of the cover's promises did come true, however: the banner proclaiming "First Issue Collector's Edition." Today, a copy of volume one, number one sells for $800 at New York's Gotham Book Mart.

Holding a copy now, the cheap newsprint yellowed and torn, one can almost feel the sixties turning into the seventies, and the Factory both resisting and anticipating the change. On one hand, there was an homage to "Peter Fonda as Scorpio Rising" and film reviews by waning Superstars such as Taylor Mead and Pope Ondine. But there were also hints of the coming disco decade, of the reactionary nostalgia for the glitz and glamour of thirties Hollywood that would swamp the revolutionary spirit of the sixties and make it all right to be stylish and irresponsible again. George Cukor, the ultimate Old Hollywood director, was worshipfully interviewed, and campy Busby Berkeley stills illustrated a think piece by future *New York Review of Books* editor Jonathan Lieberson.

True to its title, most of *inter/VIEW* Number One was tape-recorded question-and-answer sessions, transcribed with every "Ah" and "Well" intact. The tape recorder was Andy's favorite toy and tool, since the movie camera had been taken over by Paul Morrissey to make *Flesh.* While Andy was in the hospital recovering from the famous 1968 assassination attempt, he taped all his phone calls reel-to-reel at home, and when the smaller models came on the market he carried one around wherever he went. "My wife," he called it, sometimes introducing it as "my wife, Sony."

The transcription technique appealed to Andy conceptually because it seemed modern and real, two qualities he consistently valued above all others. For Andy, modern meant mechanical—silkscreen, movie camera, tape recorder, video, any machine that came between the creator and his audience. Tape recording was the literary equivalent of cinema vérité, and nobody's cinema was more vérité than Andy's. For him, directing meant putting a camera on a tripod and letting the film run. Why couldn't writing be reduced to transcribing? He had already taken the idea to its extreme with his tape-recorded novel, *a*, published by Grove Press in 1968. Nobody read it, but Andy had staked out the territory. *inter/VIEW* was the logical next step. Andy also liked tape recording because it was cheap—good writing costs good money. Any college kid could turn on a tape recorder, ask a few questions, then type up the tape.

The original *inter/VIEW* masthead listed four editors: Gerard Malanga, who now had something to do; Paul Morrissey; John Wilcock, the aging hippie publisher of the aging hippie paper *Other Scenes* (in exchange for free typesetting); and, at the bottom, Andy Warhol. Malanga was the day-to-day manager, with Morrissey hovering over his shoulder, and Andy communicating *his* ideas through his secretary and chief transcriber, Pat Hackett, who was listed as assistant editor. There was no advertising department—Brigid Berlin had apparently refused to walk in her father's footsteps.

A poet by calling, Gerard still favored the all-black look of the sixties Factory, heavy on leather, though his personality was more romantic than sadistic. He was Warhol's first art assistant/social director and the star of many early Factory films, but by 1969 he was being eclipsed off screen by Fred Hughes, a well-connected Texas dandy, and on screen by Joe Dallesandro, a disconnected New Jersey street tough. It was Malanga who came up with the artsy configuration of the *inter/VIEW* logo, which Andy liked because it was "so spacey." The official corporate moniker, Poetry on Film, Inc., was pure Gerard. He also contributed the premiere issue's only poem, an elegy to a movie star, "The Permanence of Sharon Tate."

By volume one, number four, after months of fierce infighting among the right-hand men—with Andy in the background, watching, prodding, instigating, manipulating, and denying he was doing any such thing—Malanga went to Europe and Morrissey topped the list of editors. There was also a new managing editor: the improbably named Soren Agenoux (Soren as in Kierkegaard, Agenoux pronounced "ingénue"), a film buff whom Paul had met through Terry Ork, an *inter/VIEW* contributing editor who worked at Cinemabilia, a tiny Bleecker Street shop crammed with old movie stills and posters, some of which were used to illustrate *inter/VIEW* in exchange for the magazine's sole ad.

*   *   *

When Soren called me at my parents' in the spring of 1970, he wanted a review of *Antonio das Mortes,* a wildly radical Brazilian film, which had then been seen by only a handful of people in all New York. Fortunately, I was one of them. Soren said he needed the review the following afternoon. I said he would have it and ran upstairs to my bedroom, which was still decorated with souvenirs of family vacations in Miami Beach and Montauk Point. I was certain this review was my ticket into other rooms, rooms where everything was extreme and nothing was mediocre, rooms where Art ruled and Andy was God.

I typed past midnight and got up at seven to type some more:

> I have not been to Brazil, but from 8mm movies my father has taken on business trips there, from memories of *National Geographic,* from ornate dreams provoked by the exotic word itself, Brazil has existed within my head as a savage, mysterious, brilliantined hallucination: a black nun in white habit, Amazonian lips painted fiercely fuchsia. Glauber Rocha's *Antonio das Mortes* presents a vision of Brazil which overwhelms even an imagination as excessive as my own.

My mother drove me to the railroad station. I could barely sit through classes. The subway ride downtown went on forever. I got out at Union Square and walked past the junkies to 33 Union Square West, a twelve-story gray stone building with French windows and carved balustrades. The ground-floor store was boarded up in dirty sheet metal. The chipped marble lobby smelled of urine, the cracked glass directory (Andy Warhol Films on six, *inter/VIEW* on ten) also listed the names of Saul Steinberg, famous for his *New Yorker* covers, and the Communist Party of America. I ascended to avant-garde heaven.

At the gates, looking more like Lucifer than St. Peter, was Soren Agenoux, with his stringy hair rubber-banded into a putative ponytail, his rotting teeth, his filthy fingernails, his bony body clothed in fading black turtleneck and jeans, his spiked belt, and his pointy boots. I sat on a pile of *inter/VIEW* back issues in the grubby supply-closet-sized office while Soren read my review.

He *loved* it, especially the part about the Amazonian nun. Then he told me they paid $25 per article. He must have seen disappointment cloud my face, because he hastily added, "Would you like to meet Andy?" Would I like to meet *Andy?*

We took the elevator down to the sixth floor and got out into a bare white foyer with an unpainted steel door at one end. The door had a small glass window at eye level and was locked. Soren peered through the window and knocked. After a few seconds, we were buzzed in. A few feet ahead of us, at a small Art Deco desk "guarded" by a stuffed Great Dane said to have belonged to Cecil B. DeMille, sat Andy Warhol. He was wearing a brown printed-velvet jacket, Levi's 501s, and expensive lizard boots. Only a black turtleneck echoed his sinister sixties look. He was eating lunch, vegetable purées, out of plastic containers with a plastic spoon.

He was also opening the mail, although several preppy-looking assistants were standing around doing nothing. He did it systematically. First he brought each piece right up to his pink welfare glasses and examined it intently, as if he were trying to see through the envelope or analyze the handwriting or determine the quality of the paper. Then he tore the canceled stamps off each and every piece, domestic and foreign, and stuffed them into a large manila envelope. (This, I later learned, was his "stamp collection.") As he did this he sorted the mail into separate piles. Invitations. Bills. Checks. Everything else, from press releases to fan letters, he dropped into a cardboard box at his feet. (When a box was full, it would be sealed, dated, and stored away as a "time capsule.") I was struck by the slow, methodical rhythm of his movements, the movements of a faltering child or a careful old man. At the time he was forty-two.

"Andy," said Soren gingerly, "this is the boy who wrote that brilliant review in *New Times,* the one I showed you, remember?"

Warhol looked up from his piles of mail. "Oh, hi," he said softly. He paused, then added, "Would you like something to eat?"

Andy Warhol was offering me something to eat! I was beside myself but politely said no thanks.

"Gee," he said, searching for words. "You should write a lot for us."

"I'd like to," I said, taking in the cool, clean black-and-white atmosphere of the Factory, and thinking: This is where I want to be for the rest of my life.

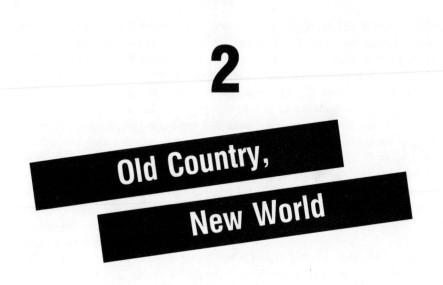

2

Old Country, New World

By 1970, Andy Warhol was already the best-known artist in the world since Pablo Picasso—the Pope of Pop Art, the High Priest of Underground Movies, Saint Andrew of the Media, with his silver halo and black leather cassock, famous for being famous. His notoriety had begun in 1962 when he shocked both the art world and the tabloid press with his Campbell's Soupcan paintings, and then his portraits of America's idols: Marilyn, Liz, Elvis, and Jackie. Next came the outrageous films that nobody saw and everybody talked about, with their amateur casts of spaced-out heiresses, hustlers, and drag queens—Superstars, Andy called them. But it was the 1968 shooting that really made him front-page news. And as soon as Andy won fame for himself, he started giving it out to everyone else, for fifteen minutes, in *inter/VIEW* magazine.

Nobody believed in the fame game more than Andy Warhol, and nobody played it better. He instinctively knew that mystery feeds curiosity, and delighted in telling interviewers that he was from different places: Philadelphia; Cleveland; Newport, Rhode Island; McKeesport, Pennsylvania. He wasn't from any of them and he managed to keep his real birthplace, along with almost every other fact about his background, childhood, and adolescence, a secret until the day he died, February 22, 1987.

Of course, it's very American to put your past behind you. On one level, Andy embodied the American dream: the immigrants' son who made it to the top by dint of hard work and new ideas, like some Horatio Alger of the avant-garde. Yet he also consistently subverted that dream, in a wry and disturbing way. The same hand that glamorized fame also delineated its emptiness. This ambiguity at the core of his work reflected the deep contradictions of his personality: Andy was innocent *and* decadent, primitive *and* sophisticated, shy *and* pushy, the eternal outsider at the center of a series of self-created In crowds. And the key to his personality, and perhaps his work, can be found in that past he so cleverly hid. Like many very American stories, Andy's really began in the "Old Country."

"I come from nowhere," Andy once said. And, for once, he wasn't lying. Ruthenia, the Eastern European land of his parents and grandparents, *was* nowhere. It can't be found on any maps—it's in the Carpathian Mountains, just north of Transylvania, at the point where the present-day boundaries of Poland, Czechoslovakia, Hungary, Rumania, and the Soviet Union meet. Its rulers—the Austro-Hungarian Empire until World War I, Czechoslovakia and Russia since then—have systematically denied the identity of its people as a distinct nationality. (The Hapsburgs liked to think of their Ruthenian subjects as "Highland Hungarians," the Czechs called them "Eastern Slovaks," and the Russians called them "Western Ukrainians" or "Little Russians.") It has always been somebody else's backyard, in constant danger of disappearing into the cracks between clashing powers and cultures, and its people were always made to feel like aliens in their own country. As one of Andy's relations put it, "In Europe, the Ruthenians were the poorest of the poor. We never even had a flag."

They barely had a language. Until 1914, school was taught in Magyar, the language of the Hungarian rulers. Ruthenian itself was a goulash of archaic Ukrainian and modern Slovak, with many Magyar, Polish, and even German words thrown in. It was sometimes written in Cyrillic letters, like Ukrainian (and Russian), and sometimes written in Roman letters, like Slovak (and English). Most Ruthenians didn't go to school, and couldn't read or write in *any* language. At the beginning of this century, the illiteracy rate in Ruthenia was between 70 and 90 percent, and there were many villages without a single literate person. Ruthenian literature was pretty much limited to folk plays performed by amateur troupes. According to Professor Paul Magocsi, one of the most popular plays tells of the Ruthenian "everyman and anti-hero, David Schrapnel, who like his more famous Czech counterpart, Hašek's *Good Soldier Schweik,* undermined the operations of the Austro-Hungarian army by his ironic and seemingly innocent stupidity." (That sounds a lot like Andy.)

The one thing that held the Ruthenians together was their church, but even that was confusing. Half Roman Catholic, half Russian Orthodox, it was originally called the Uniate Catholic Church, but was also known as the Greek Catholic Church. They recognized the Pope, but retained the Eastern Rite mass, which was said in Slavonic—yet another language for these poor people to deal with. This mixture of East and West could be seen in the architecture of the churches, which sometimes boasted a Byzantine onion dome, a Baroque cupola, and Gothic spires on the same roof. "The

churches were very beautiful,'' says novelist Gregor von Rezzori, ''because
the Ruthenians were masters of wood.'' Everything in the villages was made
of wood, including the small houses with their straw roofs and the picket
fences carved with simple, repetitious designs, like stars, crosses, and flowers. (That sounds like Andy's early commercial work.)

It was in such a village of wooden cottages and dirt streets, hidden in
the heavily forested mountain slopes, called Mikova, that Andy's parents
were born: his father, Ondrej (Andrew) Warhola, on November 28, 1886;
his mother, Julia Zavacky, on November 17, 1892. Like 90 percent of the
Ruthenians, the Warholas and Zavackys were farmers and shepherds, working the rocky wheat, corn, and potato fields for absentee landlords, raising
a couple of cows and a few sheep, goats, and chickens for themselves. One
of fifteen children, Julia took turns guarding the goats from wolves with her
brothers and sisters. The winters were bitter cold, the summers were boiling
hot, and there were frequent and sudden lightning storms. The villagers
lived in constant fear of fire. (Just like Andy at the Factory.)

Julia told her daughter-in-law, Ann Warhola, stories about whitewash-
ing their cottage every summer, ''to keep the bugs away. The children would
draw fruit and scenes in pencil on the cottages.'' They also decorated eggs,
and not only at Easter. Indeed, the Ruthenians were obsessed with eggs—
they conducted elaborate rituals involving the giving of eggs, to which they
attributed almost mystical powers, on every social occasion from births to
burials, and for introductions, dates, weddings, baptisms, even neighborly
visits. Designs were drawn on the eggs in hot wax with pinpoints and then
they were dipped in dyes made from wildflowers and berries; when the wax
was peeled off, the image emerged in white surrounded by color. (Like
Andy's silkscreening.)

According to several members of the Zavacky family, one of Julia's
grandmothers was Jewish. This was highly unusual in a part of the world
where anti-Semitism was almost built into the social structure. Every village
had its one Jewish family, who collected the landlord's share of the peasants'
produce, owned the only shop, extended credit and made loans, and controlled the liquor license given by the imperial government—the Ruthenians
liked to drink and brawl. The Jews also had the advantage of speaking both
Ruthenian and the languages of the rulers, Magyar and German. ''They were
absolutely dependent on the Jews,'' says von Rezzori, ''who were the only
ones who coped with money. Everything a shepherd dealt with shrunk or
shriveled. But interest doubled the Jews' money—without work, as the peasants saw it. So they called it 'the work of the Devil.' '' Given this background, it's not unreasonable to assume that the Zavackys' Jewish blood set
them apart from their neighbors, making them outsiders among outsiders.
(Like Andy.)

Less is known about the Warholas in Mikova. When Ondrej was eighteen or nineteen, he left for America, probably walking across Europe to a port like Hamburg or Amsterdam, like tens of thousands of other Ruthenian boys. In fact, by the turn of the century, Ruthenian emigration was so overwhelming that the sagging Austro-Hungarian Empire was worried about the dangerous depopulation of this border province. Two or three years later, in 1909, Ondrej was back in Mikova, rich by Ruthenian standards, from working in the coal mines of Pennsylvania. Blond, muscular, and handsome, he proposed to Julia. Years later, in a 1966 *Esquire* interview she did behind Andy's back, Julia recalled their courtship and wedding:

> He wants me, but I no want him. I no think of no man. I was seventeen. My mother and father say, "Like him, like him." I scared. My Daddy beat me, beat me to marry him. The priest—oh a nice priest—come. "This [Ondrej]," he says, "a very nice boy. Marry him." I cry. I no know. [Ondrej] visit again. He brings me candy, wonderful candy. And for this candy, I marry him.
>
> Wedding was beautiful, beautiful. Three-day wedding. I wear white. Very big veil. I beautiful. My husband had big white coat. Funny, funny. He had hat with lots of ribbons. Three rows of ribbons. A day and a half with my Mamma. A day and a half with his Mamma. Big, beautiful celebration. Eating, drinking, barrels of whiskey. Wonderful food—eggs, rice with buttered sugar, bread, nice bread, cookies made at home. Beautiful . . . And music, such music. Seven gypsies playing music.
>
> We married in 1909. [Ondrej] leaves in 1912. He no want to go to Army, to war. He had $160. He go to America. He runs in the night to Poland, only one mile away. He runs to Poland, then America. I stay in Europe.

There was tremendous unrest as the Austro-Hungarian Empire collapsed. World War I broke out. The Germans and Russians fought several major battles for the strategic Dukla Pass, three miles north of Mikova. For the rest of her life, Julia never stopped talking about hiding in the forest for days on end.

> My husband leaves and then everything bad. My husband leaves and my little daughter dies. I have daughter, she dies after six weeks. She catch cold. No doctor. We need doctor, but no doctor in town. Oh, I cry. Oh, I go crazy when my baby died. I open window and yell, "My baby dies." (She begins weeping.) My baby dead. My little girl.
>
> My husband in America. I work like a horse. His parents, old people. I live with them. I carried sack of potatoes on my back. I work and work. I was very strong lady. I don't see my husband nine years until 1921. I go to America, too.

In 1922, their first son, Paul, was born. A second son, John, followed in 1925. Andy was always deliberately misleading about the facts of his birth, but according to his two brothers, on August 6, 1928, a doctor delivered Andy at home in Pittsburgh. The only birth certificate that exists was filed in Pittsburgh, in 1945, when it was required for Andy's college application. This document notes affidavits sworn by Julia and an old family friend, Katrena Elachko. Her son, John Elachko, says, "My mother would never lie about a thing like that," and also points out that many immigrants of that generation, including himself, didn't have birth certificates. Andy's brothers, however, both do. Seeking further documentation, I asked them for Andy's baptismal certificate. Paul agreed, but John intervened to keep the parish priest from showing it to me. It is now in John's possession, and he won't even show it to Paul. So nagging questions still surround the event. Are the Warhola brothers really hiding something? Or just compounding the mystery their kid brother started?

When Andy was born, the Warholas lived in Soho, a working-class neighborhood overlooking the Monongahela River and the belching steel mills that blocked both its banks. Pittsburgh was the steel, aluminum, and glass capital of America then, and so polluted that the street lights had to be turned on at noon. Soho was a rough place to grow up, particularly for the children of the Eastern European immigrants who were pushing out the more established Irish factory workers, and perhaps most of all for the Ruthenians, who found their identity crisis made all the more acute in a country where the first question most people asked of newcomers was "What are you?"

"We didn't know what we were," a Warhola neighbor says. "B-a-s-t-a-r-d-s," adds her husband, "is what I always refer to our people as." Most Ruthenian-Americans seem to define their nationality in negatives: "We're not Polish. We're not Hungarian. We're not Slovak. We're not Ukrainian." When I asked the Warhola brothers what nationality they considered themselves when they were growing up, John without hesitation said, "Always Slovak." But Paul said that if he used "Slovak lingo, Mother criticized me. She said, 'What's the matter with you? You're talking like a Slovak." We always figured we were Slavish, and Slavish was a little different than Slovak."

Slavish—from Slav, not slave—was the term the local authorities came up with for these people who didn't know what to call themselves. Even their ethnic slurs belonged to somebody else. The Irish kids, who sometimes extorted small change from Paul and John on their way to the Soho Elementary School, and beat them up if they didn't have any, called them "Polacks" and "Hunkies." As in the Old Country, the Ruthenians took refuge in their church. Paul and John recall walking the two miles to the Ruthenian ghetto on the other side of town, where the copper-covered onion domes of the wooden church shone through the smog. It was called St. John Chrysostom Eastern Rite Russian Greek Catholic Church. But this convoluted attempt to clarify the confusion about who these people were only caused rich Pittsburghers to call their pallid, straw-haired Ruthenian servants "Greeks."

The Warhola house, 73 Orr Street, was a two-room tarpaper shack, squeezed into a row of two dozen just like it, facing a matching row across a muddy alley. There was no bathroom. "The commode," as Paul Warhola always refers to the toilet, "was in the center of the alley, where they had an outhouse." When Andy was two, the Warholas moved to a four-room apartment in a two-family house, around the corner on Beelen Street. "It was heated just by a pot-bellied stove," says Paul. "No bathroom, but it had a commode in the house." The landlord's son, Chester Stanek, remembers Andy as a toddler. "He was a holy terror," Stanek says. "I'll never forget the time we were standing on the front porch and he urinated on me."

Andy's father worked for the John Eichleay Company, a construction and house-moving concern. He was often away from home for weeks at a time, once for six months, working on job sites as far away as Cleveland and Hartford, Connecticut. In the early thirties, when the Depression hit hardest, he was also often out of work. But the Warholas never went on home relief. "Dad was always too proud," says Paul. "And he was very thrifty. People made fun of him for saving." John Warhola recalls his father repairing the soles of their shoes with rubber from used tires. And both the oldest boys went to work at a very early age, first selling newspapers, then carrying coal and delivering ice.

Julia also pitched in, sometimes cleaning houses for a dollar a day. She made flowers out of tin cans and peddled them door to door for a quarter apiece. And like her neighbors, she grew cabbage, beets, and carrots in the backyard, clinging to village ways in the middle of "Smoke City." One Beelen Street resident, Mary Bradenton, remembers that Julia "had a very, very sad look. She never looked happy. There wasn't a lot of chuckling, just a real slow smile. A wry smile." Mary Bradenton sometimes babysat for Andy. "He was really a handful to watch," she says, "a sprightly, rambunctious, high-strung nervous type." When Andy was four, his brother Paul took him to kindergarten at the Soho Elementary School. Andy lasted one day: a black girl hit him and he refused to go back.

In 1934, with $3,200 Ondrej had hoarded dollar by dollar, the Warholas bought a house of their own, 3252 Dawson Street in middle-class Lower Oakland. Ondrej's brother Joe bought the house next door, but Julia didn't get on with her sister-in-law. "Mary was very gabby," says Ann Elachko Madden, whose family lived on the other side of the Warholas. "Julia wasn't like that. She didn't stop and talk to everybody on the street. She wasn't cozy or intimate friends with anyone on the block."

She did confide in one woman on Dawson Street, a Jewish lady named Bessy Zionts, whose husband had a small produce business. Bessy spoke seven languages; Julia barely spoke English until much later in life. Albert Zionts recalls Julia pouring her heart out to his mother on their porch, while Andy sat on the steps listening. "She would bemoan the fact of how poor they were. And we would load her up with vegetables and fruit, and home-baked bread.'' Zionts says that Andy called his mother ''Matsuka, which means 'little mother.' We all used that name for her. She was a little woman.''

Several neighbors recall Julia going on about the death of her daughter. ''It was something that stayed with her,'' says Ann Elachko Madden. ''She was very anxious. But very interesting. A little bit different than the other women on the block. Pretty astute.'' Madden remembers Julia ''sitting in the kitchen, asking interesting questions about religion and God.'' Madden's brother, John Elachko, says, ''If you were going to kill something, a bug or a fly, she'd say, 'Loving one, don't do that.' She was a very gentle, flowery-speech-type person. She wouldn't call you whatever your name was, she would say, 'My heart, my dear, lovely one.' And she and my mother used to sing these songs from the Old Country. Most of them were sad songs. Honest to truth, our people were always sad. They were negative thinkers.''

Andy's father was even more distant from their Dawson Street neighbors, who all use the same adjectives—hard-working, quiet, good—to describe him, but can't remember much else about him. He wasn't a hard drinker like many of the other men, including his brother, limiting his pleasure to a corn-cob pipe smoked on the porch after dinner—Julia's specialties being cabbage soup, potato soup, and beet soup. John Warhola says his father was ''real strict with us,'' and Paul suggests that the reason his father didn't drink was that it cost too much.

The new brick-and-shingle house was larger but quarters were still cramped. The second floor of two bedrooms and a bathroom was rented out to boarders. Ondrej and Julia slept in the dining room on the first floor, which also had a living room and kitchen, and the three boys slept in the attic. The family bathroom was in the basement. ''My mother was always telling Julia,'' her niece Tinka says, '' 'Don't be so tight. Put on the lights!' '' And Paul says that he gave some of the money he made to Julia to send to Mikova, ''because Dad didn't believe in that and would get mad if he caught her doing that.'' There is a feeling of Julia and her boys keeping secrets from the frequently absent Ondrej.

Andy started first grade at the Holmes Elementary School, two blocks up Dawson Street. He was six, a fair-haired, sweet-faced boy, and school records show he did well in class. But in third grade he came down with a strange disease—St. Vitus's dance—a virus of the nerves, thought to be a complication of scarlet fever, that would change his looks, and his life, forever. Its most obvious symptoms were shaky limbs and blotchy skin. The other kids called him Spot. One of them, Stanley Greenfield, remembers Andy's ''cadaverous pallor.'' Ondrej started sleeping in the attic with the older boys, so that Andy could share the dining-room bed with his mother. Julia was beside herself with worry and indulged her sick child's every whim, giving him Hershey bars, comic books, coloring books, and cutout books of dolls and dresses, because she thought using scissors helped steady his hands. "Dr. Zeedick gave him a cap gun," says Andy's cousin, Michael Warhola. "And that's what he did: played with the cap gun and cut out paper dolls. Andy couldn't swing a bat." His brother Paul gave him his first camera and helped him to write fan letters to Hollywood stars, requesting autographed photos—his first collection. Shirley Temple was his favorite.

Andy loved the attention and didn't want to go back to school ten weeks later when he seemed to be better. Julia asked the Elachko boys to take him. "My brother did a couple of times," says John Elachko, "and I did also. I had to hold him, put him on my shoulder, and carry him. He was kicking, fussing, he didn't want to go." When the shaking came back in a matter of weeks, Julia blamed herself for forcing Andy to go to school and let him stay at home in bed, coloring and cutting, for many more months.

"He was her baby," says Ann Elachko Madden. "In a way, he was the daughter she never had." John Elachko adds, "He was very frail. We thought he was a little sissy, always with his mother. I can picture Andy playing on the front porch and my father would lean over the railing and try to play with him and Andy would run away." Another neighbor remembers throwing a football at Andy, when he was eleven or twelve. "Andy didn't catch it. He threw his hands up in his face."

But Andy found another way to get the kids to like him: drawing. He would sit his cousins or neighbors down on the porch or up in the attic and do their portraits. He also did still lifes of the knickknacks in his mother's immaculate living room. And, all along, he was absorbing another kind of art. Julia spent most of her free time at church, attending vespers on Saturday night and three masses on Sunday, from seven in the morning until two in the afternoon. Ondrej and the older boys only came to the last mass, but Andy almost always went to church with his mother. For hours on end, he sat and stared at the iconostasis, the screen that closes off the inner altar in Eastern Rite churches. It was covered with icons of the saints, flat two-dimensional portraits, with solid gold backgrounds, hung in horizontal rows, one after another, with no space between them. (That sounds very much like Andy's portraits.)

In the fifth grade, Andy's art teacher recommended him for free Saturday art classes at the Carnegie Museum. They were taught by the elegant and flamboyant Joseph Fitzpatrick, who took an immediate liking to the shy "Slavish" ten-year-old with the bad skin and the deft touch. "I distinctly remember how individual and unique his work was," he later told *Pittsburgher* magazine. "From the very start, he was quite original." This was Andy's first exposure to museum-quality art—and to students from less ethnic, more affluent parts of town, some of whom were dropped off by the family chauffeur. The museum sat in the middle of a park, alongside the Carnegie Library and the Carnegie Institute of Technology, on Fifth Avenue, near the limestone mansions of the Carnegies, Mellons, and Fricks. Crossing the bridge over the ravine that separated Andy's neighborhood from this neo-classical oasis must have been like going from Brooklyn to Paris. Perhaps this is when Andy first realized that art was his ticket to another world.

In 1942, when Andy was fourteen, his father died. John Elachko, whose father was the neighborhood undertaker, says that Ondrej "got very jaundiced and died from a liver infection." Julia always said it was from drinking "poison water" at a construction site in Virginia, or perhaps his liver was weakened after the removal of his gallbladder a few years earlier. His open casket was laid out at home, in the living room. "Andy hid under the bed upstairs," Paul Warhola says, "and wouldn't come down to see him. And he didn't go to my dad's funeral at Saint John Chrysostom, because my mother thought it would [lead to] a recurrence of his nervous condition." Andy was beginning a lifelong reluctance to attend memorials or funerals.

"Five days before my dad passed away," John Warhola recalls, "he says he wanted to talk to me. We sat on the back porch and he told me that he was going to go into the hospital and he won't be back. And he says that Andy's gonna be highly educated, and he says there's enough money to start him off in school. He told me to make sure the bills are taken care of and that I, you know, could take care of Mother, because Paul's gonna get married. Now Paul got married a year later. And Andy did go to college."

Paul Warhola recalls that his father had this talk with him, not John. Anyway, both helped to support the family. Julia went back to cleaning houses, at two dollars a day, until she was stricken with colon cancer two years later, and suffered through a risky colostomy operation—Andy, then sixteen, was sure his mother was going to die, too. Paul had dropped out of high school in tenth grade and worked full time at "huckstering"—buying fruits and vegetables from the downtown wholesale markets at dawn and selling them from a truck in the better neighborhoods all day and into the evening. John, who had transferred from Schenley High to a technical school, helped Paul after school and during the summers, and then took a full-time job as a Good Humor ice-cream man.

Andy helped out in the summer of 1946, though he spent as much time drawing the customers as selling them peaches and pears. His artwork earned him a $40 student prize and his first publicity: a *Pittsburgh Press* article headlined "Artist-Huckster Sketches Customers and Wins Prize." The eighteen-year-old "Andy Warhols" was quoted as saying that the "new rich" were very demanding compared to the more gracious old rich. (Sounds like a budding society portraitist.)

* * *

Andy had enrolled at Carnegie Tech the previous September, having graduated from Schenley High one year early by doubling up his eleventh- and twelfth-grade courses. Some biographies mention a scholarship, but there is no record of one at Carnegie-Mellon University, as it is now called. John Warhola says that the tuition was covered by a $1,500 postal bond their father had left for that purpose, and that Andy earned extra money that first year by working in a "dairy," making milkshakes and sandwiches. John says, "I remember him complaining, 'Geez, I had to wash dishes until three in the morning.' It was thirty-five cents an hour then." In his junior year, Andy found a part-time job more to his liking, decorating windows at the posh Joseph Horne department store. Display director Larry Vollmer was impressed by Andy, whose blossoming artistic talents were now matched by a burgeoning case of acne, centered particularly on his nose, which seemed to become more bulbous every year—"more like Julia's," as a neighbor says. His new nickname: Andy the red-nosed Warhola. Vollmer, too, felt sorry for Andy, and let him spend hours leafing through his copies of *Vogue* and *Harper's Bazaar.*

At Carnegie Tech, where he majored in Painting and Design, Andy became art director of *Cano,* the campus literary magazine, and the only male member of the Modern Dance Club. His closest friend was Philip Pearlstein, going to college on the G.I. Bill, who also seemed to view Andy with a mixture of pity and respect. "He would come over to my house to work because he didn't have room at home," Pearlstein later said in *Edie.* "There were some nieces and nephews who wouldn't let him work in peace, and they'd destroy his work. His brothers made fun of him—they thought he was strange because he was doing art." Though their styles were opposite— Pearlstein's was realistic and political, Andy's light and almost surreal—he was impressed by Andy's determination to always come up with something new.

Two anecdotes from the Carnegie Tech years show the beginnings of what was to come.

Robert Lepper, the Pictorial Design professor, gave an assignment: Go to any street, pick out a house, imagine who lives there, then draw the living room. Andy went to his own street, picked out his own house, though he didn't say so, and did a pastel of his own living room, with its maroon sofa and rug, and the radio sitting on a doily. "He left out Mother's holy pictures," says Paul Warhola, "but he put in the cross from Dad's funeral, on the fireplace where we always kept it."

In his senior year, Andy submitted the painting he considered his masterpiece to the annual exhibition of the Associated Artists of Pittsburgh. It portrayed a young man with his finger stuck up his nostril and was titled *The Broad Gave Me My Face, But I Can Pick My Own Nose.* It showed the influences of his first visit to New York's Museum of Modern Art the summer before, where he had first seen the work of Klee, Miró, Ben Shahn, and

George Grosz. Grosz was actually one of the jurors for the exhibition and he defended the nose picker against those who considered it an insult and refused to include it. Andy ended up hanging it in the Arts and Crafts Center instead, and as fellow student Robert Fleischer later told art historian Patrick Smith, people "just *flocked* to see this painting Andy did . . . it was so controversial."

3

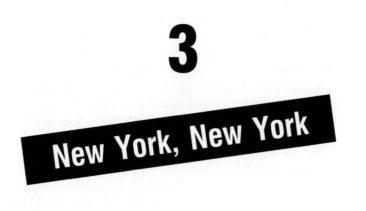

New York, New York

In 1949, Andy graduated with a degree in design and moved to New York with Philip Pearlstein, who went on to become an important realist painter. They sublet an eighth-floor walkup tenement apartment on St. Mark's Place, in what is now the East Village and was then Little Ukraine. The bathtub was in the kitchen and it was usually full, says Pearlstein, of "lots of roaches, incredible roaches." A few months later, they rented the big front room of dancer Francesca Boas's loft on West 23rd Street, and Andy sent out handmade change-of-address cards "in little envelopes filled with fairy dust" announcing, "I've moved from one roach-ridden apartment to another."

Years later, Andy loved to tell me tales of what he called "my cockroach period," and his favorite has been repeated in every book written about him. He'd never forget the day, it goes, that he finally got an appointment to show his work to Carmel Snow, the white-gloved editor-in-chief of *Harper's Bazaar.* When she opened his portfolio, he said, a cockroach crawled out and ran across her desk, and she felt so sorry for him that she gave him an assignment. It never happened—not to Andy, anyway. Philip Pearlstein says that it was *his* appointment, *his* portfolio, *his* cockroach— and that Mrs. Snow was so horrified that he didn't get the job.

The cockroach period was short-lived; Andy was an almost instant success as a commercial artist. That first summer in New York—after praying at a seven-thirty mass most mornings—he made the rounds of fashion magazines and advertising agencies, sweating in his one-and-only suit—"heavy white corduroy that gradually turned dark ivory," Pearlstein remembers. "But the moment he opened his portfolio, they loved his work." Andy had developed his trademark style of illustration while still at Carnegie Tech. It was a three-step process. He'd do a pencil sketch of the subject, displaying the same quick, facile talent that he had shown as a child. Then he'd trace the drawing on a piece of blotting paper, or even toilet tissue, in ink. And then, while the ink was still wet, he'd press the drawing onto a third piece of paper, sometimes over and over on a single sheet to achieve a wallpaper look, sometimes on sheet after sheet, producing fainter and fainter multiples of the original drawing—which he threw away. It was fast, easy, cheap, different, and modern—all the things Andy liked his work to be.

By August, he had gotten his first break: an assignment to illustrate shoes for *Glamour* magazine. They liked what he did so much they immediately gave him six more pages in the same issue, illustrating, appropriately, a feature entitled "Climbing the Ladder of Success." (The credit mistakenly read "Drawings by Warhol"—that's how Andy dropped the "a.") There he met his first two professional boosters; art director Tina Fredericks (now the leading realtor in the Hamptons) and accessories editor Geraldine Stutz (later president of Henri Bendel, now publisher of Panache Press). They recall that he was always amenable to their ideas, always on time with deadlines, always willing to revise and re-revise. And, like others then and later, they felt a bit sorry for him, nicknaming him "Raggedy Andy," because he was always so sloppily put together, and "Andy Paperbag," because he delivered his completed assignments in a brown paper bag. Andy was soon working night and day, drawing, tracing, blotting, drawing, tracing, blotting.

In the spring of 1950, Andy left the loft on 23rd Street for a rambling apartment on the Upper West Side, which he shared with a dozen aspiring young artists, actresses, and dancers, "not one of whom," he later claimed, "ever shared a problem with me." By 1951, he was making enough money to take a small cold-water apartment of his own at East 73rd and Third Avenue—and his mother came from Pittsburgh and moved in with "my little baby Andy." By 1952, Andy, Julia, and three fecund Siamese cats (Sam, Sam, and Hester), were ensconced in a five-room floor-through apartment on Lexington Avenue at 34th Street in Murray Hill, above a bar called Florence's Pin-Up. Andy was getting a lot of work—*Glamour* and *Charm* illustrations, Tiffany Christmas cards, Bonwit Teller perfume ads, Ronald Firbank book jackets, a flyer for a funeral home—and also drawing weather symbols live on television (they only showed his hands). It was never enough for Andy. From the beginning he would charm more work from art directors with little handmade gifts, special personalized drawings, limited-edition illustrated books, Easter eggs decorated by Julia.

He soon rented a second floor as a studio, and hired an assistant—first Vito Giallo, then Nathan Gluck. While he was out getting more business, they did much of the work—first just the tracing and blotting, then the drawing too. His mother did any lettering that was required, and Andy charged extra for her work. She didn't really speak English, let alone read or write it, so she made many mistakes, which Andy loved (particularly when she called Marilyn Monroe "Marlyn Monore"). If she fell behind (she also did all the cleaning, laundry, shopping, and cooking), Nathan Gluck imitated her primitive but charming script.

It was a proto-Factory, and the work produced there with the assistants was proto-Pop. Later, assistants would paint backgrounds, silkscreen, ghost write—he hated working alone. Andy always tried to keep this fact from his clients, who usually found out, and almost invariably didn't care. It seemed to make sense, and no matter how many other hands were involved in the process, the end result, everyone said, including those who did the work, was always an Andy Warhol.

It did make sense: the key common denominator between Andy's commercial art and Andy's Pop Art was a consistent questioning of the concept of the original, a consistent questioning of the concept of art itself. In both his early blotted illustrations and later silkscreen paintings, Andy put several mechanical steps between his hand and the final result, between the artist and the art. He liked to hide his essence, in art as well as life, showing the public only a cool and compelling surface image.

In 1955, he got his biggest break. Geraldine Stutz, now fashion director of the snooty I. Miller shoe store on Fifth Avenue and 57th Street, paid Andy $50,000 a year—a huge sum then—to do weekly ads in the Sunday *New York Times*. He spent his first big check on one hundred identical white shirts from Brooks Brothers. "After I. Miller, Andy was *the* commercial artist of the moment," ad man George Hartman told Jesse Kornbluth in an unpublished interview for his book, *Pre-Pop Warhol*. "He was the most successful, imitated, and adulated illustrator of fashion and style in New York," says Stutz.

In 1957, Andy won an Art Director Club Award, the Oscar of advertising, for the I. Miller campaign. In 1958, Andy's mother also won one, for a jazzy album cover. But there were disappointments for Andy and Julia too. At least once they had Christmas dinner at a Woolworth's counter.

There are many echoes of the Andy I came to know in the stories told by his fifties friends. Of course, then he hankered to be surrounded by stars and celebrities and socialites, and when I knew him he was.

A fifties friend, Buddy Radisch, told Kornbluth, "Andy was the classic star fucker, but he had nothing to contribute, he couldn't speak," and went on to describe a picnic with Garbo. Andy was invited by Mercedes daCosta, whose unabashedly lesbian autobiography, *Here Lies the Heart,* which caused Garbo to drop her, had not yet been published. Andy considered daCosta the height of elegance because not only were her shoes made in Europe, but her shoe *trees* were made by a violin maker. He was beside himself to be in the presence of Garbo, but couldn't think of anything to say to her, so he drew a butterfly and handed it to her. At the end of the day she absent-mindedly crumpled it and left it. Andy picked it up off the ground, and had his mother write across it, "Crumpled butterfly by Greta Garbo." Even then, Andy knew how to turn his rejection into an object, pain into art.

Andy had been pining over Truman Capote since the publication in 1948 of *Other Voices, Other Rooms,* with its notorious photograph of the author as a Lolitaesque odalisque, when he began sending Capote fan letters filled with stardust. Andy's first show, in 1952, was "Fifteen Drawings Based on the Writings of Truman Capote," in a rented room at the Hugo Gallery, 26 East 55th Street. He invited Capote to the opening, but the writer didn't come.

I seriously doubt if Andy was ever actually sexually attracted to Capote, but he very much wanted to be what Capote was then: provocative, cele-brated, taken seriously by the critics, asked out socially by the right people, the brilliantly witty homosexual who titillated the ladies who lunch.

Andy's hangout in the fifties was Serendipity, a combination gift shop and ice-cream parlor on East 58th Street, which opened in 1954, and launched the vogue for Art Nouveau and Tiffany lamps. "Andy started com-ing in after peddling his portfolio all day," says Steve Bruce, one of the owners. Bruce began to sell Andy's leftover advertising work—Andy always gave art directors a choice of variations—for $25 and $30 each. When the first ten sold out within a matter of days, he got Andy to do more. He was less enthusiastic about Andy's idea to sell movie stars' underwear—five dol-lars new, fifty dollars used. But he encouraged Andy to make limited-edition books, starting in 1954 with *25 Cats Named Sam and One Blue Pussy* (based on the progeny of Sam, Sam, and Hester, which were overrunning his stu-dio). Others included *The Gold Book, In the Bottom of My Garden, Wild Raspberries* (with Suzie Frankfurt, a Serendipity regular), and *Holy Cats* (credited to Julia Warhol). Bruce even let Andy have "coloring parties" there, attended mostly by handsome young men who helped put the books together and thought that hanging out with the emerging Andy Warhol en-tourage was chic. Andy would accept every party invitation he could get, including those from art directors' secretaries, because "you never know where you're going to find a job"—and brought along as many friends as he could, to ease his social awkwardness.

Buddy Radisch recalls, "Andy was consumed by his own unattractive-ness." Sometime in the middle of the decade, Andy had a nose job, though he later erased it from his memory. It didn't help in any case: though what Philip Pearlstein's wife, Dorothy, calls "the Ping-Pong ball at the end of his nose" was now smaller, his pores weren't. He later turned that experience into art. *Before and After,* one of his early Pop masterpieces, was a blown-up nose-job advertisement. And he turned his unattractiveness to his advan-tage by making himself even more unattractive—he wore pinhole glasses and

later, obvious wigs, which helped to change his image from weirdo to eccentric, becoming emblems of his unassailable uniqueness.

By the late fifties, Andy was a minor star—a highly paid, much-awarded,
rather well-known commercial artist at the center of the Serendipity scene.
But "it was a small scene," as Steve Bruce says, "very effete." A homosexual fringe scene, and Andy knew it. He didn't want to be in the middle
of the fringe, he wanted to be in the middle of the middle. He took a box
at the Metropolitan Opera, but if the social set noticed him at all it was as
"this colossal creep," to quote Frederick Eberstadt, heir to a Wall Street
fortune.

Andy wanted more: more money, more fame, more social power—to
get more fans, more boys, some love. "I want to be Matisse," he told one
friend. "I want to be as famous as the Queen of England," he told another.
All through the fifties, he tried to have his commercial work taken seriously
by showing it in galleries: The Capote show at the Hugo Gallery was followed by a group show at the Loft Gallery in 1954, and two shows at the
Bodley Gallery in 1956. All, including the last—"The Golden Slipper Show
or Shoes Show in America"—were ignored by the established art world,
dominated by macho Abstract Expressionists like de Kooning and Pollock,
and by square intellectual critics like Clement Greenberg and Harold Rosenberg. But these elaborate gold-leaf fantasies revealed much about Andy's
ambitions and desires. There were shoes dedicated to high-camp idols like
Mae West, Zsa Zsa Gabor, and Margaret Truman, but there were also shoes
inspired by the insiders of that rarefied world where fashion and society
meet, such as Diana Vreeland and Jerome Zipkin, precisely the people Andy
wanted to know and be accepted by. And there was a shoe dedicated to
Truman Capote. *Life* magazine did a spread on Andy's golden star shoes—
he had learned an important lesson of publicity: Fame attracts fame.

Little by little, Andy pulled away from the Serendipity boys and started
spending more time with a new friend he had met through Tina Fredericks.
Emile de Antonio, as Andy would explain, "was the first person who didn't
make a distinction between commercial art and fine art." He was an artists'
agent, of sorts, who helped struggling painters pay the bills with commercial
jobs. He got Robert Rauschenberg and Jasper Johns work doing windows at
Bonwit Teller for the Toscanini of window dressing, Gene Moore. "Rauschenberg and Johns could do anything," Moore says. "They did windows
you'd never guess were theirs. I kept them alive for a number of years. Once
a year at Bonwit's, I'd show their serious work—which never appealed to
me."

As Rauschenberg and Johns began to emerge as serious artists, with
shows in serious galleries like Leo Castelli, Andy, who had also done Bonwit
windows for Moore, became more and more jealous of their success. Even
after his own success in the art world, I think he was still jealous of them.

Several times in the seventies I remember him dismissing them as "staple-gun queens," Brigid Berlin's name for window trimmers. When he asked de Antonio why Rauschenberg and Johns always snubbed him at art openings—even after he bought a Johns drawing of a lightbulb for $450 in 1958 to get in with them—de Antonio told them that they considered Andy "too friggin' commercial." They signed their commercial work Matson Jones and did just enough to get by, while he was winning awards for his and making a small fortune. De Antonio added that Rauschenberg and Johns, who had once lived together, thought Andy was "too swish"—they affected a more masculine style, not as bar-brawling as Jackson Pollock's, but far removed from Andy's campy coloring parties at Serendipity.

Andy ignored the latter criticism; his gayness would become, like his very obvious wig, another badge of individuality, so out in the open that it was taken for granted. But he listened to the first part of de Antonio's advice very carefully—and decided that he would transform himself and his art into the real thing. He had been following the art scene with increasing interest through the fifties, and had built up a small collection of prints and drawings by Magritte, Miró, Klee, Picasso, Pavel Tchelitchew, and Saul Steinberg, which were haphazardly displayed amidst the Tiffany lamps and antique bentwood chairs from Serendipity in the always messy Murray Hill duplex—one friend described the décor as "Victorian Surrealist." In 1958, Andy bought a townhouse on Lexington Avenue and 89th Street, in Yorkville, then a mostly German and Hungarian neighborhood, for $60,000. Julia was settled in the basement, which had a large kitchen in the rear and a front room she used as her bedroom. Andy lived on the upper two floors, and used the first floor as a combination living room and studio. Soon he was filling it with new purchases—a cigar-store Indian, pink horses from an old carousel, paintings by Robert Goodnough and Larry Rivers, a double portrait by Fairfield Porter of Andy with Ted Carey, who may or may not have been Andy's first real boyfriend.

It was in this new house in 1960 that Andy started to produce his first real art—big, crudely painted blowups of his favorite childhood cartoons: *Popeye, Nancy, The Little King, Dick Tracy, Superman.* Some of these paintings, plus the nose-job painting, were shown in Bonwit Teller's windows in April 1961. It seems all too apt, of course, that Andy's first fine art should be shown in a department-store window. But Andy wanted to be shown in a real gallery. He wanted to be a real artist.

De Antonio was trying to help. Sometime in 1960, Andy painted two versions of a giant Coca-Cola bottle—one was full of Abstract Expressionist brushstrokes and drips of paint, the other as pure and flat as an ad. Andy asked de Antonio which he liked better; he said the second and pointed Andy on his way to his Pop Art style. He also brought potentially useful people to see Andy's work, in particular, Henry Geldzahler, the Met's young curator of Contemporary Art, and Ivan Karp, the associate director of the Leo Castelli Gallery. Karp liked Andy's work, but told him about Roy Lichtenstein, another new artist also painting cartoon subjects, who had just been signed by Castelli. Pop Art was beginning to take off in 1961 and 1962. Claes Oldenburg was selling plastic replicas of food and household products at his so-called "Store" on East 2nd Street that winter. The Green Gallery signed Oldenburg soon after, then Tom Wesselmann and James Rosenquist— and Andy was worried he'd be left out. When he wasn't picking his new friends' brains for ideas, he was begging them to introduce him to dealers— he was desperate to get a gallery and have a show, to be part of the new Pop Art pack, to show up Rauschenberg and Johns, who had become Castelli's biggest stars.

1962 was Andy's year. In January, an art-dealer friend named Muriel Latow told him that she had a great idea for him to paint but that it would cost him money—fifty dollars to be exact. Andy immediately wrote her a check and Muriel told him to paint the thing he loved "more than anything else."

"What?" asked Andy.

"Money," said Muriel. According to art historian Calvin Tomkins, she also gave him the idea to paint "something so familiar that nobody even noticed it anymore, 'something like a can of Campbell's soup.' " She didn't charge him for that one.

The next day Andy started painting singles and two-dollar bills. Then he turned his attention to the Campbell's soup can—and painted a series of thirty-two precisely rendered canvases of the thirty-two flavors available then: Tomato, Onion, Split Pea, Green Pea, Black Bean, Cream of Asparagus, Cream of Celery, Cream of Mushroom, Turkey Noodle, Chicken Vegetable, Pepper Pot, etc. They would turn out to be his ticket not only to fame but to a secure place in the history of art, his *Nude Descending a Staircase*— because in their flat, pure, shocking transformation of something so commonplace and so all-American they became icons of our culture, as Pop as art could be.

In July 1962, these thirty-two Campbell's Soupcan paintings were Andy's first show of real art in a real gallery—though in L.A., not New York. It was Irving Blum's Ferus Gallery on La Cienega Boulevard in West Hollywood—and it caused a scandal of sorts. A supermarket up the street from the gallery piled up Campbell's soup in its window and advertised "the real thing for only 29 cents a can." Andy's were selling for $100 each, and Blum only sold five, which he bought back after the show closed to keep the set intact. It was perhaps the smartest move he ever made: a year before Andy's death, Blum told me he had been offered $2 million for them; a year after Andy's death, he was offered $10 million. They are now in pride of place on permanent loan to the National Gallery of Art in Washington, D.C.—

and after all these years, still elicit that "shock of the new" of great modern art.

As usual, Andy turned the ridicule to his advantage. He took a photographer to the supermarket and got his picture taken signing the real thing. The photo was picked up by the Associated Press and wired around the world. From then on, Andy Warhol would be the man who painted the Campbell's Soupcan. In August 1962, Andy turned out his first silkscreened paintings—of Troy Donahue—followed in rapid succession by Marilyn Monroe, Elvis Presley, Elizabeth Taylor, Marlon Brando, and the Mona Lisa. Again, as with his celebrity shoe show, he was using other people's fame to make himself more famous. And like blotting, silkscreening was fast, easy, cheap, different, and modern. It too could be done with others, or by others, and called his own.

He soon hired an assistant, a Nathan Gluck for the sixties: Gerard Malanga, an art student and budding poet from Staten Island, who had spent the summer of 1962 silkscreening neckties in the garment district. Andy, the fine artist, the real artist, had made the almost miraculous transition from commercial art without sacrificing any of his original ideas, including the destruction of the original—now it was a photograph being silkscreened rather than a drawing being traced. In doing so, he made commercial art fine art, photography painting, and, depending on your point of view, either expanded what art could be for future generations, or heralded the end of art altogether. Andy himself took both views.

At last, in November 1962, Andy had his first New York show, not at Castelli as he had hoped, but at Eleanor Ward's Stable Gallery on West 57th Street. In 1963, Robert Rauschenberg sat for his portrait by Andy, and Andy also started painting the dark side of the American myth—the Disaster Paintings, which some contemporary art collectors consider his great masterpieces. Andy also did his first commissioned portrait in 1963, *Ethel Scull 36 Times*—based on poses from a five-and-dime photo machine.

In 1964, Andy had his first European show—the Flower Paintings—at the Paris Gallery of Ileana Sonnabend, Leo Castelli's ex-wife. Then Eleanor Ward gave him his first show of sculpture—silkscreened enlargements in wood of Brillo boxes, and cases of Heinz Tomato Ketchup, Kellogg's Corn Flakes, Mott's Apple Sauce. Calvin Tomkins reported, "So many people came to the opening that there was a long line on the street waiting to get in." Andy left Ward's gallery a few weeks later for Leo Castelli, who had come around after much prodding from Karp, Sonnabend, and Geldzahler, and agreed to show the Flowers. Andy was finally where he wanted to be, in the big league with the big boys.

In 1965, he had one-man shows in Paris, Milan, Turin, Essen, and Stockholm, as well as in Buenos Aires and Toronto. He also had his first American museum show in 1965, at the Contemporary Art Institute in Philadelphia. The opening was mobbed by college kids. A pattern was already being established: Andy would always be popular with young Americans, but would always have many more shows, in more important museums and galleries, receive more serious critical attention, and find many more clients on the other side of the Atlantic.

By the time of the riotous Philadelphia show, Andy was traveling with an enormous entourage, including his Superstar of the year, Edie Sedgwick, plus his own rock band, the Velvet Underground, and his own light show, the Exploding Plastic Inevitable. In 1963, he had started making silent movies with a 16mm camera—his first one in Los Angeles, titled *Tarzan and Jane Revisited . . . Sort of.* Tarzan was Taylor Mead, a fey dropout from an old Michigan family, and an Underground figure for his own film, *Flower Thief.* Jane was Andy's first Superstar, a crazy *zaftig* girl from Brooklyn named Naomi Levine. Dennis Hopper, a friend of Mead's, made a cameo appearance, and gave a party for Andy and company, inviting Warren Beatty, Natalie Wood, and Troy Donahue. For Andy, it was literally a dream come true. The Ruthenian-American staple-gun queen, the colossal creep, the perpetual outsider, was on his way inside.

Back in New York, in the large, empty former hat factory he had rented in 1963 on East 47th Street and named the Factory to play up the assembly-line approach to the art produced there, Andy began making movies every day and all night. He started at ground zero, and re-created the history of film as he went, adding motion, music, talking, scripted dialogue, plot, color, 35mm, and 3D step-by-step, through the sixties and into the seventies. His first films were so basic *(Sleep,* a man sleeping for six hours; *Empire,* the Empire State Building standing there for eight hours; *Kiss,* couples kissing in close-up for three minutes each) and so boring that once again Andy made his mark in an easy, fast, cheap, different, and modern way—and called into question the very process of filmmaking, of what a movie was. And yet, as he told me, he was "just learning to use the camera." But he was also satisfying his almost obsessive need to look, to watch; and he was slyly sending up Hollywood too. The idea for *Kiss,* for example, came from the old Hayes Office rule that forbade movie actors to touch lips for more than three seconds. More than anything, these early films gave him a reputation as a put-on artist, but they also won the Independent Film Award, the Underground Oscar.

Andy surrounded himself with Superstars, his answer to the studio system: Baby Jane Holzer, a Jewish princess from Park Avenue and Palm Beach with a long mane of teased blond hair, was his Harlow (or Bardot). Edie Sedgwick, a WASP princess from Beacon Hill and Santa Barbara, with her short silver pageboy, his Marilyn Monroe. Then there were those Catholic princesses, Viva and Brigid Berlin, zany comediennes, the Underground answer to Lucy and Ethel. And Ingrid Superstar and Ultra Violet and International Velvet—empty-headed beauties from Hoboken and Lyons and Boston, the sixties equivalent of sweater girls. And Pope Ondine, a brilliant gay amphetamine addict from McKeesport, the steel-mill town Andy said *he* was from. And Mario Montez, postal clerk by day, drag queen by night. And beautiful, empty-headed boys like Eric Emerson, Tom Hompertz, Gino Piserchio, Joe Dallesandro, who liked to take their clothes off in front of the camera and play hard to get. Gerard Malanga became a Superstar too, famous for his whip dance in *Vinyl,* and at Andy's short-lived disco, The Dom, on St. Marks Place. Not a Superstar, but their studio photographer, their George Hurrell, was another frenetic A-head, Billy Name, who covered the Factory walls in aluminum foil and sprayed the cement floor silver. Just as Andy encouraged them to change their names, they made up one for him too—Drella, half Dracula half Cinderella.

The films Andy made in the mid-sixties, including *Poor Little Rich Girl, My Hustler, Nude Restaurant,* and the epic *Chelsea Girls,* were actually seen by very few people—in those days Underground movies were literally shown underground, in cafe basements and tiny art cinemas in obscure corners of a handful of cities. But their impact was enormous. They influenced more-commercial filmmakers both in Hollywood (Peter Fonda, John Schlesinger) and Europe (Godard, Bertolucci), and because their subject matter was both forbidden and what everybody was talking about in the sixties, they were publicized all out of proportion to their distribution. After the Campbell's Soupcan paintings, nothing helped Andy's lifelong campaign to become a household name as much as his little-seen, much-talked-about movies of the sixties—until the assassination attempt.

The Factory itself became famous in the sixties as the all-night filming sessions turned into twenty-four-hour parties, where heirs from Harvard and drag queens from Harlem mixed and mingled, and much more, under Billy Name's revolving disco ball of mirrors. The drug use and orgies have been well documented, and probably exaggerated. While Andy wrote an entire book called *Popism* about the period, with the theme ''I never really knew what was really going on,'' he was at the center of this maelstrom of intrigue, jealousy, and voyeurism. And though Andy himself never took more than a diet pill then, he certainly enjoyed and encouraged everything everyone else did.

Life was a party, and more and more real stars were turning up at the wild, often spontaneous Factory bashes—Judy Garland, Tennessee Williams, Jim Morrison, Cecil Beaton, the Rolling Stones, most of Swinging London, even some of the Park Avenue swells Andy loved to lure into his version of high society, including Freddy Eberstadt and his wife, Isabel, Ogden Nash's daughter. Andy had arrived and the formal acknowledgment came in 1966: an invitation to the most exclusive and glamorous party of the decade, the Black and White Ball given at the Plaza Hotel by none other than Truman Capote.

* * *

In February 1968, a mere five and a half years after his Campbell's Soupcan show in Los Angeles, Andy Warhol had his first retrospective. It was at the Modern Museet in Stockholm, and drew the largest crowd in the history of that august institution. The catalogue, which went into second and third editions, was the ultimate Pop artifact: bound between hard vinyl covers of pink and orange Flowers were hundreds of pages of black-and-white Billy Name photographs of the sixties Factory—the parties, the movies, the Superstars, the art. There were no captions, and no real text, no heavy art criticism explaining the meaning of it all. Instead, the catalogue opened with a series of quotes, in headline typeface from an interview with Andy. Together they represented the complete Warhol image, as perfect and pure as it would ever be:

> The interviewer should just tell me the words he wants me to say and I'll repeat them after him.
> I still care about people but it would be so much easier not to care . . . it's too hard to care . . . I don't like to touch things . . . that's why my work is so distant from myself.
> Machines have less problems. I'd like to be a machine, wouldn't you?
> I tried doing them by hand, but I find it easier to use a screen. This way, I don't have to work on my objects at all. One of my assistants or anyone else, for that matter, can reproduce the designs as well as I could.
> I like boring things.
> I love Los Angeles. I love Hollywood. They're beautiful. Everybody's plastic, but I love plastic. I want to be plastic.
> If you want to know all about Andy Warhol, just look at the surface of my paintings and films and me, and there I am. There's nothing behind it.

And his most famous quote, typically always misquoted: "In the future everybody will be world famous for fifteen minutes."

Andy himself became *world* famous, front-page famous, a household name in houses where art never hung, on June 3, 1968. At four in the afternoon a Superstar reject named Valerie Solanis, author of a manifesto for a rabid Women's Lib cult called SCUM, the Society for Cutting Up Men, followed Andy into 33 Union Square West, the new Factory he'd moved to earlier that year. She waited while he took a call from Viva and when he hung up, she pumped three bullets into his chest and abdomen from a few feet away. She then shot Mario Amaya, a visiting curator, and aimed her .32-caliber automatic pistol at Fred Hughes, but it jammed. Andy was rushed to Columbus–Mother Cabrini Hospital on East 19th Street, where he was pronounced clinically dead at 4:51 P.M. His chest was cut open and his heart massaged, and then five doctors operated for five hours on his lungs, liver, gallbladder, spleen, esophagus, intestines, and pulmonary artery.

Valerie Solanis turned herself in that night, telling the police, "He had too much control of my life." Later, she explained that Andy had promised to produce a screenplay of hers, but kept putting her off. "I just wanted him to pay attention to me," she said. "Talking to him was like talking to a chair." She was put into a mental institution and eventually sentenced to a maximum of three years in prison for "reckless assault with intent to harm." She was released from the New York State Prison for Women at Bedford Hills in September 1971. At that time, Andy was still having problems with digesting and sleeping, and under the girdle he had to wear to keep his stomach muscles in place, his torso was a roadmap of scars.

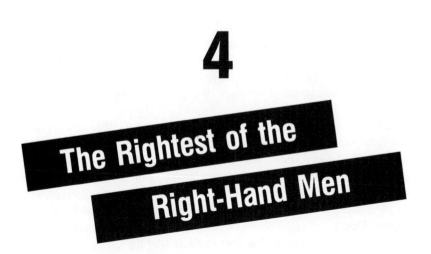

4

The Rightest of the Right-Hand Men

In the fall of 1970, six months after my first visit to *inter/VIEW* and the Factory, Andy Warhol was sitting at the same desk, eating the same lunch, wearing the same clothes—except that the black turtleneck, the last trace of the Swinging Sixties, had been replaced by a chic brown-on-navy cotton plaid shirt. The same well-groomed young assistants hovered in the background, seeming to do nothing more than keep Andy company. I hadn't learned yet that keeping Andy company was very hard work—you were expected to provide him with a steady stream of gossip, ideas, and jokes in exchange for an occasional "Gee," "Wow," or "Really." The ultimate chore was confession, which usually began with Andy asking, "What did you do last night?" and turning cold or walking away if he sensed any holding back of juicy personal details.

I had learned the names of these assistants—even the most basic information was rarely volunteered at the Factory—and that they each had a job to do in addition to having their brains picked daily. Pat Hackett transcribed Andy's tapes and got him lunch from Brownie's, the kosher health-food restaurant around the corner on East 16th Street. Vincent Fremont was in charge of Andy's checks, bills, and invoices, and opened the Factory every morning at nine and closed it every evening at seven. Jed Johnson edited Andy's movies and maintained the brownstone on Lexington Avenue and 89th Street where Andy lived with his mother, Julia. Like most of Andy's male employees, including Gerard Malanga, Paul Morrissey, and Fred Hughes, Jed had started out sweeping the floor. Two years earlier he had delivered a telegram to the Factory and was offered the job by Paul, who said, "We pay the same as Western Union, but at least you get to stay in one place all day." The hardwood floor was always extremely clean and shiny. On this particular October afternoon it was being swept by Joe Dallesandro, the muscular Superstar of *Andy Warhol's Trash,* which had just opened to surprisingly good reviews, including one by me in the *Village Voice.*

I had come to the Factory to hand in my latest *inter/VIEW* assignment, an interview with Bernardo Bertolucci, the young Italian director whose second film, *The Conformist,* was the hit of that fall's New York Film Festival. Following the *Antonio das Mortes* paean, Soren Agenoux published one or two pieces of mine each month, including an acid attack on Hollywood's idea of a hip flick, *The Magic Garden of Stanley Sweetheart,* starring the teenage Don Johnson, who was curled up nude in a fetal position on the *inter/VIEW* cover (Volume 1, Number 8; $1,000 at the Gotham Book Mart).

Thanks to *inter/VIEW,* I was quickly becoming a mini-star at Columbia Film School and at Nina Needlepoint, where I painted stitching patterns of dogs, cats, and flowers—alongside my former Georgetown classmates and future Factory cohorts Glenn O'Brien and Michael Netter—to pay for the furnished room on West 105th Street I had moved into that summer. For me the real incentive in writing for *inter/VIEW* was getting to go to the Factory. I always went to the tenth floor to see Soren, who then took me to the sixth floor, where Andy would sign my $25 checks and grope for something to say. Sometimes Paul Morrissey, who never lacked for something to say, engaged me in conversation.

"So," he would say, "is that liberal, left-wing slime Andrew Sarris still preaching his pretentious *auteur* theory to all of you spaced-out rich kids up at Columbia?" It was a typical Paul Morrissey greeting. He sat at a huge fake slate desk. Behind him were framed color photographs of four of his favorite Superstars—the most beautiful four: International Velvet, Tom Hompertz, Viva, and Joe Dallesandro. As he spat out his outrageous opinions, he tugged at his sandy brown hair, pulling out individual strands and throwing them over his shoulder. Every so often, he jumped up and Windexed some suddenly noticed smudge from the glass over the Superstar portraits. "I mean, what could be more ridiculous than the pompous, pseudointellectual notion that the director is the most important person on a movie. Everyone knows the most important person on a movie is the *star!* Everyone except those phony French foreign slime like Godard."

I had tolerated Paul's tirade until then—especially since he was the one who had told Soren to call me in the first place. But when he maligned the man who made *Weekend,* I'd had enough. "Isn't Andy Warhol the ultimate *auteur?*" I countered.

"Andy? Andy an *auteur?* You must be joking. Andy's idea of making a movie is going to the première." Paul was the only one who could get away with a crack like that—he was a partner, not an employee. He wasn't paid a salary but took 50 percent of any movie profits.

Paul Morrissey was an odd but appealing character. He was thirty-two years old but he seemed much older—perhaps because the three things he hated even more than the *auteur* theory were sex, drugs, and rock 'n' roll. He reveled in his counter-counter-cultural contrariness. Only Paul Morrissey, for example, could tell *Rolling Stone* "musicians should be heard and not seen, like children should be seen and not heard. Musicians should be heard, but not *from* or *about*. I mean, who is Led Zeppelin? Is Eric Clapton really that interesting?"

For Paul, rock stars were "drug trash," a recurring term in his rapid-fire patter, applied to everything and everyone he found morally repugnant. His original title for *Trash,* the story of a hustler who can't perform sexually because he's a junkie, was *Drug Trash,* but he decided it was too obvious. And in every conversation I had with him, he would sooner or later ask, in his high-pitched bark, "Why do you kids say you're experimenting with drugs? You're experimenting with *ill health*. Now that polio and all the other childhood diseases have been eradicated, you kids take drugs to find out what it's like to be *sick!*"

Glenn O'Brien says Paul was "an extreme prude making X-rated movies." Though Paul worshipped physical beauty, considering it a talent in itself—and featured Joe Dallesandro's chiseled torso prominently in *Flesh* and *Trash*—his attitude toward sex was decidedly Irish Catholic, i.e., repressed. In fact, I have never met anyone more stereotypically Irish Catholic than Paul Morrissey. Narrow-minded, self-righteous, guilt-ridden, and word-mad: he was almost a parody. Paul's hilarious sense of humor was also extremely Irish Catholic—black-on-black.

After a totally parochial education in the Bronx, he went to the Jesuit-run Fordham University, where he made his first 8mm one-reeler: a priest saying mass on a cliff, then shoving the altar boy off it. His right-wing views were no doubt reinforced by his first job—as a social worker on the Lower East Side, where he also bought a small house. Paul loved being close to the things he hated.

In 1965, through the Underground film scene then thriving in the East Village, Paul met Gerard Malanga, then Andy. Soon he was hanging out at the Factory, offering to clean up, and helping with the sound on *My Hustler.* By the time I got to the Factory, Paul Morrissey was definitely the rightest of the right-hand men. Rightest politically too: In that same 1971 *Rolling Stone* interview, he attacked "junk democracy" and when asked what system of government he'd prefer, replied, "Why not give royalty a chance?" His choice for the throne, he often said, was John-John Kennedy, with Jackie as regent; he brushed aside the Kennedys' liberalism because they were Irish and Catholic. "Besides," he would say, "John-John's not really a Kennedy. He's more of a Bouvier-Onassis."

He would often chuckle to himself after he made a particularly off-the-wall remark, and laugh out loud as he read his own quotes. "Did I really say that?" he'd say.

When I turned in my *inter/VIEW* articles, Paul invariably found them "too intellectual. You're letting that Andrew Sarris brainwash you." But the day I handed in my Bertolucci story, I wasn't too worried about a run-in with Paul, because I had finally connected with Andy. The week before I had run into him at Lincoln Center, waiting for a Film Festival press screening. We were both early and alone.

"Oh, hi," he said.

"Hi, Andy."

"Gee, your articles are so good. I wish I could be so intellectual."

"Paul says they're too intellectual."

"Oh, Paul's just being funny."

There was a long pause. Andy had run out of words and I had run out of nerve. Then he looked at the plastic shopping bag from Brownie's he was carrying, as if he had just realized it was in his hand.

"Oh, I know what I should do," he said. "I should take your picture."

He pulled his Polaroid Big Shot from the Brownie's bag and told me to sit on a bench with my back toward him.

"Now turn your head my way. That's right. Not too much. Look down a little. A little more. Oh, oh, that's good."

The camera was glued to his glasses and he pivoted it up and down and sideways very slightly, searching for my best angle—something I was sure I didn't have. He had chosen a bench against the window, so sunlight streamed across my face. I felt warm and wanted.

"That's good," said Andy softly. "Oh, oh, don't move now."

He snapped, pulled out the picture and snapped again. I stood up and waited beside him for my image to develop. As it did, Andy sighed, "Gee, you're a beauty."

A beauty? I looked at the pictures. It was amazing. Somehow my face had angles and bones, where I knew there were only curves and mounds. My chubby nose was aquiline. Of course, the softness of the Polaroid image, and the extreme overexposure, helped a lot.

"Oh, let me take one more. Sit in the same spot but look straight at me this time."

I did as I was told and again the result was miraculous. I looked like Elvis Presley. Before Las Vegas. I asked Andy if I could have it.

"Oh," he said, carefully slipping my beautiful image into his plastic bag. "Maybe I can give you one the next time you come to the office."

A few days later I interviewed Bernardo Bertolucci at the Algonquin Hotel. A pretty English girl translated his pronouncements: "Antonioni makes films about ashtrays." "*Satyricon* is like a big cadaver that doesn't smell." "Pasolini is so decadent in real life [that] he tries to cover it up by making his films austere." I used a bulky borrowed tape recorder, but refused to let the transcript run, à la Warhol, in raw Q&A form, insisting instead on "writing it up." It was my first interview and, visions of *New Yorker* profiles dancing in my head, I wanted to make a "literary" impression.

Several rewrites later, I headed downtown to Union Square. The *inter/ VIEW* office was not only locked but chained. Soren Agenoux and his cherubic assistant, Jeremy Dixon, were always there in the early afternoon—where were they? I went down to the sixth floor to see if they were there and found Andy eating lunch at his Deco desk. "Is Soren around?" I asked.

"Oh, uh, something happened," said Andy vaguely. "I think Paul wants to talk to you. Gee, your *Trash* review in the *Voice* was really great."

Paul also liked it. "A little intellectual," he told me, "but I liked the line about Holly [Woodlawn] looking like 'an amphetamined El Greco.' And Joe's 'Greco-Roman ass'—that was pretty funny. And it was very perceptive of you to make the comparison with *Our Lady of the Flowers*—'cause if anybody's more Catholic than Genet, it's us. We're not as perverse, though."

Then he got down to business. Would I like to be editor of *inter/VIEW*? Soren had been let go. Paul explained that Andy and he had been "too busy" to read the last three issues, "and then the other day, I started reading them and I realized Soren was putting out a silly scandal sheet."

"But I don't know anything about editing a magazine," I said, stunned. "And I've still got another semester to go at Columbia."

Paul assured me that "putting together a magazine isn't that big a deal. You just slap some pretty pictures down on the page and you and your friends from school could probably do most of the interviews. Why don't you ask Andrew Sarris if they'll give you some college credits for working for us?"

Paul also offered me a salary: $40 a week. I told him I'd think it over and gave him the Bertolucci interview, which he read rapidly. "Andy," he called across the room, "listen to this wonderful compliment Bertolucci gave you." Andy looked up from his purées as Paul read: "Everyone says in Hollywood there is psychological direction of actors, but Howard Hawks films are just like Andy Warhol films. Humphrey Bogart is always Humphrey Bogart. And Garbo always plays Garbo. It is the American independent cinema that went wrong—they are the sons who have not understood anything about the fathers."

"Gee, that's really great," said Andy.

"Isn't it? But what I don't get is how someone as intelligent as Bertolucci obviously is can call himself a Communist. It's really a joke. And why does he insist on saying 'film' and 'cinema'? It's so pretentious. You know what you have to do—every time he says 'film,' change it to 'movies.' The translator probably got it wrong anyway."

On my way out, I asked Andy if I could have one of the Polaroids he took of me at Lincoln Center. "Oh," he moaned, "I think I left them at home."

In the next few days I discussed Paul's offer with Andrew Sarris, who advised me to be careful; with Arthur Barron, the head of Columbia Film School, who approved my request to count working at *inter/VIEW* as two courses; with my father, who threatened to smash the Super-8 movie camera he had given me for Christmas if I took the job; and with my best friend from Georgetown, Columbia, and Nina Needlepoint, Glenn O'Brien, who said he'd love to be my assistant. I had tried to call Jeremy Dixon to ask him what had really happened with Soren and if he wanted to stay on, but there was never any answer at his apartment near Times Square.

Finally, I went back to the Factory and told Paul I would take the job if I was paid $50 a week. He agreed. He let me hire Glenn—at $40 a week. Those were very high salaries, he noted, for "part-time jobs." Then he announced that he and Andy were leaving the next morning for Paris to shoot a new movie called *L'Amour*. He gave me the key to the *inter/VIEW* office and the phone number of *Other Scenes*, where the magazine was laid out and typeset. He also handed me a stack of Rita Hayworth stills from the forties and fifties. "Just run one of these on every page," he said. "It doesn't matter if they go with the articles or not."

Somehow, I knew he wasn't joking.

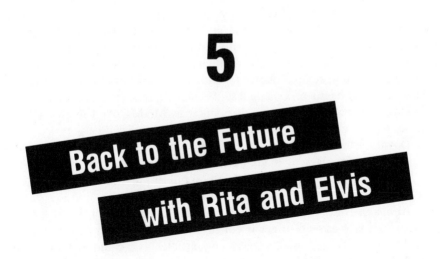

5

Back to the Future with Rita and Elvis

Putting out a magazine was, of course, a very big deal. Having an editorial assistant who loved editing and hated assisting didn't help. Fortunately, Glenn's wife, Judy O'Brien, volunteered to assist the assistant. She was the first in a long line of girls from good families who worked at the Factory for free. She was so thrilled she instantly changed her name to Jude Jade—she loved the Beatles' new song "Hey Jude." She decided this over Black Russians, the In drink at Max's Kansas City, the In bar for the Superstar set—where we instantly went to celebrate our new positions.

The Superstars, looking less than super under the red glare of the back room's only light, a Dan Flavin sculpture, greeted us with a mixture of disdain and curiosity. They were waiting to see how much coverage we gave them in the school newspaper, which is what *inter/VIEW* had been under Gerard Malanga and Soren Agenoux. We tried to appear cool and uncaring. But for us, meeting Eric Emerson (the acid-tripping onanist searching for the meaning of life in *The Chelsea Girls*) and Candy Darling (the transvestite socialite in *Women in Revolt*, the movie Paul had started shooting before he took off for Paris), was like hobnobbing with Errol Flynn and Carole Lombard at the Brown Derby.

The next afternoon we got to work. First, we carved some work space out of the mountains of back issues. (Paul had expressly forbidden me to throw any out. "Andy never throws anything out," he had said.) We plowed through the piles of unopened mail on Soren's beat-up metal desk: studio press releases, invitations to screenings recently past, and the odd Tom of Finland catalogue. There was also an envelope addressed to me. "Your first fan letter,'' Jude suggested cheerfully. It was a letter from Jeremy Dixon's mother, who wrote that her son had died the previous week. He had gone to a club, mixed too many pills with too much beer, and passed out. His buddies assumed that he had dozed off, but when they realized that he was dead, they left him for the owner to find when the club closed. It was the first time I had heard of Quaaludes, the muscle relaxant with aphrodisiac side effects, which later became as popular as M&Ms. And Jeremy Dixon was the first of my Factory friends to die of unnatural causes.

Down on the sixth floor, Pat Hackett told me that Andy also received a letter from Mrs. Dixon, thanking him for helping her son. "Did I help him?" he said, dropping the letter in a box full of press releases on his way to Paris.

Although Andy and Paul hadn't given me a deadline for the next issue of *inter/VIEW*, I wanted to get it out in time for their return from Paris. I took Paul's advice and assigned as many articles as I could to film-school friends. I also put a Rita Hayworth still on every page, tempering the arbitrariness of this by leading off with "An Untitled Adulation of Rita Hayworth" by Stephan Varble, a Truman Capote figure at Columbia. Glenn insisted on ending the issue, Malanga-like, with a poem, "a vision of st. rita"—"before color/you were golden/before I came/you were there." Jude was rewarded for fetching coffee with a bylined review of *The Mind of Mr. Soames,* starring her heart throb, Terence Stamp, and "his peach-coloured cashmere crotch." My Bertolucci interview was the only piece *not* incongruously illustrated. I knew that even Paul couldn't resist Dominique Sanda and Stefania Sandrelli tangoing, which is the still I ran from *The Conformist* in lieu of yet another ravishing Rita.

Other Scenes, where we had to do the layouts and typesetting, was definitely not our scene. John Wilcock and his bearded, beaded staff kindly showed us how to size photos and spec type, but we hated having to wait around in their dark and dirty Village basement, and we snickered every time one of them used "freak" as a compliment. We also snickered at the copy for the exchange ad *Other Scenes* ran in *inter/VIEW*, the one with the cannabis-leaf border. "*Other Scenes* can be smoked or eaten," it ran. "It's the first magazine of the grass generation."

If *Other Scenes* was hopelessly hippie, the *inter/VIEW* printer, located in a dark and dirty garage in Chinatown, was just plain hopeless. He didn't speak English and he used ink like soy sauce. The first half of our press run emerged black on black, the Rita Hayworth portraits looking like Ad Reinhardt paintings. Throwing away a couple of thousand copies meant less lifting for the circulation department, i.e., Jude Jade.

The second half of our five thousand press run, best read while wearing rubber gloves, was distributed by taxi to our four major outlets: the Museum of Modern Art lobby, the Anthology Film Archives lobby, Cinemabilia, and the Memory Shop (our second stills-for-space "advertiser"). Jonas Mekas, the intellectual guru of the Underground film movement, examined my first issue when we dropped off a few bundles at the Archives. "You have created a whole new look," he declared. Here, ironically, was a high priest of the avant-garde proclaiming Rita Hayworth stills "a whole new look." It was as funny as it was inevitable: For one hundred years, since Impressionism, the history of art had been the pursuit of the new; by 1970 it had all been done. Painting itself was dead, Conceptual Art reigned, galleries dealt in treatises, not objects. Indeed, this worship of newness for the sake of newness had overwhelmed the entire culture, from top to bottom, especially in America, the New World, where we were left with minimalist novels, wordless plays, street fashion. And Andy Warhol films: no script, no editing, no movement.

Our last stop was the Factory, where Andy and Paul had just returned from Paris. I couldn't wait for them to see the issue. Paul flipped through it quickly, making snap judgments and quips. He was particularly pleased with the illustration for an interview with Jean-Luc Godard, then in his High Maoist phase: Rita in a crisp white sailor dress. "I love it," he squealed. "It really shows how absurd the whole Commie Godard *La Chinoise* bullshit is."

Andy stood beside him. "Gee," he said, and "Oh." Did that mean he liked what I had done? He only came to life when Paul reached the inside back cover, where we had run Rita's "What Becomes a Legend Most" ad for Blackglama. "You got a Blackglama ad?" he asked excitedly. "Jude called to ask them for it," I told him, "but they didn't want to give it to us, so we ran it for free, just for fun." "Oh, I bet we get in trouble," was Andy's reply.

Crestfallen, back on the tenth floor, Glenn and Jude and I went back to stuffing issues into envelopes for our few hundred subscribers, mostly complimentary. Our biggest thrill came with the discovery that we actually had a paying subscriber in South Dakota. Before leaving at around seven, I went back down, as requested, to give Andy a few copies to take to dinner. "Gee, thanks," he said. "Uh, maybe I should take you to dinner. It's Jerome Hill and Charles Rydell. Uh, they're the new owners of *inter/VIEW*."

The new owners?

"Uh, I mean, they own part of it now. I think."

"But I'm not really dressed for dinner."

"Yes you are. Gee, that's such a pretty striped polo shirt. Did your mother get it for you at Saks?"

"Yes, but don't I need a tie and jacket?"

"Uh, it's at the Algonquin and they uh live there, so you can wear one of their jackets and uh ties."

In the taxi uptown Andy grilled me mercilessly about Glenn and Jude's marriage. "Did he marry her for her money? Oh, she married him for his money? They both have money? How great." He paused for a minute, then started in again. "Does he cheat on her? He must, right? I mean, he's so good-looking. And she's a beauty too. So they must have boyfriends and girlfriends, right? I mean, she could be a lesbian, couldn't she?"

I tried to keep him interested by telling him that Jude was jealous of Candy Darling.

"You mean Glenn has a problem!" Having a problem was Andy's code for gay. Sooner or later, he suspected everyone he ever met of having a problem. Or marrying for money.

"I didn't say Glenn has a problem," I said. "But he does have a crush on Fred Hughes. But so does Jude."

"What! They both want to go to bed with Fred?"

"They don't want to go to bed with him, they just admire the way he dresses. They think he has great style."

"Oh, c'mon. You're covering up for them. I'm going to tell Fred they have a crush on him."

We finally reached the Algonquin, thank God, and went upstairs to the suite that Jerome Hill, the elderly heir to the Northern Pacific railroad fortune, kept for the times he came into the city from his farm in Bridgehampton. We were greeted by Jerome's long-time best friend, actor Charles Rydell. Before Andy could introduce me, Charles bellowed, "I know who he is! And I've seen his first issue. I hate it. All those Rita Hayworth stills are so goddamn campy. Brigid brought it up to me this afternoon. She was going to stay for dinner until she heard *you* were coming, Andy." I hadn't met Brigid Berlin yet because she and Andy were fighting then. "Come in, Robert," bellowed Charles, "I don't really hate your first issue. It's just that Brigid was ranting and raving against all the campy faggots and she got me going. Let me introduce you to Jerome. He's the real genius in this room. Not the fruitcake you came in with." Then he bellowed out a giant laugh.

Andy laughed too, and whispered, "Isn't Charles nutty?" He meant it as a compliment.

Jerome Hill, I soon learned, was not only part owner of *inter/VIEW* and a patron of the arts but also an artist himself, who painted École de Riviera landscapes at his summer house near Cannes, and directed documentaries about growing up rich in the Middle West. Above all he was a gentleman, simple and kind. He loaned me a jacket and tie, and, even though the jacket was two sizes too large and the paisley tie clashed with my striped shirt, I began to feel more comfortable in this strange new world. Then I met the rest of Charles and Jerome's Algonquin round table.

First came Taylor Mead, another sometime Superstar who had fallen out with Andy. Like Jerome Hill, he was the scion of a major Middle Western industrial fortune, but a gentleman, simple and kind, he was not. He looked like a Bowery bum and talked like a Village waif. He spent most of dinner staring suspiciously across the table at me.

Then came Sylvia Miles, spouting the box-office figures of *Midnight*

Cowboy, the hit film of the moment, in which she played a hooker with a heart of brass. Andy resented the success of the John Schlesinger film. He said it was a "rip-off" of *Flesh,* and that Schlesinger wasted the Factory's time for days shooting the party scene and then cutting it to shreds.

"Andy," rasped Sylvia, "I loved Joe Dallesandro in *Trash.* I was thinking, we should really work together. In fact, I've got a script right here in my bag that would be perfect for the two of us. I'm carrying it around because I just came from a drink with my agent, Billy Barnes—you know Billy, he handles Tennessee—and he wanted to discuss it, and then when I told him I would be dining with you later in the evening he said . . ."

"Oh, uh, you should talk to Paul," said Andy.

Finally, with the third round of cocktails came Jerome Hill's nephew, Peter Beard. With his wife, Minnie Cushing, of the Newport Cushings. And their pet snake, all coiled up in Minnie's large straw bag. They were just back from their honeymoon in Kenya and looked as if they hadn't had time to change their clothes. Peter wasn't even wearing socks, and this was November in New York.

"Aren't they beautiful?" Andy whispered. "Don't you wish you could be that beautiful?"

"Oh, Andy," bellowed Charles, "stop acting like such a goddamn fucking faggot. No wonder Brigid can't stand to be around you anymore."

Andy said Charles was just being nutty, Sylvia said she had a great idea for a movie starring Charles and her, Peter passed around his latest photographs of dead elephants, Minnie petted her snake, Taylor stared suspiciously, and Jerome asked me if I'd like another drink. "Yes," I said. "A double vodka on the rocks, please."

I don't remember much more about that first dinner party, except that Andy started taking Polaroids of the eager Greek waiter and Charles proposed that we all—including the waiter and the snake—go back up to Jerome's suite, whereupon Sylvia announced that she had an early script meeting with a major director and needed me to escort her home. I gave Jerome his jacket back, but he insisted I keep the tie, which I still have, a souvenir of the beginning of a decade of dinner parties in hotels around the world. Somehow I hailed a taxi, dropped Sylvia off on Central Park South—"Tell Paul to call me about the script Andy wants him to read"—and made it home to my furnished room.

At precisely nine the next morning, Andy called. "You were a big hit with Charles and Jerome," he said. "Isn't Peter great-looking? And it's great the way he talks so fast. Except I never know what he's talking about. Do you think he has a problem?" Eventually he got to *inter/VIEW.* "It was pretty good," he said. "But maybe Charles was right. Doing just Rita does look too campy. But then Charles is the biggest camp of all, right? So I never know."

Had he read my Bertolucci interview, I asked.

"Oh, uh, a little bit. I think you should write less and tape record more. It's more modern."

It was a cutting remark, especially to a twenty-two-year-old who thought he was hot stuff because his increasingly frequent reviews in the *Village Voice* had prompted a letter from Seymour Peck, the Arts and Leisure editor of the *New York Times,* asking him to write for them. But I was too excited to feel hurt: This was the first time Andy had called me at home. And the first time he had expressed a direct opinion about the contents of my first issue. He added that he didn't really like Glenn O'Brien's ode to Rita Hayworth—"Poetry is so old-fashioned." He repeated all his questions about the O'Briens' sex life, then in the middle of an answer he panted, "Oh, oh, I've got to go now. Call me later if anything happens. Four-two-seven, six-four-two-oh." Then, without saying goodbye, he hung up.

It was a seductive performance. He had slighted my writing, but he had called me *and* given me his home number. That meant we were friends, didn't it? It meant that he liked me, right? It felt so cool, so hip, so *great* to turn to "W" in my phone book and write, "Andy, 427-6420, home." I couldn't wait to get to Columbia that morning to tell my film-school buddies: God called and gave me the number to heaven.

My second issue of *inter/VIEW,* in December 1970, contained a single tape-recorded interview (with Costa-Gavras and Yves Montand) among a dozen reviews and articles. And a poem. By me. It was an ode to Elvis Presley. I had put a fifties photograph of Elvis on the cover and old Elvis stills throughout the issue, capriciously decorating reviews of *Love Story, Ryan's Daughter,* and *Brewster McCloud,* as well as "Museum Film Trips" by Lil Piccard, a Dr. Ruth type who covered the artsy Jonas Mekas beat for us.

The Elvis issue was my idea, inspired by Andy's 1962 Elvis paintings. Paul had grudgingly granted his permission. He disapproved of the King of Rock 'n' Roll for overwhelming the melodious harmony of white American music with throbbing black African rhythm. I saw Elvis as an avatar of the new sexuality, and made that point visually by running a photo of Elvis in *Viva Las Vegas* opposite a photograph of Mick Jagger in *Gimme Shelter.* I theorized that many of the major sex symbols of the fifties and sixties, with their full sensual features, particularly lips, all looked alike: Marilyn, Elvis, Bardot, Jagger, Nureyev, even El Cordobes, the Spanish bullfighter. Paul had a different theory: "All the big sex symbols," he said, "have last names ending in "o"—Garbo, Harlow, Monroe, Brando, Dallesandro." The Rita and Elvis issues seemed to set off an avalanche of nostalgia for glamour in the media, fashion, and film. But, because *inter/VIEW* was Andy Warhol's magazine, nostalgia was perceived as new, the rejection of the avant-garde as the height of avant-garde. Of course, this was Paul's doing.

Paul really acted like the boss, issuing orders and opinions with an intensity and absoluteness that made it clear he *cared* what went into *inter/VIEW*. It was easy to assume that Andy, with his vague "Ohs" and "Maybes," didn't. Perhaps that's why I ignored his putdown of poetry, and his hint about taping instead of writing. I wrote a long piece for the Elvis issue on the ten best films of 1970, starting with *Trash* and ending with *Satyricon*.

Andy was much less vague and benevolent when Glenn and I brought the Elvis issue back from Chinatown to the Factory. As the previous time, he silently flipped through the issue, emitting the slightest of sighs and "Ohs"—until he reached my poem, entitled "From Memphis Tennessee Where Every Little Breeze Seems to Whisper Please Pop a Poem for Elvis." In front of everyone gathered around Paul's desk—Pat, Jed, Joe—he looked at me directly and said firmly, "No more poetry." Then he walked off without bothering to look at the rest of the issue.

He also stopped calling me at home. Since that first call in October, he had been calling me a few times a week, usually in the morning, always greeting me with, "Oh, hi. So what did you do last night?" Or, if it was night—he stayed home a lot then—"Gee, why aren't you out kicking up your heels?" I would call him too, but only if I had fresh gossip, not just about Glenn and Jude, but also about my new best friends, Charles Rydell, Peter Beard, and Sylvia Miles, or news from the back room at Max's Kansas City. I also told him a lot more than I should have about my own follies and affairs (usually one and the same thing). The fact is that Andy loved to hear gossip about *anyone,* from Candy Darling and Holly Woodlawn to my grandmother in Brooklyn. ("She moved out of your aunt's house?!? Gee.")

Whenever I called Andy, his first words were, "Oh, oh, can you hold on a minute." I knew he was quickly plugging in his telephone-taping device, but I put aside any worries I had about his recording because I sensed that if I objected there would be no more calls. Andy opened up on the phone in a way that he rarely did in person. In fact, he loved talking on the phone more than anyone I've ever known. He spent most of the morning on the phone, checking in with all the kids, and many evenings "watching TV over the phone," usually with Brigid, when they weren't fighting. And when he started keeping a diary with Pat Hackett later in the seventies, he did that over the phone as well.

Sometimes I'd run out of news to tell him and want to hang up, but he wouldn't let me, asking the same question over and over again, like a child, usually starting with *why.* ("Why did your grandmother move out?") Sometimes I had a lot to say and he'd suddenly grow uninterested, claiming that Jed was calling him or his mother needed him, or the bell was ringing, or he had to go out and was late—even though I knew by then that he didn't care about being on time. That fall I felt I was getting to know Andy on the phone, and I was upset when he stopped calling. Fortunately, Christmas soon rolled around and I was just as suddenly forgiven. Andy gave me a Cow poster and signed it, "To Robert C. with love." The next day he called to ask me where "the kids" went after the office party. "Did you stay out late? Did Glenn and Jude leave together? Was Fred there too?"

One morning in January 1971, I called Andy and told him that I had been robbed near the Columbia campus. This time, *I* taped the conversation—I had finally acquired a tape recorder and was trying it out.

BC: I was held up last night.

AW: Really . . . I mean, how did it happen?

BC: I was in a Volkswagen bus with some friends on 110th Street.

AW: 110th and Broadway?

BC: No, Amsterdam. It was outside school, we were waiting for this guy who forgot his gloves, and all of a sudden, these two black junkies were in the bus . . .

AW: They were in the bus!

BC: Yes, and they put a knife to this one guy's . . .

AW: They had knives!

BC: Yes, we didn't . . .

AW: Oh, I'm freaking out, it's just too scary. I mean, I don't feel like going out anymore, it's too crazy.

Until then, I had seen only Andy's insatiable curiosity, and a bit of his peevishness. Now, I felt the full force of his fear.

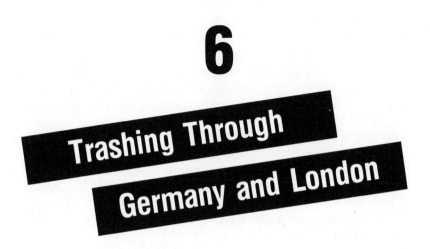

6

Trashing Through Germany and London

"Bob Cola—it's a great name, Bob."

"I don't want to change my name, Andy."

"You have to change your name if you want to be famous, Bob. It's too long now to be a famous name."

"I don't want to change my name, Andy."

"But Bob, I can't even say your name now. And you have to stop putting Robert on your articles, it's so old-fashioned."

"I like Robert better than Bob."

"Look, Bob, newspapers only have a certain amount of space to put people's names, right? And if your name is too long it doesn't fit in that space and then they use somebody else's name and that person becomes famous instead of you."

"Andy, I don't want to change my name. I want people to know that I'm Italian."

"But you're not Italian, Bob. You're American. And Cola does sound Italian. Doesn't it? Bob Cola—that sounds Italian."

"I hate Bob."

"Okay, so Robert Cola—it's a great name."

"It sounds like some soda."

"That's why it's a great name."

"So why don't I just change my name to Royal Crown Cola and get it over with?"

"Well, now *that* would be a really great name. But maybe they could sue you. Maybe it should be Royal Cola. Or Robert Crown Cola? Or Bob Royal Cola? That's a good name, isn't it, Jane?''

Andy and I were sitting in the back of a Mercedes limousine in Munich, with Jane Forth, Joe Dallesandro's co-star in *Trash*. It was the middle of February and we were on a one-week promotional tour of West Germany for *Trash,* with Paul, Fred, Jed, and Joe. I was still spelling my name Robert Colaciello. Jane yawned; Andy persisted: ''Bob has got to change his name, right, Jane?''

''He should make it Bob Kooky-Jello—that's what everybody at Max's calls him anyway,'' said Jane helpfully.

''Really, that's what everybody calls Bob?'' Andy laughed his little-boy laugh. ''That's funny, but it's too long too. Bob Cola is actually the best, right, Jane?''

''Oh, Andy, why don't you leave Bob alone? God, my tooth is killing me,'' she moaned.

''I told you what to do for a toothache,'' Andy said.

''No, what?''

''Well, first you find the biggest cock you can find, right?''

''Yeah.''

''And then . . .''

''Yeah.''

''And then you put it in your mouth where it hurts.''

''Yeah.''

''And, uh, you leave it there until the pain goes away.''

''I did that last night and it didn't work.''

''What?!? You didn't tell me you had sex last night!'' gasped Andy angrily.

''Oh, Andy, I'm just joking.''

''Was it with Fred? It had to be with Fred, right?''

''Andy, I was just joking. But my tooth really, really hurts. I've got to go to a dentist, Andy.''

''I told you what to do. There's no time to go to a dentist, Jane. We have to leave town for the next town right after lunch. What's the next town, Bob? Cologne?''

''Frankfurt. You already *were* in Cologne.''

''I was?''

This was my first trip with Andy Warhol and his entourage and I still *feel* it as if it were yesterday. When Andy invited me, I was filled with excitement, conceit, and anxiety. Germany with Andy—how cool, how hip. But would Jed Johnson finally recognize my existence? Would Fred Hughes finally stop looking down his nose at me (a nose that seemed as elegantly tailored as the Savile Row suit jackets he wore with his crisply creased jeans)? And what would I say to Joe Dallesandro (who never seemed to say anything at all)?

Actually, it was a typical Andy Warhol invitation, a last-minute quid-pro-quo paid for by somebody other than Andy. The night before they were leaving for Europe, Andy called me at home and apropos of nothing said, "Oh, you should ask Andrew Sarris if you could write an article about our trip to Germany and then maybe Paul can get the Germany distribution company to pay for your ticket. It would be good publicity for them."

Sarris referred me to Ross Wetzsteon, the *Village Voice* features editor, who liked the idea but was worried about conflict of interest. I assured him that I would be able to balance insider access with outsider distance. I'm not so sure I did in the published piece, entitled "King Andy's German Conquest":

> Andy Warhol and Company . . . began their German tour on February 17 in Cologne after a stop-over in London for the opening of the Warhol retrospective at the Tate Gallery. . . . I joined them two days later, just in time for the grand premiere of *Trash* in Munich. From there we travelled to Frankfurt, Berlin, back to Munich, back to London, back to New York. . . . All along the way, there seemed to be no limit to the number of photographers, autograph seekers, well-wishers, TV crews, interviews, press conferences, fancy luncheons, formal dinners, parties, posters, champagne toasts, handshakes, kisses, and smiles so that eventually everything—days and nights, food and drink, faces and places—merged into one frenetic whirlwind of fantasy and fame. . . . What amazed and bewildered me most about it all was how Andy, still considered something of a fraud, a freak, in this country, was greeted in Germany with an enthusiasm bordering on adoration, a respect verging on reverence.

Andy's progress through Germany was like that of a conquering kaiser. He was revered and praised as a prophet. In fact, Germany had been the best market for Andy's art since the sixties and would remain so all through the seventies and eighties. It was also the country most receptive to his movies: Three million Germans had paid to see *Flesh* the year before our tour; *Trash* would become 1971's second-highest-grossing film in West Germany, after *Easy Rider*. The Germans loved Andy's art and movies because they could read all kinds of grandiose philosophical statements into the basic neutrality of Andy's vision; they found his blank stare intellectually inspiring. And perhaps comforting; in 1971, before Fassbinder and the Neo-Expressionists, they seemed only too happy to lick up American Pop rather than deal with the depths of their own culture and history.

The night before I arrived in Munich, the *Abendzeitung* newspaper had named Paul Morrissey best director and Joe Dallesandro best actor of the year at a gala dinner. At the *Trash* première the following evening, hundreds of students rocked and pounded our limousine, the boys chanting "Andy!" the girls screaming "Joe!" Eleven hundred of Munich's moneyed and artistic elite filled the city's newest and largest movie house, the Luitpold, and went on to a champagne-and-rock bash at the giant Arriflex studios, where images of Joe and Jane were projected on the outside walls and inside the band played under a huge neon sign flashing the message "Welcome Andy Warhol's *Trash.*" Local socialites lined up behind local transvestites at Andy's table, waiting for his autograph. An *inter/VIEW* fan even asked me for *mine.* I staggered back to my grand hotel room at four or five in the morning and addressed a 3D postcard of an imperial German eagle to myself, so that I would know it all actually happened when I got back to my ungrand furnished room on West 105th Street.

Between premières and press conferences, we toured Bavaria's palaces and castles. As we made our way up the winding road to Neuschwanstein in horse-drawn sleighs, it started to snow. Andy pulled a plastic shower cap from the hotel out of his leather jacket pocket and put it on his head. "You look like an old Polish lady," said Jane, and he did. Andy grimaced, then laughed, and kept his see-through babushka on for the rest of the afternoon. He did take it off for the *Stern* photo shoot: They had arranged special permission to photograph Andy on Mad King Ludwig's gold throne. The reporter asked him what sitting there felt like. Andy, shivering amidst the stone and marble, tilted his head to one side as he thought. "I'd rather have heat than wealth," he said.

It was great copy, Andy's specialty. Yes, he usually let Paul Morrissey do the talking, but what little Andy said was always funny—and quotable. I was struck by his even temper, and the determined, good-humored manner in which he got through a week of fifteen-hour nonstop total-promo days in five German cities, with working stopovers in London before and after. "What are we doing today?" he'd ask the P.R. men from the distributors, Constantin-Film. "Oh, some interviews and lunch," they'd answer. "But I never learned how to eat and talk at the same time," he'd come back with, and then order one chocolate parfait after another and share them with the journalists. There was something so endearing about his gum chewing, his dishing and teasing, his gentle prodding, "Jane, how could you be exhausted? This is really *up there.*"

In the sixties, "up there" had been Andy's code for being high on speed, and later Brigid Berlin would tell me that Andy took one or two Obetrols, a mild amphetamine, every day until he died. In the seventies, he applied the phrase to anything or anyone he saw as important, glamorous, famous, or rich. When *Life* magazine featured Fred Hughes and Donna Jordan, another new Factory Superstar, posing in smart forties fashions, Andy sighed, "Ohhh, Donna's really up there now. You too, Fred." One night at dinner Andy insisted that I order quail—"Quail is really up there, Bob." When I said that I didn't like quail, he insisted that I order venison— "Venison is really up there, Bob." He himself ordered quail *and* venison, which he picked at, followed by *three* chocolate sundaes, which he slowly devoured, beaming and saying again, "This is really up there, isn't it, Bob?" At the same dinner he also insisted that I run back to the hotel between courses to get some issues of *inter/VIEW* for the Constantin-Film executives, who had promised to give them to a German magazine distributor. "You might not have this chance again, Bob," he told me, suddenly not so up there.

One afternoon we all set out for a quick tour of East Berlin, but at Checkpoint Charlie the East German border police seized a copy of French *Vogue* that Fred was carrying and Andy panicked. "This is too scary," he said. "You have to take me back to the hotel, Jed." Jed wanted to see East Berlin, but Andy persisted: "It's too scary. It's too scary."

After a press lunch in Frankfurt, Fred and Jed decided to check out the antique shops for Art Deco pieces, which Andy had started collecting as "props" for *L'Amour*. Jed was in a loden coat and dark corduroys, Fred in a sleek gray flannel suit. Andy looked out the window of his limousine wistfully, as they disappeared around a corner. "They're both such beauties," he said. "Fred really knows how to dress, and Jed does too. They look so good together, don't they?" His voice was full of adoration, and envy.

At the press conference in Berlin, Andy showed another side of his personality. As usual, there was a lavish buffet first, this one distinguished by a rising stallion carved out of butter. The Berlin press, particularly the female contingent, brushed aside Paul's hysterical connections between MGM stars past and Factory stars present, determined to get Andy to give them straight answers to tough questions. "Why do women always appear as vamps in your films?" "Why are all women stupid in your films?" Andy stuttered and fumbled, looked trapped and confused, and gave the same answer again and again: "Uh, we just make comedies. You're not supposed to take them seriously. It's just comedy."

His feminist inquisitors weren't satisfied. The most persistent and probing, a dramatic old lady in red, shouted out, "Mr. Warhol, was it also a comedy when you were shot by Valerie Solanis?"

Andy twisted his long, bony fingers in a tighter knot, and gave her a glare hard enough to kill. Then he averted his eyes and mumbled an unintelligible answer into his tie. The P.R. people announced there would be no further questions and the crowd began to disperse. I started toward Andy, to see if he was okay, but before I could reach him, he had made his way across the room to the dramatic old lady in red. When I caught up with him, I was stunned to hear him asking her for her address and telephone number. "Gee, if we ever come back to Germany to make a movie," he told her, "you have to be in it."

"Me in a movie," she shrieked, half in horror, half in delight. "But I'm not an actress."

"Ohhhh," said Andy, "but you're so good."

* * *

On our way back to New York, we stopped in London, where the Tate Gallery was giving a major Andy Warhol exhibit, and a major Andy Warhol scandal was brewing. The English film censor had seized a print of *Flesh* when it was shown in a London art theater the previous year, and had now forbidden the distribution of *Trash*. The English distributor thought it best for Andy and Paul to meet with the censor to petition him in person for an X rating, which would at least allow limited distribution. He was also not averse to turning *Trash* into a cause célèbre.

Half a dozen photographers were waiting for us at Heathrow, and they followed us on to the Ritz Hotel, where we gathered in the sitting room of Andy and Jed's suite, as we had in every German hotel, for tea. Andy always had Jed or Fred call room service for him: little chicken sandwiches with watercress and extra mayonnaise, butter cookies, petits fours, and chocolate sundaes. (This was before his first gallbladder attack, which would come a year later in Paris after he had eaten too much of another favorite, grilled foie gras.)

The highlight of our London visit was a reception in Andy's honor at the House of Commons. "We're really up there now, Bob," said Andy, as we entered the hallowed halls of Westminster. Our host was Sir Norman St. John-Stevas, a Conservative Member of Parliament (and later Minister of the Arts under Mrs. Thatcher), who had taken it upon himself to defend first *Flesh* and now *Trash* from the censor's bans and trims.

There were only two other guests, besides the eight of us: Edna O'Brien, the lusty and literary Irish Catholic novelist, and a Roman Catholic priest named Father Ryan, who both immediately hit it off with Joe Dallesandro. What did we talk about? Catholicism. I'm not being facetious. Sir Norman, like most English Catholics, was rather energetic and proud in his devotion to the Roman Church, and saw the censorship of *Trash* as typical puritanical Protestant behavior. Paul Morrissey, encouraging me to go on about Mary Magdalene, redemption, and Genet, pointed out, "We're all Catholic here today: Sir Norman, Father Ryan, Edna, Andy, Jane, Joe, me, you . . . Even Fred and he's from Texas where there aren't many Catholics. Only Jed isn't."

Andy was in high spirits, sipping sherry amidst the polished pomp of Sir Norman's paneled rooms. "Gee, now that we took *Trash* to Parliament," he remarked as we were leaving, "maybe we can take *L'Amour* to the White House."

It was all very "up there"—and so was I at that point. I loved the richness, the constant movement and attention, the feeling of being part of a family that I had chosen or, better yet, that had chosen me. It wasn't that I hated my own family; I have never stopped cherishing their approval and love. I just thought that they, and everyone they knew, were too normal, too average. Traveling through Europe with Andy and Jed, Paul and Joe, Fred and Jane, on the other hand, was exotic and too special. It was far away from Rockville Centre and I was thrilled to be there.

Of course, not everyone was as admiring of Andy Warhol as his newest camp follower was. A headline, "Laughing All the Way to the Trash Can," which appeared in the tabloid *Evening News* as we were departing from London for New York, came close to expressing how most people felt about Andy, his movies, and his art, on both sides of the Atlantic. *Trash,* by the way, was soon released in England, with only brief cuts of nudity; all the publicity, good and bad, helped make it a hit there.

By the end of that trip, I felt I knew Andy. I felt like his best friend, as a matter of fact. Each day he had spent a bit more time with me, joking and whispering asides to me instead of to Jane, or Jed, or Fred, or Paul. We were as complicit as co-conspirators. When we landed at Kennedy, Joe's family was waiting at the arrival gate: his brother Bobby, his wife Terry, and his three-month-old baby, Joe Jr., wearing blue jeans and jean jacket, just like his dad, and clutching a little American flag. Andy whispered in my ear, "Do you think the baby's body is as photogenic as his father's?"

My seduction by Andy Warhol—begun with the Polaroid session at Lincoln Center and the dinner at the Algonquin, then continued through a fall of increasingly frequent, increasingly personal phone calls—climaxed on the trip. There was never anything physical or romantic about our relationship; it's just that, like all those who worked closely with him, I fell in love. Not the way you do with a girl or a boy, but the way Catholics love God and nuns marry Jesus. There *was* something Catholic, something cabalistic and cultish, about the Factory and its Pope. Something, perhaps, that only those brought up in that magnificent, mysterious, and sometimes sick faith can really experience. In any case, I was more than seduced, I was converted.

I didn't even object when Andy signed my Tate catalogue, "To Bob Cola."

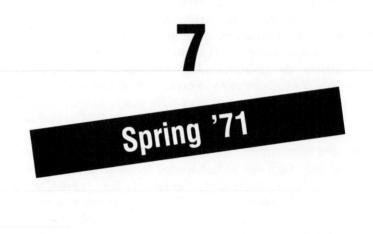

7

Spring '71

The spring of 1971 was a great time to be working at the Factory. *Andy Warhol's Trash* was still filling theaters in New York, California, and Germany; *Andy Warhol's L'Amour* was being edited; *Andy Warhol's Women in Revolt* was being shot. In April, *Andy Warhol's Pork,* the Factory's first play, opened downtown at La Mama. In May, a major Andy Warhol retrospective opened uptown at the Whitney. And *Interview,* "Andy Warhol's Film Magazine," with new, improved logo, layout, paper, and printing, raised its newsstand price from thirty-five cents to half a dollar.

The new, improved *Interview*—disencumbered of its ink-loving Chinese printer—also boasted its first cover photograph taken exclusively for us: a dreamy black-and-white portrait of *L'Amour* Superstars Jane Forth and Donna Jordan by Peter Beard. Since that off-center dinner at the Algonquin, I had spend a couple of boozy evenings with Peter. Half Tarzan, half Byron, he always carried his huge leather-bound diaries, collages of his photographs of dead elephants and famous models, with maxims, quotes, and phone numbers scrawled around, between, and sometimes over them, wherever he went. Andy was extremely fascinated by these diaries. Peter always wore the same ancient preppy rags. When he fought with his wife, Minnie, he'd sleep in his collapsing car in a deserted parking lot on Third Avenue and 13th Street, sometimes waking up to find a comatose bum or tired transvestite hooker passed out across his hood. One night, Peter and I sat up drinking gin out of plastic cups and talking, talking, talking. I remember his declaring at one point, "A beautiful woman is so much more beautiful when she's in danger—tied up to a tree or clinging to the edge of a cliff."

"Because you want to save her?"

"Because it's at the exact moment of loss that her beauty is most luminous."

That night he persuaded me to let him photograph Jane and Donna for the cover.

I couldn't wait to tell Andy the next day, but his reaction was wary to say the least. "Do we have to pay for the film?" Andy was always wary of Peter, perhaps because he too could fall under his spell—and Andy didn't like to be under anyone else's spell. "Peter is such a hustler," he would occasionally say, and accuse him of living off his uncle Jerome, or his wife.

As it turned out, Andy was right to be wary. The session was set up for a Saturday afternoon at the Factory, when it would be empty and quiet. Jane and Donna were looking forward to working with Peter, who had done fashion pages for Diana Vreeland and was known to be Veruschka's favorite photographer. Then the blood started to arrive. Cosmetic blood from Helena Rubinstein, addressed to Mr. Peter Beard, c/o Andy Warhol's Factory. That was Monday. On Tuesday, more blood arrived from Revlon, and on Wednesday a few more gallons from a theatrical makeup company. Andy was beside himself. "I told you Peter Beard is nuts!" he screeched. "Maybe you better call Peter up," said Paul, "and ask him what he plans to do with all this stuff." "Just throw it out and tell him it never got here," said Andy.

When I called Peter, with Andy and Paul hovering over me, he explained enthusiastically that he found the Rubinstein, the Revlon, and the theatrical blood all inadequate. "We might have to go with pig's blood," he said. "I think I've got a butcher who can send some down tomorrow."

"He's sending down some pig's blood tomorrow," I whispered to Paul and Andy.

Paul took the phone from me. "Hello, Peter, it's Paul. Andy was kind of wondering just what you plan to do with all this blood. Oh, you think Jane and Donna should be nude. And you're going to drip the blood all over them. Well, you know, we just had the place repainted not that long ago. And *L'Amour* is sort of an attempt to do something a little less nutty, you know, a kind of family comedy, like Lucy and Ethel go to Paris."

Peter sent the pig's blood anyway, and Andy ordered Vincent to throw it, and all the rest, out. On Saturday, Andy, Paul, Fred, Vincent, and Joe all turned up at the Factory to make sure Peter didn't try anything funny. "He better not try to throw any blood at me," muttered Donna. "I *hate* blood," moaned Jane. And Andy, who had always encouraged me to drink more whenever I went to a dinner or party with him, said, "This is all because Bob got drunk with Peter."

In the end, Peter acquiesced. No nudity. No blood.

Not every day at *Interview* was like that. There were glamorous moments: I interviewed actress Barbara Loden at home and was asked to stay for dinner with her husband, director Elia Kazan, who told me about making

East of Eden with James Dean. On another assignment, out of sheer nerves, I picked a fight with Jack Nicholson about actors versus stars. I was just spouting the Factory party line, of course, but Jack was amazingly good-natured about it—perhaps because he was both an actor and a star.

But mostly, getting out *Interview* was hard work. Though my title was Managing Editor and Art Director, I spent most of my time sizing photographs and proofreading copy. I didn't cut copy much, because we had such large pages to fill, and anyway editing wasn't really Warholian.

Helped immeasurably by Glenn and Jude, I also assigned stories, set up interviews, did interviews, transcribed tapes, opened mail, answered the phone—we didn't have a receptionist or a secretary, and sending something by messenger was considered a major expense, requiring Factory approval. We did everything but run the printing presses, and really learned how to put a magazine together piece by piece—an invaluable experience I realize now, and not one that we would have had at a large company with its compartmentalized jobs.

Then, my least favorite chore was paste-up. Long sheets of typeset copy were measured, usually by counting lines; cut with razor blades; brushed with paste across the back; then pasted down on the layout board, which was then photo-offset at the printers. The worst part was stripping in corrections—cutting, gluing, and placing single lines of copy, or even individual words, over mistakes—because the glue would get on my hands and the bits of type would smudge or fall into place crookedly and have to be picked off with the corner of a razor blade, then be reset, recut, reglued, and replaced.

One night Glenn and Jude and I were doing paste-up at *Rock* magazine (we had switched from *Other Scenes* when John Wilcock's share was bought out by Jerome Hill and Charles Rydell). It was getting very late; the layout boards were being picked up by the printer at nine the next morning. We misplaced a piece of type, the runover of some interview or other. It couldn't be reset because *Rock*'s typesetting crew had long since gone home. We searched and searched for this itsy-bitsy piece of paper, on the layout tables, under the layout tables, on the bulletin boards above the layout tables, in drawers and files and piles and pockets. I was cursing Glenn and he was cursing me and we both were cursing Andy for not spending more money on the magazine so that we could be real editors, lunching with writers, instead of goddamn manual laborers, slaving past midnight.

Finally, there was only one place left to search—the trash can, which was very large and filled with thousands of bits of glue-covered paper, not to mention the remains of sandwiches, pizza, and endless cups of coffee. I refused to do it and ordered Glenn to since he had lost the crucial piece in the first place. He refused and ordered Jude to do it. And she did. She turned the trash can over and, crying, got down on her hands and knees and started sifting through the garbage. Eventually, I calmed down and started to help. But Glenn wouldn't. He couldn't admit that it was his fault. Miraculously,

Jude found the missing piece and saved us all the embarrassment of running an interview without an end. Later, when we regaled Andy with the story as a joke (and a reproach) at yet another Algonquin dinner, he said that we should have forgotten about the missing piece. "Why do you have to have an end?" he asked.

Andy made it up to us in other ways. Every so often he would give Jude some Bakelite bracelets or pins—not as many as he gave Jane and Donna, but enough to make her feel wanted. These plastic Art Deco trinkets cost next to nothing back then, but they were just coming into fashion and Jude loved showing them off to our Columbia friends. Andy, of course, was tax-deducting them as "costumes" for *L'Amour*.

Andy gave Glenn a big thrill when he asked him to pose for the cover of the Rolling Stones' new album, *Sticky Fingers*. It was a crotch shot of a guy in jeans, with a zipper that unzipped to reveal another crotch shot of a guy in Jockey shorts. Glenn wasn't the only one Andy photographed for this project. He also shot Jed's twin brother, Jay, and his best friend, Cory Tippin, who did the makeup for *L'Amour*. When the album came out, Glenn was certain that it was he on the inside and Jay Johnson on the outside, but Andy would never say exactly whose crotch he had immortalized.

Still, Andy's attentions to me caused problems with Glenn and Jude. "We work just as hard as you do," Jude told me one night at their place, "but Andy hardly ever takes us out with him. It's just not fair." When I repeated this to Andy, he said, "I never know what to say to Glenn and then he just sits there. And Jude's too pushy. I mean, she's really beautiful and, uh, maybe we should use her in a movie. But she's not as funny as Jane or Donna. They just have that magic."

Unlike Glenn, I never just sat there. Maybe it goes back to my mother's making my sisters and me tell her our days, when we sat around the kitchen table having cookies and milk after school. She also encouraged us to mimic our teachers and other students, anything to make her laugh after a day of housework and part-time selling at Saks. I tried to oblige—perhaps that was the key to my relationship with Andy. I was brought up to respect—my parents' favorite word—authority, and I did. Andy was tape recording all the time now that Sony had come out with a smaller model, and I let him tape record in person, just as I had over the phone. He was particularly fascinated with my ability to recall conversations word for word—again, my mother's training. "Gee," he would say, "you remember everything everyone said. I should take you everywhere. If my tape recorder broke, you'd remember everything."

Unlike Jude, I never asked Andy to take me anywhere. I never asked Andy for anything. Andy didn't like people who asked him for anything, unless it was a fan asking for an autograph. He liked to give things— invitations, trips, presents of prints or little paintings—when he wanted to give them, and only then. And hold out the promise of better things to come. In his campaign to get me to start selling ads he would sometimes say, "If you work really hard, and make *Interview* make money, you can uh own part of it someday," cupping his mouth with his hand for that last part, one of his tricks.

One afternoon that busy, hopeful spring, Andy asked me if I'd like to accompany him uptown to the Whitney Museum, where his retrospective was being hung by David Whitney (a close friend of Philip Johnson and no relation to the museum Whitneys), whom artists like Jasper Johns, Cy Twombly, and Andy always consulted on the hanging of their shows. The Whitney opening was just a few days off, but Andy was still undecided about whether to cover the walls of the museum with his Cow wallpaper or not. He turned to me and said, "What do you think?" What did *I* think? As my head swelled, I found myself saying, "I think you should use the wallpaper. Your Marilyns and Campbell's Soupcans and Electric Chairs will really look different on that background. They'll look baroque."

"Baroque," repeated Andy. "Nobody's called my work baroque before. Maybe we should use the wallpaper, David. Shouldn't we?" Of course, I thought I was playing the pivotal role in a momentous decision in the history of art. Later I found out that Andy had also asked Philip Johnson, and Henry Geldzahler, and David Bourdon, the art critic for *Life,* and Fred and Jed and Vincent and Pat, and Jane and Donna and Jackie Curtis, whether he should use the Cow wallpaper or not. That's how Andy worked. He would ask almost everyone he met what he should do, what he should paint, what colors he should use, what film he should do, what Superstars he should use, as if he were taking a poll, and then he would do exactly what *he* wanted to do. This left an awful lot of people thinking that they had given an idea to Andy Warhol. But when Andy really was getting an idea from somebody else, he never let on. He never said, "That's what I should do." He just did it, and denied everything forever more.

After our meeting at the Whitney, Andy took me for hot fudge sundaes at the Schrafft's on Madison Avenue and East 77th Street, which he said was his favorite restaurant. I remembered the great TV commercial he did for Schrafft's in 1969: just a sundae revolving slowly under a rainbow of colored light gels, which made it look mouth-wateringly glamorous and Pop, as if Schrafft's had discovered LSD. "That was so easy to do," Andy told me. "And we got paid so much for doing it. I wish we could do more commercials. I have a good idea, Bob. When you go to the agencies to sell ads for *Interview,* you should tell them we'll design the ads. In the beginning we could do it for free, and then when we get bigger we could charge them extra."

"But Andy," I pleaded, "I don't have enough time to sell ads on top of everything else."

"Yes, you do. You could be selling an ad right now, instead of sitting here at Schrafft's. And you'd be so good at it, because you talk so much, and your mother's a saleslady."

"But Andy, first we have to make the magazine better and get the circulation up. It's so small that most advertisers aren't interested."

"No, it's not. Tell them it's bigger."

"I just don't have the time."

"Then tell Jude to do it." He licked his spoon like a little boy. "If she slept with those guys at the ad agencies, they wouldn't care how small the circulation is."

He was only half joking. Soon Jude Jade was selling ads for *Interview*. Or trying to anyway, *without* "paying the price."

Over the years, I sometimes wondered if Andy ever cared about *Interview*'s circulation at all. He knew, instinctively and because he would ask me to figure out the cost-per-copy every time we upgraded printers or paper quality, that magazines were lucky to break even on circulation, no matter how large. What brought in the money was ads, and from 1970 until the month he died those were the first things Andy counted every month when a new issue of *Interview* arrived at the Factory. But he refused to make the connection between increasing circulation and increasing advertising. For him, selling ads meant sending a pretty girl to the straight clients and a pretty boy to the gay clients, entertaining them at the right restaurants, getting them into the right discos, introducing them to our famous friends, paying the price one way or another. Eventually, I came to see that he was right, to a point, and helped him develop the technique of entertainment-as-selling (and selling-as-entertainment) into a minor Warhol art form. And, by the end of the seventies, *Interview* started turning a profit from its advertising.

Until then, Andy's strategy was perfectly simple and perfectly self-serving: "If we're not making money on the magazine, then we may as well use it to push the other businesses." Other businesses meant art and movies—mainly movies. What he, and Paul, wanted was a movie financed by a major studio. Andy also hoped to do portraits of the stars we interviewed, or at least more album jackets.

Since he had announced his "retirement" from painting at a show in Paris in 1965, Andy saw his art as little more than the means to make money for his movie business. Thus, he began doing commissioned portraits of collectors, politicians, and art dealers, and recycling his more successful images, like the Campbell's Soupcan and Marilyn Monroe, into lucrative editions of prints. In 1966, at the Leo Castelli Gallery in New York, Andy bid adieu to art again with a show of Silver Pillows, filled with helium, which were meant to "fly away." And when he moved from the original silver-foiled Factory of East 47th Street to 33 Union Square West, no place was set aside to paint and no Warhol paintings hung on Warhol's walls. The man who had wanted to be Matisse now wanted to be Louis B. Mayer.

Indeed, the second Factory was a little studio hoping to happen. The letterhead said "Andy Warhol Film, Inc." and the first thing visitors saw when they came through the bulletproof door was that stuffed Great Dane. At the small Art Deco receptionist's desk, where I first saw Andy eating lunch, sat Vincent Fremont, who always seemed to be reading a book about David O. Selznick. Behind that was a small open vestibule decorated with oversize framed Technicolor photographs of Gene Tierney, Norma Shearer, and Dolores Del Rio, and a John Chamberlain car-crash sculpture, the only piece of art in the entire Factory. On the left was a projection booth and on the right a narrow office where Pat Hackett typed Andy's tapes.

At the end of this vestibule, a pair of ceiling-height doors opened onto the screening room, twenty feet by forty feet, painted chocolate brown. A couple of old velvet-covered couches faced a large silver movie screen, and behind that was a giant Campbell's Soupcan made of cardboard—left over from a sixties *Esquire* cover. There was also the largest TV available in those days, a very good stereo system, and a baby grand piano, presumably for composing movie scores. And a set of twelve dining chairs by Emile-Jacques Ruhlmann, the master of French Art Deco, whose work Andy and Fred were collecting then—Yves Saint Laurent and Karl Lagerfeld were collecting it too. In fact, Fred followed their lead, and as was often the case, Andy followed Fred's. Prices for Art Deco were still incredibly low and Andy was tax-deducting it all as *L'Amour* sets and props anyway. Off to the right was a claustrophobic cubicle where Jed Johnson spent most of 1971 editing *L'Amour* on a Moviola. Further back, near the freight elevator, were a bathroom, painted black, and a locked storage room, where Billy Name had been "living" since Andy was shot—he only came out after midnight. He finally left for good in 1971, and Andy had Vincent change the lock just in case Billy decided to come back.

In the front room, opposite Paul's big black desk was another one just like it, which had been Gerard Malanga's and was now Fred Hughes's. But while Paul had Superstar portraits hanging behind his desk, Fred hung Jean Dupas posters advertising furniture and fashion shows from Paris in the twenties. For Fred, making movies was mostly about sets and costumes, an approach Andy appreciated because it meant his growing collections of chairs, old clothes, and jewelry could be tax-deducted. For Paul, movies were first and foremost about stars—his casting-agent approach also appealed to Andy, because it meant he had a reason to seek out beauties.

Andy didn't have a desk of his own. He liked to use everyone else's and go through whatever they had on it. He'd open the mail at Vincent's desk, pay his bills at Pat's, talk on the telephone at Paul's or Fred's. Between their desks and Vincent's sat the spectacular desk Fred had bought Andy in Paris, made of shiny brass with a black marble top, supposedly from the

Normandie. Andy said it was "too fancy," and "I don't need a desk." I thought he was being modest, but it was also his way of telling all the aspiring moguls who worked for him that he was the real head of this mini-MGM in the making and that all the desks were his.

Tucked into a corner behind Fred's desk was the Factory's new video equipment. Just as Andy had bought a movie camera and started making movies, then a tape recorder and turned out *a,* a novel, he now bought a videocam and monitor and announced that he was going into the TV business. Toward that end, he hired Michael Netter, my friend from Georgetown and Nina Needlepoint, who had a bit of experience with video and, just as important, was willing to work for Factory wages. Michael would come by every afternoon and shoot whatever was going on.

Paul saw the video equipment as a way of trying out ideas for movies. After the commercial success of *Trash,* both Constantin-Film and Cinema Five (which distributed it in the U.S.) were eager to finance the next Factory movie—though they weren't wild about *Women in Revolt,* the transvestite Women's Lib takeoff Paul was shooting on weekends in New York that spring. Nor were they crazy over his idea for a Civil War comedy starring Allen Ginsberg as Walt Whitman and Joe Dallesandro as the wounded soldier he nurses back to health. Cinema Five thought it was time for something really commercial.

Andy and Paul were desperate to come up with an idea. So Andy taped everyone who would let him and badgered Pat to figure out a way to transform the transcripts into movie scripts. Paul bought Vincent more Hollywood biographies, hoping he'd find the seed of a script in one of them. Whenever an *Interview* writer came by, Paul and Andy would ask if *they* had any ideas for movies. "We've got some people in Hollywood interested," Paul would say. "Oh, oh, we'll give you a percentage if they use your script," Andy would add.

I decided to write a film treatment in lieu of a master's thesis, which Columbia accepted but the Factory didn't. It was a comedy set in a Mafia nightclub in the thirties, with leading roles for Joe Dallesandro to please Paul, Candy Darling to please Andy, and Sylvia Miles to keep her quiet. I also wrote a big part for Rod Steiger, because Andy and Paul said he told them at a party how much he admired their movies. They also rejected another proposal of mine—a musical comedy based on the life of Evita Perón, with Candy Darling in the title role and a song called "There's a Charming Dictator Living South of the Equator," which Paul found funny but Andy hated. "Nobody cares about South America except you, Bob," he said.

I was momentarily disappointed, but all in all I had no complaints about working at the Factory that spring. After my graduation from Columbia in June, I told Andy and Paul that I was available "full time" and given a raise—to $90 a week. I moved to a $275-a-month studio apartment on East

76th Street, opposite the Carlyle Hotel. What's more, on April 22, 1971, I signed a contract with Dutton to write a book on Andy Warhol's films. The $6,000 advance, with one-third paid on signing, seemed enormous.

Paul Morrissey had really encouraged me to write the book. I still have the letter of recommendation he wrote for me, dated August 31, 1970. Paul helped me get an agent, Ellen Levine at Curtis Brown, and let me see all the sixties films, some at the Factory and some at Anthology Film Archives, where Jonas Mekas would often join me as I sat transfixed through hour upon hour of *Empire* and *Eat* and *Kiss*. This was a bigger favor than it seems, because in many cases there weren't any dupe prints, only originals, which are risky to project. And he let me do this before I had the Dutton deal.

Andy, on the other hand, told me I was wasting my time, that those films were too boring, that instead of writing a book I should be out selling ads—"That's the way to become rich, Bob." When I persisted no matter what he said during our almost daily phone calls, he'd say, "Oh, I have a great idea. You should do your whole book on the phone. Just tape record it. It would be so modern."

"I think the publisher wants more criticism, Andy."

"Oh, really. But criticism is so old-fashioned. Why don't you just put in a lot of gossip about Glenn and Jude."

"I think they want a lot of gossip about you, Andy."

"Oh, really. So what film did you see today."

"*Bike Boy.* I thought it was good."

"It was good. But it was a mistake. We used Valerie. That was a mistake."

It was the first time Andy had mentioned the name of Valerie Solanis to me but he quickly changed the subject. I couldn't help but feel sorry for him.

Actually, I felt sorry for Andy a lot. He looked so pale and frail, and afraid. Whenever I'd walk someplace with Andy, and he'd see someone coming toward us, a bum or a bag lady or just a leftover hippie, suddenly he'd dart into a store, any store, saying, "He looked all doped up, didn't he? Let's just stand in here until he goes by." Often I'd wonder just who he was talking about.

Feeling sorry for him was certainly part of the reason why I put up with his goading, and teasing, and coldness, with the low salary and the hard work. That, and the glamour, the proximity to fame and fortune. In some ways being close to fame and fortune is more fun, and certainly easier, than having it yourself.

Friday, April 30, 1971, was a particularly exciting day for me. I was at home packing for my move when Andy called and asked if I would take Candy Darling to the opening of his Whitney retrospective that night. "She lives right around the corner from the museum," he said. "And I already have too many people in my car—they're all calling, Viva, Ultra, Brigid,

Jackie, Holly. They all want to come with me and I'm just going crazy. It's too scary. I wish I could stay home."

Candy Darling was the most glamorous date I could have for Andy's big opening. She—I was hip enough never to call a transvestite "he"—was then my favorite Superstar, witty, striking, sweet, the Kim Novak of the Factory. I put on my most Pop shirt, white printed with red lipstick kisses, and taxied over to the East 77th Street floor-through that Candy shared with a lawyer and a garment center heir who kept her in coats and dresses. Candy was late. Fortunately, Andy was later, so we waited outside the museum for him to arrive, as Candy wanted to make her entrance with him. So did Ultra Violet, who had arrived on her own. Ultra, whose ultra-brief Factory heyday had been in the sixties, and Candy, who was the lead in the current Factory production, *Women in Revolt,* stood there on Madison Avenue trading catty remarks and dirty looks, two Superstars waiting for the studio boss.

Finally, Andy's long black limousine pulled up, and Ultra and Candy and I rushed to greet it, three steps ahead of the paparazzi. The door opened and out popped Andy—and Viva, Brigid, Nico, Holly, Jackie, Jane, Donna, and Andrea "Whips" Feldman, all jockeying to get closest to Andy. Ultra, in a dress so sheer that you could see her nipples and pubic hair, grabbed one of Andy's arms, and Andrea, in a cowboy hat and a belt with a big rhinestone heart buckle, grabbed the other. Andy's silvery wig looked different. It was longer than usual on one side and draped partially over one eye, à la Veronica Lake. Later I learned that he had new wigs with slightly different styles made up regularly. He was carrying his Brownie's bag in one hand and his Sony in the other. And he didn't look scared at all as he flashed a boyish smile for the three television crews, the score of photographers, the dozens of reporters, and the four thousand guests. He looked very, very happy.

Andy had good reason to be happy. The Whitney show, said the press release, was the last stop of "a triumphal four-star tour of world art capitals." It had originated in May 1970, at the Pasadena Museum of Art in California, and traveled to the Museum of Contemporary Art in Chicago; the Stedelijk Museum in Eindhoven, the Netherlands; the Musée d'Art Moderne in Paris; and the Tate in London, where it broke all attendance records. Andy loved the way his Cow wallpaper—a dumb magenta cow's head repeated in vertical rows on an insipid yellow background—made the Soupcans and Brillo Boxes, the Jackies and Marilyns, the Car Crashes and Electric Chairs—look different than they had in all the other museums. "We fixed it like this so people could catch the show in a minute and leave," he told *New York Times* reporter Grace Glueck, who knew that he was joking. And he was so thrilled with the opening-night mob scene, with the flashbulbs and microphones and TV cameras, that he told art critic Barbara Rose he had changed his name to John Doe. "I'm too famous," he said. "Legally?" she asked, taking him seriously. "Uh-huh," said Andy.

Rose, who wrote for *Vogue, New York,* and various art magazines, took everything seriously. Too seriously, thought Andy, who loved to put her on when he saw her and put her down when she wasn't around. "She pretends she's such an intellectual," he often said, "and that her ex-husband Frank Stella is such an intellectual artist, when everybody knows that she just writes those great things about him so all the paintings he gave her will be worth more."

But this time she got him. Her review in *New York* magazine began:

> Can a boy from a poor Czech mining family in Pennsylvania find happiness in life as the wealthy and fabulous queen of the New York art and fashion world? Apparently so, if the boy's name is Andy Warhola, alias Andy Warhol, alias—as of the opening of his current retrospective at the Whitney Museum, when he legally changed his name—John Doe.

"She called me a queen!" gasped Andy when he read it. "I hate Barbara Rose. I really do." It was the first time I had seen him upset by anything written about him. He usually laughed off his bad press, or commented favorably on how much space they had given him. He was so mad that he dismissed the rest of Rose's three-page review when in fact she went on to confirm his importance:

> As usual, Andy's timing is flawless. . . . He can afford to change his name to John Doe and still be recognized as Andy Warhol on any street corner in the Western world. His genius for manipulating the media is only part of the reason Andy is probably the most famous artist in the twentieth century. . . . Andy Warhol creates fashion, and others follow him. Merging life and art more closely than any Dadaist or Surrealist could imagine, Andy is the *Zeitgeist* incarnate. The images he leaves will be the permanent record of America in the sixties: mechanical, vulgar, violent, commercial, deadly and destructive.
>
> Dreaming the American dream, Andy not only creates but lives the American myths. . . . Last week at the Whitney, he was flanked by superstars, old and new, dressed in bizarre thrift-shop drag and enough wigs to prove that the decadence of a society can be measured by how many people are wearing other people's hair. Thronged by the press and gaping public, at last the center of attraction at his own canonization, he is the most important art object on view. For to talk of Warhol's art without talking of his life is to miss the point of his endeavor to make them literally identical. Andy's middle name should be *reductio ad absurdum.* In all matters, including the art-life dialogue, he has taken the most extreme position. While not too difficult to occupy, perhaps, the extreme position takes a genius to find these days. But Andy does it again, turning the Whitney into a boutique covered with wallpaper of cows—the stock subject of popular academic middle-class genre painting. Of course, the museum has been a boutique for a long time, and people have been treating

paintings like wallpaper even longer, but Andy spells it out with his usual cruel clarity. Stripping our cultural illusions from us, he reveals the hypocritical reality beneath the surface pretensions.

Warhol is a social phenomenon of major importance as well as an artist of real consequence, for the paintings themselves survive even Andy's own subversive tactics and remain fresh and brilliant. . . . Someday these portraits will appear as grotesque as Goya's paintings of the Spanish court. Like Goya, Warhol is a reporter, not a judge, for it was not obvious to Goya's contemporaries that they were deformed either.

"She really thinks we're still back in the sixties, with all the freaks and hippies, doesn't she?" said Paul. "Andy's portraits are more like Sargent's or Boldini's than Goya's." said Fred. "I hate her," said Andy.

Andy got his revenge a few months later when Barbara Rose interviewed him for a documentary by Lana Jokel. The interview was done at Philip Johnson's house on East 53rd Street, with the famous old architect sitting silent as an owl between Barbara and Andy, who played cat and mouse. She never caught him, never came close.

He mocked her, and everything she believed in, mercilessly. He told her he liked abstract painting, which she favored, better than "mechanical" paintings, which is what she called his art. "You can be messy and drip paint all over the place," he said, straight-faced. "It's easier. I like it better now."

She asked him what he thought of Jasper Johns, idol of the art establishment, of which Barbara Rose was, and is, a pillar. "I think he's great," said Andy.

"Why?" Barbara Rose always asked why.

"Ohhh, uh, he makes such great lunches." This brought a little gasp from the otherwise imperturbable Philip Johnson, who had arranged for Johns to invite Andy to lunch for the first time not long before. Andy smiled at the camera and added, "He does this great thing with chicken. He puts parsley *inside* the chicken."

She persisted, asking him what he thought of fame.

"Oh, it's just being at the right place or being at the wrong place. Being at the right time or the wrong time. Being in, or being out."

"How do you know if you are?"

"I don't think anybody ever knows," Andy answered thoughtfully.

"Just history," said Barbara.

Andy looked at her incredulously. "Oh, you don't believe in *history,* do you Bar-ba-ra?"

Andy was much less bothered by John Canaday's review in the *New York Times.* "Manipulation is the key to the Warhol story," wrote Canaday. "What does that mean, Bob?" said Andy, pressing the newspaper against his pink-framed welfare glasses.

8

Guns and Prayers

"Andy! How could you? You promised me you wouldn't use those tapes without asking me first!" Brigid Berlin, aka Brigid Polk, came off the elevator screaming. Andy was sitting at Vincent's desk, opening the mail. He barely looked up. Brigid kept screaming, "You promised me, Andy! How could you do this to me? My mother's been on the phone driving me crazy since seven o'clock this morning! Since the goddamn review came out in the goddamn *New York Times!*"

"We're just making you more famous, Brigid," was Andy's reply, delivered with a maddening nonchalance.

"You're nothing but a fucking faggot! You don't care about anyone but yourself! And your goddamn fucking fame! And your fucking Factory! And your fucking money!" Brigid was practically spitting in Andy's face.

He suddenly jumped up and dashed into Pat's office, closing the door behind him. Fred stood there saying, "Brigid, calm down. You know this is just the way to alienate Andy even more." Brigid started crying.

It was the middle of May 1971, and *Andy Warhol's Pork* had opened the night before at La Mama, the most important experimental theater in New York. A few days earlier, Brigid had been pushing to get into the photos as Andy arrived at the Whitney Museum. Now she was muttering through her tears that she sometimes wished Valerie Solanis had finished Andy off.

Andy Warhol's Pork was based on tape-recorded telephone conversations between Andy and Brigid about the Berlin family's private life. Polk was a name made up for Andy's films, a weak pun on the fact that Brigid spent most of the late sixties "poking" needles full of amphetamine into herself and her friends. Brigid's mother, Honey Berlin, was a strong-willed Fifth Avenue socialite who counted the Duchess of Windsor among her closest friends, and who expected Brigid to live by the Duchess's motto, "You can never be too rich or too thin." Instead, Brigid married a window dresser named John Parker and spent her $250,000 trust fund helicoptering his friends out to Fire Island Pines for lavishly wild parties. And ate.

From childhood Brigid had had a weight problem. Honey had diet pills prescribed for her, thus hooking her on amphetamines. Strangely enough, when Brigid was high on speed, she ate even more and grew fatter and fatter. Through Parker, Brigid's original "staple-gun queen," she met Andy in the early sixties. Much to Honey's horror, Andy put Brigid in his movies, most notably *The Chelsea Girls,* in which she played a character called "The Duchess," who is seen ordering drugs over the phone, torturing her lesbian lover, and poking herself right through her jeans. Honey was not amused when her lady friends called to tell her all about it, nor was she pleased when Brigid tweezered rubies out of the jeweled box the Shah of Iran had bestowed on her father, the Hearst chief. Or when she sold thank-you notes from former Presidents Coolidge and Hoover for weekends at the Berlin summer compound in Murray's Bay on the St. Lawrence River for $25 worth of speed. The Berlins were also on intimate terms with the Nixons, and this was just not the kind of thing one could talk about with Dick and Pat. Why, dear God, why, wondered Honey, couldn't Brigid and her older sister, Richie, who was no Junior Leaguer either, be more like Julie and Tricia?

Every so often, when it all became too embarrassing, Honey would call Brigid at her room in the George Washington Hotel, a glorified flophouse near Gramercy Park, and berate her in the harshest and most hysterical terms. Honey was usually tipsy and Brigid was usually high, and their conversations were straight out of Edward Albee. In the middle sixties, Brigid began taping the calls. Then she thought it was funny to call Andy and play him the tapes. Andy thought it was even funnier to tape the tapes. He was home in bed recuperating from the shooting then, so he had plenty of time to listen. And plenty of need to laugh, especially at someone else's problems.

Andy's tapes of Brigid's tapes became part of *Andy Warhol's Pork.* Of course, they were edited and put into play form by Pat Hackett, and then Anthony Ingrassia, a talented playwright and director associated with La Mama and the even more avant-garde Theatre of the Ridiculous, transformed them further in the staging. And the names were changed—the Berlins became the Porks. Otherwise, it was hard to separate fiction from reality: an overweight, oversexed, overcreative High-Society girl spends most of the time fighting with her overdressed, overimpressed, overwrought High-Society mother, shooting speed into her ass without even bothering to pull down her jeans, and talking on the phone with B. Marlow, the famous painter and filmmaker, who tapes the calls while sitting in a wheelchair.

Was it any wonder then that Brigid was screaming and crying. "Mother warned me about you" was her parting shot, as she left in defeat and despair. It was probably the first time in her life that she admitted her mother was right about something. Andy was unrepentant after she left. "Brigid's crazy," he said. "She must have taken too much speed."

"Maybe you should give her a little money," suggested Fred.

"How can we?" moaned Andy. "We're not making any money on the play." Most likely he wasn't, though *Pork* moved to London that August, where it ran for a year at the Roundhouse and inspired David Bowie to write his song "Andy Warhol Superstar"—which Andy hated. In fact, he hated it so much he always made us change stations when it came on the radio. "Can he use my name without permission?" he would ask. "Shouldn't he pay us royalties?"

If Andy refused to see the double standard, I was totally blind to it. I found the whole Brigid scene funny. I didn't like Brigid then in any case, because whenever she came to the Factory she'd ignore me or give me a dirty look. I imagined I was the enfant terrible of film criticism, managing editor and art director *extraordinaire*. And I found Brigid, in her huge men's polo shirts and bursting-at-the-seams jeans, pathetic, a has-been and an addict. Especially when she'd turn up with a pocketful of cash receipts that she'd picked up off the floor of the corner deli, where she went to binge out on chocolate cupcakes and Hostess Twinkies. Andy would pay her twenty-five cents for each receipt, and claim them as tax deductions under "Home entertainment supplies." And Brigid would waddle off with twenty or thirty dollars for another fix of speed and sugar.

Like all of Andy's "kids"—Fred, Jed, Pat, Vincent—I saw the old Superstars as annoying bores, always looking for a handout. And they saw us as usurpers, who had come between them and Andy. But we were only doing our jobs—Andy wanted to keep them as far away as possible, for fear that one of them would turn into another Valerie Solanis.

And yet he would sometimes look at us all with our short hair and clean clothes, and sigh, "Gee, it was so much more creative in the sixties. Do you think crazy people really are more imaginative? Ondine and all those speed queens used to have an idea a minute. An idea a second." He'd snap his fingers to make his point and add, "You've got to get more ideas, Bob."

There was also a scene with Viva after the opening of *Pork*. Andy taped their phone calls too when he was home in bed, and she'd call, or he'd call, and she'd talk and talk and talk, her favorite activity, usually about herself, her favorite subject. She too was furious to find out that her words had been transcribed into monologues for a character named Vulva, whose central obsession seems to be excrement, in all its various forms, from rabbit to horse. Nor was she thrilled by the fact that Vulva was played by a transvestite named Wayne County. "At least Brigid is played by a *girl,*" she screeched at Andy over the phone, shortly after Brigid's visit to the Factory. Andy couldn't, or wouldn't, handle it. "She's threatening me, Paul," he said like a scared child, and passed the phone to Paul, who told her to calm down. "At least it's not your family, like Brigid's," he said, laughing, trying to make light of it, and finding it funny too.

Viva, like Brigid, was in a state of perpetual rebellion against her rich Catholic family. Her real name was Susan Hoffman and she grew up in upstate New York. The Hoffmans, like the Berlins, had a summer house in the Thousand Islands in the St. Lawrence River—the Catholic Riviera, Viva and Brigid called it. According to Viva, her parents were not only fanatical Catholics but fanatical McCarthyites as well, who forced Viva and her eight brothers and sisters to watch the entire Army-McCarthy hearings on TV in 1953. After graduating from the local Catholic high school, Viva went on to Marymount, a Catholic women's college, and then to Paris, where she lived in a convent while studying art. She began modeling, but without much success, and soon returned home, where her parents, for reasons never really explained, put her in a mental institution. In any case, Viva always made it clear that she couldn't stand her parents and they couldn't stand her and she only used her real name to write reviews of Andy's movies for a small paper called *Downtown,* always reserving the highest praise for her own performance and comparing herself to Garbo, Myrna Loy, and Carole Lombard. And the Factory sometimes used quotes from these "Susan Hoffman" reviews in ads and on posters.

Viva had introduced herself to Andy at an art opening in 1963. Four years later, at a party at designer Betsy Johnson's loft on West Broadway, Viva had approached Andy again. *Popism* records, "She asked me if I was planning to do a new movie soon. I told her that we were shooting another one the following day, and I gave her the address so she could show up if she wanted to."

Viva wanted to—she showed up with Band-aids over her nipples, a touch Andy loved, and played a prostitute, every wayward Catholic girl's dream role. The film was *Loves of Ondine,* the same one in which Joe Dallesandro made a similarly casual debut. And just as Joe became Paul's favorite leading man, Viva became Andy's favorite leading woman. "She seemed like the ultimate superstar," he wrote in *Popism,* "the one we'd always been hoping to find: very intelligent, but also good at saying the most outrageous things with a straight-on beautiful gaze and that weary voice of hers."

But Andy lost interest in Viva after she married Michel Auder, an aspiring young French filmmaker, and dropped her altogether when she told him that *she* was taping their phone calls for *her* novel about the Underground. It was published in 1970, about the time I met Andy, and when I told him how much I liked it—Viva came across as the Joan Rivers of Roman

Catholicism—he said he hadn't read it. "I just can't go through all those nun stories of Viva's," he told me. "I've heard them so many times before. I mean, Viva's just too boring, Bob."

Brigid, Viva, Ultra Violet, Ingrid Superstar, Mario Montez, Jackie Curtis, Holly Woodlawn, Candy Darling, Maria and Geraldine Smith, Jane Forth, Joe Dallesandro, and Ondine, whose real name was Robert Olivio but who preferred to be introduced as the Pope—it certainly seems more than coincidence that the overwhelming majority of the Superstars were from Catholic backgrounds. The principal exceptions were Baby Jane Holzer, who was from a rich New York–Palm Beach Jewish family, and Edie Sedgwick, the rare representative of WASP aristocracy—which is perhaps why she fascinated Andy more than any other. "Edie's family came over on the *Mayflower*," he once told me, "and she still wasn't happy. Can you imagine? What boat did your family come over on, Bob?"

Andy's three consecutive leading right-hand men, Gerard Malanga, Paul Morrissey, and Fred Hughes, were also Catholics, though I never knew any of them to go to church. Andy himself did go to church—though not to mass and never to communion—every Sunday for as long as I knew him. He said mass took too long, and confession was impossible because he was sure the priest would recognize him through the screen and gossip about his sins, and he never took communion because he knew that it was sacrilege to do without confessing. So every Sunday he would "run to church" for a few minutes between masses, or after the last one, kneel down at the pew, make the sign of the cross, and pray. Brigid later told me that Andy was less regular before he was shot, but in the hospital he promised God to go to church every Sunday if he lived—and he kept to the letter of that promise.

Jed Johnson says he once asked Andy what he prayed for and Andy said, "Money." I think he prayed for health because he often said to me, "If you don't have health, Bob, you don't have anything. I know."

Andy was one of the first people I knew to get into health food and vitamins in a big way. The vegetable purées from Brownie's for lunch were accompanied by handfuls of vitamin C, vitamin B, vitamin E, which he bit open to spread a little oil on his pimples. He read the labels of ingredients on every jar and can and refused to buy them if they had artificial coloring or sodium nitrate or MSG or any kind of preservative. He hated vanillin with a passion—"Why don't they use real vanilla anymore?" he would say, reading the wrapper on candy bars. "I guess I can only eat Godiva." That was Andy's idea of a vice in the early seventies, after the shooting: Godiva chocolates. But he didn't actually "eat" them, or so he insisted. Instead, he'd pop a liqueur-filled bonbon, his favorite kind, into his mouth, suck its inside out, lick the chocolate a bit, and then spit the remaining mess out into a napkin, or his hand; then he licked off any goo. "I didn't eat it," he'd beam, so proud of having figured out a way to have his chocolate and not eat it too.

Well, maybe he prayed for health *and* wealth. In any case, Catholicism runs through Andy's life and work. He made a movie called *Imitation of Christ* (1966) and opened *The Chelsea Girls* with a half-hour confession scene between Ingrid Superstar and Pope Ondine, who wore black sunglasses and pressed for more details of Ingrid's first sexual experience: "Was it anal penetration? Vaginal penetration?" He devoted several pages of *Popism* to a description of Pope John XXIII's motorcade passing the original Factory, and he always said that the portrait commission he wanted more than any other was the Pope. And he loved to tell interviewers that he went to church every Sunday and loved to watch them react with surprise.

"To me his pageant has always seemed a Passion," Barbara Rose wrote in that review Andy hated, "his Catholicism a living matter and not a camp. It is possible future ages will see Andy in the image of Mary Magdalene; the holy whore of art history who sold himself, passively accepting the attention of an exploitative public which buys the artist rather than his art, which it is perfectly willing to admit is trash." *Art in America* also noted, "Warhol liberated himself as well as us by becoming a fine artist who *chose* to paint an advertisement for free—a kind of Mary Magdalene 'giving it away.' "

For me, it was the Superstars who were Mary Magdalenes—whores, hustlers, drag queens, junkies, wasted lives redeemed by the grace of Andy's art. "Andy has fed on sad, sick people," Emile de Antonio told Lana Jokel. He was right, but in doing so Andy made their sad, sick lives symbols of a sad, sick society. He not only noticed them and accepted them, filmed them and promoted them, he also gave them what they wanted most: fame, Superstardom, a small place in the history of art and film.

Henry Geldzahler discussed the Superstar syndrome with Lana Jokel, also connecting it with Andy's Catholicism: "For Andy," Henry said, "hell is a place on Earth—to be looked at, and felt, and then avoided. . . . Andy is a bit of a sadist, as well as a voyeur. He likes to push his relationships as far as they will go. . . . And if he's a voyeur-sadist, the Superstars are exhibitionist-masochists. That's why they burn out so quickly. . . . But, don't forget, there are always more candidates for Superstardom than there are Superstars."

Andy's movies, as I realized watching them for hundreds of hours in 1971 and 1972, were *real*. Andy wasn't directing, he was recording, and the Superstars weren't acting, they were confessing. Andy, of course, shied away from all such talk of Catholicism, voyeurism, sadism, and redemption. When Lana asked him about the Superstars and how he chose them, he gave his stock answer—simple, truthful, arch, and a bit cold: "We always use people who talk a lot."

But now, in 1971, the sixties Superstars were trouble, to be avoided.

The bulletproof door with the bulletproof window stood between the elevator and the reception desk. A Conceptual art piece by Keith Sonnier, consisting mostly of video cameras like the ones in banks, was hung in the vestibule in hopes that people would mistake it for a security system—Andy was suspicious of real ones, maintaining that the companies that monitored them were "actually the people who rob you." He also hoped that potential thieves, whom he assumed would be strung-out addicts, would take one look at the De Mille Great Dane and run off thinking it was a real guard dog.

In those days, Union Square was a jungle of junkies. The park was thick with heroin addicts, some nodding out blissfully, others searching frantically for their next fix, and the money with which to buy it. Friday afternoons were particularly bad because the junkies knew it was payday and that people were carrying cash. One Friday afternoon they hit the Factory. We were all sitting around, making plans for the weekend. Glenn and I had come down from the tenth floor hoping that Andy would invite us somewhere. Joe's wife, Terry, had come by with their baby girl, to show her all dressed up in a frilly outfit Andy had bought as a present.

Suddenly, two swarthy, sweaty junkies were at the front desk pointing pistols at Vincent, demanding money, demanding to see Andy. Andy must have seen them coming because he had already fled to the editing room in the back, where he locked himself in with Jed and Joe, who instinctively, like trained bodyguards, had followed him. Fred had the presence of mind to immediately give them a hundred-dollar bill, and Paul forked over that much too, saying, "This should be enough to buy what you want. Now get out of here."

The gunmen stood their ground. "We wanna see Andy Warhol," said one. "Hey, Andy, we know you're here," shouted the other. One of them grabbed Joe's infant daughter, and the other held Terry, who started screaming for Joe. "We're gonna kill the kid unless Andy comes out," the first one said, waving his pistol. Joe appeared and calmly announced that the police had already been called from the phone in the editing room. The junkies dropped the baby and ran. Andy refused to come out of the editing room until the police arrived, half an hour later.

He didn't come to work for a week after that. "It's just too scary," he told me on the phone. "I'm never going out again. But then everybody knows where I live. Maybe we should move to Europe. That's what Fred thinks we should do." What about *Interview?* I wondered, what about the movie business? "Oh, I know," moaned Andy. "It's all too complicated. I've got so many mouths to feed. Life isn't easy, Bob."

But Andy soon overcame his fear in his usual way: He went shopping. He took Pat Hackett to Klein's and bought a big bag of Dynel wigs in every style from Marie Antoinette to Afro, and every color from platinum to black. The idea, or so he said, was that he would wear them to disguise himself from Valerie, from the junkies, from the crazy, criminal world he felt was closing in on him. The ensuing scene was as unforgettable as the one that had brought it about.

"Now I know why everybody wants to go in drag," said Andy, standing in front of one of the Factory's mirrored walls, with $5.98 of chestnut brown spaghetti curls sitting on top of his own silver white wig. "How do I look? Do I look like me?" Laughter was the only possible answer: What could be more absurd than a man in a wig wearing a woman's wig?

Paul had told me that Andy had started wearing the silver wig in the mid-sixties—the actual year is in dispute—when his own hair became too thin from dyeing it silver: "He just showed up at the Factory one day with this incredible mop on his head. And since he didn't say anything about it, nobody else dared say anything about it. They all acted like it was the most natural thing in the world for Andy to suddenly start wearing this white rug with his own black hairs hanging out the back. It was just another example of the strength of his will, of his ability to get people to accept what is ordinarily unacceptable." Actually, Andy's wig was so obviously fake most people assumed it was real. They thought that if he was going to wear a wig, he'd surely have a better one—so that must be his real hair.

Andy continued trying on wigs. "Oh, it's so great," he said, now a strawberry blonde with a price tag hanging from generously flowing down-in-Dixie banana curls. He squinted through his pink-framed glasses. "Oh, I look just like a girl. A nutty-looking girl."

He looked like a spinster stenographer on her way home to the Polish part of Queens.

"Oh, I'm going around like this all the time. Then people won't bother me. Nobody bothers girls anymore. Only boys get in trouble these days," he said as a redhead. "Gee, with wigs you can change your whole personality," he said as if he hadn't been wearing one for years. "Isn't it great to be fake?" he said in an artichoke-cut ash-blonde number. And finally, "I guess I look best in light brown."

By now the entire Factory was in hysterics. And wigs. Pat and Jed and Vincent, who had to be coaxed, and I were taking turns trying on auburn Afros and lavender chignons. Only Paul wouldn't play. Andy started taking Polaroids of us and we took Polaroids of him. Michael Netter, in a Gloria Steinem, ironed-straight number, videotaped the whole charade. And immediately ran it back to cheers, catcalls, and happy little giggles from Andy, who had conquered his fear, until the next time something went wrong and violence veered into view.

Significantly, Andy let Paul Morrissey run the Factory. That meant absolutely *no* drugs or sex on the premises, which may seem like an unnecessary rule at any normal office, but which was not that easy to enforce at the new Factory, given what had gone on at the old Factory. Paul's deputy enforcer of that rule and many others was Vincent Fremont, a bespectacled young man from San Diego, who came across as a combination of Clark

Kent and Pat Boone. Vincent had come to New York in 1969 with his high school band, an all-blond surfer group called the Babies, who aspired to be "the new Beachboys." Paul took them up instantly, even inviting them to stay at his house in the East Village, where he also kept Joe Dallesandro and his family. The Babies soon disbanded and Vincent, shorn of his surfer locks, went to work at the Factory—sweeping floors, which meant that Jed Johnson could move up to film editor.

Jed was from Sacramento, California and, like Vincent, he had come to the Factory fresh out of high school, still a teenager, very impressionable and easy to mold. But whereas Vincent could be aggressive and play the cop, Jed was timid and quiet. In fact, his speaking voice was so soft that it was sometimes difficult to know whether he had said something.

Andy favored Jed above everyone else at the Factory. He liked talkers, but he liked beauties even more. Jed was smooth-skinned, naturally well proportioned, fanatically well groomed—everything Andy was not. Andy and Jed often dressed almost identically, but Andy looked like a rag doll and Jed like a statue.

After the shooting, when Andy had come home from the hospital, Jed had moved into the Lexington Avenue townhouse, to help take care of him. He had his own bedroom, and Julia, then in her seventies, was still in residence, so it seems likely that theirs was not a sexual relationship. Jed, like Andy, would go out of his way to put down the whole idea of sex as "messy" and "disgusting." He once told me, "Sex is boring enough without having to hear about it later."

Like Andy, he gave off an asexual, even ascetic aura. On the other hand, their relationship seemed to be more than mere friendship. Andy was jealous of Jed's nights out with his much feistier twin brother, Jay, and other buddies; Jed was jealous of the handsome young actors and models who approached Andy hoping to get their pictures in *Interview* or parts in a movie.

In the early seventies, Jed went everywhere with Andy, and people seemed to think that it was nice Andy had this well-mannered young man at his side. It also stopped them from thinking that Fred Hughes was Andy's boyfriend.

Pat Hackett, the third apparatchik of the Morrissey regime, was the only girl among Andy's "kids." She too represented the transformation of the Factory from an all-night party to an all-day office, from hell-on-earth to down-to-earth. Pat, who had a bachelor of arts in English literature from Barnard, prided herself on her knowledge of literary style and grammar, and she typed Andy's tapes with the reverence befitting a Faulkner or Joyce. When he started turning them into interviews for the magazine, Pat refused to be credited with "transcribed by," feeling it underplayed the sensitive process by which she cut out libelous gossip, indiscreet chitchat, and anything else that might jinx a portrait commission, movie deal, or dinner invitation, without losing the fly-on-the-wall feeling. She was brilliant at fixing Andy's sentences ever so slightly, so that he sounded less infantile, more articulate. Finally, after studying the dictionary for days, she came up with a credit she found fair and accurate: ''redacted by.'' She put the word *redacted* back into circulation.

Pat was like that: a bit nitpicky, a bit bureaucratic, but also endearing and funny. And very loyal to Andy. She saw him as a saint and swallowed his pious putdowns of sex and drugs without question. She resolutely rejected any notion that Andy's relationship with Jed was anything but platonic. ''Everyone knows Andy's asexual,'' she always said. There was no question about her own morals—she didn't drink, take drugs, or sleep around. And yet she spent several hours a day typing up Andy's tapes of Jackie Curtis and Candy Darling, and laughing out loud as she listened. In some ways, after Paul, Pat Hackett was the most eccentric personality at the Factory in the seventies.

Because of her job, loyalty, and somewhat spinsterish style—no makeup, plain white blouses, long, straight skirts, flat black shoes, ski vest on all but the hottest August days—we dubbed her Rose Mary Woods. We got a kick out of comparing the Factory to the Nixon White House, and as Watergate unfolded our little joke took on an eerie reality. Nixon taped; Andy taped. Haldeman and Ehrlichman kept everybody away from Nixon; Vincent and Jed kept everybody away from Andy. Nixon's closest adviser was a tough Irish law enforcer named John Mitchell; Andy's closest adviser was a tough Irish law enforcer named Paul Morrissey. The press hated Nixon; the press hated Andy. Brigid, ranting and raving at the George Washington Hotel, was Martha Mitchell, ranting and raving in Washington. Fred Hughes was Howard Hughes, who was rumored to be Nixon's secret campaign funder, and whom Fred sometimes claimed as a cousin. (I—who, at nine years old, campaigned for the Eisenhower-Nixon ticket with my Republican committeewoman mother—was Bebe Rebozo.)

What the Nixon White House and the second Factory really had in common was a sense of being under siege. Nixon was paranoid, and so was Andy. Nixon saw most liberals as his enemies; Andy saw most old Superstars as his enemies. And not without cause—Valerie Solanis was let out of prison in September 1971, and started phoning the Factory anonymously. Paul recognized her tough, gravelly voice. Andy would go white when these calls came in, and leave for home immediately, sending Joe downstairs first to make sure she wasn't lurking in the lobby, and take Jed with him.

9

Women in Revolt

Sometimes the seventies seem so long ago, so far away, and the lives we led then so utterly different from the lives we lead now. If I didn't have the yellowed clippings and my giddy journals, I would find it hard to believe, for example, that one night in May 1971—about the same time as Andy's Whitney retrospective—the leading intellectuals of New York gathered at Town Hall to hear Norman Mailer, Germaine Greer, and Jill Johnson of the *Village Voice* debate the pros and cons of anal intercourse.

The so-called debate was more like a three-ring circus, with Germaine Greer representing the heterosexual mainstream of the Women's Movement, and Jill Johnson championing its lesbian wing, and both of them hurling insults and obscenities at Norman Mailer, who was arduously defending the position he had staked out in *Harper's* magazine the previous month: The asshole was meant for waste, and waste alone.

In the early seventies, with Women's Lib very much the movement of the moment, and Gay Lib the coming thing, this was considered reactionary heresy, and the audience, in an array of trendy regalia from real Mao suits to YSL Mao suits, let Mailer know it. "Fascist pig!" they shouted. "Heterosexual McCarthyite! Chauvinist motherfucker!" The finale of this spontaneous piece of Living Theater came when Johnson invited two of her girlfriends onstage to demonstrate lesbian lovemaking.

"I've never seen anything so disgusting in my life," Candy Darling said to me in her best Bette Davis voice, as the women on stage tongued each other's nipples. "Real ladies don't behave this way."

In the early seventies only fake women wanted to be real ladies.

* * *

Andy Warhol's Women in Revolt took the sexual turmoil one step fur-
ther, casting Candy Darling, Jackie Curtis, and Holly Woodlawn as Women's
Liberationists. Filmed on and off in late 1970 and early 1971, it went through
a series of titles, including *Andy Warhol's Sex* and *Andy Warhol's PIGS*
("Politically Involved Girls"), which was Paul's favorite because he relished
the tagline "Only *Pigs* could follow *Trash.*" Candy preferred *Blonde on a
Bum Trip,* because *she* was the blonde. Jackie and Holly countered with
Bum on a Blonde Trip. It premiered at the first Los Angeles Filmex as *Sex,*
an homage to Mae West, but opened at a small theater in Westwood as *Andy
Warhol's Women,* an homage to George Cukor. Neither convinced Hollywood distributors that this extremely oddball comedy was in any way traditional, and it finally opened in New York, in early 1972, at a seedy movie
house on East 59th Street *off* Third Avenue, which Warhol Films had rented,
because no distributor would take it. The final title there was *Andy Warhol's
Women in Revolt,* and it was picketed by real revolting women.

The problem was not the film's title, but its basic premise, which made
a mockery of the entire sexual revolution. And, in 1971, attacking any aspect
of the revolution was taboo. The counterculture had become Culture, and
Andy, who had as much to do with that as any artist or activist of the time,
was hated all the more for betraying his avant-garde roots.

Andy, as usual, denied everything. He told Grace Glueck of the *New
York Times,* "I don't know what it's about." And added, "I think everyone's
doing such great work now. Girl artists, for instance. . . . At the last Whitney Biennial, it was the first time you couldn't tell their work from the
men's."

Fred Hughes went further: "We're for equal pay, day-care centers, free
abortions."

"And lipstick for both men and women," finished up Andy. At least
he didn't call them girls again.

But with scenes like Holly Woodlawn rimming a muscleman then
screeching, "Women will be free!" before diving back in, the denials were
not believed, so Andy blamed everything on Paul, who was only too happy
to hint that Candy, Jackie, and Holly were really playing Gloria Steinem,
Bella Abzug, and Betty Friedan.

Paul told David Bourdon (*Art in America,* May-June 1971):

Andy is despised by Gay Liberation and the Women's Revolt, whatever it is,
because Andy just presents it and doesn't take a position. An artist's obligation
is not to take a position ever, just to present. . . .

It's hard for Andy or any of the female impersonators to put down the
movement . . . because it's a subject that neither Andy nor the female impersonators have the vaguest notion about. I don't know anything about it either.

I hear a little bit about it on the talk shows—equal pay, etcetera blah blah. But the logical extension of what they obviously want is to be a man, so why not have men represent them?

Although Paul didn't come out and say it, and Andy certainly would have denied it, *Women in Revolt* is essentially Andy's revenge on Valerie Solanis. PIGS was his answer to SCUM. It was hilariously funny, a parody of parody, and nobody laughed more than Andy at screening after screening, when Candy Darling declaimed, "Women's Liberation has showed me just who I am and just what I can be." Or when a worried Holly, dragging a long red sequined scarf, turned to Jackie, in a proper black-and-white polka-dot dress, and moaned, "They're going to say we're lesbians." And Jackie snapped back, "No, they're not going to think we're lesbians. A school-teacher and a model—those are *lesbians?*"

Andy had rarely used transvestites in his movies before *Women in Revolt*. The one exception was Mario Montez, who had starred in *Hedy* and *Harlow* for Andy and in *Flaming Creatures* for Jack Smith. Still, the Puerto Rican postal worker only dressed in drag for the camera. Candy, Jackie, and Holly were almost always in drag—in the movies, on the street, and at home. After the shooting Andy was close to very few real women, that is, strong, contemporary women. He preferred the company of transvestites—and so-cialites, another throwback to the days when women lived to wear jewels given to them by men.

Maybe that's why he liked Candy Darling so much, the transvestite as socialite, the boy from Massapequa who wanted to be a Park Avenue lady. In *Women in Revolt,* Candy played an heiress lured into the movement for her money. Most of her scenes were filmed in Kenny Jay Lane's opulent Murray Hill townhouse, and the renowned costume jeweler decked Candy out in his very real-looking fakes. Candy was in her glory on the days she was shot, finally the leading lady instead of the big player she had been in *Flesh,* her previous Factory film.

Later, over dinner at Max's, she never tired of repeating her favorite line from the movie: "I'm young. I'm rich. I'm beautiful. Why shouldn't I sleep with my brother?" Then she'd take a tiny bite out of a big Max's hamburger, chew it carefully so as not to mess up her perfectly outlined lips, smile seductively as if at a camera, and do her version of Marilyn Monroe's mouthwash commercial from *The Seven Year Itch:* "I had Lim-burger cheese and bagels for breakfast, garlic dressing and Gorgonzola for lunch, steak and onions for dinner—but *you'll* never know. Because I use Kissing Sweet." The only problem was that Candy didn't have very good teeth. She called them "my fangs." (She called her penis "my flaw.")

Her dinner-table *pièce de résistance,* which I witnessed at least a hun-dred times in the three years I knew her, and which never failed to stop all other conversation, was her impersonation of Kim Novak in *Picnic.* "I want

to go to the picnic, *Mother.* '' Her eyes would fill with tears. *"Please* let me
go to the picnic.'' Then she'd snap right out of it and laugh slyly—''That
Kim. She really was something.''

Candy Darling's will was so strong, so convincing and demanding, that
even her mother always called her son Candy. Teresa Slattery's only child
was born in Brooklyn in 1946, and named James, after his father. In the
early fifties, James and Teresa Slattery divorced, a major trauma for Irish
Catholics at that time, and little Jimmy Slattery moved with his mother to
Massapequa Park, Long Island, five miles from where I was growing up in
Plainview. The process that transformed Jimmy Slattery into Candy Darling
started at the movies. As Candy later told David Bailey in a 1972 documentary for British TV:

> The first picture I saw that impressed me was *The Prodigal* with Lana
> Turner and when I was a child I used to fill up the bath tub and put blue food
> coloring in to make the water blue like in Technicolor. I used to bring all of
> my mother's plants into the bathroom and I had a yellow towel that I would
> put on my head for blonde hair, for Lana's hair. My mother had an ocelot coat
> and I used to put her coat which cost I think several thousand dollars on the
> floor of the bathroom and I would go into the blue water with the blonde towel
> on my head, and makeup . . . blue eye shadow . . . and get out of the water
> and slip into my mother's high heels, walk on the ocelot coat with the plants
> all around and . . . I was Lana Turner in *The Prodigal.* A few years later I
> discovered Kim Novak in *The Eddie Duchin Story.* I was always attracted to
> women with white hair. I thought it was the prettiest.

Sometime around 1963 or 1964, still in his teens, Jimmy Slattery started
calling himself Hope Slattery and taking the Long Island Railroad into Manhattan to hang out in the Village gay bars or to see a Fifth Avenue doctor
who specialized in hormone injections that helped turn unhappy boys into
something resembling girls. Gradually, shot by shot, Hope shed whiskers
and sprouted breasts. She became an actress, making an off-off-off-Broadway
debut at Bastiano's Cellar Studio on Waverly Place in a campy musical satire
called *Glory, Glamour and Gold.*

The playwright of this shoestring extravaganza was another boy/girl
named Jackie Curtis, a tough and brilliant street kid, who was raised by his
grandmother over her bar, Slugger Ann's, on Second Avenue and 10th Street.
It was Jackie who came up with the name Candy Darling and wrote the play
for her in one week on amphetamines. In fact, Jackie was torn between
being a writer-director and an actress-Superstar, between being a man and
a woman. Unlike Candy, who desperately wanted people to believe she was
a woman and hated being labeled a drag queen or transvestite, Jackie said,
''I got balls under my ballgown and I don't care who knows it.'' Candy was
a true believer; for her Hollywood was holy, and twentieth-century American

culture began and ended at Twentieth Century-Fox. Candy wanted to be the flawless blonde bombshell of the Fabulous Fifties. Jackie was too original for that. He/she was closer to what the seventies were about, mixups and mixtures, one day James Dean, the next Joan Crawford, or Lucille Ball. The only thing that Jackie never changed was his/her name.

Jackie and Candy were best friends, archrivals, writer and muse, director and star. They lived together on and off, first at the seedy Hotel Albert, a druggy rock-star hangout, and later in various dark walkups in the East Village. When Jackie dressed as a man, they were something of a content, complementary couple—Jackie full of energy and orders, Candy all languor and rouge. Then Jackie would put on a wig, a dress, heels, and the fireworks would start. Suddenly, they were Crawford and Davis in *Whatever Happened to Baby Jane.*

"You bitch."

"You hussy."

"Who discovered you anyway?"

"Who sells the tickets to your idiotic plays? You think they come to see *you?* Or that tramp Holly?"

"Who gave you your name?"

"My mother gave me my name. Contrary to those vicious rumors you've been spreading around town about me, I'm a *woman*—and I've got the tits to prove it."

Despite their bickering, the old-fashioned drag queen and the new-fangled boy/girl shared a truly creative relationship. After *Glory, Glamour and Gold,* Jackie wrote and directed two more plays for Candy: *Heaven Grand in Amber Orbit* in 1969, and *Vain Victory: The Vicissitudes of the Damned* in 1971.

Glory, Glamour and Gold—which Candy called *G.G.G.*—marked the theatrical debut of Robert De Niro. Jackie liked to brag that he'd "begged" for the part, so his mother, who owned a small printing company, could get the job of running up the posters and programs. De Niro played all *ten* male roles, opposite an assortment of drag queens, and his performance, Andy always said, was a tour de force.

Andy met Jackie and Candy a month or so before *G.G.G.* "One hot August afternoon during the Love Summer of '67," according to *Popism,* "Fred and I were out walking around the West Village on our way to pick up some pants I was having made up at the Leather Man. There were lots of flower children tripping and lots of tourists watching them trip. Eighth Street was a total carnival. Every store had purple trip books and psychedelic posters and plastic flowers and beads and incense and candles. . . .

"Walking just ahead of us was a boy about nineteen or twenty with wispy Beatle bangs, and next to him was a tall, sensational blonde drag queen in very high heels and a sundress that she made sure had one strap falling onto her upper arm." Jackie recognized Andy and asked him for an autograph on a paper bag from a boutique called Countdown that contained, Jackie told Andy, "satin shorts for the tap-dancing in my new play, *Glory, Glamour and Gold.* . . . I'll send you an invitation." Andy thought Jackie was funny, but he couldn't keep his eyes off Candy.

Andy and his Factory entourage attended the opening of *G.G.G.*, and after that Jackie and Candy occasionally ventured into the back room of Max's hoping to regain Andy's attention. Before he was shot he held court there almost nightly. Andy liked Max's because it was close to the new Factory, it was cheap, and he could pay his bills with paintings. The owner, Mickey Ruskin, made similar deals with other painters and sculptors, who all hung out in the front room by the bar; Larry Rivers and John Chamberlain were the hottest stars of that scene. Andy and the Superstars reigned in the back room.

Jackie and Candy desperately wanted to be admitted to the club, but they didn't become full-fledged members until the following year, when Paul put the two of them into *Flesh.* They only have one scene, but it is memorable. They sit together on a sofa, reading old movie magazines aloud, while Geri Miller, the topless go-go dancer, gives Joe Dallesandro, the wandering addict, a blowjob. Jackie mocks being shocked, but Candy, ever the lady, doesn't deign to notice. For Candy, the only thing happening on that set was the birth of her movie career.

Holly Woodlawn, the third of *Women in Revolt*'s transvestite trio, also came to Warhol Films via *G.G.G.*—though she had to wait almost three years before Paul cast her in *Trash,* which she ended up stealing. Holly liked to compare herself to Hedy Lamarr, but she actually came across as Jackie Mason impersonating Carmen Miranda. I call Holly "she" because Holly was more like Candy than Jackie, a pseudo woman, not a walking sexual question mark. But if Candy was a lady, Holly was a tramp. Holly's real name was Harold Santiago Rodriguez Franceschi Dankahl Ajzenberg. She shortened it to Holly, just Holly, after Holly Golightly, Audrey Hepburn in the movie *Breakfast at Tiffany's.* Harold hadn't read the book.

It was Jackie Curtis who added Woodlawn, evoking not only the film capital but Forest Lawn cemetery as well. And it was Jackie who launched Holly's show-biz career by putting her in the chorus line of *A Reindeer Girl,* the play that preceded *G.G.G.* Theirs was another imperfectly perfect match.

Holly Woodlawn's life story reads like a Jackie Curtis play. A passionate but flighty Puerto Rican mother, a handsome but cold German father, who walked out on his wife, and a clever but kind Jewish stepfather, who took mother and child from the slums of San Juan to the Bronx, and then to Miami Beach, where stepdaddy Ajzenberg worked as a captain at the nightclub of the Fontainebleau Hotel.

Like Candy, Holly always traced her flight into fantasy to the first time

she saw Lana Turner in *The Prodigal,* though she also claimed to be swayed
by Annette Funicello in *Where the Boys Are:* "Being from Florida, it was
only natural." At age fifteen, Harold Ajzenberg hitchhiked to New York,
metamorphosing into Holly as he made his way north. In Atlanta, he shaved
his legs. In South Carolina, he plucked his eyebrows. In Virginia, he cut his
trousers into short-shorts. In Philadelphia, a department-store cosmetic
salesman taught him to do his makeup. Arriving finally in New York, he
was a she, in a long black gown, high silver heels, and trailing "twelve
yards of black iridescent turkey boa."

Then, the way Holly has told it in nightclub routines and press releases,
she became, in rather rapid succession, a 42nd Street prostitute, a Brooklyn
housewife, a suburban mistress, a Saks Fifth Avenue salesgirl, and a high-
fashion model. No one has ever seen the tear sheets from *Vogue* or *Bazaar,*
but Holly always saw herself as a much more convincing glamour girl than
she ever was, a femme fatale instead of a figure of fun—that was part of
Holly's bittersweet comic appeal.

A few days before the fall 1970 premiere of *Trash* in New York Holly
was arrested for impersonating the wife of the French ambassador to the
United Nations and trying to cash checks in her name. How did she ever
think she could get away with it? Or was she really trying to be caught?
Andy stubbornly refused to bail her out of jail—she was transferred from
the Women's House of Detention to the all-male Tombs after the strip-
search—though on other occasions I saw him give Holly checks for a couple
of hundred dollars for rent without a question. Holly always had to sign a
receipt made out by Vincent that read "for promotion of Andy Warhol
Films," so maybe it was just that Andy thought that bail was not tax de-
ductible.

Larry Rivers ended up bailing Holly out just in time for the premiere
at the big Cinema One opposite Bloomingdale's. A few days later, after it
had sunk in that Andy Warhol Films had finally made it uptown, Holly came
to the Factory in a rage, screaming about how little she was paid and how
much the movie was making. There was some validity to her claims, and
she certainly wasn't the only Superstar to have made them. Andy Warhol
Films paid actors $25 per day of shooting, and they had to sign a release
every day, which stated that they had no claim to any additional sums what-
soever and forever. Those who refused to sign weren't given another day's
work. The threat usually worked because everyone knew there were plenty
of would-be Superstars hanging around Max's, there were no scripts that
had to be followed, and it wasn't very expensive to reshoot 16mm film.

Holly had worked five days on *Trash,* for a total fee of $125. And *Trash*
grossed $1.5 million in the United States, and at least as much in Ger-
many and other European markets. Of course, not all the gross went to
Andy Warhol Films, and no one could have predicted such success. Still, it
seemed unfair, and Andy must have sometimes sensed that it was, because

he often gave those Superstars who were in his good graces extra money for rent or a new dress or a night on the town. The key, however, was to be "in his good graces"; his largesse was based on his idea of good behavior, and he was always in control. What he hated most was when Holly demanded a percentage of the profits, which would have been a fair and logical way of recompensing contributors to highly risky projects. But Andy, Paul, and Vincent always said it would be "a bookkeeping nightmare." It would also have meant that people like Holly Woodlawn, Viva, and all the other Superstars would have had a business relationship with Andy Warhol Films that lasted longer than one day.

So Holly made scenes at the Factory, and Andy said she was "drunk" and walked away, and Vincent didn't buzz her through the bulletproof door for a few weeks until she "calmed down" and "behaved like a normal human being," until she was a good girl who would not throw a tantrum, draw a gun, and pull a Valerie.

Eventually the tension inherent in that way of working, the psychological state of siege at the Factory, became too much. Perhaps that's why *Women in Revolt* was the last Andy Warhol movie made in the old Factory style: no budget, no script, no contracts, no professionals. *L'Amour,* the other movie under production at the Factory in 1970 and 1971, represented the beginning of a new era at Andy Warhol Films: There was a budget, financed by a syndicate of art collectors put together by Fred Hughes; a script, which the money men required Paul to write before they'd sign a check; contracts, which were so complicated that they later almost led to a lawsuit; and a partially professional cast, including Michael Sklar and Max DeLys, a French actor who was a rising star in Italy, as well as Superstars Jane Forth and Donna Jordan, who played American mannequins gold-digging in Paris, i.e. themselves.

Women in Revolt was also the last Andy Warhol movie on which Andy directed—that is, photographed—some scenes. It was almost as if he couldn't let go of the old do-it-yourself, movie-a-day way of working. Perhaps it was also a tiny act of rebellion, the first sign of what was to come, against Paul Morrissey, who had seized control of the Factory camera, and thus of the content of the movies, while Andy was in the hospital, too weak to do anything but acquiesce to the making of *Flesh* in his absence.

According to Jackie Curtis, Andy picked up the camera again when he/she refused to be filmed by Paul, complaining, "He only makes Joe look good." Ed McCormack described life on the set of *Women in Revolt* for *Interview:*

> Paul asks Jackie to take her place for the shooting of the scene and Jackie ignores him. Paul takes Jackie's arm and started pulling her around like a Raggedy Ann Doll, and Jackie pulls away, with great unhand-me-you-cad flourishes of indignation. Paul turns his back . . . and Jackie slams him in the ass

with her protest sign. Paul turns around and shakes his finger in Jackie's face. . . . Meanwhile, Andy Warhol, who has apparently learned from past experience to stay well out of the line of fire, is standing quietly in the shadow of the equipment truck parked at the curb, watching them fight it out. . . . His Dilly Dally head of straw . . . is blowing in the ides of March and a small vague smile of amusement appears on his lips as he watches the conflict between Paul and Jackie, shivering visibly. After a while, satisfied that the filming is going well, Andy announces in his non-voice as soft as a ghost of a small cough that he's going back to the Factory "to get some work done."

I went back to the Factory with Andy, who suggested calling Candy, which I did. He got on an extension and told her that Jackie was "being terrible to Paul. This is your big chance to get a big scene for yourself, Candy. But you better be nice to Paul and do what he tells you and not complain and not wear too much lipstick because you're supposed to be a rich girl and, uh, rich girls don't do that anymore."

"I know what rich girls do, Andy."

"And you've got to think up some new lines, Candy. You can't keep using that same old Kim Novak stuff."

"For $25 a day, I've got to write my own lines, too?"

"This could be your big break, Candy. Oh, I've got to go. Uh, Fred wants me. Talk to Bob."

Holly Woodlawn, who had agreed to work for $25 per day again after word leaked from the Factory to Max's that *Women in Revolt* was going to be a Candy Darling vehicle because Holly was "too difficult," claimed she only worked in the movies for a pittance because "Andy Warhol could turn anyone into a star." There certainly weren't many other movie producers willing to cast transvestites. Candy Darling had flooded the producer and director of *Myra Breckinridge* with letters, pleading for the lead, but, as Candy put it, "They decided Raquel Welch would make a more believable transvestite."

Basically Candy, Jackie, and Holly had no choice but to work for the Factory, no matter how difficult Paul was, no matter how miserly Andy was.

The filming went on like this for most of 1971, a day here, a weekend there. By December, Jackie was persona non grata at the Factory; Holly had stopped coming by for handouts because she had a manager in Dallas who got her a paying part in an almost-aboveground movie called *Is There Sex After Death?;* and Candy had a big solo finale, the most closeups, and top billing in *Andy Warhol's Women in Revolt.*

Despite weekly screenings at the Factory all fall of 1971, *Women in Revolt* still didn't have a distributor. Nobody would touch it, not Cinema Five, not smaller art-film distributors like New World Films; even the Germans were wary. Finally, Andy decided to rent the Cine Malibu, a small sexploitation movie house on East 59th Street, and we launched the run with a celebrity preview on February 16, 1972. It was Ash Wednesday, and both Andy and Candy sported small black smudges on their foreheads at the dinner Fred Hughes and I had pushed Andy to give after the preview. It was in Candy's honor, and she had chosen Le Parc Périgord, an extremely conservative restaurant on Park Avenue at East 63rd Street. Andy would have preferred Pearl's or Elaine's, which were much more fashionable, and much less expensive, but Candy insisted, "I hate that artificial light at Pearl's. It's so unflattering. I don't know why all the new restaurants insist on having it. I think certain things are nice and refined and should be kept that way. You know I believe in tradition, Bob. Restaurants should have carpets on the floor, upholstered seats, and be *dark.*"

I recorded that night in my journal:

Candy was in her glory. Everyone laughed with Candy and cooed and oohed and ahed. "How witty you are, Candy." "How quick you are, Candy." "How beautiful you are, Candy."

"Oh, Candy," said Andy. "What time of the month do you have your period?"

"Every day, Andy. I'm such a woman."

After dinner, [we] walked around the corner to Scavullo's townhouse, where the real party would soon begin. Francesco whisked the group past the Pinkertons at the door and up to his bedroom, where everyone settled in to watch the TV reviews of *Women in Revolt*.

"A rip-off," said Channel 4.

"Looked as if it were filmed underwater," said Channel 2.

"It proves once again that Andy Warhol has no talent. But we knew that since the Campbell's Soupcans," said Channel 7.

Everybody laughed, Paul the loudest. Andy, taping, seemed genuinely puzzled, bewildered—he *liked Women in Revolt*. By this time the house was filling with scores of guests, many of whom made their way to the bedroom to give Candy a kiss—D. D. Ryan, Barbara Loden, Sylvia Miles. Downstairs two huge sitting rooms were filled with lilies—what else for Ash Wednesday?—and glamorosi: George Plimpton, Kenny Jay Lane, Halston, Giorgio di Sant'Angelo, Diane and Egon von Furstenberg, Countess Marina Cicogna. Gloria Vanderbilt Cooper called for an invitation and then fell ill with flu that very morning. "I want to come so badly," she cried to Scavullo. . . .

WWD's Rosemary Kent was positioned firmly at the door, ordering her photographer: "Get her—he's nobody—forget him—quick, quick, it's Silva Thin!" Silva Thin is *WWD*'s favorite drag queen, the only one permitted at Candy's party, though at the last minute Holly Woodlawn's name was put on the list. Jackie Curtis, Candy's arch enemy, stood outside in the cold, along with hundreds of other would-be crashers.

"My God, what are they giving away in there," sighed a weary Pinkerton.

"Would you believe a transvestite?" said a guest.

The next morning Andy called Candy and asked, "How was your party, Candy?"

"But Andy, you were there."

"I know, but you tell me anyway. I want to live my life through yours."

The next afternoon, about a dozen women in army jackets and pea coats, jeans, and boots were outside the Cine Malibu waving protest signs. Vincent, who stood beside the ticket booth counting the customers to make sure that Andy Warhol Films, Inc. wasn't cheated, called the Factory to describe the scene, and I called Candy. "Who do these dykes think they are, anyway?" she joked. "Well, I just hope they all read Vincent Canby's review in today's *Times*. He said I look like a cross between Kim Novak and Pat Nixon. It's true—I *do* have Pat Nixon's nose."

The White House on the Square now had its First Lady.

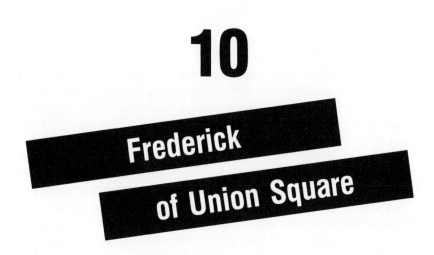

10

Frederick of Union Square

"Beauty is the hardest drug of all," I wrote after seeing *Death in Venice*. I devoted twenty of the forty pages, front *and* back covers, of the July 1971 issue of *Interview* to Luchino Visconti's film of Thomas Mann's novella about the old man and the tease. For once, Paul, Fred, Charles Rydell, and Jerome Hill all applauded. But Andy was mad. He said there were only two pages of ads and "too many pictures of the same people looking the same. I don't even think this kid is that good-looking."

"How can you say that?" countered Fred. "Marisa told me he's the best-looking boy she's ever met. The only problem was his mother was on the set and she would never let him go out and have fun with the rest of the cast."

Swedish actor Bjorn Anderssen played the boy with the smile of an angel and the heart of a statue who drives Dirk Bogarde bananas. Marisa Berenson had a small, but fabulously costumed, part in the movie.

"I thought Marisa was trying to marry David de Rothschild," snapped Andy. "She should forget about making movies and really go after him. It's much better to be a baroness than a movie star. You should tell her that, Fred. Tell her if she became a Rothschild she could have all the young boys she wanted."

"Oh, Andy," said Fred. "You're just jealous because you don't get to make movies like that."

"I am not, Fred. How can you say that to me? I thought it was the most boring movie I ever saw. It was just so long and drawn out. The same scene over and over."

That from the man who made *Empire*—eight hours in the life of a skyscraper top? And *Sleep?*

Now I wonder if Andy hated *Death in Venice* because it came too close to his own life, to his relationships with beautiful young men, to his feeling about his own strange appearance. Bjorn Anderssen, slim, cool, Nordic, looked a lot like Jed Johnson, who was perfectly capable of driving Andy bananas. And, rereading my review, which Andy claimed he couldn't understand, I realize that I was actually writing *about Andy*—though I didn't know it then, and Andy probably did.

Andy was certainly addicted to the word *beauty*. He didn't use it quite as often as the staples of his vocabulary: "gee," "oh," "really," and "great." But it was right up there with "up there." "Now, she's a beauty," or "But he's a beauty," or "That's the price you pay for beauty, Bob." Sometimes, if he was feeling blue, he'd say, "Don't you ever wish you were a beauty, Bob?" And, if he was really nervous about getting ready to go out, "Oh, I wish I were a beauty. Then anything I threw on would look good."

Conversely, Andy never used the word "ugly." The furthest he would go in putting down someone else's appearance was "funny-looking." And he always held out hope for self-improvement. "If Brigid lost a hundred pounds, she'd be a real beauty." "If Holly stopped wearing that ratty coat, she wouldn't be so funny-looking." He wanted me to have a nose job, telling me, "Then you'll be almost as handsome as Fred." He convinced me I should go to Dr. Orentreich, his dermatologist, for anti-balding hormone injections in my head, even though I wasn't balding. "But you're thinning, Bob," he said. "If you start taking the shots now you'll be okay. Otherwise, before you know it . . ." He snapped his fingers, and I found myself spending money I didn't have on shots I didn't need.

Andy was a big believer in diets, dermatologists, plastic surgery, changing hairdos, going to the right designer, exercise—anything that would help turn an ugly ducking into a swan. In the eighties, when he was in his fifties, he became obsessed with it all, but even in the early seventies, when he was in his forties, he was having regular skin treatments and facials and dyeing his eyebrows white to match his wig. And when colored contact lenses first came out about then, he rushed to his eye doctor to get icy blue ones and wore them instead of his welfare glasses when he went out at night.

I always found it most touching when Andy called somebody a beauty who was obviously not. He would look at some hideous gargoyle of a human being, with bad skin, bad teeth, bad hair, and say, "She's a beauty." He wasn't blind or being kind. It was just that by stretching the definition of beauty to the limit, he thought that—with his bad skin, bad teeth, bad hair—he might fit in too.

Andy knew only too well who was beautiful and who was ugly by the standards of a Western aesthetic based on classical ideals. His portraits transformed aging socialites into Venus de Milos, and their industrialist husbands into Florentine Davids—or, at least, into Hollywood facsimiles thereof. I remember the first time I saw him working on a portrait in the little office he had taken to paint in on the eighth floor of 33 Union Square West in 1971, when the commissions were starting to come in faster. He was crouched on the floor over a forty-by-forty-inch negative—the standard portrait-size blowup of the negative of the Polaroid that every portrait started with. The negative would then be converted into a silkscreen, which was then used to print the image onto the final portrait canvas. If this sounds complicated, it was, and various steps of the process were done by hands other than Andy's. But only Andy, in all the years I knew him, worked on the negatives—which is what I caught him doing that afternoon, much to his dismay, because he liked to keep his methodology secret, as mysterious as alchemy.

What Andy did to the negative was more like plastic surgery, though the end result was magical: beasts turned into beauties. He simply took scissors and snipped out double chins, bumps in noses, bags under eyes, the shadows of pimples, the blackness of beards. His most elderly clients were left, like Marilyn, like Elvis, with eyes, nostrils, lips, and jawlines. "God," I said, as I watched him attack a whole neck and scissor away seventy years of wrinkles, "is that how you do it?"

"Oh, oh, uh, just on this one," said Andy, aiming his shears with precision at those little lines around the mouth that come from smoking too much too long. "She does look better, doesn't she?"

Later, when I wanted to make him feel good about a portrait he was unsure of, meaning he wasn't certain that it was flattering enough, I'd say, "Andy, you should send them a bill for whatever Pitanguy charges for a face lift on top of the $25,000 for your portrait."

That's what his portraits went for all through the seventies and eighties, though the price of additional canvases of the same image in different colors started out at $5,000 and rose to $20,000 each, over the years. In those days, Andy had less than a dozen commissions a year, but he gradually worked his way up to over fifty by around 1980. All in all, it is estimated that Andy Warhol painted over one thousand individuals, most of whom took between two and four canvases each—though in 1971 a single client, Colorado businessman and art collector John Powers, ordered twenty-four of his Japanese wife, Kimiko.

Flattery sells.

Even though Andy wished everyone could be a beauty, including himself, I think he was afraid to get too close to the real thing. He didn't want his heart broken, he didn't want to lose the upper hand. Jed was the exception, the only silent beauty in Andy's inner circle. The rest of us, to one degree or other, were what Andy called "talkers," people who made their way in life on the strength of their personalities instead of their looks. Andy dreamed of beauties, but he found it easier to work with talkers—for one thing, he and his Sony always had the upper hand with talkers.

Pat Hackett says Andy chose his close associates for the qualities that he wished he had. "He wished he could type like me," she says modestly, "look like Jed, dress like Fred, have opinions like Paul, and tell funny stories at dinner like you."

Fred Hughes, curiously, was not really a beauty, not really a talker. He liked hearing gossip a lot more than he liked telling it; he refused to let Andy tape him. But his ears stuck out a bit too far, his shoulders were a little narrow, his hips a little wide, for him to count on his looks alone. No, Fred had something else, something more lasting than a pretty face, rarer than a way with words. Fred had *style*—extraordinary, remarkable, one-of-a-kind style. But Andy found a way to turn that to his own use and get the upper hand with Fred, too.

Andy's social schedule was controlled by Fred. Just as Paul did with the movies, and I tried to do with the magazine, Fred was the one who knew what Andy wanted even when Andy wasn't quite sure himself. He was the great collaborator, so to speak, of Andy's social life and art business—which for Andy were more or less the same thing. "I'm just a traveling portrait artist now," Andy started saying in interviews shortly after Fred started working with him in 1967. And to a large extent he was. "I just go where Fred tells me to go" was another of Andy's regular lines, and it was true. Fred led and Andy followed, complaining all the way there, counting his money all the way back.

I remember a typical conversation between them, in the summer of 1971. Fred came back from lunch at La Grenouille and announced that they were going to Venice for the very social first week in September. Andy said it was too expensive.

"You love Venice, Andy."

"No, I don't. It's damp. And expensive."

"You had such a good time last year at the Cipriani."

"I did? The Cipriani is so far away and it costs so much. And we didn't sell any portraits, Fred."

"So we'll stay at the Gritti. You can walk everywhere. And we did *almost* get Giovanni Volpi's last year. And he's giving a big party this year and all the Brandolinis will be there, and Anna-Maria Aldobrandini is giving a lunch for Anna-Maria Cicogna the next day and she's already asked us and I've already accepted."

"Can I bring Jed?"

"Yes, you can bring Jed. But no one else."

So they went, and Andy came back raving and ranting, "We met the

Volpis and the Dolpis and the Polpis and every lady is a *contessa* and they all live in *palazzos* and they were all pushing their daughters on Fred. But he was too busy with Loulou. You should have been there, Bob.''

"Loulou de la Falaise was there too?''

"Yeah, we invited her, but Fred didn't tell me until it was time to pay the bill. It was okay. She helped us a lot.''

"Did you sell any portraits?''

"Uh, I think we might have one. Fred says we have to go back again next year. He says it takes time to get in with this group. Fred was really great. I think he might marry Loulou.''

Fred was always "sort of engaged" to a beautiful girl from a glamorous family—Loulou de la Falaise, who worked for Saint Laurent, was the daughter of a French count whose brother, the Marquis de la Falaise, had been married to Gloria Swanson—and Andy was always predicting an imminent wedding. He wanted Fred to marry an aristocratic beauty as much as he wanted me to marry a rich widow. But in Fred's case Andy's motives weren't merely monetary.

Andy and Fred had a very complicated relationship. When I came on the scene, they seemed to have achieved a nearly perfect balance. Aside from Paul, Fred was the only person who could boss Andy around, who could tell him where to go, who to see, what to say. And Andy always asked for Fred's advice on artistic and business matters, including the movie and magazine businesses. Paul knew Fred could find backers, as he did with *L'Amour,* but he wasn't as pleased when Fred started asserting himself creatively, as he also did on *L'Amour.* I, on the other hand, was eager to get Fred involved with *Interview:* I saw him as a counterweight to Paul, who could be overbearing; and I wanted to be his friend—like everyone at the Factory, I was dazzled by his style.

And Fred was very, very clever. As much as he liked to dress up like the Duke of Windsor and go out with stars like Marisa Berenson, at premieres and openings, whenever the paparazzi pressed, Fred was quick to slip out of Andy's pictures. When Andy wanted help with an interview, someone to answer his questions for him, Fred demurred, letting Paul or me yap away at Andy's side. When journalists asked him what *his* job was, he'd tell them with a straight face, "I'm Andy's hairdresser, Frederick of Union Square.'' Andy would always laugh at this, and the journalists would write it down, and Andy would laugh again when it came out in the papers. Fred was very, very clever.

Sometimes, late in the afternoon at the Factory, when he was relaxed and a bit giddy after a La Grenouille lunch, Fred would perform his Frederick of Union Square act to amuse us. In front of the big mirrors, he'd use Scotch tape to give us all instant facelifts, eyelifts, and different hairdos. "There, that's much better,'' he'd say with a flourish as he taped away my

growing double chin. "You really are getting a champagne chin, Bob,"
Andy would chime in. He would never let Fred Scotch-tape his face or hair.
Neither would Paul.

There was no question that Fred was with Andy for the long haul. He
was a partner, not an employee; one of the kids, but a grown-up, too; Andy's
equal in a way that the rest of us were not. One day in the early seventies,
a Factory assistant came across Fred's "Last Will and Testament" while
cleaning up his desk. It was handwritten and only one sentence: "I leave
everything I own to Andy Warhol."

Born and bred in Houston, Texas, the son of a furniture salesman, Fred
was rather vague about his antecedents. But he came across as a romantic,
nineteenth-century figure—the dashing dilettante, the elegant eccentric, the
English gentleman living in Paris with his old chairs, old paintings, and old
books, the second son of a duke, making up in style what he lacked in
inheritance. "I'm *deeply* superficial" was his favorite line. He had memo-
rized all the kings and queens of England, from the Tudors to the Windsors—
and the style of chair that went with each of them. And everything he wore
was English: handmade suits from Tommy Nutter, handmade shirts from
Turnbull & Asser; handmade shoes from Lobb's. His cologne was English—
Penhaligon's Blenheim Bouquet. Even his Levi's 501s looked as if they'd
been altered on Savile Row—the seams were never crooked and there was
no extra fabric on the thighs—but maybe that was because he had them
washed and pressed every day. Fred was the first to wear jeans with suit
jackets, but when Andy adopted the style as his uniform it became known
as the Warhol Look.

Andy paid for the maid who pressed the blue jeans, and for the magnum
of champagne on the bedside table—Fred preferred to draw a token salary
of $100 a week, in exchange for unlimited expenses. And Andy broadcast
the upcoming wedding of the year, leaving Fred all the more embarrassed
when Loulou de la Falaise ran off with Eric de Rothschild. In Fred's fantasies
of old money and aristocratic womanizing, Andy had found the way to get
the upper hand. After the Loulou "engagement" collapsed, Andy started
saying, "I bet Fred marries Paloma Picasso." And he never tired of repeating, "Fred is from a really great family. He really is."

In a sense, Fred did come from a really great family. Jean and Dominique de Menil were Houston's most important art collectors and patrons.
But though they had lived there since 1941, and Dominique's family's business, the giant Schlumberger oil-equipment company, was based there, the
de Menils were not really *of* Houston. They were too European, too intellectual, and too liberal for that tough town on the bayou. And they did things
nobody in Houston ever dreamed of doing. Their cool glass-and-steel house
in River Oaks, where the neighboring mansions run the gamut from Tara to

Petit Trianon, was built by Philip Johnson, the modern architect's first residential assignment. Its plain white walls were hung with Magrittes and Dalis, not Remingtons. They commissioned the interdenominational Mark Rothko Chapel, then gradually bought up all the small clapboard houses in the surrounding neighborhood. They painted them all the same color, which became known as de Menil gray. They also funded the art department at the Catholic University of St. Thomas, where they found a freshman art-history student named Fred Hughes, and he found the family of his dreams.

"I recognized in Fred Hughes," Dominique later told Steven M. L. Aronson in *Vanity Fair*, "a young man who had not only an exceptional eye, but also an instinct for what was important, for quality. He helped me with some of my shows. And, in a way, I gave him a chance to be exposed to what was going on in the best circles of art."

"Both Jean and Dominique adored Fred," says São Schlumberger, who lived in Houston then with her husband, Pierre, Dominique's first cousin. "He was almost like a part of the family. I think it was because he was a boy who lived for art, that's all he cared about."

In becoming a de facto de Menil, Fred entered a kind of cult not so unlike that around Andy. There was also a Catholic connection. Jean was a devout disciple of the progressive Catholicism of Pope John XXIII and the Second Vatican Council; Dominique, who had converted to marry him, was even more so. The circle of plain girls from good families who surrounded her, volunteering their time to perform clerical duties, were jokingly referred to as nuns, "the Little Sisters of the Order of St. Dominique." And she herself was nicknamed "The Mother Superior." She even looked like a nun, a very important nun: severe, immaculate, erect, gray hair in a soft chignon, no makeup, even at night.

Jean de Menil, on the other hand, was something of a dandy. Family friends say he liked showing off. They also say he liked calling himself Baron de Menil. And that he was basically insecure because he thought he owed his position to his wife's wealth, even though he ran the business and he had the great eye. Fred looked up to Jean de Menil but he worshiped Dominique—and spent more time with her, arranging exhibitions and other cultural events in Houston, traveling to New York and Europe on art-buying trips. And later, if he found in Andy another Dominique, a friend at once close and cold, a boss who ruled by appearing shy and humble, he himself became more and more like Mr. de Menil—insecure about his true worth.

The de Menils helped Fred get a job at the Iolas Gallery in Paris after he graduated from St. Thomas. Alexander Iolas, a wild and wily Greek, had opened an art gallery in New York showing artists who had fled war-torn Europe—Max Ernst, Victor Brauner, and Lucio Fontana. In the sixties, he was at the height of his success, with galleries in Milan, Madrid, Mexico City, as well as Paris and New York. He was the exclusive representative of not only Max Ernst but also the other great Surrealist René Magritte. He also showed such rising European Pop artists as Jean Tinguely and his wife, Nikki de Saint Phalle. And the de Menils, who had perhaps the most extensive Surrealist collection in the world and were also buying sixties art in quantity, relied more on him for advice than on any other dealer.

The Paris job was ideal for a twenty-year-old who loved art: Fred hung shows, sold paintings on commission, met Duchamp and Cocteau, went out with Iolas to chichi collectors' parties and offbeat Bohemian *boîtes*. He even picked up the restaurant French that would serve him so well when he later went to work for "the traveling portrait painter."

Fred had met Andy for the first time in 1966 in New York. He would often hop back to Houston from Paris to help Dominique with her projects, usually stopping over in New York and staying at the de Menils' townhouse on the East Side. On one of those stopovers, he went out to Sybil Burton's discothèque, Arthur, the Studio 54 of the sixties. "Andy was with Edie [Sedgwick] and a bunch of other toffy kids," Fred recalled years later. "I went up and shook his hand."

It was a chance encounter between a star and a fan—Fred, like me, was a Warhol fan long before he met Andy; he said he had already bought a small Warhol painting while still in college in Houston. They were formally introduced a year later. Again, the setting was appropriate and historical: Philip Johnson's Glass House in New Canaan, Connecticut, at a benefit for the Merce Cunningham Dance Company, sponsored by the de Menil Foundation, with entertainment by the Velvet Underground. Fred came with a de Menil daughter. Andy came with the band. They were introduced by Henry Geldzahler. "I never saw either of them again," Henry said later only half in jest. "They . . . waltzed off into the empyrean."

When the Factory moved from East 47th Street to Union Square West in 1968, Fred had taken an apartment within walking distance. It was a small one-bedroom on East 16th Street, but it had high ceilings. Fred painted it de Menil gray, which had a slight purplish cast, upholstered everything in silver and bronze satin, and hung a few borrowed Warhols on the walls. By that time he was working with Andy full time, having started coming into the old Factory shortly after they had met in Connecticut. Needless to say, he swept the floors—sometimes in a tuxedo.

But that's not all he did. "Don't forget," he told *Vanity Fair,* "I came in with a sort of *dowry.* Being attached to the de Menils, I immediately thought of all kinds of very lucrative projects for Andy. Andy saw the silver lining." The de Menils commissioned Andy, as he described it in *Popism,* "to film a sunset for something to do with a bombed church in Texas that they were restoring . . . with the leftover money from that commission we eventually made *Lonesome Cowboys* at the end of the year and the beginning of '68."

Next, Fred persuaded the de Menils to have Andy paint their highly respected private curator, Germaine McConaghty. It was astute not to push the self-effacing Dominique into having her own portrait done first. She soon fell in line—Andy did four portraits of Dominique in various shades of gray. Then came Phillip Johnson; Sidney Janis, the 57th Street art dealer, and Jan Cowles, the wife of the publisher of *Look*. The Cowleses were close friends of Governor Nelson Rockefeller and his wife, Happy, both of whom Andy immortalized in silkscreened acrylic in 1968.

In a few years, Fred engineered the rise of Andy Warhol from the demimonde to the beau monde, and set him on the road to real riches. He launched the commissioned-portraits goldmine, drove up the sales and prices of the sixties paintings, expanded the limited-edition-print business, cultivated important new collectors and dealers, especially in Europe. "He made the connections," Paul Morrissey said later, "or if the connection was already made, he consolidated it. And he arranged for . . . the visits to the homes. That was really valuable and not what a traditional dealer could do. You know, Castelli was paying Andy $1000 a week, as an advance on the sale of paintings, but he never sold that many paintings. And most of that went to making movies. So Fred came along in the nick of time."

The portraits Fred started selling went for $25,000 and up. He also authorized Bruno Bischofberger, a Zurich dealer, to sell portraits in Europe, and Bischofberger bought eleven sixties paintings for $422,000—Andy's first jumbo sale. And at the end of 1971, Fred saved *Interview* from financial extinction by finding new backers. By then, he was still only twenty-seven years old.

Fred also made Andy something he never was before: exclusive. My earliest memory of Fred is him whispering into Andy's ear the name and address of François de Menil, one of Dominique and Jean's sons, who lived in a large, luxurious loft in the Village, and then announcing loudly, for everyone to hear, "You can bring Jed. But no one else!"

At first I thought that he was being rude and snobby, but I soon came to see that such tactlessness was actually necessary at the Factory. The *Women in Revolt* girls, and assorted other Superstars and starlets, were in the habit of dropping by in the late afternoon, and if they overheard talk of a party, or spied an RSVP card stapled into the big red appointment book Vincent kept for Andy, they took it as an open invitation. So when Andy, Fred, and Jed arrived at their exclusive private party, they were likely to find Jackie or Holly, with Rotten Rita or Silva Thin in tow, already munching the crudités.

True to form, Andy didn't make it easy for Fred to make him exclusive. I think Andy felt he got more "work" done at a party if he had more dates, kids, and Superstars working the room with, and for, *him*. "Can't I just bring Jane?" he'd ask Fred. "Okay, François might actually like her," Fred would answer, "but no one else." "Oh, not Donna, too?" "Okay, Andy,

Donna too! But *no one else!''* Then Fred would have to get on the phone to
the host or hostess and do a song and dance about how much he knew they'd
love Andy's two additional dates. And if the host said "Sorry," then Andy
would turn to Jane or Donna and announce, "Fred says you can't come with
us.''

It was a line Andy also gave me a lot. Sometimes if I seemed really
disappointed, he'd take a fifty-dollar bill out of his boot, which is where he
carried his cash, and hand it to me, saying, "Here, why don't you, uh, take
the kids out to dinner." He meant Glenn and Jude, or Michael Netter and
his wife, Madeleine. "Uh, and be sure to get a receipt.''

One night in the summer of 1971, Andy disobeyed Fred's strict order
and took me to a party at Joe Eula's. "Who's Joe Eula?'' I asked him when
he told me where we were going. "You don't know who Joe Eula is, Bob?
He's the most important person in town. He knows everybody who's anybody. Anybody who's somebody. He's really up there, Bob. This is Fred's
group, Bob. All the really chic people.''

I still didn't know who he was, but Joe Eula pinched me on the ass
when Andy introduced us. He lived in a floor-through apartment on West
54th Street off Fifth Avenue. There was a big room in front and a big room
in back and a narrow, airless kitchen connecting them, where an old black
maid was cooking up a storm, and sweating, and cursing Joe Eula: "You
ain't nothin' but a fuckin' faggot!''

"And you ain't nothin' but a fuckin' nigger, honey,'' Joe Eula cursed
back.

"Don't you honey me!''

Both salons were painted white and filled with big, white, upholstered
sofas, chaises, and chairs. There were lots of little tables that looked like
orange crates, and probably were, and on top of each one was an exquisite
white orchid plant in a plain terra-cotta pot. It was the first time I had seen
the decorating look that would go from the height of chic to Bloomingdale's
basement in the course of the seventies.

Stuck into the walls with push pins, and hanging this way and that like
works in progress in an artist's studio, were a series of fashion illustrations—
quickly executed, snappily elegant gouaches of tall, thin, exotic-looking girls
in flowing capes and scarves over sleekly tailored tunics and slacks as slim
as ski pants, everything black or red. I noticed that the girls on the walls
looked exactly like the girls on the sofas. And lounging on a chaise in one
corner, blowing smoke rings to the ceiling, was a tall, thin, exotic-looking
man, dressed entirely in black from his turtleneck to his toes, with the
exception of a long bright red silk scarf, which swirled around his shoulders
and down his torso like a very pretty snake.

I stood in the opposite corner alone—Fred had greeted me with a glare and whisked Andy off to meet someone in the other salon. I felt short, shy, and out of place. Then a fat girl in a black sequined muumuu came across the room toward me. It was Pat Ast, the Halston salesgirl Paul had cast in that year's Factory movie, *Andy Warhol's Heat.* "Hi, honey," she said. "I *lovvved* the new issue of *Interview.* C'mon, let me introduce you to Halston."

Halston was the man blowing smoke rings, and he terrified me. For one thing, Andy always spoke his name in a hushed tone. Though they were about the same age, Halston had ascended into the social stratosphere long before Andy, when he designed hats for Bergdorf Goodman in the fifties and became the favorite of ladies like Bunny Mellon, Babe Paley, and Gloria Guinness. In 1961, he did Jackie Kennedy's famous inauguration pillbox; in 1968, he started his own couture house; by 1971, he was on top of New York's fashion pack, the American equivalent of Yves Saint Laurent. And as with Saint Laurent, it was Fred who was chummy and Andy who was in awe. He always said, "I never know what to say to Halston. What should I talk to him about, Fred?"

"Dresses."

I didn't know what to say to Halston either. His Olympian grandness was intimidating. It was as if he saw himself as the fashion designer in a Hollywood movie: He was too sophisticated, too brittle, too haughty to be real. Yet, up close, he had a face as wholesome as the cornfields of Iowa, which is where Roy Halston Frowick was born. There was something likable about him, something vulnerable.

Conversation was almost impossible anyway. All the tall, thin exotic girls kept coming and going, cooing and kissing, cracking jokes and whispering gossip, falling to the floor at the foot of his chaise, jumping up to greet one another with unintelligible bursts of English, French, and Italian all mixed up. Halston said the same thing to all of them, "How are ya, darling?" And Pat Ast introduced me to this dazzling chorus line of international beauties: Marisa Berenson. Berry Berenson. Loulou de la Falaise. Elsa Peretti. Marina Schiano. Anjelica Huston. And then Liza Minnelli dashed in with Desi Arnaz, Jr. She screeched "H!" at Halston, and "Andy!" at Andy, and "Eula!" at the host. And dashed out with Desi, Jr. Perhaps because Peter Allen, whom she was in the process of divorcing, was also at the party.

It was quite a group of girls, all in their twenties then and, except for Liza, modeling. They were the girls in the gouaches, which were actually advertisements for Halston and the three other fashion designers there that night, Giorgio di Sant'Angelo, Fernando Sanchez, and Stephen Burrows. Joe Eula, "the most important man in town," I finally figured out, was a fashion illustrator. This was the chic circle into which Fred Hughes led Andy Warhol—the tight little clique that we would be part of all through the seventies. This clique—plus Mick and Bianca Jagger, Truman Capote, Jack

Nicholson, Diane and Egon von Furstenberg, Diana Ross, Calvin Klein, Diana Vreeland, Françoise and Oscar de la Renta, and European branches led by Yves Saint Laurent, Karl Lagerfeld, and Valentino—formed the new seventies society, in which fashion designers were the stars and arbiters, and the only artist was Andy.

Sometime past midnight, everyone at Joe Eula's decided to go dancing. Everyone except Halston, who was too grand, and Andy, who was too scared. The rest of us taxied to Tenth Avenue and West 48th Street, to that month's hotspot, a converted Catholic church called The Sanctuary, a refuge of sorts, where lonely white truck drivers sought solace in the company of needy black drag queens. The fashion clique found the scene amusing: the zonked-out deejay spinning soul songs on the altar, the after-hours hustlers heavy petting in the side pews, the stiletto-heeled transvestites twirling under the strobe lights that flashed across the nave. I stood there, a vodka in hand, leaning against a confessional, with Fred, who had opened up after a few more glasses of champagne and was telling me not to make *Interview* look too campy, to cut back on the Candy Darling photos, to cut out the Jackie Curtis love-life column altogether.

"Fritzie! Stop being so serious!" Elsa Peretti suddenly commanded. "Let's dance!" Fred's fashionable girlfriends always called him Fritzie and always wanted him to dance—especially since he'd gone to Arthur Murray's Dance Studio in preparation for a Rothschild ball and learned how to foxtrot, waltz, and tango. He'd steal the show at every club and party, in a suit as smooth and black as his slicked-back hair, slicing across a chaotic dance floor full of fruggers and jerkers, expertly leading Loulou or Berry.

Fred's crowd went dancing a lot in those days, and little by little he started telling me, or Glenn and Jude, where to meet them after some smart soirée, or after a business dinner with Andy. There was always a new place to dance, a momentarily well-kept secret soon to be abandoned by the In crowd when the hordes of Seventh Avenue assistants and outer-borough hair-dressers turned up.

After The Sanctuary, there was Tambourlaine, a slightly fancier place in the East Forties, which was eventually closed when a Puerto Rican drag queen was castrated in the men's room by a Cuban cocaine dealer. Then, at the end of 1971 and the start of 1972, came Stage 45, on East 45th Street, near the United Nations. Stage 45 was the one club that Andy would go to with us, because it was small and cozy, and he could sit on a banquette and still feel that he was part of the action on the dance floor.

The best night was when Helmut Berger, the star of *The Damned*, brought his director and mentor, the extremely aristocratic Luchino Visconti. Jane Forth and Donna Jordan did a torrid tango together, an homage-parody of the famous scene in *The Conformist*. They cleared the dance floor and we all sat on the banquettes applauding, laughing, shouting, "Brava, brava!" Then Cory Tippin, the handsome kid from an old Connecticut fam-

ily, who had done Jane's and Donna's makeup in *L'Amour,* wearing almost
as much rouge and lip gloss as they did, grabbed Jed's twin brother, Jay. He
was wearing makeup too, but they didn't look like drag queens—they looked
like boys who were as beautiful as girls, and they were dancing together,
very, very slowly.

"Oh, God," said Andy, "this is so great. It's like the best Broadway
show. We have to write a play like this, Bob. And put every beauty in it."
Soon enough the third act came, starring Luchino Visconti and Fred Hughes.
I'll never forget it: the old European and the young American, in identical
double-breasted black gabardine suits, elegantly waltzing to some melan-
choly Motown wail.

The next day Andy taunted Fred, "I never saw you dancing with a *boy*
before, Fred."

"Oh, Andy," Fred brushed him off, "you can hardly call Luchino
Visconti a boy. And what could I do? *He* asked *me.* I had to—out of respect
for his artistic genius."

"Oh, I know," said Andy mischievously. "But Helmut hated it. He
got so jealous. Didn't he, Bob? It was just like a scene in a play. I told Bob
we should write a play about last night."

"Well, leave me out of it, if you don't mind," snapped Fred, picking
up the phone to terminate the conversation.

Gay was not a word we used at the Factory, at least not to refer to
homosexuality. Andy preferred "has a problem." And Fred only used the
word *gay* in the old-fashioned high-society sense, to describe something
festive and pretty, as in "The Brandolini house is absolutely divine, so gay
and cozy." He picked that up from Diana Vreeland, whom he was just
getting to know then. Once, Brigid Berlin secretly taped the imperious former editor-in-chief of *Vogue* and the Duchess of Windsor lunching at her
mother's. They went on and on about the gay flowers, the gay china, the
gay curtains, and the gay Adolfo suit Honey was wearing. That's the way it
was with Fred's fashion friends; everything was gay, except the funny little
bars filled with transvestites where they went dancing night after night.

Our nonchalance was infuriating to the rising generation of liberated
homosexuals who had seen Andy Warhol as a vanguard figure. But Andy
didn't care about the correct political line; he cared about the correct style.
Like Fred, he wanted to hang out with Halston and Mrs. Vreeland, not
Allen Ginsberg and the Cockettes. In the sixties, to be openly gay seemed
daring and different; in the seventies the masses rushed out of their closets
in droves. For the Factory, the raised fist of the new liberation movement
was as uncool as the limp wrist of the fifties Fire Island set. And cool was
the Factory style long before Fred Hughes got there.

What Fred brought out was a sophisticated "European" attitude of dismissing the doctrinaire and making an art of ambiguity. And that's what I liked too—all mixed up. Although it all got a little too mixed up the day my mother accidentally encountered Candy Darling. I had taken my mother to see Andy's retrospective and she surprised me by liking it, especially the Electric Chair paintings, which she saw as an endorsement of capital punishment. Then, just as we were about to leave, the giant doors of the Whitney elevator slid open and out stepped Candy, in a trenchcoat and dark glasses, her platinum tresses dripping wet from the rain. "Well, fancy meeting you here, dear," she said.

"This is my mother, Candy," I said.

"Oh, I'm so happy to meet you, Mrs. Colacello," said Candy. "Your son is a very talented writer and a marvelous human being."

"Thank you," said my mother. Later she confided, "I feel sorry for somebody like that, who's so confused they don't know if they're a man or a woman. He or she or whatever you call it looks like something the cat dragged in. I mean, you can't tell me that's a happy person, Robert. And I hope to God and the Blessed Virgin that you don't end up like that yourself. Did you see the shoes? They were falling apart. This is what you call a Superstar? I'm not even going to tell your father. He'll get himself all worked up. You're *not* spending a lot of time with people like that, are you, Robert?"

I told her I wasn't.

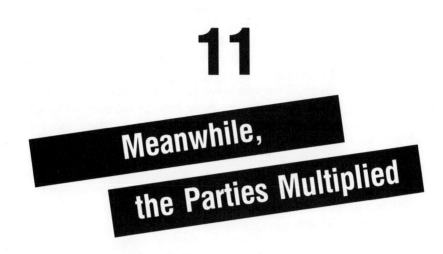

11

Meanwhile, the Parties Multiplied

On November 23, 1971, the New York *Post* announced: EDIE, ANDY'S STAR OF '65, DEAD AT 28.

"I never understood Edie," Andy told me as we taxied uptown at the end of the day, which was actually a week after Edie Sedgwick died of "acute barbital intoxication." "Even when she had a drawerful of amphetamines at home," he said, "she still would steal a few more from another one of the girls." But he didn't make that much of the death of his most famous sixties Superstar; he acted as if it were just another passing detail in his long business day. Death was not something Andy liked to contemplate.

And there were no tears shed at the Factory that day. Edie Sedgwick was as remote to most of us as Jean Harlow. Viva called and ranted, Brigid came by and raved, but Andy floated above their gory gossip on a cloud of "Gees" and "Reallys." "I never really understood Edie," he repeated forever after when her name came up. "I mean, she was beautiful and talented and from a glamorous family, but she thought she was nothing." And then he'd tell the story of the stolen pills again, a parable in the gospel according to Andy, as if it somehow explained everything, including his lack of understanding, his rejection of responsibility, his inability to mourn.

I was already starting to count the deaths by overdose in Andy Warhol's world: Jeremy Dixon, the angelic *Interview* assistant; Steven Piven, a talented actor in *Pork;* now Edie Sedgwick.

Without knowing it, after only a year and a half, I was overdosing on the wonderful world of Warhol myself. Working too hard, playing too hard, burning my candle at both ends like an old cliché. I was smoking too much pot, drinking too much vodka, going to too many parties, downing dangerous quantities of Tuinals and stingers. My love life was less than zero, but I confessed every last minus into Andy's silent Sony.

And I was always broke. I even went back to Nina Needlepoint part time that fall—a "humiliation," as I scribbled in my journal, followed by "MONEY MONEY MONEY." I resented having to do that, on top of editing and art directing Andy's magazine and doing half the interviews and movie reviews in it for an extra $25 apiece. There was never enough time to research my Warhol film book, let alone write it. And my old friends Glenn and Jude were constantly on my back, clamoring for higher salaries, better invitations, more power. So I gave in to an idea of theirs: Glenn would take over as managing editor and art director while I worked on my book; my new title at *Interview* would be special contributing editor. It was a step down, but also a way out.

And it dovetailed perfectly with the plans of Fred Hughes, who was secretly negotiating the sale of the Jerome Hill and Charles Rydell shares to Peter Brant and Joe Allen, his new best friends—and Andy's new best clients. Peter Brant and Joe Allen were in their twenties and ran their fathers' rapidly expanding newsprint company. Bruno Bischofberger, Andy's new Swiss art dealer, was also part of the complicated transaction, which involved the exchange of paintings, the publication of the Electric Chair prints, tax write-offs—a typical Fred Hughes deal. And Fred's name went on the masthead as editor, above those of Paul Morrissey and Andy Warhol.

And now that I was free of the drudgery of *Interview* paste-up and newsstand delivery, I couldn't resist Andy's suggestions to organize a screening at the Factory, or to arrange an invitation for him, plus five, to a movie première—especially when he added, "If they say we can have that many tickets, you can come too." It was a chance to learn how the party and publicity game was played by the greatest player of the century, Gertrude Stein and Elsa Maxwell notwithstanding. And it meant getting closer to the real center of power at the Factory, which was not the *Interview* editorshop, or the director's chair on the movie sets. It was Andy's big red appointment book.

On New Year's Eve, 1971, I spent the morning at Nina Needlepoint working to pay for my Christmas presents, the afternoon at Anthology Film Archives watching part of Andy's *24-Hour Movie* for my book, and the evening at an extremely swell bash—Beluga on Flora Danica china, Dom Perignon in Baccarat crystal—given in her East Side town house by a rich Indian dowager named Bachu Dinsha, a friend of my new best friend, Adriana Jackson, a wise and mischievous Milanese aristocrat, and her husband, Brooks, the Iolas Gallery partner in New York. Through Adriana, I had arranged for Andy, Jed, Candy, and Sylvia to be invited—Fred was going to Halston's. It was the first Manhattan house I'd been in that was entirely occupied by one person, not counting the cook, butler, maid, and chauffeur. And I was feeling "really up there" now.

An old Georgetown buddy, Chris Murray, had a different take on Bob Colacello at the New Year. He was in New York for the holidays and had come by my apartment one night for a reunion with Glenn and Jude and Michael and Madeleine. My Georgetown and Columbia friends noticed that I had started talking like Andy—I was saying "Oh" and "Uh" at the beginning of every sentence—and that every place I went with Andy was "really up there," and that everyone I met with Andy was "a beauty." After a couple of hours of listening to my Andy anecdotes, celebrity chitchat, party itineraries, gay-bar scandals, and financial woes, Chris cracked a joke that made us all laugh. "You know," he said, "since Bob came to New York City and went to work for Warhol, he's lost his morals, lost his money, and now he'll lose his mind."

Maybe Chris Murray was right; maybe I was losing my mind. My days seemed like one long telephone call, reliving the previous night's social roundelay, planning that night's and the next's. And the intrigue was tricky. For example: Candy Darling had been tossed out of her East Side setup by the garment center heir and moved into the West Side duplex of Samuel Adams Green, an art-world friend of Andy's from the sixties, who had curated the riotous 1965 show in Philadelphia, not a favorite of Fred's. Sam saw me as his way back into the Factory social orbit and suggested that I help him give a dinner for Nureyev. He'd get Nureyev, Monique van Vooren, Lily Auchincloss, and the McKendrys, if I got Andy and Paul—without Fred. I wasn't sure if I should do that, but I was under pressure from Candy to be nice to her new patron, and Andy agreed when I broached the idea. "Fred will probably be in Paris anyway," he said. Fred was not in Paris anyway, and was not at all pleased when Sam Green persuaded John and Maxime McKendry to bring her daughter, Loulou de la Falaise, who was not in Paris either. And when Sam suggested that we now needed a young man to balance out his two tables for eight and I suggested my new friend Robert Mapplethorpe, Fred really hit the roof. Then Andy announced, a few hours before we were due at Sam's, that he might not go after all.

The day I was organizing this Vietnam Peace Conference of a dinner, April 17, 1972, my appointment book noted that the first one-third of my Warhol film book was due at Dutton—though I had written only the introduction. At 2:30 that day, I was scheduled to interview Ultra Violet for the book. At 5:30, I was expected at a Polish embassy reception. At 8:30, Larry Rivers was staging an "opera" at the Whitney Museum, to be followed by a hot-dog-and-jazz party at his East 14th Street loft.

I spent the morning at *Interview* arranging a shipment of 180 pounds of back issues to Bruno Bischofberger in Zürich; discussing a Naty Abascal (then a big model, now the Duchess of Feria) photo session with Peter

Beard; attending a meeting with a Mr. Cal Costly regarding the distribution of *Interview* in Stamford, New Haven, Hartford, and Boston. What was I doing there, six months after I had stepped down as managing editor? As special contributing editor, I was theoretically under no obligation to do anything but interviews, film reviews, and the new "Smalltalk" column I was writing, but in reality I couldn't avoid the managerial side of the magazine.

Glenn needed help, which he sometimes requested, sometimes demanded, and sometimes resented—our relationship had become rocky. I didn't like being bossed around by my former assistant; nor did I find it easy to stop being bossy myself. "Stabbed in the back by Glenn," I melodramatically scrawled in my diary on March 16, 1972, "even sooner than I expected!"

What made matters worse was the fighting between Glenn and Paul Morrissey, who then expected me to deal with Glenn. Both were hot-tempered, neither was capable of compromise, and Glenn confused being provocative with "editorial independence." He delighted in telling the boys in Max's back room that he'd hired Fran Lebowitz on the spot because she'd brought him a nasty review of *Women in Revolt* that she had published in *Changes,* "a magazine with a readership of fifty-three," as Fran put it. Glenn thought this was "gutsy." Paul thought it was a good reason not to use Fran. She began writing for *Interview* early in 1972, and her generally nasty film reviews quickly evolved into a column called "Best of the Worst," which Paul referred to as "Worst of the Worst." Andy didn't like Fran either. For one thing, she always went mute around him. She later told me that she was sure if she got too close to him *before she was famous,* "my sense of humor would somehow become Andy Warhol's sense of humor."

"Who does she think she is?" Andy always said of Fran in those days, especially after he found out that she refused to learn to type and instead dictated her handwritten pieces to Glenn or Jude. "She's not that good. She just does that New York Jewish comedy that everybody does. We should drop her."

Despite the personality clashes, *Interview* made considerable progress after Glenn O'Brien took over. His first issue, February 1972, was a Marilyn Monroe special; March 1972 featured James Dean in all his tough, confused splendor. But his third issue, in May 1972, really opened the magazine up in a big way, adding sections on art, music, books, and fashion. This last was key, because that's where the advertising was. Our first fashion spread was dazzling: a Halston interview by Pat Ast illustrated with Joe Eula sketches of Halston and his girls, including Pat, the Berenson sisters, Loulou de la Falaise, and Elsa Peretti. It was chic and hip and exclusive and the fashion pack loved it.

Then Joe Eula asked to have his original drawings back. They were to be delivered to Halston, he said, who had apparently bought them and was planning on having them framed. The only problem was that Glenn had misplaced the drawings. When we finally found them under some pile of rejected layouts, they were crumpled and a bit torn. We tried to flatten them out, but there was nothing to do. Finally, it was left to me to take them uptown to Halston. I tried to leave the package with his receptionist, but Halston told her to show me right in and greeted me with an effusive proclamation of *Interview*'s inevitable rise to the top of the fashion-magazine heap. "I sent a copy over to John Fairchild," he said, referring to the fearsome titan of *Women's Wear Daily*, "with a little note attached that said, 'Watch out!' And I've been giving them out to the ladies when they come in for their fittings—you know, Lily, Mica, Chessy, like that. Everyone *adores* the story, darling. And what really makes it work are Joe's fabulous drawings, don't you think?"

I passed the fabulous drawings in an *Interview* envelope across the black lacquer desk. Halston was dressed all in black and surrounded by white orchids. He slid them out. "Is this your idea of a *joke?!?*" he screamed. "These drawings are *ruined! How dare* you treat the work of a *great* artist with such careless *disdain!* Get *out!* And be sure to tell your Andy Warhol that he's not the *only* important artist in town! Get *out!* Get *out!*"

Fred went right to work repairing the damage, sending orchids to Halston and Joe, and persuading Andy to send Cow posters or something. Glenn refused to write an apology note, so I did. Andy actually found Halston's tantrum more amusing than insulting. He tape recorded my retelling of it, of course. One thing did worry him: Halston's note to John Fairchild. "Halston was really being mean," Andy insisted. "He knows John will get mad if he thinks we're really going into fashion and then he'll tell all the designers not to give us ads. How much do you bet that's what happens, Fred?" Fred dismissed Andy's worrying as paranoia. But Andy, who had started out in fashion magazines and fashion advertising, probably knew what he was talking about.

The improved contents of the May 1972 issue also boasted a completely new look—starting with the cover, in color for the first time. The Art Deco *Interview* logo was dropped. So was the limiting tagline, "Andy Warhol's Film Magazine." In their place, *Andy Warhol's Interview* was splashed in bright blue-and-red handwriting, like a giant signature. The cover photo, Donna Jordan by Chris von Wangenheim, was also awash in color—red lips, turquoise eye shadow, yellow hair—airbrushed onto the original black-and-white photograph by our new cover designer, Richard Bernstein. He remained the designer, and that remained the look, with slight permutations, of every *Interview* cover for the next fifteen years. The overall effect was of an Andy Warhol portrait autographed by Andy Warhol—though Andy's hand had never touched the page.

Fred Hughes had worked out the perfect solution to the conflict of interests between Andy and *Interview*'s new backers. Peter Brant and Joe Allen saw Andy as *Interview*'s primary asset: They wanted his name on the cover above the title, and big; they didn't see why Andy shouldn't design the cover himself. Andy told me that he didn't want to design the cover because "it would never come out right and I would go crazy." He also thought it was tacky to feature his name so prominently on the cover of his magazine. Fred didn't believe in either the perfectionist or the modest line; he thought Andy was being cheap with his time and talent. Peter Brant and Joe Allen, he reminded Andy more than once, were not only providing the magazine with newsprint and picking up its monthly losses, but also buying Warhol paintings directly from the Factory, from Leo Castelli and Bruno Bischofberger, and at auction. Andy kept saying, "Oh, I know, Fred. I know. But I just can't do it. I just can't do it."

And so Fred turned to Richard Bernstein to create a Warhol front page for the Warhol magazine without Warhol. Bernstein, a talented young graphic artist and habitué of Max's back room since the late sixties, was dating Berry Berenson at the time we hired him, so he was wrapped up in the new seventies fashion scene. Conveniently, he was influenced by Andy artistically; and, more important for *Interview*'s purposes, he was in awe of Andy personally. That made him malleable to the endless requests for revisions from Fred or Glenn or me, many of which actually came from Andy. The cover was the one page of *Interview* that Andy always saw *before* publication.

I remember a meeting at Bernstein's studio in the Chelsea Hotel, with Fred, Glenn, and me all trying out various styles of handwriting, and patching bits together. We also fiddled with the angle of the cover photograph and the positioning of the date and price. And then we brought the final paste-up back to the Factory for Andy's approval. He gave it a mildly enthusiastic "Gee, great." And then, the minute Bernstein left, said what was on his mind: "It looks a little too much like me, Fred." When the May issue was printed, Andy decided that his name should be smaller than the word *Interview* for June. By July, it was big again, to please Peter Brant and Joe Allen, whose belief that prominently displaying the Warhol name would increase newsstand sales was slowly but surely proving correct.

It was also because of pressure from our new investors that Andy started doing interviews for the magazine. He soon realized that it was a great way to meet movie stars, and loved doing them so long as he had one of his Factory cohorts along to "ask the real questions."

One day in May, Andy, Robert Mapplethorpe, and I went to see Rudolf Nureyev in rehearsal with the Royal Ballet at Lincoln Center. When I had called Nureyev to arrange the appointment for Andy, the regal Russian had requested Mapplethorpe's presence. It was the beginning of a comedy of errors. And a triple ego war.

Robert Mapplethorpe, whom I'd seen with his girlfriend Patti Smith on the New York poetry scene, had called me after my *Village Voice* review of *Robert Having His Nipple Pierced,* an Underground movie he was in. We had become fast friends, despite Candy Darling's warning "Everyone knows he's a sicko." I published his work for the first time in *Interview,* even though it annoyed Paul, Andy, and Fred. Andy disliked Robert, just as he disliked Fran, because he hardly talked in his presence. In fact, neither would utter a word in his presence. Robert told me that he was afraid that Andy would steal his art ideas, "like he did with Brigid." Of course, some would say, Robert's early mix of photography and painting derived directly from Andy.

In the long taxi ride from the Factory to Lincoln Center, Andy didn't say a single word because he was furious that Robert was carrying a Polaroid Big Shot camera, just as he was. Robert fought silence with silence, while I chattered on brightly like a Washington socialite seated between the ambassadors of Iran and Iraq. When Nureyev entered the fray it was more than I could handle; I just stood in the wings taking mental notes for *Interview* and my diary. The battle royal started like this:

WARHOL: What color are your eyes?
NUREYEV: The interview is canceled.

To make sure that his edict was obeyed, Nureyev pressed the off switch of Andy's Sony. He claimed that I had never told him that we were coming to interview him. It was one of the first times that Andy had done an interview for the magazine, after months of pressure from the Brants, Fred, Glenn, and me. He was nervous to start off with and now he was angry as well. He put his turned-off tape recorder back into his plastic shopping bag from Brownie's and pulled out his Polaroid Big Shot, popping its blinding flash—one, two, three times—at Nureyev. Then he slid the film out of the camera quickly and slipped the developing photos into his jacket pocket, his prize captured. But Nureyev demanded to see the results. The first shot was a handsome portrait, as was the second—Nureyev signed both for Andy. Détente at last, I thought.

But when the third Polaroid was developed, revealing a tight closeup of Nureyev's crotch, the Royal Ballet star had a Russian fit. He sneered and snarled and growled like a Tartar tiger, and clawed the offending image out of Andy's hand and flung it to the floor. Andy knelt to pick it up. Nureyev put his foot down on it. Robert aimed *his* Polaroid at Nureyev's foot on Andy's photo. Andy gave Robert a nuclear look. Nureyev grabbed Robert's camera, yanked out the photo, and crumpled it into a useless, gooey wad.

"Don't you like your foot?" Robert had the nerve to ask.

"My foot, yes," replied Nureyev, tapping the tip of Robert's nose, looking hard into his eyes, and smiling for the first time since we arrived. Then, in his gray T-shirt and a burnt-sienna leotard, he spun away from us and into his dance exercises, stretching and arching his taut body. Andy and Robert took more Polaroids, each as if the other wasn't there. Nureyev looked every photo over and tore most of them up.

Pop. Pop. Pop.

"You don't really want this one, do you?"

Rip. Rip. Rip.

Pop. Pop. Pop.

"I look schizophrenic in this one, no?"

Rip. Rip. Rip.

After a while, the rehearsal began in earnest and the Royal Ballet company, at close range and out of costume a pretty motley crew, paraded around the stage. Andy said his first words since Nureyev had shut off his tape recorder: "Rotten fruit."

Then, suddenly, Nureyev leapt, and leapt again, and again and again and again in a stunning circle of leaps, each one held for an instant of breathtaking suspension, a flash of beauty fixed in flight. Andy melted: "He's so great. I didn't know a person could be that great. He should be in movies." Andy was clutching the bits and pieces of his ripped-up Polaroids. So was Robert Mapplethorpe.

Andy called me at home that night. "We would have got a real interview out of Nureyev if you hadn't brought that awful Robert Mapplethorpe along," he berated me.

"But Nureyev asked me to bring him, Andy."

"But it's your fault they even met because you got him invited to Sam Green's dinner for Nureyev. You should be trying to get Jed invited to dinners, not Robert Mapplethorpe."

"I did get Jed invited to that dinner. You said he didn't want to go."

"I never said that. You never told me he was invited."

"All right, Andy. But listen, Robert was a big hit at that dinner. Lily Auchincloss found him fascinating."

"It would be a lot better, Bob, if Lily Auchincloss found Jed fascinating," said Andy, ending that conversation.

I was beginning to discover that it wasn't easy being Andy's assistant social director. One of the ongoing difficulties, which grew worse over time, was the Jed Johnson situation. It wasn't hard to get Jed invited anywhere; everyone thought he was attractive and sweet. The hard part was getting him to go. And when he wouldn't, Andy preferred to pretend that Fred or I forgot to tell him that Jed was invited, rather than to admit that Jed wanted a night off from his housemate and boss. Rejection, especially romantic rejection, was something Andy simply could not deal with, so he denied that he had been rejected, or that there had ever been any romance at all. For Andy, asexuality was not only a cover, it was also an escape.

Sometimes the diplomatic dance between Andy and potential *Interview* subjects got very complicated. Particularly with people who were "big stars" but whom Andy nevertheless disliked. Yoko Ono began badly with Andy when trying to enlist his support for her 1972 "This Is Not Here" exhibition at the Everson Museum in Syracuse, New York, on John Lennon's birthday. He took her to tea at an old haunt, Serendipity, and asked me along. Heading uptown in her limo, she started asking for favors, never the way to Andy's heart. She expected him at the upstate opening and she wanted him to get Jasper Johns, Robert Rauschenberg, and Larry Rivers too. She justified her pushiness with attacks on the male-chauvinist art establishment's oppression of struggling female artists. "But I thought your family owned a bank," teased Andy. "Even rich women," said Yoko, "can be oppressed, Andy." "Oh really." At the ice-cream parlor she ordered one of everything on the menu and told him how much it would mean to John if Andy was there for his birthday. "Oh really," Andy said again, promising to attend, "but only if you tell me how big John is." "How big?" "You know, down there." "Now, Andy, I'm trying to be serious."

This was a standard conversational ploy of Andy's, asking women the size of their husband's cocks. Most of them blushed, or tittered, or told him, but not Yoko. Mrs. Lennon was not amused. Andy said he'd go anyway, but I knew he wouldn't. He got Fred to call David Whitney and Leo Castelli to try to get the other famous artists. They all said no. As did Andy at the very last minute, saying Jed was sick. So he sent Holly Woodlawn and Silva Thin in his place, and I took Candy Darling, and she promised not to call Yoko a "Japanese beetle" to the press.

Although he said he "never knew what to ask" during the interviews he did for the magazine, somehow Andy always got to the heart of the matter, usually in an indirect, roundabout, seemingly fumbling way.

The sickly child who'd written to Shirley Temple for her autograph still thought Hollywood was heaven and treated stars like saints. And this adoring, quasi-groupie approach of Andy's often led his subjects to let down their guard and give away more of themselves than they did with any other interviewer. Talking to Andy, they thought, was like talking to a worshipful fan, not a reporter—but a fan who was also a star, and therefore an equal. He asked such cute, harmless questions, like "What's your favorite color?" The kind of questions a child might ask, they thought, not realizing that, as Sony rolled on relentlessly, these children's questions sometimes make adults look foolish.

* * *

For the June issue, Andy tape recorded John and Yoko. Andy began
with another of his specialties, not a dumb question but a non-question,
which nonetheless put the subject on the spot.

> ANDY: We thought maybe you could just talk to yourself on the tape and
> ask yourself your questions.
> YOKO: Oh good idea!

Mr. and Mrs. Lennon proceeded to discuss, at great length, their problems with the United States Immigration Service, which had refused their
request for permanent-resident visas because John had once been busted for
marijuana possession in England. Yoko asserted that John was being perse-
cuted because of his involvement with the peace movement. John compared
his case to that of Charlie Chaplin. Andy listened.

John Lennon asked Andy if *he* had ever voted. "Well, if you vote you
have to go to jury duty," answered Andy, not answering at all, though the
assumption the reader probably made was that Andy never voted. It was a
hip, cool, cynical answer in keeping with his image. As was the advice he
gave the Lennons on their visa problems: "Why don't you give some money
for Nixon's campaign?"

Andy didn't follow his own advice. That fall, he donated a series of
prints to the McGovern campaign—and ended up on Nixon's enemy list. He
let his liberalism out of the closet—and paid for it with endless IRS audits,
or so he was convinced. Andy believed in *every* conspiracy theory, even
those that contradicted each other. Fear was as much a determining factor
in his politics as it was in the rest of his life. Fear, and love of money, which
is another form of fear.

Politics, after all, combines two of the themes that interested Andy
most: power and fame. At about the same time he was interviewing John
Lennon and Yoko Ono, he was starting a new series of "real" paintings, as
opposed to commissioned portraits, his first since his "retirement" from
painting in the middle sixties.

It began with an idea from Bruno Bischofberger, who had been pushing
Andy to go back to painting, as had Fred. Bruno's idea was that Andy should
paint the most important figure of the twentieth century. As a large part of
Bruno's clientele was German, Hitler was ruled right out. On the other hand,
Franklin Delano Roosevelt didn't seem likely to sell well among the St.
Moritz set either. Bruno and his staff researched the history books, brain-
stormed and pondered: Who? Finally, he came up with the perfect subject:
the man responsible for both the technological richness and the technological terror of life in this century.

He flew to New York to present the idea in person. "I've got it," he told Andy. "Albert Einstein! The most important person of the twentieth century!"

"Oh," said Andy. "That's a good idea. But I was just reading in *Life* magazine that the most famous person in the world today is Chairman Mao. Shouldn't it be the most *famous* person, Bruno?"

Bruno was horrified. "A portrait of a Communist leader did not seem like something easy to sell to Gunther Sachs or Stavros Niarchos, I told Andy," he says. "But Andy pointed out that Nixon had just been to see Mao, and if he was okay with Nixon, he would probably be okay with people like Gunther and Stavros too."

Andy wasn't apolitical; he was ruthless. Mao was a brilliant choice, and Andy's timing was perfect. The Mao paintings, when they were exhibited a year later in New York, Zürich, and Paris, were greeted with universal acclaim. They were controversial, commercial, and important, just like the man they portrayed and the man who painted them. And they were all about power: the power of one man over the lives of one billion people.

Mao Tse-tung, it might be noted, was the *only* political figure Andy ever painted of his own volition. Except, come to think of it, Nixon. Andy's contribution to the McGovern campaign was an edition of 350 signed and numbered prints with "Vote McGovern" scrawled across the corner of an electric-orange-and-hot-pink portrait of a particularly tricky-looking Dick.

Meanwhile, the parties multiplied. On the rare night that I stayed home, I was overwhelmed by feelings of depression and confusion. I wanted to run away from Andy and the Factory and New York and write my book in peace and solitude. I was mad at myself for turning over power to Glenn only to be stuck with at least as much work and a lesser title. I wondered what I was doing at all these parties with people twenty years older and twenty times more successful than me. Did they like me, or were they using me to get to Andy? Did he like me, or was he using me to get to them?

I felt trapped, in over my head, and lonely. So I went to another party, and felt important because I was among important people. And like Andy, like Sylvia Miles, Ruth Ford, Candy Darling, I rationalized that I was meeting people who could help my career, that going to parties was work. Sometimes it was. Candy was cast in Tennessee Williams's *Small Craft Warnings* after she impressed the playwright at his birthday party. And I was asked to write for *Harper's Bazaar* by its features editor, Barbara Goldsmith, at Ruth Ford's dinner. She set up a meeting with the new editor-in-chief, James Brady, who had been John Fairchild's right-hand man at *WWD*. They said that since I went to so many parties why not write up some for them?

I didn't know it then, but I was witnessing social history in the making. All the elements of the fashionable new society that would dominate the decade, and merge with the rich Reaganite group in the eighties, were there:

the Park Avenue ladies in their designer dresses; the European titles flocking to New York for freedom and kicks; the beautiful Brazilians; the trips to Manila, where Imelda and Ferdinand Marcos set up a jet-set court; the movie stars and the models and the photographers, always the photographers; the loud music; the late dancing; the fabulous flowers, which by the end of the eighties would make most society parties look like Mafia funerals. And, between the lines, the homosexuality, the drugs in offices and bathrooms, the mindlessness of our merriment, the cruelty of a world where beauty and style and money were all.

Parties, parties, parties, all winter, all spring, all night.

The premiere of *Cabaret,* with everyone from Gloria Vanderbilt Cooper and Mayor Wagner to Desi Arnazes, Sr. and Jr., in attendance, and everyone from the von Furstenbergs to the O'Briens following Michael York around at the "divinely decadent" party at the Plaza afterward.

The premiere of *A Scarecrow in a Garden of Cucumbers,* starring Holly Woodlawn, who arrived in a long white limo with live white doves attached to her wrists, flapping, squawking, excreting. "How Holly," said Candy.

Jerome Hill's off-to-Cannes dinner party at the Algonquin, where Andy, William Burroughs, Terry Southern, and Larry Rivers sat in a row, like some Mount Rushmore of Hip, and Brigid Berlin burst in with a radio broadcasting Nixon's massive bombing of Hanoi. Everybody said it was the end of the world, except Burroughs, who had already passed out, and Andy, who was deep into dessert—a "snowball" of ice cream covered in coconut and vodka.

The David Hockney opening at the André Emmerich Gallery, followed by a bash at Michael Findlay's loft, one of the first in SoHo, where Elsa Peretti and Taylor Mead did a tipsy tango to the new disco version of "Respect Yourself," and the boys in Halston danced with the boys in Stephen Burrows as if they were at a gay bar instead of a respectable art-world party.

A posh pasta party at the Italian embassy for an Iolas Gallery artist from Milan named Lydia, who made giant cocks in gold. Andy took John and Yoko, who badgered Ambassador Vinci about their U.S. visa problems.

My twenty-fifth birthday dinner at Sam Green and Candy Darling's duplex, with Robert Mapplethorpe and John McKendry, Sylvia and her beau, Rudolf Martinus, Ruth Ford and Dotson Rader, the Jacksons, Scavullo, Andy, Paul, and Jed, but—again—not Fred. Glenn and Jude were asked for after dinner, and Andy, as a joke, gave me a rhinestone necklace, which a *Daily News* reporter who was writing "A Day in the Life of Andy Warhol" described as diamonds. My father, an avid *Daily News* reader, called bright and early the next morning. "Why would a man give a man a diamond necklace?" he wanted to know.

"They're rhinestones, Dad."

"It says right here in the *News* that he gave you a diamond necklace, goddamn. One of the guys in the office already asked me about it."

"Tell him not to believe everything he reads, Dad."

My mother was more worried about my health: In April I had been diagnosed with a severe case of anemia. My blood pressure was just slightly above coma level. I knew something was wrong when I fell asleep at a Patti Smith reading at John and Maxime McKendry's—not an easy thing to do given the way Patti read and the way the McKendrys entertained. I had been passing out quite a bit in March and April, and at the oddest times and places, such as the porn theater I went to one afternoon with Robert Mapplethorpe. Finally, I went to see a doctor recommended by Francesco Scavullo. Dr. Josue Corcos was a dapper Moroccan bachelor who attended to the King of Morocco's sisters when they were in town. He told me that the anemia was the cause of my depression, and that vertigo, along with dizziness, faintness, and exhaustion, were all symptoms. So I hadn't lost my mind in New York City, just my red blood cells. I had to go to Dr. Corcos's office for vitamin B-12 injections every day for two weeks, then three times a week for another two weeks, finally tapering off to once a week by the end of May. And eat red meat every day. And sleep as much as I wanted whenever I wanted.

My mother rushed into the city with homemade lentil soup, for iron, and meatball stew and piles of frozen hamburgers and steaks. "And stop going out so much," she nagged. "Do you hear me? Stay home for a change and eat the lentils I made for you. Invite a friend over and broil a nice sirloin steak."

"But, Mom," I persisted, "I have to go out for work."

"Forget work. Get yourself better first."

12

A Pile of Rocks

In the end, Adriana Jackson saved me. I had met Brooks and Adriana Jackson when Paul shot the last scene of *Heat* in their apartment on Second Avenue in the Fifties. Their pet ocelot, Trumba—Italian for mixed-up—the child they didn't have, was also in the scene with Sylvia, Joe, and the others. As a young woman from a good Milanese family, Adriana had studied painting, won prizes, had shows. They had a fantastic art collection—the fruit of Brooks's twenty-five years with Iolas: several Magrittes and Max Ernsts, and a major Picasso gouache. A few nights after we'd shot the scene there, a terrible electrical fire swept the apartment, engulfing the silk-lined walls. Brooks saved Trumba, Adriana saved the Picasso, suffering third-degree burns on both hands from the red-hot gilt frame. Bandaged and on painkillers for many weeks, she never complained or blamed Andy and the Factory, even though the fire might have somehow been caused by the film equipment.

Adriana saw herself as my surrogate mother. She was always telling me, "You're just like all the Americans of your generation: very intelligent and totally ignorant. You must come and spend a summer with me in Italy. First, you meet some whores. Then, I introduce you to the countesses." Perhaps she was my surrogate Auntie Mame. She knew I had to get away from Andy and the life I was leading. So she arranged a business trip to Mexico for all of us and then announced that I was staying there with her for the summer to recuperate and work on my book. It was hard for Andy to protest, because she had also arranged for me to sell my first commissioned portrait on that trip.

The victim, which is what we half-jokingly called Andy's portrait clients, was Maria Luisa de Romans, the wife of the Italian ambassador to Mexico. An heiress to the second-largest fortune in Italy, after the Agnellis, she was also an artist herself. She had had an exhibition of paintings at the Iolas Gallery in New York that spring, and Adriana had made sure that Andy and I were always seated near her at dinners then. She didn't speak English, but she was able to understand Andy telling her, over and over, that he thought her paintings were "just greaaat."

Maria Luisa and I communicated in Spanish, and at one of the dinner parties in her honor she told me that she was having an exhibition at the Museum of Modern Art in Mexico City that June and wondered if Andy and I would like to join Adriana and Brooks as her guests for the opening. "Does invited mean first-class tickets?" Andy asked me when I told him about Maria Luisa's suggestion. "Can I bring Jed? And Fred has to come too. And you should get her to agree to have her portrait done before we agree to go." Adriana persuaded Maria Luisa that the expense of four first-class plane tickets and rooms at the best hotel in Mexico City would be nothing compared to the prestige and publicity Andy's presence would bring her.

It didn't hurt matters when I rushed up to Maria Luisa's suite at the Regency with a tape recorder and interviewed her for *Interview,* though Glenn later refused to give the story more than a half page. As for the portrait commission, Adriana thought it would be more diplomatic to wait until we were in Mexico to bring it up, and Fred agreed, despite Andy's whiny objections.

On June 7, 1972, we flew to Mexico City—Andy, Jed, Fred, and I, plus Brooks, Adriana, and Trumba. On the flight, Fred had a long heart-to-heart with Adriana, which she later repeated to me. She touched a raw nerve when she told him that she remembered him when he first came to the Iolas Gallery in Paris. "You were so full of hope and creativity then," she said, "and now you only think about business. It's a little sad, no?" Fred told her that he had discovered that he was good at business and that what he really wanted out of life was to make money, lots and lots of it. He said he planned on making his first million by the time he was thirty, which was only two years off, and by the age of forty, he would be as rich as Howard Hughes, and as important an art collector and patron as Jean de Menil. "*That's* creative," he declared. "Do you really think Andy will let that happen?" Adriana asked. "Of course, because I'll make him very rich, too," Fred answered. "I already have made him a lot richer than he was before I came along."

As for Andy in flight, he sat beside Jed poring over every last page of the *New York Times.* I found this fascinating, because he made a point in every interview he gave of saying he never read anything but movie-star biographies, and because he asked me every morning when he called, "Is there anything in the paper I should know about?" Now, he managed to find an obscure item on a back page about an outbreak of typhoid fever in Mexico. "There's a plague in Mexico," he immediately leaned across the aisle to me. "We have to get the portrait right away and leave as soon as we can."

He wasn't kidding. The minute we landed at the Mexico City airport, where Maria Luisa awaited us with two long limousines with Italian flags waving from their hoods, and a Mexican TV crew, Andy whispered in my ear, "You have to pop the question right now, Bob. You and Adriana should go in the car with her and pop the question, and I'll go in the other car with Fred and Jed."

"It's too rude, Andy."

"No, it's not. *She* has the TV crew here already, doesn't she?"

For the next three days and nights, at the black-tie museum opening and the stiff diplomatic lunches and dinners before and after, Andy taunted me with the same directive: "Pop the question now, Bob. You're not here to have fun, Bob. You're here to work." He even got Jed on my case. "There's ten percent in it for you," Jed pointed out to me as the three of us rode in yet another embassy limo to yet another embassy party. "Ten percent of $25,000 is a lot of money, Bob," Andy added helpfully. I didn't dare say that I'd assumed I'd be getting twenty percent, like Fred. "Just get Maria Luisa in a corner at this dinner," Andy instructed, "and pop the question. She loves you, Bob. I'm sure she'll say yes."

Finally, after a week of Andy's nagging and my resisting, Fred popped the question—on the dance floor of the French ambassador's residence. Maria Luisa agreed to have four portraits done for a total of $40,000. I offered to waive my commission, but Fred said that since I had made the contact and arranged the trip, he would make sure that Andy gave it to me. He also proposed to the Jacksons that if they brought two more clients to us, Andy would do Adriana's portrait free.

The next day, Andy rushed right over to the Italian ambassador's residence with his Big Shot, popped about a dozen rolls of Polaroids, and caught the next plane out with Jed and Fred. "We'll see you in a couple of weeks, Bob," he said in farewell. "Maybe you can get some more portraits while you're here from Maria Luisa's rich Mexican friends."

"Leave Robertino alone, Andy," Adriana chimed in. "He's coming with me to Puerto Vallarta for the summer. He needs to rest. And write!"

"Oh, really," said Andy. "See you in a couple of weeks, Bob."

As much as I needed a rest and wanted to write, I was actually sorry to see Andy leave. I felt that we were closer than we had been before we came. It was the same feeling I'd had after the trip to Germany. Part of it came from spending time together all day every day, but Andy also relaxed a bit on trips. He didn't have to worry about Valerie Solanis lurking or deal with the demands of his Superstars. His fame, and his fear, were a little less intense away from New York, and he let down his guard, if only slightly.

He was also helpless in hotels, or pretended to be. He was afraid to call room service on his own, terrified when a maid knocked on the door if he was alone, beside himself if he had to answer his phone and it was a reporter or a fan, though he managed to deal with dealers and clients, charming them with gossipy tidbits and avoiding business entanglements with "Oh, let me ask Fred when he gets back."

In Mexico City, Fred and Jed usually went to museums and antique shops after lunch, leaving me to go back to the Camino Real Hotel with Andy. Typically, Fred found a huge Courbet landscape, for a mere $250, in some junk shop, whose proprietor had no idea what it was. As much as Andy loved to shop, he was always anxious to get back to the hotel to call Vincent in New York, "to see if any checks came in the mail." These calls could go on for an hour or so, with me just sitting around reading Mexican magazines.

One day, as Andy went on and on, I slipped away to my own room to nap. The phone rang. It was Andy. "I don't know how to turn the air conditioner off," he moaned. "Could you come and do it for me?"

I found him sitting on the terrace, pulling hairs out of his arm. I shut the air conditioner off and turned to leave. "Gee, thanks," Andy said softly, as he came back into the sitting room. "Oh, no, now I let in a moth. Do you think you can kill it? I can't kill anything." I murdered the moth and turned toward the door again. "Uh, shouldn't we order something from room service?" said Andy plaintively.

"I thought I'd take a nap."

"You don't want to sleep."

"I sort of do, Andy."

"Gee, I wonder where Jed is? It's getting so late." He sounded so lonely. I hesitated for a moment; I really was tired and wanted to sleep. Andy stood in front of the mirror over the sofa.

"I look so terrible," he said.

"It's the light."

"No, it's not. It's me."

I stayed and called room service, ordering Andy's afternoon favorites: tea, chicken sandwiches, sundaes. And we talked. I don't mean that Andy turned on his tape recorder and I talked. This time we had a real conversation, and Andy told me things he had never told me before.

"It's just so hard to get up in the morning. It would be so much easier to stay in bed all day, wouldn't it? I have to take, uh, a pill to get going. I just don't have any energy since I was shot."

"What kind of pill?"

"Oh, uh, just a little Dexamyl. It's nothing."

He told me, "Life isn't easy, Bob. I had to sell fruit on street corners to get through school, you know. It wasn't easy."

We had visited the great Mexican artist Siqueiros at his studio the day before, and as we spoke, Andy flipped through the catalogue of a recent exhibition that Siqueiros had signed to him. He stopped at a reproduction of a late abstract painting. "Anybody could do this," he said. "I mean, he could turn out hundreds of paintings a day like this. He just puts on the base. Then takes it off. Then goes crazy a little. It's just action paintings. Anyway, Pollock was much better. Pollock was a great painter. I wish I had a Pollock. This is nothing. But his wife was funny, wasn't she? Do you think she's a lesbian? She could be a lesbian, right? She's tough."

I wasn't surprised in the least by Andy's off-the-wall sexual speculation. That was typical, everyday Andy. But I was almost shocked to hear him say what he really thought about another artist's work, especially something so negative and analytical and, in my opinion, right. Andy didn't talk about art; it wasn't cool. If asked, he said everything was great, or mocked the questioner, as he did with Barbara Rose.

That afternoon Andy also told me, "I think American Indian art is the greatest art. It's so simple and beautiful. And it doesn't matter who made it."

I'm sure he really meant it and that the Andy I saw that day was the real Andy: wistful, touching, unhappy, and smart. Another afternoon, a newspaper reporter came to interview Andy in the same hotel room and got the fake Andy: cool, coy, campy, and dumb. The *Excelsior* headline ran: IRONICO, ANDY WARHOL, DICE: "NIXON, EL MEJOR PRESIDENTE PARA EE UU" (The Ironic Andy Warhol Says, "Nixon Is the Best President for the U.S.A.")

REPORTER: What is the meaning of your art?
WARHOL: It's decorative.
REPORTER: And your films?
WARHOL: Comedy. The art's comedy too. And a little bit of politics.
REPORTER: What do you see as the political situation in America?
WARHOL: It's changing.
REPORTER: In what way?
WARHOL: Angela Davis went free.
REPORTER: What does that signify?
WARHOL: New politics.
REPORTER: What do you mean?
WARHOL: More crime.
REPORTER: Who do you favor for president?
WARHOL: Nixon's just great.
REPORTER: Why?
WARHOL: He travels so much—like a movie star, a Superstar.
REPORTER: Why is this?

WARHOL: I guess he likes to be on TV. He's good friends with Bob Hope, Ronald Reagan, Bing Crosby, Frank Sinatra and Shirley Temple.
REPORTER: Why do you talk in monosyllables?
WARHOL: It's easy to translate.

Well, maybe the fake Warhol wasn't so dumb.

Another afternoon, like typical tourists, we visited the shrine to the Virgin of Guadalupe, Mexico's patron saint, in the poor northern part of the city. Lines of penitents, in crowns of thorns, their bare backs bleeding or scabbed from self-flagellation, crawled on their knees across the vast stone square toward the enormous church. In awed silence we entered the cool, dark shrine. Thousands of votive candles flickered in memory of the dead before at least a dozen side altars, and a wide center aisle of marble swept grandly to the almost grotesquely rococo main altar, dripping with some of the gold that had brought the Spanish *conquistadores* to Mexico five centuries before.

We stood there, both appalled and dazzled, not knowing quite how to behave, like tourists or believers. Then Andy said in a hushed voice, "I think we should kneel." We followed him to the last pew, through what he sometimes called "all the Catholic things"—taking holy water, genuflecting, kneeling, praying, making the Sign of the Cross after each step of the Roman ritual. It was the first time I had been in a church with Andy, and I realized then that his religion wasn't an act, something that sounded good in a cover story.

We took one more excursion during our stay, to the Aztec pyramids at Teotihuacán. Andy didn't want to go at all but came along because he also didn't want to stay alone at the hotel. "It's just a pile of rocks," he kept saying, as our big black limousine with the Italian flag waving from its chrome-trimmed hood headed down the highway. After forty-five minutes, we arrived at the dust-choked little village, a country crossroads of adobe huts. The entire population, perhaps a hundred people, seemed to be congregated in front of the only store in town, watching the only television set in town. The legendary pyramids, centuries old, loomed above.

"I told you it was just a pile of rocks," said Andy, pointing at the pyramids. "You can see it from here. Why do we have to get out?"

"*Andy,*" we scolded in unison, "we came all this way! Stop being silly."

"I'll wait in the car," he insisted. "It's too hot. And it's just a pile of rocks."

We left him alone with the chauffeur and walked through the village to the pyramids. The tallest is about twenty stories. It *was* too hot, and at that altitude—central Mexico is about 7,000 feet above sea level—we were finding it difficult to climb and breathe at the same time. But we kept going, panting all the way, until we reached the pinnacle. There we were greeted by an urchin peddling a broken bit of clay. "Eet's a genuine pre-Columbian antique. Only one dollar, meester, *please.*"

We couldn't help but laugh and think that maybe Andy had been right after all. It was just a glorified pile of rocks, a tourist trap with a souvenir seller on top. We couldn't wait to tell him about our letdown and give him the "genuine pre-Columbian antique." But we were greeted by another surprise when we got back to the car. The limousine was surrounded by the entire population of Teotihuacán, who obviously found it and its occupant much more fascinating than whatever had been on TV. They had encircled the car and were pointing through the windows and laughing at Andy, whose face had turned a vivid crimson from embarrassment, anger, and fear. To make matters worse, the chauffeur was worried about the car overheating, so he had turned off the engine, and the air conditioning. Andy, who never sweated, was sweating right through his Brooks Brothers seersucker jacket, and twitching.

We felt guilty and a little frightened ourselves as we cut through the mob and got into the car with Andy, who didn't find our story or our souvenir in the least amusing. As we drove off, he said one last time, with vengeance in his voice, "It's just a pile of rocks."

A week or two later, Brooks, Adriana, and I were lolling around the pool of the villa they had rented in Puerto Vallarta, watching Trumba chase frogs. "You know," said Adriana, shaking her head, "I will never forget that scene at the pyramids and that poor man sitting there sweating with all those *cretinos* pointing and laughing. But, you know, I think he would have rather died from the heat and the embarrassment than admit he was wrong and come with us to see the pile of rocks. It's really amazing how strong his beliefs are underneath all the joking and posing. He didn't want to be contaminated by the beauty of an ancient civilization. It might disturb his ridiculous, fanatic belief in *the new.* No, my little Robertino, this is not a man with whom you can even *have* an argument—let alone think of winning.

"Better you stay here with me."

And so while the Jacksons and Trumba took their siestas every afternoon, I sat at my typewriter trying to decipher Andy Warhol's films. I'd scrutinized the thirty or so silent movies (1963–64), the thirty or so "talkies" (1964–66), and twelve of the seventeen or more features (1965–72), from *My Hustler* to the as-yet-unreleased *Heat*—and had also interviewed a slew of Superstars—including Brigid, Nico, Jackie, Candy, Eric, Jane, and Donna—as well as Paul, at great length, twice, and Andy, over the phone, once. I was more overwhelmed by it all than when I had begun the project a year earlier. What did it all mean? And how could I explain it?

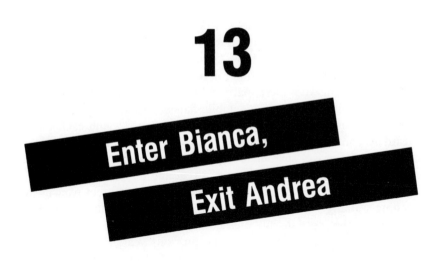

13

Enter Bianca, Exit Andrea

I'd been in Mexico for six weeks, my anemia was better, Trumba was getting on my nerves . . . and then the phone rang. It was Andy. "Don't let him pull you back," Adriana warned me as she passed me the receiver.

"Oh, hi, Bob," he said. "Everybody misses you. When are you coming back to work?"

"I'm working on my book, Andy."

"Oh, I know. Uh, everybody misses you. Oh, and the Erteguns are giving a big party for Mick Jagger's birthday and Fred could get you invited too."

He told me in a rush that Charles Rydell and Jerome Hill were staying in the South of France for the rest of the summer, and they had loaned their farm, Windy Hill, in Bridgehampton to Lana Jokel, who was editing her Warhol documentary there, and had agreed to let me stay there too, to work on my book on Andy. "And we'll really help with your book, we really will," Andy told me. "So get on a plane quick, or you'll miss Mick's party—oh, I forgot, Bianca Jagger is dying to meet you. She's Fred's new best friend and we told her all about you, and she's dying to meet you. So get on that plane tomorrow."

Sure enough, five nights after returning from Mexico, I was dancing with Bianca Jagger at a backwoods roadhouse in Bridgehampton called the Millstone. The Millstone was the hip place to go on Saturday night back when the Hamptons were the hip place to go on the weekends. Its aura of forbidden fruit attracted a fast crowd of celebrities and sophisticates: Terry Southern, Francesco Scavullo, Jackie Rogers, Giorgio di Sant'Angelo, Liz Smith, du Pont divorcée Frances Carpenter, Spreckels sugar heiress Jill Fuller and her ex-Superstar husband Gino Piserchio (Holly Woodlawn had been both the best man *and* the matron of honor at their 1970 Aspen wedding). Most of them were there that hot July night, including Larry Rivers, who arrived on his Harley with his nubile fiancée Diana clinging to his love handles. Guys in Levi's 501s and pink Lacostes danced with each other to "I Heard It Through the Grapevine," and cruised around the back "garden," a patch of gravel surrounded by a stockade fence where the air was sweet with marijuana. Inside it stank of sweat and poppers.

All action stopped when Bianca, in a white Saint Laurent pantsuit with a matching walking stick, strutted in on the arm of Fred Hughes, in a dark suit jacket and the most sharply creased Levi's on earth, followed by Andy and Jed. She and Mick had married the previous year, but they had been living between London, Malibu, and the South of France, and the New York In crowd was dying to see the woman who had caught the biggest male sex symbol since Elvis. *"She looks just like Mick,"* everyone seemed to whisper at once.

And then, suddenly, I was dancing with Mick Jagger's wife—thanks to Andy. "Isn't it exciting?" Andy said to me. "I told you Bianca was dying to meet you. You know how she got Mick, don't you? Whenever he called her in Paris for a date, she told him she had an appointment with the hairdresser that she couldn't change. I mean, he would be in Germany or someplace on a tour and say he had a few hours to fly to Paris and she would say no, she had to go to the hairdresser. This is what Fred says, anyway. It *is* hard to get an appointment with the right hairdresser in Paris. Why are you laughing, Bob? It *is!"*

The first thing I did Monday morning back in the city was call Barbara Goldsmith at *Bazaar* and get an assignment to cover Mick's birthday bash for them. When Andy found out, he announced that he was taking Polaroids of it for *Vogue.*

After the tumultuous Rolling Stones concert at Madison Square Garden, Atlantic Records owner Ahmet Ertegun and his decorator wife, Mica, gave their party for Mick in the rooftop ballroom of the St. Regis Hotel. Oscar and Françoise de la Renta had worn earplugs to the concert, and at the party Françoise went around saying, in French, that the birthday boy looked like an ape. They and most of the other "Fortunate Four Hundred" invited to the party left the concert early and by eleven had limousined to the hotel, which was besieged by unfortunate thousands trying to crash. Zsa Zsa Gabor and Huntington Hartford actually did crash, to Mica Ertegun's horror. Zsa Zsa told Judy Garland's daughter Lorna Luft, "You know, darlink, it's a good thing your mother died before her career began to wane." Candy Darling and I sat at a table with Andy, Truman Capote, Lee Radziwill, and

Peter Beard. As the Muddy Waters Blues Band took over from the Count Basie Orchestra, Fred kept announcing that July 29 was his birthday too. Andy gave his Polaroid camera to Ronnie Cutrone (Glenn's assistant) and Pat Hackett so they could do the *Vogue* photo popping for him: Dick Cavett POP Chessy Rayner POP Woody Allen POP George Plimpton POP Jann Wenner POP Jane Holzer POP Ossie Clark POP Tennessee Williams POP Bob Dylan POP POP POP.

Andy had arranged the "special entertainment"—Geri Miller, the stripper from *Trash,* jumping out of the birthday cake in her birthday suit and twirling her tits. This was followed by entertainment arranged by Ahmet— a half-dozen black old-timers from Bourbon Street, tap dancing. Marion Javits, the Senator's wife, was horrified. "Everything we fought for for all these years," she sobbed out loud as she fled, "has just gone down the drain."

Sometime after two in the morning, Mick and Bianca arrived. He was in a white denim suit and a tweed cabbie's cap; she was in a black-and-white polka-dot dress, with black gloves, black shoes, black walking stick, and a few black feathers in her hair. Some guests brought gifts to their table, everything from an American Indian turquoise-and-silver bracelet (from Andy) to a gold box filled with cocaine (from no one knew who). Both items were just beginning to become trendy.

The party went on until six in the morning as the sun came streaming through the ballroom curtains, with neither Park Avenue nor the Factory kids eager to leave. It seemed to be the beginning of so many things, and the end of so many others. *Bazaar* titled my piece "The Decline and Fall of Nescafé Society or Next Week We Play Pompeii." A few days after the party, political columnist Harriett Van Horne, who was not at the party, wrote about it in the New York *Post*. Shocked by reports of the presents, the black tap dancers, Geri Miller's twirling siliconed tits, the all-pervading "decadence," she noted, "In the perfumed twilight of the Roman Empire unspeakable things went on. Are we entering that same twilight?"

We were.

That weekend, I took my typewriter and files to Bridgehampton to continue working on my opus Warholus. Windy Hill was more an estate or a compound than a farm, though home-grown corn and other garden vegetables were served at lunch and dinner. There was a large Victorian main house, filled with Tiffany lamps, a modern guest house, servants' quarters, a barn or two, a pool, a pond, and a gazebo, all set on about a hundred acres of woods and pastureland north of the Montauk Highway on the road to Sag Harbor. I was happy there, working during the week, playing on the weekends.

Giorgio di Sant'Angelo had rented a large modern ranch house over-looking a swan-filled pond in nearby Wainscott, and one Saturday in August he gave a posh little dinner. I had downed several vodkas-on-the-rocks when someone offered me a thick white tablet with an indentation down the middle and the brand name Rorer embossed along the curve of one side, officially a "muscle relaxer," unofficially the aphrodisiac of the seventies. I swal-lowed the Quaalude with a swig of Stolichnaya, and when I came to I was sprawled on the floor. Glenn and Jude practically carried me out, into an ice-cold shower. Then someone gave me a revival pow-der, something even trendier than Quaaludes, and also a first for me: co-caine. I hadn't quite got the proportions right, or the sequence, but it was my first taste of the Disco Decade's favorite cocktail—Stoli-coke-and-'lude.

One Sunday, Paul Morrissey called from Montauk and invited us out to see the new place he and Andy had bought. It turned out to be an im-pressive, if understated, compound of five white clapboard houses built in the thirties sitting at the end of a long and winding private road on about twenty acres of unspoiled land directly facing the open sea. It was known locally as "The Church Estate" after the original owners, an Idaho family who only used it a couple of weeks each September, when the bass fishing was best. Andy and Paul had paid $235,000, fifty percent each, and it is now worth nearly twenty times that.

Talk-show host Dick Cavett and his actress wife, Carrie Nye, lived in an impeccable Stanford White house about a half mile to the west, toward Montauk Village. Peter Beard had just bought a small stone cottage about a half mile to the east, next to the Montauk Point Coast Guard base. Across the Montauk Highway was an immense dude ranch, where you could rent horses to ride over the dunes to totally deserted white sand beaches. It was the Factory answer to Hyannisport, and that first summer it even housed Kennedys, much to the delight of Andy, Paul, and Fred.

Jackie Kennedy Onassis's sister, Lee Radziwill, had rented the largest of the five houses—five bedrooms, high-ceilinged living room, and cozy, old-fashioned kitchen. (The others were usually inhabited, in descending order, by Paul, Andy and Jed, Fred, and the caretaker and his wife.) Jackie (and her children, Caroline and John-John) had visited Lee (and her chil-dren, Anthony and Tina) several times that summer, and Andy loved to joke about putting up "gold plaques" that said "Lee slept here" and "Jackie slept here."

Lee spent a lot of time that summer supervising the rescue of Grey Gardens, where her eccentric Easthampton cousins, the Beales, lived. There had been a public outcry over the house's crumbling, varmint-infested con-dition and overgrown yard. Jackie and Lee were paying for all the work. Maxime de la Falaise McKendry, who was a regular house guest of Gior-gio's, had met a boy at the supermarket who claimed to be the best friend of the Beales. She persuaded him to take us along the next time he visited them on Georgica Road, and I took along my new little Sony tape recorder, just like Andy's.

Grey Gardens didn't look at all bad from the outside. It had been freshly stripped, sanded, and painted. Lee was doing a good job, given the incredible decay into which the house had fallen—and the incredible state of mind into which her cousins had fallen.

Little Edie Beale, about sixty years old, greeted us shyly. Her shaved head was wrapped in a brown silk scarf, which matched her brown turtleneck and brown skirt, brown stockings, and brown boots. She looked like an Islamic nun with an Irish drunk's face—white skin, red nose, very red, off-register lipstick. She led us upstairs to meet her mother, Big Edie Beale, about eighty years old and not shy at all. Big Edie was propped up in her bed in her bedroom, which had not yet gotten that Radziwill touch. A tree branch extended into the room through an open window to the middle of Big Edie's bed, and squirrels and raccoons climbed in to eat potato chips and pretzels. The bedcover was a trash heap of cracker boxes and candy wrappers, half-eaten tins of tuna fish and cat food, spilled milk, assorted other droppings, and piles of old *Confidentials* and new *Enquirers*, all with Jackie covers. Big Edie looked like an old Indian chief, with a mane of untamed white hair shooting out from her once beautiful features, and her still bright blue eyes.

"You're wearing *my* scarf!" she screamed at Little Edie as we walked in. "Jackie gave that scarf to me! Take it off this minute!"

"No, she didn't!" Little Edie screamed back. "She gave me all the *brown* Valentinos, and she gave you all the *black* Valentinos. This scarf is *brown!*"

"It's *black!*"

"It's *brown!*"

"It looks like black to me!"

"It's BROWN BROWN BROWN!!!"

To us, Big Edie was the picture of hospitality and charm, offering us snacks from her bed, which we politely declined.

I couldn't wait to call Andy in the city and tell him about the great tape I had for *Interview.* He said we'd better ask Fred. Fred said we'd better ask Lee. Lee said we'd better not.

But she agreed to let me interview her for *Bazaar.* Editor James Brady was even more pleased when I told him that Lee suggested using a Peter Beard photograph with the story. Like the rest of New York, he had heard all about the secret romance between Lee and Peter at Andy's house in Montauk—though Andy swore he hadn't told a soul, and told every soul he'd told that he hadn't, usually accusing them of telling him. I was one of those souls, so I know how Andy's gossiping worked, though I was still amazed at his ability to deny what he had said five minutes after he had said it. And to lie with a liar's face in a liar's voice—and insist he was telling the truth.

A little later, the Maysles Brothers, who'd shot the Rolling Stones' fateful Altamont concert as *Gimme Shelter,* began filming the Beales for their movie *Grey Gardens.* It had started as Lee's idea.

On Friday, August 11, 1972, Andy called Windy Hill from Montauk. I assumed he was going to invite us out, but began to wonder when I heard Lana muttering, "Oh, my God, my God." She hung up and repeated the conversation to me verbatim, as if in a trance. She said Andy made small talk at first. How was her editing going? Had we seen much of Larry Rivers? Who was coming out for the weekend? She asked him how he was enjoying his new summer house. "Oh, I hate it here," Andy answered. "When you get between the sheets at night, it's just dampsville. And I'm so bored because it costs so much to call New York that Paul won't let me talk to Brigid." When Andy and Brigid "watched TV together" over the phone, one call could last as long as prime time.

Then there was a long pause. Finally, Andy said, "I have some bad news." "What?" Lana asked a bit frantically, afraid it had to do with Jed, to whom she was close since they had edited *Heat* together. Andy blurted it out: "Andrea kicked the bucket."

Andrea Feldman, who played Sylvia Miles's crazy daughter in *Heat* and who sometimes called herself Andrea April or Andrea Whips or Andrea Warhol or even Mrs. Andy Warhol, had committed suicide. She was twenty-four years old and had killed herself by jumping from a fourteenth-floor window at 51 Fifth Avenue at four-thirty in the afternoon with a can of Coke in one hand and a rosary in the other.

She had first come to the attention of the Factory in 1967, in the back room of Max's Kansas City, by sitting on a Coke bottle and belting out "Everything's Coming Up Roses." She called her porno parody of Ethel Merman "Showtime." Andrea was a disturbed and lonely girl, whose well-to-do parents couldn't handle her. Her exhibitionism was extreme, even by Superstar standards; her outrageous public acts were obvious calls for help. And attention. Which is what Andy Warhol gave her. He not only turned his relentlessly voyeuristic camera on her, legitimizing her exhibitionism with an aura of stardom, first in *Imitation of Christ,* then in *Trash* and *Heat,* he also brought her to chic parties and glamorous openings, encouraging her to "Do Showtime, do Showtime . . . c'mon Andrea, give us a show."

"I'm sitting on top of the world," Andrea would sing, as she threw her skirt up and tucked a bottle inside her—a champagne bottle by now. Yes, Andy gave Andrea the attention she craved, and for that she worshiped him. "I'm Andy Warhol's biggest Superstar," she screamed at the Pinkerton guards who wouldn't let her into the party at Tavern on the Green after the Broadway opening of *Jesus Christ Superstar.* It didn't get her into the party, but the *Daily News* photographer snapped her making a scene, and when one of his pictures ran the next day, Andrea crowed. "That Sylvia Miles think she's a big star," she said. "Well, I don't see her picture in the *News* today!"

Andy tried to help Andrea sometimes. Don't take drugs, he would say sometimes. Don't lose so much weight, he would say sometimes. You look so pretty in pink lipstick, you shouldn't wear blue anymore, he would say, prodding her in a more normal direction. Unfortunately, you can't turn an exhibitionist on and off at will. Not even if you are Andy Warhol. Showtime became all the time for Andrea. And it made her crazier and crazier. Especially when Andy stopped watching.

In her last days, after she had come back to New York from Paris, where *Heat* had opened that summer, before the American premières scheduled for Los Angeles and New York that fall, she wore black lipstick and starved herself down to eighty-five pounds and took whatever drugs anyone offered. She was obsessed with Catholicism, thinking that Andy had rejected her because she was Jewish, and posed for a photograph wearing a crown of thorns with her palms turned to the camera to show self-inflicted stigmata. Then her mother and stepfather left for California. Her best friend, the considerably saner Superstar Geraldine Smith, refused to see her. Her boyfriend walked out. And when she came to the Factory, begging for money, talking for hours on the phone, reminding everyone over and over that she, not Sylvia Miles, was the star of *Heat,* Andy hid in his little side office and had Vincent send her away. I too was happy when she went away and the screaming stopped. I always thought her just a spoiled brat and never found "Showtime" funny.

Still, it was a shock when Andy called Lana with the news. And he was obviously feeling guilty or was at least showing guilt. "I really should have helped her more," he said. "She used to call me every night at two in the morning and ask me for help but I didn't know what to do. Then, three nights ago, she didn't call. It must have happened then. I thought she would be all right when the movie came out. Why didn't she wait for the movie to open? She was so good in it. It would have helped her. She was so good in California, and then when we saw her in Paris she was getting so skinny. I guess something was wrong then. She always went crazy when her parents went away. She hated to be alone. I wonder if she was taking drugs. She looked so skinny."

What was really strange about Andrea's death is that nobody called the Factory with the news for three days. Andrea had jumped on Tuesday, August 8, a few days after the tenth anniversary of the death of Marilyn Monroe, with whom she identified, on what many of us back then, perhaps including Andrea, thought was Andy's birthday. It was almost as if all the old Max's crowd were so mad at Andy and the new Factory that they had not wanted to tell us. On the Friday morning, Andrea's stepfather had called Vincent to say that her funeral would be held that afternoon at the Riverside

Memorial Chapel. When Vincent, stunned, asked for more details, Andrea's stepfather would only say, "It was a terrible thing." Vincent called Andy. Andy called Lana and me.

In the next few days, just how terrible a thing it was became more and more obvious. Andrea had apparently made dates for that afternoon with half a dozen guys she had gone out with, including the poet and diarist Jim Carroll, so that they would all be down on the sidewalk when she flew out the window. In a *Village Voice* obituary that ran the following week, Geraldine Smith mentioned a note, "addressed to everyone she knew, saying she loved us all, but 'I'm going for the bigtime, I hit the jackpot!' " In the back room of Max's the old Superstars were saying that Geraldine had been kind in print—the note wasn't to everyone and it wasn't about love; it was to Andy and it was very, very nasty.

That same week, Andrea's last interview, "conducted July 29th, 1972" by Greg Ford, was submitted to *Interview*. Glenn wanted to run it, but both Paul and Fred made it clear that would not be appreciated. Somehow I got a Xerox of it—one can hear Andrea's desperate confusion, the love and hate and need she had for Andy. And Paul. And the scrap of fame they gave her.

> They just throw you in front of a camera—they don't care what you look like. And they just use you, and abuse you, and step on you, and they don't pay you anything. I am very depressed about the whole thing, because I know I'm a damn good actress and I've been brought down by Warhol and I've been mistreated by them. And Paul Morrissey told me I was the best actress he ever had.

Andy took all this in—the gossip, the obituaries, the posthumous interviews—and said very little. Soon it was September, time to go to Venice for the film festival, where *Heat* was making its Italian premiere. Before he left, he called to say that he wanted to take me along, but Fred thought there were too many men going as it was: Andy, Paul, Jed, and himself.

Andy also said that he had been thinking about Andrea and wondered if she wasn't "being really creative" when she killed herself. "It's like she deliberately made her suicide a comedy," he said. "Oh, I've got a good idea for a movie: suicide as a comedy. It is a good idea, isn't it, Bob?" At times like those I hated Andy. How could he turn something so sad into a joke?

But then I remembered he was just using humor to mask his fear, to deal with the thing he could never deal with: death. And I remembered the shooting and how close he had come to death himself. It's amazing how much I forgave Andy because of that—and I wasn't there when it happened. I didn't give him mouth-to-mouth resuscitation like Fred. I didn't help him recuperate like Jed.

14

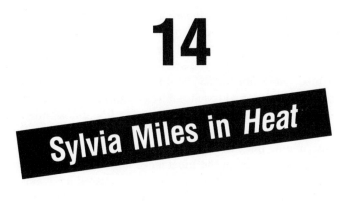

Since I'd first met her at the Algonquin, Sylvia Miles had still been dining out on her 1969 Oscar nomination for *Midnight Cowboy,* while desperately seeking the role that would clinch her stardom. Finally, in the summer of 1971, she had been cast as the female lead in *Andy Warhol's Heat,* the Factory's idea of a Hollywood movie. I had got her the part. But if she had been using me to get closer to Andy and Paul, I had been using her to go to better parties and meet bigger stars.

Sylvia knew everyone and went everywhere. Her philosophy was: "You never know who you might meet who might give you a part." Sylvia often took me on her nightly nights out—to movie premières, theater openings, gallery openings, boutique openings. If it opened, she went. I was only too happy to escort her, especially to places where Andy hadn't invited me, like the premiere of *Cabaret.* He only had two tickets, and he took Jed, but it was nice to surprise him with my presence, to show him I could get invited without him, and to hear him say, "You're here, Bob? Gee, you're really getting up there."

In any case, Sylvia Miles was a natural for the Factory, another one of a kind, full of character and charm. She dressed like a Las Vegas showgirl and played chess like a Russian champion. This was the year of hot pants and bullet belts, and Sylvia would loop the latter around the former, add a low-cut halter, tights, and boots, and go to dinner at Lee and Anna Strasberg's with Joanne Woodward and Ben Gazzara.

"See," she said, the first time I picked her up at her studio apartment on Central Park South, showing me her clippings collection. "The top drawer is the late fifties and early sixties when I was doing all that intellectual off-Broadway stuff like *The Iceman Cometh* at the Circle in the Square in 1957 and Jean Genet's *The Balcony,* and *Matty and the Moron and Madonna.* . . . Then comes the middle sixties, when I went Hollywood and did things like *Parrish* with Troy Donahue—did you see it on the *Late, Late Show* the other night? Then this whole drawer is just 1969, because that's the year I did *Midnight Cowboy* and I got so much publicity from all over the world. And then the bottom one's the current stuff, but see it's almost filled up, so I don't know what to do. Get a bigger chest of drawers, I guess. Either that or a bigger apartment. But I'm kinda attached to this view.''

Sylvia's apartment was on the nineteenth floor facing the park and she had a small breakfast table and two dining chairs pressed up against the wall of windows. ''I made the chairs myself,'' she told me. ''They're French. I can also do Early American and Spanish. I learned how at my father's furniture factory when I was growing up in the Village.'' Sylvia actually carried her most recent reviews and tidbits around with her, wrapped in Saran Wrap, in her shoulder bag.

''Voilà!'' says Sylvia in *Heat,* giving Joe Dallesandro a tour of her thirty-six-room Hollywood mansion. ''If there's anyone you'd like to impress, you could do it here.'' Sylvia plays Sally Todd, ''a minor, practically unknown, fading Hollywood movie star''—to quote her ex-husband, a producer played, Factory-style, by producer Lester Persky. Her nearly empty hilltop house is the last symbol of past status, but it's a step up for Joe, who plays a long-forgotten child star, a former Mouseketeer, trying to make a comeback in rock 'n' roll.

If *Women in Revolt* represents Andy's rejection of the more aggressive side of the Women's Movement; if *L'Amour* portrays Andy's desire to gold-dig his way up the Art Deco altitudes of Paris society, a wish-I-were-there postcard to the Rothschilds and the Saint Laurents; then *Andy Warhol's Heat* is his answer to Hollywood, his no-thank-you note for the invitations he never received from MGM and Paramount, Columbia, Warner's, and Twentieth Century-Fox.

The New Hollywood in *Andy Warhol's Heat* was a sleazy motel, frequented by has-been hustlers, sadistic lesbians, and moronic porn stars who masturbate by the pool, and run by a grossly overweight, sexually voracious tyrant in a ponytail and a muumuu (wonderfully played by Pat Ast, whose couture muumuus were made by her boss, Halston). The only escape from this sun-bleached insane asylum is that haunted Hispano-Hollywood horror on the hill, the mortgaged-up manor of the formerly famous Sally Todd. (Actually, the house was formerly Boris Karloff's.) That's where Joe ends up, in bed with his hostess. He's pursued there by her emotionally disturbed daughter, played by Andrea Feldman, another denizen of the motel, where she shares a room with her baby (played by Joe Jr.) and a girlfriend who uses other women's bodies as ashtrays.

Andy didn't go to Hollywood for the filming, which lasted two weeks in July 1971. But he had his ways of keeping a degree of control. Paul called the Factory every morning before they started shooting. And Jed called Andy every night at home with a private report of the day's activities. What's more, Andy barraged Sylvia, Andrea, and Pat with late-night calls from New York, stirring things up long distance. As usual, he knew exactly what he was doing. The three actresses were meant to hate each other—they were all, in the typical Paul Morrissey schema, after Joe—and after Andy's calls they did. He made Sylvia jealous of Pat's Halston muumuus. He made Pat jealous of Sylvia's star billing. And, as we've seen, it didn't take much to drive poor Andrea crazy.

One night after Sylvia got back from Hollywood, Andy took her and me to dinner at Lüchow's, the famous old German restaurant on East 14th Street, to discuss additional love scenes to be shot in New York. Walking around Union Square Park on our way to meet Sylvia, Andy said, "We've got to get Sylvia to do something different. I don't know what, but it can't be the same old love scene with Joe's ass going up and down over and over again." Over sauerbraten and red cabbage, he asked Sylvia, "What could be different and new and a little bit strange for you to do with Joe? I mean, I like the scenes you did out there, but it is a lot of shots of Joe's ass going up and down."

Sylvia looked pained. "What do you mean, a lot of shots of Joe's ass— I assume my face is visible in some of the shots too?"

"Oh, it is. You look great, Sylvia. Doesn't she, Bob? But we need some more scenes, uh, doing something different. Something, uh, more modern."

"I hope you're not talking about a blowjob, Andy, because I'm not sure I want to do that on screen. In fact, I know I don't."

"You mean you would do it off the screen?"

"Now, Andy." Sylvia licked her lipstick. "You know how much I love and respect you and Paul and Jed and Robert and everything you all do at the Factory, and how good I'm sure this film is going to be for my career. But I've got a reputation to protect, you know. I am a professional, you know, Andy. I'm not Pat Ast, who's basically a saleslady at a boutique. Or Andrea-whatever-she's-calling-herself-this-week. I'm not a nut, Andy."

"Oh, Andrea's not a nut. Is she, Bob?"

"All right, let's leave Andrea out of this," said Sylvia. "The point is that I've got a professional reputation to protect, which many professional people, including my agent, Billy Barnes, who also happens to be Tennessee's agent, warned me I might be risking if I wasn't careful about what I do in this film. Which, don't get me wrong, Andy, I'm absolutely thrilled to be in. It's just that . . . a blowjob isn't even very avant-garde. Right, Robert?'' Sylvia never called me Bob.

''Oh, I know it isn't,'' whined Andy with an edge. ''I never said you should give Joe a blowjob. That's not new and different. It's got to be something more peculiar. Something people will talk about.''

''I'm not a transvestite, Andy.''

''There's gotta be something, uh, something funny that people will remember.''

''Well, you know, Andy, there are only so many things you can do in bed. A man and a woman, I mean.''

''Oh, really? Like what?''

''I'm not going to sit here in Lüchow's and list them for you, Andy.''

Andy was furious with Sylvia after we dropped her off uptown. ''Who does she think she is? If we were still working the old way, with cheap film, we could cut her out and put somebody else in. That's why I think it's always better to use our own new kids.''

Andy changed his mind about Sylvia after he saw the dailies of the additional love scenes shot in New York. She had found something different and peculiar to do, something more modern than a blowjob: She brought Joe Dallesandro's beefy hand to her mouth and sucked his stocky fingers one by one.

Andy was beside himself: ''Oh, now this is great. Oh, Sylvia really is good. I mean, it's like a baby sucking, uh, somebody else's finger. It really is great. It really is peculiar. This is the best scene. You have to use it a lot, Paul. Don't cut it too much, Jed. Uh, do you have Sylvia's number, Bob? I'm going to call her.''

He did, right then, and sang her praises, which Sylvia, like all of us, couldn't get enough of, even if it was for sucking fingers. The real point was that Sylvia had done what Andy wanted, even though he wasn't quite sure what that was himself. That's how Andy worked. He prodded and he poked, he nagged, turned cold and mean, dropped hints and clues—until the actor, or director, or editor, or co-author, or assistant silkscreener, figured out what Andy wanted to express, but couldn't.

Andy asked me to help organize the New York premiere of *Heat*, on October 5 at the Lincoln Center Film Festival. He told me that he and Fred had to be in Europe on that date ''to do some work for Bruno Bischofberger''—the work turned out to be commissioned portraits of the German industrialist Gunther Sachs and his then wife, Brigitte Bardot. ''We'll pay you for it,'' Andy said, determined to get me back to work at the Factory, especially as assistant social director, the capacity at which he thought I was most useful. Why not? I reasoned—I could use the money, it would be fun to make the list, and it would just be for a couple of weeks anyway, and then right back to Bridgehampton and the book.

Sylvia was very happy to hear that I was making arrangements for what she considered *her* big night. Even though she had already enjoyed triumphal receptions at the Cannes and Venice film festivals, every giddy moment of which had been recounted in vivid detail back in the New York *Daily News* by Rex Reed, she still wanted to make a big splash in her hometown—and get yet another full-page rave from Rex. Indeed, as far as Sylvia was concerned, every showing of *Heat* anywhere should be heralded with klieg lights—and reviewed by Rex:

> The film is like an open wound, and Sylvia is a kind of cross between Lana Turner and Gloria Swanson in ''Sunset Boulevard,'' eating her way through the movie like an emotional barracuda and leaving everyone around her for fishbait. The film is such a milestone in her career that everything else in her life is now referred to as ''B.H.'' (Before ''Heat''). It cost only $50,000 to make—a far cry from all the waste and hoopla of her previous film, Dennis Hopper's ''The Last Movie''—but it has finally made Sylvia a star.

Unfortunately, after Andrea Feldman's suicide, Andy, Paul, and Fred decided that *Heat*'s New York opening at the Film Festival should be a ''quiet number,'' a decision not at all to Sylvia's liking, and she enlisted her archrival, Pat Ast, in her effort not to let Andrea's ghost haunt ''our premiere,'' as Sylvia put it. La Ast, who had Halston whipping up his most magnificent mumu yet for *her* big night, couldn't have agreed more. The two of them called me several times a day to try to reverse the Factory decision. When that didn't work, they lobbied the most patient man ever to do public relations for movie stars, John Springer, who handled everyone from Joan Crawford and Bette Davis to Elizabeth Taylor and Richard Burton. They got him so enthused that he came up with the brainstorm of inviting another of his glamorous clients to this remake of *Sunset Boulevard,* Gloria Swanson herself. Sylvia *hated* that idea. No, Gloria Swanson, or any other big star, would not be asked after all.

Well, Jack Nicholson and Warren Beatty were invited, but they were friends and potential leading men for Sylvia now that she was a leading lady. And Rex Reed, Eugenia Sheppard, Suzy, Rosemary Kent, Francesco Scavullo, Giorgio di Sant'Angelo, Diane and Egon von Furstenberg, Ruth Ford and Dotson Rader, Tennessee Williams . . . Sylvia was constantly calling with ''just one more name.'' And that name's date.

''All New York is here,'' said a festival regular, according to *Village Voice* reporter Arthur Bell, who went on to note:

> Sylvia Miles made her entrance to Alice Tully Hall with director Paul Morrissey and co-star Joe Dallesandro, ''It's the greatest moment of my life,''

she said, before I asked. One must take her seriously now. Carole Lombard with schmaltz boleroing in and out of bed with Joe as George Raft in a ponytail. Chemistry.

The lights go on. A baby spot shines on an opera box where Sylvia and Paul and Joe are joined by other members of the cast. A standing ovation, and an announcement that there'll be a panel discussion with Sylvia and Paul Morrissey and Otto Preminger. Sylvia slinks to the stage. She slowly, seductively, slips off her fur. The panel begins. Otto Preminger isn't sure about the picture. *Heat* doesn't represent Hollywood as he knows it. Retired movie stars are decent. There are no decent people in *Heat*.

Elia Kazan, in the audience, states from his seat that he found the movie moving and especially enjoyed the area of mystery where motivation is not explained and over-simplified. Paul says his direction is really non-direction and it's an easy road to keep direction out of his films. Characters are cast to type and left to their own devices. "When you cast the young man who masturbated [Eric Emerson], did you audition him?" asks Preminger. . . .

We all got a big laugh out of Preminger's line later, at "the small subdued" party that I persuaded Candy Darling to hostess at Sam Green's. As Arthur Bell's *Voice* report continued:

Holly and Zouzou and *Women's Wear Daily* crowd under a Lichtenstein and *After Dark* and Alice Cooper and Tally and Bob Colaciello and Scavullo and Warren Beatty and Rex and Lauren Hutton and Jack Nicholson, sip and smoke and small talk. Sylvia holds court on a couch. . . . A press agent says *Heat* got the biggest reaction ever in the ten years of the festival. Tally Brown says her wig is made of cotton candy. Holly Woodlawn says she loves everybody and kisses Jim Jacobs. Eric Emerson says he can get a hard-on at a moment's notice, which makes his *Heat* work cinema vérité. John Springer says, "Don't we have good times." Jude O'Brien says she's leaving for Japan tomorrow. Paul Morrissey says Andrea Feldman loved performing more than anybody he ever knew. Sylvia Miles stands on the stairwell and says, "Ask me if it was worth it. It was. Every bit of it." And the press agent to my left says, "What movie is that from?"

Of course, I was thrilled to find myself mentioned in the same sentence with Jack Nicholson, Warren Beatty, Lauren Hutton, and Alice Cooper, as were my parents in Rockville Centre and my grandmothers in Borough Park.

Andy came back from doing Brigitte Bardot's portrait in Europe and said that I'd done such a good job that he thought I should fly out to Los Angeles with them the following week, for the Hollywood preview of *Heat*. Why didn't I see if I could cover it for the *Voice*, he suggested, and they would see if the producers would cough up an extra plane ticket and room at the Beverly Hills Hotel for me. It was my first trip to Hollywood.

The "special celebrity preview" of *Heat* at the Directors Guild was, in Paul's words, "a great occasion for comedy."

All afternoon, producer Herb Pickman had been assuring Andy that "lots of big stars" were coming to the preview, and bit player John Hallowell had been calling too, with hourly star-watch bulletins: "Rita's coming. Lana's coming. Lucy's coming." But now, as the Directors Guild lobby filled with hordes of P.R. people from all the studios who wouldn't finance a Warhol movie, Andy was feeling let down. "Oh, there are *no* big stars here," he moaned. "I'm going back to the hotel."

Then, in rapid succession, Lorne Greene, George Cukor, and Rona Barrett arrived, and Andy felt better. He took Polaroids of each, in lieu of shaking hands, and said, "Oh, gee," when they said they were happy to meet him, quickly followed by, "Oh, do you think you could sign my Polaroid?"

Rona positioned herself between Andy and Sylvia and wasn't about to budge. Unfortunately, for the first time since I'd met her, Sylvia had too much to drink, and was hiccuping loudly. I steered her to the bar to get a glass of water. She started winking at the handsome young bartenders. A professional autograph hound, the kind that crash openings and hang out by stage doors collecting multiples of celebrities' autographs to sell or trade, approached Sylvia for her autograph. After she signed his book, I asked him what her autograph was worth on the open market. "Not much," he said. And Andy Warhol's? "Even less."

Meanwhile, Ann Miller tap-danced in and Andy took Polaroids of Ann Miller tap-dancing in and Ann Miller signed Andy's Polaroids of Ann Miller tap-dancing in. He had also collected signed Polaroids of Russ Tamblyn ("You missed Russ Tamblyn, Bob. He's a big star."); Goldie Hawn, in an old leather jacket, jeans, and a peace-sign T-shirt; and Lucie Arnaz, holding hands with her then beau, Jim Bailey, who was famous for his "impressions" of Judy Garland, Peggy Lee, and Barbra Streisand, but who was never to be called a "female impersonator," let alone a transvestite. Andy was fascinated by this Hollywood version of Jackie Curtis, and happy with his growing collection of signed star photographs.

Andy used the word "star" in the broadest sense possible, to encompass anyone who had ever appeared in a movie, play, TV show, radio show, fashion show, ballet, opera, or any other type of performance, no matter how obscure, for any length of time, no matter how brief, and including anyone who was or had been married to anyone who had. "Gee, Christina Kauffman is so beautiful," he sighed over his Polaroid of the ex-Mrs. Tony Curtis arriving. "Who?" I asked, and got the same reply I always got whenever I asked who somebody was whom nobody had ever heard of but him: "You don't know who Christina Kauffman is, Bob?!? Christina Kauffman is a big star!"

Suddenly, a swarm of paparazzi flew in from the klieg-lit boulevard, shouting in unison: "Mae is coming! Mae is coming! Mae is coming!"

"Mae West is coming!" gasped Andy.

"You didn't tell me Mae West was coming!" rasped Sylvia.

"Yes, I did," piped up Paul. "I told you to wear an uplift bra."

A long black stretch limo bearing a bevy of Mr. America contestants had pulled up outside the Directors Guild, but when the platinum-topped Raisinette of a woman squeezed between these slabs of beefcake saw the waiting photographers, she waved to her chauffeur to drive on. Was it really Mae West? Later a rumor circulated that she had driven around the block, changed into a brown wig, and walked back to the theater unnoticed. As much as Andy wanted to believe it, even he had his doubts. "What did she do with the six musclemen?" he wondered. "Do you think she left through the fire exit before the movie was over?"

Heat was a big hit with the Hollywood crowd. Rona told Sylvia she was a cinch for an Oscar and Sylvia hiccuped her thanks. George Cukor, the famous director and Paul's idol, told Paul it was a great film, and Christopher Isherwood, the famous writer, posed for and signed a whole roll of Polaroids for Andy. Ann Miller did another little tap dance and pronounced *Heat* "kicky." Lorne Greene found the film "funny, but don't ask me why." Only Lucie Arnaz and Jim Bailey were unenthusiastic. He thought *Heat* was "unbelievable," and she concurred. "I can't say I liked it. The characters were too strange."

"But her boyfriend's a drag queen," Andy kept muttering.

"Impressionist, Andy, impressionist," Paul jokingly reminded him.

"Listen, Paul, I know a drag queen when I see one, and she's got a lot of nerve calling our movie strange."

"Oh, well," said Paul. "It's nice to have the stars' kids, but it would have been nicer if big Lucy had come."

Somehow, even though *Heat* cost somewhere between $50,000 and $100,000 to make, took in about 2 million in the United States alone, and was praised by the established critics from Cannes to Venice and from New York to Los Angeles, the studios remained unimpressed. And Andy knew it, and I think he knew why. As he told Joyce Haber, the powerful gossip of the Los Angeles *Times,* at lunch, "We like Hollywood so much, you know. We've always wanted to work here. It's been our dream. But they think we're putting them down."

15

The "models" included Lily Auchincloss, Candy Darling, Nan Kempner, Pat Ast, Berry Berenson, Lauren Hutton, Jane Holzer, Kitty Hawks, China Machado, Donna Jordan, and Jane Forth, cradling her newborn baby by Eric Emerson, a boy they named Emerson Forth. It was Halston's fashion show at the 1972 Coty Awards presentation ceremony at Lincoln Center, and Andy, at Halston's request, and with considerable help from Joe Eula, had produced it. Andy's bright idea: to have the models cooking breakfast on stage, which had been outfitted with the latest in kitchen appliances from General Electric. It was almost surreal to see Mrs. Kempner, who kept the best cook in town at home on Park Avenue, flipping a fried egg over easy, trying not to get any grease spots on her floor-length, red sequined Halston sheath. Andy's favorite part: the smell of bacon fat wafting through the audience of fashion grandees assembled in the Mitzi Newhouse Theatre, which Diana Vreeland pronounced "the most optimistic fragrance in the world!"

Thanks to Fred I was a dresser, alongside the eligible young Baron Eric de Rothschild, Revlon heir John Revson, and Michael Butler, the multimillionaire aviation heir and producer of *Hair*. Our enviable "job" was to help the modeling socialites, Superstars, and fashion editors, and a few of Halston's favorite working models like Karen Bjornson and Nancy North, in and out of their dresses. Most were braless, and between changes a rising star from the Netherlands, Apollonia von Ravenstein, was shimmying and shaking for the bachelor dressers.

I had landed in New York that morning on the "red eye" from Los

Angeles, and was surprised when Fred asked me to take part in the Coty fun. It was also the first time we had had a real talk on the phone. He wanted to know "everything" that had happened on the Hollywood trip: Had Paul driven me crazy? Had Andy been nice to me? Had I finally had enough of Sylvia?

So I was quite full of myself at Halston's party after the Coty Awards, dancing up a disco storm simultaneously with a beautiful model named Jennifer Lee (who went on to marry and divorce Richard Pryor) and Prince Egon von Furstenberg, and later at Max's Kansas City downing vodka stingers with Candy and Eve Orton, the fashion editor of *Harper's Bazaar,* who assured me that her editor-in-chief, James Brady, loved my pieces on Mick Jagger and Lee Radziwill and wanted more.

The next morning, Scavullo called with the news that the adventurous James Brady had been replaced by cautious Anthony Mazzola. Then my literary agent, Ellen Levine, called to say that Dutton didn't like my first 150 pages and wanted a complete rewrite before they'd advance me any more money. Screw Dutton, screw *Bazaar,* screw freelance writing, I fumed, heading downtown in a taxi I couldn't afford: I'm still special contributing editor of *Interview,* Fred is finally being really friendly, Jed had suggested making a movie together when we were in Hollywood—I'm going back to the Factory full time and for good.

My new salary was $125 a week and I was basically back where I'd been before Mexico and Bridgehampton: overseeing my former assistant at *Interview,* who had no desire to be overseen. "You've got to do something about Glenn," said Paul, who had had a big fight with him over how many Joe Dallesandro photos to run in our *Heat* special issue. "See if you can get Glenn to be more amenable to Paul," said Fred, who was tired of mediating their frequent disputes. Fred hated problems and Glenn was becoming a problem.

It's too bad that Glenn wouldn't, or couldn't, defer to authority. In the year or so (spring 1972 to summer 1973) that he was managing editor and art director, *Interview* kept getting bigger and better, more varied and stylish. In addition to discovering Fran Lebowitz, Glenn had expanded the contributing-editors list to include bright young journalists like Lisa Robinson (on rock stars), Scott Cohen (on sports stars), and John Calendo (on old Hollywood stars). He signed up the well-connected Joan Juliet Buck, a movie producer's daughter who had been to school in England with Anjelica Huston, as London correspondent, and added a page of "London Smalltalk," which recorded the monthly doings of the Zandra Rhodes/David Hockney set. The colorful R. Couri Hay, another new contributing editor, was the scion of the Hay Whitney Hays, and the best friend of Candy Darling's hairdresser, Eugene of Cinandre. Couri's specialty was thrusting a tape recorder into the face of someone like Frank Sinatra at a movie première and shouting, "I'm R. Couri Hay from Andy Warhol's *Interview.* What did you think of the movie, Frank?'' Andy always called him E. Couri Hay, just to drive him crazy.

Glenn also started a Hollywood "bureau," in the person of Susan Pile, Pat Hackett's closest friend, and a former Factory transcriber, who had moved to L.A. and gone into P.R. We used whatever friends and contacts we had, and when we put all our friends and contacts together, we came up with some pretty good things. That's partly why it was so important to get along with Andy, Paul, and Fred: They had the best contacts. Thanks to Fred, for example, Lee Radziwill interviewed Mick Jagger in Montauk and Bianca Jagger interviewed Yves Saint Laurent in Paris.

Andy interviewed Bianca—we were all very big on Bianca, especially when we noticed that her picture on the cover sent sales up. Thanks to my growing friendship with Scavullo, he did a spectacular cover shot of Bianca, in a black cloche trimmed with white feathers and a veil and long black gloves with a big diamond ring worn over them, and four more pages of fashion shots inside—all at great expense in assistants, hair, makeup, printing, and retouching, and all for free. Scavullo wasn't the only big-time studio photographer who was willing to do this for us; Bill King, Chris von Wangenheim, and others did too—they liked the fact that we usually ran their photographs full page, and our page was very large, and we hardly ever put type across a photograph.

Scavullo got us Dali, Giorgio got us Lena Horne, Halston got us Lauren Bacall, and Adriana Jackson got us Romano Mussolini, the jazz-pianist son of Il Duce. Well, only my grandmother in Brooklyn thought that last one was a favor. Even Geri Miller stopped twirling her tits long enough to come up with an intimate, at-home chat with Peter Boyle, "King of Unreleased Movies." Andy interviewed Ryan O'Neal and his eight-year-old daughter, Tatum, who had just starred in her first film, *Paper Moon.* She pestered Andy to call up Candy Darling and ask her over. The first thing Candy said to Tatum was "Gotta cigarette, kid?"

Andy also interviewed Jim Bailey when he came to do his impressions at Carnegie Hall. "The show was great," Andy told him. "But I think you're great as a boy. I think you should just forget the other stuff and go on as a boy." Lorna Luft had apparently convinced Lucie Arnaz that the Warhol crowd wasn't so strange, because she invited us to another opening of Jim Bailey's, at the Waldorf-Astoria's Empire Room. We sat at the front and center table with "the family"—Lucie; her brother, Desi Arnaz, Jr.; his fiancée, Liza Minnelli; and her half-sister, Lorna. When Jim came out as Judy, Lorna jumped up and down in her chair, screeching, "Liza, he's just like Mama! He's just like Mama!"

Our "Gala Christmas Issue" had Andy dressed as Santa on the cover, aiming his Big Shot at black super-model Naomi Sims, who sported a big red poinsettia behind her ear. Inside, the interviews ran the gamut from Bette Davis to Ron "Superfly" O'Neal, plus director Frank Perry, writer

James Purdy, artist Lucas Samaras, designer Clovis Ruffin, musician Curtis Mayfield, soap-opera actor Tom Fucello, and Princess Christina of Sweden. Jack Nicholson covered the New York Film Festival for us. And Fran Lebowitz's monthly column tore into the movies:

> *The Unholy Rollers* is AIP's Sistine Chapel. It is that rare a work: a perfect bad movie. It stars Claudia Jennings as Karen. For Claudia and Claudia alone they make orange pancake that streaks. She looks best under neon light. Miniature golf was invented with her in mind. Fifties rock expresses fully the depths of her soul. She is the real Raquel Welch.

There was also a Diana Ross centerfold by Bill King in that December issue. We just put in everyone famous, interesting, talented, and/or beautiful whom our assorted contributors and friends had met that month. Reading an issue of *Interview* then was like hanging out in the back room of Max's Kansas City or going to a private party at Halston's salon. It was becoming the inside chronicle of celebrity life in the seventies. There was no other magazine quite like it, though one could see the influence of the *Village Voice, Rolling Stone, WWD, Modern Screen,* and *Sixteen.* But unlike those publications, we didn't separate avant-garde culture, rock 'n' roll, fashion, movies, and TV, which were all rising and mixing in the seventies. We mixed and rose with them, little by little.

Our investors, Peter Brant, Joe Allen, and Bruno Bischofberger, were pleased enough with *Interview*'s progress to spring for better paper—smooth, white-coated stock instead of rough, low-grade newsprint. We were printing about twenty thousand copies a month, not bad considering the first issue print order of only one thousand three years earlier.

Advertising was up, too. Though still far from a profitable level, it had multiplied from that one-eighth-of-a-page trade ad from Cinemabilia into six or seven full pages a month (at $800 a page), mostly from movie and record companies. This was largely due to the tireless efforts of our new director of advertising, Sandy Brant, Peter's stylish wife. We didn't see much of Peter, but Sandy came in early every morning and kept calling the advertising executives at the movie and record companies until they gave her appointments. She then sat in their offices and kept talking, in her soft-spoken, unfailingly polite, but very persistent way, until they gave her ads.

Sandy's assistant was a frizzy-haired brunette named Susan Blond. Typically, she was a serious painter at the Whitney Museum School when Andy lured her to *Interview*'s advertising department with party invitations. "The best part of my job," she says, "was being in that video soap opera that Andy was making up at Maxime de la Falaise's with Candy Darling and Geri Miller. It was called *Phonies.* "

Andy had been searching for a way to do something fast, easy, cheap, different, and modern in television ever since he'd bought video equipment the year before and put Vincent Fremont and Michael Netter in charge of "the video department." Actually Andy, as usual, wasn't sure what he wanted to do with TV, and, as usual, was constantly polling his friends and associates for ideas. When I told him about Marshall McLuhan's observation that the word *phony* entered the language after the invention of the telephone, and that "People are phony on the phone," Andy saw a new way to use an old idea. "Let's just do a TV show on the phone. It can be people calling each other up and fighting." He loved the idea of people fighting on TV, just so long as he wasn't in the middle of it.

"But Andy," I protested, "you said I should do my book over the phone, and *Pork* is all phone calls; it's the same old thing."

"No, it's not," argued the artist who saw no reason why he shouldn't do a dozen paintings of the same subject in a dozen different colors, and then do prints of the same thing. "One's a book, one's a play, and one's a TV show."

Once they started videotaping, with Charles Rydell and Brigid Berlin as the fighters, Andy soon had a new idea for a title, *Nothing Serious,* and a new idea for combining the fight with interviews, soap opera with a talk show. And instead of just fighting on the phone, why not fight over the dinner table, and have celebrities come to dinner to talk about their new projects, while the regulars fought. And the dinner table could be Maxime de la Falaise McKendry's, because she was writing a food column for *Vogue,* which she had hopes of expanding into a TV show, à la Julia Child. Andy's idea was that Maxime could give recipes, when she wasn't interviewing and fighting. That was it. To make Andy Warhol's *Nothing Serious:* Take one-quarter of the Julia Child show and mix with one-quarter of the *Honeymooners,* add one-quarter of *As the World Turns* and one-quarter of the Johnny Carson show, stir in some singing and dancing, garnish with aspiring Superstars, serve very cool. The day after each shooting when it was all played back at the Factory, we'd realize that it was just too amorphous and amateurish to make it into anything viable. *Nothing Serious* was really nothing serious.

Sometimes I wonder if Andy wanted it to work. I wonder if any of it— the video projects, *Interview,* even the movies, anything other than the art and the selling of the art—was meant to be serious. Paul was serious about the movies, Glenn and I cared about the magazine, Vincent was committed to coming up with a TV show that worked—but was Andy? He certainly never minded the typos and other mistakes in *Interview.* "Why do you have to spend so much time proofreading?" he'd always ask. He liked things to be "bad," he liked things to be "boring"—concepts that may or may not have worked in the realm of art, but were not of much use in the movies, magazines, or television. Sometimes I found this attitude refreshing; other times it was just discouraging. If Andy didn't really care whether anything came of our efforts, then how should we? Maybe all these side businesses were just a way to keep himself busy, to surround himself with creative young people, to put friends on the payroll, to run up expenses and tax deductions against the art profits, to promote the sale of art and make Andy more famous, to spend the days and kill the nights, to ward off his fear and anxiety and emotional distress, to not be alone.

Or maybe Andy genuinely believed that if we took ourselves too seriously, fretted and sweated and tried to be professional instead of just doing it fast and easy and cheap, the end result would be stale and dull instead of turning out different and modern, magic and new.

Certainly everything Andy did, including the commissioned portraits, provided the perfect framework for nonstop social life—and the perfect excuse for nonstop social climbing. *Nothing Serious* is a good example. As a TV show it was a dead end. But our friendship with Maxime, which grew out of it, wasn't. And it was at her real dinner parties, not the ones we videotaped, that I met—and Andy and Fred got closer to—many of the social stars of the seventies and eighties.

Maxime was researching a book of medieval cooking. That meant she'd find ancient recipes in the archives at the Cloisters for dishes like twelfth-century Russian borscht—skinned ducks boiled in beet soup—and try them out on us. And she didn't like it at all when she found bits of dark, fatty duck meat left at the bottoms of our bowls. "I hauled those ducks in from Long Island myself," she said, scowling, "so you'd best clean your plates. If you want to be asked back, that is." She always questioned her guests at the end of each meal and we always told her how delicious everything had been, secretly wishing that she were researching a book on twentieth-century French cooking. Still, everyone went to Maxime's—the Erteguns, the Rayners, the Kempners, the Ryans, John Richardson, Boaz Mazor, Kenny Jay Lane—everyone that *WWD* nicknamed the Cat Pack.

At one of Maxime's dinners I was seated next to Diana Vreeland, which, in the Cat Pack, was like being seated next to the Queen of England. It was the first time I had met this legendary figure, whose name Fred and Andy were always invoking in tones of awe and worship. "She looks a little like an Egyptian mummy come to life," I wrote in my diary. There was something hieroglyphic about her incredibly erect posture and sharp dramatic gestures, her long-sleeved black cashmere tunic and wide ivory cuffs, and her ink-black hair sleeked back around her ears like a Pharaonic helmet. Others have compared her to a cigar-store Indian, noting her Apache nose and the deep red rouge slashed up her cheekbones and across her forehead like warpaint. Her grand and far-flung style suggested lost empires—Babylon and Cuzco, Moghul India and Czarist Russia. Though, at seventy-two, she was anything but old and decrepit, or old-fashioned and nostalgic.

The conversation that night at Maxime's was sprinkled with names like

Agnelli, Niarchos, Rothschild, Guinness, and Paley. I sat there and listened as a whole world was conjured up: the heavenly world of international High Society, where Aristotle Onassis was Zeus, and the Duchess of Windsor was Aphrodite. It was a world where the all-purpose adjective was "divine," the most popular form of address was "darling," the standard gesture of greeting was two quick kisses two inches away from one another's cheeks. A world of ladies who lunched at the five L's—La Grenouille, La Caravelle, La Côte Basque, Lafayette, Lutèce—and who were photographed by *WWD* on their way in and on their way out. A world where In and Out meant good and bad, right and wrong, where it was more important to be on the International Best Dressed List than in the *Social Register.* It was the world that Andy had finally conquered, after two decades of campaigning. In the fifties, as a fashion illustrator, he was on the fringe of their group, bringing them surprise presents in their offices at *Bazaar* and *Vogue*—D. D. Ryan, Gloria Schiff, her "Toni Twin" sister Consuelo Crespi, Lily Auchincloss, and Chessy Rayner all worked at one or another magazine with Mrs. Vreeland. In the sixties, Andy and his tinfoil Factory were objects of curiosity for the more adventurous—Mary McFadden, Mica and Ahmet Ertegun, Kenny Jay Lane, Freddy and Isabel Eberstadt all went to parties there, usually at the invitation of Jane Holzer.

Now, in the seventies, Andy was finally getting really in with them. Sometimes at the end of the Factory day, while I was helping him find a taxi on the corner of 17th Street and Park Avenue South, he'd invite me to a party that Jed didn't want to go to with him. He'd keep me waiting outside his front door, on Lexington Avenue, while he hurried to get ready. A few times, when it was really cold or raining hard, he let me into the outer vestibule, but he always closed the inner door behind him. "I'll be right out," he'd say. "I've got to talk to Jed for a minute." Or "I've got to see if my mother's okay."

I remember one party in particular, a smart Park Avenue cocktail party given by a smart couple who were, and still are, leading lights of High Society. All the way there, Andy told me again and again, half seriously, half ironically, "Now this is going to be a really up-there party, Bob. This is the group that really counts. This is Society, Bob." It *was* chic and stylish. The ladies were kissing Andy on both cheeks and asking him if he was going to Paris for a Rothschild ball, to which he replied, "Gee, I don't know. I think maybe Fred is." The men seemed to be evenly divided between husbands and escorts. It was fun to stand at Andy's side among the rich and famous, as he whispered out of the side of his mouth: "She's the one with the money," he said about the hostess, and "He's really after you, Bob," he said about the host. He said it was "a mixed marriage—you know, fags with dykes."

As soon as we were in the elevator, I started to tell Andy what I thought about the party, but he signaled me to stop. "They give the elevator men big tips to tell them what their friends say,'' said Andy as soon as we were out on Park Avenue. ''But wasn't that great, Bob? Everyone was there. That was really it, Bob.''

We had our first office Christmas party at the Factory in 1972, for the kids, some of our friends, and the favored Superstars—Candy, Sylvia, Pat Ast, Geraldine and Maria Smith, Donna Jordan, Jane Forth, Eric Emerson, Joe Dallesandro. It was a cozy ''family'' affair, with Moët et Chandon champagne and little Joe Jr. chasing baby Emerson Forth around the floor. Andy gave everyone Electric Chair prints, which were worth about $200 each then. I gave Andy my Beales tape from that afternoon at Grey Gardens, the one Lee told Fred she'd rather we didn't run. Andy was thrilled—''Gee, what a great present, Bob''—and put it in a time capsule with everybody else's presents, which were mostly jokes in any case. Only Pat Hackett came up with something he took home to use: a case of Heinz ketchup.

Andy gave himself a dog for Christmas, a black dachshund puppy he named Archie, after Archie Bunker, the lower-middle-class loudmouth on the new sitcom *All in the Family*. He carried it around in his arms at the office party, whispering into its ear, ''Talk, Archie, talk. Oh, Archie, if you would only talk, I wouldn't have to work another day in my life. Talk, Archie, talk.'' The funny thing is, I think he was really serious.

16

Roman Candles

Andy was in Rome a lot in 1973, co-producing *Andy Warhol's Frankenstein* and *Andy Warhol's Dracula,* with Carlo Ponti, Sophia Loren's husband and then the most important producer in Italy, and acting in *The Driver's Seat,* opposite Elizabeth Taylor. He loved Rome. It was his kind of town: gossipy, fashionable, starstruck, "soooo glamorous." The swank nightclubs were clogged with movie stars like Ursula Andress, Elsa Martinelli, Florinda Bolkan, Maria Schneider, Helmut Berger, and Hiram Keller, and the newsstands were bursting with scandal sheets, like *Oggi, Due Mille,* and *Eva Express,* which chronicled, often inaccurately but always dramatically, their romantic ups and downs, ins and outs. It was a recherché fifties kind of scene, the last days of the end of an era, before the oil crisis and the Red Brigades. Starlets still received diamonds and rubies from producers. Contessas still furnished gigolos with Maseratis and Alfa Romeos. And everybody knew every detail of each other's private lives and discussed them endlessly over long, late lunches and longer, later dinners. Andy's kind of town, all right. What's more, as he put it, "They let dogs eat in all the restaurants, and Archie loves pasta."

Andy, Archie, and Fred commuted between New York and Rome that spring while *Frankenstein* and *Dracula* were being shot at Cinecittà. Paul, Jed, and Pat Hackett, who was helping Paul with the scripts that Ponti had insisted on, lived in the rented Villa Mandorli off the posh Appia Antica, next door to Valentino's. It was a tough schedule: Ponti had given them eight weeks, and an $800,000 budget, to shoot both movies back to back. It was the first time the Factory crew had worked in 35mm—instead of 16mm—

and the first film, *Frankenstein,* was shot in 3D—you could barely make a move without everything going out of focus. This meant that every shot had to be very carefully choreographed in advance, which severely crimped Paul's improvisational style. When it came time to start *Dracula,* with time and money running out fast, 3D was abandoned.

These were the last two Factory films that Paul Morrissey directed and the last two Factory films Joe Dallesandro starred in. I heard about the infighting on the set from Andy and Fred, and from Monique van Vooren, who starred in *Frankenstein,* and Maxime de la Falaise, who starred in *Dracula.* It was the same kind of infighting that had ruined *L'Amour,* which finally opened in early 1973 and flopped.

Paul was very much in charge on *Frankenstein* and *Dracula;* it was the success of *Heat* that had led Ponti to finance the films in the first place. But Paul depended on Jed to edit and on Pat to help with the script, and they both chafed under his high-handed direction. Paul never suggested, pro-posed, or hinted. He ordered. And then, as often as not, he changed his mind, and ordered the very opposite, in the same shrill manner. That's what got to Jed. He'd edit a scene the way Paul wanted it and then Paul would hate it and tell him to do it another way, only to have Paul hate that and tell him to put it back together the way it was originally. This might be normal for some director-editor relationships, but the Factory wasn't a normal movie company, Paul wasn't a normal director, and Jed wasn't a normal editor. And Andy was always available to listen to Jed's complaints, either in person or over the phone, and to take his side, which didn't help. ''Paul is being so mean to Jed,'' he'd tell me, after a long night of long distance.

He also listened to Pat's complaints about Paul. She felt she was being treated like a secretary, when she was not only writing a large portion of the dialogue but also coaching the actors after hours. Maxime told me that it was Pat, not Paul, who gave her the most direction, who stayed up late going over the next day's lines with her, rewriting so they came out more naturally. But Maxime also respected Paul for the way he held the overall structure together. And that wasn't easy, with an all-Italian crew and a poly-glot cast that included Udo Kier, the German actor who played Count Dra-cula; Joe Dallesandro, who played the stake-wielding hero; one of Ponti's spaghetti starlets; and Maxime, the medieval cook, making her movie debut. Maxime was quite believable as an impoverished aristocrat hoping one of her five unmarried daughters would attract the wealthy count from Transyl-vania. Her consort was played by Vittorio de Sica, the venerable Italian director. *Dracula,* as it turned out, was his last appearance on screen, and he almost stole the movie. The other scene stealer was Roman Polanski, the Polish director, as a *taverna* lounge lizard who beats Count Dracula at cards.

Dracula had its moments, but it wasn't one of Paul's best. It lacked the kind of pathos and biting social observation that gave the humor of *Trash, Women in Revolt,* and *Heat* their depth and edge. Perhaps Paul, and Andy,

Jed, and Pat, were too American, too Pop and camp, to do justice to this Central European legend. You can't send up what you don't have down.

Andy Warhol's Frankenstein, despite the 3D, was equally two-dimensional: funny but not much else. Both films were commercial successes by Factory standards in the United States, Europe, and, for the first time, Japan. *Frankenstein* alone took in $4 million in the United States according to *Variety,* and as much as $20 million worldwide (though these figures were disputed by Ponti, and the Factory sued). And if the film itself lacked social significance, its opening at Cinema One, on Third Avenue in New York, made some kind of social statement, with the likes of Lee Radziwill, Pat Lawford, Nan Kempner and Lily Auchincloss, plus John Phillips, Bianca Jagger, and Halston, all sitting in the dark in those special 3D glasses. Somewhere, in one of Andy's time capsules, there's a photo of that audience; he should have silkscreened it into a mural.

Frankenstein employed much the same cast as *Dracula,* including Udo Kier as the villain and Joe Dallesandro as the hero who kills him. But one of Ponti's *spaghettini,* the redhead, was replaced by another, a blonde, and Maxime de la Falaise was swapped for Monique van Vooren. Monique was the kind of character that exists only in Fellini movies: hyper-sophisticated, hyper-dramatic, hyper-hysterical. Tall, buxom, and blonde, she even looked like Anita Ekberg in *La Dolce Vita.* She claimed to have discovered Hiram "Satyricon" Keller and to have lost many of her admirers to her close friend and frequent Manhattan house guest, Rudolf Nureyev. She was always heartbroken, but she never missed a party.

During the filming, Monique took it into her head to fall in love with Paul. When Andy heard, he started calling her every night to ask how her seduction of the notoriously inhibited Paul was going. Andy would reassure her that Paul "didn't, uh, like boys, or anything, he was, uh, just shy with women." He told her to really go after him.

This was all Monique had to hear. The next day, she was batting her eyelashes, hiking up her skirt, and leaning over to reveal her cleavage, all aimed at Paul. He paid her no mind, as this was pretty much the way she always behaved. That night Andy told Monique that Paul was typically Irish-Catholic, very strict and serious, not the type to have a quick fling with his leading lady. Monique took to wearing a big gold crucifix, saying the rosary between takes, and going on about her Catholic girlhood and convent education. And although Paul never succumbed to Monique's nunnish charms, on several occasions since I have heard him say, "You know, Monique is not the decadent sophisticated European jet-set type she makes herself out to be. She's actually quite serious and devout."

I hated hearing about all these Roman goings-on secondhand; I wanted to be there. Finally, in July, Giorgio di Sant'Angelo invited me to accompany him and his assistant, Jay Johnson, for a one-month Roman holiday. Jed and Paul were still in residence at the Villa Mandorli, wrapping up post-production on *Frankenstein* and *Dracula*. Andy gave me permission to go and said we could stay at the villa. He gave me a few hundred dollars, in brand-new hundred-dollar bills, admonishing me to "bring back lots of receipts." I think he liked the idea of my checking up on Jed, and on how he was getting along with Paul.

My month in Rome was everything a vacation should be. We slept late, took lunch by the pool, shopped on the Via Condotti, came home for a nap, went to late dinners in fun restaurants and smart apartments, then stayed up late perambulating around the Piazza Navona or dancing at Scarrabocchio. Every other day or so, Andy called to get a full report, although I was becoming better at editing what I told him, and I'm sure he sometimes wondered if the chaperone hadn't turned into the ringleader. And when he pressed too hard—"You were out how late? Was Jed there too? Did you ask that rich kid, Aldo Palma, for his portrait yet?"—I'd yell into the phone, "I'm on vacation, Andy!" "You're always on vacation, Bob," he'd mutter back, and hang up.

One day, Giorgio decided that he was going to give a party to thank all the Romans who had given parties for him. "But no pasta," he pronounced. "I want to have an American party. Hot dogs and hamburgers, ketchup and mustard, sauerkraut and watermelon." The cook was totally perplexed. She finally figured out that hamburgers were flattened-out meatballs, but where was she to find frankfurters in Rome? Someone eventually found some at an American army base. We gave up on the sauerkraut. (Now, of course, there's a McDonald's on the Via Veneto.)

I had another bright idea: why not invite Paulette Goddard and Anita Loos? I knew they were working in Rome on Paulette's life story, *The Perils of Paulette,* because Paulette had told me they would be when we first met her a few months earlier.

The party was slated to start at nine, which in Rome means come at ten. Not Paulette. On the dot of nine, a big black Mercedes came rolling down our graveled drive, and out they stepped. Paulette was in a figure-hugging white dress and white high heels. She wore only three colors—white, pink, and red—because they reflect light, giving a glow to the skin. It was an old Hollywood trick, and Paulette was first and foremost an old Hollywood star. Anita wore a black Chanel suit, made especially for her in miniature. And she had retained her trademark hairdo from the thirties, a bob with bangs.

I saw their arrival from my upstairs bedroom window and hurriedly finished dressing. Giorgio was still in his room, changing his hair color, something he did as often as other men shave. Jay Johnson and his sister, Susan Johnson, were locked in the bathroom, doing their makeup. Jed was in the kitchen, trying to persuade the cook not to fry the hot dogs in olive oil and garlic. Only Paul was there to greet our star guests. As I dashed downstairs, he was already listing, and praising, every movie the former Mrs. Charlie Chaplin had ever appeared in, from *Modern Times* to *Babes in Baghdad,* and every movie Anita had written, from *Intolerance* to *The Greeks Had a Word for It.*

It was an hour before Giorgio descended from his dyeing salon, also in white. He too charmed Paulette and Anita with tales of seeing all their movies when he was growing up in Argentina. Jed was still in the kitchen, trying to persuade the cook not to put breadcrumbs and oregano in the hamburgers. Jay and Susan were still upstairs doing their makeup. Our Roman guests had yet to arrive. And Paulette and Anita were hinting that they hadn't had a thing to eat since noon.

By ten-thirty, Paulette was really hungry, Giorgio and Jed were in the kitchen trying to calm the cook, Susan and Jay were *still* doing their makeup—and our Roman guests all arrived in one big bunch, pouring out of a motorcade of Mercedeses and Alfa Romeos: Valentino, Giancarlo Giametti, Lucia Curia, Elsa Martinelli, Willy Rizzo, Daniela Morera, Max DeLys, Florinda Bolkan, Countess Marina Cicogna, Franco Rossellini, Count and Countess Crespi, Hiram Keller, Nando Scarfiotti, and Audrey Hepburn's husband, Dr. Dotti, all chirping away in a mad mélange of Italian, French, Portuguese, and English, creating a huge commotion in our entrance foyer. Paulette was momentarily diverted, as they all told her how much they loved all her movies.

Then, like something out of an old slapstick farce, down the stairs came Susan Johnson, crying hysterically, mascara dripping down her teenage cheeks, followed by a roaring rush of water—a tidal wave! Jay had sat on the edge of the old porcelain sink to get closer to the mirror; the sink had collapsed and was now a gushing geyser. In seconds, the foyer was awash, the Romans were slipping and sliding on the tile floor, Jed was trying to fight his way up the stairs against the flood, Paul was shouting at the maid and cook to get some mops, Giorgio was looking for the number of an emergency plumber, and I was trying to placate Paulette, who was screaming that she wanted to leave, that she was starved, that her shoes were ruined, that she had never been to a worse party in her life.

There was only one thing preventing her departure: Her Mercedes was blocked by other cars, and everybody was too agitated to figure out which car was whose. But Paulette was screaming, "Move that car! Get me out of here!"—so somehow Jed, Max DeLys, and I literally lifted a Ferrari out of the way, and Paulette and Anita took off, never, I felt sure, to be seen again by us.

After we'd mopped up, Jed and Jay had a fight, and Jed stormed out. Jay ran after him, pleading, "Don't do it!" "Don't do what?" I asked, as

I tried to calm him down. "I can't tell you, but it's all my fault. I'm always ruining everything. I wish I could be good like Jed, but I can't. Please, Bob, you have to make sure he's all right."

I found Jed at the nearby villa of Andrew Braunsberg, the producer who had helped put together our Ponti deal. Jed was in bed, in his clothes, sobbing. "Maybe Andy's right," he said. "Life is too hard."

"It'll get better," I told him. "You'll see. You'll get to direct your own movie soon. I'll talk to him about it."

"Andy doesn't care."

"Yes, he does. And you've done so much already."

"Life's too hard."

I went back to our villa. The cook was proudly passing a platter of hamburgers *all'olio* and frankfurters *oreganato* or vice versa. Jay was crying on Naty Abascal's shoulder and Susan was crying on Paul Palmero's shoulder, or vice versa. Sometimes it seemed like everything and everyone in our particular world was vice versa, upside-down, inside-out, starting with Andy. I had another vodka, another line of Roman coke—it was just coming in there too—and forgot about Jed and Jay, Paulette and Anita. The next morning, Paulette called on the dot of nine to thank me for asking her to Giorgio's party. It was the best party she'd ever been to, she said. Anita had loved it. She'd sat up all night writing down everything that had happened, and now they had the final chapter of *The Perils of Paulette*. "And that girl," Paulette said, "that beautiful Botticelli girl who came down the stairs in tears, with the water coming down behind her. Anita said it was like a scene in a movie, and it was. And it was so sad. It reminded me of me, when I was her age and suffering so with Charlie.

"Now be sure to call me in New York this fall," she added. "I'll be at the Ritz Tower after the fifteenth of September, and I'd like to see more of you and Paul Morrissey and those handsome young twins, and, of course, Andy. I hope you're going to call him and tell him he missed the party of the year."

A few days later Andy called me. "I'm coming over in a few days," he said, "to act with Liz Taylor in Franco Rossellini's new movie. Why don't you wait there for me? You can come on the set with me. You can watch Archie."

Archie went everywhere with Andy, to work, to dinner, to parties, and to Europe. He had already crossed the Atlantic ten times, on Andy's lap, never in the hold. (Later, Andy got a second dachshund, named Amos, and Archie stayed home.)

Andy arrived in Rome on Sunday, August 5, with Archie on an Hermès leash. On the flight over, he had read Norman Mailer's Marilyn Monroe book. Was it good? I asked. "I never knew Marilyn had so many abortions.'' Who but Andy Warhol would read Marilyn Monroe's biography in preparing to meet Elizabeth Taylor? He was worried about the script. ''You've got to find out if I have any lines. I hope not. Oh, is there any steak for Archie?''

On Monday he read the script. Or rather, he had me read it for him. I told him his lines: ''Let's go, let's go. I fear I am dangerously late.''

''That's not the way I talk,'' said Andy. ''They should make it the way I talk.''

''Gee,'' said Andy, ''I knew Liz Taylor was short, but I didn't know she was *that* short.''

It was eight-thirty in the morning, Tuesday, August 7, at Rome's Leonardo da Vinci Airport. *The Driver's Seat,* based on Muriel Spark's novel about a psychotic German *hausfrau* who flies to Rome in search of the perfect lover—and killer. That was Elizabeth Taylor's part. She briefly considers as a candidate the character that Andy played, to quote the script, ''a rich creep of undisclosed nationality and occupation.'' ''Gee,'' said Andy, ''my first movie and I'm typecast already.'' It was just a cameo, but Andy was taking his billing very professionally. ''Tell them,'' he told me, ''not to say 'guest star.' I want to be listed as 'and introducing.' ''

Now, here we were, on location and on time, which meant getting up at dawn, for Andy's first day of shooting. The only problem was that nobody else was on time, not the crew, not the director, Giuseppe Patroni Griffi, not the producer, our friend Franco Rossellini—just this short, stocky, dark-haired woman pacing back and forth at the other end of the empty terminal. She looked like Elizabeth Taylor, but we couldn't be sure from that distance. ''That must be her,'' Andy said one moment. ''That can't be her,'' he said the next. ''Oh, where is everybody? Why are we the only ones here? Do you think the movie was called off? Maybe Liz had a fight with Franco. Or is that Liz over there? Why won't she say hello? Oh, Archie, I'm all washed up in the movies before I even started.''

''Maybe you should go and see if that is Liz Taylor,'' Andy was telling me, over the roar of jetliners taking off and landing, as it approached ten-thirty. I was saved from this awkward task by the arrival of a couple of crew members, who introduced themselves, and then the lady in question: She wasn't Elizabeth Taylor, but her Italian stand-in, who walked through the scenes so shots could be set up without Miss Taylor's presence (which, we would soon learn, was not always guaranteed on her movies).

The stand-in told us that this was her eighth Elizabeth Taylor movie. Andy said, ''Gee, we thought you were short. I mean, we thought Liz Taylor was short. I mean, what do I mean, Bob?'' ''Andy means,'' I imaginatively translated from English to English, ''he thought you actually were Elizabeth Taylor because you look just like her; you're so pretty.'' It didn't matter;

the stand-in didn't understand English. The minute she was out of earshot, Andy whined, "Why don't I have a stand-in to walk through my setups, instead of having to get up in the middle of the night. Huh, Bob? Did you ever think of asking Franco that?" I hadn't.

There was still no sign of the real Elizabeth Taylor when Franco Rossellini arrived at two in the afternoon and called lunch. "That woman will be the end of me," he announced dramatically as he led Andy, Archie, and me into a fast-pasta restaurant overlooking a busy runway.

Franco was the bachelor nephew of Roberto Rossellini, the pioneer neo-Realist director who is perhaps best known in America for his affair with Ingrid Bergman. Franco loved to refer to "my aunt Ingrid" and knew everyone in the Italian movie business on a first-name basis—Anna (Magnani), Sophia (Loren), Carlo (Ponti), Federico (Fellini), Luchino (Visconti). And, as this *dolce vita* world was the playground of the original fifties and sixties jet set, he was also on first names with such luminaries as Marella (Agnelli), Marie-Hélène (de Rothschild), Rosemarie (Marcie-Rivière), and Cristina (Ford). It was Franco Rossellini who first introduced Doris (Duke) to Imelda (Marcos) in the sixties, and, for that matter, who first introduced Andy to Imelda a bit later in the seventies. He was fast, funny, bitchy, bright, stylish, a little bit lazy, the Roman's Roman.

That day, over spaghetti alla Bolognese airport-style, Franco went on about Jackie and Ari and Maria (Callas, of course, whom he had starred in his movie version of *Medea,* directed by Pier Paolo Pasolini). "You know," he said, "people think that Maria was a prima donna, very difficult and insecure and demanding, but she was nothing, nothing at all, compared to Elizabeth Taylor. This woman will be the end of me, I tell you. You know how many times I called her at the Grand Hotel this morning? Every hour on the hour since nine this morning. And does she even come to the phone for me? No, I get the hairdresser telling me Miss Taylor is not feeling her best, Miss Taylor is looking a little puffy—it's costing me tens of thousands of dollars for every hour we don't shoot, and Miss Taylor is looking a little puffy! Oh, well, this is the price we pay for the stars, right, Andy? I must warn you, Andy, whatever you do, don't call her Liz. She hates to be called Liz. It's always Elizabeth and only Elizabeth. Like the Queen."

Andy was all ears, and tape recorder.

"And another thing, Andy, don't take that tape recorder around her."

"Oh, really," said Andy. "It's a good thing you're here, Bob, you can be my tape recorder. Bob remembers everything everybody says. It's really great."

Now it was Franco's turn to say, "Oh, really," and Andy quickly added, "But we don't let him print it."

Just as we were about to ask for the dessert included in the prix-fixe lunch, the waiters dropped everything and pulled out signs from behind the bar, proclaiming ON STRIKE! and DOWN WITH RICH TRAVELERS!

"Does this mean we don't have to pay?" asked Andy.

"No, it means we don't get dessert," answered Franco, adding, "Now, it's three o'clock. Let's see if Elizabeth Taylor has honored us with her presence. Did I tell you how much it's costing me to keep her at the Grand Hotel? Forty thousand dollars a month! She told me she didn't want to be paid for the movie, just expenses, which I thought was a good deal, until I found out that expenses meant a seven-room suite at the Grand Hotel. One for her, one for the secretary, one for the hairdresser, the wardrobe mistress, the dogs, and you should see what the dogs did to that room! They had to move all the furniture out and cover everything with newspapers; there was no other way. I mean, do you think Elizabeth Taylor is going to walk her dogs down the Via Veneto? And the secretary and the hairdresser and the wardrobe mistress can't do it because they have to be with her, because God forbid she should be without her entourage for even a second. But the final straw was when she went to Bulgari and started charging jewelry to her room at the Grand Hotel. I had to draw the line. I mean, you can carry this just-expenses business just so far."

At four in the afternoon, Elizabeth Taylor sauntered onto the set, followed by her secretary, her hairdresser, and her wardrobe mistress. She didn't look puffy, she wasn't that short, and her eyes really were purple. She was already costumed in the one dress her character wears throughout the movie, a pink, green, yellow, orange, and blue print Valentino that more than met the script's requirement for something "garish and vulgar," and was said to have cost $22,000, including four copies to rotate during shooting. Her hair was teased up and out—the script again—but she still looked beautiful, "really beautiful," as Andy put it.

Her secretary and her hairdresser were a pair of Mediterranean musclemen named Ramon and Gianni, in matching tight white T-shirts and tight white trousers, accessorized with red patent-leather belts, shoes, and shoulder bags. Every so often, between takes, Ramon would pull a mirror out of his bag and hold it up in front of Elizabeth's face; then Gianni would pull a teasing comb out of his bag, and hand it to Elizabeth, who would fitfully tease her own hair higher. She looked almost mad when she did that, though one couldn't be sure if she was just in character or almost mad.

"Gee," said Andy, "why don't you carry a mirror and comb around for me, Bob?" "Because," I replied, "I'm carrying Archie around for you, Andy." We were standing off to the side, watching Elizabeth get to work, which she did almost immediately. All she had to do, said Griffi, was follow the X-marks taped to the floor. Much to Franco's relief, she was perfect on the first take: She walked through the terminal with two hundred extras, all supposedly coming off a plane from Hamburg; she screamed her best *Vir-*

ginia Woolf scream as an "Arab terrorist" cut through the crowd, and "fainted" convincingly when he "stabbed" a man in front of her.

It all happened so fast and looked so real that Andy, who hadn't read the script, thought it *was* real, and panicked. "My God," he blurted, "Liz is still Jewish, isn't she? We better get out of here." Elizabeth was still Jewish (out of loyalty to her third husband, Mike Todd), and Andy's paranoia wasn't totally unjustified: The Athens airport had been turned into a bloody battlefield by Arab terrorists only a week before, and the waiters' strike, which seemed funny at lunch, had spread throughout the airport. Electrical wires had been cut, we had to use a generator to continue shooting, and the constant din of arriving and departing jumbo jets did nothing for our nerves. Even little Archie developed a case of the shakes.

When the take was finished, Franco signaled for Andy and me to come and meet Elizabeth, who gave us a quick hello and then turned toward her trailer, set up just outside the terminal's wall of windows, like a little cottage from Hollywood. "Ah, Elizabeth," coughed Franco, "perhaps Andy would like to have a little drink too." She invited Andy to her trailer. That left me standing there with Archie in my arms. "Uh, oh, oh," said Andy, "can Bob bring my dog too?"

"So long as he doesn't piss on my carpet," snapped the most famous movie star in the world, marching ahead.

"Gee, Bob," whispered Andy as we followed. "What a great opening line. I mean, that's the first thing Elizabeth Taylor said to me. You've got to remember it for my memoirs."

The second thing that Elizabeth Taylor said to Andy was that she had called the Factory in the sixties to ask if she could have a print of his famous portrait of her and was refused.

"It must have been a mistake," said Andy. "But why don't I take some Polaroid pictures and make a new portrait of you?"

She was so busy searching for his hidden tape recorder she barely replied. Or was she afraid it would cost her money? Andy tried again. "It would be great if I could take a few Polaroids and do a new portrait of you, because the other one was from newspaper photographs and this would be better and uh . . ." I could see his mind calculating, "And . . . uh, I could give you one." He wasn't really giving anything away; he no doubt could sell a whole series of Liz II paintings and prints. But Elizabeth didn't, or pretended she didn't, understand. Andy tried one more time, but she cut him short with "I'm too puffy to be photographed today."

Then she gulped down a Debauched Mary, her name for a drink that was "five parts vodka and one part blood," and launched into a diatribe against lesbians in the movie business, all of whom, she seemed to think, were after her. "That fucking dyke!" she screamed about someone we knew.

"Oh, she's really nice," said Andy, trying to be loyal.

"Nice! I'll tell you what that bull dyke did to me. I was on my death-

bed—this is when I had to have the tracheotomy because I couldn't breathe—
and Richard was at my side, holding my hand, day and night. And that bull
dyke released a photograph of Richard dancing with her dyke girlfriend on
Ari Onassis's yacht from three years before, as if he were dancing with her
then—she didn't tell them it was an old photograph—while I was dying in
the hospital! You call that *nice?*''

"She did that?" asked Andy, getting nervous. "Oh, I can't believe it.
It must have been a mistake. The magazine must have done it or something.''

"*Time* magazine doesn't do things like that intentionally. Your dyke
friend tricked them into it, and I want you to let her know that I know what
she did.''

"Oh, oh, uh, really.'' Andy was really nervous now. "Oh, uh, Bob
will. He knows her better than I do.''

Later, Andy said to me, "Do you think Liz Taylor is a lesbian?" I told
him that I thought she'd made it clear that she was anything but. "Then why
were they all after her?" he persisted. "I mean, maybe they knew that's
what she wanted.'' That's the way Andy's mind worked. He was often convinced that people were saying the opposite of what they meant. Maybe
because he often did so himself.

Lesbianism in Hollywood somehow led Elizabeth to the Kennedy family, and an evening that she and Richard Burton had spent with Bobby Kennedy, years ago. Bobby had challenged Burton to a "Shakespeare contest"
and won. When she talked about Burton—they were in the midst of their
first divorce—it was with a mixture of affection, anger, and remorse. She
seemed so unhappy about the whole thing. Andy was all ears, and no tape
recorder—he had slipped it to me and I had hidden it in my inside jacket
pocket, turned off. Nonetheless, Andy was thrilled: Not only was he hanging
out with Elizabeth Taylor, but she was talking about his favorite subject,
sex, and even using four-letter words.

With a remarkable memory for dates, places, people, and dialogue, she
recounted the long and torturous history of her illnesses, accidents, and
operations. "Feel my back,'' she suddenly commanded Andy, who was
startled but followed orders, gingerly. "No, lower . . . lower . . . *there.*
Can you feel the crushed vertebrae?''

Andy said he could, and then startled me by announcing, "Now I'll
have to show you my scars.'' He loosened his tie and unbuttoned his shirt.
He was wearing, as always, the medical girdle that had held him together
since the shooting. His upper torso crisscrossed with the scars of stitches.

"You poor baby,'' said Elizabeth Taylor softly, "you poor baby.''

An assistant knocked on the trailer door and said that the crew was
ready for Miss Taylor's next shot. When Elizabeth saw the way it had been
set up, she refused to do it and marched off for the day, followed by Ramon,
Gianni, and her wardrobe mistress, a beleaguered Italian woman with pins

in her mouth. "It just doesn't work," Elizabeth told Franco, "and anyway, it's close to six and I don't work after six." Even Griffi agreed that she was right about the shot, and the alternative she had suggested turned out to be much better, the flow of characters simpler, the background more dramatic. "Gee, she could be a director," said Andy admiringly. "Are you out of your mind?" snapped Franco Rossellini, who was furious. "She arrives at four in the afternoon, and then she has the nerve to tell me she doesn't work past six! That woman will be the end of me."

The next day, Andy decided to "be late like Liz." Of course, when we arrived at 11 A.M., everyone was already there, including Elizabeth. Andy was whisked into Makeup, where his wig was smoothed down, and even trimmed a bit, while he sat there shaking. He wanted a lot more makeup than they wanted to put on him.

While I held Archie, Andy went through his scene several times with Miss Taylor's stand-in, then with Elizabeth herself. He changed his opening line from "Let's go" to "C'mon, girls," and "I fear I'm going to be dangerously late" to "I'm late." Andy handed her the book she had dropped in the confusion of the terrorists' attack and ran off with his entourage. She screamed, "He's afraid of me! Why is everyone afraid of me?"

This dull bit of business was repeated through four master shots, four sets of closeups of Elizabeth, and four sets of closeups of Andy, a dozen times in all.

Finally, Andy got me to ask her secretary, Ramon, if she would like to come to the villa for lunch the following day. Ramon asked her, and she said yes. "Oh, good," said Andy, "we'll take some Polaroids then." Only if she didn't still look puffy, Elizabeth said.

The following morning when I told the cook that Elizabeth Taylor was coming for lunch, she enlisted the aid of nearly every other cook on the Appia Antica, luring them with the promise of serving the star. Soon a half-dozen of them were busily preparing their specialties, from *lasagne al forno* to chicken *cacciatore*. One of them told me in broken English that she had been hired by Eddie Fisher years ago, when he had rented a villa on the Appia Antica and was still married to Elizabeth. Unfortunately, she explained almost tearfully, she never met Miss Taylor, because the one and only time she came to the villa, "she and Mista Fisha hava bigga fight in the middle of da night and she run away before I can serva da breakfast." This time, she told me, she was going to be sure to get her autograph. Meanwhile, Andy Braunsberg was calling every *principe* and *principessa* he knew to ask them for lunch with Elizabeth Taylor.

By one, when she was expected, everything was ready: the lasagne, ravioli, ziti, spaghetti, cavatelli, and gnocchi, the chicken, veal, lamb, beef, sole, shrimps, and lobster, the bourbon and vodka, the *principes* and *principessas,* Eddie Fisher's former cook and her autograph book, even Anna Karina, actress wife of director Jean-Luc Godard. But where was Elizabeth? Then it was two o'clock. But where was Elizabeth? And then it was three o'clock. But where was Elizabeth? The *principes* and *principessas* were offended. The half-dozen cooks were on the verge of tears. "Are you sure you told her today?" asked Andy. "No, I told her tomorrow, which is today." "Well, maybe she thought tomorrow was tomorrow." Andy and I were fast degenerating into what he called our "Abbott and Costello Show."

Elizabeth arrived at three-thirty, without explanation or apology. Ramon and Gianni were two feet behind her, in their matching white and red. She was dressed casually, for lunch in the country: blue jeans, a purple T-shirt with mirrored embroidery à la Marrakech circa 1966, assorted gold chains, and an American-flag ring made of diamonds, rubies, and sapphires, a gift, she said, from Gianni Bulgari. "Isn't it a giggle?" she said. "Oh, it's just great," sighed Andy.

"This is the way she dressed to meet Sophia," Ramon informed us, talking about Elizabeth as if she weren't there. "Madame Ponti wore a Dior suit with a Dior handbag and Dior shoes."

"And Dior gloves!" screeched Elizabeth in delight. "Can you imagine? She was standing at the front door of her own house, waiting to greet me, in *gloves!*"

"Oh, I know," said Andy. "She was wearing gloves when we went there for lunch too. But she's really great. Really great."

Elizabeth coughed and asked for a Jack Daniels neat. Then when everyone else went into the dining room and the half-dozen cooks marched out with their half-dozen pastas, she said she wasn't hungry and just wanted to sit outside with us. She consumed several more neat Jack Danielses. I was afraid to go into the kitchen: I was sure I'd find the half-dozen cooks slitting their dozen wrists.

Andy suggested that Elizabeth should direct films because she knew so much about setting up shots and lighting and dialogue and she, flattered, said that was her ambition. She told us that she always worked for a percentage of her films. "I own ten percent of *Virginia Woolf,* and that's the highest-grossing black-and-white film ever made. And I just bought seventy-five percent of *Around the World in Eighty Days* from the Todd children." She smiled shrewdly. "I'm going to re-release it every year at Christmas."

"Gee," sighed Andy. "Maybe you should be a producer and a director." He paused, and added, "Uh, do you think we could do some Polaroids now?"

"Oh, Andy," said Elizabeth, "you are sweet. But don't you think I'm looking awfully puffy?"

"No, you look great. Doesn't Liz, I meant Elizabeth, look great, Bob?" I said she did.

"I tell you what, Andy. We'll do the photographs when you come back in October to shoot your other scene. Okay?"

Just then, a friend of Braunsberg's arrived, a perfectly nice associate producer who had worked in Puerto Vallarta on *Night of the Iguana,* when Richard Burton's romance with Elizabeth Taylor was at its height. At first she was happy to see him, and they reminisced. But the more they talked, the more Elizabeth insisted that he call Burton, who was also in Rome, staying at Carlo Ponti's villa. "He won't take calls from me," she said, fighting back the tears, "but from you he would."

The friend resisted, she persisted. She became obsessed with the idea. She dragged him into the library, begging him to call. A minute later, she let out a blood-curdling scream and came running back to the terrace. "I'm no easy lay," she shouted. "I'm no easy lay. That motherfucker tried to put the make on me," she sobbed. "I'm crying on his shoulder and he tries to grab me." This was turning into a real Elizabeth Taylor movie and Andy wasn't sure he wanted a part in it anymore.

She pulled Andy by the hand and walked into the garden. He followed obediently, looking back at me like a lost kid. She led him to a corner framed in hedges, and they sat down on wrought-iron chairs on either side of a table. I couldn't hear what they were talking about—well, Elizabeth was talking, and Andy was listening—but I could see what they were doing: she was picking the leaves from the hedge, Andy was wringing his hands and every so often signaling me to come. But I was stuck with Ramon and Gianni, who acted as if we were all having a perfectly normal afternoon.

Elizabeth kept picking leaves and piling them on the tabletop, until it was covered and the hedge was bare. Eventually, I walked over and asked her if she'd like a drink. She looked at me with purple eyes full of anger, and I retreated. Andy called softly, "Oh, Elizabeth is staying for dinner. Maybe you should tell the cooks." I headed for the kitchen, where the half-dozen cooks sat dejectedly, dividing up the leftovers. "Miss Taylor is staying for dinner," I announced, and they suddenly turned giddy, like death-row inmates who've just been pardoned. I told them we'd sit down to eat at eight.

A few minutes before eight, Miss Taylor disappeared into the servants' bathroom, off the kitchen. We sat down at the dining table and waited. And waited. And waited. The cooks hovered in the doorway, desperate to serve the twice-slaved-over meal. Ramon and Gianni took turns knocking on the bathroom door, but she wouldn't let them in, and she wouldn't come out. Somehow, somebody called a doctor, who arrived in a black car with a black bag. Apparently, she let him into the bathroom and slipped away with him, not saying goodbye. We just heard his wheels crunching over the gravel, and saw Ramon and Gianni jumping in Elizabeth's car and hurrying after them. Andy and I were left sitting at the dining table, facing a sad-eyed staff and a vast overcooked feast. "Gee," said Andy, completely perplexed. "She has everything: magic, money, beauty, intelligence. Why can't she be happy?''

The following day, before we left for New York, I arranged to send two dozen long-stemmed red roses to Miss Taylor at the Grand Hotel. On the card I wrote: "Dear Elizabeth, I think you're the greatest. Please take care of yourself. Love, Andy.'' I was proud of how well I could adapt my handwriting to Andy's, how well I could forge his signature. On the plane, in first class, Andy held Archie up to his face and said, ''Wouldn't it be great if I could marry Liz? Then we'd really be on easy street, wouldn't we, Archie?'' Archie silently nibbled the caviar Andy was feeding him.

In October, Andy, Archie, Fred, and I flew back to Rome to shoot his ''big love scene with Liz.'' It wasn't really a love scene, just a weird exchange between Andy and Elizabeth in the mysteriously empty lobby of the Cavalieri Hilton. Andy did have a ''long speech,'' at least, long for Andy— ten whole sentences in a row—which made absolutely no sense. The opening line was ''The King is an idiot.'' ''I'll never be able to do this, Bob. This is a twenty-thousand-dollar speech. And I'm working for free. You've got to try and make it shorter.''

Andy's big scene: He took his place on a couch in the Hilton lobby. The assistant director shouted, ''Scene 242, Take One,'' just like in the movies. Miss Taylor came running in and noticed Andy sitting there. ''Remember me?'' she said. That was Andy's cue. He opened his mouth and stuttered, ''The King, the King, the King . . .'' Elizabeth sat down on the couch with Andy and took his hand, telling him how she lost a $20,000 Fabergé cigarette case on her way to the beach the other night. Andy fluffed his lines again, she sat down again, took his hand again, and told him how someone stole $55,000 worth of jewels from her in London. No go, Andy a blank. She took Andy's hand and told him how Richard Burton left a suitcase containing $3 million worth of jewels at the Geneva train station, but got it back.

Andy just couldn't do it. She ordered two Debauched Marys, ''to relax the memory.'' Andy's memory was more than relaxed, it was completely supine. Finally, she suggested that Andy write out his lines in his own hand on large cue cards, which he did, and the filming went on through master shots, cutaways, closeups of Miss Taylor, closeups of Andy. When it was all over, several hours later, Andy looked as drained as I'd ever seen him. ''I was so awful,'' he said, ''but Liz was great. She held my hand and told me all about her jewelry problems. She always refers to Before the Diamond and After the Diamond, B.D. and A.D. Isn't that great?''

Andy added, ''Oh, she said I could take Polaroids of her tomorrow.'' But the next day, Ramon called and told me that Elizabeth ''looks much too puffy.''

* * *

A few days after our return from Rome that October, Andy called me at home one morning to announce that he and I would be escorting Lee Radziwill and her sister Jacqueline Kennedy Onassis to the Brooklyn Museum that afternoon. I had never met the former First Lady, and was far from nonchalant. Andy wasn't nonchalant either; he was worried—about his "chauffeur," Bobby Dallesandro. Bobby, who copied his brother Joe's street-cowboy style but lacked his charisma, was supposed to drive Andy to and from work. He usually managed to make it to Andy's house by noon, but he often had an excuse for why he couldn't wait for Andy in the afternoon—a night class at Queens Community College, a sick aunt who had to be taken to the doctor, something wrong with the station wagon. Andy was always threatening to fire him, but Paul would intercede, and Andy would take a taxi uptown.

"I told him to clean up the station wagon," said Andy, "because he was going to have Jackie O in it, and he said, 'Who?' Can you believe it? So I had to spell it out for him: Mrs. Jac-que-line Kenn-e-dy O-nas-sis, the wife of Pres-i-dent John F. Kenn-e-dy. I think he finally got it. Oh, why can't I have a normal chauffeur like everybody else? I'm sure Bobby is going to be late, and I just know he's going to get lost."

Bobby was late, he did get lost, and his idea of cleaning up the station wagon was throwing the piles of fast-food packaging, empty beer cans, and old coffee containers, not to mention a used condom or two, from the floor in the front to the storage area in the back. He wasn't a bad guy, just a bad chauffeur.

After Bobby picked us up, we went to Lee's apartment, where she and Jackie were waiting in the lobby. It was raining and they were in identical tan trenchcoats, with almost identical kerchiefs around their heads. They hopped in the back seat—Andy and I were squeezed up front with Bobby—and we headed toward Brooklyn.

After the usual greetings, Mrs. Onassis's first words were: "So tell me, Andy, what was Liz Taylor like?" I couldn't believe it. Here was the only person in the world who was more famous than Elizabeth Taylor and she wanted to know what Elizabeth Taylor was like. Her first question was right out of an *Interview* interview. And what's more, it was asked in the voice of Marilyn Monroe! If Marilyn Monroe had gone to Foxcroft and Vassar, that is. The same girlishly sexy breathiness. It was a revelation, of sorts.

"Oh, gee," said Andy. "She was great. She held my hand and told me about B.D. and A.D. It was great." The back seat was silent. Then Andy pressed the playback button on his human tape recorder, and I reeled off a somewhat censored version of Andy's Elizabethan adventures, starting with an explanation of those initials—Before the Diamond, and After the Diamond. Every so often, I'd pause and let Andy pipe up with a punchline.

Meanwhile, Bobby Dallesandro had decided to take a "short cut" to the Brooklyn Museum, which involved a lot of zigzagging through the high-crime side streets of Bedford-Stuyvesant. Andy was getting more and more fidgety, especially since every corner seemed to have a stop sign, and a crowd that invariably recognized Jacqueline Kennedy Onassis sitting in the back seat of this beat-up old station wagon. We drove through a stretch of slum known as Little Haiti, with rundown stores with names like Port au Prince Deli and Pétionville Pawnshop. Jackie said she loved Haiti, and told us about the primitive painters whose fee was based on what you wanted in a painting: $50 for a house, $25 for each tree, another $25 for each cow, pig, or dog.

"That sounds a lot like the way I work," noted Andy, honestly. "I love it when people tell me what they want me to paint. Maybe I should do portraits of people with their dogs, and charge extra for the dog. Isn't that a good idea, Bob?"

Jackie and Lee laughed. They seemed to be having a good time, despite the winos peering through the windshield at every stop sign. When we finally got to the museum, I noticed something else about Jackie, and the way she dealt with her almost oppressive fame. She simply acted as if it didn't exist, as if those murmuring admirers were pointing at someone else. Like a thoroughbred in blinders, she kept her eyes fixed on the goal, always looking straight ahead at the Egyptian artifacts on display, never at the hub-bub her presence was causing. It wasn't a haughty or arrogant attitude, but it did keep people at a respectful distance. I could hear them whispering about her—"Is that her sister? Is that a Burberry raincoat? Who's the guy in the wig?"—but no one asked her for an autograph or came too close. They treated her more like a saint than a celebrity, and it had a lot to do with the way she carried herself.

I also noticed something about the relationship between Jackie and her younger sister. Lee seemed to know everything there was to know about the exhibition. "Oh, look, Jackie," she would say, "that bowl is just like the one we saw in the Cairo Museum." She could list the Pharaohs and the dates they ruled. She seemed to have the mind of a curator, and the taste of an aesthete. Jackie looked at her the way a pupil looks at a teacher, intently, taking it all in. Lee talked, Jackie listened. Lee led, Jackie followed. And there was no sign of their reputed competitiveness. On the contrary, they seemed to have complementary personalities.

By the end of the afternoon, I saw Jackie's first question about Liz Taylor in a different light. She wasn't being silly, or dumb, or starstruck. It was a deliberate disarming ploy, her way to let us know that she was like any other normal person, curious about the same things we were, anybody was. She wasn't lost in the stars at all.

Was Andy? That's much more complicated. I think he was in the six-ties, as his fame swelled his head with a feeling of omnipotence, and the shooting brought him down to earth again, with a frightening, eye-opening thud. And I think that he eventually lost his way once more in the last few years of his life.

But until then, his sense of reality was razor sharp. Yes, he'd gush over Elizabeth Taylor's diamonds and Paulette Goddard's rubies, but whenever he came across that De Beers ad in a magazine, he'd ask, "A diamond is forever *what,* Bob?" Yes, he collected diamonds himself, but he didn't show them off; he hid them at home. They weren't status symbols for him to show off, but investments to ward off his dire fear of poverty. His gushing over stars, and the minor celebrities he called stars, was as much an act as Jackie's question about Liz, designed to disarm and charm and relax. It was funny, it was normal, it made Andy accessible. But in private, his usual response to a star he had met was not "Gee" and "Wow" and "Great"—it was "Who does she think she is?" Eventually, he even said it about Jackie.

17

It's All Work

There they were on *New York* magazine's February 5, 1973 cover: Prince and Princess von Furstenberg, in black tie and silver lamé, smiling triumphantly at the camera under a red banner proclaiming them "The Couple That Has Everything." Egon and Diane were both twenty-six years old, rich, beautiful, sexy, and sought after. But, as *New York*'s zinger put it, "Is Everything Enough?" Nothing was ever enough in New York in the seventies, and the von Furstenbergs' openly open marriage—and separate Park Avenue apartment for their two young children—exemplified the hedonistic restlessness of both the city and the decade.

Diane and Egon had married in 1969 and moved to New York the following year. The *New York* writer Linda Francke called them "a contemporary version of someone's American dream: young immigrants, hardworking, raising a family, entertaining and being entertained, knowing everyone and being known." They were a new kind of immigrant: rich, fashionable, well connected, and they landed in the middle of rich, fashionable, well connected New York Society.

By 1973, they had been joined as New York residents by a giddy horde of glamorous immigrants from Europe and Latin America, including Egon's aunt Suni Agnelli Rattazzi, and her daughter Delfina; movie producer Dino de Laurentiis, his movie-star wife Silvana Mangano, and their teenage son Frederico. Countess Marina Cicogna, Florinda Bolkan, Franco Rossellini, and his niece Isabella Rossellini all moved into the Hotel Meurice. This group quite naturally melded with their friends who were already settled in New York—Giorgio di Sant'Angelo, Naty Abascal, Monique van Vooren,

Marina Schiano, Elsa Peretti. And there were the constant commuters from Rome and Rio and Bogotá—Valentino, Lucia Curia, Helmut Berger, Pilar Crespi, and her new husband, Gabriel Echavarria.

It was also the year of Watergate. At the Factory, we teased Pat "Rose Mary Woods" Hackett about "the missing eighteen minutes" on one of Andy's tapes for *Interview,* and she gave a hilarious impersonation, in her quilted vest, of Nixon's secretary explaining how her automatic foot pedal really did it.

Then Nixon's "enemies list" was leaked to the press, with Andy's name on it as McGovern's biggest financial supporter—they calculated his "donation" at $350,000, the 350 limited-edition posters he had done at $1,000 each, when his actual cost had only been a few thousand dollars. Andy immediately blamed Fred for letting himself be talked into doing a McGovern poster in the first place. "We're gonna get audited now, Fred," Andy started saying, and sure enough the IRS did audit his 1972 returns, and kept on auditing Andy for the rest of his life. On the advice of his lawyer and accountant, Andy stopped tape recording his lawyer and accountant. It also became a little harder for a while to get Andy's wife, Sony, invited along—1973 was not a good year for tape recorders.

(Strangely enough, when Nixon resigned in August 1974, Andy was suddenly sympathetic to his plight. "I don't think he's guilty," Andy said. "He was just performing for the tape." Even I said this didn't make much sense. "Yes, it does," Andy persisted. "Nixon needed good tapes so he could make a lot of money off his memoirs. Did you ever think of that, Bob?" No. "Well, why didn't he just burn the tapes? What was he saving them for? For Swifty Lazar, that's what." Maybe Andy's mind worked like Nixon's, or vice versa. It wasn't the first time *that* thought had run through my mind.)

The rich new immigrants didn't fret about such things. Like the poor old immigrants, they had come to America for freedom. Not freedom of religion, or freedom of speech, but freedom of class, and freedom of fun. Not the right of public assembly, but the right to wear their jewels in public. They wanted to drive around town in their Mercedeses without having a hammer and sickle scratched into the hood the minute the chauffeur wasn't looking, or, perhaps, *by* the chauffeur. They wanted to get rid of their chauffeurs and drive themselves. They wanted to see sides of life they could never see at home, and meet people they could never meet in Rome. They wanted to shake off the inertia and fear of closed-off Old European society and wallow in the carefree energy of the open-ended New York mix. And, most of all, they wanted to go out—every night, all night.

And guess what well-known New York artist was waiting for them with open arms, a loaded Polaroid, a magazine in need of a niche to call its own, and a staff of presentable young men who just happened to like to go out every night, all night, too?

* * *

After Wednesday, June 13, 1973, there was a place for us to go all night every night: Le Jardin opened with a special performance by Candy Darling at midnight, singing "Give Me a Man" to an audience that included lightweight boxing champion Chu Chu Malave with fashion illustrator Antonio Lopez, The Happy Hooker Xaviera Hollander with a fleet of happy hustlers, and actor Sal Mineo with a large all-male entourage plus actress Jill Haworth, whom he was supposedly marrying.

Like Studio 54, for which it was a sort of preview, Le Jardin was located near Times Square, an outpost for swells in the middle of Manhattan's raunchiest district, off Broadway on West 43rd Street next to Nathan's Famous Hot Dog emporium. Like Studio 54, it had an upstairs and a downstairs, occupying the basement and the penthouse of the Hotel Diplomat, then a crummy single-room-occupancy haven for junkies and winos. Like Studio 54, it was lavishly decorated, with silver lamé banquettes off the dance floor downstairs, and gold palm trees and black lacquer walls upstairs. Like Studio 54, it was famous for its handpicked waiters and bartenders, who wore basketball shorts and matching satin tops, which they usually took off. Like Studio 54, balloons were let loose from the ceiling to heighten the frenzy of the dancers, who were usually already frenzied enough from the amyl-nitrate "poppers" that were passed from nose to nose with casual abandon. And like Studio 54, everybody danced with everybody else, boys with boys, girls with girls, busboys with socialites, in groups and alone, it didn't matter, so long as you danced, which in those days meant jumping, jerking, twisting, twirling, shimmying, shaking, conga lines, chorus lines, anything but cheek to cheek. The songs that really hit the spot: "Feel the Need in Me" and "I'll Always Love My Momma."

One of the best nights at Le Jardin was the joint birthday party Scavullo and the Factory gave for Sean Byrnes and Vincent Fremont. Maxime de la Falaise McKendry and Nan Kempner drove the photographers wild by jitterbugging together. Fred Hughes twisted solo with his latest fashion accessory stuck in his mouth, a big fat Havana cigar. I also remember several nights when Vincent and I would want to leave and Fred would scream, "I'm your *boss* and I *order* you to stay!" We did.

When the rest of us went on to Le Jardin or the Tenth Floor (which we called the Popper Palace), Andy nearly always went home. And, bright and early the next morning, he'd called Fred or Vincent or me, to find out what he had missed. "Did Andy torture you this morning?" we'd ask each other, meaning his relentless grilling as we struggled to recall where we'd been a few hours earlier, who else was there, who wore what, who said what, who did what, and, most important to Andy, who went home with whom. Sometimes, just to get him off the phone and sneak in an extra hour of sleep, we'd snitch on each other—and then Andy would be very happy and hang right up and call that person and, with sworn testimony in hand, torture them.

I was sure it was Andy calling early in the morning on Saturday, April 14, 1973. I had been out until four or five, showing the town to Bianca's brother, Carlos Macias-Perez, an aspiring photographer who wanted to meet models, and I was in no mood to be harassed by Andy at 8 A.M. Still, I answered the phone, first because Andy didn't give up after a few rings, and second because you never knew when he might invite you to lunch with someone glamorous.

But it wasn't Andy. It was Vincent. Andy was in the hospital after an attack of kidney stones at Elsie Woodward's dinner the night before, and Fred was there talking to the doctors and would call me when he had more news. I stayed in all day, waiting for Fred's call, worried sick about Andy, thinking about how fragile he seemed, fretting that he had fallen ill on Friday the thirteenth.

At seven, Fred called and said that Andy had pulled through, it was gallstones not kidney stones, but they weren't going to operate, they didn't think Andy could take that, they'd try and treat him through diet and rest. Fred said that he thought Andy should "retire to Switzerland and paint." He pressed this idea for a while afterward, but as much as Andy liked Switzerland, he liked New York better. "Fred," he said, "think of the phone bills I'd have calling you kids on the other side of the ocean."

"We'd take turns staying with you," Fred said.

The day after Andy's attack, Diana Vreeland told me, "I have never seen anything like it in my life, and I've seen a *lot!* Andy arrived with Fred and literally crumpled to the floor in the most excruciating pain *imaginable!* Somehow, we got him into the bedroom and onto the bed, and we called for an ambulance, which in New York is like sending out for *Chinese food*— they take for*ever!* Andy was *writhing* in pain, but quiet as a lamb. And what really touched me was to see how gentle Fred was with him, holding his hand and telling him that everything was going to be all right. But he was scared, Fred was. Very scared indeed."

I was scared too. I couldn't imagine a world without Andy. By 1973, I was spending more time with Andy than with anyone else, and no one else was as interesting, stimulating, and challenging. Paul, Fred, and Jed had been in Rome so much that year, making *Frankenstein* and *Dracula,* that Andy fell back on me for company. "You're so easy to be with," Andy would say after a night out in New York, or after that horrific day in Rome with Elizabeth Taylor. "You're so good, Bob, so funny." Such compliments had all the more impact coming from someone who usually blamed you when things went wrong and said nothing when they went right. He even began to confide in me about his personal life. On the plane back from

Rome in August, he told me about a boy who wanted to go to bed with him. "He lives right around the corner," Andy said wistfully. "But what do you do? It's just another person to think about. Just another problem." Another time, he said, earnestly, "Why is it you can never get it up for the one you really love? I mean, if you didn't care you could, but if you do care, you can't."

Of course, I had been confiding my personal life to him, sometimes not so willingly, since almost the first day I met him. And to his tape recorder. Still, when he opened up to me, I was touched and flattered. I knew that it was harder for him, that he had more to lose. In short, my boss had become my best friend, in my mind at least. And in his? Maybe it was "just work."

Andy had a very peculiar attitude toward "work." He wanted to make money, and to keep it, but he also couldn't relax, hated vacations, dreaded having time on his hands to think about "problems," by which he almost always meant something to do with love. At the same time, he was a bit lazy, a bit of a procrastinator. He didn't get to the Factory until lunchtime, didn't start painting until four or five, and then wanted to have people around, to make work "fun." But the minute it really became fun, he turned it back into work, to keep control.

So working with Andy was fun, but having fun with Andy was work. And going out with Andy was "getting ideas," "getting portraits," "selling ads," "finding new people for *Interview,*" "bringing home the bacon," and never forgetting to ask for the receipt.

One night Andy and I went to Rex Reed's private screening of MGM's compilation *That's Entertainment.* Some of the original stars were at the screening, and afterward Andy was as excited as a kid. "Myrna Loy said hello to me. *Myrna Loy,* Bob." I didn't quite share Andy's fetish for Myrna Loy and when I responded with a blasé shrug, he suddenly turned on me, hissing that if *I* worked harder *we* could be turning out movies like MGM used to in the old days. "Don't you want to see your name in lights, Bob?" he taunted me. "I'll give you drugs, Bob, if that's what it takes to get you to work." Then, realizing what he had said, he softened his tone markedly, and added, "Maybe I should take drugs. Judy Garland took drugs. We have to work all the time, Bob. Success doesn't just come out of thin air, you know."

I asked him if his Pop Art success in the sixties was the result of a lot of work. He gave me a straight answer. "No," he said, "the success was just being in the right place at the right time. But it was a lot of work *after* it happened. A lot of paintings." And then he reminisced about the sixties in a way he never would when I asked him to for my Warhol films book. "I slept three hours a night," he said, laughing a little. "I dragged myself to the office around eleven. Painted. Made movies. Took the kids to dinner. When we had the nightclub [the Dom, on St. Marks Place], we had to go there until four in the morning. Did the lightshow. Then went to Chinatown for supper. Got home at seven. Crawled into bed. After the nightclub [went out of business], we sat all night in the maze at Max's. It was all work.''

After the Rex Reed screening we went to a dinner Brooks and Adriana Jackson were giving after an Iolas Gallery opening, looking for potential portrait clients. There weren't any. But Adriana was always trying, and she did line up several portraits for Andy over the years. It was always all work.

Before the screening Andy and I had been at the Carlyle to see São Schlumberger, who was visiting from Paris. Andy took Polaroids for her portrait, while I made her laugh, and unpacked the film and threw away the used batteries—this was usually Fred's job, but he was in Europe, lining up more portraits. It was all work.

When I finally got home, around one-thirty, I decided to make a list in my diary of all the portraits that I knew Andy had done in the previous two and a half years, 1972 through mid-1974:

Marella Agnelli; Luciano Anselmino (an art dealer from Torino); Brigitte Bardot; Leo Castelli; Maria Luisa de Romans; Eric de Rothschild; Sylvia de Waldner; Graziella (an Italian mystery woman); David Hockney; Brooke Hayward Hopper; Iolas; Katie Schlumberger Jones; Ivan Karp; Nan Kempner; Mrs. Maslan (of Minneapolis); Steve Mazoh (art dealer); Jason McCoy (Jackson Pollock's nephew); André Mourgue (Iolas's friend); Mrs. Max Palevsky; Lee Radziwill; Man Ray; John Richardson; Hélène Rochas; Yves Saint Laurent; Ileana Sonnabend; Valentino; Diane von Furstenberg; . . .

I left out Gianni Agnelli; Stavros Niarchos; Baron Heini von Thyssen; Henry Geldzahler; Frances and Sidney Lewis, the Richmond, Virginia, owners of the Best Food Stores chain; and Kimiko Powers, who had twenty-four portraits of herself in a kimono. At $25,000 for a single portrait plus $5,000 for each additional one—most clients took two, many four, and a few eight or ten—and not counting trades, the total income was well over a million dollars.

I'd had very little to do with it, except for the Maria Luisa de Romans deal, and even in that case it was Fred who "popped the question." Fred was always popping the question then, and more often than not getting yes for an answer. That was the basis of his power at the Factory: He brought home the most bacon by far. Andy was never satisfied, though. He was constantly prodding me to pop the question, too.

Andy pressed me to get Bianca's portrait, because she told him how grateful she was to me for showing her brother a good time in New York. "You see, Bob," Andy told me, "it's all work. Now the next time Bianca mentions her brother, Bob, you've got to jump in and pop the question." I'm sure that Fred had already popped the question, but Andy believed the more question poppers the merrier.

Dealing with Bianca wasn't easy in any case, because it also meant dealing with Mick. Whatever one wanted, the other didn't. After we put Bianca on the *Interview* cover in January 1973, we thought it would be great to do a Mick cover. But he wouldn't do it, because, Andy suspected, we did Bianca first. Instead, Mick told us that he'd only do it *with* Bianca, but when I told Bianca that, she said, "Watch out for Mick. He's very devious." He probably thought we wouldn't put the same person on a cover twice in one year, but if it were up to Andy, we'd put the same person on the cover every month—so long as they sold. And we all—Andy, Fred, Paul, Jed, Glenn, Richard Bernstein, Scavullo, I, unanimous for once—couldn't get enough of Bianca, which was probably what was making Mick so jealous.

Bianca called early in December 1973 and said that she wanted her portrait done as a Christmas present from Mick. "We want something wild and different," she mushed in her best Managua-goes-Mayfair accent. "I mean, maybe this is too silly, but maybe Andy could paint us together as king and queen."

"King and queen of where?" I asked.

"Bob! You are spending too much time with Andy."

The next day, Andy got back from a trip to Paris for the big French-American fashion gala that Marie-Hélène de Rothschild had organized, and I couldn't wait to tell him that Bianca wanted a portrait. "Tell her to fork over some money," he snapped. "She's nothing but trouble."

The big art-world event of 1973 was the Scull auction at Sotheby Parke Bernet, on October 18, at which one of Andy's early sixties paintings went for $135,000, breaking his record. Andy was happy, but not that happy: A Jasper Johns went for $250,000, breaking the record for any contemporary work sold at auction, a de Kooning for $180,000, and a Barnett Newman for $155,000. The total sale, for fifty lots, was over $2.2 million, an enormous sum then. As oil went up, and the dollar went down, money was fleeing into gold, diamonds, and art, and Andy was into all three, and getting more so every day.

The Scull auction was a turning point in art-world history: It was the first time the public at large, not just dealers and collectors, attended and followed an auction of contemporary art, with people fighting to get into Sotheby's the way they would fight to get into Studio 54 a few years later, with several TV crews recording the hoopla. It was the first time women artists protested an art event, because not one of the fifty works was done by a woman, and the last time artists, led by Robert Rauschenberg waving a placard reading "SCULL'S A PIG!," protested the commercialization of their work by collectors. In many ways, it was the beginning of the art boom that seems to know no end today, and of the hyping of auctions. It really was the triumph of Pop.

Andy didn't begrudge the Sculls the profits they made on the paintings they had bought for a few hundred or a few thousand dollars in the sixties, and he certainly didn't stand outside Sotheby's waving a placard denouncing collectors. He stayed home and waited by the phone for Fred to call with a report of how his paintings sold. And the very next day he dragged one of his early sixties works out from under a pile of rolled-up canvases at the Factory. It was his first Campbell's Soupcan painting, or so he said, not one of the photographically rendered series he did for his first show at Irving Blum's gallery in Los Angeles, but an earlier attempt, sketchier, less purely Pop. He showed it to me and said I should ask Adriana Jackson if Iolas might be interested, for $100,000. "It's a nothing painting," he said, "but it's the first." Adriana brought down a Milanese dealer who said he had "secret Lebanese clients"—everyone was suddenly trying to sell art to the Arabs—but he didn't really understand why such a small painting was worth that much. A few weeks later, Andy asked David Whitney down to take a look and also dragged out a Flower painting from 1964, blue and yellow on a light forest-green ground, with an unpainted white end. "The white makes it more abstract, doesn't it?" asked Andy, hopefully, because he was still convinced that abstract art brought higher prices. "No," said David, whose opinion Andy valued extremely highly, "just harder to take." "Oh," said Andy, rolling it up.

In January 1974, the Museum of Modern Art had a big Marcel Duchamp show, and we all went to the opening. Standing in the lobby, which had hundreds of black umbrellas hanging upside down from the ceiling, Halston said to Andy, "Duchamp started everything, didn't he?" Andy said, "Oh, I know." "And finished it, too," added Halston. "Oh, I know," said Andy again. Duchamp, perhaps the greatest of the Dadaists, had made his mark in 1917 by signing a urinal and declaring it "Ready made" art.

Andy never denied the major influence Duchamp had on his work and he owned one of the limited-edition urinals Duchamp did in the sixties. When he got bored in a restaurant, or wanted to charm potential clients, he did what he called "my Duchamp number"—and signed the spoons, forks, knives, plates, cups, ashtrays, and gave them away. Except Andy never used the word *signature*—it was always *autograph*. That was the difference between Dada and Pop.

Andy didn't go to many art openings in the seventies, or see many artists. Perhaps he was still nervous about his contemporaries. Perhaps he thought they would steal his ideas or turn their noses up at him. Most of those he did see were more friends of friends than friends of Andy's. Larry Rivers was a friend of Charles Rydell's, and then mine and Vincent's. David Hockney was usually brought to the Factory, when he visited New York, by Henry Geldzahler. Marisol was Halston's friend. Andy liked Roy Lichtenstein and his wife, Dorothy, and Arman and his wife, Corice, but he didn't see either couple very much, though he did both couples' portraits as trades. He did see a lot of the Iolas Gallery painter known as CPLY, whose primitive style was halfway between Surrealism and Pop, but he was keenly aware that the painter's real name was William Copley, that he was an heir to a San Diego newspaper fortune and a major collector of contemporary art; over the years he bought several Warhols. Andy was also friendly with other Iolas Gallery artists, such as Harold Stevenson, who had a small part in *Heat,* and Marina Karella, a provocative sculptor, who was married to H.R.H. Prince Michael of Greece, the ex-king's cousin. The Iolas Gallery artists in general were rather social: Stevenson moved from Paris to the Dakota in 1972 and gave fancy Sunday teas; Marina and Michael of Greece moved from Paris to Park Avenue a few years later and gave Saturday-night soirées, mixing the raffish and the royal; CPLY was a big party giver too.

Andy adored Iolas. As Adriana Jackson said, they were both ''monsters''—spoiled, selfish, overgrown children who lived according to their own whims with little thought of the feelings or wishes of those around them. A onetime ballet dancer, at seventy Alexander Iolas could have passed for a Warhol Superstar. He didn't quite go around in drag, but he came close in his flamboyant turquoise and emerald satin suits, with platform shoes covered in the same fabrics, and full-length fur coats thrown over his shoulders like capes. His conversation was equally Warholian: sex and gossip, gossip and sex. He liked to create rivalries among his associates and saw the embarrassment of those he considered inferior as a form of entertainment. Underneath the flashy, playful exterior, however, was the acquisitive and discerning vision of a great collector, and the quick mind of a Levantine money changer. Iolas was actually born in Alexandria, Egypt, and his true passions were antiquities, Picassos, gold, diamonds, and cash of any denomination. We dubbed him Alexander the Greek, and years later he commissioned a series of prints from Andy of Alexander the Great.

Andy generally preferred the company of dealers to artists, and not only because they could sell his work. Dealers tend to collect as well, and Andy was much more interested in talking about what to buy, where to buy it, and for how much, than about art history or theory. That's why, for example, he had more to say to Ivan Karp, who collected Americana with such excessiveness that he eventually purchased an entire upstate New York village, than to Leo Castelli, who tended to talk about art as ideas. That's also why he liked Bruno Bischofberger and his wife, Yoyo, so much, because they collected Art Deco jewelry, and later fifties furniture, with the same passion that Andy did. And he also had an immediate, and lasting, rapport with Bruno's young associate, Thomas Ammann, who was flying back and forth from Zürich to New York quite frequently in 1973 and 1974. Andy and Thomas would go shopping together for old watches. We all liked Thomas a lot, and more than any other nonemployee he became part of the

Factory family, one of Andy's kids. "It's great to have a kid who picks up the check for a change," Andy sometimes said.

There was one artist who genuinely fascinated Andy, in the same way that movie stars and models did: Dali. It wasn't that Andy liked Dali, or his work, that much. He was taken with Dali's scene, which was not unlike his own in the sixties, and with Dali's wife, Gala, who had no equivalent in Andy's world, or any other. Gala was a Tartar from Central Asia, and the great heartbreaker of the Surrealist set in Paris in the twenties, dropping Paul Éluard for Max Ernst, and Ernst for Dali. Though she was eighty-two years old when I first met her, she still came across as a beauty: slim, erect, smooth-skinned, with the same jet-black hair in the same French roll that she had in Dali's thirties and forties portraits. Andy was determined to do her portrait too; he never pursued anyone harder and longer than he did Gala.

Andy and Dali had been introduced by Ultra Violet in the sixties, and though neither of them saw much of Ultra anymore, they went on seeing each other through the seventies. Dali spent every fall and winter in New York, at the St. Regis Hotel; he moved on to the Hotel Meurice in Paris in the spring, and spent the summer at his house beside the Mediterranean at Cadaques, Spain. More than any other artist, Dali lived the life of an international *grand seigneur.* Though Andy was catching up fast.

Andy first took me to tea with Dali in April 1973. Dali's teas were regular Sunday-afternoon events and had nothing to do with Darjeeling and crumpets, everything to do with champagne and strumpets. They were always held in the King Cole Bar of the St. Regis, beneath the 1906 murals by one of Andy's favorite painters, Maxfield Parrish, and were followed by dinner at Dali's favorite restaurant, Trader Vic's in the Plaza Hotel. That afternoon, as usual, his guests included ten or twelve starving young beauties of both sexes, and Pandora, the star of the Cockettes' movie, *Luminous Procuress,* who looked like Edith Sitwell in drag. "I never know," Andy often said, "whether I copied transvestites from Dali, or Dali copied transvestites from me."

Dali himself, in a gold brocade dinner jacket, was attended by an elegant middle-aged Spanish lady, whom he introduced as "King Louis the Fourteenth," and our young disco-dancing friend Juan de Jesús, whom he introduced as "the Crown Prince." Neither was wearing a crown. Dali carried a gold-topped scepter, waving it in the air whenever he wanted to make a point, which was often. He rose to greet Andy and waved for us to sit at his table. I was just back from Colombia *(Heat* showed at the Cartagena Film Festival) with about fifty five-cent prints of the Virgin Mary, each a half-inch square and encased in cheap blue, pink, green, or yellow plastic. I thought they'd be the perfect present for Andy, plastic, multiple, and Catholic, but he suggested giving them to Dali instead. Dali loved them.

And then Gala made her entrance, in a black Saint Laurent tuxedo, accompanied by a stringy-haired blonde youth in hippie sack shirt and pants, whom Dali, with a flourish of his scepter, announced as "Jesus Christ Superstar!" This time the connection wasn't just in Dali's imagination; the boy had starred in a European production of the musical, and was now rumored to be Gala's lover. Dali kissed Gala on each cheek and she sat down with us. Then he showed her my gift, which she immedately threw into the ashtray, saying, "How dare you bring Dali *plastique!*" The next thing to go into the ashtray was Andy's tape recorder. "No tape Gala, no photo Gala!" she shouted at Andy, who started trembling. Still, he managed to slip out, "Oh, gee, you look so beautiful. Can't I do your portrait?"

"Gala only pose for Dali," she shouted.

"But, uh, mine would be different from Dali's."

"Mucho more expensive, you mean."

"No, no, we can trade."

"Gala no trade great painting of Dali for *photo* by you. Gala hate photos!" Both Gala and Dali were in the grand habit of referring to themselves in the third person. Andy gave up, with a weak and futile "Oh, really." He really looked hurt, like a child told that Santa was not coming this year.

Perhaps Dali noticed; he offered Andy "a magnif-ico i-dea." "Oh, what is it?" asked Andy, his hopes slightly lifted. Dali said that Andy should paint a triptych of Clara Petacci, Eva Braun, and Eva Perón, with "La Petacci" in the middle, hanging upside down, "naked and *muerta* like they find her with Muss-o-lini." "Oh, really," said Andy again, this time meaning, "Is he for real?" Dali pounded his scepter and declared, "*Sí, sí, sí!!!* Dali even give you the *título:* 'The Three Great Whores of the XX Century' "—that's how he pronounced it, "ex-ex."

"Oh, are you doing any new art?" asked Andy.

Dali said that he was putting "effigies of Mao Tse-tung and Marilyn Monroe," in vegetable emulsion, "on lee-tle white beans, and you swallow, and at thees *momento* is possible commun-i-on with Mao and Marilyn together in your sto*mach.* Only—you take no whiskey."

Andy said, "Oh really" for the third time, and picked his tape recorder out of the ashtray, which was the signal to leave. Outside the hotel, he said to me, "I never know what Dali is talking about. Do you think he was making fun of me? He was, wasn't he? But I don't care, he's just being entertaining, right? Oh, I wish I could get Gala's portrait. If I could only sneak one photo . . ."

The next day Dali called the Factory himself and asked for "Bob Valpolicella." Jane Forth, who was playing receptionist after *L'Amour* flopped, told him, "You mean Bob Kookyfellow," and passed the phone to me. "Dali invite Warhol and Valpolicella to the lunch *para el* brain *de* Alice Cooper *en* La Goulue, *mañana* at one o'clock sharp!" and hung up. He was having a show of holograms at the Knoedler Gallery, one of which was titled

"Alice Cooper's Brain." Andy wouldn't go, saying, "Gala never goes to
lunch. She's too tired from staying up all night with her young boyfriend.
Do you think she gets all her energy from all the yogurt they eat where she
comes from? Maybe I should eat more yogurt, Bob."

I went to the lunch. Andy was right. Gala wasn't there, nor was Jesus
Christ Superstar. But King Louis the Fourteenth and Crown Prince Juan de
Jesús were, and Dali gave me a title too, Count Valpolicella. At either end
of the L-shaped table for twenty were Candy Darling and Poutassa de la
Fayette, whom Dali anointed the Queens of the North and the South. Alice
Cooper arrived mid-meal—which consisted of lamb chops, and only lamb
chops. This was Dali's way of thumbing his royalist nose at that year's liberal
cause, a meat boycott organized for much the same reason as the grape
boycott and the lettuce boycott. He even made a point of blessing the platters
of red meat with his gold scepter. Seated at an adjacent table were a couple
of real royals, Prince Rainier and Princess Grace of Monaco, aghast. After
lunch, Dali and his drag court filed across Madison Avenue to Knoedler's
for a press conference covered by the American, French, Spanish, and Japanese networks, and the unveiling of Alice Cooper's brain, which, like most
holograms, was only visible at certain angles.

The following fall, like clockwork, Dali returned to the St. Regis, and
Andy returned to tea, still pining for Gala's portrait. Once again Dali, in
brocade, and Gala, in black, were accompanied by Louis XIV and Jesus
Christ. And Crown Prince Juan and the starving young beauties, and Pandora, who was rumored not to be a drag queen after all, and Holly Woodlawn, in a reverse-drag tux of her own. Halston floated in with his coat over
his shoulder, Iolas-style. "Gee, Bob," said Andy, "why can't we get a setup
like this." It seemed to me we had. Dali's British business manager, whom
he introduced as *El Capitán del Dinero* (the Captain of Money), told Andy
he could be making seven million a year by doing plates, coins, prints, and
books like Dali. Gala wasn't as forthcoming. "I'm not interested in your
doing my portrait," she said, "because you're not a technical enough
painter."

A few days later, Andy arrived at the Factory in a huff. He had been
shopping his way downtown, as usual, and had popped into F.A.O. Schwarz
and bought himself a teddy bear, strolling down Fifth Avenue with it, un-
wrapped, under his arm. "I know I was putting on airs," he said, "by
carrying the teddy bear, but I just felt like it. And then I ran into Gala by
the St. Regis and as soon as she saw it she wanted it. She kept saying, 'It's
for Gala, no,' and pulling at it. And I was pulling it back, but she grabbed
it and wouldn't give it back. I mean, what was I supposed to do? Hit her?
Oh, I hate her. Why won't she let me do her portrait?"

And the fall after that, when Dali and Gala returned, I lunched with
them at La Grenouille, hoping to land her portrait for Andy. Dali was on
his royalist kick. He asked me if I knew any talented young artists, and

when I said no, he said he didn't either because it's "impossible" to have artists in a democracy. He said that when the monarchy is restored in Spain, art will thrive again around the court of the king. That seems to have happened, but his next prediction remains surreal: He insisted that the kings of Greece and Albania would be back on their thrones sooner than anyone thought. Mao, he said, was a "modern monarchist," because he knew that the cult of personality was necessary to lead large numbers. Ceaucescu of Rumania, he added, was also a modern monarchist, because "he bring back the scepter to Rumania," and he pointed to his own golden scepter. I agreed with every word he said, and then popped the question. "No," he replied, "the strength of Gala it is in her privacy. Gala *never* is pho-to-graphed!" To soften the blow, he told me his favorite artist in the world was Dali, "and next Andy Warhol."

As Andy's painting studio on the eighth floor became too crowded, he started painting on the floor in front of the small Art Deco desk where I was working in the screening room, which was also filled with time capsules, thirties furniture, rolled-up Maos, stacks of Electric Chair portfolios, etc. In the remaining patch of floor space Andy would unroll a canvas and paint, talking to me while he did. It was a sign of trust. A couple of years earlier, when I had happened to walk in on him working on the eighth floor, he had stopped what he was doing, and had responded to my questions about his technique with the utmost vagueness. So I carefully recorded the first time I saw him painting in front of my desk:

Monday, December 31, 1973: After three years finally get to see AW really paint. The outline of the face is traced from blowup of photo negative onto tissue and then tissue is placed over carbon, which is over raw canvas, and retraced by pressing carbon outline onto canvas. Then A slaps paint (acrylic) on with a large brush, more like housepaint brush than artist's brush, rarely cleaning brush, as he switches from area to area and color to color. He also uses hands, especially fingers, to create texture, gesture, blend colors. He doesn't clean hands much either, so colors merge, appear here and there, disappear rather arbitrarily. After it dries the photo negative is silkscreened (by Alex Heinrici at his own studio) onto the painted canvas.

A: Want to fingerpaint, Bob?
B: If I do one more thing for you, Andy, I'll go crazy.

18

Factory Disputes

The more time I spent with Andy, the more I answered him back, because I realized that he liked it, or at least respected me for it, the way he did Paul and Fred. That was one of Andy's strengths: He wasn't surrounded by yes-men. And sometimes I had to answer back, out of self-defense. I was very wary of being enlisted as an art assistant then, because Andy had started telling me that my hands were my best feature, that my handwriting was "so artistic," that I held a pen "the way a painter does." One day he even told me, "You could probably be an artist, Bob." He didn't mean I should quit working for him and go off and paint for myself, he meant I should help him paint. But, as I told him that day he started painting in front of my desk, if I did one more thing for him, I'd go crazy.

As *Interview*'s special contributing editor, I was doing one or two in- terviews of my own every month, setting them up, researching them, transcribing them, editing them, and proofreading them. I accompanied Andy on most of his interviews and asked many of his questions—Pat Hackett did the transcribing, editing, and proofreading. I was also setting up interviews by friends and celebrities, from Candy Darling to Delfina Rattazzi, and often transcribing, editing, and proofreading them. I was writing most of the "Smalltalk" gossip column, which dovetailed with my second Factory position, assistant social director. That entailed arranging Andy's social life when Fred was in Europe, and sometimes when he wasn't, inviting press and celebrities to screenings and lunches at the Factory, helping to organize parties, and whenever possible negotiating to get them for free. It meant going to lunches, cocktails, dinners, parties, screenings, and openings with

Andy, covering them for *Interview,* getting ideas and hustling portraits all along the way. We were also on the verge of signing a contract with Harcourt Brace Jovanovich for *The Philosophy of Andy Warhol,* of which I was to be the ghostwriter. And I was still helping Vincent out on the endless *Nothing Serious* video pilot.

So no, thank you, I didn't want to fingerpaint.

My pay: still $125 a week, $6,500 a year, and when I complained about not having enough money to live on, Andy would say, "If you sold some portraits, you'd make commissions, Bob."

"But I can't take Andrea de Portago out to dinner and convince her to convince her mother to get her portrait done, and then make her pick up the check, Andy."

"Well, if you stayed home more often and wrote some scripts, your name would be in lights and you'd be on easy street, Bob."

"I hate my apartment."

"Your apartment is great. It's on the best street in New York."

"I know, but it's only big enough for one person, or two people who are very close."

"You know two people who are very close?"

I'd laugh and give up, or in this case write the line down for the philosophy book.

At Christmas that year, Andy gave me a $250 bonus, in cash, three fifties on top, and one hundred singles to make it look like more. No art. Vincent handed me a check for an extra week's pay. I gave Andy a Bergdorf Goodman tie, with BG embroidered all over it, which he loved and wore every day for the next six months, and also a blowup poster of four Instamatics I had taken of him and Elizabeth Taylor, which he loved and put in a time capsule.

Meanwhile, the Glenn problem was driving everyone crazy, except Andy, who saw office intrigue as entertainment, real-life soap opera. Glenn was now feuding with our star cover photographer, Francesco Scavullo, and with Giorgio di Sant'Angelo, who had hired and fired Jude. She and Glenn were fighting too. Andy thought I should weave the O'Briens' marital saga into a script called *Modern Marriage.* And when it got further complicated by the role of fledgling disco star Grace Jones, he said, "If you had written down everything that happened to Glenn and Jude like I told you to when you kids first started here, you'd have a great novel now, Bob." He meant *he'd* have a great novel.

Andy didn't want Glenn fired, not only because he basically liked Glenn but also for the same reason he never wanted anyone fired—he was sure they'd react violently and come and get him. So Fred came up with the usual Factory solution: Glenn wasn't fired, but someone else was hired to do his job: Rosemary Kent, star reporter.

Fred told Glenn that Rosemary wasn't going to replace him but work with him, although she was given the title of editor-in-chief. Rosemary saw Glenn as "production manager." This charade lasted for one issue, August 1973, and then Glenn quit. Glenn was soon hired by Jann Wenner to run *Rolling Stone*'s new New York office. Unfortunately, Glenn made Jude—who had come back to *Interview* after Giorgio dismissed her—quit too, and years later he said she never forgave him. In any case, they divorced not long after.

Rosemary Kent, like Fred Hughes, was originally from Houston, Texas, but they may as well have been from different solar systems. Fred was pure de Menilville; Rosemary was plain Cowtown, and proud of it. Fred was slim and elegant; Rosemary, in her own words, was "fat and happy" and thought it would be great fun to do a special fat-and-happy issue of *Interview,* by which she did not mean lots of ads: "Why not use the power of the press to bring back that Rubenesque look?" Fred never talked about his private life, not even when Andy taunted him about it; Rosemary, encouraged by Andy, took great delight in graphically describing her entire erotic history in vivid detail. Worst of all, Rosemary's favorite word was the word Fred hated most—*professional*—and whenever Fred disagreed with her about some aspect of the magazine, she'd scold him with, "Well, ah just don't think youall are being very professional." Then she'd sob, "Ah just can't take working in this amateur-type atmosphere."

Andy had loved going out with Rosemary when she was at *WWD:* She was bright, she was funny, she talked dirty for his tape recorder, and she put his picture in the paper he most wanted to be in then. But once Peter Brant hired her, at an enormous salary, and caved in to her demand to be called editor-in-chief, a title no one before or after got at *Interview,* Andy started referring to her as "the Big Cheese." As in, "You've got to do something about the Big Cheese, Bob. She wants to put Dyan Cannon on the cover. And Elliott Gould. And when I said we should be putting beauties on the cover, she told me I was being unprofessional. Do you believe it? She told *me* that."

I believed it. She told me it was unprofessional to write about Candy Darling, Sylvia Miles, and Monique van Vooren, so I stopped writing "Smalltalk" altogether. She insisted that Fran Lebowitz do tape-recorded interviews and Fran quit. She attacked Marina Schiano at a cocktail party at the de la Rentas for "only" giving her YSL earrings that Christmas, instead of a silk blouse like she had the year before, "when I was still at *WWD.*" Somehow, in the midst of transforming *Interview* into a "professional publication," she found the time to write what she called "a real juicy story" about Mick and Bianca for *Viva,* and Bianca called me and said Mick had walked out when he read it, blaming it all on her. Rosemary's second-favorite word was "juicy."

She interviewed Peter Beard and asked him lots of "juicy" questions about Lee Radziwill, and Lee called me and said Peter was so depressed about it could I possibly try and tone things down? Then she sent Barbara Allen, the pretty young wife of *Interview*'s co-publisher, out to Montauk to do photos of Peter for the story, and when they clicked, she encouraged Barbara to leave Joe for Peter. "Barbara married Joe for all those YSL dresses," Rosemary told me, "and now she regrets it. She and Peter are perfect for each other." But what about Lee? "Who cares about Lee?" Andy was beside himself. He saw everything going down the drain: *Interview*'s backing, the rent from Montauk, afternoons with Lee and Jackie.

But Rosemary's biggest fiasco, and my biggest headache, was *her* fight with Scavullo. Nobody had clamored more for the hiring of Rosemary Kent than Scavullo and his stylist Sean Byrnes. But the minute she had the job, all hell broke loose. It was over her wedding (to Henry Meltzer, an equally fat-and-happy architect), set for the fall of 1973, at Scavullo's house in Southampton.

Scavullo told Rosemary she could invite 75 guests; she had already invited 225-and-counting. He wanted a sedate seated luncheon on a Sunday afternoon; she wanted a wild buffet hoedown that went on all night. They both came to me to complain. Rosemary sobbed that Scavullo was being "cruel"; Scavullo screamed that Rosemary was being "monstrous."

"I've already invited half the state of Texas to this wedding and now I have nowhere to have it," she wailed.

"I'm not going to have my beautiful house in the country destroyed by her ticky-tacky friends," he shouted.

"He'll never do another cover for *Interview* again!" she decreed.

"I'll never do another cover for *Interview* again!" he agreed.

Fred backed Rosemary, because he'd never liked Scavullo; Andy backed Scavullo, because he was working for free; and I somehow negotiated a ceasefire. As for the wedding, Rosemary and Henry rented out an abandoned bank in Tribeca, which was then still known as the Lower West Side, but they didn't bother to have it vacuumed or dusted. Andy brought Paulette Goddard to please Rosemary, but she wouldn't sit down in her white suit, and made Andy take her back uptown after five minutes. Rosemary was "really hurt." I stayed on for the square dancing, not to mention the performing chimpanzee on roller skates, which Giorgio di Sant'Angelo (who had designed her "cowgirl" wedding gown) dubbed "Rosemary's Baby."

In early December, Peter Brant and Joe Allen called a meeting. "Everyone acting very Wall Street," I wrote in my diary:

> . . . sitting around the oval table, sipping sherry (Fred's chic touch), discussing circulation, advertising, and cost figures. Joe Allen says we're losing $2500 per week. AW: Gee, the paper is getting bigger, we used to lose only a few hundred. Rosemary sticks her foot in it by asking for more money for good writers. *Professional* writers. Fred objects to that word for the thousandth time. Expounds his theory of frivolity (as an anti-depressant) and dilettantism. I back

him up with perhaps too strong an attack on Rosemary's choice of writers. I
even bring up the *WWD*-copycat complex.

The next day, Andy told me that my remarks were "really intelligent."
Fred said that I was "a little harsh," especially the *WWD* cut. "Bob's right,"
said Andy, defending me. And I was: Leo Lerman, the features editor at
Vogue, had told me that everyone at Condé Nast was calling Rosemary
Kent's *Interview "WWD Jr."*

John Fairchild had apparently also taken note: He banned Andy from
being mentioned in *WWD* then (and evermore). Andy was upset, saying that
he knew we should never have hired Rosemary. Fred said it was Andy who
wanted to hire her in the first place, and Andy said it was Fred. Finally they
agreed to blame it on Peter Brant. Fred rationalized that being dropped by
WWD was a blessing in disguise, because too much social coverage was bad
for Andy's image as an artist. Andy didn't seem convinced. Wasn't all coverage good coverage? And didn't *WWD* reach just the right audience for a
society portraitist?

Things got worse. Rosemary slammed the bulletproof door in my face
when I told her not to run a hideous photo of Sharon Hammond, a beautiful
young Park Avenue hostess at whose parties we were meeting good portrait
prospects. She had a knack for choosing the one bad shot on a contact sheet,
and blowing it up real big. A few weeks later she hung up on Fred when he
asked her to be more civil to Vincent. The next day, after Joe Allen had
reported that monthly losses were now up to $12,000 and ordered a cutback
of editorial pages, Rosemary threw out a Scavullo fashion spread and an
interview by Andy.

Rosemary was just too "professional" and "juicy," too fat and happy,
for us. Beyond matters of style and personality, she just didn't understand
the complicated interlocking relationships between Andy's various businesses. *Interview* was meant to further Andy's other interests, not derail
them. And Rosemary had become increasingly frustrated. She was the editor-
in-chief, the Big Cheese, but everywhere she turned there were bosses: Andy
and Fred, Peter and Joe, Vincent in matters of money, Pat Hackett when it
came to Andy's interviews. Peter and Joe had also hired an associate publisher named Carole Rogers, who had been circulation manager of the *Village Voice,* and who quarreled so badly with Rosemary that their husbands
almost came to blows one day and Vincent had to run upstairs to separate
them. Scavullo was the bossiest of all, because he worked for free, and,
even though I was still only special contributing editor, Andy and Fred
expected me to "supervise Rosemary." Vincent once said that Andy let
everyone make up his or her job and find their own niche. The problem
was, everyone made up the same job and found the same niche: boss.

The only boss who wasn't around as 1973 turned into 1974 was Paul Morrissey. When the *Interview* masthead was reshuffled in the August 1973 issue—Rosemary's first—Andy and Fred were no longer editors but president and executive vice president. Paul, who had also been an editor, was dropped. By whom I don't know, because I was in Rome then, as was Paul.

When he got back in late 1973, he didn't come to the Factory regularly anymore, and often had a young lawyer named Richard Turley call in for his messages. Perhaps he didn't feel welcome. Pat Hackett was furious with him because he didn't give her the credit she felt she deserved on *Dracula* and *Frankenstein*. Jed was balking at the idea of making any more movies with him and more than ever wanted to direct a movie of his own. Vincent, who had been almost completely under Paul's wing before he went to Rome, had become much closer to Andy. And to Fred—Vincent even started having suits made at Fred's New York tailor, Everall Brothers, and smoking a cigar. Vincent was a boss now, too, with his own video projects. The truth is, with Paul away, we had all become bossier.

In January 1974, Paul flew out to Hollywood to try to sell a western called *West,* not unlike *Lonesome Cowboys,* with Mick and Bianca in the Joe and Viva roles. Bianca was game, but was Mick? He seemed more interested in another Paul Morrissey idea, *Caligula,* which also interested Franco Rossellini and Gore Vidal. They eventually ended up doing it without Mick or Paul, financed by Bob Guccione, the publisher of *Penthouse*—and suing each other forevermore.

Paul kept calling from the coast, prodding me to come up with movie ideas *quick.* He said he had a meeting with Ray Stark, who thought *Dracula* was "Third Avenue camp." "Hollywood wants clean movies," Paul said Ray said. I came up with an instant idea for Mick and Bianca and football-star-turned-movie-actor Jim Brown: a simple love triangle, in which Bianca has to choose between black and white, macho and androgyne, the cleancut world of sports and the decadent world of rock. No. How about a World War II movie, I said, with all the men in the army and all the women working in an arms factory at home, and the men are all weak (Max deLys, Helmut Berger, Hiram Keller, Taylor Mead), and the women are all strong (Maxime de la Falaise McKendry, Sylvia Miles, Florinda Bokan, Brigid Berlin). No.

"What about Sherlock Holmes?" Andy said—Princess Mdvani owned the rights to Conan Doyle's works and wanted Andy to produce a modern version. Paul said he had already told Ray Stark, who wasn't interested.

Andy was still pressing for me to write *New York* (based on Fellini's *Roma), Modern Marriage* (based on the O'Briens), and his latest idea, *Times Square* (based on Le Jardin). Once he came in with a pile of *National Enquirers,* and said that Pat and I should write a script based on the headlines. Pat tried harder than I did.

"Why doesn't Paul come in?" Andy wondered one day, going uptown in a taxi from the Factory. I said I didn't know. "Well, why is Richard Turley calling for his messages?" I didn't know that either. Round and round we went, in circles of ambiguity, and most ambiguous of all was the relationship between Andy and Paul. "I think it's only a matter of months before Paul Morrissey leaves Andy, or vice versa," my diary records on November 30, 1973. "I think it's a good thing." They drifted away from each other over the next year, though it was hard to say who was leaving whom. There wasn't a fight, or a divorce, just a permanent trial separation. But I was wrong about its being a good thing, at least for Andy. The only movie made after Paul's departure was *Andy Warhol's Bad,* in 1976, directed by Jed, with a screenplay by Pat—based on those *Enquirer* headlines. And while it wasn't that bad, it wasn't that good.

Back then, I had high hopes of working with Jed and Pat. We spent a lot of time together coming up with ideas and going out in search of inspiration. One night in November 1973, when Andy and Fred were in Paris, Jed and I went to dinner at the Jacksons', and then decided to check out Max's Kansas City, which neither of us had been to since Le Jardin opened. He suggested going up to Andy's house first, to get Andy's Mercedes. In the four years that I had known Andy, I had yet to see inside his house, so I was very curious.

Andy's house, 1342 Lexington Avenue: There's a big Cy Twombly blackboard painting in the foyer. The first floor is divided in two rooms, both rather clubby feeling, crowded with American primitive artifacts, old iron cows, roosters, sheep, old portraits, old quilts over old couches, and a couple of wooden Indians near the stairway. Jed made me promise not to tell a soul I had been there.

Andy had a new idea for a Broadway play, a musical based on Lou Reed's new album *Berlin.* One night in January 1974, Andy and I went to dinner with Lou Reed at Reno Sweeney's, a new cabaret-style restaurant in the Village, to talk things over. Lou's opener was, "I want *you,* Andy, *your* ideas—not Paul's or Brigid's." He glared at me across the table—he didn't want my ideas either. It was a very difficult dinner, with Lou hesitant to tell too much about *his* ideas, afraid Andy would steal them, wary, like Robert Mapplethorpe and Fran Lebowitz. He did explain the psychology of the lead character a bit: He only shows emotion when he's out of speed, Lou said, and when his drug dealer makes it with his girlfriend but not him. When the girlfriend commits suicide, he can only describe and feels nothing. Was this the Lou Reed story then?

He's so skinny, small, hair cut very short, little silver shirt, jeans, pea coat, nothing starlike at all. He took us to the Ninth Circle "to see the kids I'm talking about." There was one kid who caught Lou's eye—very young (17?), dark hair around his face, eye shadow. Everyone else looked like extras in a movie about decadence in . . . Berlin. Ugly, bearded, painted, bruised, bandaged, strange. A couple was dancing and we couldn't figure out if it was two girls, two boys, a boy and a girl. We couldn't figure out if another was in blackface or really black. Everyone seemed depressed, and when they laughed, it was mocking. Only the kid seemed enthusiastic (for his own decline?). People kept coming to our table and saying hello to Andy, rather respectfully, which was funny considering how degenerate they all looked. I think Andy was enjoying himself, getting ideas, not paranoid at all. Lou just sat there numb.

And yet we never had another meeting with Lou Reed, who said he was off to Amsterdam for a "tryst."

Now I can understand Lou Reed's reluctance to have his brain picked clean by Andy, but then I agreed with Andy when he told the kids at the Factory, "Gee, Lou was acting so strange last night, right, Bob? He was really mean to Bob, right Bob? And he really hates Paul and Brigid, right, Bob?" And I didn't see that by taking Andy's side I was only making it more difficult to protest when Andy wanted to pick my brain clean.

One of the ways he did that was through what he called the "Fantasy Diary." When he first proposed it, I wriggled out of it, but after *Vogue* decided to publish my "Liz and Andy" Rome diary, he became increasingly insistent. "I'll tell you everything I do," he said, "and then you just make it up from there. Just make it up. Just turn the pages out. And put in lots of sex and philosophy." "Who does he think he is now," I asked *my* diary, "the Marquis de Sade?"

I had been keeping a diary since almost the first day I met Andy. Sometimes I'd write it late at night, sometimes when I got up. A typical morning entry began, "I am extremely hung-over and don't remember much of yesterday," and then went on for three detailed pages typed single space. Andy knew and would occasionally ask offhandedly, "Are you still writing your diary? Oh really." Then, after the IRS started auditing him in 1972, he started dictating an Expenses Diary to Pat Hackett, at first when he came in every day, and later over the phone—that's what eventually grew into *The Andy Warhol Diaries,* published posthumously.

So starting in September 1973, once a day, I tapped out the Fantasy Diary—wildly exaggerated versions of Andy's days and nights. He told me he went to lunch with Philip Johnson and David Whitney one Sunday: I wrote about the three of them riding in a white Cadillac convertible, cruising down Fifth Avenue, David driving, while Andy and Philip threw Godiva chocolate-covered cherries, Andy's latest craze, at their cheering fans. He told me he had stopped in at Jolie Gabor's costume-jewelry shop on Madison

Avenue: I made up an orgy at Madame Gabor's, including most of Park Avenue society, all squishing around on a floor covered in Godiva chocolate-covered cherries. In the Fantasy Diary, a French-American fashion gala in Versailles ended up with Marie-Hélène de Rothschild slapping Hélène Rochas in the Hall of Mirrors, while Halston's models did high kicks on the runway, and the titles in the audience threw—yes, Godiva chocolate-covered cherries.

At the time, I was reading Nigel Nicholson's book *Portrait of a Marriage,* in which he, his parents, Harold Nicholson and Vita Sackville-West, her mother, Lady Sackville, and his brother, Ben Nicholson, all sit down to meal after meal and then all go to their rooms and describe meal after meal in their diaries. It struck me that this was what the Factory was turning into—with Andy and Pat doing the Expenses Diary, Fred trying to keep one going too, and me doing the Fantasy Diary, which I would give to Pat, who kept it in a box in her office, then going home and writing my own diary. I was beginning to despair, however, that my diary was losing its energy, not to mention its individuality. Andy, my diary records, "read Fantasy Diary and liked it a lot. Now he wants to take me shopping for underwear and write fifty pages on it."

Then along came a literary agent named Mrs. Carlton Cole. Roz Cole was Patrick O'Higgins's agent and he introduced us to her at a holiday brunch given by Sharon Hammond's mother, Ellen Lehman McCluskey Long. Roz told Andy that he should write his autobiography. He told her that I was writing his biography, referring to my Warhol films book, which Curtis Brown had sent to five or six publishing houses since Dutton dropped it, with no luck. Roz was very quick on her feet: "Well, why don't you write your *philosophy*. I mean, if anyone has a philosophy, it's got to be you." Andy loved that idea—hadn't he been telling me to put "lots of philosophy" into the Fantasy Diary? Of course, his idea of philosophy was going shopping for underwear, and musing on love and sex along the way—and why not? "Philosophy is anything, Bob. Just make it up."

So I stopped writing the Fantasy Diary—I was running out of things to do with chocolate-covered cherries anyway—and started writing the proposal for *THE Philosophy of Andy Warhol,* which we delivered to Roz Cole at the beginning of February 1974. We were very insistent on that capitalized *THE*—we saw it as the real title and the perfect follow-up to Andy's 1968 novel, *a.*

Andy said I would own part of the book. I was pleased with the prospect of making some real money; Roz was talking about a $50,000 hardcover advance, and $150,000 for the paperback. But I was also a bit blue about my films book going nowhere and suddenly writing a book for Andy instead of about Andy. I didn't want to be just a ghostwriter, so Ellen Levine, my agent at Curtis Brown, and I were talking about new ideas for a book of my own. And Andy, in his way, was trying to help. A phone call from him on December 11, 1973, shows how:

AW: Oh, Bob, this is [a rich young European I had slept with once]. I really miss your cock.

BC: Hi, Andy.

AW: Oh, Bob, I'm soooo hot for your cock.

BC: Hi, Andy.

AW: Oh, we have a book for you to do, Bob. Princess Marconi.

BC: Who?

AW: Don't you know who she is, she was the sister of . . . the one who married . . . and her brother married . . . [he meant Princess Mdvani, whose brother, Prince Mdvani, was one of Barbara Hutton's husbands].

BC: American?

AW: No, Georgian, from Russia.

BC: She really wants a book?

AW: Yeah, she wanted Patrick O'Higgins to do it but Paul talked her into using you. I'm going to tape her—*Reminisces*—and you can do her biography.

BC: But, Andy, my books are going to be just like your books.

AW: Noooo. I'm doing Paulette [Goddard]. You're not doing Paulette, are you?

BC: No, my agent was up though and she's going to try and get Candy.

AW: You're doing Candy?

BC: If my agent finds out that Bantam really wants it.

AW: Why don't you shove it up your agent—then she'll really work for you.

BC: What about Mrs. Vreeland's biography? Fred said he was getting me that.

AW: Really? Oh, see, I want to tape her *Reminisces* too.

BC: You mean for one book called *Reminisces?*

AW: No, different books: *Paulette Reminisces, Mrs. Vreeland Reminisces, Princess Marconi Reminisces.* . . . We're all going to make a fortune on books this year.

BC: I wish I could think up something new to do.

AW: Have you thought about work? That's new, Bob, work. I mean, you could have a play by now.

BC: I know, it just seems that these things take so long. I want things to be fast.

AW: Well, you can dance fast, you can come fast, you can whip off pages fast. . . .

BC: But that's just the Fantasy Diary, because I know no one will see it except Pat Hackett.

AW: But you should write everything like that, fast and cheap. Just do it and then you'll have something.

19

Candy Dies

"I have to make a comeback, Bob!" It was Candy Darling calling, in August 1973, and she sounded desperate. So far, it hadn't been a good year for "the blonde of blondes." Even though she'd had a critical and box-office success with Tennessee Williams's *Small Craft Warnings* the year before, she couldn't find work, or at least the kind of work she wanted. The one job she had done since the Williams play was *The Death of Maria Malibran,* a German TV movie directed by Rosa von Praunheim, a rising avant-garde filmmaker. But Candy didn't want to be avant-garde; she wanted to be Kim Novak.

She was offered the "Harlow" part in the movie version of *The Beard,* by director Donald Cammell, but it required her to perform fellatio on "Billy the Kid," and she turned it down. "It's hard enough to give a blowjob in real life," she said, "let alone on the screen."

She was hoping to get the Joan Crawford role in the Broadway revival of Clare Boothe Luce's *The Women,* but it went to Lainie Kazan, then to her understudy. Andy's response was that I should write a play for Candy, Sylvia, Maxime, and Monique called *The Bitches.* Even Candy's hopes to be a party-scene extra in *The Great Gatsby* remake came to nothing.

That spring, Sam Green had given a dinner for John Schlesinger, who was casting *Day of the Locust,* hoping he'd like Candy. But Schlesinger was more taken by a photograph on Sam's wall of a newer blonde, Cyrinda Foxe, who was making waves among the Max's Kansas City set by dropping David Bowie for David Johansen of the New York Dolls (who later became Buster Poindexter). The next day, hiding her disappointment, Candy called Cyrinda herself to tell her the good news. "But I can't see John Schlesinger," Cyrinda fretted, "not with these pimples!" Candy couldn't resist. "Listen, darling," she cooed, "that's why he wants you instead of me."

Sam Green, I believe, had also got Candy the job singing at Le Jardin, when it opened that June. It paid $1,500 a week, though half of that went back to the club to pay for the band and other expenses. But it was a regular income, and Candy moved out of Sam's and into a questionable but modern hotel on Seventh Avenue. Unfortunately, Candy wasn't much of a singer, and the jet setters at Le Jardin wanted to dance, not sit still and listen. Candy was out of work within a week, and now she had no place to live. Sam couldn't really be blamed for not taking her back in; the last time he had, she came for a week and stayed for a year.

But poor Candy—on top of everything else, she wasn't feeling well. She thought it was an ulcer, and took to drinking milk instead of vodka stingers. And she drifted. Sometimes she stayed with her mother; sometimes she stayed with her hairdresser, Eugene of Cinandre. She was still as beautiful, maybe more so, thinner and paler. She took to dyeing her hair a little less platinum, a little more "pink champagne," as she called it, and dressing even more conservatively, always in black or brown.

One night, to cheer her up, I took Candy to dinner at the Italian embassy. She wore a plain brown Valentino cocktail dress, and Adriana Jackson, who loved this sort of caper, lent her some proper pearls. The old Italian baron she was seated next to thought he had finally found a real old-fashioned fifties sex symbol in the age of Women's Liberation, and whisked her back to his suite at the Hotel Pierre. They drank champagne and danced the cha-cha, but Candy begged off going any further for fear he'd have a heart attack when he discovered that she was a he. The next morning, he sent her six dozen long-stemmed red roses with a note begging her to return with him to Rome. Candy called Adriana in a panic: "What do I do now? The poor man thinks I'm a regular Anita Ekberg. He kept whispering in my hair as we danced about finally meeting a woman who loves being a woman."

On another night, perhaps the swan song of Max's Kansas City, which was being killed by disco, Glenn introduced Candy Darling to Divine, the three-hundred-pound transvestite star of *Pink Flamingoes*. "Smalltalk" dubbed it "A Summit Meeting" because, to everyone's surprise, the two blonde bombshells formed an instant mutual-admiration society. Glenn recalled that Divine said to Candy, "I'm such a big fan of yours," and Candy said to Divine, "I'm such a big fan of *yours.*" Then Candy imitated Divine's best lines, and Divine imitated Candy's best lines. They talked about everything from Watergate to leg waxing—"and where to get size-11 high heels," Fran Lebowitz remembers.

When Scavullo invited me out to Southampton for Memorial Day weekend, I asked him to invite Candy too. Geraldine Smith was also asked, and on the way out, she started talking about Andrea Feldman's suicide the previous summer. Geraldine said Andrea had left a note for Andy and it said, "You ruined my life and everyone else's." She went on and on with the gory details: Andrea landed on her feet. Her body was crushed from the waist down. They amputated the bottom half of her body for the funeral and had a half-closed casket.

Candy wouldn't say a word against Andy, though she too had her reasons to be upset with him and the Factory, for passing her up when the parts were doled out for *Frankenstein* and *Dracula*. I remember telling her that Carlo Ponti said they had to use as many Italians as possible and Candy retorting, "Maxime de la Falaise is Italian? Monique van Vooren is Italian?" I mollified Candy by saying that I was still trying to get Andy to do my Evita idea, starring her.

On the way back to the city, we had another conversation in the car, about beauty and how to keep it. "Men stay better than women," Candy said. "I don't know why that is." Was she having doubts about spending every cent she made on hormone injections and electrolysis? Candy continued wistfully, "It was easy to be beautiful in the sixties. A ton of make-up was chic. Now you have to be a real beauty in a real way, or you're out."

"You have to look like Tatum O'Neal," said Scavullo, trying to lighten things up. But Candy took his quip seriously. "Like Tatum, right, like Tatum," she said, sounding further and further away.

In September, Candy was taken for tests to Columbus–Mother Cabrini Hospital, the same small Catholic hospital where Andy had been taken when he was shot. "Why don't you write my bio now," she asked me, "before it's too late?" She had somehow managed to get a private room, and the nuns had taken to her immediately. When I told her that the guard at the reception desk had referred to her as "Mr. Slattery," she called him up and turned on her charm to convince him that only "Candy Darling" was to be used. "No one knows that other name except me and you. It's our little secret," she purred. Then, hanging up and turning to me, "You gotta know how to deal with these types." She had interviewed model Lauren Hutton for us the week before, and had the tape ready for me, neatly labeled in lavender ink. "Now, don't let that Rosemary Kent change everything around. I'm trying to get Hedy Lamarr to do an interview too, and I don't want her messing things up."

The tests went on for three weeks. Candy did her best to be cheerful when I went to visit, chatting about other interviews she wanted to do, and asking after Andy. We both knew that he would never visit her in the hospital, especially *that* hospital, but he always sent presents with me, anything she asked for: a shower cap, a special brand of toothpaste, Tic-Tac mints.

On Tuesday, October 2, 1973, I called Candy from the Factory and asked her if she wanted anything. She eked out the sentences in short gasps, "Yes. More juice. The sweet kind. I crave sweets." I went to the hospital, bearing more gifts from Andy: expensive note paper, expensive chocolates.

She was spitting up phlegm when I arrived. I noticed today how white she was. Ghostly. Candy called for a nurse and as soon as she arrived I left. Candy said, "Tell Andy to call me. And no more presents. I don't need presents." It was the first time she didn't put up a good front.

The next morning, I called Andy, and told him how badly Candy was doing and that she wanted him to call her. "Oh, I can't, Bob. I just can't. What's wrong with Candy, anyway? I mean, do you think she really has cancer or something?" I said that her doctor wouldn't tell me anything. "I know about doctors, let me tell you," said Andy. And then he found an excuse to get off the phone. I realized Andy wasn't going to be of any real help. It wasn't that he didn't care. He just couldn't cope.

I called Maxime, who with the Jacksons had been paying for bills not covered by Medicare. Maxime had also enlisted Nan Kempner. It was touching to see these grand society ladies going out of their way to help an impoverished drag queen. Maxime suggested calling Dr. William Cahan, the cancer specialist at Memorial–Sloan Kettering Hospital, and the husband of *Vogue* editor Grace Mirabella.

I called from the Factory, as Andy hovered over me. Dr. Cahan said that he would look into Candy's case, to see if anything could be done that wasn't already being done at Columbus–Mother Cabrini. He said he would need Candy's clinical history, X-rays, and biopsy sample, and that I should have her mother authorize the transfer. Andy hovered over me through the call to Candy's mother too. Teresa Slattery appreciated what we were trying to do, but she didn't think there was much hope. Candy didn't know it, but the doctors had told her that Candy had leukemia and a malignant tumor in her stomach. I hung up the phone and told Andy. For the first and only time in the seventeen years I knew him, I saw him cry.

That night, Andy and I went to dinner at Brooks and Adriana's. The star guest was Gina Lollobrigida, in a gold brocade suit and matching shoes, and what looked like a big bouffant wig, chestnut-colored. "She looks like the wife of the French consul going to dinner at the English consulate," said Maxime. Andy hated her, star or no star, and when she heard we were going to Rome the next week, and suggested we take the same TWA flight, Andy shot her down: "TWA goes on to Israel. You might get hijacked. Did you ever think of that?"

Gina held up the Polaroid I had taken of her with Andy. "Look at me," she said, "with Death."

"If only Candy were here," Maxime said, "to put this one in her place."

"Oh, I know," said Andy. "What's that great line, Bob, that Candy always says to the other girls, you know, when they're going to the bathroom?"

"Mention my name and you'll get a good seat."

Dr. Cahan called me a few days later. Along with other specialists at Memorial–Sloan Kettering, he had reviewed Candy's case, and there was nothing they could do for her that wasn't already being done at Columbus–Mother Cabrini—radiation and chemotherapy. I called Candy and told her the best doctor in New York said she was having the best treatment. Within days, Candy was worse. She couldn't talk on the phone and didn't want visitors, because the treatments had made all her hair fall out. Sam Green said that she had two or three weeks left. But then Candy went into remission. She was released from the hospital in the middle of November, just in time for her birthday on the 24th. She was twenty-seven years old, one year older than me.

There was a birthday party at her friend Jeremiah Newton's apartment in the Village. Candy arrived an hour and a half late, wearing a chic black-sequined dress and a matching beret to cover her hairless head. We told her how great she looked. "I know," she joked, "I finally have that swanlike neck I always wanted. I'll tell you one thing, there's more hair under this beret than under Andy's wig." She sat on the only sofa in the room and we sat on the floor at her feet and she opened her presents—negligees and dressing gowns, plastic jewelry, perfume, movie-star biographies, and a TV from Andy. Candy was ecstatic; she didn't have one at her mother's. "I feel very lucky to have so many friends. And I know if I die, it will hurt not only me but a lot of other people. That's why I'm going to live—for all of you."

Candy went to parties every night that week, as if it were her last. I saw her at Le Jardin, shaky but gorgeous in one of Maxime's outfits. Maxime was holding Candy up with one arm and her husband, who had a broken leg, with the other. Nan Kempner and I went to help, and the five of us formed an impromptu chorus line, kicking our legs for the camera. *WWD* ran the photo the next day, and Andy was happy—maybe the ban was being lifted. And Candy, exhausted, carried the clipping back to her bed in Massapequa Park.

One night, when I got home, there was a letter in my mailbox addressed in lavender ink.

Jan. 30, 1974

Dearest,

Forgive me for not calling you regarding the book, but I have been very ill again—one week of severe headaches and now along with everything else I have Bell's Palsy. My right hand and right side of my face have become paralyzed. I can not close my right eye. My mouth goes to one side and when I eat the food goes all over my lips. I am very weak most of the time. I can not call you as I am afraid the phone co. will turn it off. I can not pay the bill as everything has to go to medical expenses. No Medicaid. Tom Eyen asked me to be in his play *2008 1/2* and even advertised me in *Village Voice* and I heard a lot of people asked for money back for they did not see me. I would do it if he gave me money but I'm afraid of how I would appear in front of public. Don't know what I'd do without the T.V. the Factory gave me. It's a blessing. All I do is watch it. Of all the pain killers I have, the best thing is Anacin— imagine. Nothing else to say but please write or call. (Don't forget the shut-ins!)

Love to all,

Candy

X X X

I called Candy the next day from the Factory and found out how much the phone bill was; Andy agreed to pay it. I remember him coming to the phone and saying, "Oh, hi, Candy, I hope you feel better," and then scurrying back into Pat's office.

Soon Candy was back at Columbus–Mother Cabrini.

Tuesday, March 5, 1974: Visited Candy at the hospital with Adriana. Candy looked like Joan of Arc in Bresson's film. Incredibly thin. Hair grown in short and dark. A slight mustache like a shadow. Perfect facial bones and skull. One eye cloudy. One arm bandaged in plastic—paralyzed. Her voice deep, speech slow, everything from the throat, between coughs—"Aren't you going to kiss me?" Her mother, Teresa Slattery, a small Irish woman with red-brown hair, in a purple knit pantsuit, white blouse, black boots, glasses with slightly pointed frames. She was feeding Candy bouillon she had made, putting it into a syringe, and then emptying the syringe in Candy's mouth.

A few days later, Candy died. A feeling of complete emptiness engulfed me, as if the floor had fallen out. Then the phone began to ring. It was the *New York Times* calling about the obituary. Margot Rivera saying that Geraldo was going to do a big spot on Candy on the evening news. Giorgio di Sant'Angelo saying that if Candy's family wanted he would contribute the beaded black dress that Candy always loved for her to be laid out in. Maxime telling me about her visit with Candy the day before she died. A doctor had told her, "When you get better, I'll take you out to dinner." "Yeah," said Candy, "we'll go to Nedick's." The strangest call was from Jackie Curtis, Candy's mentor, onetime friend, and lately bitter rival. Jackie was inviting me to the revival of *Glory, Glamour and Gold*. "Did you hear about Candy?" I asked. "Yeah, she died." What did it all mean?

That's what Andy wanted to know when he called: What did it all mean? Put it in the book, Bob, he said, this is philosophy. Then, rushing through the sentence like a child admitting guilt if it means he'll get his milk and cookies, he said, "I guess I should have called Candy more." He also told me to find out if the family needed any help with the funeral. And to send flowers. "You wouldn't want to go, would you, Andy?" "Oh, Bob, I just can't face it." He wasn't whining. He was pleading.

Candy was laid out in the same room where Judy Garland had been. The big arrangement of white chrysanthemums, orchids, and lilacs I had chosen was to the right of the open casket, with a note I had written: "To Candy, love forever, Andy." Vincent had given me an Andy Warhol Films check for $500 for Mrs. Slattery, who was wearing a black satin suit, a string of pearls, and a black pillbox hat, and sweetly greeting Candy's fans and friends with "Hello, I'm Candy's mother."

Candy's father was also there, a small but solid Irish worker, with rough hands and a long-ago-broken nose. He said he called his son James, and that's the way he wanted him buried. Candy's mother frowned. It was a strange wake, with Candy's family, an older brother, an aunt and uncle, some cousins, in navy suits and black dresses on one side of the room and Candy's friends from the Theatre of the Ridiculous and La Mama and Max's Kansas City in feathers and sequins and boas on the other. I briefly looked at Candy in the casket, embalmed, looking like the transvestite she never looked like in life.

After the eulogies by Julie Newmar, Eugene of Cinandre, and R. Couri Hay, as the mourners gathered on the sidewalk outside Campbell's Funeral Home, a huge black Rolls-Royce turned the corner from Madison Avenue into East 81st Street and paused beside the hearse at the very moment Candy's casket, closed at last, was being slid into it. The Rolls was driven by a smartly uniformed chauffeur, and sitting in the back seat, all alone, was an elegant old woman in white—white fur, white veil, white gloves. Gloria Swanson.

20

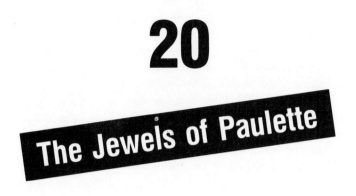

The Jewels of Paulette

Nostalgia—which I've always thought started when Paul handed me those Rita Hayworth stills—was all over New York in 1973 and 1974. Everything old seemed new and everything new seemed old, and the way to the future seemed to be through the past. Andy and entourage were at the Josephine Baker and Maria Callas comeback—the former a hit, the latter a flop—as well as at the comeback of Sal Mineo, in a Broadway play called *The Children's Mass.* We were convinced it was based on the Holly Woodlawn story, especially since the lead character kept saying everything was "absolutely flawless," which is what Holly said about everything. Holly was in the audience, too, and Andy was very nervous about seeing her for the first time since the fights over money during the making of *Women in Revolt,* but she behaved absolutely flawlessly and was thrilled to have a play based on her life, even if it dwelt on drugs, booze, hustlers, and murder. "It makes me a legend," Holly reasoned, "like Marilyn Monroe."

Even Holly went nostalgic in 1973, launching a cabaret act at Reno Sweeney, itself a takeoff on a thirties-style nightclub. Now that Andy and Holly had made up, we went to see her night after night, taking our uptown friends and European art dealers to hear Holly belt out her big number, "Cooking Breakfast for the One I Love," waving a frying pan in one hand and a spatula in the other. The opening act at Reno Sweeney was a new old group called Manhattan Transfer, two guys and two girls like a barbershop quartet spliced with the Andrews Sisters. The real Andrews Sisters came back too, in early 1974. So did Ricky Nelson, at the Bottom Line. Andy and company went to those openings too.

One night in April 1973, Andy passed up dinner with Joan Crawford for dinner with Marshall McLuhan, and was furious with himself for making the wrong choice. The man who said that the medium was the message, and that television would eliminate books, wouldn't talk with Andy's tape recorder on. "I thought he knew about machines," Andy said. "Oh, Bob, it was soooo boring. And to think I missed Joan Crawford for that."

But by the fall of 1973 Andy had his very own Old Hollywood star to take to all those nostalgic openings: Paulette Goddard, who had starred with Joan Crawford in the 1939 movie version of *The Women.*

Andy had first met Paulette in spring 1973 at the opening of the Metropolitan Museum's Gold Show, featuring everything from a seventeenth-century 24-karat Saint Sebastian to the gold-lined helmet the astronauts wore to the moon. It was the perfect place to meet a woman famous for her passion for gold and diamonds, rubies, emeralds, and sapphires—a passion she shared with Andy.

Andy had been working on a feature for *Vogue,* using Polaroid's latest camera, on the most beautiful women in America, and John McKendry, the Met's curator of photography and prints, had suggested that he photograph Paulette at the Gold Show opening. Andy was delighted, Paulette was delighted; the only problem was getting them together that night. When Paulette was upstairs, Andy was downstairs, and when Andy was upstairs, Paulette was downstairs—and each refused to ascend or descend for the other. So I was ascending and descending the Met's very long, very marble staircase, trying to get them both in the same place at the same time. After three or four round trips, just as I decided to give up, there they were, together, talking and laughing.

Paulette was a walking Gold Show in herself: wearing a body-hugging gold lamé gown with an Egyptian tombful of gold around her neck, studded with big rubies. And she still wore her red hair the way she did in her first great hit, Charlie Chaplin's *Modern Times.* She told us Charlie had given her the trademark hairdo by dunking her head in a tub of water and leaving it the way it came out: in a straight, close pageboy, with bangs over her forehead that gave her a perpetually young and sportive air.

Her attitude, now, however, was more haughty than sporty. When Andy took out his Polaroid camera, she refused to pose, saying she had never agreed to, even though John McKendry had assured us that she had. And when she was at last persuaded to change her mind, she insisted on posing full face, even though Andy asked her to pose in profile. They disagreed, and they kept on disagreeing for the rest of the decade. And I spent the rest of the decade in between them, trying to get them together—which they somehow always did on their own, just when I least expected, just when I was about to give up.

"Who does Paulette Goddard think she is?" Andy said later that night. And a minute later, as he peered closely at her rubies in his Polaroid: "Gee, she really is the greatest, isn't she?'' Paulette had told Andy, ''You don't break rules, you just don't have rules.'' And Andy had asked me, ''Was that a compliment, Bob?''

Despite their prickly first meeting at the Gold Show that spring, and the disastrous party in Rome that summer, Paulette couldn't wait to get together with us, she said, when she returned to New York in September. Paulette spent half the year in Europe, based at her Swiss lakefront villa near Locarno, which had been left to her by her third husband, Erich Maria Remarque, the novelist who wrote the world bestseller *All Quiet on the Western Front.* Between Charlie Chaplin and Remarque, Paulette had been married to the actor Burgess Meredith for two years in the forties. *''Burgess,''* she always said, pronouncing his name with disdain, ''was the biggest mistake of my life. It cost me all my beautiful Picassos and Braques. Oh, how I cried. But I got more. Yes, I did.''

A few days after she got back to her aerie in the glamorous Ritz Tower on Park Avenue at East 57th Street, Andy, Fred, and I took her to dinner at La Caravelle. We were seated at the first table, just inside the door, thanks to Paulette, we thought. A few tables down sat John Fairchild, with Condé Nast chief Alexander Liberman and his wife, Tatiana, Oscar and Françoise de la Renta, and Marina Schiano. They kept waving at us, and Andy was sure that was because of Paulette too. ''Maybe John Fairchild will take the ban off now,'' Andy said, explaining to Paulette about the Rosemary Kent mess. ''You don't need that kind of publicity, Andy,'' she said. ''You're the most important artist in the world. Why, in Switzerland, everybody knows that. Even my Italian maid.''

''Oh, really,'' said Andy.

''I told Andy the same thing,'' said Fred, ''but he never listens to anything I say.''

''I do too, Fred. That's all I do. Listen to whatever you say. Oh, that's Fred's wife down there, Marina Schiano. They're married but they don't live together.''

''That's the best kind of marriage to have,'' said Paulette. ''I call it a maître d' marriage. Not too much romance, just someone to take care of all the boring stuff, like dealing with the servants, the menus, the reservations. That's what Erich used to do for me. He wrote all morning and in the afternoon he took care of all that.''

''Well, Marina certainly doesn't do that for me,'' said Fred.

''But you do it for her, and isn't that nice,'' said Paulette.

''No,'' said Andy, ''Fred and Bob do it for me.''

Paulette was wearing a typical Goddard getup: a svelte white dress—for the glow—and the most remarkable diamond necklace any of us had ever seen. Hanging from a chain of two-karat diamonds were at least a dozen larger diamonds in ascending size from five karats to twenty karats, and each one was a different shape: round, oval, oblong, square, pear, marquise.

Andy was transfixed. "I never saw a necklace like that," he said. "Why are they all different shapes and sizes?"

"They're all my old engagement rings," Paulette explained matter-of-factly. "I always sent back the setting, and kept the rock."

"You did! Oh, how greaaaaat. Isn't that greaaaaaat, Fred? Isn't that greaaaaat, Bob?" Three long greats meant he meant it.

Andy was enchanted, but also very wary. "Do you think she's looking for a new maître d', Bob? I should never have told her that I collect diamonds, too. Now she'll expect me to send her an engagement ring, so she can send it back without the rock. Oh, I bet she just wants a book out of us, right? She did say the book with Anita Loos wasn't working out. *The Perils of Paulette* is a terrible title, isn't it, Bob?"

"Well, I can think of a better one."

"What?" asked Andy.

"*From Chaplin to Warhol,* by Paulette Goddard Remarque." It was my turn to torture him a bit.

"Oh, Bob," he wailed. "She does want to marry me! You have to let her know that I'm married already." Then he quickly added, "To Archie."

Andy wasn't being entirely paranoid, or self-aggrandizing. Remarque had only died in 1970, and other than her aging mother, who lived on Second Avenue, Paulette didn't have any family, any children, and, it seemed, had few friends, other than Anita Loos. And they *were* having problems with their book, or at least Paulette said so. "Anita's trying to portray me as one of the girls," she had said at dinner.

"What girls?" asked Andy, edging his tape recorder closer.

"Oh, you know, Garbo, Dolores del Rio, Mercedes da Costa . . . that whole group."

"You mean," Andy spluttered, "uh, lesbians?"

"Now, Andy," Paulette scolded, "I'm surprised to hear a man of your sophistication, an artist, use a word like that. Only psychiatrists use those boring clinical words—homosexual, bisexual, oedipal. In Hollywood, we said someone was single-gaited, or double-gaited, and they were, believe me, they were."

Andy saw more and more of Paulette that fall, but always with me along. One of the things that terrified him about her was the way, as he put it, "she walks around in broad daylight with all her jewelry on. What if she's *mugged,* Bob? Does she think I'm going to defend her?" But, of course, Paulette's jewelry was a big part of her attraction for Andy. They could go on for hours about it. She claimed that different stones had different physical effects on the body: "Rubies warm the blood, sapphires cool it" was one maxim of hers. He was fascinated by the three rings she always wore on one finger, her "everyday diamonds," she called them: a rare blue diamond, a rarer yellow diamond, and the rarest pink diamond, each the size of an almond. "Gee," Andy told her, "Liz Taylor's diamonds aren't as good as yours."

"That's why she started That International Rumor about me," snapped Paulette. She said it with capitals, as if it were the title of a movie: *That International Rumor.*

"What International Rumor?" asked Andy eagerly.

"Never mind," said Paulette. "If you haven't heard it, I'm not going to tell you."

Andy was sure that Anita Loos must be trying to put the International Rumor into *The Perils of Paulette,* and that's why Paulette was growing increasingly disenchanted with the project. He was equally sure that it had something to do with Dolores, Mercedes, and Greta.

In November, *Dracula* was ready to be screened for the press—it came out before *Frankenstein,* because the 3-D took longer to edit. Andy brought Maxime, because she was the star, Fred brought her daughter Loulou, and I brought Paulette. She loved it. Over dinner at Pearl's later, she said that Joe Dallesandro was "a born star," but suggested that he take ballet lessons to learn to move more gracefully for the camera. "It magnifies everything, you know," she said. "I ran away from home when I was fourteen, to study ballet. I worked to pay for the lessons. And it was a great help with Charlie's movies, which were all movement—movement and mime. Joe should study mime, too." We promised to pass the advice along.

Paulette also said that stardom had just come to her. "I was obliged to be a star, because I was married to Charlie Chaplin." At another dinner, at Elaine's, I repeated that line to Alexis Smith, then starring in *The Women* on Broadway. "I'm sure Paulette did a little something to become a star," said Alexis. "Moved ever so slightly. Just a fraction of an inch." As I told Andy on the phone later, "Our lives really are becoming like some Clare Booth Luce play!"

"Oh, I know," he said, cracking his bubble gum into the receiver, like a contented kid. "It's really great the way you got us together with Paulette, Bob. She's the best, Bob."

Around New Year's the *Daily News* predicted that Andy Warhol and Paulette Goddard would marry in 1974, and Andy wasn't thanking me at all. "I can't marry Paulette," he whined, as if the newspaper item were a directive from on high. "She'll outlive me. She will, Bob."

Sometimes Andy was less worried about her wanting to marry him than he was about her wanting to marry me. Was that part of her technique? For Christmas she had given me an expensive black cashmere scarf, leaving it with the doorman at the Ritz Tower for me to pick up. "She didn't leave one for me?" Andy asked when I told him about it. "She brought caviar to the Factory Christmas party for you," I said. "That wasn't for me, it was for the office." "So then why did you take it home?" "I gave it to Archie."

A few days after New Year's, Paulette called me at home and said that I was her "favorite beau" and that she wanted to give me Erich Maria Remarque's nutria-lined raincoat, but it was in storage in Zürich. We spent the following weekend going to museums together, including a Pop Art show at the Guggenheim. Andy was beside himself when I gave my report. "You're *my* maître d', Bob," he said. "Andy, I was teaching her about your kind of art." "Oh, really, did you sell her a portrait? What are you waiting for, Bob?" "She already has her portrait by Diego Rivera." "She does? Well, maybe we should take her to lunch next Sunday. Why don't you call her right now and ask her? Tell her it's on me."

We had lunch at the Regency Hotel, Paulette, Andy, Jed, and I. Andy brought Paulette a *two*-ounce bottle of Joy, the most expensive perfume in the world then, with a note that said, "Have a really smelly New Year." Paulette started talking about Chaplin: "Charlie always told me, 'Don't play it, *be* it.' You know, Max Eastman and Upton Sinclair ruined Charlie, by intellectualizing what he did, and then he couldn't do it anymore. That's what's so great about you, Andy. You don't intellectualize what you do, you just do it. I mean it. Bob took me up to the Guggenheim last week to see your pictures and I got that immediately. I really did."

"Oh, gee, really," Andy was spluttering. I could tell he was getting ready to make a move. "Well, the intellectuals never liked my work. I guess it's not abstract enough for them." He was stalling. "Oh, gee, you know, Bob told me that you're still having problems with Anita Loos on your book."

"Oh, I am, Andy, I am. Anita has my life all mixed up with hers and it wasn't that way at all."

"Uh, well, we were thinking that since we just tape record and you can say anything you want in the tape recorder, maybe we could do your book with you. Couldn't we, Bob?"

I said we could, as we were pretty sure this is what Paulette wanted anyway.

"Oh, Andy," Paulette sighed, as if he'd just given her a big engagement ring for her necklace. "Would you? I think that's a great idea. I'm going to call up Bill Jovanovich first thing tomorrow morning and see if he'll agree to it. He knows I'm fed up with Anita."

The next day, Paulette called me and said that Bill Jovanovich, of Harcourt Brace Jovanovich, and an old friend of hers, was all for our book, and as soon as she "let Anita down *gently,*" and we worked out the contracts, we could start.

"Why do we have to wait for the contracts to start?" Andy asked. "We already have enough tapes for a few chapters, right?" I said that Paulette had made it quite clear that she didn't consider anything she had said so far on the record. "Oh, let's just keep seeing her, and she'll never know which tapes we did before the contract and which ones we did after, right?" Right.

The day after that, the *Enquirer* called the Factory, saying they had heard that Andy was seeing a lot of Paulette Goddard. I asked Andy what I should tell them and he said, "Tell them I left Liz Taylor for Paulette." I told the *Enquirer* that. "Well, what's the exact nature of their relationship?" the reporter wanted to know. "Breakfast, lunch, and dinner," I replied. Then I called Paulette, thinking I better prepare her for the *Enquirer* headlines. "When I get off the phone I'm going to have a good hoot," she said, "but I don't want to waste your time now listening to me laugh." "What does she mean by that, Bob?" asked Andy. "Oh, I bet she's really mad."

The three of us started going to all the fashion shows together: Halston, Giorgio di Sant'Angelo, Oscar de la Renta. Paulette and Andy would always get front-row seats and I'd be seated next to them, which would make Rosemary Kent furious, because she'd be further down the runway or in the second row. Paulette would carry on a conversation throughout the show, "in that voice that carries," Andy would later say. "It's so embarrassing, right, Bob?" But it didn't carry over the disco music all the designers were starting to play, and Andy's tapes were undecipherable. Had Paulette figured that out?

To thank us for introducing her to all our designer friends, Paulette introduced us to her Old Hollywood and high-society friends. We went to lunch at La Côte Basque with Maria Cooper Janis and her mother, the former Mrs. Gary Cooper, now Mrs. Rocky Converse, wife of Southampton's number-one physician. Andy wanted to talk about Gary Cooper, but Maria wanted to talk about her ESP paintings and Uri Geller bending her keys. Andy was fascinated, but not as much as he would have been about Gary.

Paulette took us to a party at Raffles, the private club in the basement of the Sherry Netherland, given by Earl Blackwell. Andy sat between Eugenia Sheppard, the diminutive fashion and society reporter for the New York *Post,* and the equally diminutive Anita Loos, which made him nervous because he wasn't sure if Paulette had told her about the switch in co-authors yet. "She looks like an eighty-two-year-old little girl," Andy said of Anita later. "She's adorable. And she told me all this good stuff about Paulette. I think I know what the International Rumor is now, but I can't tell you because you'll tell Paulette."

Last Tango in Paris (which Andy thought was based on his 1968 *Blue Movie)* was the talk of the town, and Paulette wanted to meet Bernardo Bertolucci. So Andy and I got them together for drinks at the Pierre Hotel one afternoon. It was the most interesting time we had with her in this pre-book-contract period, when she thought everything was off the record, and Andy pretended he didn't know what that meant. Paulette told us about the meeting of Chaplin and Cocteau, on a slow boat to Japan in the thirties. "They *hated* each other," she said, "and it was a very slow boat."

She also said that Chaplin had wanted to be a writer, a serious writer, "more than anything else in the world. He got tired if people expected him to be Charlie Chaplin at dinner parties; he wanted to be taken seriously. And then Upton Sinclair and Max Eastman came along and convinced him he was serious and that was the end of him. And our marriage. Life with Charlie became unbearable. He would get up in the morning with that long face, write until lunch, and after lunch tear up everything he wrote in the morning. And then he'd take it out on me."

Later, Bertolucci told us that he was sure Paulette made this all up "to get her revenge on Chaplin, by making him seem the failed writer. She's something, this woman, no?" We thought she was something too, and looked at each other with dollar signs in our eyes, thinking we had a surefire bestseller in Paulette's book. When she finished with Chaplin and Cocteau, she got onto Diego Rivera and Trotsky in Mexico City in the forties.

Paulette didn't say she had an affair with Rivera, but she sure made it sound that way. She talked about the portrait he had painted of her, and their long lunches and dinners with Trotsky, who was in exile in Mexico. She claimed that she and Rivera were on their way to Trotsky's house the day he was assassinated by Stalin's henchmen. "As we approached the house in our car," she said, "we saw a car full of thugs with their fedoras pulled over their faces parked outside the gate. Diego said, 'Duck, Paulette, duck!' And he stepped on the accelerator and home we went."

"And then what happened?" asked Andy.

"And then we never saw Trotsky again," said Paulette. "You know, Trotsky had something that very, very few people have: the power of concentration. You have it, Andy. You pretend not to. But I've watched you. And I know you do."

"Oh, I got it," Andy said, "when I went on this round-the-world trip with a friend in the fifties. I got it in Bali, actually, when I saw people burning the dead and dancing."

The day after Valentine's Day, 1974, I organized an instant "picnic" lunch at the Factory for Christopher Isherwood and his artist friend Don Bachardy, inviting Paulette, Anita, and Maria Cooper Janis. Paulette pitched in with a pound of caviar, saying, "I've never been to a picnic. Except in Indochina."

"When were you in Indochina?" Andy wanted to know. So did Sony.

"When General Patton took me during World War II."

"You *knew* General Patton?" asked Andy.

"Of course I did. I knew a lot of generals. I'll tell you all about it when we start the book."

"Oh, can't we start today?"

"There are too many people for me to concentrate properly."

"Thank you for lunch," said Anita Loos on the way out, "and good luck with your book with Paulette. You'll need it."

Paulette had let her down *gently*.

21

Paris (and *Philosophy*)

"Now you're really going to see a palace, Bob."

Andy and I were in Paris, on our way to a lunch in his honor at the Baron Alexis de Redé's Palais Lambert on the Île Saint Louis. We had arrived a few days earlier for the opening of Andy's Mao exhibition, on February 22, 1974, at the Musée Galliera, along with Fred Hughes, Peter and Sandy Brant, David Whitney, who hung the show, and Paloma Picasso.

It seemed like I'd seen nothing but palaces in Paris, starting with our hotel, the Crillon, where we had an endless suite of rooms smothered in gold brocade, which Fred told me had been occupied by the German high command during World War II. The Musée Galliera had been the palace of a rich Italian family in the eighteenth century, Fred said. Andy's paintings had never looked more spectacular: the four twenty-foot-high portraits of Mao hung side by side in the epic grand hall, which had been covered in Andy's delicate white-and-lavender Mao wallpaper—overwhelming icons of twentieth-century revolution set in the faded splendor of the *ancien régime*. The smaller salons had also been wallpapered and filled with medium-size Mao paintings, the Mao prints, and, in one room, one hundred miniature Mao paintings, which looked like so many Oriental postage stamps.

Everyone we'd visited lived in some sort of palace too: Yves Saint Laurent and his partner, Pierre Bergé; São Schlumberger and her husband, Pierre; Count and Countess Brando Brandolini, who owned half of the seventeenth-century *hôtel particulière* on the Rue du Cherche-Midi where Andy and Fred had recently purchased an apartment previously owned by Violet Trefusis, girlfriend of Vita Sackville-West. We had gone to see how the decorating work was progressing, and the high ceilings, ornate wood-work, and marble baths with gold fixtures made it look pretty palatial to me.

"Oh, I know," said Andy, "but the Baron has a real palace, with footmen in funny white wigs and everything. You won't believe your eyes, Bob." Andy cracked his chewing gum before discarding it in the ashtray and added, "And the Baron was adopted. You could be adopted too, Bob. If you played your cards right. And stopped chasing after all those crazy young beauties." He wasn't proposing to adopt me himself.

Andy was a little let down when we drove into the cobblestoned court-yard of the Palais Lambert. The footman who scurried down the stone steps to open our taxi door wasn't wearing a white wig or gold livery, just a plain black uniform and his own gray hair. "Why isn't he all dressed up, Fred?" asked Andy. "They only get all gussied up for the big balls, Andy," Fred explained. "This is just a normal little lunch."

I had never been to a normal little lunch quite like it. The Palais Lam-bert, with its colossal crystal chandeliers and acres of red damask, looked like Versailles. The dining room, where twenty-two of us ate at one long table off gold plates with gold knives and forks, looked like the Hall of Mirrors. A footman stood behind every other chair in case a napkin dropped. I half expected Marie Antoinette to float through the double-height, double-width hand-painted doors, but instead in floated her seventies incarnation, Baroness Marie-Hélène de Rothschild. "Her husband, Baron Guy, really owns this place," Andy whispered to me in a rush. "And now she wants to get rid of this nice old blind American lady who lives downstairs and stick the Baron de Redé down there, so she can have this apartment. She's sort of mean," Andy rushed on, while Fred gave us cautionary glances, "but we're trying to get her portrait and I really like her a lot, so be sure to tell her how great she looks."

Fred kissed her hand; Andy said, "Oh, hi, you look great, this is Bob, who helps us with *Interview.*" The Baroness de Rothschild was followed by the Princess de Polignac; the Baroness de Waldner; Bettina Graziani, the Aga Khan's last flame; Virginia Chambers, the soon-to-be-evicted down-stairs neighbor, in very dark glasses; and Irving "Swifty" Lazar, the leg-endary Hollywood literary agent. Yves Saint Laurent and his "family" were all there too: Pierre Bergé, who ran his business; his muses, Loulou de la Falaise and Betty Catroux; his spokeswoman, Chilean-born Clara Saint, and her beau, Thadée Klossowski, the handsome son of the painter Balthus.

This Paris circle made the New York fashion world seem downright plain, even boring. It wasn't only the Proustian *richesse* that was overwhelm-ing, but also the Proustian intrigue and backbiting. Nobody ever seemed to say anything nice about anybody else, not even their greatest friends. We saw the Saint Laurent–Rothschild group almost exclusively that week, be-cause if we had seen any other they would have stopped seeing us. In New

York you could mix and mingle. But in Paris the only things that were mixed were the marriages, and they were very mixed indeed. Otherwise, you had to stick with one clique.

After lunch Andy told me: "In Paris, it's who's *not* invited that counts. Now who wasn't invited to lunch? The Brandolinis. They were In the last time we were here, why are they Out now, Fred?"

"They're not Out, Andy. You can only fit so many people around one table."

"But that was a really big table, Fred. And Hélène Rochas? Where was she? I thought she was the most In. How did she get to be Out, Fred?"

"She's out of town, Andy, that's how. Did you have too much champagne at lunch, or something? I wish you wouldn't fill Bob's head with such garbage. You never get it right, anyway."

"Yes, I do, Fred, because I get it from you. Oh, Bob made a big faux pas at lunch. I forgot to tell you. He told Loulou that we saw São. She's not part of the Yves Saint Laurent group, Bob. She's part of the Givenchy group."

"You didn't say she's having her portrait done, did you, Bob?" asked Fred. I said I sort of had. "Oh, no, this is all I need! I already have Pierre Bergé on my back because Marina let it slip that you did Valentino."

"She's *your* wife, Fred," said Andy.

"I know she's *my* wife, Andy," said Fred.

"How much do you want to bet, Fred, that São doesn't go through with her portrait when she hears that we did Hélène Rochas?"

"Well, she won't hear, unless *Bob* tells her!"

"We're never going to get Marie-Hélène, Fred. She hardly looked at me at lunch. She talked to Yves the whole time, in French. I told you we should've done her first."

"Andy, you're driving me crazy. I got you Eric de Rothschild first, didn't I? I can only work on so many people at the same time. If we don't get Marie-Hélène, we don't get Marie-Hélène, and that's that." Fred stormed off to his room, muttering under his breath, "I told you so, I told you so, I told you so . . ."

"Gee, I guess Fred's cranky," said Andy, unfazed, "because you kids stayed out so late last night, kicking up your heels at Club Sept." Club Sept was the hottest night spot, Paris's Le Jardin. All the most beautiful models went there for dinner upstairs and dancing downstairs, every night into the wee hours. The king of the club was Antonio, the hottest fashion illustrator since Joe Eula. If he liked a girl, it was a pretty sure thing that the fashion magazines and fashion designers would too. He had launched the careers of Pat Cleveland and Apollonia van Ravenstein, sweeping them up from the dance floor to the runways of Saint Laurent and Halston, and now his latest discovery was Jerry Hall.

"Did you meet anybody cute at Club Sept after I left?" Andy asked.

"Did you meet anybody cute at Club Sept after I left?" Andy asked. No. "Did Fred?" No. "Oh, I had the oddest conversation with Clara and Thadée in the taxi home, but I can't tell you about what, because Fred will get mad. He says I can't tell you anything, because you talk too much, Bob. You have to learn to talk less, especially in Paris. Thadée's father gave them another drawing and they want to sell it to me. Should I do it?"

"Is that what you're not supposed to tell me?"

"No, it's something much worse. I mean, it's just the Yves Saint Laurent group is so nutty. Like, Thadée is Clara's boyfriend, right? But then . . . Oh, I better not tell you. Oh, I know what I should do, call up Pat in New York and give her the expenses. These trips don't cost peanuts, you know, Bob. Gotta bring home the bacon." Andy got to Pat in New York: "And then we took a taxi to the Baron de Redé's to talk about Marie-Hélène's portrait, twenty-five francs . . ."

When he got off the phone, his face brightened as he said, "Should we call Fred's room and tell him São just called to cancel her portrait?"

"Why don't you leave Fred alone, Andy? He works so hard for you."

"No, he doesn't. He stays up all night kicking up his heels and drinking a lot of champagne. Your champagne chin is getting worse, Bob."

"Andy, you know that all the entertaining Fred does brings in a lot of business."

"Oh, really. Gee, should we call room service and order up some hot chocolate and chocolate cake and chicken sandwiches and tea and whatever else you want, Bob?"

"I can't eat another thing, Andy, after that enormous lunch."

"Oh, I know. But I didn't eat anything. It all had too much butter and cream. It's all bad for my gallbladder. Let's just get some chocolate cake, okay?"

"But that's bad for your gallbladder too, Andy. What's the point of taking your pill every morning and not eating lunch, if you come back to the hotel and eat chocolate?"

"I don't eat it, Bob! I just put it in my mouth and spit it out."

I called room service. Eventually, Andy went to his room to lie down before yet another dinner with the Saint Laurent group. I liked the Saint Laurent group, but I wasn't sure if they liked me. It was hard to tell who they liked, except each other, and even then I wasn't sure. Yves hardly talked, except in whispers and in French. Pierre never stopped talking, in barks and in French. They knew that Andy and I didn't speak French, and they could speak English, but, said Andy, that's the way the French are. Loulou was nice one minute, not the next. Clara was always nice, always laughing, but did she also laugh behind your back? And Thadée was like Yves, the weak, silent type. Or so it seemed. I wondered if Yves and Pierre had an Andy-and-Fred act going, and if when no one was around, Yves drove Pierre crazy, as Andy did Fred. Everyone said that Yves was so pure and sweet and fragile, but I wasn't so sure. That's what they said about Andy, too, wasn't it?

I went into Andy's room—he was asleep, snoring slightly, on top of the gold brocade bedspread. He was also fully dressed, which wasn't that unusual, as even at night he slept in his blue Oxford shirt, girdle, jockey shorts, and knee-length support hose, so that only a short stretch of leg was exposed between his socks and shirttails. Now he had his expensive Parisian cowboy boots on too, and I thought I'd slip them off to make him more comfortable. He awoke in an instant, with a start. "What are you doing, Bob?" he squealed, as if I were about to murder him. He took them off himself. Had I ever touched him before? I don't think I'd ever even shaken hands with him.

I retreated to my own room, with its gold brocade bedspread, gold brocade curtains, gilded furniture, gilded woodwork, crystal chandelier, crystal vase filled with white tulips on a gray February day. I stared out the high French doors at the expensive view: the Place de la Concorde, the Seine, and, across the river, the Boulevard Saint-Germain, with the Eiffel Tower off to one side. It was our last night in Paris, and I couldn't wait to get home to my tiny Manhattan studio with a view of the studio across the street.

And yet, the minute I got back, I couldn't wait to go on another five-star trip with Andy.

The opportunity came soon enough—an invitation from Franco Rossellini to the world première of *The Driver's Seat* in Monte Carlo in May. "Everyone will be there, darling," Franco said, "Ursula, Elsa, São, Rosemarie . . ." He meant Andress, Martinelli, Schlumberger, and Marcie-Rivière, the Swiss socialite legendary for her multiple marriages and multiple fortunes. "And don't breathe it to a soul, but I think I have Ari *and* Stavros coming, except one doesn't know the other is coming." He meant Onassis and Niarchos, who were bitter rivals. "All my friends from all over the world are coming to support me," he went on, "because would you believe that those so-called intellectuals who run the Cannes Film Festival turned down *The Driver's Seat*—which is a masterpiece, I tell you, a masterpiece!—and those idiots chose some piece of shit by Franco Zeffirelli as the official Italian entry instead?" The two Francos were also bitter rivals. "So you know what I did? I picked up the phone and I called my old friend, Princess Grace, and arranged to have the première of my film on the same night they show the Zeffirelli film in Cannes. And, as you know, darling, when Grace and Rainier invite, the entire Côte d'Azur comes. There's not going to be a star left in Cannes that night! Rex Reed has already told me he is coming to *my* premiere. Don't you think it's divine?" Franco got to the point: "Now, of course, I want Andy to be there. And you too, my darling Bobino, because without you holding Archie all those days, we could never have shot Andy's scenes, let's face it, darling.''

What about Elizabeth Taylor? Would she be coming too? With or without Richard Burton?

"Who knows what those two are doing," Franco snapped. "One minute they're remarrying, the next minute they're splitting up again. It's a big bore, and, *entre nous,* if it wasn't for the publicity, I wouldn't care if she came or not. Now, be sure to tell Andy that I'm sending two *first-class* tickets, *round trip,* because I know how he is. And I'll see you in Monte Carlo. *Ciao, bello.''*

I was sure Andy would say yes—free tickets, Onassis and Niarchos, another chance, perhaps, to take that Polaroid of Elizabeth Taylor—it was the perfect setup. Andy said, "Oh, really," which meant, "What's the hitch?" He paused to make me suffer a bit and added, in an uninterested tone, "Well, maybe we can go. Let's ask Fred. Maybe he can line up some portraits for me to do in Europe at the same time. Maybe it would be a good way to get some work done on the *Philosophy* book. We can tape a lot. Why don't you call up Paulette in Switzerland and see if she wants to meet us in Monte Carlo? I bet Franco would love that. And why don't you call Franco back and see if he'll send her a free ticket too. And what about Fred? Can't Franco send him a ticket?'' Traveling with Andy, like going out with Andy, was work.

In March we had signed two book contracts with Harcourt Brace Jovanovich, one for the *Philosophy* book and one for the Paulette book. They were to be titled *THE* and *HER,* respectively. (And if and when Andy did an autobiography, that would be called *ME.*)

Andy had said he would give me "part" of the Philosophy book advance, to get me going on the proposal and outline. When it was accepted, he agreed to give me "half," but he wouldn't let the lawyers put that in the contract. He said HBJ might "get mad"—a ridiculous excuse as they knew of my involvement all along. I tried to change his mind, but he always came back with "Don't you trust me, Bob?" When HBJ paid out the first half of our $35,000 advance upon signing the contract, he gave me my share in dribs and drabs. Finally, Roz Cole said she needed a letter from Andy authorizing her to pay my share of future income directly, and Andy gave in, probably thinking there wouldn't be any future income.

"I love doing the *Philosophy* project," I wrote in my diary. It was so much easier being a ghostwriter than a real writer. When the "I" wasn't me I could coast along at the typewriter, instead of worrying over every syllable. I plunged right into Chapter One: "Existence"—Andy getting up in the morning, dragging himself out of bed, tiptoeing across the minefield of chocolate-covered cherries on the floor, looking at himself in the bathroom mirror, trying to answer that eternal question: What is Being? It was Andy's idea to cull phrases from the Factory clippings scrapbook to describe what he saw in his mirror: "the affectless gaze . . . the wasted pallor . . . the childlike, gum-chewing naïveté . . . the slightly sinister aura . . . the long bony arms, so white they looked bleached . . ." Journalists had had a field day with Andy over the years and now, typically, he was going to use it all himself.

When I finished the chapter, I handed it to Andy. He counted the pages, as he counted the ads in *Interview,* and said, "Only twelve?" He took it home that night and read it over the phone to Brigid Berlin, taping her reaction. Then he gave the tape to Pat Hackett, telling her to "make it better." So now the ghostwriter had a ghostwriter, Factory-style. A literary assembly line was set up: Bob to Andy to Brigid to Pat to Andy to HBJ, with a quick stop at Fred's desk, to make sure we didn't put in anything "funny" about Lee Radziwill or Jackie Onassis. (Another assembly line was set up for the Paulette book. A friend of Fred's, Christopher Hemphill, a young scribe from an old family, was hired to redact those tapes. Paulette to Andy-and-Bob to Chris to Fred for the Lee-and-Jackie check to Andy-and-Bob to HBJ.)

Pat ended up writing more of the *Philosophy* book than I did, and I ended up paying her half of my half of the advance. She deserved a percentage of its future income as well, but Andy absolutely refused to consider it. Andy liked to set his collaborators against each other. As Pat put more and more time, effort, and ideas into the *Philosophy* book, she became increasingly dissatisfied with her deal. Eventually, she decided if she couldn't have more money, she wanted more credit—a byline. When she proposed that to Andy, he gave her a curt turnoff, and she made the mistake of screaming at him, then bursting into tears. "Pat's freaking out," he moaned, scurrying out of the cubicle they shared. "You've got to do something, Bob. Pat's going crazy." It was Andy's standard last recourse, and just in case I missed the implication, he added, "I don't know *what* she might do." When it came to doing business with his Factory workers, Andy played every emotion.

I did calm Pat down, not by giving her more of my share—I felt I deserved what I was getting, especially in light of my Factory salary—but by promising to pitch her idea for a book on the Factory in the sixties to Roz Cole and HBJ. I did, and that idea became *Popism: The Warhol Sixties,* by Andy Warhol and Pat Hackett.

The Paulette Goodard book, *HER,* was another complicated story. Andy had said I would get "part" of that too, but again, when it came time to draw up contracts, he balked, this time blaming it on Paulette. At one point, he said "all the money" I was getting for the *Philosophy* project was "really for helping with Paulette," since "Pat is doing your job for you," ignoring the fact that *I* was paying Pat. He loved to tangle everything up, until you felt so roped in you just gave up. He eventually agreed to give me 10 percent of his half of the $50,000 advance. Paulette got the other half, and Andy wanted me to ask her for 10 percent of that too. I didn't.

And while we negotiated, we worked. A few days *before* we signed the *HER* contract, Paulette, Andy, and I had met with a major magazine editor to line up a first-serial-rights sale. Paulette turned on the charm and out poured a waterfall of Old Hollywood gossip. "Oh, yes, I dropped George Gershwin for Clark Gable," she splish-splashed, "wouldn't you?"

A few days *after* signing the contract, Paulette, Andy, and I met for lunch at the Regency Hotel, along with Sony, her twin sister Sony Colacello, and her older cousin, Motorola Goddard. Paulette wanted three tape recorders "for protection." There were also three sirloin steaks on the table, medium rare. Unfortunately, Paulette's Old Hollywood gossip had suddenly turned more medium than rare. Whenever Chaplin came up, Paulette would say something short and vague, and then freeze her face into a frown, as if it were too painful to go any deeper. Andy hadn't helped matters, admittedly, by starting off lunch with "Well, now that we're really working, tell us what we really want to know: How big was Charlie's cock?"

Despite this foreboding beginning, we went ahead with a celebratory lunch at the Factory with Mr. and Mrs. Jovanovich and Steven M. L. Aronson, our very able editor at HBJ. Paulette brought her "picnic provisions," champagne, caviar, and Brie. Not to be outdone, Andy showed up with his "office entertainment supplies," pâté de foie gras, prosciutto, and pastries from the swank Dumas bakery. After our guests left, I bought the afternoon New York *Post* and there was our lunch, already written up in Eugenia Sheppard's "Inside Fashion" column, with a long quote from Paulette explaining, as only she could, how the book project came to be. "It was the year of the white fox," she told Eugenia. "I was always wearing it, long, short or just a stole, and Andy *is* the white fox, blond, pale and silent."

"I don't think Paulette wants a book, Bob," said Andy. "I think she wants to marry me. This was the engagement lunch. I just hope she doesn't expect an engagement ring. Or a white fox."

Just before Paulette left for her usual summer in Switzerland, Andy and I went by her apartment to give her a little Sony like ours. She promised that she would make tapes and send them to us, if we promised to make copies and send them right back. There was more champagne and caviar— was this whole thing a ruse for Paulette to deduct her daily staples? And then Paulette insisted we kiss her goodbye. Andy gave her a peck on the cheek, but from me she demanded a kiss on the lips. "You're the only one I let kiss me on the lips," she said. "Again, but harder."

"Paulette doesn't want a book," Andy said when we were back on Park Avenue. "She wants to marry you. Maybe you should. Then I wouldn't have to give you ten percent. You'd be on easy street."

Within forty-eight hours, Paulette's lawyer sent Andy's lawyer a side letter to the HBJ contract: "Paulette Goddard Remarque and Andy Warhol agree that neither author shall have the right to use the tapes thereof without the prior written approval of the other and that each author shall receive a copy of each tape." I persuaded Andy to sign. "She's nuts," he said, "if she thinks I'm really going to do this."

"You know what I like. Long sleeves, décolleté, red or white. Maybe pink, but *pale* pink, like champagne, not bright pink, like Valentine's Day wrapping. No chemise! You know the look I mean. Andy knows. If it's good for the girls you put in *Interview,* it's good for me. Size ten. Byyyye." It was Paulette, asking us to pick out some dresses for her from YSL's Rive Gauche boutique. We were in Paris, she was in Switzerland, and in a couple of days we would all be in Monte Carlo for *The Driver's Seat* premiere.

Paris was wonderful the second time around. It felt more familiar, less forbidding. We were at the Crillon again, to which I had quickly grown accustomed. Clara Saint took us to the Rive Gauche boutique but we couldn't find anything for Paulette—Yves wasn't doing red or white that season, and his pink was a no-glow salmon. With my first *Philosophy* check, I bought a Fred-like black suit for the Monte Carlo première.

In the afternoons, Andy and I worked on the *Philosophy* book—with me reading from Chapter Two, "Sex Is Work", Andy popping candy in and out of his mouth. It was a terrible chapter and Andy, I noted, "tore it apart with amazing clarity of vision sometimes, fumbling abstract intuition other times, always making it better." He told me that the book should have more "nutty lines." He said it should be funny, but not too funny, so that people couldn't be sure if we were serious or not. "I think Mr. Jovanovich is an intellectual," he said, "so we have to put some serious stuff in there, Bob. You don't want to give the money back, do you?" And he quickly came up with a serious Warholian line: "I can start things, but I can't stop them." What's more, it was true.

Most nights we went to dinner at Club Sept with Clara and Thadée, or Jay Johnson and his model friend Tom Cashin, who were now living and working in Paris. Andy always left right after dinner, but Fred and I stayed on downstairs, dancing with the models. I couldn't believe that drinks cost ten dollars each. Fred paid.

Almost everywhere we went, Andy insisted on bringing an odd American boy named Rodney Buice, a friend of a friend of a friend. Rodney was a painter. He did forty-by-forty silkscreen portraits of movie stars and society figures, for $500 instead of $25,000. Otherwise, it was difficult for the untrained eye to tell the difference between a Buice and a Warhol. Andy thought this was "greaaaaat." Fred thought that Andy's clients might be at best confused, and at worst infuriated, if they saw Rodney's work, especially on the recommendation of Andy. But that was the whole point of having Rodney around, to torture Fred, to make his job harder. Fred put his foot down when Andy wanted to drag Rodney along to lunch at Pierre and São Schlumberger's for the unveiling of her Warhol portrait.

The Schlumbergers lived in a vast private house called the Hôtel Luzy, near the Luxembourg Gardens. It had everything, from a Matisse odalisque to a Motown discothèque. And things mostly seemed to come in twos: a blue drawing room and a green drawing room, an upstairs dining room and a downstairs dining room, a large library and a small library, matching chests of drawers from Marie Antoinette's boudoir, a pair of Picassos, a second Matisse. Yet São seemed so casual about it all, dismissively waving her hand with its giant Golconda diamond on one finger and a giant Burmese ruby on another, when I praised the Rothko and the Kline and the Bonnard and the Monet. She was more excited by her latest acquisition: her portrait by Andy. He had done something special for São: Instead of four panels of the same pose in different colors, he had done two of one pose and two of another, full face and three-quarter view. And he had "really painted," which was his code for de Kooning-like gesture. Unlike so many of his society portraits, it wasn't flat and two-dimensional.

Neither was the subject. São Schlumberger was one of a rare breed: a rich woman with a mind of her own. Half Portuguese, half German, she refused to follow the Paris pack, no matter how much that made the other ladies tittle-tattle. She loved her couture and her jewels as much as they loved theirs, but she also loved art and artists. The Schlumbergers were said to have an annual income of several million dollars, and while São didn't mind showing it, she also didn't mind sharing it. She supported the museums in Paris, and was active on MoMA's International Council. She helped finance, to the tune of several hundred thousand dollars, some of Bob Wilson's elaborate avant-garde productions. All of that impressed Andy but he also liked São because she wouldn't censor what she said when Sony was around. And she said a lot.

São and Pierre, whose first wife had died, married in 1961. Six years later he suffered a massive stroke. Now he walked with a slow limp and hardly uttered a word. But when São walked into a room, he perked up, and chattered away with her in some unintelligible tongue.

Though we'd met when Andy did the Polaroids for her portrait at the Carlyle, São seemed to take special notice of me that day, laughing at my jokes, agreeing with my opinions of people in Paris, asking questions about *Interview*. Andy and Fred started teasing me about it the second we were out the door. "São likes Bob," Fred said. "I can tell. Did you see the way she looked right at Bob when she said, 'See you in Monte Carlo'?"

"Oh, I know," said Andy. "You should marry her, Bob."

What about her stricken husband?

"He won't be around forever," said Andy. "And if you marry São you can get her to have her portrait done by me."

But we had just unveiled it.

"Oh, I know, but you can convince her to have me do a new one every year. I could show her hairdos change. It's a great idea, Bob."

"Oh, there's going to be a cat fight in Monte Carlo," said Fred, "between São and Paulette over Bob."

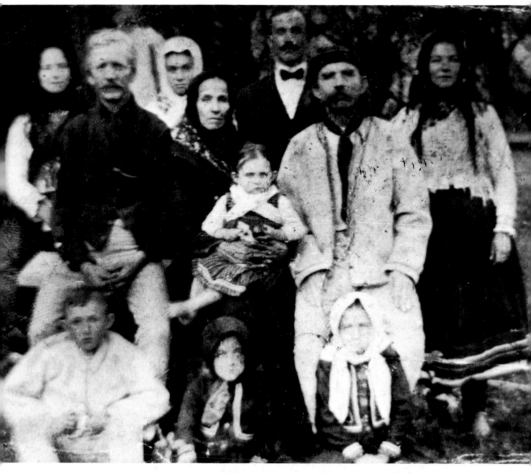

Ruthenian roots: Andy's mother, Julia Zavacky Warhola *(back row, far left),* with her family in their Carpathian Mountain village, before World War I. (Courtesy Amy Passarelli)

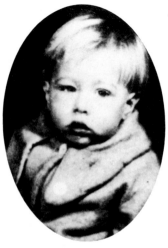

"He was a real holy terror," a Pittsburgh neighbor said of Andy, here at age three. (Courtesy Amy Passarelli)

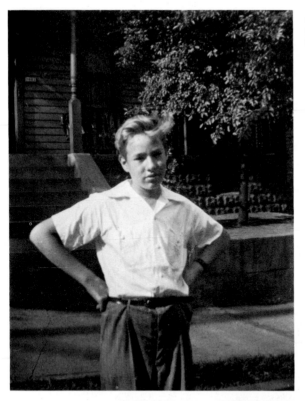

Andy, about age thirteen, in front of the Warhola house on Dawson Street. (Courtesy Paul Warhola)

Julia with her three sons—Andy, age seventeen, Paul in his Navy uniform, and John—and her first grandchild. (Courtesy Paul Warhola)

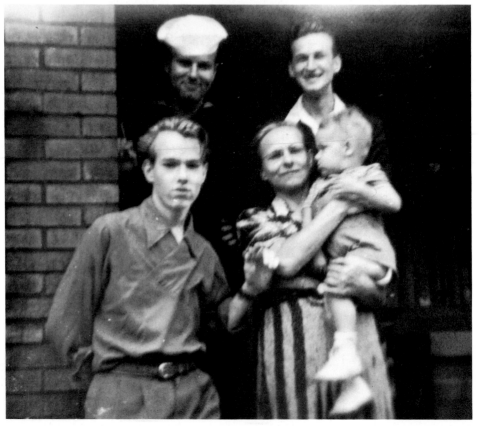

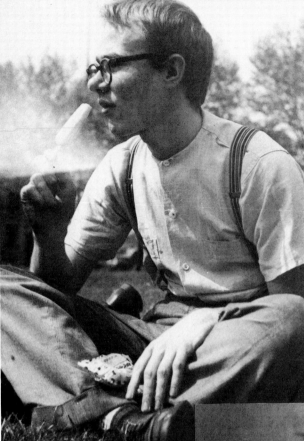

Andy at Carnegie Institute of Technology (now Carnegie-Mellon University), circa 1948: "If someone asked me, 'What's your problem?' I'd have to say, 'Skin.'" (Photo Philip Pearlstein, © 1989)

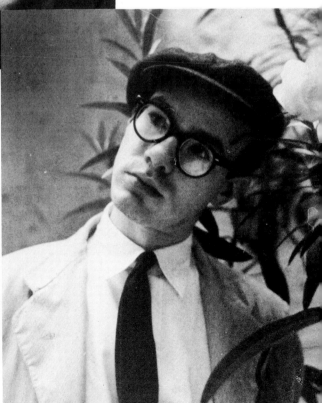

Andy in New York, 1952, at the beginning of his success as a fashion illustrator. (Courtesy Nora Zavacky)

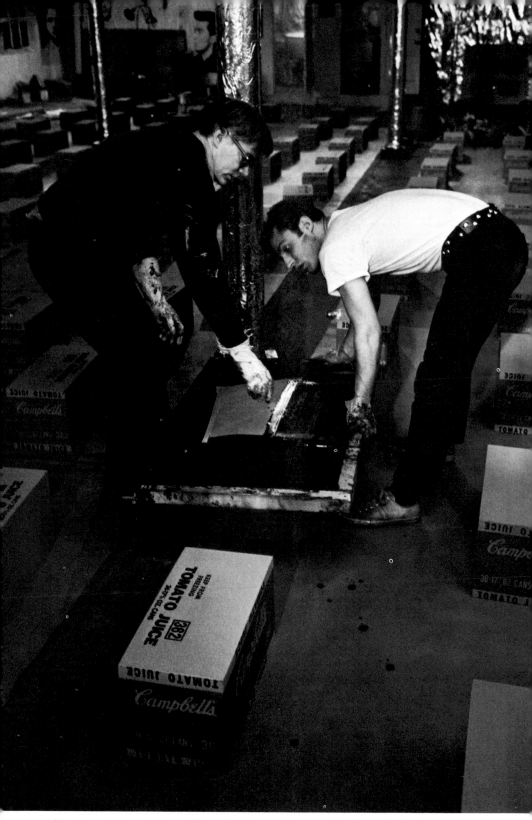

Mass production: Andy and Gerard Malanga silk-screening *Campbell's Tomato Juice* sculptures at the silver-foiled first Factory, 1964. (© Ken Heyman/Black Star)

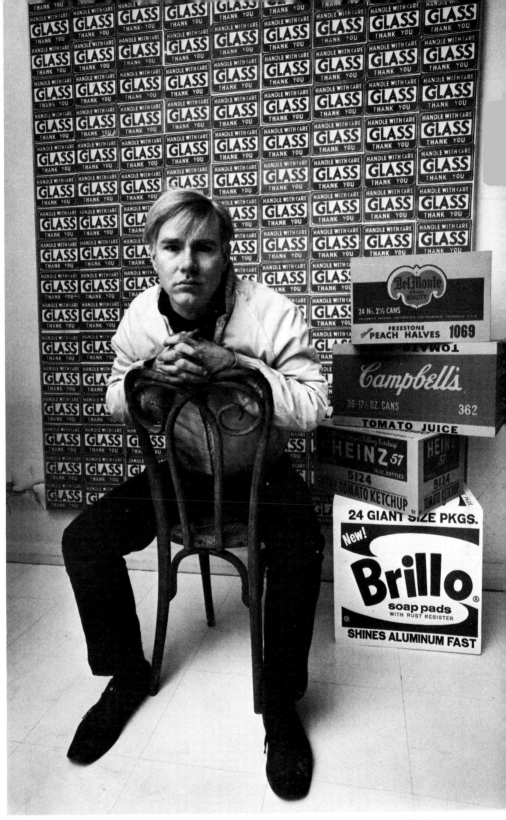

Pop meister: Andy at the Stable Gallery, New York, 1964. (© Ken Heyman/Black Star)

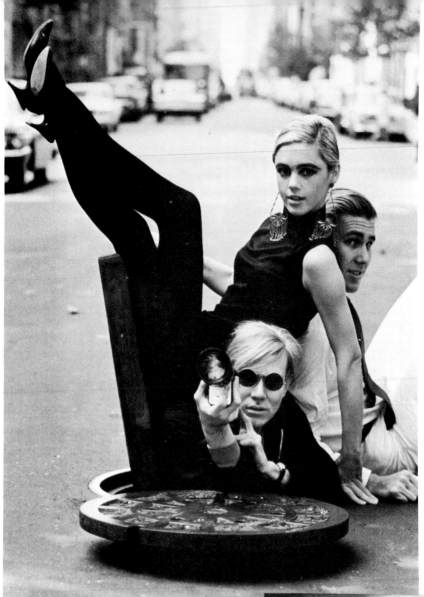

Underground moviemakers: Andy,
Superstar Edie Sedgwick, and Chuck
Wein, 1965. (© Burt Glinn/Magnum)

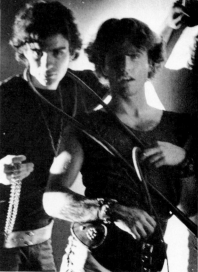

Whip dancers: Ronnie Cutrone (left) and
Gerard Malanga performing in Andy's
traveling multimedia show, The Plastic
Exploding Inevitable. (Courtesy Suzan
Cooper Gallery)

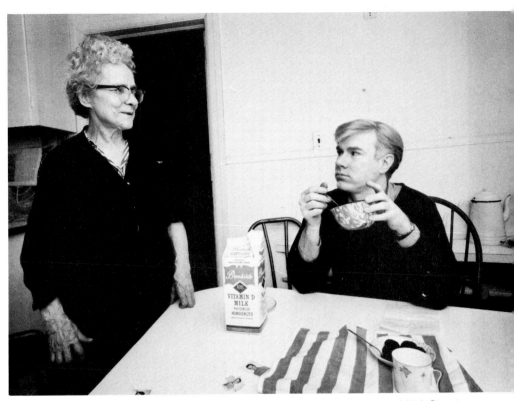

Mama's boy: Julia serves Andy breakfast in the house at Lexington Avenue and 89th Street, 1964. (© Ken Heyman/Black Star)

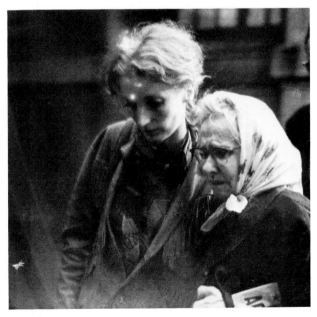

June 3, 1968: Viva, left, comforts Julia at the hospital after Andy was shot by Valerie Solanis. (Courtesy Suzan Cooper Gallery)

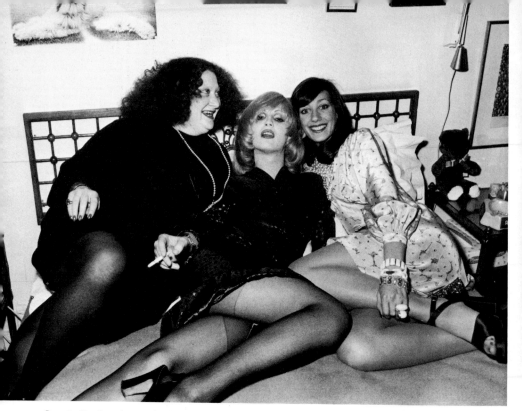

Candy Darling *(center)* with Pat Ast *(left)* and Marisa
Berenson *(right)* at Scavullo's 1972 Ash Wednesday
party. (Archive BC)

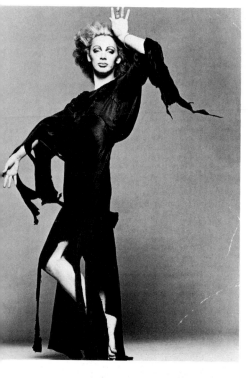

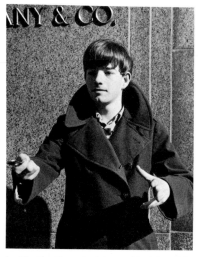

Jackie Curtis out of drag. (Archive BC)

Holly Woodlawn in drag. (© Frank
Kolleogy)

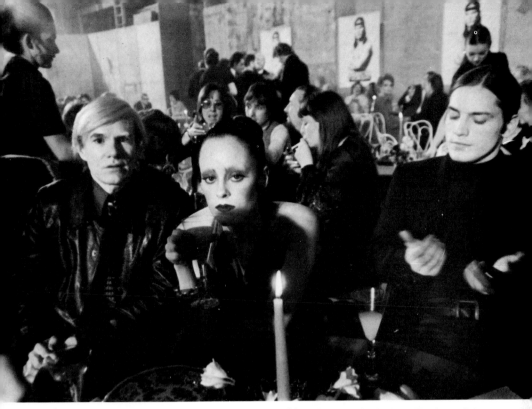

Munich 1971: Andy, Jane Forth, and Joe Dallesandro at *Andy Warhol's Trash* premiere. (AP/Wide World Photos)

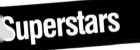

Andrea Feldman (aka Andrea April, Andrea Whips, and Andrea Warhol) and me a few months before her August 1972 suicide. (Archive BC)

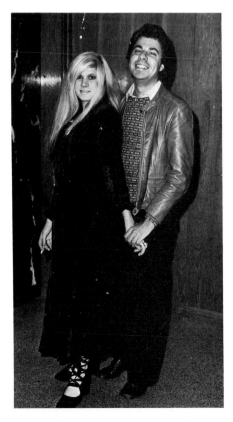

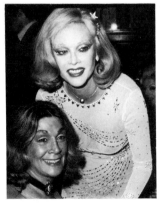

Sylvia Miles *(left)* starred in *Andy Warhol's Heat*; Monique van Vooren starred in *Andy Warhol's Frankenstein.* (Photo Robert Hayes)

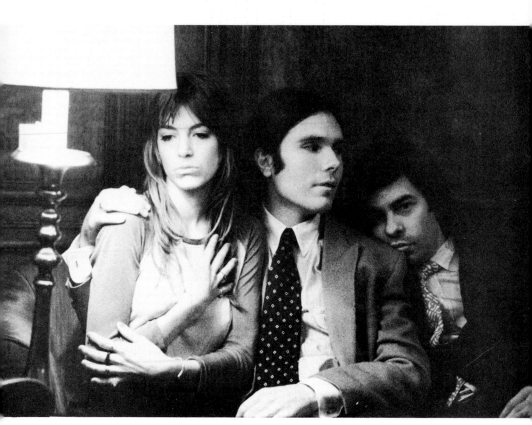

Jude Jade, Glenn O'Brien, and me at the Algonquin Hotel, 1972. (© Peter Beard/Visions)

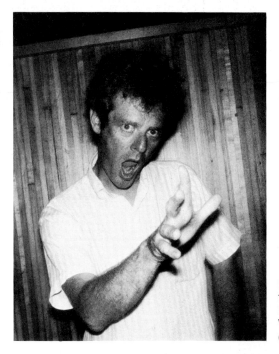

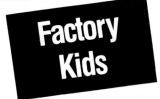

Factory
Kids

Paul Morrissey directed Andy's
films and ran the second
Factory, at 33 Union Square
West, from 1969 to 1974.
(Photo Bob Colacello)

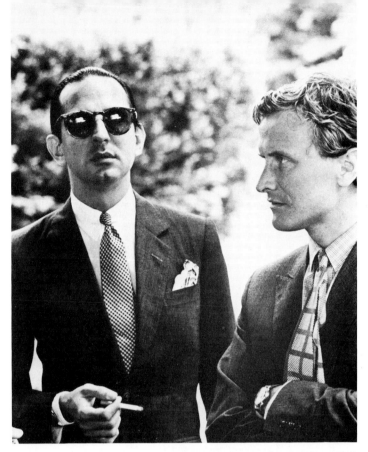

Fred Hughes *(left)*, president of Andy Warhol Enterprises, with art dealer Thomas Ammann. (Archive BC)

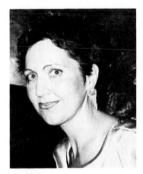

Pat Hackett, Andy's redactor, screenwriter, coauthor, and diarist. (Photo Paige Powell)

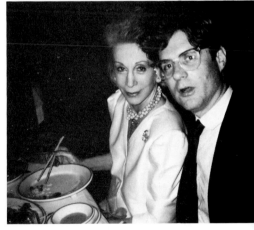

Vincent Fremont, vice president, secretary, and treasurer of Andy Warhol Enterprises, with *Interview*'s Washington correspondent, Ina Ginsburg. (Photo Paige Powell)

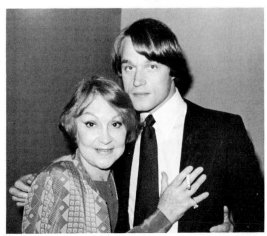

Jed Johnson, Andy's film editor/director, decorator, and housemate, with hostess Adriana Jackson. (Photo Bob Colacello)

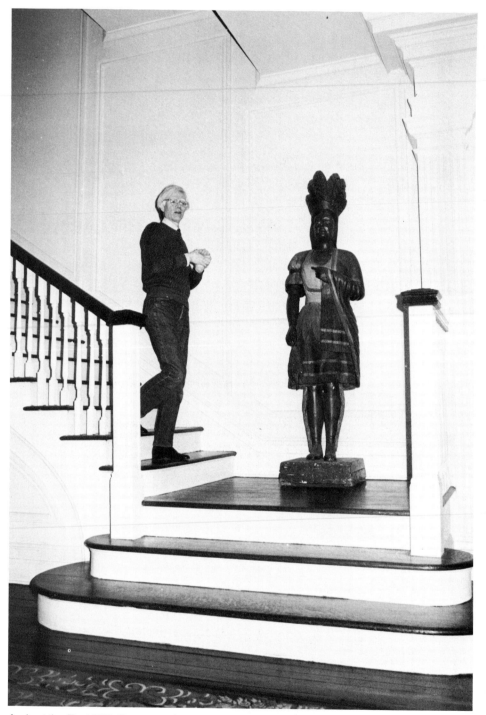

Andy at the East 66th Street townhouse he bought in 1974. (Photo Bob Colacello)

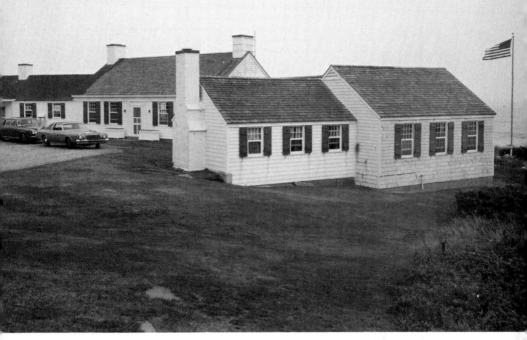

Jackie slept here: the Montauk compound Andy and Paul Morrissey bought in 1972, and later rented to Lee Radziwill, Mick Jagger, and Halston. (Photo Bob Colacello)

The art deco sitting room at 57 East 66th Street. (Photo Paige Powell)

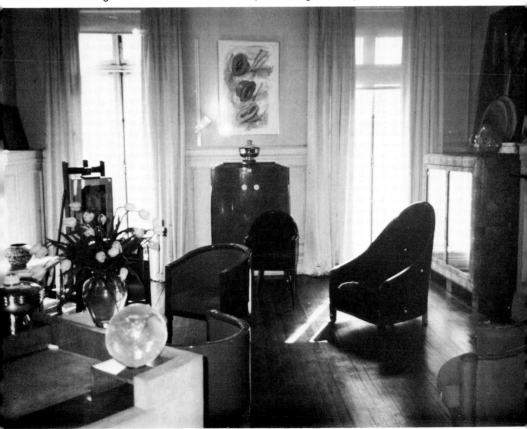

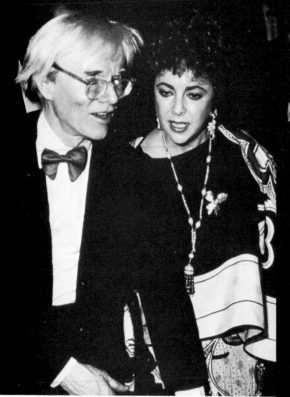

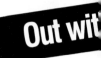

Andy with Elizabeth Taylor at the opening of *The Rink*, 1984. (© Ron Galella)

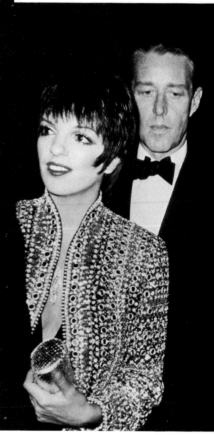

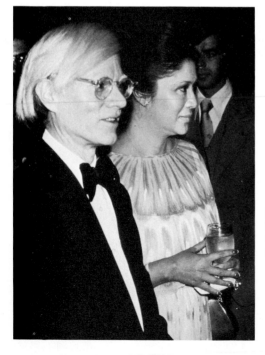

Andy with Imelda Marcos at the opening of Diana Vreeland's Russian costume exhibit, 1976. (© Ron Galella)

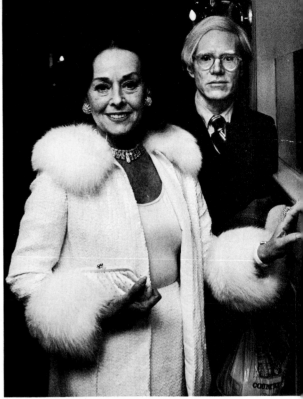

Andy with Paulette Goddard and the famous diamond necklace made from her old engagement rings at the opening of *Full Circle,* 1973. (© Ron Galella)

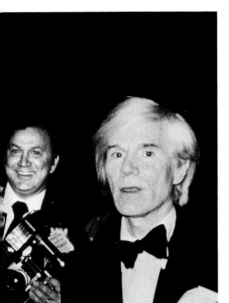

Andy with Liza Minnelli, Halston, and Ron Galella at the opening of *The Little Foxes,* 1981. (© Betty Burke Galella/ Ron Galella)

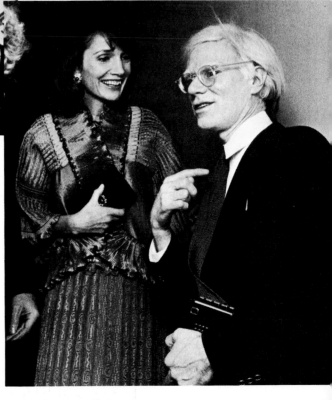

Andy with Lee Radziwill and his "wife," Sony, at the Costume Institute opening, 1975. (© Ron Galella)

German artist Joseph Beuys autographs a catalogue for Andy, circa 1981. (Photo Bob Colacello)

Larry Rivers *(left),* with collector Francois de Menil, was one of the few artists to socialize with Andy in the seventies. (Photo Bob Colacello)

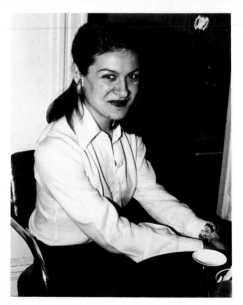

Early Paloma: Picasso's daughter was one of Andy's favorites and not only because of her father's fame, circa 1975. (© Christopher Makos)

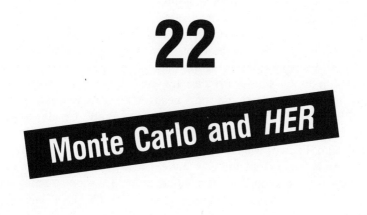

22

"Get out of my picture, Bob." It was Paulette. In Monte Carlo. Standing at the top of the long marble staircase that descends into the marble lobby of the *belle époque* Hôtel de Paris. Swathed in white fox stole, over a white Lurex gown, with blinding blue-white diamonds at all the vital points—ears, throat, heart, wrists, fingers. At the bottom of the staircase were a hundred paparazzi, lured from the Cannes Film Festival by Franco Rossellini's cast of thousands, including Onassis, Niarchos, Ursula, and Liz sans Dick. They had just bombarded Elsa Martinelli as she arrived through the front door on the arm of her husband, furniture designer–fashion photographer Willy Rizzo. Paulette was waiting for them to turn around and focus their cameras on her.

Far from having a cat fight with São Schlumberger over me, Paulette was annoyed that Andy wasn't here instead of me. He had gone to a pre-première reception given by Rainier and Grace at the palace, with Liz and Franco. Paulette wasn't asked because she had turned down a request to appear on Monaco TV the day before, saying, "I never do TV." When it was explained that Princess Grace was going to be on the same program, Paulette cracked, "Well, she has to; it's her country." So I was Paulette's date and Fred was sent to fetch São. We had introduced them over tea that afternoon and they had hit it off. São had admired Paulette's "everyday" pink diamond ring, and mentioned an English duke she had almost married for his fabulous collection of pink diamonds. "Isn't that something," Paulette had gasped. "I almost married his father for the same reason. But I decided that no amount of pink diamonds was worth it." "I decided the same thing about the son," São had said.

The première was a *paparazzi* dream, or nightmare. Franco even let them into the theater, and as the lights went down and the credits went up, they were still snapping away in the dark at the stellar first row: Stavros Niarchos with his son Philip, Princess Ira von Furstenberg, Countess Marina Cicogna, Hélène Rochas and her beau Kim d'Estainville, Rosemarie Marcie-Rivière and her fifth husband, Elsa and Willy, Ursula, Sylvia Vartan . . . Prince Rainier and Princess Grace sat in a box above it all, with Elizabeth and Franco, who seemed to be getting along just fine for the cameras. Andy was complaining in my ear that Grace had been "cool" to him, which he blamed on Paulette's snubbing her TV show. "I mean, I can't go on TV because I'm saving myself for my own TV show, but who does Paulette think she is?"

He whined even more when he appeared on the screen, "I look terrible. I told you to tell them to put more makeup on." He had to laugh, though, when he opened his mouth and out came "The King is dead," in Italian. Paulette loved the movie and she loved Andy in it, or so she said. "You were born for the screen," she told him. "Didn't she say the same thing about Joe Dallesandro in *Dracula,* Bob?" whispered Andy. "Who is she trying to kid?" We went on to the dinner at Regine's club, New Jimmy'z, which wasn't seated except for the royal table, which we weren't seated at. Andy blamed that on Paulette too. He wanted to leave the minute we got there, and did after a half hour, with Paulette, São, and their jewels. I ended up at the Tip Top pizzeria at three in the morning, with Kim d'Estainville, Hélène Rochas, Bettina Graziani, and Marina Cicogna. As we munched our slices, in waltzed Their Serene Highnesses, Grace and Rainier, who sat down at the next table and ordered spaghetti.

The next morning, Andy was waiting for me with a tape recorder. "This is work, Bob," he said. "You're not on vacation. Even though you act like you are, staying up all night kicking up your heels." I said I had been trying to get Marina's portrait, and Bettina's portrait. "And what were you and Fred doing the night before, when you stayed out all night at Jimmy'z?" Trying to get Onassis's portrait. It was the standard line for the standard lecture. "I hope Fred got a receipt." Onassis paid, I replied.

Jimmy'z had been deserted that first night, except for Ari Onassis and his court: Franco Rossellini, Elsa Martinelli, Willy Rizzo, Roberto Shorto, and, intriguingly, Philip Niarchos, son of Stavros. Onassis's marriage to Jackie was close to an end, the jet set said, and I was shocked by his appearance: so old and weary, with his eyelids held open by bits of Scotch tape, because of a rare disease of the eye muscles. There was only one couple on the dance floor, both tall, blond, slim, obviously Scandinavian, obviously entranced with each other, wearing identical red polo shirts and slacks. Roberto Shorto, a Brazilian whose sister was married to the art-collecting Baron Heini von Thyssen, bet Onassis a bottle of Dom Perignon which was the boy and which was the girl. Then he got up and pinched the boy's tit, saying, "We were wondering if you were a girl." The Scandinavian socked him one, propelling him across the dance floor and into my lap.

The trip's main purpose was to tape record Paulette morning, noon, and night, to get the book done, "fast and easy and cheap." Well, it wasn't that cheap—the Hôtel de Paris cost about $300 a night for a room. And it wasn't easy either. The first thing Paulette eliminated was mornings. She said she had to have her bath, her walk, her time to change for lunch. Andy suggested taping her doing all those things, but she wasn't having any of that. So we spent mornings in Andy's room, taping each other for the *Philosophy* book. After a few days, Paulette eliminated nights too. She said she had to get her beauty rest, and we went out to dinner too late. "But everybody goes to dinner late in Europe," said Andy. "But I'm not everybody," said Paulette. So we spent the rest of our nights hanging out at Jimmy'z with Fred's latest flirt, an aristocratic young French woman named Ariel de Ravenel. Next to go were afternoons. Paulette said she had to have her walk, her nap, her time to dress for dinner. "But you're not going to dinner," said Andy. "Not with you I'm not," said Paulette. So we spent our afternoons wondering what Paulette was doing at night without us. Andy liked to imagine that she was having a secret lesbian affair with a woman we'd met at Ariel de Ravenel's mother's house.

That left lunches. Those weren't easy, or cheap either. But they were fast. No matter what we asked, Paulette seemed to find it "too psychological" or "too banal," and good reason to skip dessert and dash off to her afternoon constitutional, leaving Andy, me, and Sony with a few lines about whether Beluga was really better than Sevruga, or whether Harry Winston was really better than Van Cleef and Arpels. When Andy wanted to be positive, he would say, "Well, that's what the book should be about, two celebrities going around talking about caviar and jewels and furs. Shouldn't it, Bob?" When he wanted to be negative, he would say, "I hate her, Bob. This is all your fault for inviting her to that party in Rome."

It was all the more frustrating because we knew there was a great book in the Paulette Goddard story. She wasn't just a retired movie star, she was a real femme fatale, a woman whose personal life was more interesting than anything she had done on the screen, though *Modern Times, The Great Dictator, The Women, Reap the Wild Wind, Kitty, The Diary of a Chambermaid*, and twenty-five other (mostly) hit films were nothing to sneeze at. As far as we could tell, from hints she dropped and tales we heard from people who knew her, she had been involved with some of the major figures of the century, including George Gershwin, Henry Wallace, General George Patton, Diego Rivera, and Willy Brandt, then the chancellor of West Germany.

"Oh, I must get back to my room," she said one day as she rushed off from lunch, "Willy's calling to tell me how the mark's doing." "The mark?" asked Andy. "The Deutschmark, Andy. I've got to know whether I should turn them into Swiss francs in the morning." "Now we know what she does with her time," said Andy.

"If only she would tell us *something*," Andy kept sighing, longing for stories like those Jerry Zipkin had told us about Paulette before we left for Monte Carlo—Jerry and Paulette had been on the same Beverly Hills–New York–South of France circuit for a long time. "Oh, Paulette was a crackerjack," Jerry said. "She was famous in those days for never going on a date for less than a pair of ruby clips." His best story was about Paulette and Dietrich, who had also been in love with Erich Maria Remarque. In fact, he said, Erich was having a hard time choosing between them until Paulette called him in Switzerland, where he was with Dietrich, and issued an ultimatum: her or me. Erich sent Dietrich packing and Paulette joined him in Switzerland to prepare their wedding. But Dietrich had left a hat in the guest-room closet, just to be sure that Paulette knew she had been there first. The punchline was that Paulette saved the hat, and wore it to a party a year or two later at which she knew Dietrich would be. It sounded like the Paulette we knew.

At one lunch, Andy came up with the idea for us to make a list of "all the big Hollywood stars you knew and then we'll read them off and you say one thing about each one." Paulette approved. We made the list and went to lunch again. We started off gently. Lucille Ball? "One of the funniest women on the screen." Well, we knew she didn't really know Lucille Ball. Myrna Loy? "Now, she was funny too, but not many people knew that." A little better, we thought. Marion Davies? "Well, Marion was one of the most beautiful women on the screen." But could she act? asked Andy. Or was she just there because of William Randolph Hearst? "Oh, Andy, let's not make this book banal. You're an artist." He dropped a big one: Greta Garbo? "Well, Greta was one of the most beautiful women on the screen." Now he had it: Marlene Dietrich? "I saw a lot of Marlene. She was one of the most beautiful women on the screen too. They all were. That's what was so *marvelous* about Hollywood then."

Andy was desperate. Fred and I almost enjoyed watching him being tortured for a change, which made Andy even more desperate. He came up with another ploy: "Maybe if I buy Paulette an expensive present, she'll talk." We went to the Cartier branch around the corner from the Hôtel de Paris. The most inexpensive "expensive" thing we could find was a gold swizzle stick for Paulette's champagne, at a little over a thousand dollars. "Does it come in silver?" asked Andy. "We don't sell silver in this store," said the salesman. "Let's get out of here, Bob," said Andy.

We went to Yves Saint Laurent's boutique instead, which was run by his father, who gave us a big greeting. Andy had been asked by a journalist at the premiere who was the most exciting person he had met in Monte Carlo and he had answered, "Yves Saint Laurent's dad." We picked out six of YSL's silk blouses, which cost about two hundred dollars each. That was the year they had bows that tied at the collar. When Andy presented them to Paulette at our next lunch, she gushed like a little girl. "A present for *me?* Oh, Andy, how sweet. I adore presents. How did you know?" Then she announced that the bows would have to be cut off. Did we think Yves's dad could have it done? "But, but, Paulette," said Andy, "that's the whole point of these blouses. I mean, that's the style." "I know it is, Andy," said Paulette. "But where will I wear my jewelry? Under the bow? Or over the bow? It won't look right either way."

"Oh, I hate her," Andy kept saying as we waited for room service that afternoon. "She's the worst."

Meanwhile, Fred was working on the Smiths. Hans and Kardi Smith, the Danish fertilizer king and his wife, a dynamo from Hamburg. The Smiths had recently acquired the grandiose estate of the former King of Montenegro, just next door to Kim d'Estainville's old family house in Cap Martin, a few miles outside Monaco. They had also recently acquired an art gallery in Monte Carlo's only strip shopping center, where they were giving Andy a show of his new Hand-Colored Flower Prints, which were based on Japanese flower arrangements, and look like nothing Andy had ever done before, or since: soft and dainty. Andy called it "My Palm Beach show," and was sure it would be very commercial among the people who never bought Warhols, which it was.

Fred was trying to persuade the Smiths to have their portraits done. The Smiths were trying to persuade Fred to invite all his swell friends to the big ball they were giving after Andy's opening. They particularly wanted their next-door neighbor, Count Kim d'Estainville, who was the biggest snob on the Côte d'Azur, and his steady house guest, Hélène Rochas, who was the second-biggest snob on the Côte d'Azur. Kim and Hélène wouldn't come, but Fred persuaded Kim's sister, Countess Giordano, to come instead, and the Smiths agreed to let Andy take Polaroids of them a few hours before the ball.

We brought Paulette to the ball too, which delighted Kardi Smith. "So she's good for something," said Andy, who had had it with her. In fact, Kardi was so delighted that she loaned us one of her two Rolls-Royces, the white one, to bring Paulette in—"like a big movie star, *ja?*" said Kardi. And Andy softened; after all, it was a dream come true, arriving at a ball in a white Rolls with a glamorous movie star in diamonds. "Gee, you look great," said Andy. "Now which necklace is that?"

The Smith house was situated high above the Mediterranean, with marble terraces and staircases zigzagging down from the house to the sea. Dinner was served on the uppermost terrace, and the entire setup was strung with tiny white lights. Paulette was seated next to Andy and as far as I could tell they were having a good time. Then a slightly tipsy older man tapped her on the shoulder and said, "Pardon me, Paulette Goddard?" in a thick French accent. "Yes," said Paulette, "do I know you?" "Not really, but you saved my life," the old Frenchman answered. "Well, how did I do that?" Andy edged Sony closer. "Well, it was in World War II and I was a soldier at the front and it was terrible, the bombs, the fighting, the war. I was ready to give up on life and throw myself at the Germans' guns. And then another soldier told me the famous story of you and Anatole Litvak at the Brown Derby and how you . . ."

"Oh, he did, did he? I think it's time to go, Andy."

"No, no, no," the Frenchman went on. "It was a beautiful story and you should be proud of it, because it inspired me and so many other soldiers to fight, to live . . ."

"I'm glad it did. And now if you'll excuse me, I think it's time to go, Andy."

Andy wasn't moving, and the Frenchman wouldn't stop. "But it's a wonderful story, the way you went under the table and . . ."

Paulette screamed, "Get me out of here!" Then she jumped up and started running down the zigzagging staircase toward the sea. Andy grabbed Sony and ran after her, and I ran after him, and the Frenchman ran after us all, pleading, "I didn't mean to insult you. You saved my life! When I heard this story of a big movie star giving a blowjob under the table at the Brown Derby, I thought there was a reason to live." Paulette was running with her hands over her ears now, and I was right behind her. Andy had fallen back a bit, to tape record what the old Frenchman was saying.

When we all got to the bottom, Paulette turned around and started running up the zigzagging staircase, and I chased after her, while Andy comforted the old Frenchman by the sea. He was in tears. He had finally met the woman who saved his life and she had run away from him. Paulette wasn't in tears, just fit to be tied. "Get me out of here!" she screamed at me again. Kardi Smith produced the other Rolls-Royce, the black one, and Paulette and I rode back to the Hôtel de Paris in silence. At last, she said, "So now you know the International Rumor, the one Elizabeth Taylor likes to spread about me. And it isn't true, not one bit of it. It's so silly, really."

Andy called me when he got back to the hotel. "Paulette was really mean to that guy," he said. "He was just a crazy fan. That's not such a terrible story. I think I heard it years ago. But it was with another movie star and another movie producer and the guy went under the table, not the girl. Did you tell Paulette that all the kids used to do that at Max's?" I told him that Paulette had said that was the International Rumor, but he didn't believe it. He said it wasn't bad enough. "Maybe *she* was going out with Dietrich, not Erich. Did you ever think of that, Bob?"

On top of all this, the Grand Prix trials started, at five-thirty every morning, right under our windows at the Hôtel de Paris. Fred said that Kim and Hélène had invited Andy and Paulette to watch the actual race from their front-row table on the Hôtel de Paris terrace, which was not only the best place but also the best table. Andy said we could stay a couple of more days. Unfortunately, the Hôtel de Paris said we couldn't, though they extended Paulette's reservation, and found a room for Mick and Bianca Jagger, who checked in the same day we checked out. "Mick's somebody," Andy said, "and I'm nobody." He sounded like he meant it.

Andy and I went to a new high-rise condominium where the Smiths kept an extra apartment, and they loaned Fred another apartment they had in another new building. Staying in the same hotel as Andy was one thing, but staying in the same apartment with him was another. There was no escape. Andy was always there, from the moment I woke up until the moment I went to sleep, nagging me to work harder. And as the race cars roared by our windows there at 5:30 A.M. too, there was more time to work—to think up trick questions for Paulette and to tape record *Philosophy* riffs about "champagne chins and beer bellies."

Andy approached writing the same way he approached painting or making movies: quantitatively. It was never "Write the Sex chapter." It was "Let's do a ninety-minute tape for the Sex chapter." No, Andy. "Okay, let's do forty-five minutes. Just one side." Okay, Andy. So Andy said, "Sex is nothing," and I talked for forty-five minutes about the sex lives of my friends and myself, and then, realizing what I had done, spent another forty-five minutes begging Andy not to drop some choice tidbit at the Grand Prix lunch.

That was another comic disaster. No sooner had we accepted the invitation from Kim and Hélène than Paulette announced that she had accepted an invitation from Massimo Gargia, a playboy whom everyone called Count Mozzarella for some reason, to lunch at his table, with ex-Empress Soraya of Iran, and that she expected Andy to sit with *her*. He did, and I sat with Kim and Hélène, who made a point of noting that it must be difficult for Andy to see the race from a table so far back.

After the first course, I went over to Andy and told him that I thought it would make a world of difference if he came over to say hello to Hélène, not immediately, but in five or ten minutes, and give her one of his bet stubs. "Say you bought it for her, and you hope she wins," I said. "Gee, thanks, Bob," said Andy, "that's a really good idea. I wish you were at this table with me. I can't go to these things without you or Fred. I do everything wrong. I called Soraya's lady-in-waiting Soraya's mother, and everybody laughed at me. Then I asked if a lady-in-waiting was like a maid, and they all laughed again.''

As instructed, Andy came over in a few minutes, with a bet stub signed, ''To Hélène, Love Andy.'' When he returned, Kim said, ''Say what you will, but Andy Warhol is a real gentleman. I'm sure it was Paulette Goddard, who's just a typical Hollywood type, who was impressed by Soraya, not Andy.''

23

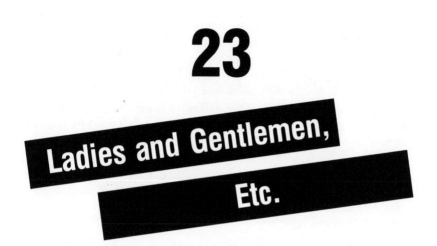

Ladies and Gentlemen, Etc.

Paulette went back to Switzerland. Andy, Fred, Ariel de Ravenel, and I were driven through the Alps to Turin, or Torino, to see a protégé of Iolas whom we called Anselmino of Torino, because he looked more like a hairdresser than an art dealer. Andy had done an edition of one hundred prints of the Man Ray portrait for him and he had slipped in an extra thirty trial proofs. Andy complained, but he signed them the morning after we got there. Now Anselmino wanted to commission a larger edition of prints, and maybe paintings too. His idea: drag queens. Andy said drag queens were out, but Anselmino persisted, suggesting portraits of Candy, Jackie, and Holly. Andy said Candy was dead, and Jackie and Holly would drive him crazy, asking for more money every time they heard one had sold. "Can't you think of another idea?" said Andy. Anselmino said he would.

At dinner, Anselmino pushed his drag-queen idea again. His argument was constantly interrupted by the alarm going off on his parked Mercedes. He said it was Communists trying to rob it and sent his assistant, Dino, out on the street to chase them. Then he returned to his *idée fixe:* They shouldn't be beautiful transvestites who could pass for women, but funny-looking ones, with heavy beards, who were obviously men trying to pass. "Well, maybe we could do it," said Andy eventually. "We can put a wig on Bob. He has a heavy beard." "Bravissimo," said Anselmino of Torino.

"I'm not doing it," I said, the second Anselmino was out of sight.

"But I'll give you one," Andy said, careful not to specify one what— big painting? little painting? print? autographed Polaroid?

"I don't want one."

"You can give it to your mother."

"Andy!!!!!" I screamed across a deserted seventeenth-century piazza.

"Leave Bob alone," said Fred, trying to calm things down.

"Maybe Ronnie Cutrone can do it. He has a heavy beard," said Andy, stirring things up again. Ronnie Cutrone, a budding artist, who first came to the Factory as a dancer with the Velvet Underground, had been promoted to Andy's art assistant in 1973, when Glenn O'Brien left *Interview*.

We fought all the way to Paris, Andy telling me it would be fun to have my portrait done in drag, me telling Andy I really didn't want to be immortalized quite that way. At last he said, "Oh, I know what we should do. We should get those nutty-looking drag queens from that awful place we went to that night, remember? The one with all the blacks and Puerto Ricans, where I was robbed. What was it called?"

"The Gilded Grape."

"What a great name. Well, you can go there and get the drag queens for me, because I can't go there, it's too crazy. And those drag queens are so dumb they won't know they're posing for me, so we won't have to pay them a lot. Unless you tell them it's me, Bob."

"I won't tell them it's you, Andy."

"Well, we have to be careful. You never know. And I was robbed there. But we'll be on easy street if this deal with Anselmino goes through."

The Gilded Grape was a bizarre little bar on Eighth Avenue and West 45th Street, frequented by black and Hispanic transvestites (average height: six feet two) and white truck-driver types (average weight: 275 pounds) who picked them up. We'd visited it a few weeks earlier with Kenny Jay Lane and a group of titled Parisians, sightseeing. But the people they had come to stare at stared at them. The ladies tucked their necklaces under their collars and turned their rings wrong way around. Andy hid his Brownie's shopping bag, containing the usual Polaroid camera, film, flashbulbs, and tape cassettes, plus chapter one of the *Philosophy* book, under his chair. That was the last he saw of it.

Now we were on our way to Paris, where Marie-Hélène and Guy de Rothschild were giving a garden party at Ferrières, their weekend castle, to celebrate the engagement of their son, David, to Olympia Aldobrandini, the beautiful seventeen-year-old daughter of Count and Countess Aldobrandini of Venice. As we turned the last curve of their ten-mile driveway, we saw a fifty-foot portrait of David and Olympia hanging from the parapets. "Why didn't they ask me to do their portrait, Fred?" asked Andy. "It's a nineteenth-century painting they blew up," Fred explained, "and they just cut the heads out and stuck photos of David and Olympia on top." "That's what I mean," said Andy. "They could have just stuck my portraits on top. Did you ever think of asking Marie-Hélène that?"

A brigade of footmen dressed up like the Vatican's Swiss Guards lined the staircase, and just inside the entrance a footman asked your name, then

passed it to a second footman, who bellowed it out: "La Princesse de Polignac . . . le Prince de Furstenberg . . . le Prince et la Princesse de
Beauvau-Craon . . . le Comte d'Estainville . . . Madame Hélène Rochas
. . . le Baron de Redé . . . Monsieur et Madame John Heinz . . . Made-
moiselle Bettina Graziani . . . Ses altesses royales le Prince et la Princesse
Michel de Grèce . . . le Baron et la Baronne de Waldner . . . le Comte et
la Comtesse de Brandolini . . . Monsieur Andy Warhol . . . Monsieur Bob
Colacello . . ." It did give me a bit of a rush.

Marie-Hélène, in a flowered chiffon garden-party dress by Saint Laurent,
stood at the head of the receiving line, with her hairdresser, the legendary
Alexandre, right behind her, adjusting the pearl-tipped pins that kept her hairdo
up. Next were Baron Guy, Olympia in a white cotton garden-party dress by
Valentino, David, and the Aldobrandinis. We shook hands with them all and
went through the château to the rear entrance, over which another fifty-foot-
high portrait of the engagement couple hung. "It's a multiple, Fred," said
Andy, "just like my portraits. And I could have made them look so much
more beautiful. David looks fat." Fred dashed off with Ariel.

Just then a pack of paparazzi poured out of the house and into the
garden, pursuing Jackie Onassis, sans Ari. "Hi, Andy," she shouted breath-
lessly as she hurried by, looking for a hideout. "She didn't say, 'Hi, Bob,'
Bob," said Andy. I was feeling a bit out of place as it was. My new black
YSL suit had been perfect for the premiere in Monte Carlo, but was too
formal for a garden party. Andy was wearing a black jacket over his blue
jeans—the same thing he had worn everywhere from the Baron de Redé's
lunch to Princess Grace's reception. "I'm not dressed right, either," he said,
to reassure me. Then he added, "But I'm an artist, so I can get away with
it, right?" to throw me off again. Fred was wearing just the right thing, an
impeccably cut white suit. "Fred always looks right," Andy pointed out,
in case I hadn't noticed.

Despite the teasing, I enjoyed being with Andy at this kind of up-there
extravaganza. He didn't miss a trick and he brought it down to earth.
"There's Sydney Chaplin. Should we run over and ask him if Paulette was
a good stepmother? Oh, and look, there's poor Virginia Chambers. Do you
think she came to ask Marie-Hélène not to evict her? That's the Vicomtesse
de Noailles, the really old one over there. She was in Proust and Cocteau
loved her. You know, Bob, you went to college. I wish she would trade me
some furniture for her portrait. Should we run over and pop the question?
God, doesn't Michael York look handsome? But his wife never lets him out
of her sight for a second. That's Marc Bohan over there, you know, from
Dior. The one counting his dresses. He must be upset because everybody's
in Saint Laurent, right? That funny-looking lady in the black hat is Mrs.
Lallanne. She and her husband make those sheep that everybody collects.
It's *art,* Bob, isn't it? Remind me to ask Fred if we should ask them to trade.
There's Egon with Princess Minnie. I can never say her name right. It's

something like Bobo-Crayon." It's Beauvau-Craon. "Everyone says Egon
wants to marry her, now that Diane's going out with that Italian TV guy.
The one with the Polish name. There's Philip Niarchos. Should we say hello
to him? I wonder why he didn't bring Mary Russell, you know, the fashion
girl we met in Monte Carlo. Oh, I know, because Giovanni Volpi is here,
and Mary just broke up with him for Philip, or maybe Giovanni just broke
up with her for Marina Schiano. Oh, don't tell Fred I told you that. Oh, did
you get a load of São's brooch, the one that looks like a bunch of flowers—
diamond flowers, Bob. I love the way it blows in the breeze. It must be an
old Cartier. Or maybe Van Cleef. You could be on easy street, Bob. But she
was with Pierre. He never comes to these things. This must be really important, right? But then the first person I ran right into was Count Mozzarella, so maybe it's not. And *we're here,* so how important can it be, right?
Oh, let's do who's not here—that's how you can tell if it's a good party or
not, by how important the left-out people are. Givenchy isn't here and he's
important, right? Marisa Berenson isn't here and she's important, right?
Well, she's not here because she went out with David before Olympia came
along, so that's different. . . . Oh, I forgot to tell you the best thing. When
you went over to the bar to get a drink, I had the best time with that snotty
French kid who used to be in love with Robert Mapplethorpe. He told me
that Bettina's new boyfriend used to fuck his wife, while he hung out on
street corners picking up boys. Isn't that great? You've got to do our *Modern
Marriage* script, Bob. And he told me that he had to do it every night with
somebody different. Isn't that fascinating? I told him I had to do it every
night with nobody different. Is that a good line for the *Philosophy* book,
Bob?''

    That was Andy: standing at the edge of an up-there party, chattering it
down into the gutter, then lifting it up again and turning it into work. People
always asked me, "What do you and Andy talk about at parties? I can never
seem to get him to utter a word." Now they know.

    Unfortunately, we were no longer staying at the Hôtel Crillon. The
apartment on Rue de Cherche-Midi was ready. Well, the gold faucets only
ran cold water, and the double-height French windows facing the Brandolini's garden were covered with sheets, as were the sofas and chairs, and there
were no lamps, just candelabras, lots of them, and candles, lots of them
too. Fred considered this quasi-decorating job, which he did mostly himself,
"romantic." Andy considered it a lot cheaper than putting the three of us
up at the Crillon. I hated it, especially since Fred had a chic little bedroom
done in hand-painted paneling on the top floor, and Andy had a sumptuous
big bedroom done in gilded paneling on the first floor, and I had a disgusting
little bedroom done in cement paneling in the basement, right under the
glass-tiled floor of the dining room, which Andy stomped on early each

morning to wake me up. "Time to get up, Bob. We're late for lunch," he'd shout, around 8 A.M. And to make matters worse, from my point of view, the first appliance we bought was a typewriter. "Time to type up the Sex tape we made in Monte Carlo, Bob. Why don't you just sit down at the typewriter and type up fifty pages real quick on *Modern Marriage,* Bob?"

And while I typed, Andy sat there chewing gum, popping chocolates in and out, rattling on about whether Fred was really in love with Ariel and how I should call São and seduce her into commissioning the history of her hairdos. "Just stick it to her, just stick it in her," he'd go on, proud of his play on words, insisting that I write it down to stick in the *Philosophy* book. If he told me I could be on easy street once, he told me a million times—there was no one like Andy to take a tired cliché and turn it into a broken record.

Did he mean what he was saying? Or did he just like to hear himself talk? Was he filling some desperate hole of loneliness? Or torturing me into submission? Did he need to believe his kids were the sought-after Romeos he wasn't? Or was he trivializing our personal lives so that he could keep control? It was so confusing, and when I wasn't laughing at the absurdity of it all, I wanted to cry or scream or shout, and sometimes I did. But that meant Andy won, and the one thing Andy always wanted was to win. When I said I wanted to stay in one night and curl up with a good book, instead of going to yet another dinner at yet another fancy restaurant with yet another variation on the In group list, he said, "You gotta live life to write it, Bob." When I went out and lived life one night, all night, he said, "You're never going to be a writer, Bob, because you're more interested in kicking up your heels."

After two and a half weeks on the road with Andy—Paris, Monte Carlo, Torino, Paris again—I was ready to go home. Or anywhere, as long as Andy wasn't there.

A month later, Fred proposed my going along on another European trip—more and more, he liked having me there to free him from constantly attending to Andy. Fred made this trip sound like a vacation: two weeks in July on the Italian Riviera. Andy was going to be "artist-in-residence," Fred said, "at a really up-there artists' colony run by a marvelous old Swiss woman." He hadn't been there himself, but Paloma Picasso and Nicky Weymouth were coming along as Andy's "art assistants—think of what fun you'll have with those two." And when I wasn't having fun with the girls, I'd be dreaming up clever new maxims for the *Philosophy* book with Andy. He made it sound like Aristotle and Plato going off to summer camp with Jane Russell and Marilyn Monroe.

But where was *he* going to be while *I* was having so much fun in the sun? "I'll be just down the road," he explained, "stirring up some business in Monte Carlo. I suppose I'll have to spend a lot of time with Hans and Kardi Smith. It's just over the Italian border, this art colony, in a little town called Boissano. I'm sure it's charming. And when you finish up there, we'll have a few nights at Jimmy'z kicking up our heels.'' Andy's clichés were catching.

Boissano, a little town with one church and one pizzeria, was two hours further from Monte Carlo than Fred had estimated. And the artists' colony really was up there—halfway between the beach and the mountains, too far from either for a cooling dip or a refreshing hike, among hills covered in fruit orchards and swarming with flies, which had a peculiar habit of drowning in our wine glasses. As for that marvelous old Swiss woman, she served us polenta three times a day and forced us to share every meal with the paying guests, who asked questions like "Why did you paint Marilyn Monroe's lips orange?"

The artist and his three assistants resided in one large dormitory room, with one small bathroom, above the "museum," which housed a (Pablo) Picasso, a Chagall, a Magritte, and a Miró, which meant it was locked up tight at night, from the outside, with us in it.

Fred had been right about one thing: Nicky Weymouth and Paloma Picasso, who hardly knew each other before Boissano, were both fun. Otherwise they were opposite in almost every way. Paloma was dark and low-key, Nicky was fair and high-strung. Nicky, who later briefly married Kenny Jay Lane, lived in London near the Jaggers and the Gettys. She gave constant parties, drawing everyone from David Hockney to Lady Diana Cooper. Paloma was doing her first collection of jewelry, for the Athens goldsmith Zolotas, a friend of Iolas. And she had just starred in her first (and only) movie, an artsy French-Czech horror called *Immoral Tales*. She played a Countess Dracula type, and Andy never stopped teasing her about the ads featuring a naked Paloma in a tub of virgins' blood. Paloma just laughed, a great laugh, big and crackly and real.

Andy had a thing about Paloma. And Paloma's father. As we sat around on our cots in the museum dormitory, he'd grill her for hours about her father, with Sony propped up on a pillow. What was Picasso really like? Nice? Mean? Funny? Smart? Did he paint as soon as he woke up, or did he wait until later in the day? How long did it take him to do a painting? How many did he do in a week? A month? When Paloma came up with a number, Andy would moan, "Oh, I've got to paint more. I've got to paint faster." It was all about quantity, including the question Andy could never resist: How big was his cock? Paloma laughed that off too. Andy persisted, "I mean, didn't you ever take a bath with your father when you were a little girl?" "Yes," said Paloma, "in blood."

Andy couldn't get enough. What did he eat, what did he wear, how much money did he make? Paloma said that her father liked making money and liked spending money, especially on comfort and luxuries for himself.

She said one of Picasso's favorite guests was Jean Cocteau. "He would bring my father all the latest art-world and society gossip from Paris. My father liked to hear about those people, though he didn't like to see them. My brother Claude and I liked Cocteau a lot too. He was good with children, like you, Andy."

"Oh, really? I'd rather be like your father."

Paloma only talked so much about her father to please Andy. She wasn't the sort of celebrity child who bragged; neither did she recoil at his name. Her father was her father, and that was that.

Andy was sure she was much more affected by her father than she let on, and a couple of years later when he met her husband-to-be, Rafael Lopez Cambil, an Argentine playwright, Andy said the same thing over and over. "He looks just like her father. That's why Paloma fell in love with him."

At the end of our first week in Boissano, Andy had had enough. "Call Fred and tell him to come and get us," he ordered. "I'll give the money back, if I have to." Now, *that* was a new line. Fred came scurrying down the coast, full of stories about how hard he had been working in the restaurants and discos of Monte Carlo. We wanted to string him up from a fruit tree and let the flies finish him off.

Fred had Anselmino of Torino along, who had a portrait for Andy to do in Genoa on the way to Monte Carlo: a twenty-year-old Italian ballerina, whom Andy had never seen before and never saw thereafter. It always amazed me when people commissioned Andy cold like that. And as more and more dealers in Europe pushed the portraits, there were more and more clients whose total relationship with their portraitist was fifteen minutes. Anselmino had another present for Andy that day: He had lined up the financing, several hundred thousand dollars, for the Drag Queen series, and a museum to show it in, the Palazzo di Diamante, a municipal art center in Ferrara. As we sped down the coast to Monaco, Andy begged me to pose in a wig. "We'll just put on a little makeup," he promised. "Anselmino wants your beard to show. Don't you, Anselmino?" Anselmino said "Sí," and so, after the excruciating boredom of Boissano, did I.

That night, we celebrated Fred's thirty-first birthday and our freedom with a long table of Riviera rich kids at Le Pirate restaurant. It was the most expensive on the entire Côte d'Azur because after dinner everybody would throw their plates and glasses over their shoulders, smashing them Greek-style. As the rich kids got into it, Andy started calculating the cost—$5 a glass, $10 a plate. "This is going to be expensive, Bob," he told me. "Don't throw anything. It's too silly." I picked up the kerosene lantern on our table. "What are you doing, Bob?!?" And I threw it over my shoulder. Everybody screamed, especially Andy. His bill, with an extra $150 for the lantern, came to $2,000.

*   *   *

I did pose for Andy when we got back to New York, in a blonde wig. Fortunately, Andy decided it was unusable. Ronnie Cutrone, Vincent, and I found most of the models at the Gilded Grape. We would ask them to pose for "a friend" for $50 per half hour. The next day, they'd appear at the Factory and Andy, whom we never introduced by name, would take their Polaroids. And the next time we saw them at the Gilded Grape, they invariably would say, "Tell your friend I do a lot more for fifty bucks."

When the paintings, retitled Ladies and Gentlemen, were shown in Ferrara in 1975, Andy took me along for the opening, and for a minute I wished that my portrait had worked out: They looked so stunning in the High Renaissance Palazzo di Diamante. It was Andy's second-most-beautiful exhibition, after the Maos at the Musée Galliera in Paris. The left-wing Italian art critics went wild, writing that Andy Warhol had exposed the cruel racism inherent in the American capitalist system, which left poor black and Hispanic boys no choice but to prostitute themselves as transvestites. At the press conference in Ferrara, a reporter wanted to know if Andy was a Communist. In Italy in the mid-seventies, the expected answer was yes. "Am I a Communist, Bob?" said Andy. "Well," I said, "you just painted Willy Brandt's portrait, but you're trying to get Imelda Marcos." "That's my answer," said Andy, as the translators scratched their bearded chins. But back at the hotel that night, he said, "Maybe I should do real Communist paintings next. They would sell a lot in Italy." Thus was conceived the 1977 Hammers and Sickles series.

The Ladies and Gentlemen, or Drag Queen, paintings, like so many of Andy's great seventies works, were never shown in the United States. Two years after his death, however, one large painting was auctioned at Christie's New York from the estate of Jean-Michel Basquiat, fetching the highest price of anything in that sale: $176,000.

"I think it's Spiro Agnew, Bob." Andy and I were waiting for our flight to Paris in Pan Am's first-class lounge at JFK, in October 1974. So was the former Vice President of the United States, who had resigned in disgrace the year before, followed by Nixon that August. They were the two most reviled figures in American politics at the time, but that wasn't going to stop Andy. Or me. Fred was off checking some rolled-up portraits through customs, and Jed was getting us drinks from the bar. "Gee, I never knew Agnew was so handsome," said Andy. I knew what he was getting to: "Why don't you go ask him for his autograph, Bob?" I said I didn't want to bother him. "Uh, it could mean a raise, Bob."

I gulped down two Courvoisiers and, with Andy's Magic Marker and my *Time* magazine in hand, headed for Agnew. "Excuse me, sir," I fumbled, "but I'm traveling with Andy Warhol and we're big admirers of yours, and we were wondering if you would give us your autograph." I held out the Magic Marker and the *Time* magazine. Agnew gave me a stern look. "I'd be delighted to give you my autograph, but not on that magazine." How could I forget that it was *Time* that had led the charge against him?

I ran back to where Andy was sitting, and said I needed another magazine. "How about *Modern Screen?*" "As long as it's not political." "Here, hurry, before Fred gets back. And see if he'll write, 'To Andy.' " I ran back to Agnew, who produced a gold fountain pen from his gray suit. "Do you think you could put, 'To Andy'?" "My pleasure," he said, signing his name with a flourish, across the cover photograph of Liz Taylor and Richard Burton, together yet again.

Andy was in seventh heaven. I could do no wrong for at least twenty-four hours. Fred was furious. "Why are you and Bob sitting there like two cats who just drank the milk?" he wanted to know. Then he noticed Agnew on the other side of the lounge. "Andy! You got Bob to go over and ask for his autograph, didn't you? Andy! If Hitler came back from the dead, you'd get Bob to ask for his autograph, wouldn't you? And you'd do it, Bob, wouldn't you?"

"You never let me ask people for autographs, Fred," said Andy.

"Oh, God," moaned Fred, "I can see this is going to be a great trip."

"You wouldn't let me ask Rebozo that time at the Crillon, you wouldn't let me ask Tricia Nixon at Trader Vic's, you . . ."

"Andy!!!!"

In Paris, we went to the Cherche-Midi apartment, still exquisitely undone, Fred Hughes style. "Isn't Fred ever going to get the furniture upholstered?" I asked.

"This is chic, Bob," said Andy. "It's the old-money look."

"I wish we could have the new-money look."

"Oh, I know," sighed Andy, "hot water."

"Broadloom."

"Instead of splinters in my feet."

"Lightbulbs."

"Instead of worrying about Fred passing out with the candles burning."

"Can't I stay in a hotel, Andy? I hate that room in the basement. I hate pissing in the sink."

"Pissing in the sink is chic, Bob."

"Isabel Eberstadt told me about a very reasonable hotel right between here and São's house. I could get the smallest room."

Andy gave in, and from then on I usually stayed at the Hôtel de l'Abbaye when we came to Paris, sometimes as often as ten times a year, to and from Germany, Italy, Belgium, and Switzerland. On this trip, for example, we were on our way to Milan, for the Iolas Gallery opening of the Man Ray portraits and prints. And Paulette was meeting us there, to get some work done on the book, which had been on hold while she summered at the Villa Remarque.

In the meantime, there was plenty to do in Paris. Every morning, I'd stop at the bakery across from the apartment and buy fresh rolls and bread, enough for an army, because Andy always said it wasn't enough. He liked to have extra to throw to the pigeons in the garden. He'd make his own toast and slather it with fresh fruit jams from Angelina's—no butter, it was "bad for the gallbladder"—standing in the kitchen shivering in his shirttails and socks. Then he'd climb back into bed with his breakfast, and moan and groan about how hard it was to get going in the morning, all the while coming up with people for me to call about ads, covers, lunches, dinners, interspersed with admonitions to ask Fred first. "You better wake Fred up," he'd say. "But be careful because I think he has somebody in bed with him. I heard noises when he came home in the middle of the night." I'd shout up to Fred, who would stagger down the stairs alone.

We were usually out of the apartment by noon, shopping our way to lunch. Andy seemed to know every antique-jewelry shop on the Left Bank, and he'd pop in and out of them, asking if they had any "really big brooches from the forties, maybe citrine or, uh, aquamarine?" Big was always better with Andy and he'd rather have a huge garnet than a tiny ruby, though he'd take that too, in trade for art, if he could. After buying the latest jackets and shirts, more for Jed than Andy, at YSL's men's boutique on the Place Saint Sulpice, we'd taxi over to the Right Bank and hit the Faubourg St. Honoré and the Avenue Montaigne: first the dog store for Archie's present, usually a new hand-tooled leather collar; then Guerlain for Andy's perfumes, usually special tuberose and narcissus blends; Cerruti for Jed's polo shirts; Hermès for Fred's briefcases; Fauchon for Andy's candies; Weston on the Champs Élysees for their Italian cowboy boots; and on to the Ungaro and Valentino boutiques for men, where we got good discounts and we all bought blazers and corduroys—except Fred, who had even those made to order in London or New York. Everywhere we went, Andy handed out copies of *Interview* and I tried to come up with a polite way to ask for an ad on top of the discount.

In the afternoons, the apartment would turn into the Paris Factory, and we'd have meetings over tea and champagne with William Burke, Fred's Paris art assistant, and Joel le Bon, *Interview*'s new Paris correspondent. Photographers and models came by with their portfolios, and we'd dream up *Interview* assignments for them. Andy wanted to use everybody, but Fred and I were more selective. Clara Saint would bring reporters from *Marie Claire* or French *Vogue* and we'd all sit around making up answers for Andy, which Clara would then translate into French, emitting little squeaks of laughter when she realized what she was actually saying. And Andy would call Vincent in New York: "Did you turn the faucet in the bathroom off?

Did you make sure those girls up at *Interview* put their cigarette butts out? Did you get the check from Anselmino yet? Fred, we didn't get the check yet. You better call Milan and say we're not coming.''

The check came, and we went on to Milan, where everyone was waiting for Andy at the Iolas Gallery—including fifty paparazzi and Paulette Goddard, looking icy in a white fox cape fringed in matching foxtails, and a white sequined suit with Dali's diamond-and-ruby "Lips" brooch pinned to the lapel. "Ohhh, I've always wanted one of those," sighed Andy, zeroing in on the Dali. He handed Paulette a miniature Mao painting wrapped in a page of *Interview,* and when she saw what it was, she melted. "Oh, I've always wanted one of these." The book was on, and so was Sony.

Paulette, Andy, Jed, and I piled into a chauffeured Mercedes and went on to Andy's second Milan opening, of the Hand-Colored Flowers, at the Galeria Multi-Centro, chased all the way by fifty paparazzi. As Andy and Paulette stepped out of the car, Jed stepped on Paulette's dragging cape, tearing off a foxtail or two. He picked them up and gave them to her, and it was one of those cases where honesty didn't pay. "My poor little babies," she cried, stroking the torn-off tails as if they really were her pets, or kids.

There was a fur shop across the street, and before we knew what was happening, Paulette was heading for it. Andy, Jed, and I, plus the fifty paparazzi, dashed across the street after her. "I'd like to try on that coat in the window," Paulette ordered the salesgirl, pointing at a white Russian lynx. "That's the most expensive fur there is," whispered Andy nervously. "What if Paulette wants me to pay?" Paulette tried it on and asked for the price. "Sixty million lire," said the salesgirl. "Seventy-five thousand dollars," said Paulette, with her calculator mind. "That's not bad for white Russian lynx. It's the most luxurious fur in the world."

"Oh, I know," said Andy, as white as the coat. Paulette pirouetted in the triple mirror. Andy turned a whiter shade of pale. "Well," said Paulette, "whattaya think, Andy?"

"Oh, uh, it's a little short," said Andy, "isn't it, Bob?" I said it was. Jed said it was. The salesgirl said that was the style this year. You could have heard a foxtail drop, if it hadn't been for the paparazzi pounding on the window, shouting for Andy and Paulette to come out. Paulette pirouetted one more time. "It *is* short," she said, sliding out of the coat. "That was a close call, Bob," whispered Andy, regaining some of his normal color, off-white.

Andy had met his match in Paulette. Like him, she was an expert psychological torturer, a master manipulator of the first rank, a world-class hoarder of gems, gold, cash—and, in her case, furs. "I always say," she always said, "if you get one great fur coat every year, in twenty years you'll have a great closet." And Andy always said, "I hope she doesn't think this is the year she's getting one from me." Paulette had met her match in Andy.

We were in Milan three nights, and every night a fashionable industrialist gave a party full of industrious fashionables in an ancient palazzo decorated in the most up-to-the-minute style. Under gold-leaf ceilings there were sleek suede banquettes, oversized stainless-steel coffee tables bearing exotic orchids in terra-cotta pots, all-white Fontana canvases artfully slashed and torn. Andy and Paulette always sat together, with Sony as a chaperone, wooing and cooing over her jewels, the modern art around them, the white truffles that the rich Milanese grated with abandon over everything from pasta to salad. Clever Daniela Morera, *Interview*'s new Italian editor, got them all to advertise: The Milanese designers were our first real advertising base. She also got Armani, Versace, and Krizia to have their portraits done by Andy.

At one of these parties, Anselmino's artist sidekick, who called herself Carolrama, announced that she was a palm reader and tried to take Andy's hand. He recoiled, saying that he had a better idea: She should read Paulette's for the book. "And then she'll do yours, Andy, to go with it," said Paulette. "Oh, okay," muttered Andy into his button-down collar. Carolrama took Paulette's hand in hers, and with Daniela Morera translating and Andy taping, pronounced her "strong, cynical, and cruel—to others and to yourself." Then it was Andy's turn. "Oh, Bob will do it for me," he said, "and in the book we'll say his hand was mine."

That was the beginning of the end of *HER*. Paulette had been opening up in Milan, telling Andy sparkly Aldous Huxley and H. G. Wells stories. But after Andy got me to have my hand read as his, she went back to talking about where to get the best caviar in Milan, the best foie gras in Zürich, the best smoked salmon in New York. Paulette and Andy were too equally matched for creative collaboration, which obviously requires give and take, not tit for tat.

24

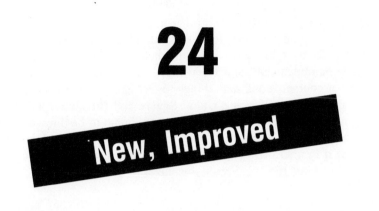

New, Improved

Paul America had been a silver-Factory Superstar. Tall, blond, and handsome, he had appeared in a single movie (like Valerie Solanis), playing the title role in *My Hustler,* shot on Fire Island in the summer of 1965. Now, nine summers later, he was back, pressing the buzzer at 33 Union Square West, an alumnus coming to call. He was buzzed in on the strength of his name, but the minute he came through the bulletproof door we knew it was a mistake. He was unrecognizable: huge, bearded, beer-bellied, in overalls and faded flannel shirt, wild eyes roving until they met Andy's and locked into a terrifying stare. "Oh, hi," said Andy, "gee." Paul America stood there, staring. "Oh," said Andy gently, "I'll tell Pat you're here." He walked toward the back room as quickly as he could without running. Paul America stood there, staring at Andy's disappearing back, like a ticking time bomb. And then he turned and left. And Vincent shouted, "You can come out now, Andy."

It was time to move on. We needed more space, we needed more security. In August 1974, we found both just across Union Square, at the corner of Broadway and East 17th Street. The third Factory occupied the entire third floor of 860 Broadway, a six-story brick building that curved with the corner and extended through the middle of the block to East 18th Street, where there was a rear entrance with a freight elevator and a second staircase. This meant that Andy could escape undetected if disgruntled Superstars and off-the-wall fans came knocking at the bulletproof door we took across the square with us. We also installed a proper security system in the new place, with closed-circuit TVs, instead of trying to pass off Keith Son-

nier's conceptual video sculpture as high-tech protection. We tried to get the
landlord, who was Larry Rivers's brother-in-law, to hire an armed guard for
the lobby, but he said the other tenants would object, and Andy said it was
too expensive for us to hire our own. Nonetheless, we were leaving the place
where Andy had been shot, and we all felt less afraid.

Andy, of course, found new things to fret about in the new space: the
curving wall of windows facing Union Square and Broadway, which let in
lots of light and air, might also allow a rock or bomb to be thrown from the
street. "It's only three floors up," said Andy, "and everybody can see right
in and know if I'm here. Did you ever think of that, Fred?" That didn't stop
Andy from making the windowsill his favorite place to sit and read the
newspapers.

Another "security" measure, which only Fred Hughes could have
dreamed up, was to hire foreign receptionists. Jane Forth, who retired to
have a second child, Branch Emerson, was replaced first by Frank Waill, a
Parisian friend of the Beauvau-Craons whose French was far superior to his
English, and then by Laura Moltedo, a Venetian friend of the Rattazzis who
took the job to *learn* English. This ruse actually worked: The troublesome
old Superstars stopped calling after having to spell their names four or five
times before Monsieur Waill announced that Monsieur Warhol wasn't in,
and when Signorina Laura answered the phone with *"Ciao,"* most of the
nut cases assumed they had the wrong number and hung up.

The move's only downside was moving itself. There were two basic
problems: Andy didn't want to hire professional movers, insisting that "you
kids" were perfectly capable of lugging things like the brass-and-marble
Normandie desk across Union Square, past the junkies and winos, in the
middle of August. When we said we weren't, he said we were lazy, and he
didn't want to move anyway. He also expected us to carry the hefty sofas
and chairs, the baby grand piano, the giant Campbell's Soupcan, the movie
screen and projectors, the video and editing equipment, the desks, filing
cabinets, bookshelves, and typewriters, the rolled-up canvases, stretched
portraits, and hundreds of portfolios of prints, the thousands of back issues
of *Interview,* and all the tenth-floor office furniture, plus the alpine stacks
of corrugated boxes filled with Polaroids, Sony tapes, manuscript pages,
financial and legal records, old magazines and books, canceled stamps, used
batteries, movie stills. . . . That was the second major problem, Andy didn't
want to throw anything out.

Vincent suffered the most through this ordeal, as Fred was off to Monte
Carlo again in August, Pat Hackett and I were out in Montauk rushing to
meet a September 15 deadline on the *Philosophy* book, and Jed had his
hands full at home. As moving day approached, with Andy still insisting that we could do it all ourselves, Fred landed from the Côte d'Azur and
overruled him. In retaliation, Andy wouldn't hire painters for the walls
that Fred had designed to separate *Interview* from the Factory proper. "I

never wanted walls,'' Andy said. ''You'd rather have all the messengers who come and go to *Interview* watch you paint?'' asked Fred. ''I could paint behind a screen,'' replied Andy. ''Right, Andy, you do that,'' said Fred, leaving to check out the work on the new place. ''You should carry something if you're going across the street, Fred,'' said Andy. ''It'll be one less thing for the movers to move. They charge by the hour you know.'' ''I *know, Andy!!''*

By the end of September, everything was in its place in the new Factory. Off the elevator was a small bare vestibule, and through the bulletproof door was another larger one, where the alleged Cecil B. DeMille Great Dane stood beside a massive white marble 1920 console, and over that hung an Art Deco poster by Jean Dupas advertising a 1925 furniture exhibition in bold letters: *Palais de la Nouveauté.* Twin sets of tall glass doors, designed by Fred, with raw wood frames and sleek brass handles, opened to the *Interview* offices and to the Factory. On the Factory's vast black reception desk, made by combining the two fake slate tops and their supporting file cabinets from the old Factory, sat a large wood bust of Leonardo da Vinci, said to be the figurehead of an old ship. At either end sat Frank Waill, making Holly Woodlawn spell her name out for the tenth time, and Chris Hemphill, typing up the tapes of Paulette Goddard in Monte Carlo.

To the right was a gilded Art Deco salon suite—sofa, two armchairs, and pouf—designed by Maurice Dufréne in 1925, and upholstered in tapestry by Jean Beaumont. Beyond that, at the far end of the front room, was Fred's office, partially hidden behind high black screens made from the same fake slate. It looked more like a decorator's shop than a manager's office. His desk was always buried under mountains of chic clutter, his latest finds from the *antiquaires* of Paris, rolled-up American Indian blankets, pyramids of marbled paper boxes from Venice, portfolios of old photographs and fashion illustrations, bills, contracts, date books, letters, engraved invitations . . . ''You've got to clean your desk up, Fred,'' Andy would say when a crucial document was missing. ''Lady Ann Lambton is coming from London to do it for me'' was Fred's typical reply.

To the left of the reception desk was the *Normandie* desk with a phone for Andy, who continued to use everybody else's phone and everybody else's desk, especially Vincent's. Vincent's office looked very much like a manager's office, with a wall of file cabinets bursting with legal documents and tax records. Andy never nagged Vincent about cleaning up his desk because the mess was usually made by Andy. There was always an open cardboard box on the floor, a time capsule in progress. In fact, Vincent's ''private'' office was the antechamber through which everyone passed on their way to the dining room.

This was the *pièce de résistance* of the third Factory, where Andy and Fred could finally show off all the treasures from their Paris shopping sprees, the Art Deco masterpieces that Andy called ''used furniture'' and ''*L'Amour* props.'' The former tenant of this Factory had been Sperry & Hutchison of S&H Green Stamps, and their chairman had built himself a splendid office with an antique pink marble fireplace and carved oak paneling brought over from a baronial English estate.

It was the ideal setting for the large oval dining table of Macassar ebony and burled amboyna, and the twelve birch armchairs upholstered in red leather, all by Emile-Jacques Ruhlmann. There was also a Ruhlmann sideboard, with a white marble top, that we used as a bar. Hanging above that was a late nineteenth-century Orientaliste painting in a Carlo Bugatti frame, which matched a Bugatti pedestal done in the same Moorish-fantasy style. The fireplace was set in an alcove, and as there was no way Andy was ever going to allow a fire to be lit, Fred blocked it with several Somali ancestor-worship poles, and above the mantelpiece he hung an enormous moosehead, an office-warming present from John Richardson, who had himself received it as a gift, but couldn't get it through his door. The only other painting in the room was ''The Wind,'' a lush Scottish Victorian oil of two girls leading a goat through a forest.

That was the essence of Fred's decorating style: Nothing matched and yet it all worked. His final touch was a crucifix made of pink seashells from South America, which he hung over the utilitarian medicine cabinet in the small bathroom off the dining room—the Factory bathroom, we called it, as opposed to the *Interview* bathroom off the entrance vestibule. That one had a couple of closed stalls and a urinal, which Andy was afraid to use ''because you never know who you might run into in there.''

Behind the dining room, heading toward 18th Street, was the combination Xerox room–kitchen, with all-black appliances that took months to come from Italy; the projection booth, where the reels of Andy's early movies were stored; and the forty-foot-long screening room, which came to be known as the middle room, as we weren't making any movies to screen. There were more Art Deco treasures lined up against the walls of this room: twelve cast-iron chairs by Edgar Brandt; and a pair of display cases from a defunct Philadelphia department store, which Andy left mysteriously empty. Invariably, visitors asked what they were, until Andy put a stuffed lion in one and a stuffed owl in the other, and then visitors asked if Andy had a thing about dead animals.

At the far end of the middle room was a floor-to-ceiling door, and behind that, stretching seventy or eighty feet to 18th Street, was the largest room in the new Factory: the storage area, which housed everything from the time capsules, neatly labeled and shelved in chronological order, to an eighteenth-century American door and frame in peeling pale blue paint. Andy said it was his favorite piece, because ''You can go in and out of it and still go nowhere.''

To the left of the storage room was Andy's painting studio, an empty stretch of space with a sink in one corner. Further back was more storage, for paintings and prints, and then the freight elevator. Off Andy's area was Pat Hackett's office, a bleak cubicle facing an inner alley, where she typed the diary and scripts. Then, heading back toward 17th Street, came my office, which, like Vincent's, was more like a hallway than a private room. It had two doors: one from Andy's area, and one to the *Interview* office. *Interview* staffers used it as a shortcut to the Xerox machine, and Andy used it as a shortcut to the *Interview* office. There was a window with bars on it, facing the alley, and my semicircular Art Deco desk. I dragged one of the Brandt chairs in from the screening room to use as a desk chair. Andy often told me to be careful with it, although the red leather seat was already peeling and the rest of it was iron.

The *Interview* office was long, narrow, and dark. One wall was lined with the metal shelving from the old tenth-floor office, collapsing under the weight of back issues, and the other, facing the grim alley, was lined with beat-up old desks, real "used furniture." There was a small, airless mailroom to one side, and then the reception desk and the tall glass doors that opened to the vestibule, across which one could see the Factory reception room, with its beautiful decor, open space, and bright light.

The third Factory was laid out like a circle and as you went round it, you passed through the quarters, each with its own mood and style, of the various businesses in the Factory family, with *Interview* still the poorest relation, and Andy Warhol Films, Inc. more estranged than ever. There were no mirrored walls for Superstars to preen in, just long stretches of white walls to lean paintings against. Despite a quadrupling of space, there was no place to put the framed photographs of Joe Dallesandro, Viva, Tom Hompertz, and International Velvet that had hung over Paul's desk in the second Factory; they were stuck in the unused projection room for good.

Paul didn't have a desk at the third Factory, nor did he have a title in the new company Andy formed. The new stationery, and the lobby directory at 860 Broadway, said Andy Warhol Enterprises—or AWE for short. Andy was chairman, Fred was president, and Vincent was vice-president, secretary, and treasurer. Andy Warhol Films, Inc. henceforth existed only as the copyright owner of the movies that Andy and Paul had made together. And Paul was gone.

Also gone was Joe Dallesandro, who stayed in Rome after the success of both *Frankenstein* and *Dracula* in Italy, making spaghetti westerns for $100,000 a picture. His brother Bobby was gone too; Andy had Vincent tell him that he could no longer afford a "chauffeur" with the rent on the new place. His fate had been sealed the afternoon his car broke down in the middle of the intersection of Fifth Avenue and 42nd Street, with Andy and Paulette, covered in diamonds, sitting in the back seat. "We had to jump out in all the traffic," Andy said, "and all the 42nd Street people were looking at Paulette's fur coat, and she was screaming at me, and I was screaming at Bobby . . ."

Rosemary Kent didn't make it across the square either. She was fired on June 11, 1974, in what we called "the coup d'état." The final battle was over the cover of the special English issue we were doing that summer: Fred wanted Charlotte Rampling, the elegant English actress he had fallen for in a big way at one of those Rothschild balls; Rosemary wanted her fat-and-happy English bulldog, Sedgewick's Boogie Woogie. After a meeting with Peter Brant, who had been pushing for Rosemary's dismissal for months, Fred said that he would do it "at the first convenient moment." That came while he was conveniently in Paris, and the task fell to Rosemary's arch-enemy, associate publisher Carole Rogers. After Vincent had the locks changed first thing in the morning, Carole called Rosemary at home and told her, "on behalf of Peter, Joe, Fred, and Andy, I'm calling to say that your services are no longer required at *Interview.*" Andy was sitting nearby, reading the papers, as if he had nothing to do with it. Later he said, "I'm sure Rosemary's going to sue. We should never have given her a contract."

When Fred came back from Paris, he appointed me editor, and Peter Lester, a young Englishman who had come over to help on the special English issue, managing editor. Within a month, Peter Lester complained that his title sounded "too businessy" and Fred agreed to give him my title, and I was given the title executive editor. As Andy and Fred expected me to "run" the magazine, I thought I should be called editor-in-chief, but Fred said that title had been forever tainted in Andy's mind by Rosemary Kent. Actually, executive editor, with its "businessy" ring, turned out to be rather accurate, as it soon became evident that I was not only held responsible for editorial content but also advertising sales and promotion. In simplest terms, I was once and for all the boss at *Interview,* and, along with Fred and Vincent, one of Andy's three right-hand men at the third Factory.

Soon, I came up with an idea for a column called "Excerpts from the Diary of Andy Warhol." Pat and I worked on a sample column, and when we showed it to Andy, he thought it was a great idea, saying every name we mentioned would have a reason to buy the magazine, and every restaurant or shop we mentioned would have a reason to advertise. But he crossed out his name and scrawled "BC" over it. That's how my column, "OUT: Excerpts from the Diary of Bob Colacello" was born. It was the first time I was called Bob in print, not Robert, and just as Andy dropped a vowel, I did too. We came up with "OUT" because the whole thing was so "In" it was ridiculous. Most people didn't get it and referred to it as "Out and About" or "Going Out," or "Way Out."

I came to see it as a parody of "Jennifer's Diary" in the British *Harper's & Queen,* in which an ancient society matron follows Princess Margaret and the Duchess of Kent from garden party to tea party to charity gala, recording in excruciating detail what they wore and ate, but never what they said. I liked to put in what people said, as well as wore, ate, and *drank,* and although Princess Margaret eventually made it into "Bob Colacello's

OUT,'' I was usually recording the party doings of the Empress Vreeland and His Highness Halston.

Andy critiqued the first column for me: "Leave my name out," he said. "And instead of putting in gossip put in ads, like what perfumes everybody was wearing." He said his favorite day in the first column was the one where I just listed fifty names, from Mick Jagger to Ronnie Cutrone's girlfriend, Betsy Jones, who had been at Stevie Wonder's party at the Delmonico Hotel, and left it at that. "Every one of those people will tell ten friends their name is in the paper," said Andy, "and ten times fifty is how much?" Five hundred. "Gee, Bob, your column might really make *Interview* big. Just stick in every name you ever meet and every brand name they're wearing. And no gossip. We can't afford to get anybody mad at us yet."

My new job and title came with a new salary from Motion Olympus, Inc., the company Peter Brant and Joe Allen had set up as owners. It was $150 a week, in addition to the $125 a week I had been receiving from Andy since 1972, which was raised at the end of 1974 to $150, making my combined salary $300 a week, or $15,600 a year. I was also given a $450 Christmas bonus, in a straightforward check. I spent half of it, $225, on an antique Japanese wood box for Andy.

Looking back at my financial records and tax returns for the years I worked at the Factory is depressing. In 1974, for example, I had over $5,000 in unreimbursed business expenses, and as I still wasn't on payroll, no pension or medical insurance plan. It was same story for 1975 and 1976. In 1977, my salary was raised to $450 a week, or $23,400 a year, and I was finally put on payroll and given an expense account. I was probably the highest-paid person there, except perhaps for Vincent. Fred's salary was still $100 a week; everything else was expenses and commissions. These were large, of course, but often he had to beg Andy to pay him what was owed when it came in, rather than stretch it out into lots of smaller payments. Andy always had an excuse when it came to money. Back in the summer of 1974 it was the increased expenses of the new office, and the high cost of buying and furnishing his new house.

Andy also moved that year—to a six-story brownstone at 57 East 66th Street, between Madison and Park avenues which he bought in early 1974, when real-estate prices had plummeted in the recession brought on by the oil crisis. He paid $310,000 outright, because he didn't believe in mortgages. Andy didn't have to do much renovation beyond removing wall-to-wall carpeting and interior repainting. He kept the old kitchen and the old bathrooms just the way they were. Jed, who moved with him, was in charge of the decorating, though Fred also advised and consented.

Andy constantly complained about how much money Jed was spending, even though the style he had chosen, American Empire (Early Nineteenth-Century), was still completely undiscovered and, for the most part, unwanted. Most of the pieces Jed bought cost between a couple of hundred and a couple of thousand dollars. One room, the second-floor library, was done in Art Deco with pieces Andy already had. Still Andy went on, almost daily, about "the fortune" Jed was spending "like water." Of course, once it became known that Andy Warhol's house was done in American Empire, and that Yves Saint Laurent had asked Jed to do his new Hotel Pierre apartment in the same style, the prices started climbing and never stopped—until certain individual pieces Jed had bought for Andy came to be worth as much as his entire decorating job.

Andy's move sparked a chain reaction: Fred moved into Andy's old house on Lexington Avenue at 89th Street, and Vincent moved into Fred's old apartment on East 16th Street, within walking distance of the Factory, which he dutifully opened and closed every day, checking every faucet and every ashtray, as Andy fretted and made him double-check them. No one was more patient with Andy than Vincent, or more loyal. Even among ourselves, he would never talk against Andy, or take any side but Andy's, though he would sometimes try to get Andy to change his mind when he was being particularly obstinate. Vincent was reliable, practical, and hard-working, which made him the logical choice for all his new corporate titles, even though he was only twenty-four at the time. For me, the key to Vincent's nature was something he told me one night at Le Jardin, between dances with a very pretty Halston model. "I wouldn't even attempt to fall for a beauty unless I had one hundred thousand big ones in the bank."

Andy had tried to talk me into moving into his old house, the one he'd never let me into, "rent free." But I sensed that would be the trap of traps, having my boss as my landlord. Andy nearly didn't let me inside his new house either. A few nights before the big Factory move, Andy, Fred, Jed, Vincent, and I had a "board meeting" dinner at Quo Vadis on East 63rd Street, the favorite restaurant of Diana Vreeland, Lee Radziwill, and Jackie Onassis. After dinner, Fred and I walked Andy and Jed home. When we got to the house, Andy said, "Oh, uh, oh, goodnight," and started fumbling for his keys. Jed shrugged his shoulders, as if to say, "What can I do?" But Fred put his foot down. "Andy," he snapped, "you mean you're not going to invite Bob in to see the house?" "It's late, Fred." "Andy, Bob is the editor of your magazine, he picks you up to go out night after night, you are not going to keep him standing in the street like you did uptown." "Oh, okay, do you want to see the house, Bob?"

. . . tour of Andy's new house. Very *stately.* That's the best word for it. American primitive portraits in the front hall. Upstairs, one Deco salon, one American Empire. On the third floor, A's bedroom with a canopy bed—dark brown silk canopy. Next to the bed: two crucifixes, two alarm clocks, a box of dog biscuits. Green wood shutters. FH: "This is the way a gentleman should live."

Andy and Jed often fought about letting friends into the house. Jed, naturally enough, wanted to have friends over, for fun, and also to show off all his hard work. His bedroom was also on the third floor, in the back, rather severely done in Mission oak. I could understand why Andy didn't want word of where he lived to get out, but he pushed it to the extremes of paranoia. It took six months to get Lee Radziwill invited over, two years before Andy would have Diana Vreeland for a drink. Both women had Andy to dinner countless times at their apartments, so it was a bit awkward when they expressed curiosity about Andy's house and he pretended he didn't know what they were getting at. I wanted Andy to ask Paulette Goddard, but he wasn't going to let *her* see how well he lived—"Then she'll really want to marry me," he said. He didn't want people to see how rich he was, especially people who might be potential clients. He said they'd stop feeling sorry for him, and stop buying his art. I once asked him why he didn't have any of his own art in his house. He said it would be "corny."

When Diana Vreeland was finally allowed into the house in 1976, Andy took a picture of her sitting on a new acquisition: an Egyptian Revival chair, with a gilt eagle back and gilt lion legs, that resembled a throne, fit for the Empress of Fashion. Fred wanted Andy to paint Diana's portrait, for history's sake really, but he told Andy it would be in exchange for her society introductions and *Interview* advice. Andy said she never actually *sold* anyone a portrait of his, or an ad, so she didn't deserve a "commission." He also said, "Oh, now Diana's going to tell everyone what my house looks like and they're all going to want to see it, and I just can't, Fred, I just can't."

Sometimes, when I was too tired to sit at the typewriter, I dictated "OUT" to Brigid Berlin and paid her $25 to transcribe it. One Saturday, she dropped off a column. She had never been to my cramped East 76th Street studio before, and the minute she arrived, Dali called and asked Brigid if "Count Valpolicella" was in. Brigid couldn't miss the irony of it all. "You're writing your Society column and Dali's calling you a count," she said, "and there's your broom between the refrigerator and the wall." It was ridiculous, and a little sad when I thought about it, which wasn't often: the difference between the glamorous life I was leading in my column, and the life I had at home.

So, in February 1975, I rented an airy three-room apartment in the Leonori, at 26 East 63rd Street, a turn-of-the-century residential hotel that had recently been renovated. The rent was $450 a month, almost twice what I had been paying, so there went most of my new *Interview* salary. The living room, bedroom, and kitchen had all been freshly painted white, and I got Andy to give me a leftover roll of Mao wallpaper, and had window shades made. Andy also gave me a fake Venetian console for the foyer wall. Fred gave me a real Art Deco table for the same exact spot. My mother contributed a carpet sweeper, even though I didn't have carpeting. "Wall-to-wall is always nice," she said. She also brought me a box of salt, for good luck, as did Adriana Jackson, Mariana Schiano, Elsa Peretti, and Delfina Rattazzi. For a long time that was my spice shelf: five boxes of Diamond Crystal iodized salt.

Now that Andy and I lived three blocks apart, we saw even more of each other, though Andy had his ways of reminding me that proximity didn't necessarily mean closeness. Shortly after moving in, I came down with flu, my temperature soaring in the middle of the night. I didn't have any aspirin, and when it hit 103 degrees, I panicked and called Andy about two in the morning. "You can't call me this late," said Andy. "I thought Jed could come around the corner with some aspirin," I said. "But what if he gets what you have and gives it to me?" was Andy's reply. Jed picked up on an extension and promised Andy that he would leave the aspirin with the doorman, to avoid the risk of infection, but he actually did come up to see if I was all right, and I promised not to tell anyone he had.

The next day, Andy called to see how I was feeling and to blame my flu on "too much partying," making sure to mention every party I'd be missing during my recuperation. The usual Warhol sympathy call. Then he started in on another of his campaigns: to get me to go to his doctor, Denton Cox. "He's a great doctor, Bob. He has a big Rolls-Royce." "Is he going to examine me in the car, Andy?" "It won't cost you anything, Bob. I'll pay." "Andy, I already go to your accountant, your lawyer, and your bank. I'm not going to your doctor!" "But I'll pay, Bob." "Right, and you'll ask Dr. Cox to send you my urinalysis the next morning!"

"Wake up, Bob. It's time to go shopping. My ship came in." That was Andy's way of saying that a check had arrived from Anselmino of Torino, or Alexander the Greek, or his new art dealer in Bonn, Herman "the German" Wunsche. And the minute his ships docked, Andy turned into the drunken sailor of shopping, bingeing out on everything from Fiestaware to diamonds. In 1975, Andy moved up from the Mercedes to a new black-and-brown Rolls-Royce Silver Shadow—Jed was under strict instructions to say Andy had traded it for art. The following summer he acquired a second Rolls-Royce, a rare old station wagon, for Montauk (though it was in such fragile condition it never left the Southampton mechanic's garage).

After I moved, he started calling me almost every morning to "go shopping on the way to work." As Ivan Karp has said of Andy, "He was one of the helpless collectors. Helpless. He had to find something every single day.'' Andy was a shopping junkie, hooked on hoarding. Some things he used, like his Fiestaware, or displayed, like his cookie-jar collection in his glass-fronted kitchen cabinets. But most things were stuck in closets in the shopping bags they came in, or buried in the rapidly growing stacks in the vast Factory storage area.

Andy had two regular shopping routes from his house to midtown, where he grabbed a taxi to the Factory. The first was the ''junk shop'' route, down Second Avenue from the Sixties to the Fifties. One shop on this route was Sarsparilla, where Andy bought hundreds, if not thousands, of Walt Disney's original acetates, the individual hand-painted frames of the cartoons: Mickey Mouse, Donald Duck, Snow White, Cinderella. I remember his turning down *Fantasia,* because it wasn't the ''real'' Disney style. Another day, in another shop, he picked up a wolfhound rug, stuffed head and all, for almost nothing, because the owner wanted it out of the shop. ''It's repulsing the customers,'' he said. Andy took it down to the Factory and added it to his collection of stuffed animals, which he was Polaroiding for what became his Cats and Dogs shows in London and Kuwait.

Andy's second regular walk, the jewelry route, took him from Fred Leighton's antique jewelry shop on Madison Avenue in the Sixties, where he bought Mexican turquoise-and-silver pieces, some ornate Indian jewelry of the Moghul era, and Art Deco diamond, emerald, and sapphire bracelets, among many other things. The next stop was usually Seaman Schepp's, on Park Avenue at 58th Street, where he bought forties brooches, bracelets, and rings with huge semiprecious stones, often competing with Diane von Furstenberg and Marisa Berenson for the same pieces. Sometimes we stopped in Tiffany's to check out the latest Elsa Peretti designs, which he never bought there because he could get them wholesale or trade them from Elsa herself.

The last stop was what Andy called ''The Street of Dreams''—West 47th Street between Fifth and Sixth avenues, otherwise known as the Diamond District. Andy's favorite shop there was a tiny hole in the wall, owned by a man called Boris Tinter, who had a hook instead of a left hand. When Andy walked in, Boris would say, ''I have something special I've been holding for you,'' and out from under his counter would come a diamond bracelet or a string of pearls, hanging from Boris's hook. On the corner of 47th and Fifth was the big Diamond Exchange, a sort of supermarket of gem dealers, all in yarmulkes, all greeting Andy as if he were their best friend. He only took me there once and we rushed right out, Andy saying, ''Gee, they're so aggressive in there.'' I'm sure he realized it was a mistake to let me see how well the diamond dealers knew him. Andy looked at jewelry the same way he looked at his mail: He held it right up to his eye and studied it closely, murmuring questions about karats, facets, cuts, flaws, color, brilliance, and ''d-quality.'' He knew exactly what he was doing.

I asked him what he did with his jewelry, and he said he put it on

Archie and Amos and they played together on the bed. And, gradually, he started wearing it—under his clothes where it couldn't be seen—a diamond necklace under a turtleneck, for example. One of his jewelry-collecting cronies, Joan Quinn, recalls Andy wearing a gold-and-crystal David Webb frog inside his jacket, and when she spotted it and said she had wanted to buy it from a Madison Avenue shop they both frequented, Andy said, "Oh, I got a really good deal." She also remembers the "piles of old high-school graduation rings that Andy used to buy by the pound on 47th Street."

Barbara Allen remembers Andy in Paris in the mid-seventies, "wearing this beautiful Art Deco diamond bracelet, which kept slipping out from under his shirtsleeve. I asked to see it and Andy took it off and I put it on and then I said that I was going to wear it for the night. Andy got *really* nervous. He *hated* me wearing it, but I just wanted to tease him, to give *him* a hard time for a change. He followed me around all night checking to make sure that I still had it, and he was so *relieved* when I finally gave it back to him."

Shopping with Andy, like doing anything with Andy, was both enjoyable and a bit of a chore. As much as he wanted a companion to share in the experience, he couldn't help being competitive and secretive. Bruno Bischofberger once introduced him to a dealer in American Indian rugs. Andy was delighted to see a stack of forty or fifty rugs. He made the dealer show him each one, listening carefully to what he said about their quality, origin, style, etc. When the exhausted dealer reached the bottom of the pile, Andy, thoroughly educated, announced he was ready to go, and Bruno, thoroughly embarrassed, hurriedly bought two or three rugs. The next time Bruno was in town, he visited the dealer, who told him that Andy had come back that afternoon and bought the ten least-expensive ones, at four or five hundred dollars each. "I guess he didn't want me to think he was rich," Bruno says. "But actually I thought it was another example of Andy's biggest flaw as a collector. He always wanted a bargain, when actually he would have been smarter to buy the one great rug for $5,000 rather than the ten cheapest. Because the great things go up, and the bargains stay bargains."

Joan Quinn agrees. "When we'd go shopping together, he'd always come back. He wouldn't buy in front of me, because he wouldn't want to take the cash out, or make the deal, or bicker and dicker, which is what he did when he went back. He never bought on the spot. He didn't want me to know what he was collecting, but he always wanted to know what I was collecting."

On one of my first shopping expeditions with Andy, he talked me into buying a Maxfield Parrish print. He said that he would buy it, but he already had several Parrishes and the price, $90, was a bit high, "but it'll probably go up." I said that it really didn't go with my apartment. "It doesn't have to go, *Bob,*" countered Andy, in a tone that suggested I was a philistine fool. "It just has to go *up.*" It did go up, to the top of my closet.

Another "collection" that Andy got me started on was what he called "Mafiaware"—black glassware with scalloped edges from the Depression era. "It's a bargain," he said, "and your mother will love it." "My mother's not in the Mafia, Andy." "She's not?" He bought me the first two pieces, a creamer and sugar bowl, for five dollars, and whenever he found more he'd get Vincent to buy it for me as a birthday or Christmas present. The one time I served something to my mother on it, she said, "Why would you want *black* dishes? It reminds me of those real *gavones.*"

For Andy, however, collecting had nothing to do with decorating. Fred had decorated the Factory and Jed had decorated his house, and, little by little, Andy undecorated both places with his bags and boxes, stacks and piles, collections, possessions, investments, hedges against inflation and fear.

25

A Small Work of Art

People kept stopping Andy on Park Avenue, asking for his autograph, as we headed toward Seaman Schepp's one Saturday. "It's Archie that does it," claimed Andy modestly. "They only recognize me when I'm with him." Walking a dog might have made Andy seem more accessible, but the truth was that Andy's fame was expanding rapidly in the mid-seventies. The more he went out the more he got his picture in the papers; he met more and more famous people, which got his picture in the papers even more. Celebrity is a circle and Andy was now in the middle of it, spinning happily along.

And since the moves to the new Factory and the new house, he seemed to have his fear under control. He didn't cower or tremble when a bum, or a black man, passed anymore, and he signed autographs for anyone who asked. "Oh, I know what I should do," said Andy. "I should start carrying a pile of *Interview*s with me and sign those when people stop me. It's a great idea, Bob, isn't it?" It was, but I suggested that Andy give away back issues, not current ones, so as not to compete with newsstand sales. He was thrilled with his idea, as if he had finally figured out a way to simultaneously deal with his fame and spread it. It was nice but pushy, generous and self-serving. It connected him to his fans, but also put something between them and him. He could hide behind the magazine and not have to talk to them. They could curl up with the magazine at home and get to know him better. It was one of those perfect Warholian gestures, a contradiction that worked. By monitoring the insert cards, we also knew it gradually sent up subscription sales.

Andy's life now settled into the daily routine he would follow until his death: doing his diary on the phone with Pat in the morning; shopping his way downtown; arriving at the Factory in time for lunch with clients; painting in the afternoon; a long evening hunting more clients at openings, dinners, and parties; always handing out *Interview;* snapping photos; tape recording; and making sure always to get a receipt everywhere he went. On Sundays he dashed in and out of church, but he certainly didn't rest. Once a month or so, to break up the routine, there were safaris to the capitals of Europe, as well as to Washington, D.C., and Hollywood.

These were exciting days and nights for Andy and the Factory, a golden age of creativity and expansion, perhaps even more frenetic and glamorous than the silver nights of the tinfoil-Factory era. New York too was making a comeback, regaining the allure it had had in the sixties, and we were right in the middle of the new society and the new nightlife. Toward the end of the seventies and during the eighties, Andy and the Factory went through several major crises, but from 1975 until 1978 everything was going up.

Interview, in particular. I soon stopped shopping with Andy, except on Saturdays, because I couldn't wait to get to work, no matter how late I'd been out the night before. There was a new sense of mission, camaraderie, and fun at the new office. While Carole Rogers concentrated on expanding local and national distribution, Fred and I put together the editorial staff. Diana Vreeland sent us her star volunteer—she had a small army of fashion-mad kids working for free at the Met's Costume Institute, just as she'd had at *Bazaar* and *Vogue.* ''I haven't met anyone who cares, really *cares,* about the difference between *peau de soie* and *soie de gazar* as much as this chap does since . . . well, since *me!''* she said.

André Leon Talley was a graduate of Brown University and the Rhode Island School of Design, but we told him he had to answer phones as well as cover the fashion shows. (Just as everybody at the second Factory had to start out sweeping floors, everybody at *Interview* had to work their way up from the receptionist's desk.) On his first day of work, a hot Monday in August 1975, André turned up in khaki safari shirt and Bermuda shorts, with matching knee socks, topped off by a hunter's helmet from Abercrombie & Fitch, looking every inch the Kipling colonial in Kenya—except that André is black and as tall as a Harlem Globetrotter. We dubbed him André de Interview, because he often answered the phone with a festive *''Bonjour!''*

André was actually paid a small salary, but Andy loved Diana Vreeland's concept of volunteers, and Fred found a ready pool in the growing number of ''English Muffins'' landing in New York from London. They were the British equivalents of the rich young Italian immigrants who had landed the year before, and were soon to be followed by the ''French Fries.'' Most of the English Muffins seemed to pop right out of the transatlantic toaster and into Fred's house on 89th Street, and Andy thought that in exchange for room and board it was only fair that they volunteer some time to his favorite charities: Andy Warhol Enterprises and *Interview* magazine.

So Lady Ann Lambton came in most mornings—late mornings—to straighten up Fred's desk, which meant adding her mess to his. And Catherine Guinness, the Stout heiress, came in most mornings—late mornings—to proofread *Interview,* which meant she changed "color" to "colour" and "center" to "centre" and someone else, usually me, had to change everything back. I finally remonstrated with her, "This is *not* an *English* magazine! And when are you going to get it through your head that Minnelli has two n's and two l's, and Rattazzi has a double t and a double z?''

"Well, as far as I'm concerned," snapped Catherine, "you have far too many foreign names in your column."

That did it. "Listen, Catherine," I shouted, "I don't care if you're working for free or not. I am ordering you to take that Robert Mapplethorpe photograph off the wall." Catherine had hung over her desk the raunchiest Mapplethorpe I have ever seen, of three men engaged in bloody torture, and Carole Rogers shielded her eyes every time she passed it. Catherine had a comeback; rich kids who work for free usually do: "Robert has just been to photograph the Archbishop of Canterbury, you know." It was true.

Of course, Catherine and Ann weren't at the Factory for their clerical skills. Their real function was to help entertain the clients, a job they plunged into with almost missionary zeal, enlivening the dullest advertising lunches and elevating portrait-pushing dinners to heights of hilarity.

That still left me, however, with no one on the editorial staff who could actually do things like type. Catherine pecked a word a minute, André Leon Talley preferred to communicate good news in gold ink and bad news in purple ink, and Peter Lester, who was talented but extremely turf-conscious, considered such tasks beneath him. Finally, along came the person who had as much to do with the success of *Interview* as any of us: Robert Hayes. For starters, he could type. What's more, he *would* type. And read proofs, size photos, style cover shoots, deal with photographers' fees and fits and fetishes. Robert Hayes was the essential inside man—loyal, hard-working, reliable, and intelligent—freeing me to dash from lunches to parties to Europe with Andy and Fred; wine and woo the stars and the advertisers; get ideas; set directions; run into the office to dictate columns, bark orders, give lectures, pep talks, and pats on the back; and run out again.

I first met Robert Hayes in late 1974, at a SoHo loft showing of rock 'n' roll photos by Christopher Makos. Afterward, I took Chris and Robert to dinner at Ballato's and it was the beginning of a long association with the Factory for both of them. Chris, a Californian in his late twenties, was brash and ambitious. He was doing covers for *Circus* magazine then, but he very much wanted to get his work into *Interview,* and I soon started giving him assignments. His stark, graphic black-and-white style worked well on newsprint, which tends to soften photographs that are too subtle or complicated.

He had previously worked as a part-time dog sitter for Tennessee Williams (until he locked the playwright's best friend in a closet at the Hotel Élysée, while he entertained a pal with room service). Chris was starstruck, enthusiastic, wily, and wild.

Robert was just the opposite: steady, cautious, guileless, and a bit unsure of himself. He was a few years younger than Chris and had only been in New York for a year. He was from New Brunswick, in Canada, and had graduated from McGill University in Montreal, but the only work he could find was selling shoes at the posh Mario of Florence shop. I happened to mention that the biggest problem at *Interview* was that nobody wanted to type. A few weeks later, I asked Chris how Robert was doing and he said he'd enrolled in a typing course at the Katharine Gibbs Secretarial School after work. Impressed, I hired Robert as an editorial assistant the day he finished the course. Within a few months, I promoted him to assistant editor, and by the end of 1976, when Peter Lester was transferred to Los Angeles as West Coast editor, Robert became managing editor.

At the end of 1975, we hired Marc Balet as art director. A Pratt Institute graduate and Prix de Rome winner, Marc had a natural feel for the clean, simple look that Andy, Fred, and I all favored. And he was the best friend of Fran Lebowitz.

The day after Rosemary Kent went, I called Fran and asked her down for lunch to try to get her back. She listed her demands: a raise from $25 to $50 per column, retention of her copyright, and permanent placement on the last editorial page, with a guarantee that no ad would ever share her space. We would have to type her column, but she would proofread and edit her own copy, and oversee her layouts. I agreed immediately—though I did persuade her to let me leave the copyright symbol off the page, for fear of inflaming other contributors. (We also needed Fran to drive the layouts to the printer in far-off south Jersey, which she had done in the Glenn O'Brien era for $25 plus all the food she could eat. She wanted that fee doubled too, and I agreed again, as nobody else seemed to have a valid driver's license, and nobody wanted to spend six hours round trip on the turnpike without Fran cracking one-liners all the way.)

I made one suggestion: that Fran expand her new column to cover more than movies. Fran readily agreed, as she was banned from most movie screenings because of her old column, "Best of the Worst." She thought it might be broadening to be banned from fashion shows and book-launching parties as well, and came up with a new name for her new, improved column, "I Cover the Waterfront."

"A salad is not a meal," she wrote in her August 1976 column, titled "Food for Thought and Vice Versa," "it's a style." And: "Large, naked, raw carrots are acceptable as food only to those who live in cages eagerly awaiting Easter." And: "Brown rice is ponderous, overly chewy, and possessed of unpleasant religious overtones." Fran did columns on "Earth and

Other Negative Shoes: A Legitimate Complaint'' and ''Polyester, Vinyl, Acrylic & Others of Their Ilk: A Complaint.'' She was against SoHo before most people had even heard of SoHo. She was actually the perfect antidote to the relentless trendiness of the rest of the magazine. And her back-of-the-book complaints balanced Andy's cheerleading cover stories. He loved everything; she hated everything.

Andy was doing at least one interview in every issue now, usually the cover story. No matter who the subject was—Ginger Rogers, Dustin Hoffman, Cher—he found a way to talk about perfume and jewelry, because that's what interested him most, and he wanted to mention potential advertisers. Andy's interviews were as much portraits of him as of his subject.

ALFRED HITCHCOCK: But today of course, with the Age of the Revolver, as one might call it, I think there is more use of guns in the home than there is in the streets. You know? And men lose their heads.
AW: Well, I was shot by a gun, and it just seems like a movie. I can't see it as being anything real. The whole thing is still like a movie to me. It happened to me, but it's like watching TV. . . .
AH: Yes. Yes.
AW: So I always think that people who do it feel the same way.
AH: Well, a lot of it's done on the spur of the moment.
AW: Well if you do it once, then you can do it again, and if you keep doing it, I guess it's just something to do. . . .
AH: Well, it depends on whether you've disposed of the first body.

When Andy ran out of questions, which was often, the interviewee sometimes interviewed him.

LEE RADZIWILL: Did you go to church today, Andy?
AW: Yes, but I only stayed a minute.
LR: This is pretty personal, but do you ever take communion? And go to confession before?
AW: Well—I never feel I do anything bad. But I do take communion sometimes.
LR: Do you give up things for Lent?
FRED HUGHES: He gives up things for his figure.

This was one of the rare times Fred accompanied Andy on an interview. I went with Andy on almost all of them, often letting Pat convert some of my questions into his. It seemed normal by then, having my words printed as Andy's. Andy always said, ''I'll ask a few Eugenia Sheppard questions, Bob, and then you've got to come up with the Edward R. Murrow ones for me.'' Only Pat and those of us who were there know what Andy actually said, and what she said he said. Pat was also very adept at ''fixing'' Andy's questions and comments, so they made a bit more sense to those unable to differentiate between ''Oh, really,'' to which Pat might append ''I'm not sure about that,'' and ''Reallllly,'' which she'd follow with ''how exciting.'' She also unraveled his sentences, which tended to get convoluted when he went beyond ten or twelve words, as if English were his second language. And because Andy gossiped so much during his chitchats with the stars, she came up with the device of inserting cryptic lists to indicate that time had passed and things had been discussed that the reader wasn't allowed to hear. An example from the Hitchcock interview:

> Fonda's collapse
> Burton's breakup
> (wait for elevator)
> still in the hospital
> Franco Rossellini
> (into the elevator, ride down)
> Monte Carlo
> Princess Grace

At first we did them in the star's hotel suite or at whatever restaurant he or she chose. But after we were asked to leave ''21'' because Burt Reynolds wasn't wearing a tie and wouldn't wear the one they gave him, we stuck to Quo Vadis, which was more tolerant—and on the ground floor of my building. Andy asked all the stars the brand name of everything they were wearing, including fragrance, but once they realized we were ''mentioning'' it in the magazine, they mostly made a point of saying they didn't do ''free endorsements.'' So Pat was reduced to asking me what I wore, and she'd redact in, ''BC is wearing a gray tweed jacket from Saks Fifth Avenue, YSL corduroy trousers, a blue shirt, a green wool vest from De Noyer . . .'' Andy ''endorsed'' Levi-Strauss's 501s every month. And we never got a Levi-Strauss ad.

Andy rarely went to the cover shoots, but there was one he didn't want to miss: Bette Midler's. She pulled him in front of the camera with her, which he loved, and we ran the photos inside, which he said he hated. Cover sessions took so much time, often lasting all day and into the evening, starting with an hour or two, or three, of hair and makeup, depending on how big a prima donna the cover girl was—or the hairdresser and makeup man were. Most of the covers in 1975 and 1976 were photographed by Chris von Wangenheim (Fred's favorite) or Bill King (Peter Lester's favorite).

People magazine editor Richard Stolley had some famous rules about what covers sell best: Young is better than old, pretty is better than ugly, movies are better than music, music is better than TV, and anything is better than politics. The *Interview* twist: *Only* young, *only* pretty, movies are best, but music, fashion, and society are also good, and anything, even politics, is better than TV. The one TV star we put on the cover in the seventies, Shaun Cassidy, bombed. Our readers didn't watch TV, they went to discos. We did want Diana Vreeland on our December 1975 cover, but she herself laid down that law: "Nobody picks up a magazine with someone *my* age on it!" After that, when we put older stars on the cover we did them the way they looked when they were younger: We used a thirties publicity shot for Ginger Rogers, and a forties Dali portrait for C.Z. Guest. And when we did Dustin Hoffman, who wasn't pretty, we sandwiched him between models Lisa Taylor and Beverly Johnson, who were—and it still didn't sell. The all-time worst seller was a bearded Brad Davis. I wanted to make him shave, but Robert Hayes said that was going too far. After it sank on the newsstands, I had a new rule: no beards.

Late one afternoon in early 1975, Andy, Fred, and I tried to figure out who to put on the next few covers. Looking over the sales figures for the previous year, we realized that our best sellers were also our best friends: Liza Minnelli, Cher, Raquel Welch, Ryan O'Neal, Jack Nicholson and Anjelica Huston (together and separately), Mick and Bianca Jagger (separately). We decided to start repeating them, though not more than once a year, and thought of other famous friends we hadn't done yet, like Diana Ross, Diane von Furstenberg, and Elizabeth Taylor, all of whom became hit covers within the next two years.

It was a breakthrough and it confirmed our instinct to make *Interview* a reflection of Andy's celebrity-studded world, and to be what we were rather than trying to be what we weren't, which had been Rosemary Kent's mistake. We stopped competing with other magazines, and forgot about scoops and exclusives. We were sitting on the most exclusive scoop of all: the opportunity to document life among the rich and famous from the inside. The only thing we could do was also the one thing *only we* could do. Suddenly our biggest liability, lack of distance, was our biggest asset, proximity to the stars. We didn't have to provide our readers with objective journalism; we were letting them into the party.

My first post-Rosemary issue, August 1974, had launched our "Millionettes-of-the-Month" series, with interviews of Paloma Picasso, Nicky Weymouth, and Federico de Laurentiis. Now, for our February 1975 issue, we decided to do a complete Millionettes special with Marisa Berenson on the cover, photographed and interviewed by her sister, the new Mrs. Tony Perkins. Inside there was a two-page list, surrounded by party shots, of all the young Agnellis, Astors, Brandolinis, Berlins, de Menils, Flicks, Kempners, Kennedys, Niarchoses, Portagos, Radziwills, Rattazzis, Tennants, and Vreelands, among others, identified by age and vocation ("Princess Minnie de Beauvau-Craon, 21, art expert"; "Christina Onassis, 24, gay divorcée"; "the Prince of Wales, 22, the Duchess of Windsor's great-nephew''). At the end of the list was an admonition: "How to be a millionette? Work hard, play hard, make it all look easy. If you don't have a million, act like you do. When you marry, marry a millionaire." Priscilla Rattazzi called from Sarah Lawrence to say she couldn't go to the cafeteria anymore without someone asking her to pick up the check.

There was also a "Hollywood Kids" subsection: interviews with Roc Brynner, Jeff Bridges, Deirdre Flynn, Francesca Hilton, Dore Schary's daughter Jill Robinson interviewed by Brigid Berlin, Maria Cooper Janis by Dena Kaye. And a poem, also called "Hollywood Kids," by Carrie Fisher, daughter of Debbie and Eddie, then age seventeen:

> Be kind to children of movie stars
> Driving around in their foreign cars
> Their sun-tanned, sun-glassed faces
> Their petty smooth disgraces
> They fell from a golden womb
> Only to collide with a precocious gloom.

Newsweek picked it up for their Newsmakers section, and for once Andy didn't complain about putting poetry in *Interview*. A few months later, *Time* did a cover story on "The New Beauties," borrowed liberally from our Millionettes list and crediting us liberally too. When two more of our Millionettes, Delfina Rattazzi and Linda Hutton, ended up on the covers, respectively, of the *New York Times* spring fashion supplement and *Town and Country,* we knew we had arrived.

The *Wall Street Journal* took note of the whole new direction since Rosemary's departure, in a long article by their cultural commentator, Benjamin Stein, titled, "What Bianca Wore at Diana's Party":

> Originally patterned somewhat after *Women's Wear Daily, Interview* has gradually evolved a format and style so superficial, so utterly concerned with the fluff and trivia of life that it makes *WWD* look like *Commentary.* But appearances here are deceiving. . . .
>
> In a sense Andy's magazine is just like Andy's art. Its very superficiality says something heartrending about the despair of most people's lives . . . in a sense [that] makes every issue of *Interview* a small work of art. And anyway, at a slightly less anguished level, it's awfully funny.

Carole Rogers immediately whipped up handouts for potential distributors and advertisers, headlined: "Every issue of *Interview* is a small work of art," the *Wall Street Journal.* Under that she quoted them quoting me:

> "We're trying to reach high-spending people . . . not necessarily people who earn a lot of money, but people who spend a lot of money . . . the trend in our society is towards self-indulgence and we encourage that."

"Gee, Bob," said Andy, "you really could sell ads." That was always Andy's major concern, and I agreed—it was crucial and I could do it, but first I had to get the editorial right. Fred was much more supportive of this strategy than Andy. He had been a big help on the Millionettes issue—it was his word—and we collaborated closely on several other theme issues in 1975.

The "April in Paris" issue had an Antonio drawing of Brigitte Bardot on the cover and inside everything from "The Philosophy of Yves Saint Laurent" to "I Cover La Waterfront." We did a special Puerto Rico issue in August, with an Antonio drawing of Rita Moreno on the cover and inside everything from "Chatting with Chita [Rivera]" to "I Cover El Water-front."

The "Photography" issue in November was one of our last attempts to be "serious," and in the end it confirmed that so-called serious people would never take Andy Warhol's magazine seriously, that all-out frivolity was the way to go. We originally wanted Richard Avedon, who was having the first exhibition of his photographs at the Marlborough Gallery, to be on the cover. But when I called him, he turned us down, saying he didn't think he "should be associated with a magazine that put Cher on the cover." It was the first time anyone had said no to our cover. Andy was furious. "He used to photograph Cher for *Vogue,*" he said.

We put off a cover decision and gathered photographs, starting with a couple that Fred pulled out from under the piles on his desk: a Cecil Beaton portrait of Gary Cooper and a James Abbe portrait of Fred and Adele Astaire. Andy coughed up his Man Ray study of a swimmer's back, telling me to "be careful" with it at least twenty times. Man Ray was Andy's favorite, so we decided to put on the contents page a portrait of him on his eighty-fifth birthday by Chris Makos. The Sonnabend Gallery allowed us to run a David Hockney landscape across the centerfold. Brooks Jackson gave us a rare Edward Steichen of Iolas as a Balanchine dancer, and Horst kindly contributed his 1953 shots of Maxime de la Falaise McKendry as a Schiaparelli model. Peter Beard contributed dead-elephant photographs from his book in progress, *Nor Dread, Nor Hope Attend,* and Francis Bacon allowed us to print his comments on them as captions. Robert Mapplethorpe brought us a witty shot of a leather keychain hanging from a banana, and persuaded Sam Wagstaff to let us publish sixteen photographs from his fledgling but already important collection.

It was shaping up as a great issue, but we still didn't have a cover shot. And then Veruschka dragged Ara Gallant down to the Factory. Gallant had been the hairdresser and makeup man on many of the *Vogue* shoots Avedon did in the sixties, and he was still a major star of the beauty business. He had started taking his own photographs a few years before, but he was shy about showing them, terrified of rejection, afraid nobody would take him seriously. Veruschka wanted us to see Ara's striking shot of her taking a picture of herself, holding the camera up to her face like a mirror. It had elegance, style, and impact. We decided to use it right then and there. It was perfect, Andy, Fred, and I all agreed, and it had been taken by Avedon's former hairdresser.

We used Ara for almost all our covers after that. He knew a lot about lighting, composition, and styling, having learned from working with the masters, Avedon and Vreeland. And he not only took the picture, he also did the hair and makeup, simplifying life for us and speeding up the shoots for the stars, who all loved working with him because he made them look so beautiful. In some cases, such as Catherine Deneuve and Faye Dunaway, he even got them for us.

John Springer told me at a 1976 party that after *Time* and *Newsweek* the magazine his clients most wanted to be in was *Interview.* "It's the one publication," he said, "where they always come out sounding just like they do in real life, and looking better." It was the basic formula that Andy reminded me of every so often: "The interviews can be funny, but the pictures can't." He knew only too well that almost everybody loves the sound of his or her own voice, and almost nobody loves the way he or she looks. When Richard Bernstein brought a cover in, I'd look at it quickly and then take it over to the Factory side to show Andy. His most consistent comment was "Can't Richard retouch it more?" Sometimes he'd say, "Her nose looks too big. Tell Richard to just take a scissor and cut the bump out, and then airbrush over it with a little brown to make it look straight." Or "Gee, now this is a great cover. It doesn't even look like her. It's soooo *glamorous.*"

New York magazine called *Interview* "the ultimate fanzine: friends writing about friends in articles that looked like the ads," and when they asked Andy who read it, he answered, "Our friends. And whoever's on the cover." It was funny, and true, and it worked. In the mid-seventies our real circulation began to catch up with our claimed circulation, and more and more of our interviews were being done by our friends, much of it free, for fun. Anjelica Huston did Mae West, Patti Smith did Jean Moreau, Polly Bergen did Giorgio di Sant'Angelo, Delfina Rattazzi did Lina Wertmuller, and Victor Hugo was "received" by Prince and Princess von Furstenberg— separately. Florinda Bolkan made an "Homage to Luchino Visconti."

Fred and I often looked through his old *Vanity Fair* collection, with their "Impossible Interviews." In our magazine, it seemed, no combination was impossible: "Kojak vs. Viva," "Gore Vidal by Monique van Vooren," "Leni Riefenstahl by Bianca Jagger." When Lally Weymouth published her serious historical work, *1876: The Way They Were,* we sent her good friend Halston to dress her *and* interview her, and they told each other how much they loved her mother, Kay Graham, the owner of the *Washington Post.* When the Duchess of Bedford published her biography, *Nicole Nobody,* we sent her daughter, contributing editor Catherine Milinaire, to interview her. *Interview* editorial policy and Factory social life were on parallel tracks now, just as Andy had always wanted.

More friends signed on as regular contributing editors. Lance Loud, the son of *An American Family,* whom we met through Chris Makos, started a monthly music column called ''Loudspeaker.'' J. Paul Getty III became our L.A. correspondent, and Firooz Zahedi, the nephew of the Iranian ambassador, covered Washington, D.C., for us. Barbara Allen did a shopping column called ''Good News.'' Between bouts of stretching canvases for Andy, Ronnie Cutrone did his ''Art in View'' page. Another new feature was ''Viewgirl'' and ''Interman,'' full-page photographs of beautiful young aspiring models and actors, preferably from good families. Diana Vreeland's favorite young photographer, Patrice Calmettes, who lived in Paris, sent us titled teenagers from France, Italy, and Spain, and when one of them didn't have a title, he gave one.

Brigid Berlin did in-depth interviews with Clifford Irving, Christopher Cerf, and Billy Baldwin, as well as President Ford's dog's astrologer. Maxime de la Falaise McKendry's pieces included ''Oshima Uncensored,'' ''Larry Rivers on Mom, Death, Sex and Art,'' and ''Alain Robbe-Grillet: Is He an Onanistic Agronomist?'' The real Brenda Starr of our staff, however, was Bianca Jagger, whose September 1975 White House interview with Jack Ford, the President's son, put us on the map in a big way.

Our special Politics issue in July 1976 also showed us that political stories get picked up in the national press more than any others. Like so many *Interview* ideas, it started out with a telephone call from a friend. Earl McGrath, the right hand of Ahmet Ertegun, called to invite Andy to a fundraiser for Governor Jerry Brown of California, who was running for President. Andy and I went, and he taped Jerry Brown's speech and took a few Polaroids, and Earl persuaded the handsome young Governor to let us do it as a cover story. Meanwhile, Spiro Agnew was touring the country to promote his novel, *The Canfield Decision,* and he had the publicist from his publisher, Playboy Press, call me about an interview, because he remembered us from the Pan Am Clipper Club. So now we had a Democrat and a Republican.

Two more friends called with ideas. Daniela Morera wanted to interview Mussolini's far-left great niece, the leading photographer of interior design in Milan. And Cuban-born Paul Palmero, who had just been an Interman, thought we should do Batista's far-out son, a popular disco dancer on the Le Jardin–Club Sept circuit. We ran their stories side by side: ''Maria Vittoria Mussolini: from Uncle Ben to *Casa Vogue''* and ''Fulgencio Batista Jr.: from Havana to Nirvana.'' Now that we had the Italian Communist and Cuban Fascist bases covered, all we needed was a dash of Middle Eastern monarchy, and Firooz Zahedi brought that. He was on his way to Iran with Elizabeth Taylor, and would bring us back a color centerfold of Elizabeth in a *chador*—a low-cut, sequined *chador*. He also gave us another photo of Elizabeth at the foot of the Lincoln Memorial, which we ran on the contents page. The press made fun of it, of course, but they certainly wrote about it. And within a few months, Elizabeth Taylor was a senator's wife.

Andy was of two minds about our covering politics. His official political position was neutrality, and he was afraid that, even if we joked about politics, people might not get it and think we were taking sides. Somebody might be offended, he worried, and cancel a subscription, or worse yet, cancel an ad. When he was in that frame of mind, he'd point out, "Politicians don't advertise, they ask for handouts. Fashion designers advertise. Jewelry designers advertise. Book people advertise—well, not that much. That's why when you do an author you should say what perfume they're wearing. Perfume advertises the most. And cigarettes and liquor. Can't we have everybody smoking and drinking in every photograph, Bob?"

But Andy also saw politicians as the biggest stars of all, famous people who had power—and who liked their portraits to hang over the seat of power. He knew that when they were running for office they wanted portraits as contributions, as McGovern had in 1972, and Carter would in 1976. But once they were elected, they needed official portraits, paid for from official funds, just like Israeli Prime Minister Golda Meir, who commissioned Andy in 1975, and West German Chancellor Willy Brandt, who sat for him in 1976. "If we could only get President Ford's portrait," Andy told me, "we'd be on easy street. Because they could commission one for the White House, and then one for Congress, and one for the Supreme Court, and then one for every embassy in every country. Did you ever think of that, Bob?" When Andy was in this mood, he was all for putting politics in *Interview*. He worried less then about losing ads, if it was too funny or not funny enough, on the right side or the wrong side, so long as it helped Andy Warhol become the official portraitist to the leaders of the world, a kind of Karsh of Pop.

Portraits and ads. Ads and portraits. Portraits and ads. Ads and portraits. Ads, ads, ads. Portraits, portraits, portraits . . .

26

Portraits and Ads

Sales of both were going up, up, up at the new Factory, and many deals were closed in the paneled dining room over box lunches from Brownie's. Lunch, which usually started at one and often lasted until after three or four, was the centerpiece of Andy's day, when his kids and his clients gathered round the Ruhlmann table, and all his businesses intertwined in a tense and giddy tangle of work and play. At one end of the table, Andy would be taping a Viewgirl from Los Angeles or an Interman from Milan about their latest sexual adventures, or telling a reporter from Chicago that his Philosophy was: "Not doing it is the most fun of all." At the other, Fred would be negotiating with an art dealer from Düsseldorf, or popping the question to a parvenu from Peru. In the middle, I'd be spinning the Elizabeth-Taylor-in-Rome tales yet again, for an advertiser from Madison Avenue or Seventh Avenue, with a hearty guffaw track courtesy of Lady Ann Lambton. At first, we only had as many guests as fit around the table, but eventually our lunches grew into parties, the social crossroads of Park Avenue and SoHo, *le tout* Paris and *haute* Hollywood. Lunch at the Factory was an international status symbol, like Rolex watches or the Concorde, as obligatory a stop on the Grand Tour of Manhattan as a night at Studio 54. Brownie's soon gave way to salmon and caviar sandwiches from William Poll, Diana Vreeland's favorite gourmet shop, or, when Andy cracked down, pasta salads from Balducci's, the best Italian deli in the Village. We always served cocktails and red and white wine. We never hired waiters. Andy said, "Artists don't have servants." So we were the waiters, and everyone remarked how charming it was when Andy got up and refilled their glasses.

One of our first get-togethers in the new place was a secret lunch in October 1974 for Leni Riefenstahl, Hitler's favorite filmmaker, and the Tanzanian foreign minister, organized by Bianca Jagger and Peter Beard. *Triumph of the Will* and *Olympia*, Riefenstahl's documentaries of the 1934 Nuremberg Nazi party conference and the 1936 Berlin Olympics, were recognized classics taught in every film school, but she was still an ostracized and controversial figure, despite the fact that she'd been acquitted of collaboration after the war. Bianca had met her when the London *Sunday Times* magazine asked the Jaggers to pose for a cover, and Mick flippantly told them he'd only pose for Leni Riefenstahl, thinking they'd never go for it. They did, and Bianca and Leni became fast friends. "She was one of the great beauties of the day, another prejudice to overcome," Bianca wrote in *Interview* when Harper & Row published Riefenstahl's *Last of the Nuba*, her book of East Africa photographs. "She had to prove, always, that a beautiful woman can do anything, that a beautiful woman is not necessarily dull and spoiled, that a beautiful woman can be intelligent and original."

"I think Bianca's talking about herself," said Andy, who agreed to have Leni to lunch more out of curiosity about her friendship with Bianca than out of curiosity about the Nazis or the Nuba.

The Tanzanian foreign minister turned up at the Factory with a phalanx of security men, who searched the place while he waited in his limousine. Andy loved the secrecy and the security, saying, "Gee, if we always had diplomats down, we'd always have guards." And Leni managed to charm him too, bringing him a signed copy of her book, and taking him through it page by page, pointing out the "elegance" of this Nubian's back or the "strength" of that Nubian's legs, answering Andy's questions about their makeup and their jewelry. "She's great," he said after she left. "She doesn't care about politics. She just cares about beauties." He could have been talking about himself.

Another early lunch guest came to play a bigger role in Andy's world, and Bianca's: Jerry Hall. Antonio brought her to the Factory hoping to convince us that she would make a great *Interview* cover. The minute she opened her big beautiful mouth and said in a big beautiful drawl, "Ah want to marry a millionaire, so ah can have caviah any time of the day or night, and take nice, long champagne baths," Andy was convinced. I was against putting an unknown on the cover at that point. We compromised, and made her the Viewgirl of the September 1975 issue, which coincidentally had Bianca on the cover.

In January 1975, Diana Vreeland came to check out "Andy's new place" and pronounced it, "Divine! Divine! Divine! Oh, Andy, I'm *so* happy for you, and for *the boys* too. You must all be so *inspired* by this *marvelous* new space! New vista! New light!"

"New bills," said Andy.

I remember Diana's advice about *Interview:* "Don't give people what they want. Give them what they *never knew* they wanted."

It was the difference between following trends and setting them. Andy, Fred, and I all agreed *Interview* should do the latter, though Andy interpreted Diana's advice to mean we should put unknowns on the cover, and Fred and I wanted to keep stars on the cover until the magazine was strong enough to sell itself no matter who was on the cover. And that meant improving the quality of our paper and contents, widening distribution, stepping up promotion, spending more money. So we had to sell more ads, and more portraits to cover the losses until we did. That's what most of our lunches were really about: selling ads and selling art, often in tandem, one hand washing the other. Paintings always just happened to be leaning against the walls in the Factory reception room, and you couldn't miss the stacks of *Interview* in the foyer on the way in or out.

One day in 1974, Halston came to lunch and bought ten miniature Mao paintings, for about $2,000 each. It was the beginning of a long business relationship between him and Andy. He also asked Andy to do his portrait, and came to the Factory a couple of months later for the "unveiling" lunch and was so pleased by Andy's depiction that he agreed to advertise in *Interview* for the first time. We all had another Stolichnaya, and Halston's Venezuelan-born window dresser and close friend, Victor Hugo, came up with the idea of making a bow tie cut out of caviar and photographing it for the ad. It ran on the March 1975 back cover, and where Halston led, others followed. Between December 1974 and December 1976, our advertising pages doubled, with most of the increase in the fashion category.

Our big breakthrough in the wine-and-spirits category came from another lunch: with Eric de Rothschild, who had been Andy's first portrait client in Paris, back in 1972. We were dying to get Château Lafite Rothschild ads, but to make it seem less premeditated, Fred also asked Eric's old friend, retired Superstar Jane Holzer. Then Leo Castelli's wife and partner, Twoiny, called to ask when she could bring Marion Goodman, of Multiples, Inc., by to see the Drag Queen paintings. Fred invited them too, figuring that they'd be impressed by our glamorous friends, and our glamorous friends would be impressed by their seriousness. We talked about Paloma Picasso, the Gilded Grape, everything but the dual purpose of the lunch: selling art and ads.

When Jane brought up her recent Palm Beach visit, I had my cue and showed her the latest issue of the *Palm Beach Social Pictorial,* which called *Interview* "so avant-garde not even the avant-garde knows what it's about." Now Andy had his cue: "Oh, you should show Jane the article the *Wall Street Journal* did on the magazine." Not Eric, Jane. She laughed all the way through it, especially at the part making fun of the Diana von Furstenberg interview by Victor Hugo, hooting, "I *love* Victor's stories, they're hysterical''—and Eric couldn't wait to grab it from her. By the end of the lunch, *he* suggested advertising in *Interview,* but wondered what image would be right. Now Fred had *his* cue and said it should just be their label, on a plain white ground, and designed the ad on the spot. We were so afraid that, if Eric took it up with their agency in Paris, it would take months before they came up with a campaign they considered appropriate, or nix the idea altogether.

In the meantime, Vincent had taken Twoiny and Marion into the middle room to see the Drag Queen paintings, hinting that they might advertise more in *Interview* too, and I left for a meeting with Diane von Furstenberg's advertising manager, Bob Loeb. When I'd made the appointment, I'd let it drop that Victor Hugo was designing Halston's first ad for us, and at the meeting I started off with the Rothschild news. ''You know,'' said DVF's ad man, ''*Interview* reminds me of *The New Yorker* in the forties. I think it has the right ambience for the DVF image''—and gave me two pages for Diane's new perfume, Tatiana.

Diane von Furstenberg, by the way, had had her portrait done shortly before Halston, in 1974, and Jane Holzer had hers done shortly after Halston, in 1975, just after the Rothschild lunch. Then Halston commissioned Victor Hugo's portrait, to thank him for designing his ads, and Andy gave Halston a rare discount, to thank him for letting Victor put *Interview* in the window of his Madison Avenue boutique—every month when a new one came out, he'd have the mannequins reading it.

It all clicked. And kept on clicking: Rothschild wine led to Lillet apéritif, which led to Cuervo Gold tequila, which led to Wyrobowa vodka—and no more Stolichnaya at lunch. Lillet was another important breakthrough, because the ads came from the agency, not a friendly client. They exacted a high price: First they wanted us to weave in mentions of Lillet in Andy's interviews, sending us a case to pour while we taped. Then they gently suggested that Lillet made a nice substitute for vodka and champagne at lunch, sending us another case to serve while we sold. And why not, they proposed, have a cocktail party at the Factory and only serve Lillet, to turn all your trend-setting friends on to this all-purpose, all-hours apéritif. We did, inviting our trend-setting friendly clients—Marina Schiano of YSL, Elsa Peretti of Tiffany, Bob Loeb of DVF Fragrances. Lady Ann Lambton almost blew the account by breaking into the Moët et Chandon hidden in the kitchen, and slipping some to Maxime de la Falaise McKendry, who was supposed to be weaving Lillet into her medieval menus for *Vogue.* And Andy had had to endorse Lillet to get the ads in the first place.

Andy loved endorsing products. Our first regular advertising contract had been from Pioneer Electronics, featuring Andy and Archie, surrounded by stereo speakers, turntables, and tape recorders, under the headline: ''Andy Warhol's unfinished symphony.'' Vincent had arranged that deal, partially in exchange for a sound system for the new Factory. Along with endorsements, Andy loved trades. When the Lillet people first presented their idea—checks from chic Parisian places like the Georges V and Maxim's for "two Lillet on the rocks" signed "Andy Warhol"—Andy enthusiastically agreed. As soon as they left, he said that I'd have to sign his name for him, "because you have such artistic handwriting and if I do it, everybody will know how to forge my autograph."

The Lillet people soon had another idea: They wanted us to line up Diane von Furstenberg and Marisa Berenson for the campaign. I did that too. I had quickly learned that *Interview* didn't have "the numbers," or circulation, and what numbers we did have were not "ABC audited." So instead we sold ambience, image, art direction, promotion, public relations, social connections, endorsements. If an advertiser wanted it, Warhol, Hughes, and Colacello were at their service. Other magazine owners and publishers might perform some of these services for clients, but most editors avoided almost all of them. We really didn't have a choice: The magazine had to survive.

Peter Brant was getting tired of the losses, and in August 1975, when Fred turned to him for help in financing *Bad,* Peter said he'd give it if he could get out of *Interview.* They made the swap—another complicated deal that I was not privy to, though I believe it involved some paintings—at the end of the year. We took Motion Olympus, Inc., off the masthead page and put on Interview Enterprises, Inc. I was a little upset that I wasn't asked to be an officer of that company—indeed, I wasn't even told who was—but it passed. Whenever I was upset about *Interview,* especially selling ads, Andy would allay my agitation by telling me, "If you work harder, Bob, the magazine could really be big, and then you'd be on easy street." If I was really fed up, he'd softly add, "Maybe we could give you part of it then."

Selling advertising also helped me become a better editor: It forced me to focus on what kind of readers we wanted and how to get them, to see the magazine as a complete process, with editorial feeding circulation, circulation feeding advertising, advertising feeding editorial, rather than separate parts working against each other. That didn't mean doing everything the advertisers wanted, though we did a lot, and Andy would have had me do more. It did mean that a certain kind of reader led to a certain kind of advertiser and vice versa. And in explaining the magazine's editorial policy to advertisers, I was also formulating it for myself—defining it in sharper, clearer terms, giving it direction, identity, finding not only its niche in the market, but also its place in the culture. There was another thing I liked about selling advertising: Success could be measured in dollars and cents, pages and half pages and quarter pages, and like Andy, I was soon counting them and measuring totals against the previous year's. I liked the feeling of building something from the ground up.

And I wasn't the only one doing it. Everyone pitched in: Fred pressured the art galleries, like Castelli and Sonnabend, and they'd come through when they could. He'd also keep after Marina Schiano, who finally coughed up a double-page spread from YSL. Vincent kept Pioneer renewing their contract and used it to bring in their competitor, JVC. Carole followed up on many of the contacts we made socially and made sure clients paid, which was often the most difficult part of selling ads. She also ran a team of roving salespeople, sending them off to the boutiques Barbara Allen mentioned in her column and the record companies that Sandy Brant and Susan Blond had developed. Susan had moved on from a P.R. job at United Artists to a bigger one at Epic Records, where she kept the pressure on for us, and then we used the ads she got us to get ads from the competition. Even Brigid Berlin came through with a full page from her mother's favorite designer, Adolfo, for the December 1976 issue, saying it was the Berlin family Christmas present to Andy. She had been listed under Advertising on the masthead for two years already, because Andy was sure just having the Berlin name there would bring in the advertisers who remembered her father from Hearst.

We pegged our December 1975 issue to the theme "Fashion as Fantasy." It was a big success, hitting a new high in ad pages, including Valentino, Gianni Versace, Issey Miyake, and Roberta di Camerino, all for the first time. We put Tatum O'Neal, aged twelve, on the cover in an Oscar de la Renta turban. Inside, Andy taped "Ryan's Daughter on Seventh Avenue" and Barbara Allen photographed Tatum trying on outfits in the de la Renta, Halston, Calvin Klein, Anne Klein, and Albert Capraro showrooms. It was one more of those catchy stories that were picked up by the gossip columnists from coast to coast. And in editing it, and selling ads for it, I came up with a line we used for a long time, to keep the two separate in our minds and the clients'—"Interview is *not* a fashion magazine, it's a *fashionable* magazine."

Meanwhile, the lunches went on, more ads and portraits were sold, and we learned from our hits and misses. The hits usually happened when the guest of honor wasn't obviously there for business—and then we used our glamour guest to lure the clients.

Sometimes we had the wrong guest of honor, and everything went wrong. Sometimes we had misses that turned into hits. Sometimes we had misses that stayed misses, like the time Fred and I got our wires crossed, and he invited the King of Sweden, who brought his court, and I invited Fulgencio Batista, Jr., who brought his joint. Nobody bought anything at that lunch. Sometimes the most successful lunches were solo lunches, when we had a single guest down and got to know him better, like Calvin Klein, who took his first page in *Interview*'s February 1976 issue and gradually evolved into our biggest advertiser.

Another solo guest, neither a potential ad nor a potential portrait, except perhaps in the very long run, was one of Andy's favorites: Lorna Luft, then age twenty-one. Andy always liked Liza, but he loved Lorna. He felt more comfortable with her just as he was chummier with Bianca than with Mick, or Victor Hugo than Halston. Lorna held another attraction for Andy: She was one hell of a talker, a veritable fountain of gossip, who hadn't yet learned when to turn it off because she was still so young. "I saw Bianca every day in L.A.," she said that day—the Rolling Stones were on tour. "She called *me* when she flooded her suite at the Beverly Wilshire—yeah, she let the tub run over, the usual thing—and I said, 'Should I come over with a plumber or a plunger?' So I rushed right over, and Bianca told me the best dish: Barbra Streisand asked her agent, Sue Mengers, for two tickets to the Stones concert and Bianca got them and then Barbra never showed up, never called, never wrote a note of apology—can you believe it?"

"Uh-huh," said Andy, "she wouldn't even consider our offer to star her in Patrick O'Higgins's *Madame.*"

"Playing a whore or what?" asked Lorna, ready to start another rumor.

"Noooo," said Andy, "playing Madame Helena Rubinstein, a Russian Jewish princess. So how was the big Diana Ross party for Mick? Bianca hated it."

"Well," said Lorna, taking a deep breath and then running with it. "First of all, Diana had four security checkpoints, for five hundred guests, so it took *forever* to get into the place, and *then* the security men kept asking people to stay *out* of the house and to stay *in* the garden, because 'the children are sleeping'—can you believe it? I mean, send the children to a hotel for the night, right? I mean, I was sitting on the piano . . .''

"You were sitting on the piano!"

"Yeah, with Liza and Bianca, and the security men asked *us* to go outside—can you believe it? And Bianca said she would, but 'Miss Ross' would have to ask her herself. Don't you love it? And then Liza told Mick that he was the best and he said, 'Ah, shucks,' and it was just so cute, oh, I wish you could have been there, Andy. Oh, but I've *got* to tell you about going to the Stones concert. I went with Liza, Jack [Haley, Jr.], Raquel, Ron Talsky, and Bianca, and when we appeared the crowd went wild and this cherry bomb landed right at Bianca's feet!"

"Did it go off?"

"No, Andy, don't be silly. Oh, did you see me on the cover of the *National Star* with Burt [Reynolds]?"

"Yeahhhh, you looked greaaaat. So is Burt as great in bed as they say he is?"

"Andy! I do like Burt, but we're just friends."

"Yeah, sure. I bet you gave the *Star* the pictures, Lorna."

"Andy, I did not! I didn't give them an interview either. They made my quotes up."

"All right, Lorna. So give us an interview, all dirt, and we'll put you on the cover. Won't we, Bob?"

As much as I liked Lorna too, I had to remind him that Lorna had been on the cover just a few months before.

"You mean she didn't sell?" said Andy.

"No, Andy, I mean we have to wait awhile before we put her on again."

"Oh," said Andy. "Bob's terrible, isn't he, Lorna?"

Andy gave away a cover at almost every lunch, and I usually took it back. Lorna just laughed it off, and went on with the gossip she fed Andy like candy. "Did I ever tell you about the time Marilyn Monroe asked me, 'Do you love me, Lorna?'—I mean, I was just a kid, right? And I said, 'I love you, Marilyn,' and she said, 'But do you like me, Lorna?' You know, Marilyn and my mother were best friends."

"THEY WERE? Lorna, you never told me that!" Andy sounded as if he were having an orgasm. "God. What did they talk about?"

"I don't know."

"YOU DON'T KNOW?"

"Well, we didn't have tape recorders in those days."

"Oh, God, I think I forgot to turn my tape over. Oh, I did. Oh, Lorna, you've got to say everything all over again, just like you said it the first time."

The real selling lunches were the "unveiling" lunches. In September 1975, Andy unveiled Joe MacDonald's portrait. Joe was the leading male model of the seventies, and he used his earnings to collect Art Deco and Pop Art, which Andy always told him was "so smart." The other guests were all friends of Joe's—David Hockney, Henry Geldzahler, and Robert Mapplethorpe. Andy had invited Sue Mengers too, thinking she'd sign up Joe MacDonald for the movies. He was often doing things like that, trying to help, but often doing just the opposite, because he would press so relentlessly—"You have to make Joe a movie star, Sue. He's so great. He really is." And he'd press just as relentlessly for the next young hopeful that walked into the room, so that people rarely took his recommendations seriously.

We wanted to have an unveiling lunch for Mick Jagger's 1975 portrait, too, but, as usual, Mick was wary of being used and said no. He came down to look at it alone, and Bianca arrived a little later and left a little earlier in her own limo, their movements, like their marriage, increasingly out of synch. Andy had done several versions of Mick's portrait, as he often did when he thought a subject might interest other collectors, or was rich enough and egotistical enough to take more than had been ordered. Mick, known for his frugality, restricted his choice to the three most flattering—and we kept unveiling the ones he didn't choose at lunches he wasn't at. Edmund Gaultney, the director of the Freeman-Anacker Gallery in New Orleans, asked if he could show the leftover Mick Jaggers. Fred asked Mick for permission, and when the show opened two months later, he asked Edmund to advertise it in *Interview*. Fred was attaching that condition to more and more art deals: In the same issue, March 1976, we had an ad from the Max Protech Gallery in Washington, D.C., for a show of the Drag Queen prints, and in the June 1976 issue, another one from the Coe-Kerr Gallery for the joint Andy Warhol–Jamie Wyeth show, "Portraits of Each Other." Portraits and ads, ads and portraits.

The Warhol-Wyeth exchange had an important effect on Andy's image: It alienated him even further from the serious art establishment, critics like Clement Greenberg, Harold Rosenberg, and Robert Hughes, artists like Robert Motherwell, Jasper Johns, and Frank Stella, and, most important, their temple of worship, the Museum of Modern Art.

Many of the portraits Andy did in the first two years at the new Factory, 1975 and 1976, have the same look: soft and pastel, with faraway eyes, lost under azure, mint, or lavender shadow—Mick Jagger, Joe MacDonald, Roy Lichtenstein, Marilyn Karp (the art dealer's wife), Marcia Weisman (the sister of Norton Simon), Doda Vorodis (a rich Greek friend of Jerry Zipkin), Tina Freeman (a young Coca-Cola heiress from New Orleans), Carole Coleman (another Louisiana heiress, whose Warhol portrait was supposed to cheer her up, but who committed suicide shortly after it was delivered). Andy's portrait style tended to run in cycles, so that for certain years there is a uniformity, broken occasionally by a portrait of someone he knew particularly well, or who so impressed him it provoked a new response.

The last portrait Andy painted at the old Factory in 1974 was of his mother, Julia Warhola, who had died two years before, though Andy avoided telling anyone about it, including Jed. Julia had been in a Pittsburgh nursing home for nineteen months before she died, at age eighty, on November 28, 1972. Andy had avoided mentioning that fact, too, and Jed was under strict orders not to say a word. Andy paid for the nursing home, but never visited her there. He called her every day and she begged him to come see her. "She *hunted* for him, under the dressers, in the basement," his sister-in-law Ann Warhola later told me. "They found her out on the highway looking for him." Andy paid for her funeral, but he didn't go to it. "He was afraid of death," Anne Warhola said.

Andy often said the same thing about death that he said about sex—it was "abstract." And that's how he painted Julia, her photographic silkscreen image faint and faded under layers of squiggles and squishes, gobs and goops, painted on by her son's fingers.

Now, in the new Factory, he abandoned fingerpainting and the more complex, gestural style of the 1972–74 portraits, for a cleaner, smoother, simpler look—the difference was not unlike that between the two spaces in which he painted, the older cluttered and cramped, the new clear and spacious. Although Andy was not about to admit it to Diana Vreeland, he *was* inspired by the open vastness of the new space. For Andy, space was a void to be filled, and just as he stepped up his morning shopping sprees, he also stepped up his afternoon painting sprees. It may have been so that the latter could pay for the former, but I think it went a little deeper: Now that Andy had a studio to paint in, he became a real painter again.

Every day after lunch, and on most Saturdays and some Sundays, Andy was in his backroom studio for three or four hours, painting away. Ronnie Cutrone would premix colors and prepaint backgrounds, but often Andy would ask him to do it over or would do it over himself, remixing the colors and repainting one background on top of another. He often added a bit of black to even the lightest colors, so that his pastels weren't flowery, and his candy colors came out more like Necco wafers than M&M's.

He wasn't only painting commissioned portraits by any means, though some of his other work was commissioned by a dealer before he started it. In any case, he was painting more than he had since the mid-sixties, and with the same intensity and prolificacy. After the Maos, which he painted through 1974, came the Drag Queens (Ladies and Gentlemen) in 1975, the Cats and Dogs into 1976, and the Skulls that same year. The Skulls were eerie and glamorous relics from the grave, some bright yellow and magenta, others black-on-black, always one of Andy's most masterly color schemes. Andy painted every subject until he had exhausted his range of appropriate, and inappropriate, color combinations—he thought about color a lot, more than he did about composition or light or line, it seemed to me. And he painted each subject in a series of sizes, from ten feet tall to ten inches square, or from jumbo economy size to individual size, like detergents in supermarkets. He also did several versions of each size, four or six or eight of the largest, ten or twelve medium-size, twenty or thirty smaller ones, and a hundred miniatures.

They were priced, then, from $8,000 to $80,000, though dealers paid half that and friendly collectors usually got about one-third off when they bought directly from the Factory. We called that our "wholesale" price, just as when you buy directly from a designer's showroom. Andy's regular dealers didn't like it, but they knew if they protested too loudly, Andy would just do more business through his irregular dealers.

The quality dealers, like Leo Castelli, Bruno Bischofberger, and Thomas Ammann, were constantly begging Fred to get Andy to curtail his quantity, often pointing out that paintings weren't prints, though they knew full well that Andy was trying to prove the difference moot—that was what Pop Art was all about, wasn't it? Still, they would chant in chorus, "Tell Andy there's a limit to what the market will bear. Enough is enough, enough is enough." It was a futile effort, and some of them backed him when he did prints of the same subjects he painted: the Drag Queens and Mick Jaggers in 1975 (each in editions of 250 portfolios of 10 prints each), and the Skulls in 1976 (50 portfolios of 4 prints). He also did drawings of the same subjects he painted and printed. He would pin a piece of heavy vellum stock on the wall, project the image through a slide projector, and trace over the projection onto the paper in pencil. All in all, it was an incredible outpouring.

And while Andy painted, we were all at our desks in the front of the Factory and the *Interview* office, working on his magazine, his books, his TV and movie projects, his exhibitions and social schedules, his publicity and image. Every so often, when he finished a painting or got a call he wanted to discuss with one of us, he would toddle out of his studio in his high-heeled cowboy boots, like a kid in his mother's shoes, and head for our desks, where we sat holding things down, in anticipation of that big kid, our boss, making a mess and turning everything upside down.

Sometimes Andy would stop at Carole Rogers's desk and ask her, apropos of nothing, "How much money do we make on each issue we sell?" It was a legitimate question for the owner of a magazine, particularly one that was losing money, to ask the associate publisher. But when Carole said she'd have the figure for him by the next morning, he'd switch to gossip about the other *Interview* staffers, as if he really didn't care about the figures, and then complain to me that she wasn't "doing her job." He'd ask to see layouts and make no comments, beyond "Gee," or "Oh," and then tell me that Marc Balet wasn't doing his job either.

What he really meant was why wasn't I hovering over everybody at *Interview,* driving them on, as he would have been had he not been painting. If I explained that I was on the phone—Andy often talked at me while I was so engaged—with John Springer or Bobby Zarem, trying to line up a cover story, he'd say, "Oh, I forgot to tell you. I told Victor Hugo he could design the next cover instead of Richard Bernstein. He's getting us *ads,* Bob." And then he'd toddle off, like the bad kid from next door, who just knocked down all your building blocks. Except he was supposed to be the father.

At times like these I turned to Fred for support. He almost always took my side, marching back to Andy's studio and telling him to give me a break and forget about making Victor Hugo cover designer, or putting Lorna Luft on the cover again, or trading Calvin for clothes instead of getting paid for his ads, or any of the countless other "great ideas" Andy got in his nervous moments between paintings, when he saw his domain expanding and feared he was losing control.

At the end of the working day, which was the beginning of the working night, Andy and I usually taxied uptown together. More often than not, it was close to seven and I was always in a hurry to get home and change for dinner, and Andy was taking his time because he didn't change for dinner. He also had to put Vincent through the ordeal by fire and water before we could leave, checking and rechecking the sink in his painting area, the *Interview* bathroom and the Factory bathroom, and the sink in the kitchen, for drips that might turn into floods, and all the ashtrays from the 17th Street side to the 18th Street side and back again, for ashes and butts that might burst into flames in the middle of the night. It wasn't unusual for him to "just run to check the back sink" and stop and make a phone call once he got there, while Vincent and I buzzed him on the intercom and then went back and pulled him away.

Then there would be another five-minute wait while Andy went back into the Factory bathroom to "make sure I look all right." Five minutes more would be spent waiting for a taxi on the deserted corner of Park Avenue South and 17th Street, with Andy loaded down with his Brownie's bag, a stack of *Interviews,* and a shopping bag or two of whatever he had picked up on his way to work that morning. I always offered to help carry the load, and he always said, "That's okay."

In the taxi, during the twenty minutes or so it took to get uptown, Andy and I had our daily "meeting." I'd fill him in on *Interview* and the book business: the upcoming *Philosophy* tour ("Make it short, Bob"); the on-going *HER* project ("Paulette will never talk, Bob"); and the new deal we made with HBJ in 1975 for *Popism: The Warhol Sixties* ("I don't understand why Pat has to have her name on the cover, Bob"—"Because she's writing the book, Andy"—"Oh, really?"). Andy nagged me about helping Vincent revive the *Nothing Serious* TV project, which had been stalled since we moved, mainly because Vincent was so busy running a much bigger office. "I'm not a TV director, Andy. I've got a magazine to get out." "Oh, really?"

And we talked about whom to pop the question to at the two or three or four parties on our schedule that night. And how *I'd* be on easy street when all those ships came in, unless I ran off and married whichever rich client's wife Andy was insisting was in love with me, and then we'd both be on easy street, because I'd spend all her money on his art. When he got to Park and 63rd Street, I'd jump out and Andy would shout behind me, "Don't forget to pick me up in half an hour."

27

Imelda

"Hurry up, Andy. We're going to be late for Mrs. Marcos."

"Should I bring her the new *Interview?*"

"Yes."

"Did you write anything bad about her in 'OUT'?"

"No."

"Do I look all right?"

"Yes." His wig was askew, but if I'd told him that, he'd be back in the Factory bathroom for another ten minutes, and Fred was already in the elevator, holding the door open, barking, "Let's go! You can't keep a First Lady waiting." I held the bulletproof door and Andy rushed through, his Brownie's bag in one hand and Archie in the other. "Should we drop Archie at home first?" he asked. "There's no time," snapped Fred, "and he'll help break the ice. Dogs always do."

"Archie," said Andy, stroking his pet under the chin, "you're going to meet Mrs. Marcos. Oh, if you'd only talk, Archie, we wouldn't have to do things like this."

In November 1974, after a year of not-so-subtle hinting by us, Franco Rossellini had finally arranged for Andy to get together with the wife of the President of the Philippines, over tea in her suite at the Carlyle Hotel. The year before, she had electrified the art world by asking for prices at the Francis Bacon retrospective at the Metropolitan Museum. When told that the Met paintings were actually not for sale but that there was a Bacon show on at the Marlborough Gallery, Imelda had immediately motorcaded down to 57th Street, and, the buzz was, snapped up twenty large canvases at

$200,000 each. She was really bringing home the Bacon—and also, that same trip, according to a Bulgari associate, a million-dollar diamond.

Unfortunately, Franco had been called back to Rome on *Caligula* business and Andy was nervous about meeting the "Iron Butterfly" without him. "Franco could have popped the question," he said in the taxi. "Relax, Andy," said Fred, "these things take time. We've got to get to know her first."

"We might not have *time,* Fred," said Andy. "They could be thrown out of the country tomorrow. Did you ever think of that?"

"I read the newspapers, too, Andy," said Fred. "Fix your hair."

"God, what do I have two hairdressers for?" Andy teased. And tortured: "Well, if you won't pop the question, Fred, Bob will. Won't you, Bob? You're good at politics. You went to Georgetown Foreign Service School." He was already unwrapping his Polaroid film, to increase the pressure on me to pop the question the first time I met the First Lady.

Andy was always in a rush to pin down a potential portrait, but he was particularly anxious about this one. It could be the big break in his campaign to become the official portraitist to the leaders of the world. And, unlike President Ford, or any other leader of a democratic nation, Imelda Marcos really could order up scores of her silk-screened likeness, for every cabinet member's office, governor's mansion, and ambassador's residence, fulfilling one of Andy's fondest fantasies: the single commission that miraculously multiplied ad infinitum. And then, wouldn't President Marcos want *his* portrait, too, to hang side by side with the First Lady's in every post office, train station, and national-bank branch in the land? And once the Marcoses set the trend for official portraits by Andy Warhol—so flattering, so easily reproduced—wouldn't the Pahlavis and the Saudis, Hassan and Hussein, the King and Queen of Thailand, all follow? And how about Imelda's new best friend, Mrs. Mao Tse-tung? Why, Andy had her husband's portraits in every size and color, just sitting there at the Factory, waiting to be shipped to China the minute the check came in the diplomatic pouch. "And think of how great my diary would be, Bob," Andy sometimes said, "when we get to meet all these kings and queens." Right, and ask them about the size of the royal cock.

The one thing that worried Andy about hanging out with this group, aside from losing his limousine-liberal clients, was their tendency to attract assassins. Mrs. Marcos, for example, had already been stabbed in the arm by one of her Filipino subjects. Andy didn't want to be there, popping Polaroids, when the bullets sprayed. But then, what if the Marcoses were killed or toppled *before* getting Andy started on this imagined merry-go-round of monarchs and potentates commissioning portraits by the dozens, or hundreds, or thousands? There *was* a Communist insurgency in the Philippines and martial law had been declared in 1972. So we had to hurry and pop the question right away, and just hope that there weren't any crazed revolutionaries with machine guns lurking in the lobby of the Carlyle. As Jerry Zipkin had advised Andy a few nights before, "Never get in an elevator with Imelda. And if you have to, always let her get out first."

When we got off the elevator on the 34th floor of the Carlyle Hotel, we were confronted by a U.S. Secret Service post, set up between Imelda's suite, 34b—the one where President Kennedy had always stayed, noted Fred—and suite 34a, which was owned by Henry Ford II, whose second wife, an Italian jet setter named Christina, was one of Imelda's most intimate friends. The Secret Service men checked our passports and then announced us—by walkie-talkie—to their Filipino counterparts, who were standing a few feet away. "Gee," whispered Andy, "this is glamorous. And scary. I better not tape, right?"

The Filipinos checked our passports again and opened the door to Imelda's suite, where a video crew was waiting, with its bright lights on, to record our entrance. "They've got us on film now," whispered Andy. "We're linked with her for good, so we better get her portrait, Bob." Still being videotaped, we moved into the center of the sitting room and admired the view of Manhattan, Queens, *and* New Jersey, while noting the names on the cards attached to the flower arrangements set up on pedestals: Jerry and Betty Ford, Nelson and Happy Rockefeller, Henry and Nancy Kissinger, Hugh Carey, Abe and Mary Beame, David and Peggy Rockefeller, Dick and Honey Berlin. . . . "Gee, Brigid's parents really are up there," said Andy. And after a beat, "Can you see my pimples in this bright light?" When the camera crew started taking Polaroids of us, Andy really got worried: "They're putting us on file, Bob. And when the revolution comes, the Communists will find our pictures. This is all your fault, Bob."

Then Mrs. Marcos swept in from the bedroom, tall, dark, and handsome, with her soft half-Oriental features and hard jet-black pompadour, a kind of cross between the middle-aged Merle Oberon and the juvenile Elvis Presley. She was wearing a simple black dress, set off by a big Bulgari diamond pin, which immediately caught Andy's eye. She waved away the camera crew imperiously, telling them, "*Please.* Let us get to know each other first." She turned to Andy and explained, "It's the Filipino TV. They are making a documentary of my trip to America and Mexico, where I have to go to buy some oil." She made it sound like cooking oil, ordinary, as if she were a housewife dashing to a corner bodega called Mexico. "What can I do?" she went on in a voice that was simultaneously very feminine and very strong. "They follow me everywhere I go with their cameras and their lights, because the Filipino people can't get enough of me. They want to know everything I do, everyone I see. . . . I am their star. Their star and their slave."

"Oh, gee," said Andy. "We brought you our magazine."

"But you won't write in it that I am extravagant," said Imelda, "will you? I don't know why the American press always writes that I'm extravagant. Do I look extravagant?'' She had conveniently covered her diamond pin, all twenty karats of it, with the copy of *Interview*.

"Oh, no," said Andy, stuck now that he couldn't talk about the one thing they had in common: jewelry. After a long dead pause, he added, "Gee, isn't Franco Rossellini great?"

Imelda agreed that he was, but she wasn't in the mood for gossip. Instead, she launched into a long speech about art, full of platitudes and clichés (but no suggestion that she was aware that Andy painted portraits), finally concluding that artists brought people together, just as she was trying to do in her travels, to bring nations together and join the East and the West. Every time she said East she turned her head one way and every time she said West she turned the other, East, West, East, West, and we turned ours with hers, until we were dizzy, and stifling yawns. The Philippines, she said, was ideally positioned to play the go-between for the East and the West, because it was neither one nor the other, but both. She often used "I" when she meant the Philippines, and "the Philippines" when she meant I. This, she said, is what she had told Mrs. Mao Tse-tung on her recent trip to China, and Mrs. Mao, she said, agreed.

"Oh, gee," Andy said, "I think the way the women dress in China is great, all the same. I love uniforms. But then I think the fashion business is such a great business because it gives so many people work, you know, changing from long to short so you need new clothes every season, and uh, oh . . ."

"Well, I do not want to appear immodest," said Imelda, "but I think I have changed the course of fashion in China—by wearing a dress. I wore the national dress of the Philippines, which has butterfly sleeves. Today I am wearing Dior, because this is a private event, but in public I always wear the national dress, because I want to promote the Filipino fashion industry. And many Chinese women told Mrs. Mao that they thought my dresses were very pretty and that they were thinking of how nice it would be to wear dresses sometimes. And Mrs. Mao said maybe."

"Oh, really? She said maybe. Gee, that would be a big change, wouldn't it, Fred? Oh, Fred's on the Best Dressed List. Aren't you, Fred?"

Imelda wasn't interested in Fred, or me, only Andy. She barely noticed Archie-the-icebreaker, though when her children emerged from another room they went right for him. "This is my daughter, who has the same name as me, but we call her Imee," said Imelda. "She is enrolled at Princeton University, in New Jersey. And this is my son Bong Bong, whose real name is Ferdinand the Second, after his father. He is enrolled at Oxford University, in England." Bong Bong was wearing an embroidered see-through shirt, which his mother explained was "the national shirt of the Philippines."

"Oh, Mommy," squealed Imee, "this dog is *adorable.*"

"Well, then," said Imelda, "Archie must come to the Philippines and we will introduce him to our dogs. We have thirty dogs and they live in a doghouse, which is really more like a dollhouse, behind our palace in Manila. Well, I must say goodbye now, and have a little rest. I was up until seven in the morning with my next-door neighbor, Cristina Ford. She is such a fun girl.''

"Gee, oh, uh,'' sputtered Andy, terrified that whatever he said would come out wrong. Finally he hit upon a polite but still somewhat inquisitive formulation. ''That's late.''

"You know,'' said Imelda, ''I only need two hours of sleep a day. This is God's gift to me. Because it allows me to have the time and the energy to serve the people of my country.''

The second we hit the street, Andy said, ''God, is she a phony. What does she mean, the Filipino TV just can't get enough of her—she owns the TV there, doesn't she? And did you notice, she only invited Archie to the Philippines? Why didn't you say something, Fred? And you too, Bob? You both just sat there and I had to do all the work.''

"She barely acknowledged our existence,'' I replied.

"She lost me when she started in on that East-meets-West bullshit,'' said Fred. ''And did you get a load of the way she told us that Princeton was in New Jersey and Oxford was in England, in case we didn't know?''

"What a phony, right?'' said Andy, laughing a bit.

"I'd forget getting *anything* out of her,'' said Fred. ''She'll never have her portrait done, take my word for it.''

"She'd make a great portrait though,'' said Andy, not so willing to give it up. ''She really is beautiful, and I could make her more beautiful. And what did she mean about being up all night with Cristina Ford? Was she trying to tell us something, Fred?''

"I know what's coming next, Andy, and I don't want to hear it,'' said Fred, turning up Park Avenue.

"Don't you love it when Fred gets grand,'' said Andy, turning down Park with me. ''Oh, we should've gossiped more with her, right?'' he said, analyzing what went wrong and how to correct it. ''But I guess she wanted to be serious and stiff for the cameras, right? You should ask her for lunch at the office, Bob. And then she can let her hair down, and we can tell her the Liz Taylor stories. That's probably why she likes Franco so much, he tells her movie-star stories. And we can show her my portraits of Mrs. Agnelli and Mrs. Rochas Perfume and Mrs. Schlumberger Oil and, uh, oh, Mr. Mao, right? I bet she's fun when she lets her hair down. Today was just an act. We've got to see her again. Call her up tomorrow.''

I wasn't sure she even knew my name, so I sent flowers instead, from Andy. I wrote a note, thanking her for her kind hospitality and asking her to lunch, and then Andy copied it out in his own hand, which he only did for first ladies, and very big clients. In response, a secretary called and invited Andy to tea again, at the Chinese Mission to the United Nations,

where Mrs. Marcos was showing the Filipino TV documentary of her trip
to China. It didn't sound like the sort of place where she could let her hair
down, or where we could tell Elizabeth Taylor stories, but at least she wanted
to see Andy again. He and I took a taxi from the Factory in the late afternoon, passing through Times Square, where we were jolted by the news
flash atop the Allied Chemical Tower: ONE DEAD, ONE HOSTAGE AT FILIPINO
EMBASSY IN D.C. We listened to the details on the taxi radio—just minutes
before, a guerrilla had rung the bell at the embassy in Washington, shot the
butler in the head, and was holding the ambassador, who was the uncle of
Mrs. Marcos.

"Should we just go home?" wondered Andy. "And tell Imelda we got
the address wrong?"

"I don't think Communist guerrillas will attack the Communist Chinese mission," I reasoned, torn between a twinge of fear and that 10 percent
commission check I saw somewhere over the Imelda rainbow.

"Politics is so confusing," said Andy, sighing. "And work is so hard,
isn't it, Bob?"

The Chinese Mission to the UN was housed in a former motel near
Lincoln Center—"with their own Chinese restaurant and their own Chinese
laundry," as Andy put it, immediately getting the point: They never had to
leave the premises. The Communist mainlanders had replaced the Nation-
alist Taiwanese in the China seat at the UN in 1971, and were still rather
wary of the wicked ways of the West. Indeed, we were among the first New
Yorkers to be asked to their mission. We weren't so sure it was an honor
when we saw the half-dozen New York City police cars parked out front.
"This is too scary," murmured Andy as our passports were inspected first
by the U.S. Secret Service, then the Filipinos, and finally the Chinese.

Once inside, we found ourselves in a large room, decorated in a motel-
modern style, with a large group of Chinese men, all dressed in identical
gray Mao suits. "How do you tell the diplomats from the servants?" Andy
wondered. "Here comes a servant," I said, as a Chinese man approached
with a lacquered tray holding lacquered cups, which we assumed was tea.
"Coca-Cola?" he asked. "This is too nutty," said Andy. "Here comes a
diplomat," I said, as another Chinese man approached with his hand out.
He led us to a smaller room, decorated in a slightly more opulent motel-
modern style. There, between a Chinese man and woman in identical gray
Mao suits, sat Imelda, in the national dress of the Philippines, looking worried. "It must be the ambassador and his wife," Andy murmured. "Their
suits are better cut." It was Ambassador and Mrs. Wah. Imee and Bong
Bong, in national dress and national shirt, were there too, also looking
worried. It was definitely not the day to pop the question.

The seven of us—Imelda, Imee, Bong Bong, Ambassador Wah, Mrs.
Wah, Andy, and I—proceeded to the screening room, the former ballroom
of the former motel. It was decorated with row upon row of former motel-

ballroom chairs, gold steel upholstered in gold vinyl. Over the portable movie screen hung a very large portrait of Chairman Mao. "That could be mine," whispered Andy. We all sat in the front row in the otherwise empty room, and waited for the Chinese servants to figure out how to run the portable movie projector. "Is this glamorous, Bob?" whispered Andy. "I mean, here we are with the First Lady and the First Son and the First Daughter and the Mr. and Mrs. Ambassador and just us, nobody else. So it must be glamorous, right? But then they can't get the projector to work, and it's just like the screenings at the old Factory, right?"

"Don't make me laugh, Andy, please."

Imelda gave us an imperious look, and Andy shut up, and the lights went down and the movie went on, and then I really had a hard time not laughing, especially when I looked over at Andy, who would roll his eyes, ever so slightly so only I could tell, and smile devilishly, ever so slightly so only I could tell. The Filipino TV documentary turned out to be Imelda's home movies, with a voice-over narration done by the same fellow who narrates golf tournaments on television, in a hushed and reverent whisper, describing in words the very same image that was on the screen, in case anyone was blind: "And now the First Lady of the Republic of the Philippines, Imelda Romualdez Marcos, is landing in her own Philippines Air Boeing 707 at the Peking Airport. And now the First Lady of the Philippines, Imelda Romualdez Marcos, is stepping out of her own Philippines Air Boeing 707 at the Peking Airport, accompanied by her son Ferdinand Marcos II, affectionately known as Bong Bong. The First Lady of the Philippines, Imelda Romualdez Marcos, is wearing a beautiful example of the national dress of the Philippines, in a beautiful bright yellow, and Bong Bong Marcos is wearing a beautiful example of the national shirt of the Philippines, in white embroidered with red, blue, green, and yellow. And now, six thousand young Chinese schoolgirls, waving red and yellow streamers, are welcoming the First Lady of the Philippines, Imelda Romualdez Marcos, accompanied by her son . . ."

Ten minutes later, there was a cut to the next scene, tea with Mrs. Mao, that same afternoon, the narrator emphasized, noting that Mrs. Marcos didn't even have time to change her national dress. Mrs. Mao was wearing a gray Mao suit (even better cut than Ambassador and Mrs. Wah's). According to the narrator, the two first ladies "agreed to try and solve the problems standing between the two countries." And then Mrs. Marcos ran right off to tea with Chou En-lai, immediately after tea with Mrs. Mao, the narrator emphasized, with no time to change her national dress. Premier Chou was wearing a gray Mao suit (very well cut) and he too agreed to try and solve the problems standing between the two countries. That night, Mrs. Mao gave a state banquet for Mrs. Marcos, and all the Chinese wore gray Mao suits and all the Filipinos wore national shirts and national dresses, Mrs. Marcos having finally found the time to change into a bright blue one. The next day, Mrs. Marcos went to Shanghai, where two million Chinese in gray Mao suits waved at her motorcade and admired her bright pink national dress.

This went on for seven cities, seven airport arrivals, seven motorcades, seven banquets, and at least seven changes of national dress. I had to keep nudging Andy awake. He perked up, however, for the finale: Imelda's audience with Chairman Mao, who hadn't been seen much in public since the Nixon-Kissinger visit two years before. The reason why was apparent in this film: He could barely stand up. In fact, when Mrs. Marcos presented her hand to be kissed, he would have fallen right past it to the floor if Mrs. Mao hadn't pulled him back up from behind. Mrs. Marcos was so touched by his effort that she started crying, ever so delicately, into the national handkerchief of the Philippines, which, as the narrator noted, is also hand-embroidered. She shed a few more tears when Chairman Mao kissed Bong Bong on the cheek and nearly fell over again. Mrs. Mao yanked him up, and beamed at Mrs. Marcos, who beamed back. They looked as if they had just closed a major deal, and Chairman Mao looked as if he didn't know where he was. "He's going to die any minute," whispered Andy.

Three hours after we'd sat down in the screening room, we bid Imelda, Imee, Bong Bong, and the Wahs goodbye, Andy assuring them that it was "one of the best movies I ever saw." When we had cleared the three sets of Secret Service men, Andy said, "Did you see the way Mrs. Mao looked at Mrs. Marcos? I bet she's giving her lots of rubies, because China has Burma now and that's where the best rubies come from." Andy wasn't strong on geopolitics, but he understood the politics of gems. He also added, "Imelda must really like us, if she asked us to something that small. Send her more flowers and write her another note about lunch, and I'll copy it again first thing tomorrow."

Imelda responded with another invitation: to the opening of the Filipino Cultural Center, at 556 Fifth Avenue. Andy and I were greeted by another security nightmare: a couple of hundred demonstrators screaming, "IMELDA GO HOME!" while police on horseback pushed them back, so that the limousines could get through. We jumped out of the taxi a block away and weaved our way through the crowd of protestors, onlookers, paparazzi, and police, Andy illogically trying to hide behind a copy of *Andy Warhol's Interview*. "Don't lose me, Bob," he whimpered. Inside, there was a line to get through the security check and a big woman in a big red velvet gown, bellowing, "I *am* Mrs. William Randolph Hearst, Jr.!" "Patty's mother," said Andy, putting a few more feet between him and her, just in case the Symbionese Liberation Army should arrive.

After a fifteen-minute wait, we finally made it into the inner sanctum, where a stage had been set up for a show of Filipino national fashions. Imelda was sitting front and center, of course, with Ambassador Wah at her side and Cristina Ford right behind her. She was pleased to see Andy, "but

not *that* pleased," as he put it on our way back to our third-row seats, and
she barely remembered me, even though she'd seen me three times in six
days now. As the show began—lots of butterfly sleeves, see-through shirts,
and Filipino men in sarongs dancing with flames—we could hear the chanting mob on the street: "IMELDA GO HOME! IMELDA GO HOME!" Andy
clutched his Brownie's bag, full of still-unwrapped, still-unused Polaroid
film, and said, "This is really glamorous. And really, really scary." The
single "really" meant not really, and the double "really" meant really.

We had one more go at the Imelda Marcos portrait, four months later,
in March 1975, when she returned to New York, after a whirlwind tour of
the world's capitals, with a few brief stops in her own. "I met so many
wonderful heads of state," she told us over dinner at Trader Vic's, "and
some very nice first ladies, too." She loved that term, "head of state,"
dropping it so often during the meal that Andy was convinced that that's
what she wanted to be herself, that first lady wasn't enough for her any
more. "If I were her husband," he said later, "I'd be more worried about
her than the Communists. It does sound great—'head of state'—doesn't it,
Bob?"

This time Franco Rossellini was in town. He'd been on part of her world
tour with her, he arranged the dinner, and he assured us she "adored Andy."
He had called me the day before and said that Imelda wanted to give a
"small, intimate dinner for a few close friends like you and Andy. But you
must bring glamorous dates, because you know how these first ladies are,
they just can't see *anybody*. I was thinking maybe Princess Radziwill and
Princess von Furstenberg. Shall you call them, or shall I, darling? And then
for the daughter, sweet little Imee, we must think of someone Imelda would
approve of, someone from a good family, rich, handsome, intelligent . . ."

"How about Vincent Fremont?" I suggested, knowing Andy always
liked to have as many employees along as he could.

"Vincent is sweet," said Franco, "but I had more in mind a Philip
Niarchos, who unfortunately is in St. Moritz, or a Mick Flick, who unfortunately is also in St. Moritz . . ."

"How about Lupo Rattazzi, Delfina's brother?"

"Bobino, you're a genius! He's handsome, he's charming, and Imelda
worships the ground the Agnellis walk on—let's call him up right away."
Lupo, unfortunately, couldn't come until after dinner, so Vincent sat in for
him at dinner, and when Lupo finally arrived, he and Imee started talking—
and didn't stop for the next five years. Andy was sure that that alone would
endear us to Imelda forever, but it didn't, perhaps because nothing else about
the dinner clicked.

Mrs. Marcos was on the phone with Cristina Ford when we arrived in
her heavily guarded suite at the Plaza Hotel for drinks before dinner. We
had brought the two princesses, Lee Radziwill and Diane von Furstenberg,
as requested, but Imelda kept talking on the phone, while they stood there,

admiring her new Francis Bacon triptych with a very jealous Andy. When she finally hung up, Imelda greeted us and then turned to Franco Rossellini and said, "You know, Franco, it has been driving me crazy for days now: When we went to the coronation of the King of Nepal, why did they say the Katmandu Airport wasn't big enough for my DC-10 and make me switch to my DC-8 in Calcutta? Because I am sure that when we landed in Katmandu, Prince Charles was arriving in a DC-10!" Lee Radziwill raised an eyebrow and muttered to Andy in a stage whisper, "Oh, get off it. Who's she trying to impress? My brother-in-law owns an airline." "She owns a country," whispered Andy back.

Meanwhile, my date, Diane von Furstenberg, was stage-whispering to me, "She really is like Evita Perón, she really is." I was sorry I'd brought it up on the way to the Plaza. I still don't know if she overheard these comments, because she was so busy chatting with Franco about the coronation, and, in the background, Van Cliburn was playing the piano. Van Cliburn was the most famous concert pianist in the world then, but Imelda had managed to seduce him into playing cocktail music for her. His mother— a Texan of the Rosemary Kent, rather than the Fred Hughes, school—was there too, in the foreground, complaining about going to Trader Vic's. "Ah hate that foreign food! Whah cain't we go to the Oak Room, where I cain git my favorites: tomato soup and prime rib." It was a bit like *Beverly Hillbillies* meets *The King and I,* with Imelda as Yul Brynner.

Andy, Vincent, and I sat there, like The Three Stooges, making faces at each other—Andy trying to signal that one of us should pop the question and Vincent and I signaling back to forget it. Rounding off this totally mismatched cast of characters were a roly-poly middle-aged man whom Franco introduced as the Filipino Banana King, and Imelda's lady-in-waiting, who fretted over little Imee, who fretted over the new ring her mother had given her that afternoon: It had a five-karat diamond set off by one-karat rubies, emeralds, and sapphires. Imee thought it was too little. "It's a lovely ring for a girl your age," said the lady-in-waiting. "I'm not that young anymore," said Imee. "Oh, can I see?" said Andy, slipping it off her finger and holding it up to his eye.

Over dinner, Imelda talked about the difference between the East and the West, turning her head back and forth, with the whole table following, which was rather dangerous on those Trader Vic's drinks, the ones with seven kinds of rum and a gardenia on top. Imelda explained, as Lee raised her eyebrow and Diane whispered, "Evita," that in the East people care about the Three Parts of Life, the Material, the Mental, and the Spiritual, while in the West, they only care about the Material.

At that particular moment, we were all trying very hard not to stare at Imelda's very large emerald necklace. We were also all trying very hard not to notice the surrounding tables occupied by Filipino musclemen dressed up as admirals, generals, and colonels, with lots of medals and gold braid—

and guns. And then Lupo Rattazzi arrived and Franco Rossellini realized, like a good superstitious Italian, that we were thirteen at one table. I think he meant it as a signal for Vincent to leave, but Princess Radziwill and Princess von Furstenberg took it as their cue instead, and kindly suggested that Andy and I wouldn't have to escort them home if Mrs. Marcos loaned them one of her spare limos.

Andy saw his portrait chances departing with them and said they should wait a minute, because we were going to Le Jardin. Imelda was thrilled, she had heard so much about Le Jardin and was dying to go, but the princesses weren't and left in one of her limos. After we piled into another with her, a muscular Filipino with a holster under his jacket came knocking on the window and informed Mrs. Marcos that Le Jardin was a security risk. "My Secretary of State forbids me to go to Le Jardin," she told us, "so we shall go to Hippopotamus instead."

Hippopotamus had seen better nights. It was deserted, and while little Imee and Lupo Rattazzi slow-danced into a long romance, we all sat there, because Imelda wouldn't dance with Vincent or me, only Andy, and Andy didn't dance.

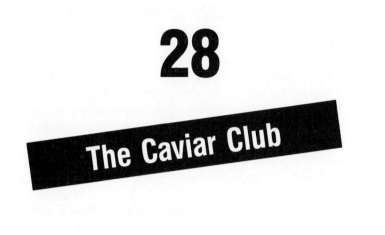

28

The Caviar Club

Andy never did get Imelda Marcos's portrait. But there were other rainbows to chase on his nightly runs up and down Fifth and Park avenues, from cocktails at Nan Kempner's to dinner at the Iranian embassy to coffee at John Richardson's to Elaine's for a nightcap—or two. After Regine's opened around the corner on Park and 59th in May 1976, Andy would often stop in on his way home, "just for a minute to see if anybody good is there." Good meant rich and famous, and a minute meant an hour—or two.

Andy was now accepting almost every "good" invitation he received. "Just in case," he'd say, and "You never know"—where the pot of gold might be. Often that meant three dinner parties in one night, with Fred covering one, Vincent a second, me a third, while Andy and Jed dashed from bash to bash. Andy actually preferred this to sitting through a four-course meal, especially if he was stuck next to a lady who wouldn't let him tape. He liked to "appear" at as many parties as possible, increasing his chances of being mentioned in the next morning's columns, which was his favorite way to start the day: reading about himself. It also kept him from getting "too involved," as he put it, at any one place, though it sometimes miffed the hostesses. When I mollified them by explaining Andy's other social obligations for the evening, they'd invariably ask, "How does he do it?"

One of his tricks was to eat a good square meal at home before he went out: roast chicken or turkey, mashed potatoes, puréed turnips, parsnips, or cauliflower, all washed down with fruit juice mixed with Perrier. Sometimes he'd finish off with an apple or a pear, always peeled, just in case washing hadn't removed the pesticides and even though he had bought it from Perrone's, the most expensive market on the East Side, where the fruit wasn't supposed to have pesticides. Everything had to be the best and fresh, never frozen. He told me that he liked "white foods because they look clean." He favored purées because solid vegetables were too hard on his torn-up intestines, which is also why he avoided lettuce and other roughage. And he tried very hard not to put too much butter on his mashed potatoes, because he always worried about another gallbladder attack. His restricted diet was another reason why formal dinners were difficult for him: The fancy food was too tempting and it was awkward to pass it all up. Hostesses minded that almost as much as they minded his coming and going in the middle of the meal.

Andy's predinner dinners were prepared by his new Filipino housekeeper, Nena, who came to work and live at Andy's house in the middle of 1975, after Jed made it clear that he couldn't be a movie director, interior decorator, *and* maid. ("Andy says I should be going out and directing movies and bringing home the bacon," Jed once told me, "but how am I supposed to do that if I'm always cleaning up after the messes he makes?") She was soon joined by her sister Aurora, because keeping up a house of that size was an awful lot of work. Andy was awkward around them at first and unsure of how to refer to them, stumbling over "the maids" and finally settling on "the girls." They were capable, hard-working, quiet, and discreet. And little by little he adjusted to having them around and even grew rather fond of them. Once, when we were off to see Imelda, he told me, "Nena said to be careful around Mrs. Marcos; many Filipino people don't like her. She was worried about me. Isn't that sweet?" He'd call them every day when he traveled "to make sure everything is all right" and always brought them back expensive perfumes and scarves from the airport boutiques. Still, he pretended that he never really wanted servants, just as he never really wanted to live in a big house, that "it was all Jed's fault that I have all these bills to worry about, all these mouths to feed. Those girls look little, Bob, but they eat a lot. I bet they are having parties while I'm out trying to make a buck. They *could* be."

Andy's other trick for getting through three or four social stops in one night was having his employees do all his social work for him. We worked the room for Andy. We popped the question for Andy. We even ate the food for Andy, who passed things he couldn't eat onto our plates, so he wouldn't be embarrassed when the hostess or the waiter noticed he hadn't touched a thing. Fred kissed the ladies' hands upon arrival, Vincent flattered them on their dresses or their figures, I whispered jokes in their ears, and Andy said, "Oh, hi. Gee."

Andy would find an old friend or a young beauty or the one *wrong* person in the room, the oddball cousin, the penniless divorcée, the ostracized social climber who'd pushed her way into the party, and talk exclusively to him or her, especially if that person was a talker who would pour his heart out to Sony, while Andy just sat there and listened, occasionally asking the one *wrong* question, like a kid who noticed the one false note in a situation: "Does your uncle, the host, really like your aunt? Or does he like boys? You can tell me." Almost invariably, the oddball cousin not only told Andy, but also told the uncle or aunt what Andy had asked, and then Fred or Vincent or I would have to clean up the mess in the morning.

Sometimes the hostess or the rich visitor from Paris she thought would be perfect for an Andy Warhol portrait would ask me why Andy was ignoring her and I'd go over to Andy and try to suggest that perhaps he should circulate a bit. I had to be really careful about how I phrased it, because if I came across as too bossy or snobby Andy would retaliate with "Gee, this is the most interesting person here, Bob. You should really do a big interview on her." And then there would be another mess to clean up in the morning, when the one wrong person called to make an appointment for her cover story.

Usually when I suggested that the potential portrait client could use a little personal attention from her potential portrait painter, Andy would tell me, "That's what you're here for, Bob. Tell her to hurry up and commission me while she still looks good." The one wrong person would always find that funny and would always repeat it too. And I'd walk back across the room to the one right person and tell her, "Andy said he loves your new dress, your new husband, your new apartment, your new Rubens. . . ." If she was a difficult sort, or stone sober, or stone drunk, she might come back with "Well, then, why doesn't he tell me himself?" And I'd answer that Andy was very shy and not very verbal, a purely visual person who could only really express himself in his work, and that when he said "Gee" or "Great" it really was a major effort, and a major compliment. Sometimes Andy actually would be helpful and walk back across the room with me, and say "Gee" and "Great" a lot, while I "translated" his baby talk into grownup conversation.

And sometimes he'd really surprise me and hit it off with the one right person, usually if he sensed he could ask the one wrong question and get away with it. Why was he so unreliable, and even downright unhelpful, especially after moaning and groaning in the taxi to the party about how we had to bring home the bacon this time, as if our lives depended on it? Part of it was his Ruthenian social awkwardness, part of it his constant fear of rejection. But a *big* part of it was his need to harass those closest to him, to keep us on our toes, to make us earn our keep, to remind us that we were there because of him. He hated it when "Fred gets on his high horse" or "Bob gets too big for his britches," as he would put it to each of us about the other. And God forbid that we should have a good time at a business dinner, or worse yet, begin to think that we were asked somewhere just because somebody liked us. Like a mother whose worst nightmare is an empty nest, Andy wanted his kids to be popular but unloved, confident but insecure, to be the life of the party but not to upstage him. The contradictions compounded until it was very hard to know which Andy wanted more: success or control.

I didn't dwell on such thoughts back in the high party years between 1975 and 1978. Instead, while Andy was home replenishing his energy with a home-cooked meal, and putting on another layer of pimple cream, and not changing because "artists aren't supposed to dress up and I'll never look right anyway," I was home changing because "you gotta look good for the ladies, Bob," and shaving for the second time that day, and replenishing my energy with the only thing in my refrigerator: a bottle of chilled Stolichnaya.

"Andy Warhol is still going to parties in great style," Eugenia Sheppard noted in her syndicated column of September 26, 1974. "At Iranian Ambassador to the U.N. and Mrs. Fereydoun Hoveyda's dinner the other night, Andy arrived with no less than eleven people in tow, including Lee Radziwill, in a black sequined pants suit; Diana Vreeland, in lots of ivory jewelry . . ."

We nicknamed the Iranian embassy the "Caviar Club," and Andy was invited there about once a month—we had been introduced by the Italian Ambassador to the UN, Piero Vinci, and his wife, Maria Laura, before they were transferred to Moscow. Like the Vincis, Ambassador Hoveyda, a former film critic, and his young German-born wife, Gisela, sought out cultural figures to spice the usual diplomatic, business, and social mix, and that was one of the reasons their embassy was the hottest ticket among the UN missions. Other regular guests were Elia Kazan and Barbara Loden, Shirley MacLaine, Gail and Sidney Lumet, Bob Wilson, Marion Javits, and Louise Nevelson—though Andy, as usual with artists, "never knew what to say to her." Just as predictably, he felt more comfortable with Karl Lagerfeld, who was always a guest of honor there when he was in town because he had known Gisela since childhood.

During the 1975 New York Film Festival, the ambassador asked us to a big dinner for his old *Cahiers du Cinema* pal, François Truffaut, and Andy was pleased when the French filmmaker told him that the sixties Warhol movies had influenced his own work, adding, "though they influenced Godard more." Andy was also pleased when Bob Wilson, the rising star of the avant-garde, told him, "You're my idol." Andy replied, "I hope tonight's not the night I fall off my pedestal."

He was less pleased by my conversation with Ambassador Wah at a dinner for Prince and Princess Sadruddin Aga Khan. "Why would Andy Warhol," the Chinese ambassador wanted to know, "paint Marilyn Monroe with an orange face?" I said that Andy was being abstract. "In China," he replied, "art is never abstract." "I hope you didn't tell him I painted Mao with a green face, Bob," said Andy.

Ambassador Hoyveda was happy for Andy to bring his entourage—which could be anyone from Diana Vreeland, Lee Radziwill, and Paulette Goddard, to Mick Jagger, Hiram Keller, and Alice Cooper, plus Fred, Jed, Vincent, Lady Ann, Catherine, Barbara Allen, and, occasionally, Archie—who sat on Andy's lap, licking up the fish eggs.

Iranian embassy dinners were always impressive, and slightly absurd, which made it all the more enjoyable for us: the five-pound bowls of Imperial Gold caviar, said to be "even better than Beluga," the place cards embossed in gold with the imperial lion, the gold-framed photographs of the imperial family in their gold crowns. The townhouse at 1033 Fifth Avenue was one of the largest in the city, and its spacious pale blue salons reeked of official power and wealth, though the geometric mirror mosaics gave it a shot of exotic glitz. We all grew quite fond of the ambassador. His paisley brocade dinner jackets and purple bowties, his pipe puffing and collage making, his genial and witty after-dinner tales undercut the pomposity of the imperial thrust. And we grew even fonder when, some sixteen dinners later, in January 1976, he passed the word from Teheran: Her Imperial Majesty Empress Farah Diba wanted Andy to come to Iran and paint her portrait.

"Really?" said Andy, eyes bright, voice brighter. "Let's go there right away and do it." Then he lowered his voice and muttered to me, "Before something happens."

One week later, something did happen: The *Village Voice* accused Senator Jacob Javits of "sleeping with a highly paid foreign agent"—meaning his wife, Marion, who had recently taken an $80,000-a-year consulting job with Iran Air. To make matters worse for the popular Jewish senator, the *Voice* portrayed the Shah as an enemy of Israel, ignoring the fact that he had guaranteed its oil supply as part of the fragile Mideast truce Kissinger negotiated after the 1973 war. It was the opening salvo in the ensuing campaign the *Voice* led in the American press against the Pahlavi regime. "How much do you want to bet," said Andy, "that we don't get to do Farah Diba's portrait now? And it will all be Marion's fault."

Marion resigned her Iran Air job, but the dinners went on and we kept going to them. There were dinners for the Smithsonian's Islamic Art Institute, for Regine, for Nureyev. After the publicity over the "Marion Hari Scandal," a pair of New York City cops were stationed outside, which made Andy a trifle nervous, but our trip to Iran was falling into place, and we were meeting more and more useful people at the embassy. Such as Nima Farmanfarmaian, a young Iranian writer whom Vincent dated for a while, who happened to be Eugenia Sheppard's assistant, and who also happened to mention Andy in the column every other day.

Another stunning Iranian we met there was Mercedes Kellogg, the

young wife of Ambassador Francis Kellogg, Nixon's special liaison for the
refugees from Southeast Asia. We also met John Kluge, the chairman of
Metromedia, and later, in the eighties, the second-richest man in America
(according to *Forbes* magazine), who showed interest in Andy's TV show.
Vincent and I hurriedly wrote him a treatment, which was hurriedly rejected. A more lasting friendship, and business relationship, developed with
paper king Chris Gilman and his wife, Sondra. The Gilmans were serious
collectors and Andy ended up painting both of them and their two children.

      Paulette Goddard, who was one of Andy's more frequent Iranian em-
bassy dinner dates, loved going there because she could wear her major
jewelry and feel safe—once the ambassador lent Paulette his bodyguard to
escort her diamonds, rubies, and emeralds home. At a dinner on Valentine's
Day 1975, she was wearing what appeared to be half the mineral wealth of
Burma, provoking Lena Horne to say, "I'd love to steal a ruby." "I bet you
would," said Paulette. "This is just like a movie," said Andy, "we've got
to put it in the book, Bob."
      We were still taping Paulette for the book everywhere we went together,
though in early 1975 the title had been changed when HBJ discovered a porn
novel called *Her*. Our book was now *Her, Him and Them*—we realized that
Paulette would never sit down and have a heart-to-heart with Andy, so it
had to be a book about everyone Paulette met with Andy. At an embassy
dinner for the Shah's twin sister, Princess Ashraf, and the ambassador's older
brother, Prime Minister Amir Abbas Hoveyda, we taped an entire chapter
of *Her, Him and Them*. Senator Charles Percy of Illinois recalled meeting
Paulette back in the forties as a Chicago college student who won a date
with her in a studio promotion. "And you were so adorable," said Paulette,
"the perfect gentleman." "Well, I was so intimidated," said the senator.
"You were covered in diamonds, like the big Hollywood star you still are."
"Well, I don't know about the last part," said Paulette, "but I *am* still
covered in diamonds."
      Andy was happy with this new "cast of thousands" approach, and he
had me set up another "scene" for the Paulette book soon after: lunch at
Lutèce with the Hoveydas and the Dalis. Paulette was wearing her Dali lip
pin "to please Dali," which did not please Gala. *Her* first shot was to grab
Andy's tape recorder and shove it into the vase of flowers in the middle of
the table. Andy fished poor Sony out and hid her under the table.
      Then I made the mistake of crossing my legs and slightly tapping Gala's
leg in the process. "You kick Gala!" she grunted, and punched me in the
arm. "Punch her back!" snapped Paulette. It occurred to me that Gala
would probably be nicer to me if I did, so I gently hit her arm. Andy was
shocked, Dali laughed, and Paulette shouted, "Harder! Hit her harder!"
Gala and I exchanged a few more blows, hers much more forceful than mine,

and when she realized I wasn't going to let her have the last punch—even though Andy was harping, "What do you think you're doing, Bob?"—she threw her arms around me and gave me a big kiss. "Bravo!" declared Dali, waving his scepter to bless our reconciliation, as Andy gingerly lifted Sony out from under the table.

Then everyone got down to business: Paulette tried to interest the ambassador in buying her collection of antique Persian rugs, the ambassador tried to interest Dali in donating a painting to Teheran's new museum of modern art, Dali tried to interest Gisela in donating money to the Dali Museum in Cadaqués, Gisela tried to interest Andy in buying tickets to her benefit for Bob Wilson, Andy tried to interest Gala in letting him paint her portrait, and Gala tried to interest me in ordering two plain poached eggs, as she was, instead of the Lutèce *plat du jour*. "What a great lunch," said Andy on our way down to the Factory. "I just hope the tape didn't get wet. Maybe if I punched Gala too, she would let me do her portrait."

"I couldn't believe the way Paulette was encouraging me to hit Gala," I said. "I was just being funny, but Paulette really meant it."

"Oh, I know," said Andy. "There's something wrong with Paulette lately."

Not long after, Paulette asked me to help her clear out her storage bin at a Second Avenue warehouse. She said there might be something there for my apartment and that I could take anything I wanted. I liked a thirties silkscreen of a deer and a doe and Paulette stunned me by making me write out a "loan agreement," explaining that it had been a gift from King Vidor, so she didn't feel she could actually give it to me. "Let's get out of here," she snapped, even though we'd barely begun to sort through the old furniture and bric-a-brac. "It's depressing me." As I walked her back to the Ritz Tower, she told me, in code, what was really depressing her. "I have an appointment with a surgeon tomorrow," she said. "Get the picture?" I didn't, but she refused to discuss it further.

"Oh, God, it must be something terrible if she won't tell us," said Andy when I told him. "But you should tell her that she has to work even harder on the book now, just to keep busy."

In the month before her mystery operation at the end of March 1975, Paulette wouldn't talk about the book or her problem. She wouldn't see us either, always saying that she had to see "the surgeon," and then rushing to hang up. We found out the date of the operation from Anita Loos, but the hospital said no calls were allowed. Anita told us when Paulette was being discharged, and Andy went with me to Fernando Sanchez's showroom to pick out a rose satin negligee and robe to send her at the Ritz Tower. He even wrote the card in his own hand: "Get well soon. We miss you. Love, Andy and Bob."

When Paulette called to thank us a few days later, he hurriedly passed the phone to me, saying, "You've got to convince her she should talk about her operation for the book. It can't be all caviar and diamonds. Tell Paulette she can buy a lot more caviar and diamonds if we have a bestseller." It might have helped Paulette to talk about it—whatever it was—and it might have made a bestseller, but at the time Andy's pressing seemed heartless. Soon he was asking, "Did you ask Paulette when we could start taping her recovery?" Paulette wouldn't see Andy, or tape, or talk about the book, for the rest of April and most of May.

Paulette finally swept back into Andy's life at the end of May, making a grand entrance in red Halston chiffon and that big engagement-ring necklace. It was at the Factory dinner for São Schlumberger, the first and almost the only time that Andy allowed a party there at night. He had Ronnie Cutrone hang the Cats and Dogs paintings, because he knew that São had a weakness for both, and sure enough she did end up buying a big Cat painting for her new house in Cap Ferrat. We hired two Pinkerton guards for the lobby and a fleet of waiters, despite Andy's suggestion that Ronnie man the gate and the rest of us work the tables. The fifty guests included Jack Nicholson and Anjelica Huston, Faye Dunaway, Carroll Baker, Diana Vreeland, Jerry Zipkin, the entire Halston group, and Larry Rivers.

Some of our younger friends turned up after dinner, along with a woman who could often be found at hipper parties in the mid-seventies, discreetly exchanging hundred-dollar bills for small packets of aluminum foil. Andy hardly noticed her presence. He was too busy taping Paulette. "She drank so much vodka," he told me after she left, "and I did too." "Did you get her to talk?" I asked. "Oh, yeah. She told me that her doctor was the meanest man she ever met in her life, and that her operation was the worst thing that ever happened to her—but she didn't say what it was."

The next day Paulette called me and said to tell Andy "all the operation business is off-the-record. I had a *ski accident,* and that's that." Her capacity for denial seemed as enormous as Andy's—another way in which they were perfectly matched.

Paulette just didn't want to work, especially on a book about herself. The movie star whose intelligence had lifted her above the usual vulgar vanity was now wallowing in self-pity about the beauty she was convinced she had somehow lost for good. Andy was worried about her, and worried about the book, which was due in six weeks, on July 15, 1975. He and I worked every weekend at the Factory or his house, going through the manuscript: almost six hundred pages redacted down from our twenty-five taping sessions by Chris Hemphill, who had organized some chapters by themes, such as "Caviar" and "Gems," and others by scenes, like the one with Senator Percy or the lunch at Lutèce.

When we handed in the pile of transcripts, Paulette was already packing for her six months in Switzerland, and Andy was already saying he was not giving back the money if they hated it.

They hated it.

When Paulette returned to New York in the spring of 1976, Andy wanted to tape some more, but her heart wasn't in it. She had physically recuperated in her villa by the lake, but she never really recovered psychologically: She didn't want to face her life, she wanted to forget it. Her relationship with Andy took on a quality not unlike that between the aging movie star in *Heat* and her movie-producer ex-husband: I'll come to your openings if you come to mine. Paulette and Andy went to everybody's openings, were photographed together, and made all the papers, as famous couples always do, and then didn't see each other until the next opening.

One night in May 1976, we went to Janet Gaynor's opening at the Wally Findlay Gallery. *This* was the kind of art opening Andy liked in the seventies. The retired actress, whom he remembered from the 1937 version of *A Star is Born,* brought out all the big stars from the twenties to the fifties, from Lillian Gish to Betty Furness. Paulette was besieged by fans in their fifties to their seventies, some wearing as much jewelry as she was. While she signed autographs, out of duty not joy, Andy and I wandered off to look at Janet Gaynor's Renoiresque peonies and petunias.

"The paintings are so bad," Andy said, "but I bet they go up. Look how big she signs her name. It's like buying an autograph and then you get the flowers thrown in, right? Sometimes I wonder if I should be with this kind of gallery and make a lot of money quick, but Fred says that's the wrong way to think. Oh, look, there's Irene Selznick. Let's go ask her about Paulette."

The elegant widow of David O. Selznick, and daughter of Louis B. Mayer, told us the *real* reason why her late husband didn't use Paulette in *Gone With the Wind.* Paulette had told us that Chaplin wouldn't release her from her exclusive contract with his company. But Irene Selznick said, "This was going to be the biggest *family* movie ever made and David wanted to *see* Paulette and Charlie's marriage certificate, because the rumor in Hollywood was that they had never made it official. Charlie told us that they had been married by the captain of a ship off the coast of Shanghai, so there was no certificate. David decided it was too big a risk to take and that's when the great search for Scarlett O'Hara began. Paulette was heartbroken, and she never forgave Charlie, but it wasn't because he wouldn't let her out of her contract; it was all about the missing marriage certificate."

Suddenly, Paulette was at our side. "Hello, Irene," she said coldly. "Hello, Paulette," said Mrs. Selznick even more icily.

"That woman has always hated me," Paulette growled, as Irene turned her back. "She's a bitch, and she always was."

Paulette was acting stranger and stranger. She was never the most patient of people, but after her operation the slightest delay drove her to distraction. If we were five minutes late in arriving at the Ritz Tower, she'd drive off to the theater without us and leave our tickets at the box office. "Well, I guess we have to find a taxi," said Andy one time, "now that my rich girlfriend has stranded us." It soon became "*your* rich girlfriend," after HBJ rejected our revised manuscript and Paulette refused to have a third go at it. "It's all Paulette's fault," Andy said, "because she never really talked. And that's *your* fault, Bob, because you didn't pay the price."

Andy had a similar seesaw attitude about Fred's intensifying friendship with Diana Vreeland. Andy was both proud that one of his kids was the Empress of Fashion's favorite courtier, and envious that *he* wasn't on her arm, particularly at her annual imperial pageant each December, the high point of the Manhattan social season, the Metropolitan Museum of Art's Costume Institute Ball. He always made Fred pay for his own ticket.

When Diana invited Fred to three dinners in one week, Andy said, "You can't go out with Diana every night, Fred. You have to go out with me sometimes, you know." When she didn't invite Fred to a dinner, Andy said, "I guess Diana's dropping you, Fred. You better pay more attention to her." He approved of Fred's going to Japan with her in 1975 "because she's invited by the head of Sony and that might be good for business." He disapproved of Fred's going to Russia with her in 1976 because "there's no business in Russia; she just wants Fred there to carry her bags." His biggest worry, repeated often, was that "Diana's filling Fred's head with funny ideas." He meant that she made Fred feel that he was not just Andy Warhol's hairdresser. And when he really got out of control, he'd accuse Diana, in her late seventies, of "wanting to go to bed with Fred," in his early thirties.

To alleviate Andy's resentment, Fred encouraged Diana to ask Andy out with her on his own. It never really worked. Their dates started out well enough, because while Andy was always late, Diana was always later. But they usually ended up badly, because Diana liked to linger at parties, chatting until the wee hours, and Andy couldn't wait to get on to the next party, or go home. He often left without her, asking someone else to take her home, and she'd call him the next morning and, as he put it, "scream at me." Sometimes he'd add, "She really is funny," and sometimes, "Who does she think she is?"

Andy's real ambivalence was about Diana herself, and it probably went back to the fifties, when she was *Bazaar*'s extremely social fashion editor, and he was their sometime illustrator, "Andy Paperbag." They went about their business in entirely opposite ways, Andy and Diana, and yet they were alike. They both had to be in charge, but Diana was openly dictatorial and made no bones about it, while Andy was a closet control freak, who deviously pretended he didn't know what was going on and claimed, "I just follow my hairdresser around." Andy and Diana also shared a need to be surrounded by what he called "beauties" and she called "attractive young people," but while Andy sat there like the eye of the storm, silently turning his tape recorder in the direction of whoever was talking, Diana talked up a storm.

"Dietrich," she declared one night at dinner, "is not a woman, not a man, but a *phantom."* She paused dramatically, and lowering her voice to a deep hush, added, "as could only come out of Central Europe." Then she snapped back to her sharp editress voice. "Of course, I *adore* Central Europe, simply adore it." And ended in an almost poetic chant: "Munich. Zürich. Salzburg. Vienna. *Buda-PEST!"* Another long pause, followed by an invasive question, *"You're* from that part of the world, aren't you, Andy?"

And, as always, an evasive answer: "Oh, I'm from Pennsylvania."

"Oh, Bob," she went on that night, "you're so lucky you're a *wop,* because when a wop walks into a room, it lights *up."* "What lights up," I shot back, "the room or the wop?" Diana loved that. "Oh, Bob, you're too much. Isn't he, Andy? You know, you're so lucky to have these boys." She often reminded him of that, and he rarely appreciated it, though we did.

Another night she pronounced: "There is no such thing as an ugly *duchess."* And another she explained why Valentino was a great designer. "He understands *opulence,* in the *Oriental* sense—*real* luxury," she intoned imperially. "Why, he rang me up from Rome the other day just to say he was thinking of having his *yacht lacquered RED!* Now, *that's* taste."

Red, of course, was Diana's favorite color, and she painted it on everything from her front door to her cheeks, which she "rerouged" after dinner, the way other women put on more lipstick. Her second-favorite color was purple, which she used to accent the reds in her apartment and her wardrobe, both of which were opulent, in the Oriental sense. Yet for all the real luxury in her style of dressing and decorating, there was also a sense of simplicity and comfort, just as under all her pronunciamentos and italics there was a straightforward and cozy woman, who knew how to enchant men.

Diana had been a widow since 1969, and her sons lived in Rome and Los Angeles; her grandsons, whom she doted on, passed in and out of New York on their way from Europe to the Far East. So we Factory "boys" helped fill the void—she always called me "My boy around the corner." Diana also had her favorite "girls"—Marisa Berenson, Penelope Tree, Marina Schiano. She preferred strong, independent women—"It's whimpering women I can't take!" When I complained to her about Bianca's demands about her *Interview* cover shoot for the Jack Ford issue, saying she expected magic, Diana replied, "Magic doesn't come to those who don't expect it."

"What a great line," said Andy. "Diana really does say the greatest things." And yet, he also said of her, on several occasions, "She doesn't know what she's talking about. She just makes everything up." He went back and forth. They were not, in any case, a compatible couple. Diana liked to touch, to feel, to take your hand in hers, to put her arm in yours, all the normal things that Andy couldn't deal with, that made him back off. She often mistook his physical pulling away for a gesture of personal distaste, and it made her mistrust Andy, which he sensed, making matters worse. "Diana doesn't really like me," he told me once, with resignation, not envy, in his voice. She never disputed his genius as an artist, and she adored his fey, funny side, but there was a latent ambivalence in her feelings toward him that was almost as strong as his toward her.

The best thing Diana ever did for Andy, as far as he was concerned, was to have him to dinner with the Duchess of Windsor, in May 1975. Andy was so excited about meeting her that he brought her a small Flower painting (from the 1964 series), which the Duchess mistook for a box of candy and kept trying to open.

Andy had given Diana a tape recorder for Christmas six months earlier, and she took it out of its case for the first time after the Duchess of Windsor went home. "Tonight's the night," she told Andy, "that you teach me how to use this thing." But the batteries had gone dead and Diana didn't have any others in the house and, incredibly, Andy didn't have any in his bag. He could have taken the batteries out of his tape recorder and put them in hers, but that would have meant that whatever was said would be on Diana's tape, not Andy's.

Despite the underlying ambivalence and mistrust between the Empress of Fashion and the Pope of Pop, it was her stamp of approval that put him in the middle of Park Avenue society in the middle of the seventies. It was Mrs. Vreeland, more than anyone else, who *pushed* Andy, and Fred and me, by introducing us to her swell friends at her small dinners and by bringing us to the small dinners of her swell friends.

29

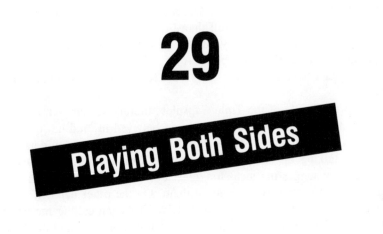

Playing Both Sides

One of Diana's swellest friends was Jerome Zipkin, a real-estate heir in his sixties and New York's most ubiquitous man-about-town. At one point in the fifties, Andy had sent Jerry daily drawings and notes—"Happy Monday," "Happy Tuesday," "Happy Wednesday," etc.—hoping to turn a distant acquaintance into a close friend. And he saw him here and there on the cocktail-party circuit in the early seventies. But he didn't begin to get close to Jerry until the night in February 1974 when Diana Vreeland asked Andy and me for drinks before Patrick O'Higgins's birthday party at Elsie Woodward's. Jerry was Diana's date, and the four of us piled into his 1953 marshmallow-and-licorice Cadillac, driven by an ancient "colored" chauffeur who called his boss Mr. Zippers. It was only twelve blocks from 550 Park Avenue to the Waldorf Towers, but Jerry managed to fill us in on half of Hollywood, *le tout* Paris, and a good chunk of Gotham in the short ride. He must have liked the way we laughed, because he pronounced us his "new best friends."

One hot Saturday night in July 1975, Jerry asked us up to his place for drinks, way up in the Nineties, "on the hem of Harlem," he said. It was the first time either Andy or I had been there. His sprawling prewar apartment, done in various shades of green and gold, was crammed from the living room to the bathrooms, from floor to ceiling and wall to wall, with paintings, drawings, prints, sculptures, objets d'art, knickknacks, mementoes, books, magazines, newspapers, and framed photographs of everyone from Cardinal Spellman to Lynn Revson, including his close friends Governor and Mrs. Ronald Reagan. "Geeee," said Andy, genuinely flabbergasted, "you have even more stuff than I do."

"I bet you don't have every Sunday *New York Times Book Review* section going back to 1957," snapped Jerry.

"No, but I have every New York *Post* front page since 1968," replied Andy.

It was the Battle of the Time Capsules, literary vs. tabloid.

Jerry also pushed people he liked and believed in, and he soon started pushing us, introducing us to potential clients, suggesting our names for party lists, talking up Andy and his boys and their work. Like Diana, he was constantly suggesting ideas for *Interview,* and like her he never brought them up a second time if we ignored them. On the other hand, if we liked an idea of Jerry's, he set it up immediately. He began calling me up at the Factory to order gift subscriptions, for the Patiños in Paris and the Marches in Madrid, the Hales in San Francisco, the Bloomingdales in Los Angeles, the Dudleys in Nashville, the Wyatts in Houston, and eventually the Reagans in Washington, D.C. When I sometimes offered to put his friends on our complimentary list, he'd have a fit and lecture me, "Is that any way to run a business?"

Andy was fascinated by Jerry but was also "scared" by him, and he sometimes worried that "one morning Jerry will wake up and decide that I'm out." It was an admission of how insecure Andy really was, because Jerry was well known for being stubborn and not mercurial. Once he made up his mind about someone, it took an earthquake to change it. And he liked Andy.

That year, Andy also finally became a real friend of another idol to whom he had sent daily notes and drawings in the fifties: Truman Capote. Andy had attended Truman's Black and White Ball in the sixties, and they got to know each other better through Lee Radziwill in the early seventies, but it wasn't until April 1975 that Andy felt comfortable enough just to call Truman up and ask him to dinner at Trader Vic's. Truman came alone. Andy brought Vincent, Chris Makos, Robert Hayes, and me.

"This reminds me of the dinner party Elvis gave me in Las Vegas," cackled Truman.

"You had dinner with Elvis?" Andy said, swooning.

"Uh-huh. In his suite at Caesar's Palace."

"In his *suite?*"

"Uh-huh. Jus' little ol' me and big ol' Elvis . . ."

"Oh, God."

". . . and seven hillbilly boys from Memphis, Tennessee. Which is *why* I say that *this* dinner reminds me of *that* dinner."

Warhol's hillbillies guffawed, but not too hard.

"Except Elvis also invited one woman," Truman continued. "Guess who?"

"Uhhhhmmm . . ." Andy couldn't.

"Doris Duke!"

"*Doris Duke.* Oh, God."

"Uh-huh. Apparently Doris and Elvis go way back."

"You mean . . . ?" Andy was beside himself: Could it be that the richest woman in America and the King of Rock 'n' Roll were romantically linked?

"I *mean,*" said Truman, pausing for effect, "whatever you want me to mean."

Thereafter, Andy always uttered the same line after his meals with Truman: "I never know what to believe—do you think Truman makes it up as he goes?"

That night, Andy was also doubtful when Truman said that he had received a letter from the imprisoned Charlie Manson. "He wants me to write an article in the *New York Times,*" Truman said, "correcting the portrayal of his personality in *Helter Skelter.* Isn't it incredible?"

It was, and Andy asked, "He wrote you that?"

"Uh-huh. I have the letter right here in my pocket," said Truman, patting his pocket for effect. "But I can't show it to you, because that would be an invasion of privacy. Guess who Manson's prison sweetheart is?"

"You mean he has a boyfriend in jail?" Andy found that hard to believe too.

"That's exactly what I mean," said Truman, "and he's the prettiest murderer on Death Row."

Truman said Death Row the way most people say Hotel Ritz, but Andy wasn't impressed. Nor did he share Truman's fascination with beautiful killers.

Andy was delighted, however, with Truman's praise of his *Philosophy* book. "I loved it, Andy, I really did," he said, "because it was done with style and charm."

"Oh, gee," said Andy, turning pink. That "gee" meant do I tell him Pat and Bob wrote it, or not? We had sent Truman galleys, hoping he'd give us a quote for the ad campaign and a few days after our dinner he called one in to me: "Acute. Accurate. Mr. Warhol's usual amazing candor. A constant entertainment and enlightenment." As I jotted it down, Truman told me to "make sure those periods aren't changed to commas. And it must be used in its entirety, or not at all. I slaved for *hours* to get it just right and I don't want some copygirl cutting it up." Then he chuckled, as if to say, Believe that one and I'll tell you ten more. He also went on, as he had at dinner, about his new "novella" coming out in the June 1975 issue of *Esquire,* titled *Mojave.*

When *Mojave* appeared, Andy found it "boring," as did almost everyone else. No doubt sensing the reaction, Truman said that it was actually the first chapter of his long-awaited "Proustian" novel, *Answered Prayers,* and as such meant to be "the lull before the storm. And believe me," he added, "my next chapter is going to be a *hurricane,* the likes of which you've never seen. It doesn't take place out in the desert, but right smack in the middle of one of the favorite New York restaurants of all the people we know and love."

"La Côte Basque 1965," which appeared in the December 1975 issue of *Esquire,* really did blow up a storm. The victims included not only its jet-set subjects, but also, in the end, its author. "Society's sacred monsters are in a state of shock," wrote Liz Smith in *New York* magazine. "Never have you heard such gnashing of teeth, such cries for revenge, such shouts of betrayal and screams of outrage." The Paleys, the Whitneys, and Jan and Gardner Cowles, she noted, "have drawn the line against Truman." Lady "Slim" Keith, Caroll de Portago, and Pamela Harriman were "incensed." Peter Glenville pronounced Truman "utterly ignoble," Gloria Vanderbilt said she'd spit on him if she saw him, and Nedda Logan declared, "that dirty little toad is never coming to my parties again." Leading this Park Avenue posse was none other than Andy's new best friend, Jerry Zipkin, who told Liz Smith, "Truman is ruined. He will no longer be received socially anywhere. What's more—those who receive him will no longer be received."

When our other new best friend called from the Coast, where he was starring in Neil Simon's movie *Murder by Death,* Andy told him, "It was greaaaat." Then he hung up and told me, "Don't tell Jerry that Truman called." When Jerry asked him what he thought of "La Côte Basque 1965," Andy said, "I tried to read it, but I couldn't. I just can't read." No one was better at playing both sides than Andy.

Shortly after Truman's bombshell exploded, Andy and I had dinner at Le Périgord Parc with one of the leading ladies in one of the biggest scandals exposed in the *Esquire* piece, Elsie Woodward. Indeed, her daughter-in-law, Anne Woodward, had jumped out the window the day before it had been published, some said because she saw an advance copy and couldn't take having the old story about murdering her husband dredged up again.

The nonagenarian Mrs. Woodward was the picture of mourning chic, in a black broadtail suit with a matching pillbox hat. We talked about everything but *Esquire,* until Elsie's constant companion, Patrick O'Higgins, brought up an interview with Truman in the Sunday *Times,* about the Neil Simon movie. "What I don't understand," said Elsie, "is why anyone would give him a movie role. He doesn't have a very good speaking voice." Andy tittered nervously, and said nothing until Patrick changed the subject again. He wasn't about to risk the date he had with Elsie for Kitty Miller's New Year's Eve party—*the* Society New Year's Eve party since the fifties, and one Andy had been trying to get invited to for almost as long. Later, as I walked him home, he said, "Did you notice that Patrick says Truman's name, but Elsie always says 'he' and 'him.' That's the way you have to be in life, Bob. Really, really cool."

Andy was not only good at being in the middle, he *liked* being in the middle. He let me run "Capote: Answered Questions" in *Interview*—based on a lecture Truman gave at NYU when he returned from California—but I had to cut out any references to specific Society enemies of Truman's. I could leave in Truman's dig at Gore Vidal, because we were running Monique van Vooren's interview with Gore in the same issue, in which he said, "I sat down on what I thought was a pouffe and it was Capote." Monique invited us for dinner after the taping session and Andy couldn't wait to tell Gore, "Oh, I know what you should do. You should go on the road with Truman and Tennessee and do imitations of each other, because you all do each other so great, and have big fights on stage, and end up in Madison Square Garden. You could all make a fortune. You really could." Gore Vidal stood there, wondering for a while, and then took Andy's "great idea" one step further. "We have to have Norman Mailer as the referee," he said, "to tell us what it's like to be manly."

"When will you stop playing both ends against the middle?" Maxime de la Falaise McKendry screamed at Andy at Adriana Jackson's dinner for Max Ernst, in February 1975. Maxime was furious because Andy had brought along the owner of Knoedler's, who had just let John Richardson go as director of the gallery, and she considered that disloyal. "You're too commercial," she continued in a loud, lecturing tone, "and it's going to catch up with you one of these days." Andy didn't like to be yelled at, and he turned around and headed for the door. Adriana and I chased after him and found him waiting for the elevator, red-faced with embarrassment. "Come back," said Adriana, "it's my house, not Maxime's, and any friend of yours is welcome, even another art dealer."

"I was just trying to get everybody to be friends," Andy said, when I dropped him at home. He wanted to be everybody's friend, and to go to everybody's party, and he couldn't understand why everybody else didn't too. He loved to watch people fight and feud and compete, but he hated to choose sides or remain loyal or get involved. As the sixties Superstars' books started coming out in the seventies, it became apparent that this was the thing about Andy that drove them craziest. He wanted to rise above the fray, and do everybody's portrait and get everybody's ad. The only time he did take sides was when he had no choice: when one side rejected him, or when Fred, Jed, Vincent, and I all ganged up on him and forced him to show some loyalty to a close friend or major client, and even then, Andy sneakily sent out feelers across the street.

So, shortly after bringing John Richardson's former boss to meet Max

Ernst, he went to John Richardson's to meet Francis Bacon. The art-lined walls were punctuated with the odd stuffed animal, and Bacon tried to draw Andy out. "Would it be too presumptuous," he asked, "to request a visit to your workshop?" "Oh, uh, no," said Andy, darting his eyes around the room, looking for a rich kid to talk to instead. When Bacon turned up the next day, Andy was as aloof as he usually was with other artists. Was he feeling insecure, jealous, or more likely just afraid to open up around the competition? Andy could be extremely competitive; he just didn't want anyone else to be, or have anyone else's rivalries get in *his* way.

He went to dinner parties at Diana Vreeland's red-on-red apartment and cocktail parties at her former boss Alexander Liberman's white-on-white townhouse. And he sent Diana a red poinsettia at Christmas, and Liberman's wife, Tatiana, who was Russian Orthodox, a white poinsettia twelve days later. And he sent Diana hot pink peonies for Easter, and Tatiana white lilies for Russian Easter.

Andy's holiday flower list was growing at a rapid pace in the middle seventies, almost as fast as his social life was. We added another thirty names to his original list of twenty useful hostesses and journalists. And Andy was also adding holidays, "the ones when people don't expect a present," he said: Mother's Day, Father's Day, the Fourth of July, Halloween, and Thanksgiving.

One new addition to Andy's gift list was C.Z. Guest, another swell he met at Diana Vreeland's. Andy adored C.Z. because she talked faster than he could tape her, sent him orchids from her greenhouses in Old Westbury, and trusted him with her two children, teenage Alexander, and Cornelia, who was eight when Andy met her in 1975. C.Z. considered Andy a "good influence because he's a worker—and that's what it's all about these days: work, work, work." He was also impressed by the fact that C.Z. and Winston Guest, the legendary polo player and Phipps Steel heir, were "old money."

Andy was much less taken with Pat Buckley. The night we met her, the wife of the conservative columnist William F. Buckley, Jr., was holding forth on her exchange with Rose Kennedy the night before. "Don't get me *started* on Rose Kennedy," she started. "That *horrible* little woman said to me, 'Patsy'—how *dare* she call me that—'Now, Patsy, you must tell Bill to be nice to Teddy in his column.' I told her, 'I wake up every morning and tell Bill to *go after Teddy.*' But *Rose* pressed on. 'Patsy, you don't seem to understand. I want you to be nice to Teddy.' I couldn't take it a second longer, so I told her, 'Now get this straight, Rose. I think Teddy would be the worst thing to happen to America!' "

Everyone laughed at Pat Buckley's story, except Andy. "She's so mean," he told me later. "No, she's not," I said, "she's just got strong beliefs and sticks to them." "You like her, Bob, because she has the same strong beliefs that you do. I think she's *scary.*"

Françoise de la Renta was another strong-minded woman Andy found scary. He tried to like her, and he very much wanted her to like him, and she tried, too. Françoise could be warm and charming and very, very funny, but to all those qualities she brought a wicked haute-couture edge. "How's your hernia, *mon chéri?*" she once asked coming through the door of a friend's apartment, assuming that he had already informed his other guests of his medical condition. Andy was terrified that she'd turn to him and ask if he was still getting gas from eating beans. Like Andy, Françoise played both sides of the street. Only she could get away with working for Condé Nast, as a contributing editor at American *Vogue* and *House & Garden, and* be the best friend of *WWD*'s John Fairchild. Andy was sure that if she would only hop on his bandwagon a caravan of commissions would follow—and he'd get his picture back in *WWD* as well.

"Shouldn't we invite Françoise?" he always said, when we were planning one of our grander Factory lunches. "And no other woman," he sometimes added. He thought the perfect lunch to ask her to was the one we gave in April 1976, for five ambassadors from the United Nations. "But we already have Paulette coming," I said. "Oh, God," said Andy, "they'll hate each other." So we put Françoise at one end of the table and Paulette at the other, and the Iranian, Italian, Irish, Spanish, and Chinese ambassadors in between. Françoise kept saying that everything was "marvelous," "fabulous," and *"très, très chic,"* but later we heard that she said we had "all the wrong countries."

So Andy wasn't too thrilled when Fred announced, in October 1976, that Françoise had asked to use the Factory for a big dinner. "She'll have all the right people," Fred said. "And she'll say everything we do is wrong," said Andy. "I told her our only condition was that she do everything," said Fred, "that it should be her party, not ours." "Then why are we doing it?" asked Andy. "You can't say no," said Fred. "It's for Pierre Bergé, Hélène Rochas, Kim d'Estainville, and Cristiana Brandolini." "Oh, God," said Andy, "I just know they'll all end up never speaking to us again, and it will be all Françoise's fault. You watch, Fred. Just watch."

Françoise invited Fred and Andy, but decreed that no one else from the Factory staff be invited except Catherine Guinness and me. "Not even Jed?" asked Andy. No, said Fred, and Jed was getting bored with these dinners anyway. "Not even Vincent?" asked Andy. No, said Fred, and Vincent didn't fit in with this crowd anyway. "Well, then I'm bringing Archie as my date," said Andy. No, said Fred, leave Archie home that night, please. "I have to have a date, Fred," said Andy, "at my own dinner." Fred reminded Andy that it wasn't *his* dinner. "I hate Françoise," said Andy.

Was that the reason he told Ronnie Cutrone to hang the Skull paintings on the walls that afternoon?

After Diana Vreeland, Tatiana Liberman, and Irene Selznick walked through the door, he wished he hadn't hung the Skulls after all. "These are the wrong paintings," he said, "for the right people." Then came Annette Reed, Lally Weymouth, Louise Melhado, Diane von Furstenberg with her new steady from Hollywood, Barry Diller, Barbara Walters, Grace Mirabella and Dr. William Cahan, the Kempners, the Erteguns, John Richardson, Drue Heinz, and Marietta Tree. "This is so glamorous," Andy sighed. "I guess Françoise really does know how to get the good group. Oh, *God,* here comes Betty Bacall." When John Fairchild strode up to him and said hello, Andy was almost unable to speak. "Gee, uhm, would you like a drink?"

By the time dinner was served in the middle room, which looked like a tomb, with red votive candles, white gladiolas, no windows, and four large Skull paintings, Andy was miserable. On one side he had Candice Bergen, who told him, "I'd like to be friends with you, but I'm afraid of your tape recorder." On the other he had Françoise, who scolded him for eating. "You never do," she said, "why are you tonight?"

The funereal atmosphere wasn't helped by the lack of music, which Françoise had forbidden, because "it makes people stay late." And, sure enough, the minute coffee had been served, Françoise asked me to help her "get rid of people. Remind them it's a Monday night," she said. I decided that the best thing to do was get rid of myself, and as I headed for the elevator, Andy asked me where I was going. "Françoise wants everyone to leave," I explained.

"But why would she go through all this trouble," he asked, truly perplexed, "so everybody could go home at eleven-thirty? I'll never understand society, Bob."

"Goodnight, Andy."

"How much do you want to bet," he said with a knowing smile, "*WWD* doesn't write it up?"

His prediction came true: They ran photos of everyone but Andy, and said the party took place in "a downtown artist's loft." He didn't mind being put down in print, so long as they spelled his name right; but putting him down and not spelling his name at all, that got him where it hurt.

It was time to take sides. "Why don't you call up that Eleanor Lambert lady," said Andy a few days later, "and ask if she's free for dinner tonight? Isn't she on the outs with Fairchild? Maybe she'll help us get ads." Eleanor Lambert, the powerful fashion publicist, said she was having dinner that night with Lynn Wyatt, the wife of the Houston oil and gas tycoon. So I proposed letting us take the two of them out and she agreed. Andy was thrilled: Eleanor might mean ads, and Lynn Wyatt might mean a portrait.

At La Côte Basque, Andy was quite taken by Lynn. She was both a beauty and a talker, and told Sony all about her new acquisitions from the Paris couture. "Ah bought two Givenchys, several Saint Laurents, and a few Diors," she said. I could see Andy's eyes totting up her bill and converting it into portrait panels. "Did you buy any of those big new taffeta ballgowns from Yves?'' Lynn said she had bought one and it was so huge and came wrapped in so much tissue paper that ''it took up one whole suitcase.''

"Well, what you should do," said Andy, "is put the dress in one suitcase and the tissue in another." That was one of Abbott's better punchlines, except nobody got it, including Costello.

30

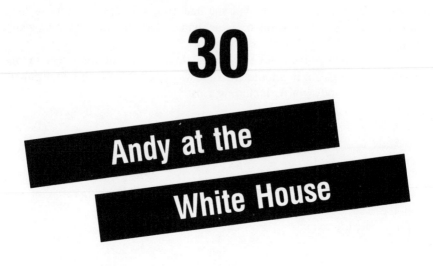

Andy at the White House

"He must be dyeing his eyebrows," said Jed as I pounded on the bathroom door in our Watergate Hotel suite, worried that Andy would be late. "That's how you can tell that Andy's really impressed by where he's going," Jed explained, "when he dyes his eyebrows."

Sure enough, an hour and a half after he had locked himself in the bathroom, Andy emerged with one very white eyebrow and one very black eyebrow. His wig was well combed, his cover cream was well applied, and he looked rather elegant in his white tie and tails. "The pants are too itchy," he said, "so I left my blue jeans on underneath. That's okay, isn't it?" I said it was. "Is it okay to bring my tape recorder?" I said it wasn't. "Do I smell okay? Did I put on too much?" He stank of tuberose, lavender, and sandalwood, but I assured him that his homemade fragrance was fine. "Oh, God, I'm so nervous," he said. "I wish you kids could come with me."

Andy was going to the White House for the first time in his life: President and Mrs. Ford had invited him to the May 15, 1975, State Dinner for the Shah of Iran. He had insisted that Jed and I take the Metroliner to Washington with him, and now he insisted that we ride in the limousine with him too, "right up to the front door." But when we got to the White House gate, the guards said we couldn't go any further without invitations. "What do I do if Betty Ford asks me to dance?" Andy wailed. "Or the Empress?"

"You can't say no," teased Jed, jumping out of the car.

"You'll never get her portrait if you do," I added mischievously.

"Wait up for me," said Andy. "It'll end early. I *hope.*"

As the limousine drove in and Andy waved to us through the rear windshield, we couldn't help but smile at the thought of his "getting everything wrong," as he had put it. "He looks so cute," said Jed. "Doesn't he?"

Back at the Watergate, we settled in for a night of room service and TV with my old Georgetown buddy Chris Murray, and waited. And waited. And waited. When Andy didn't turn up by one, we assumed he had gone on to another party with someone he'd met at the White House, but by two we were beginning really to worry: Had he lost his car? Forgotten the hotel? Was Andy really as hopeless on his own as he pretended to be? Maybe it wasn't an act.

And then Andy, feeling no pain, tottered in. "Oh, God," he said, "I had the best time. It was just so up there. So *glamorous*. And I had to run from the Red Room to the Green Room to the Blue Room because the Empress was following me and I was so afraid she was going to ask me to dance. . . ."

"She was *following* you?" I interrupted.

"Well, she kept ending up in whatever color room I went in and I didn't want to take any chances, so I kept changing colors. But she was really, really kind and sooo beautiful. Oh, God, you should've been there, Bob. You would've loved it. First, these really, really good-looking Marines . . . oh, wait, let me get my tape recorder and then I'll tell you everything from the beginning."

As he dashed to the bedroom, he suddenly stopped to pull off his suit pants, revealing the Levi's 501s underneath. Only Andy, I thought. In a second he was back with Sony, and trying to tell the story in order:

"Oh, and Bobby Zarem was there," he began.

"Bobby Zarem?" I liked Bobby Zarem, he was a great P.R. man, but he wasn't the first name I expected to hear in a description of a state dinner.

"Uh-huh," said Andy. "He came after dinner because Ann-Margret gave a command performance and she's his client. And Allan Carr was there too, because he's her manager. I should've said you and Jed were my manager and P.R. man and you could have come after dinner too. Allan was great. He helped me hide out from the Empress."

I asked him if Betty Ford had asked him to dance.

"No, she didn't care about dancing with me. She was dancing with Fred Astaire."

"Fred Astaire was there?"

"Yeah, and he looks just like an older Fred Hughes. He does, Bob. Oh, and Bob Hope was there and Pearl Bailey, and Suzy, who looked really great, and Merv Griffin, but he made a faux pas because he arrived at the door the Shah was supposed to arrive at instead of arriving in the basement like the rest of us."

"What?"

"Okay, let me start from the beginning. First the car pulls up to this door with an awning and it looks glamorous and everything, but it's really the basement. And this beautiful girl asks you your name and then this good-looking Marine takes you to the staircase and then another good-looking Marine takes you up the stairs and then he leaves you and another good-looking Marine brings you into the big room where you have drinks and then they don't play 'Hail to the Chief' because that's what Nixon did and suddenly the President and Betty and the Shah and the Empress are just there in a row and another Marine takes you up to them and another Marine asks your name and he tells it to another Marine who tells it to the President who says, 'Hello, Andy.' It's so glamorous the way they do it and every Marine is better-looking than the other one. Really good-looking. Oh, and I forgot, when you're still in the basement, just before you come up the steps, another Marine announces your name really really loud to the press and I was really embarrassed because I felt like I should be standing there with my camera taking pictures behind the rope like them, right? But I mean, they know, right, that just because you go to the White House doesn't mean you like that President, right? Did I say the President looked tired? I don't think he knew who I was. Oh, and the Shah was cool to me. But the Empress said how much she had heard about me from Ambassador Hoveyda, so he really is our friend and you have to remember to get me to send him a little painting or something when we get back to New York, Bob.''

"So who were you sitting between at dinner?"

"Oh, that was really glamorous. Nancy Kissinger. But she just drank milk, I guess she has an ulcer, and smoked. God, she really smokes. And I didn't know what to say to her. And on the other side I had this really great funny little lady whose husband owns a bank in Texas and she was wearing this dress she made herself out of a lace tablecloth. I mean, isn't that nutty? Your husband owns a bank in Texas and you're invited to the White House and you make a dress from a tablecloth. I mean, I really liked her and she kept saying it was an antique tablecloth, but I mean, can you see São doing that? Or Marie-Hélène de Rothschild? I mean, Americans really are different than Europeans, right? Oh, and Ambassador Zahedi was at that table too, I told you that, right? And he was really, really nice and drew this map of where the best caviar comes from for me to give to Paulette. I have it right here in my pocket. I hope it's not too crumpled up. Oh, God, it is, Bob. What do I do now? Put it in a time capsule? She'll never know, right?''

"What were the toasts like?"

"I can't remember the *toasts,* Bob. I'm not like you. I'm lucky I remembered Nancy Kissinger's name. Oh, but I almost forgot the best part. Susan Ford came after dinner with five boyfriends in blue jeans. And she's really a beauty and I told her I had blue jeans under my pants and she didn't believe me, so I just unbuttoned one button to show her. Do you think she'll tell her father that I was being funny or something? I'll probably never be invited back, right? And I made another faux pas, I think, when I told her that her five boyfriends were one more handsome than the next one. I'll never be invited back, right? And actually, when I think about it, my favorite part was the Marines—I mean, one taking you ten feet, then another taking you another ten feet, then another another ten feet, and another and another and . . . uh, it's a really glamorous way to get from the door to the table, Bob, let me tell ya. I mean, you really know you're in the White House after that.''

Jed had wandered off to bed, and Andy suddenly said, ''Oh, I forgot to tell Jed that all the furniture in the Red Room and the Green Room and the Blue Room is American Empire. I mean, it looked just like my living room. So I guess Jed really does know what he's doing. Should I wake him up and tell him? No.''

''Well, it is after three,'' I said.

''Oh, God. We have to go to bed, Bob.'' He jumped up and headed for his bedroom and with his back moving from me said, ''Gee, thanks, Bob, for bringing me to Washington. We should come more often.''

Two months later, Andy was back in Washington and at the White House again. We went with Bianca Jagger to interview Jack Ford. The story was partially told in our 1979 book, *Andy Warhol's Exposures.* What was left out reveals quite a bit about Andy's relationship with Bianca.

It began when Andy and I had a late dinner at Elaine's with Bianca, who was making mysterious noises about David (Kennerly, White House photographer and Ford family friend) and Jack and Mick and the Rolling Stones concert in Washington the following night. She had a way of creating suspicion as she sought to allay it, sometimes just to tease Andy—and Sony. ''Listen,'' Andy told her, ''if you're such a good friend of Jack Ford and you're such a good friend of ours, you'd get us invited to the White House to interview him.'' ''Andy, you're being so aggressive,'' said Bianca, pretending to be shocked, ''but since you're making this a test of my friendship, I will do it.''

In the morning the White House called to invite Andy for lunch with Jack Ford, and Mick and Bianca, on the *Sequoia,* the Presidential yacht. Andy was ''too nervous'' to call them back, so I called for him, while he whispered, ''Tell them I can't go without you and Jed.'' At 4:30 A.M., Bianca called to say that we should get to Washington as soon as we could in the morning. The *Sequoia* was out, but the interview was on, and she was trying to get us invited to lunch at the White House first.

We caught the 9:30 A.M. Metroliner and arrived at the Sheraton-Carlton by one. We found Bianca, in a white terrycloth robe, being made up by Pierre Laroche. Between strokes of blush and mascara, he stepped back and snapped Polaroids for Bianca's approval. She showed us her lunch-at-the-

White-House outfit: a yellow silk dress with matching bonnet and platform sandals. "Gee," said Andy, "it's beautiful. What time is lunch anyway?" "I'm not sure, Andy," moaned Bianca at her sexiest. "Bob should call David Kennerly at the White House for further instructions."

"How much do you want to bet," snipped Andy, as we headed back to our suite, "that Bianca forgot to tell them we were coming? Oh, I hate her. She made us rush down here and now we're not even going to lunch. She just wants to have lunch with Jack without us. She's rotten. And this hotel is a dump."

He was still in a snit when a White House car came for us at three and Pierre Laroche—in a silver Mylar jumpsuit accessorized with a silver skull earring, a silver skull necklace, and saddle shoes—hitched a ride. "I'm only authorized to bring three gentlemen to the White House," said the driver, trying not to cough on "gentlemen"—as Andy turned pink. "Mrs. Jagger needs me there to retouch her makeup," said Pierre Laroche—as Andy turned red. "May I ask what you have in that package?" said the driver, nodding at the large cardboard box wrapped in brown paper that Pierre was carrying—as Andy turned crimson. "A dress from Giorgio di Sant'Angelo and the shoes that go with it," said Pierre—as Andy gave me a kick that meant, "Do something." I explained that we were from *Interview* magazine and were doing a photo session with Jack Ford and Mrs. Jagger and that Mr. Laroche was Mrs. Jagger's hairdresser. "Stylist," said Pierre. We drove in silence toward 1600 Pennsylvania Avenue. Pierre tried to draw Andy out by showing him the Polaroid camera and Sony tape recorder he had in his satchel. "Just like yours," said Pierre. "Oh," said Andy. A short "oh," followed by nothing, was the most killing comeback in Andy's vocabulary, the Warhol equivalent to "Drop dead."

It was all a bit ridiculous in the end. As Jack and Bianca sat there, with the Washington Monument in the distance, Dirck Halstead took pictures for *Interview,* David Kennerly took pictures for the White House, Andy took pictures for Andy, and Pierre Laroche took pictures to check Bianca's makeup.

Eventually, Bianca decided to change into her Giorgio di Sant'Angelo, a stunning black cocktail dress of stretch Lycra embroidered with rhinestones. While Pierre Laroche helped her in Lincoln's Bedroom, Jack gave us a tour of the second floor: the Yellow Oval Room, the Diplomatic Reception Room, the Treaty Room, the Queen's Bedroom, "where Queen Elizabeth II, or whatever, stayed." Andy and Jed drooled over the American Empire furniture, and at one point Andy asked Jack if he was "interested in furniture at all."

"Once again, Andy," he shrugged, "I'm one of the people who, if I can't put my feet up on it . . ."

"Is that Victorian?" asked Andy, pointing at a settee.

"I wish I had the curator along," said Jack.

When we got to Lincoln's Bedroom, he knocked on the door eagerly, no doubt dying for the art-and-antiques tour to be over and the photo session with Bianca to begin. But Pierre shouted through the locked door, "One more minute," and Jack was stuck with us.

When Bianca was finally ready, and quite beautiful in her glittery black dress with a black beret that had once belonged to Marlene Dietrich, she and Jack posed in the light by the window, with his hands gently around her waist, and her eyes looking sweetly into his. Then he said he had to go to a meeting with his father in the Oval Office and left us in Kennerly's hands. "God," said Andy, "he's sooo cute. And isn't it great when you say, 'My Dad,' and it's the President? And did you notice that he kissed Bianca on the lips when he said goodbye?" Bianca, meanwhile, had thrown herself on Lincoln's bed, and was smiling for the cameras. "Do we have to leave?" she asked, only half joking. "Oh, I know," sighed Andy. "Don't you wish you could stay?"

He wasn't mad at Bianca anymore. But he would soon be calling her names again, after the Rolling Stones concert at the Capital Coliseum in Maryland that night. In the confusion at the end of the show, we lost Bianca and she hopped on the group's special bus back to Washington, which she had never told us about, and we were left waiting for another two hours, until the pack-up crew gave us a lift to the hotel. That set Andy off again: "She's the worst. I'm never speaking to her again, and you can tell her that for me, Bob."

And yet she had been "our really great friend," when she'd suggested that the Stones rent Montauk as a base during their American tour. Andy's opinion of Bianca at any given moment was typical of his mercurial estimation of most of his friends: He loved them when they were giving him his way, and hated them when they weren't.

31

Philosophy on Tour

In September 1975, Andy made a major cross-country tour to promote *THE Philosophy of Andy Warhol: From A to B and Back Again,* covering eight cities in sixteen days. He took along a pack of "B's," as the local papers invariably dubbed Fred, Jed, Lady Ann Lambton, and me. Archie was scheduled to come too, but at the last minute Andy had an anxiety attack about his getting stuck in the hold, even though I showed him our itinerary from the travel agency, with "Archie confirmed" next to every flight. "I wish I could stay home with Archie," he whimpered. "Why can't you just do the tour for me, Bob? You got me into this in the first place."

I hadn't fully comprehended what I'd gotten myself into by ghostwriting the book, until Andy was photographed for the cover of *New York* magazine, which had bought the first serial rights. They posed him in a closet, sitting at a typewriter, under a headline that read: "ANDY WARHOL'S GREATEST SECRET: HE LIKES TO WRITE." It finally hit me then—I was part of a big lie, and while it had lined my pockets, it robbed my ego of any hope of recognition. Pat Hackett probably felt even more ripped off: Nine chapters were wholly hers; four were mostly mine; one, "The Tingle," was Brigid's, and all three of us had worked on the prologue. But there was no question of taking Pat on the tour. "She might start saying she wrote it," said Andy. So one ghost had to sit at home, while the other ghost went on the road to lie some more.

The book promotion had actually begun months before publication, when Andy went out to HBJ's warehouse in New Jersey to sign six thousand copies of the first printing. It was Andy's idea. The HBJ people had been so let down when he told them that he wouldn't make any TV appearances, he'd said, "What if I sign every book?" They were incredulous, but Andy said he meant it, and they came up with the sales gimmick of offering "signed copies" to stores that placed their orders by a certain date.

So, on a Friday in May, Andy and I were driven out to Saddle Brook, where high stacks of books and an assembly line awaited him. It was a very Warholian scene: One kid took a book from the stack, a second opened it to the right page, a third held it as Andy scrawled "AW" in black magic marker, a fourth whisked it away, and a fifth restacked it. When we left, Andy asked, "How many books do you have here?" The manager said eighteen million. "God," said Andy, "don't you wish they were all our *Philosophy,* Bob?" "And you could be signing them for the rest of your life," I answered. "Oh, I know. Wouldn't it be great?" In July, when the orders exceeded the copies already signed, Andy went back and did six thousand more.

Then came a week of promotional parties in New York, just before the tour started. Leo Castelli gave the official publication party in his SoHo gallery, a gesture that touched Andy. He was less touched by the conspicuous absence of Leo's other star artists—Rauschenberg, Johns, Lichtenstein, and Stella. My diary records only one artist, David Hockney, with Henry Geldzahler as usual; two writers, Fran Lebowitz and Jonathan Lieberson; and enough interior decorators to furnish every loft in the neighborhood. Bianca's date was another President's son: Roberto Somoza of Nicaragua, age sixteen. She was Andy's best friend again, because that meant more publicity for his book party.

The next afternoon, Andy signed books at the Madison Avenue Bookshop. There was a long line of fans and pals, and it moved very slowly, because in addition to inscribing each book to each buyer personally, Andy also did a drawing on the title page—a soupcan, banana, heart, or flower. When he found someone "cute," he flipped through the book and scribbled something every fifty pages or so, little surprises to be found later. And for people he knew, he sketched a stylized penis or vagina, though when someone asked what the latter was, he answered, "elephant ears." I tried to rush him a bit, but he persisted in asking each person's name and then asking me, "How do you spell 'Jane,' Bob? How you do spell 'Tom,' Bob?" And then he looked up and saw another old friend from the sixties, Ethel Scull. She nagged him about not being invited to any of the parties that week, which Andy blamed on me. That was when Andy realized that *anyone* could turn up at these advertised public appearances. "I hope we have bodyguards on the road," he said.

Our first stop was Baltimore, where two thousand fans mobbed the Museum of Fine Art to see Andy. The majority were clean-cut and preppy, with a good number of smart suburban housewives, loaded down with Warhol posters and catalogues, knowing these items would be more valuable once signed by Andy. People expected so much of a simple signature, from financial gain to an aesthetic blessing, and they waited so long and so patiently to come near him to get it. They wanted him to sign their hands, their arms, their foreheads, their clothes, and their money. They brought cases of *real* Campbell's soup cans for him to autograph, and old Velvet Underground albums, paperback copies of *a,* early issues of *Interview,* Liz and Marilyn posters from the sixties. One young man opened a *Penthouse* centerfold and politely asked Andy, "Could you sign it on the crotch?" A teenage girl knelt on the floor in front of him and pleaded, "May I kiss your pen?" He autographed everything they brought, except a dachshund—it reminded him of Archie, he said, and wouldn't so much as initial its tail, though the owner begged. At least half the crowd had cameras to take Andy's picture and the other half wanted their pictures taken with him. He did drawings in hundreds of *Philosophy* books. For John Waters, the Baltimore-based director of *Pink Flamingoes,* he drew a barrage of elephant ears.

The only time he showed any sign of annoyance was when someone turned up with the Campbell's Soupcan shopping bag that the museum was selling in its gift shop. "I don't get anything on this," he told me. "Find Fred and tell him to complain."

Fred had fled the crush, to try to find the house where the Duchess of Windsor had been born. Jed had gone with him because he thought there might be some antique shops near Wallis Simpson's birthplace. Lady Ann stuck with Andy and me. In her dark glasses and commanding English accent, she relished the role of keeping the jostling fans in line, getting their names and spelling them out to Andy. Despite the large numbers, he still insisted on signing each and every book, can, and dollar bill to its bearer. "They came all the way for us," he said, when I tried to get him to speed up the process by sticking to simple autographs. He also scolded me when I told people they could only have a free copy of the new issue of *Interview* if they bought a book. It was as if he were trying to stay on the good side of the surging mass. When we arrived, he had immediately spotted "the nut," a guy in black who stood at the edge of the museum lobby, glaring at Andy with some weird anger in his eyes. He continued to glare for the entire three hours we were there. "I'm really glad," said Andy every so often, "that this big fat armed guard is standing right behind us, Bob."

That first day in Baltimore was typical of the days to come in Ann Arbor, Chicago, Minneapolis, Los Angeles, San Francisco, Houston, and St. Louis. In every city, Andy did book signings in galleries and museums, as well as bookstores, and in every city we went to dinner with potential portrait clients, most of whom were duds. We kids went to the Le Jardin of every city—every city had one by 1975—while Andy went to bed early and woke up early the next morning, and gave each of us a lecture about staying out late, then tried to get us to tattle on the others. "Did Bob smoke pot?"

"Did Jed meet anyone?" "Did Fred go to Ann's room when you got back to the hotel?"

In every city, while Andy signed books, with Lady Ann spelling at his side, Fred met with the director or curator of the local museum, Jed checked out the local antique shops for American Empire or Art Deco props, and I arranged for *Interview* to be sold at the local "international" magazine shop—it was still a foreign publication in Middle America.

And in every city Lady Ann left her sunglasses at the book signing and Andy had to buy her a new pair. He didn't mind because she helped him through the half-dozen interviews he gave in every city and played along when he introduced her as "my fiancée, Lady Ann Lambton."

Andy considered these interviews "torture," especially when he was asked the question he hated most: "Are you rich?" As "business art" was one of the prime credos of his *Philosophy,* variations of that question came up in almost every city. Andy always answered "No," or pointed to the paint spots on his shoes and made a funny face. It was interesting to see how journalists responded to his book. The older ones from big-city dailies tended to take it, and everything Andy said, with a very large grain of salt. But the kids from college papers seemed to get the joke and take it seriously at the same time. Andy went blank when a reporter from the University of Illinois presented him with honey in a squeezable plastic bottle. "You wrote in your book," the earnest student explained, "that honey should come in ketchup bottles, so I thought you'd like this." "I better read the book again," Andy said after the kid had left, "and find out what Pat put in. Oh, why can't I remember anything, Bob? It's like my mind has this button that just goes erase." "That's a line in the book, Andy," I pointed out.

What was most amazing in every city was the size and scope of the turnout for Andy's public appearances. He never sold less than 150 books at a signing, and sometimes he sold twice as many in the usual two-hour stretch.

In St. Louis, Andy was put on display in the corner window of the Stix, Baer, Fuller department store, with a table piled with books and Lady Ann, in her latest pair of shades, beside him. Giant speakers blasted the Velvet Underground's "Heroin" out into the downtown streets, and soon a large crowd had their noses, and their cameras, pressed against the window, as Andy sat there, like a mannequin, or a robot, signing away. The voyeur was on exhibition, the outsider was inside, the former department-store window dresser was now famous enough to dress a department-store window with his mere presence. It was one of those strange Warholian twists on the American Dream—and only the blacks passed Andy by.

Andy noticed that blacks *never* came to his book signings, in any city, including New York. And on the single occasion when an ill-dressed youth said he couldn't afford to buy a book, Andy bought one for him, and then listed it in his expenses as, "Book for poor kid—$7.95." But most bookstores and art galleries are on the right side of the tracks, and Andy noted over and over "how rich America is." Ann Arbor, he said, "has that rich look—big white houses with beautiful big lawns." His first impression of Chicago, coming off the airport expressway into the heart of Michigan Avenue's "Miracle Mile," was "Gee, it's so beautiful—big, clean, and rich-looking."

He tended to equate the beauty and wealth of a city with the number and size of its skyscrapers, but was always let down when we actually stayed in one and the windows didn't open. It was a quandary: The old hotels were rundown, the new hotels were inhuman. And room service was lousy in all of them. "The eggs they put in the pancakes are probably fake," he explained. "And the club sandwiches have fake turkey and the chocolate cake has vanillin instead of vanilla." Andy solved the problem by ordering only steak, sometimes even for breakfast, even though it was bad for his gall-bladder. "What I don't understand is this is such a rich country, so why can't we have good food?"

In Minneapolis, we stayed at the Marquette Inn in a spectacular high-rise complex designed by Philip Johnson, one of those charmed people, like Truman Capote and Jerry Zipkin, whom Andy worshipped and envied. "This is greaaat," he said, as we were checking in. The rooms were quite something: Andy's had red velveteen walls, white mesh curtains, red-and-white wall-to-wall shag carpeting, and one of his orange-and-yellow semi-abstract iridescent Sunset prints over the bed, which was covered with a red chenille bedspread. He noticed that the matchbooks were printed with the line "700 Rooms with Andy Warhol Originals" and wanted me to call Fred's room and ask him "why we weren't getting paid for that." I suggested calling Marina Schiano, who was in town opening a YSL boutique, instead. She said that her room was a green version of Andy's and that she had to wear sunglasses in it, because the rug was "vibrating."

"Oh, I have a good idea," said Andy. "Let's call David Whitney and tell him how much Marina hates her room." David Whitney was Philip Johnson's closest friend. "Tell the truth" was the way Andy started the long-distance call, "Philip designed these rooms as a joke, right? I mean, they look like Oldenburg's room at the Museum of Modern Art. No, I like it. No, I really do. The kids hate it. Marina Schiano is here too and she said she had to wear sunglasses because her room is so bright. And Fred hates the whole building, but he only likes old rundown hotels. I love it. My prints look so great. Tell Philip I'll give him a good price if he wants me to do more for his next great building."

Andy's art dealer in Minneapolis was very much in the tradition of

Alexander the Greek, Herman the German, and Anselmino of Torino. In fact, Gordon of Minneapolis *was* a hairdresser. Gordon Locksley started out "dressing heads for Clairol," as he put it. "And then I opened my own beauty parlor and I entertained the ladies so much with my imitations of all the movie stars that they encouraged me to open my own nightclub where I could do my imitations on stage and all the ladies came and made it such a success that I started buying Pop Art for the walls and then all the ladies started wanting Pop Art for their walls so I started selling art and that became such a success that I opened my own art gallery. And now the ladies go to my beauty parlor in the morning and my art gallery in the afternoon and my nightclub in the evening." Gordon called his story "The History of Hairdressing in Minneapolis," and Andy loved hearing it so much he made Gordon repeat it every time he introduced him to one of us.

The line waiting for Andy at the B. Dalton bookstore in Minneapolis was typical, including the obligatory funny-looking boy who had come all the way from Fargo, North Dakota, to complain about never getting his back-issue order from *Interview*. But Andy noticed something different about this line: "Who are those two old ladies holding hands back there, Bob?"

They did look odd—in their matching black babushkas, bulky black overcoats, thick black stockings, and klutzy black shoes—for Andy Warhol fans. But they smiled so sweetly and waited so patiently they couldn't possibly be Valerie Solanis types disguised in grandma drag. Andy acted as if they were. "They're getting closer," he said as the line moved forward. "Who are they, Bob?"

Finally it was their turn. Andy looked up and said, "Oh, hi," like he did with every book-buying fan. But they weren't holding books, they were holding hands.

"Hello," one of the ladies said tentatively. "I am Mrs. Gregory Warhola. And this is my sister-in-law, Mrs. Robert Warhola. We are from the Carpathian Mountains. What part of Czechoslovakia are you from?"

"Oh," said Andy. "Uh."

"The Carpathian Mountains?" Mrs. Gregory Warhola repeated hopefully.

"Oh," said Andy. "Uh, where is that?"

"In Czechoslovakia? What part of Czechoslovakia are you from?"

"Oh, uh, Pittsburgh."

"But your parents . . . ?"

"They're from Pittsburgh too. Oh, this is Bob Colacello, the editor of our magazine *Interview*. Would you like a copy?" He quickly signed one each. The little old ladies looked bewildered as they walked off, hand in hand, with *Interview* under their arms. And Andy went back to signing the fronts of T-shirts, the backs of jean jackets, and lots and lots of Campbell's soup cans.

*   *   *

Andy was thrilled when we landed in Los Angeles. We checked into the Beverly Hills Hotel, where he could finally order something other than steak. He had the same suite as the last time he was there, in 1972, for the première of *Heat,* and a big bouquet was waiting on his coffee table from Sue Mengers.

The hotel was crawling with stars. Bobby De Niro was at the next table at lunch in the Polo Lounge. We crossed paths with Dustin Hoffman in the lobby, and when Steve Lawrence and Eydie Gorme rushed by to join him, Andy couldn't keep himself from gaping. Art Linkletter was lolling by the pool, and Neil Sedaka was being paged.

Lorna Luft soon turned up and took us to Liza's house high in the hills. Liza was married to Jack Haley, Jr., then, and they were just hanging out at home, Liza in a yellow sweatshirt, Jack in a "Chicago" T-shirt. Raquel Welch, in white jeans, turned up with her boyfriend, Ron Talsky, also in jeans. Liza whipped up daiquiris in the kitchen and Jack called out for Kentucky Fried Chicken. "This is so glamorous," Andy whispered to me. "I mean, it's not like seeing the stars all dressed up at a première in New York. It's really being at home with them on any old night in Hollywood." We loafed around the bedroom—"The bedroom, Bob!"—watching Lorna in *McCloud.*

Andy did five book signings in as many days. At the Margo Leavin Gallery he sold over four hundred books, because clever Margo had called all her clients and offered them "signed Warhols for $7.95." At the Pickwick bookshop on Hollywood Boulevard a hopped-up "Valerie type" threatened to rip Andy's wig off his head; we crowded around protectively. At Hunter's Bookshop in Beverly Hills the turnout was saner. At her Beverly Hills house, Dolly Bright Carter, a trustee of the Los Angeles County Museum of Art, served cocktails to the invited collectors and socialites, most of whom bought three or four books each. "Why can't every book signing be like this, Bob?" said Andy. "In a rich house with rich people who buy lots of books for their rich friends." The last book signing was at the Cedars Sinai Hospital. Andy didn't want to do it at first, but Marcia Weisman, who was the hospital's chief fundraiser, assured him that it would be in the lobby, not a ward, and that the book buyers would be her lady friends from the fundraising committee, not patients.

Andy tried to squeeze in a little movie business in L.A.—he still had hopes that a Hollywood studio would finance one of his movies, and in 1975, he hoped it would be *Bad.* He told me to call Federico de Laurentiis, who was working in Hollywood for his father, Dino, but Federico asked me to write a script for him before I could ask him to read the *Bad* script. I politely declined and he politely asked me to send the *Bad* script to him, but nothing ever happened. And Brooke Hayward took Andy and Fred to lunch with Dan Melnick, the president of MGM, but MGM did not produce *Bad* or any other Andy Warhol movie.

Andy was destined to be disappointed in Hollywood. He always just missed. Producer Ray Stark wasn't home when his daughter Wendy took us to see his collection, and even the note that had come with Sue Mengers's welcoming bouquet had read, "Wish I were here, but business called me out of town."

Still, Andy said Los Angeles was his "dream city" and "maybe we should buy a house here and use it as an *Interview* office." I certainly agreed, as did Fred and Jed. But none of us, especially Andy, would ever have dreamed of living in San Francisco after the day we spent there. Squeaky Fromme had attempted to assassinate President Ford there the day before we arrived, and Andy wasn't calmed down by the death-threat note that awaited his arrival at the Fairmont Hotel and Tower on Nob Hill.

We had a Pinkerton guard at his book signing that afternoon. The turnout was sizable and fairly typical, with a few more Cockettes and other drag types than any other city, but not that many. But even the guys in jeans and windbreakers seemed to have chips on their shoulders. They wanted to know why Andy hadn't "come out" in his *Philosophy* book, why he'd "sold out" to business art, why he didn't do more for "the movement" and "the revolution." Andy just murmured, "Oh, I haven't?" and signed as fast as he could, though he still did his little drawings, still tried to deflect aggression with charm. One particularly belligerent fellow in a work shirt came up to Fred and me and demanded to know why we were wearing ties. "The tie is a symbol of capitalist oppression," he insisted, "and Andy *used to* stand for liberation. You guys are nothing but a bunch of Fascists."

After dinner at Trader Vic's, Andy went back to the hotel with Ann, and Fred, Jed, and I went out in search of the local Le Jardin, but there wasn't one in San Francisco, supposedly the most liberated city in the country then. All the gay bars were strictly gay bars, and unless you dressed like a clone they wouldn't let you in. Clones, of course, didn't wear ties.

In Houston, we received a warmer welcome. It was, of course, Fred's hometown, and he took great pride in squiring us around, pointing out the houses of the leading families, explaining the social distinctions between the better residential districts: River Oaks, "where everybody lives now," and Montrose, "where the grand old families used to live."

"Where did your family live?" Andy asked Fred.

"They used to live downtown. They used to *own* downtown. Well, a good part of it anyway. And my grandfather quite stupidly sold his property on Main Street a year or two before the boom."

"Gee," said Andy, "downtown does look bigger and better than ever before. Lots of new skyscrapers since the last time we were here, Fred. Actually, I think Houston has the prettiest skyline, because all the new buildings don't have flat roofs."

"I knew *you'd* love them," said Fred, laughing. *"I* think they're hideous."

"You're laughing now, Fred," said Andy. "But you could be collecting rent from them if your grandfather was smart."

Thanks to Fred, Andy had a great four days in Houston. Though Dominique de Menil was out of town, Fred arranged a book party at her house, and Andy was beside himself as Fred's old school chum, Marion Wilcox, filled him in on the cast of characters. "That's Camilla Blaffer—the Blaffers are Humble Oil, now Exxon. That sweet old lady is Nina Cullinan—she donated the new Mies van der Rohe wing to the Houston Museum of Fine Art."

"The whole wing? Oh, God, this is so glamorous."

"There's Pierre Schlumberger, Jr.—your friend Sāo's stepson. He's talking to Sisi Kempner—no relation to your friend Nan. These Kempners own the Imperial Sugar Company and they live in the company town, which is called Sugar Land."

"The whole town? Oh, God, this really is glamorous."

"Here come Balene and Sanford McCormick of the McCormick Oil and Gas Company—they just bought two de Koonings."

"They did? Should I pop the question?"

"I'd wait until the second time you see them. Oh, there's Theodore and Caroline Law—she's a Humble Oil heiress too. They just bought a Picasso."

"Oh, I'm going to pop the question. People who like Picasso like my work too."

He stayed in a state of rapture through Harry Hurt III's party for Red Armour, a polo star, the following night. "You know it's really rich when they play polo," he said. "Really rich and really butch." And he became positively ecstatic at the Bayou Club, where we were invited to watch the Wichita Falls vs. Tulsa polo match the next day. The Bayou Club, the exclusive bastion of Houston's Old Guard, had a members' barbecue following the match, with a band called the Hickorys, and screwdrivers served by the pitcher on picnic tables out behind the simple clapboard clubhouse. Andy was impressed when Marion Wilcox told him that Will Farrish III donated the polo field—"The whole field?" And impressed again when Humble Oil heir Joe Hudson gave him a tour of the stables and introduced him to his Argentine horse trainer—"Horses are really rich, and horse trainers from Argentina are even richer." But he was happiest sitting under the shade of a big old oak tree, with a borrowed baseball cap shielding his face from the last soft rays of the afternoon sun, watching the children of Houston's aris-

last soft rays of the afternoon sun, watching the children of Houston's aristocracy playing tag. "They're the most beautiful young children I ever saw,"
he said. "Every one's a Barbara Allen."

And on the plane back to New York, Andy decided that "Houston was
the most glamorous time we had. But isn't it odd that we were in Houston
four days, and we never once saw Fred's family?"

One week after our return from Houston, we were back in another
American city that Andy found "really glamorous": Washington, D.C. Andy
had been invited to one of the ten housewarming parties Vice President
Nelson Rockefeller and Happy were giving at the new vice-presidential residence. When their social secretary had called she'd said that Andy could
bring a guest, and he'd said, "Give her your name, Bob, because you're a
Republican, and also you can set up a book promotion in Washington for
the same date."

Rockefeller seemed interested in, and comfortable with, Andy in a way
that few politicians ever were. There was a lengthy receiving line, and the
moment it ended, he sought Andy out and, putting his arm around him like
an old friend, said, "C'mon, Andy, I'll take ya upstairs to see the Max Ernst
bed. They're making a hell of a fuss over it down here in Washington."

They were: Every reporter we ran into asked Andy what he thought of
Rockefeller's spending $35,000, of his own, not the government's, money
on a bed, and Andy told them all that he thought it was "too little." When
he actually saw the Surrealist masterpiece in the vice-presidential bedroom,
he told the Vice President he thought it was "realllly greaaaat." There were
enough *l*'s and *a*'s to make me think he meant it, but not enough for me to
be sure. The bed came complete with a mink bedspread and a mirror suspended over it from one of the bronze-snake bedposts, a small mirror, more
like something out of a dentist's office than a bordello. Andy couldn't resist
murmuring, "I didn't know it had a mirror."

"I knew you'd get a kick out of that," said Rockefeller.

"Gee, the mink bedspread must be worth the price alone, right?" said
Andy.

Rockefeller chuckled and said, "Andy, you never cease to amaze me.
Keep up the good work. I've got to go pay some attention to all those
politicians downstairs. Nice to meet ya, Bob. I'll keep an eye out for the
magazine." He was so smooth, and so sincere, or so it seemed, this patri-
cian politician who made us feel we artistic New Yorkers were above all this
Washington game playing. The minute he was out the door, Andy peeked
behind the lacquer screen that was attached to the headboard. "Oh, look,
Bob," he said, pointing to the pair of pajamas and a nightgown neatly folded
on the floor behind it. "I guess they really sleep together."

* * *

The *Philosophy* book was published in England in October 1975, and London was the last stop on our promotional tour. It made the bestseller list in London. And the Fleet Street papers had a heyday with Andy, especially when it leaked out that Lord and Lady Lambton, Ann's parents, would be giving him a party on our last night in London. The Lambtons hadn't had a party since his lordship, who had been Minister of Aviation in Heath's Conservative government, was forced to resign in the friskiest scandal since the Profumo affair. There were those, including Ann, who said Lord Lambton had been set up by the Labour opposition, and there were those who said he was the raciest rake in British High Society. Andy believed both sides completely, and couldn't wait to meet Ann's parents.

The party was everything Andy liked a party to be: a big bash in a big house with big names, and lots of beautiful young rich kids running up and down the stairs, and spilling the beans on each other to Andy and Sony. Lady "Binty" Lambton, Ann's mother, greeted us in a ruffled blouse and flowered skirt covering a figure as robust as Jayne Mansfield's, with a teased-up pile of hair to rival Elizabeth Taylor's or Holly Woodlawn's. Andy shyly handed her a *Philosophy* book, which she immediately tossed behind a set of old encyclopedias on the bookshelf, saying, "I throw all my most valuable possessions back there." Lord Lambton, looking like a cross between David Niven and Cary Grant, wore a gray suit so well cut you hardly noticed it and very dark Ray-Bans, very hard not to notice, at night, indoors. He thanked Andy for "taking such good care of Ann in America," and Andy told him, "Ann was the best bodyguard we ever had. She really worked hard."

It was pure Evelyn Waugh, particularly since none of the participants found it the slightest bit odd. "Well done, Andy," said Ann. "My parents really liked you." The Lambtons' "security man" was a moonlighting young fireman, and their guests, sprawled out from the garden to the attic, included the Marquess and Marchioness of Dufferin and Ava, Lord and Lady Lichfield, Princess Elizabeth of Yugoslavia, Gunther Sachs, Lucien Freud, Keith Moon, Martin Amis, J. Paul Getty III, and a woman in rubber named Jordan, who worked in a King's Road boutique named Sex.

"Now this is class!" said our agent, Roz Cole, after being introduced to Lord Weidenfeld and Lady Harmsworth. Then a girl with pink hair flew by with a boy in a pink dinner jacket and she wasn't so sure what it was. The party literally went on until dawn, and Andy spent a long stretch of it sitting on a sofa in the corner with the octogenarian Lady Diana Cooper, often called "the Diana Vreeland of London," and the teenage Charlie Tennant, sporting the rich punk look—orange suspenders and one earring. At five in the morning, the belle of the ball, Caroline Kennedy, who was taking summer art courses in London, was still waltzing with Mark Shand.

"They look so beautiful together," said Andy, of the late president's seventeen-year-old daughter and the twenty-seven-year-old heir to one of England's largest construction fortunes. "But if this gets in the papers," Andy continued, "I just know that Jackie's going to blame it all on me."

A photograph of Caroline and Mark leaving the Lambtons' made page one of the London tabloids, and Jackie called Andy the day we got back to New York, wanting to know what was going on. "She said I never should have invited Caroline to a party like that," Andy told me, "but I said I didn't invite anybody, Ann did."

32

Bad Behavior

One night in March 1976, in exchange for ads in *Interview,* Andy was co-hosting a promo party I'd arranged at the Time-Life Building with Terry Ellis, the president of Chrysalis Records. It was called for nine, and by ten, Fred, Jed, Vincent, the entire *Interview* staff, and I were there—wondering what had happened to Andy. He was having dinner first with Catherine Guinness, and she had promised me that she'd get him to the party at a reasonable hour. My stomach twisted when she arrived without Andy at ten-thirty, and when she told me he had gone home to bed it tied itself into a double Windsor knot. I found a phone and called him, begging him to come. "I'm too tired," he said. "But it's *your* party, Andy." "It's *your* party, Bob. Go back to work."

I downed a vodka to work up the courage to tell the president of Chrysalis that Andy wasn't coming. Fortunately, I ran into Fred first, who said he would call Andy. I stood there as he tried to reason with Andy, who obviously wasn't budging. "Why are you doing this to Bob?" Fred pleaded, and then turning to me, said, "He hung up on me." We both headed back for the bar, where we found Vincent, who said he'd go to Andy's to try to get him to come.

While we waited, having reassured everyone, especially the president of Chrysalis, that Andy was on his way, Fred and I tried to figure out why Andy was "torturing" me. The reason, we decided, was pretty obvious: I was leaving for a week's vacation in a couple of days. Andy hated vacations almost as much as he hated raises. And to make matters worse, I was going with a real friend, Kevin Farley, not an advertiser or a potential portrait. As

Andy had put it when I first asked him for the week off, "I'm not paying you to just go anywhere with anybody."

When he finally arrived with Vincent, he said, "Oh, hi, Bob," as if it were perfectly normal to show up two hours late for a party he was hosting. "Gee, what a great party," he added. Then he made a beeline for Linda Stein, the wife of the president of Sire Records, saying, "She could get us Elton John's portrait. Did you ever think of that, Bob?"

In the spring of 1976, Andy was also turning the screws on Fred and Jed pretty regularly. The problem was *Bad*. The Factory's only seventies movie not directed by Paul Morrissey had started shooting at the end of March 1976, in a rented studio on East 19th Street, with Jed directing a screenplay by Pat Hackett. Carroll *(Baby Doll)* Baker had been cast as the lead, with Perry King, the star of *Mandingo,* as her criminal son. Some of the Factory kids, past and present, got smaller parts: Susan Blond, Barbara Allen, Geraldine Smith, and Brigid Berlin, who just couldn't stay away from Andy.

We had already tried to get Vivian Vance to play the lead: a put-upon middle-class housewife with an unemployed alcoholic husband, a nymphomaniac daughter, and a kleptomaniac son, who does electrolysis in her kitchen to pay the bills. Pat's script for *Bad* was an extension of Andy's idea to make a movie out of *Enquirer* headlines. There was even a deranged mother who threw her baby out the window. It was, of course, a far cry from the *I Love Lucy* show, but we thought Vivian Vance would be perfect for the part and we also thought we'd have a chance to get her because her husband, John Dodds, an editor at G. P. Putnam's Sons, was an old friend of Andy's from his book-jacket-designing days in the fifties.

Vivian Vance had thought differently. "I'd love to do it, Andy, I really would," she'd told us over dinner at La Caravelle. "But you must understand that for all those people out there I'm still Ethel Mertz, Lucy's next-door neighbor and the nicest woman in America, and that's why I can still go into any dinner theater in the country and get paid $20,000 a week, because all my nice fans in their mink stoles want to see Ethel Mertz be nice. I *hate* being nice and I *hate* my fans and I *hate* their mink stoles! But I love making $20,000 a week anytime I want, you know, to buy a new Cadillac, or a sable coat. And as much as I love you and I love the script and I love the boys and girls who work with you, Ethel Mertz just can't star in *Andy Warhol's Bad* and still expect to go out to those dinner theaters and get that $20,000 a week. I'm sorry, Andy, I really am." We were sorry too. It had been one of the best performances we had ever seen, full of the bitter passion that would have been perfect for the part.

Our second choice for the lead in *Bad* had been Lana Turner. We were quite certain she was right for the part, though Andy was skeptical after meeting her at a party. "She'd be too difficult," he said. "We'd have to do everything the way she wanted. She's just like Paulette, without the dia-

monds." The one actress we knew not to ask to be in *Bad,* even though
she'd have been great if she'd only let her Brooklyn roots show, was Paulette.

    The *Bad* story started back in 1973, when we met Robert Stigwood and
one of his young right-hand men, Jeff Tornberg. Stigwood had produced
Jesus Christ Superstar; he was the manager for the Bee Gees; he had a
private plane, a yacht, a castle in Bermuda, a penthouse triplex in the San
Remo on Central Park West, decorated by Mica Ertegun and Chessy Rayner;
there was even talk of a merger between the Robert Stigwood Organization
and Ahmet Ertegun's Atlantic Records. He was not an easy man to get to
know. He maintained his cool but pleasant distance, while letting his entourage do most of the talking for him. Andy, of course, was jealous: Stigwood
always served Dom Perignon at meetings, even in the middle of the day.
His young associates didn't have to pour it, as we did; they had proper
servants in proper uniforms to do it for them. We were all a little jealous of
the Stigwood organization.
    All through 1974 and early 1975, AWE and RSO edged closer to a *Bad*
deal. Fred and I were going to be associate producers, and Jeff Tornberg the
executive producer. But just when we thought everything was set, everything
started changing. Stigwood was worried about Jed's being "too soft-spoken
to direct," or so Jeff Tornberg said.
    In March 1975, Robert Stigwood made his final decision on *Bad:* No,
with no reason why given. We were sure it had something to do with disa-
greements between him and Jeff Tornberg, especially since Jeff had called
Andy that morning and invited him over for "strawberries, cream, and a
cloud with a silver lining." The silver lining was that he was now available
to work at AWE. Fred wanted to "give Jeff a chance." We actually took a
formal vote on it, the only one ever at the Factory, all of us sitting around
the Ruhlmann table in the dining room, raising our hands. Andy, Jed, and
Pat voted against Jeff, Fred voted for him, and I abstained. I wasn't sure I
wanted to get mixed up in the Factory movie business after all. Somehow,
Fred's one vote constituted a majority, and Jeff Tornberg stayed on as executive producer—another *Bad* problem.

    Now, a year later, Jed's dream of directing was coming true, but Andy
made that a problem, too. As much as he wanted Jed to succeed, he also
couldn't help being jealous. For months, while we tried to raise money after
Stigwood pulled out, Andy had been telling me that he wanted Jed to have
a big hit. "Jed really is a hard worker," he often said, and just as often
added, "It would be nice to have somebody else bring home the bacon for
a change." I was present at parties when he "begged"—his word— movie-
producer friends like Franco Rossellini and Lester Persky to coproduce *Bad.*

The problem with begging, especially at parties, is that people wonder why you're so desperate. The more Andy went on about Jed's being "the best director and the best movie editor and the best decorator, he really, really is, I really, really mean it," the more people wondered what was wrong with Jed, and why Andy didn't back him with some of his own money.

Money was another problem. The film was budgeted at $1.2 million, and Fred persuaded Peter Brant to finance it. But Andy made that a problem too. On one hand, he was worried because Peter had pulled out of *Interview* in exchange for backing the movie, which meant Andy had to cover the magazine's monthly losses, now running at about half of what they were under Rosemary Kent, approximately $5,000 to $6,000 a month (two or three portraits a year was the way I looked at it, and he was now doing two or three a month). On the other hand, Andy also fretted about "Peter taking over" and "losing control to Peter." He told me, "If Peter ever gets mad, he can just dump all the paintings he owns in auction and ruin my prices. We're just too involved. I mean, it's like Peter is my boss now."

Fred bore the brunt of Andy's anxiety about the Brant business. "Don't forget whose side you're on" was one of his regular sendoffs when Fred was going up to Greenwich to see Peter and Sandy, or taking them out for a night on the town. "Andy, I'm just trying to keep everything going," Fred said once, "and believe me, pleasing Peter Brant *and* you is *not* easy."

It certainly wasn't. Just as shooting was about to begin, Peter demanded that Andy put in $200,000 of his own money. Andy refused. Fred went back and forth between them, trying to get one or the other to give in or compromise and split the amount. But Peter felt that Andy had to show some faith in his own people, particularly in Jed, and Andy felt that Peter was "being mean," especially to Jed. The rest of us watched with horror. Why wouldn't Andy budge, we wondered? And, more disturbing, if he wouldn't help Jed, who would he help? At the last possible moment, when it became apparent that Andy wasn't going to invest a cent, Fred saved the day. He put in the $200,000—his "entire life's savings," Andy told me, smiling. I was shocked that Andy let him go through with it, and disgusted, and from then on I always made a point of saying that I worked for Andy Warhol *and* Fred Hughes.

Fred, true to form, played the *Bad* drama down. He said that Andy really was under financial pressure, and that he himself was just making a normal investment in a project he believed in. I shouldn't go on about how horrible Andy had been, Fred said, nor about how wonderfully he had behaved. "It's not really my life savings," he said, "just some Schlumberger stock the de Menils gave me years ago." It was all part of his gentleman-of-the-old-school act: stiff upper lip, never explain, never complain.

It was a hard act to pull off and, more and more, the actor was slipping out of his role. One night during this *Bad* period, Andy, Fred, Marina Schiano, and I went to a cocktail party at Earl Blackwell's for Mary Martin. Actually, Andy and Fred had gone directly from the office, and I had gone to pick up Marina. When we arrived, they berated us for being late and "missing all the big old stars." We had actually missed Douglas Fairbanks, Jr., Rex Reed, and Barbara Walters. Mary Martin, Lillian Gish, Gloria Swanson, Maureen Stapleton, Bricktop, and Paulette were all still there or just making their grand entrances.

In the taxi to our second party of the evening, Marina set Fred off by mentioning that Countess Marina Cicogna had turned down the Mary Martin party "because it was too early and she grew up with all those stars anyway." Fred blew his stack and said that Countess Cicogna could go jump in the Grand Canal. "Fred," said Andy, "she's one of our best friends." "Listen, Andy," said Fred, "I remember the time five years ago when she wouldn't let me and *you* come to a party of hers in Venice, and you were saying how much you *hated* her." "I *never* said that, Fred. How can you say that I did?" "Give me a break, Andy! *Give me a break.*"

"Oh, Fred's drunk," said Andy, and then proceeded to invite Marina Schiano to go on our next three business trips, just to really send Fred up the wall. By the time we arrived at our next party, Fred was giving the finger to both his wife and his boss, and while Marina tried to calm him down, Andy just giggled and said to me, "Why is Fred always in such a bad mood lately, Bob?"

But Andy was in a bad mood lately, too, or, rather, *Bad* was having a strange effect on his behavior.

In late March, just as Jed finally started shooting *Bad,* Andy, Fred, and I went to dinner at Elaine's with Averil Meyer, Linda Hutton, Mark Shand, Harry Fane, and J. Paul Getty III—Millionettes one and all. After dinner, Andy surprised me by going downtown with the rest of us to the Barefoot Boy, a tiny disco with huge speakers that our crowd took over between the closing of Le Jardin in early 1976 and the opening of Hurrah at the end of the year. I was also surprised by how much he was drinking, and how late he was staying, and how little he minded when I went to the bathroom every fifteen minutes with the Getty boy.

In the middle of April, when Jed was still shooting *Bad,* Andy took him to Delfina Rattazzi's party for Arnold Schwarzenegger and Bob Rafelson, the star and director of *Stay Hungry.* It was mostly Millionettes that night too: Lupo Rattazzi and Imee Marcos, François de Menil, Andrea de Portago with Paul Simon. For no apparent reason, Andy decided that a young Colombian named Andreas Echavarria was "Mr. Rich Right." When Maxime de la Falaise McKendry invited us all back to her place for an instant supper, Jed said he was going home, but Andy said to me, "Let's go, and bring Mr. Rich Right.'' And on we went, from Maxime's to Infinity, another downtown disco, ending up at the Barefoot Boy, where, once again, Andy got drunk, stayed until four, didn't mind my bathroom detours, and chatted up everyone who approached him. ''They're all so young and so cute,'' he said. ''But Mr. Rich Right dropped me, Bob. I've got to find another one. Somebody to pay the bills. Somebody to bring home the bacon. Life's expensive, Bob. Really, really expensive. And love is cheap. Really, really cheap.''

A few nights later, Andy wanted to go on and on again. We started out at a cocktail party at Calvin Klein's sleek new pad overlooking the 59th Street Bridge. It was for Carrie Donovan of the *New York Times,* one of the most powerful fashion journalists, and every fashion designer in town was there—Bill Blass, Oscar de la Renta, Giorgio di Sant'Angelo, even Halston, who considered Calvin an upstart. Andy took pictures of department-store bigwigs for ads. At one point, he told me, both Marvin Traub of Blooming-dale's and Kal Ruttenstein, then of Bonwit Teller, said they wanted to advertise in *Interview,* ''but since each one heard the other one say it, how much do you want to bet neither one does it? Oh, there's Gerry Stutz. She gave me my first job. Should I go ask her for our first Bendel's ad?'' That was the old Andy, all work. But later that night the new Andy, all play, came out again. We went to a big dinner at Regine's which went on until 2:30 A.M., and then Andy wanted to go on to Elaine's with Bianca for a nightcap, even though he was drunker than I'd ever seen him.

Jed finished shooting *Bad* in June, and edited it all summer. In September, we had the first screening, and everyone said they loved it, though no one jumped to pick it up for distribution. The next night Fred gave a Factory family dinner at home for Thomas Ammann. Diana Vreeland was there, and Marina Schiano, Andrea de Portago, Vincent with his new girlfriend Shelly Dunn, Chris Makos, and Robert Hayes. We toasted Jed with champagne and then headed downtown—Robert and I stopping off to pick up cocaine on the way, the rest going directly to the Barefoot Boy, where we all danced until the closing hour. All, that is, except Andy, who had dropped off Diana and gone home early. That's pretty much how it was after *Bad:* When Jed went out late, Andy went home early, and when Jed went home early, Andy went out late.

''You missed Liz Taylor last night,'' Andy told me one Sunday morning in June 1976. ''I mean, *Elizabeth.* She yelled at me for calling her Liz.'' According to Andy, his one-time co-star was also having a pretty bad spring. After her 1975 remarriage to Richard Burton ended in a redivorce, she had briefly reconnected with Henry Wynberg. Now she was involved in a highly publicized and highly complicated romance with Ardeshir Zahedi, Iran's bachelor ambassador in Washington. In fact, Andy had spent that Saturday

night at Zahedi's Waldorf Towers apartment with her and his nephew, Firooz
Zahedi, who had called his cousin, Nima Farmanfarmaian, who had called
Andy, to come over for TV dinner from room service. Andy said that he
thought she was unhappy because Ardeshir was getting nervous about her
getting serious. "And she asked me if she could use Montauk, because she's
broke and has nowhere to go. How can she be broke? I said yes, because
she was so sweet. We were watching this horror movie on TV and she was
holding my hand. But then Nima had Chris Isham there and he took a picture
and Elizabeth let go of my hand. So that was the end of our affair."

Not quite. The following Thursday, Andy and I arrived late at Elsa
Peretti's all-white penthouse, where a bon-voyage bash for Valentino was in
full swing. Much to our surprise, there was Elizabeth, in a big white caftan,
with her big white diamond ring, all curled up on a big white ottoman, with
Kevin Farley, the friend I'd taken that *verboten* vacation with a few months
back. He was now working at Iolas Gallery and had come with Barbara
Allen that night, but when Federico de Laurentiis moved in on Barbara,
Miss Taylor moved in on Kevin. And within five minutes of our arrival, so
had Andy. "Gee," he said, "Kevin's such a beauty. We should put him on
the cover with Elizabeth. I'm going to tell him if he gets us an exclusive that
we will."

Big fat joints of Brazilian marijuana were being passed around, and
Elizabeth took a big fat puff and led Kevin out to the balcony, where they
started aiming chocolate-covered strawberries at passing pedestrians twenty
floors below. Then they went into the bathroom for a very long time—it was
like a scene from the Fantasy Diary for real. Andy was beside himself, and
begging me to take pictures for him through the bathroom window on the
balcony. "God, Elizabeth must really like Kevin," he said, "they've been
in there forever. I wonder what they're doing, Bob. Do you think they're
making out? You've got to stick my camera through the window and find
out."

We could hear Elizabeth cackling through the door, and later Kevin told
me that she had been telling him about her love and health problems and he
had been telling her he really wasn't interested, which made her laugh even
louder. When they finally emerged, Elsa led me into the bathroom, "to try
out my new mouthwash," she announced, "the most fantastic lavender you
ever tasted." Her mouthwash turned out to be a bottle of coke.

Meanwhile, Marina Schiano was snapping a shot of Elizabeth and Kevin
back on the ottoman. "Look at her, even for an Instamatic she poses like a
star," said Marina, adding to Elizabeth, "You must have been in a bad
mood when I first met you, because you were awful, but tonight you are
fun, you're stoned, and you look great *even* stoned." It was Marina's instant-
intimacy routine, and one that most big stars fell for, because few people
have the nerve to pull it off. But Elizabeth leaned over to Kevin and stage-

whispered, "What's this bitch carrying on about?" And Andy off-stage-whispered to me, "She's letting Marina take a picture. You've got to take a picture for me." But I lacked Marina's nerve, and still remembered the glare Elizabeth gave me that crazy day at the villa in Rome, when I tried to come between her and the bush she was stripping clean.

Sometime past midnight, André Leon Talley suggested that we all go to a black disco on Eighth Avenue called Othello. Elizabeth allowed herself to be persuaded by Valentino. In the limousine there, she was busily hand teasing her hairdo higher, and putting eyedrops in her purple eyes. When Kevin asked her for some, she cracked, "With those eyes you don't need eyedrops." Andy shot me a look of total ecstasy: He loved being in the middle of an Elizabeth Taylor romance, especially when somebody else was playing the male lead. And as Elizabeth and Kevin boogie-woogied at Othello, while black girls clapped and hollered, Andy told me, "God, Kevin really is a greaaaat dancer. We really should put him in the magazine." He was a bit let down at 2 A.M., when Elizabeth announced it was time to go home and asked Valentino to take her. He wouldn't be able to call Kevin for a morning-after session with Sony.

A week later, we found ourselves at the Museum of Modern Art's annual Party in the Garden. As the seventies went on, it got wilder every year. People went from smoking pot in the open air to sniffing poppers as they danced to disco music, and by mid-decade Victor Hugo was hip-hopping with another boy next to Martha Mitchell and her Wall Street date. When Fred, Catherine, and I arrived at this year's bash, Chris Hemphill said that Halston and Elizabeth Taylor had been at Lily Auchincloss's dinner before the party.

But we couldn't find Halston or Elizabeth or Andy, who had gone to Carroll de Portago's dinner, at the garden party, so Catherine and I decided to go on ahead to Charlie O's, where Lester Persky and Bobby Zarem were giving yet another party. Just as we were about to give up and go home, in walked Andy in a burst of flashbulbs, with Halston and Elizabeth, who went straight to the ladies' room for half an hour, until Lynn Redgrave was dispatched to fish her out. She was in a great mood when she finally joined Andy and Halston at the table that Lester and Bobby had cleared for them. She laughed as I shouted, *"Basta! Basta!"* at the paparazzi and laughed again when I told her that the only one who persisted was Robin Platzer from *Interview* and "I fired her for the night." Andy laughed too and said, "What a great idea, to fire someone for one night." And after Elizabeth and Halston departed at one-thirty, we went on to Regine's, where Andy spent the next hour telling me that Elizabeth Taylor was "the most wonderful person" he'd ever met. "She really is, Bob, she really is. And she's coming to lunch at the Factory tomorrow and letting me take Polaroids for the new portrait I'm doing of her."

"Is she going to pay you?" I asked.

"It doesn't matter, Bob," Andy shouted above the music. "She's Elizabeth Taylor."

Elizabeth Taylor didn't turn up for lunch the next day, but she invited us up to the Waldorf Towers for drinks that evening. She was still staying at the Zahedi suite, and the ambassador was still in Washington. "I bet he's trying to dump her," Andy said on the way uptown, "because she's Jewish and that would make too many problems for the Shah. And she can't convert to Moslem because she'd never make a movie again, right? God, life really is hard. And the bigger you are, the harder it is. I mean, Elizabeth finally met Mr. Rich Right and she can't marry him because she's the wrong religion. Aren't you glad you're not a big star, Bob?" I said I was, adding, "Poor Liz." "Elizabeth, Bob, Elizabeth. Oh, I bet I never get her portrait."

When we arrived, she was talking on the phone and somehow managed to get tangled up in the long cord as she talked and walked. "That cord doesn't want to let go of you," I joked. "At least something doesn't want to let go of me," she said. She was wearing a caftan from Iran, lots of gold chains, and her big diamond ring, and when she disentangled herself from her phone, she apologized for missing lunch. She said she had a cold and had taken some cold tablets that knocked her out. Andy didn't bother to take his Polaroid, all loaded and ready, out of his plastic bag, knowing full well that her explanation was leading right into her usual "too puffy" excuse. Halston arrived and she offered us all some Iranian Imperial Gold caviar, which gave Andy an opening to say that we were going to Iran soon— the trip was scheduled for July 1976—to do the Empress's portrait. Liz deftly switched the conversation to the English royal family, and told a very funny story about the time Richard Burton couldn't remember the Queen Mother's name when he had to introduce her to someone and she said, "I think the two words you are grasping for are Queen Elizabeth." "But that's her daughter's name," said Andy, playing dumb. "It's her name too," she said. "Get your queens straight, Andy," she hooted.

Andy had forgotten about her portrait for the moment. He was too busy trying to turn his tape recorder on in his jacket pocket, without Elizabeth noticing. The phone rang and her secretary told her, "Elizabeth, I think you want to take this one in the bedroom."

"You mean it's Ardeshir," she said with another hoot, and Andy gave me another one of his ecstatic looks from the fan who stepped into the soap opera. He also let Sony out of his pocket for a little air.

Afterward, giving me a lift uptown, Elizabeth told me how much she liked Andy. "He's a real artist," she said, "and such a kind, gentle, sweet, funny man. Please tell him I really am sorry about lunch today. Maybe we can do the photographs out at his house in Montauk. The natural light might be nice, don't you think? God knows, I need all the help I can get."

She didn't pose for Andy in Montauk, or anywhere else ever, though they were friends until his death. I don't think she was being bitchy or difficult about it, or playing power games with Andy, à la Paulette. In fact, she was so relaxed in Montauk that she joined in our softball games and ran around the bases like a big, happy kid. But the more I saw of her, the more I realized that she just didn't want to have her portrait done again. Maybe she didn't want to wake up every morning and face her face. Maybe she preferred to be remembered the way Andy had painted her in 1963. Andy, who painted himself every three or four years, couldn't understand why anyone wouldn't want a portrait done, particularly by an artist as flattering as he was. "I could make her look so great," he said again and again. In October 1976, when she married Senator John Warner of Virginia, Andy saw it as another opportunity to talk her into posing: "*Everybody* has their portrait in Washington, don't they, Bob?"

Liz, Imelda, Gala—those were three portraits that Andy always wanted and never got. He wanted them for different reasons: Gala was art history, Imelda meant money and power, and with Elizabeth Taylor he was chasing the stars, as he had been since the age of eight.

33

On the Road Again

Despite, or perhaps because of, the *Bad* mess back home, Andy, Fred, and I were constantly traveling in 1976. In February alone, Andy's art business took us from Birmingham, Alabama, to St. Moritz, Bonn, and Naples. In "The Pittsburgh of the South" Andy received the key to the city at a "Bicentennial Ball" at the Birmingham Art Museum. An Andy Warhol Room had been set up, with twenty small paintings borrowed from the Factory, and, for some reason, an early Charlie Chaplin movie projected on one wall—some Alabamians thought it was an early Andy Warhol movie. In St. Moritz, Andy took Polaroids for the portrait of Inga Rodenstock, the wife of the largest German eyeglass manufacturer, and had a small show of "Selected Works: 1960–1975" at the Bischofberger Gallery. In Bonn, Chancellor Willy Brandt, puffing a Churchillian cigar, sat for his portrait at Herman the German's Wunsche Gallery. Andy told him, "Oh, uh, Paulette Goddard really loves you." The Chancellor, taking another puff on his cigar, affirmed that he did indeed know Paulette. "She is," he said, "what I believe you Americans call a smart cookie."

Andy made an important purchase in Bonn: The new Minox 35EL was the smallest camera then available that took full-frame 35mm photographs, and it had a sleek, all-black, James Bond look. I bought one too, and we both took the same first picture back at the Hotel Bristol: a room-service still life. As I recall, I took mine seconds before Andy took his.

In Naples, Andy had another small show of selected works at the Lucio Amelio Gallery. One afternoon, as we took matching photos of the Bay of Naples, Andy said, "We should do a photography book together, Bob. We've

got to take photographs wherever we go from now on. It's work now, Bob.''
That's how our next book, *Andy Warhol's Exposures,* started.

Our frequent flights continued: to New Orleans in March for the Mick
Jagger painting show at the Freeman-Anacker Gallery; to Jacksonville, Florida, in May for the Gilmans' portraits; to London in July for the Cats and
Dogs show at the James Mayor Gallery, and then on to Teheran for Farah
Diba's portrait; to Seattle in November for the Warhol Retrospective curated
by Charles Cowles at the Museum of Fine Art, and then on to Los Angeles
for Marisa Berenson's wedding to Jim Randall, which we photographed for
a chapter in *Exposures.*

Andy always started off ''dreading'' these trips, whining that he wanted
to ''stay home with Archie'' and worrying about ''what Jed's doing while
I'm away.'' But once he was airborne, he forgot his fretting in the newest
movie-star biography, and once he landed, he was happy to be someplace
other than New York, at least for a few days. Then the calls to Vincent in
the office and Jed or ''the girls'' at home increased from one a day to three
or four, and the whining started again. ''Can't we leave a day or two early?''
he invariably asked Fred as we entered the second week, and often Andy
and I would leave for New York without Fred, who was only too glad to
''clean up the loose ends'' and have a few days in a foreign port to himself.

The only trip Fred didn't come on was to Las Vegas, in April 1976. It
was a day or two after that big fight at Earl Blackwell's party, and Fred
canceled out of it at the last minute. That left Catherine Guinness, then still
fairly new in the Factory family, and me, to accompany Andy to Las Vegas,
where he was delivering finished portraits to Paul Anka.

Surprisingly, Andy hated Las Vegas, and by the end of our three-day
stay he wasn't too fond of Paul Anka either, though the crooner did take all
four portraits and used one of them on his next album, titled *Portrait,* for
which he paid an additional fee. Andy was hurt, really, because Paul and
his wife, Anne, hadn't invited us to their house. ''They didn't want their
kids to see us,'' he said. That was always the test for Andy: When people
kept their children away from him, he took it to mean that, deep down, they
believed all the awful things written about him and considered him a creep.

Paul Anka put us up at the new MGM Grand Hotel, which billed itself
as ''a $100 million fantasy starring 2,100 rooms and suites and featuring the
world's largest casino,'' thinking Andy would love it because the halls were
lined with enlarged photographs of Dietrich, Garbo, Bette Davis, and Joan
Crawford, and the MGM lion, in brassplate, was affixed to the door of every
room. Andy hated it for all the usual reasons and then some: fake turkey in
the club sandwiches, ''so I can only eat steak''; windows that only opened
an inch, ''so you can't jump out when you lose all your money''; a sunken
circular bathtub in the middle of his bedroom, with a wall of mirrors behind

it, "so I never stop seeing myself"; purple shag carpeting in his living room, "so deep and hairy they can never get it really clean, Bob. I guess I can never take my socks off in this room." When he looked out at the commanding view of "the Strip," with one casino hotel after another, each surrounded by an epic parking lot, all plunked down in the middle of the hot, hazy desert, he said, "Do you think Robert Venturi was on drugs when he wrote that book about how great Las Vegas is? Or maybe it is prettier at night, when the lights go on." At night, when the lights went on, he said, "It's sort of pretty, but it's not Paris, Bob."

What he really hated about Las Vegas was the gambling. "The minute you leave your room," he complained, "you're in the casino. I mean, from the elevator to the front door is all casino, right? Even the desk where you get your key is in the middle of the casino." Andy didn't gamble so much as a quarter in a slot machine the whole time we were there, and if Catherine and I stopped to try the machines, he rushed us on. "These people look so desperate, Bob," he said. "You don't want to end up like them, do you? C'mon, Catherine, let's go to the room and see what's on TV."

He didn't much like the casino's clientele, who were mostly middle-aged, middle-class middle Americans, with a few Japanese and Mexican tourists, the latter being the only ones vaguely well dressed. "We haven't seen one beauty yet," Andy pointed out, adding that the middle Americans "all dress unisex now." That wasn't what the auto workers and housewives from Michigan and Ohio would have called it, but the men's "leisure suits" were exactly like the women's "pants suits"—polyester, collarless, bellbottom, bright blue or dim beige. "And they all wear chains around their necks," said Andy. "The men and the women. No ties. And white patent-leather shoes. The men and the women. And tease their hair. The men and the women." I noted that they all looked like they had just thrown their third mortgage on their split-level house on the roulette wheel, and lost it. "Oh, I know," said Andy. "Don't you wish you were back in Monte Carlo with the rich kids, Bob?"

Andy thought the live MGM lion in the cage by the pool, which you could pose with for five dollars, "looked drugged." There was a line to get in the MGM Theater, which was showing the Marx Brothers in *Go West,* and one kid on it recognized Andy and asked for his autograph. He was followed by the rest of the line, most of whom asked Andy, "Who are you?" after he signed his name for them. At the MGM newsstand and souvenir shop, where we proposed leaving a stack of *Interview*s to give away free, the cashier said, "I'll *try.* This place isn't too hip, you know."

The Ankas took us to the Circus Maximus restaurant in Caesar's Palace, where the waiter introduced himself: "I am Florian, your captain for the night." Andy got drunk on the exorbitant Montrachet Paul Anka ordered and tried to pass his Boeuf Wellington onto my plate when Anne Anka wasn't looking. After dinner, we played twenty-one in Caesar's casino, which also engulfed every square foot between the elevators and the front door. That is, we played, and Andy watched. Paul Anka gave Catherine and me one thousand dollars each, which we rapidly lost. "You should've slipped it in your pocket, Bob," said Andy. "That would have been too rude, Andy. He gave me the money to play with him." "No, it wouldn't have been. They give him the money to give you, just so they can say he was there."

The following evening, the Ankas took us to the Ah So restaurant in Caesar's Palace. Andy got drunk on the exorbitant sake Paul Anka ordered and tried to pass the "fried everything" onto my plate when Anne Anka wasn't looking. When a "card-trick expert" named Jimmy Grippa, who said he had served in the Italian infantry in World War I, began pulling cards out of Andy's pockets without warning, he turned sullen. He turned fuchsia when a few hundred-dollar bills came flying out of one pocket—they weren't part of the trick. After dinner, the Ankas arranged for us to catch the "Hallelujah Hollywood!" floor show back at the MGM Grand. We thought it would at least be campy, but as Andy said, "It's so bad it's not good."

On the flight back to New York, Andy and Catherine drank quite a bit, and to the astonishment of the other first-class passengers, began poking and pulling each other's arms, and grabbing and twisting each other's hands, like three-year-olds. They were shrieking and giggling and yelling, and then Andy actually hurt Catherine by pressing her ring into her finger until it bled. "Silly goose!" she squealed, finding that the funniest joke of all. Andy quieted down at the sight of blood, and told Catherine several times how sorry he was.

A dozen little girls in gold brocade robes greeted us at Teheran International Airport and pinned pink roses to our lapels. "God," said Andy, "this is like Imelda Marcos arriving in China, Bob."

Andy, Fred, and I, with Nima Farmanfarmaian, our Iranian friend from New York, as guide, flew from London to Teheran on July 5, 1976. A Mercedes carried us through the dense traffic, and denser smog, past the new highrises and newer construction sites in the heart of Teheran's new midtown business district. But Iran's modernity was a halfway thing. From his sleek, but vaguely shoddy, orange-on-orange room at the Hotel Inter-Continental, Andy tried to call Vincent at the office in New York, only to be informed by the hotel operator that international calls required an appointment made several hours in advance.

"I hope we can see the Empress right away," Andy said, "and leave."

That night, we headed uptown for dinner at Nima's stepfather's house. On the way we passed vast tracts of suburban subdivisions so new that the neat, small lawns in front of the neat, small houses were still in the sprouting stage. It all looked suspiciously identical to Levittown, Long Island—and indeed most of the area was being developed by Arthur Levitt. Uptown, one hour north of downtown, the Pahlavis had erected an extravagantly contemporary sixties palace on the piney slopes of the snow-tipped mountains that ring the hot, dry city, and the rich followed them northward into palaces of their own.

Abol Farmanfarmaian's house was typically uptown: low-slung, sprawled-out, ultra-modern, like a place on Mulholland Drive, above Beverly Hills, decorated like any plush suburban villa anywhere in the West, but with sudden bursts of forgotten native beauty—a Qajar painting hung among a wall of Minimalist prints, a Persian carpet thrown across the patio, a gold mosaic dragon set in the bottom of the pool, under the Plexiglass bridge. Abol, or rather his servants, fed us the typically uptown dinner: a "Western course" of filet mignon and salad, followed by a "Persian course" of lamb and chicken kebabs over sour cherry and saffron rices. On the table were baskets of thin, dry bread, pickled almonds and onions, and an eggplant-yogurt dip. The meal began, as did every meal we had in uptown Teheran, with a seemingly bottomless bowl of Imperial Gold caviar. Technically, Abol explained, Imperial Gold was available only to the royal family and high government officials, but at $50 a kilo it was well within the means of most uptown residents. The second grade, Pearl Grey, was found mostly in better restaurants. "Anything vaguely black," Abol concluded, "forget about it."

We consumed vast amounts of Imperial Gold in the next three days, while waiting for Farah Diba to return to the capital from Meshed, an ancient city near the Afghan border where she was dedicating a new hospital and several schools. We also devoured a lot of Pearl Grey, which room service supplied for only nine dollars a half pound—it became Andy's substitute for petit fours and phone calls.

Uptown social life seemed rather Mulholland Drive too: lunch in T-shirts and jeans by the pool, dinner in evening gowns and jewels by the pool— surrounded by torches and lit with spots. We mostly saw aunts and uncles and cousins of Nima's—Teheran's old-money set. Some of them had ties to the old Qajar dynasty, overthrown by the Shah's father in 1926, but while they were perfectly capable of making the sort of remark that French aristocrats whose titles go back to the Bourbons make about French aristocrats whose titles only go back to Napoleon, they also did business and mixed socially with the new rich who came up with the Pahlavis. In fact, without Nima's background profiles, we could never have told the old group from the new: They all seemed more American or European than Middle Eastern, and they all preferred talking about the couture houses of Paris or the discos of New York, rather than about oil prices or human rights. And I never once heard the word "Shiite," though the Ayatollah Khomeini was only three short years away.

On our second night in Teheran, Prime Minister Amir Abbas Hoveyda, the older brother of Ambassador Fereydoun Hoveyda, invited us to a large formal dinner in honor of Prime Minister Bhutto of Pakistan. It was held in the rose-scented garden of his grand old palace downtown. "History embraces our nations!" Bhutto almost shouted at the end of his speech, and *le tout* Teheran jumped to their feet and applauded. Bhutto was overthrown the following year, and later executed. Hoveyda held power two years longer, but faced a fundamentalist firing squad before Bhutto.

Andy was bored. Fred went on about the beauty of the old downtown houses, which he pointed out were 1940s copies of 1910 Roman houses, "which of course were copies of 1870s Paris houses." Andy became more interested when Nima said that most of the downtown residential district had been built by "Granddaddy Farmanfarmaian," who had left one million dollars to each of his thirty-two grandchildren.

He really perked up when he got back uptown to the Key Club, a swank private disco rumored to be secretly owned by the Shah's twin sister, Princess Ashraf. Andy sat on a velvet banquette, telling a royal nephew he could be an Interman and asking him if he'd like to have an affair with Marion Javits.

Two nights later, His Majesty's Chief Minister, Mr. Bahadory, confirmed Andy's appointment with Her Majesty, who had finally returned from Meshed, for the following morning at the imperial palace. Unfortunately, he said, Andy could only bring one "assistant," which meant he had to choose between Fred and me. Nima was expected too, as she knew Farah Diba and would help smooth things out.

Andy left the decision up to Fred, who decided he would go instead of me, even though I had arranged the commission and the trip. I tried not to sulk as I rang room service for a double order of Pearl Grey. When Andy got back from the portrait sitting, he knocked on my door, and very sweetly told me he wished I had been there, "because you would have known what to say to her, Bob." I asked him what it was like, but couldn't get him to say anything beyond, "She was really, really beautiful and so was her palace." He said it several times, louder and louder, and that's when I remembered that he was sure our rooms were bugged.

On our last day in Teheran, we visited the old bazaar, and realized finally that we weren't in Los Angeles. The bazaar itself was impeccable, with its stalls of exquisitely displayed spices and silks, iron and silver, copper and gold. But the streets around it were hot and dusty and lined with open sewers. There were heaving crowds everywhere, and the young men had their heads shaved, to prevent lice, Nima said, and the young women were in chadors, even though the Shah didn't like that, Nima said. Two or three times a dark anonymous face hissed as we passed.

Then we went to see the Crown Jewels, in the basement vault of a downtown bank. The moment Andy passed through its portals, he was in paradise.

"This is His Majesty's crown," the guide began. "It weighs four kilos—gold, diamonds, rubies, and emeralds—and was made by Van Cleef and Arpels for His Majesty's coronation in 1967. This is Her Majesty's crown. It weighs three kilos—gold, diamonds, rubies, and pearls—also Van Cleef and Arpels 1967. This is the old Reza Shah's crown. It is so heavy it had to be suspended from the ceiling when he wore it. . . .''

In the middle of the room was the legendary Peacock Throne: 50,000 karats of precious gemstones set in sixteen sections of solid gold so that it could be taken apart to be moved to the palace. Along the walls, in glass cases lit with tiny spots that intensified their natural glow and glitter, were: the largest ruby in the world—one hundred karats; the largest collection of pink diamonds in the world; velvet trays full of loose emeralds, rubies, sapphires, yellow diamonds, blue-white diamonds; necklaces, bracelets, earrings, brooches, rings, more crowns, coronets, and tiaras.

Andy, when he regained his speech, said he was most taken with a solid emerald snuff box, seamed in diamonds, which the guide noted ''was valued at five million dollars—ten years ago.'' ''It's like sculpture,'' Andy said. He also got a high on the ''pickle barrels'' in one corner, filled to their brims with big baroque pearls. I was most interested in the six-foot globe of the world made for the Shah's father: The seas were covered in emeralds and the continents in rubies, except for Iran, which was paved in diamonds. ''Gee,'' said Andy to the guide at the end of the hour-and-a-half tour. ''Thanks a lot. This was the best time we had in Iran. Or anywhere.'' The guide made his day even sweeter when she thanked him, saying, ''Our last visitor was Elizabeth Taylor. She has a very big diamond ring, but you know more about stones than she.''

It was a successful trip: Farah Diba ordered eight portraits for the palace in Teheran, two more for the main office of Iran Air and the National Bank of Iran, and another two for the embassies in New York and Washington—twelve in all, for a total fee of $190,000. I received 10 percent, my first big commission. And Andy's dream of the perpetually multiplying portrait seemed to be coming true.

34

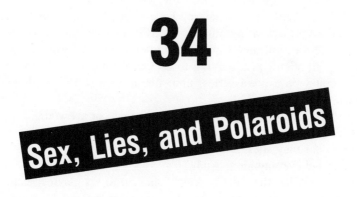

It was eleven-thirty on a spring morning in 1977 when I arrived at the office, horrendously hung over from the previous night's blitz of vodka, coke, and Quaaludes, but I *wasn't* seeing things. That was a hairy arm stuffed up a hairy anus in the Polaroids neatly arranged across the top of my desk. My shelves were lined with other Big Shots of more predictable penetrations: oral-genital, anal-genital, oral-anal—all male on male, and in extreme close-up. Even on my chair there were half a dozen shots of an engorged penis entering a mustachioed mouth. Andy had been at it again: photographing sexual acts between street hustlers and call boys arranged by Victor Hugo, Halston's friend. It was all for art's sake, of course: the Torso Series, as the paintings made from these photographs came to be called. But around the office we referred to these works in progress as the Cocks, Cunts, and Ass-holes Series—very light on the cunts.

It wasn't the first time that Andy had left the results of one of his Polaroid orgies to dry in my office, but I wanted it to be the last. When Andy arrived an hour later I gave him a piece of my mind. "Am I supposed to have an advertising meeting in here with these cocks all over my desk? What about the girls who work here?"

Andy was nonplussed. "Just tell them it's *art,* Bob. They're land-scapes."

"They might resemble landscapes when you get done with them, Andy, but right now they look like porn pictures and I'm sick and tired of finding them on my desk every other morning. What if Jed happened to come by the office, or if Pat saw them and told Jed?"

"Oh, he's already mad at me, so it doesn't matter."

"Well, you have to do what you have to do, but can't you *please* do it in the back room, *not* in my office." I was trying hard not to shout.

"Oh, we did, but then I put them in here so Victor wouldn't steal any. I mean, it's all Victor just wanting to do these things, and I thought, well, maybe it could be a good series, and, uh, it's really Victor—I don't have that much to do with it."

"Andy, is Victor going to sign the paintings, or are you?"

"It is a good idea, Bob. You know it is. I mean, look at this—can you believe how far they stick their arm up their ass?"

"I can believe anything, Andy."

He was holding the "fist-fucking" shot up to his glasses, examining it as if it were some exotic new gem discovered in the jungles of Brazil. "I mean, it's so, so . . . so abstraaaact."

A few days later, my office was strewn with genitalia again, and this time I shouted at him that I'd tear his "landscapes" into a thousand pieces and then they'd really be "abstract." More and more, he seemed to be going out of his way to provoke me, as if he wanted me to have a temper tantrum, as if he liked me to look bad in front of the rest of the staff, while he stood there like an unfairly chastised little boy.

I wasn't the only one, however, shouting at the boss, and coming in later and later, with heavier and heavier hangovers. Fred was even angrier by day, and even more blitzed by night. I recorded one night in October 1977, at Hurrah, that typified what was going on between Andy and Fred then. Andy and I were already at the club with Halston, Victor, and Barbara Allen, when Fred came in with Thomas Ammann. He was obviously drunk, which in Fred's case meant he assumed the grand theatrical gestures and deep commanding voice of Diana Vreeland. He tore off his jacket and whirled around the dance floor with Barbara.

Then, looking completely disoriented, he staggered toward me, and in an almost tearful voice, said that somebody had stolen his jacket. "I can't go on anymore," he said. "People are always stealing things from me. I'm always losing things. I just can't go on. You've got to help me, Bob." I asked him where he'd put his jacket, and he said on the banquette near Andy, but Andy said he hadn't seen it. I started searching for it in the dim disco light. "It's not here," Andy insisted. "Fred's so drunk he lost another jacket." Finally, I made Andy stand up, and there it was: Andy had been sitting on it.

"I think it's strange," Jaime Frankfurt told me one night when I was in a complaining mood, "that the two top men in Andy's organization are so miserable. I think Andy definitely has something to do with it." Jaime was the son of Andy's old friend Suzie Frankfurt, and Fred's assistant at the time, so his words had some weight.

I lit another joint and changed the subject.

*   *   *

Diana Vreeland had her own take on what was going on with "Andy and you boys." We dined together tête-à-tête at Ballato's and she began by tearing into Andy for taking six weeks to say yes to her invitation to the Saul Steinberg opening at the Whitney Museum. "*Maybe,* as you might have gathered, Bob," she said, "is not a word of which I'm enamored. I'm very much a yes-or-no kind of girl." I tried to defend Andy, but she was having none of it. "That's the trouble with you boys! You protect Andy, you guide Andy, you talk for Andy, you write for Andy, you do business for Andy, you give Andy all your ideas—well, what does Andy do? He takes much too much from Fred and you, Bobby, and it's not *good.* That's why he's not avant-garde anymore. I don't mean this as a slight to Fred or you, but you're not *artists.* Andy has to stop relying on the two of you for everything and come up with something from his own head again."

The next day when I told Andy that Diana had said he wasn't avant-garde anymore, he shot back, "Did you tell her about the Piss Paintings?"

More formally known as the Oxidation Series, these were Andy's way of declaring himself in the vanguard again. With his unerring sense of timing about his own career, he knew that his traveling portrait-painter act had taken him far enough down the road of conservative commercialism, and that the moment had come to shock again. The Piss Paintings, which he began doing in December 1977, along with the Torso Series, which he had started earlier that year, were meant to do just that.

It was also a message that Andy was hearing from some of his dealers, most of the critics, and Ronnie Cutrone, the sole Factory worker who actually hung out at the artist bars of SoHo and Tribeca, where Andy's portraits of Mrs. Maslon of Minneapolis and the Empress of Iran were not exactly considered trail-blazing works. There was never any thought at the Factory of abandoning the commissioned-portrait business—that would have been financially impossible in any case. But Andy realized that he needed to be perceived as a real artist, even a way-out artist, for that most bourgeois of businesses to flourish. Part of the appeal of having one's portrait done by Andy, as opposed to a traditional society portraitist like Alejandro Vidal-Quadras, was that it was thought to be a bit daring, naughty, and intellectual.

Evidence was also mounting that when Andy tried his hardest to be commercial he had his biggest commercial flops. The Cats and Dogs Series, commissioned by the James Mayor Gallery in pet-loving London, bombed when they were shown there in 1976, and bombed again when Mayor arranged for Andy to bring them to Kuwait in January 1977—though that might have had more to do with the fact that most Arabs don't believe in representational art. Andy had already been paid several hundred thousand pounds by Mayor and his backers, so he wasn't left holding the kitty litter. But that kind of fiasco did nothing for either his market or his reputation.

The 1977 Athletes Series, a vast number of paintings and prints of sports stars commissioned by Richard Weisman, the investment banker son of L.A. collectors Freddy and Marcia Weisman, also bombed. Andy was paid $800,000 for the portraits of Muhammad Ali, Rod Gilbert, Ron Duguay, Vitas Gerulaitis, Dorothy Hamill, Willie Shoemaker, Tom Seaver, Chris Evert, Pelé, Kareem Abdul-Jabbar, and Jack Nicklaus. The last, claimed Andy a bit wistfully, "didn't even know who I was." They were shown in New York, London, Toronto, and Cologne, but everywhere the art critics yawned and the sports fans wondered why Andy had painted O. J. Simpson in pistachio and cantaloupe. Finally, eager to recoup some of his investment, Weisman arranged a joint show with the Peter Max of sports portraiture, LeRoy Neiman. Andy and Fred, feeling guilty about the money they had already banked, had no choice but to agree. Again, such exertions did nothing for Andy's prices or stature.

Andy's most successful show in 1977 was of his least obviously commercial series, the Hammer & Sickles, at the Daniel Templon Gallery in Paris. These were a tongue-in-cheek response to the Marxist analysis of his work by Italian art critics. In Andy's hands, the tough symbols of Communism were turned into stunning still lifes, beautiful enough for capitalist titans like Gianni Agnelli to buy for their palatial walls. The show sold out, despite—or perhaps because of—the opening's being invaded by three hundred Parisian punks in leather, rubber, chains, and razors. Templon served raspberry sorbet and a dry Chablis. The punks used the former to scrawl "HATE" and "WAR" on the gallery walls and chugged the latter so rapidly that they were soon vomiting it all over the gallery floor. Andy hid out in an inner office, and when a couple of young nihilists began peeing pink sherbet and white wine in the vicinity of her bejeweled shoes, São Schlumberger coolly said, "I think I'd better get going to my dinner at Versailles." When I told Andy, still in his hiding place, he laughed a little and then said, as if noting a new look at the couture collections, "Pee is getting big, Bob."

Andy, who saw everything as fashion, was not only right but was also putting things into their proper context: piss and punks and leather and whips were all the rage among the sexual extremists of the late seventies, and sadomasochism was *le dernier cri* of the sexual revolution that was sweeping the West from the Berlin Wall to the Golden Gate Bridge. The women's and gay-liberation movements had convinced large numbers of people that sex wasn't a sin but a right, and whatever inhibitions they had left got washed away in the flood of Third World drugs sweeping First World cities. And it was not just the major cities, at least not in America. Tom Wolfe, who also sees everything as fashion, summed it up in a 1977 article, titled "The Sexed-Up, Doped-Up, Hedonistic Heaven of the Boom-Boom 70s":

By the mid-1970s, anytime I reached a city of 100,000 to 200,000 souls, the movie fare available on a typical evening seemed to be: two theaters showing

Jaws, one showing *Benji* and eleven showing pornography. . . . Two of the eleven would be drive-in theaters, the better to beam the various stiffened giblets and moist folds and nodules out into the night air to become part of the American Scene.

In New York, always in the lead, the public orgy had begun way back in 1970, at the Continental Baths, which was now Plato's Retreat, where heterosexual swingers copulated openly in the pool, sauna, steamroom, showers, and bar. Homosexual adventurers had hardly been disenfranchised, however: By 1977, Manhattan boasted at least a dozen thriving gay bathhouses, though they were considered a bit passé compared to the backroom bars of the far West Village, where leather and rubber, bondage and discipline, masters and slaves, indeed every sort of kink and fetish known to man, ruled from midnight to daybreak, when the cobbled old streets and crumbling old warehouses were given back to the traditional commercial activity of the neighborhood: meat packing.

The most fashionable haunts of the sexual fast crowd were the Anvil and the Toilet. The Anvil was famous for its fist-fucking stage show. The Toilet featured tubs and troughs where naked men lay for other naked men to urinate on them. It was like a Robert Mapplethorpe photograph come alive. This was what Andy's Piss Paintings and Torso Series were really all about: what was going on. He hadn't anticipated the times—Mapplethorpe did that. His specialty was sensing the times as they happened, and it enabled him not only to join the latest trend but to leap to the head of the line.

Andy only went to the Anvil once, so far as I know, and he never went to the Toilet, though he also once went to the Eagle's Nest, another West Village leather bar, where he was fascinated, he told me, by a man who urinated in an empty beer bottle and left it on the bar for someone else to drink. "They were all fighting over it," he said, adding that all-purpose adjective for not making moral judgments, "It was so abstract." I was with him the night he went to the Anvil, in early 1977, before he had started either the Torso or Oxidation Series. We had dinner at Ballato's with Bianca, Andrea de Portago, Steven Aronson, and Archie, and afterward we decided to see what the talk around town was all about. We piled into Bianca's long white limo and directed the driver to the corner of West and 14th streets.

It was barely eleven o'clock, which in the far West Village meant everyone was still at home, slipping into his studded dog collar. The front of the Anvil was empty, except for two or three patrons and a big black stud dancing on the bar, totally naked, unless you counted his three gold cock rings. Gingerly we stepped into the pitch darkness of the back room. That was completely empty, though, as our eyes adjusted, we could make out the stage, with its chains and shackles, racks and stretchers. "Gee," said Andy, clutching Archie, "I wonder if anyone we know was strung up there last night.'' He speculated about a certain editor, a certain dancer, and a certain writer who often wrote bitchy things about our crowd.

We wandered back to the front room, where there were now four patrons, and the same black hulk bouncing his balls to Thelma Houston's ''Don't Leave Me This Way.'' Andrea wanted to leave immediately, Bianca was tittering nervously, and Andy stood there, trying to look without us seeing him look. Then the dancer strutted his stuff to our side of the bar and started doing disco knee bends in front of Andy's face. That's when Archie gave his shaft a lick, and the bartender, in full leather, asked us to leave. It became one of the standards of our Abbott and Costello act: Archie getting us thrown out of the Anvil, the perfect Andy Warhol anecdote, in which the supposed decadent is revealed as an awkward innocent after all.

It's always difficult to pinpoint the moment that an idea jells into art in the artist's mind, and even more so in Andy's case because he was a walking Gallup Poll, asking people for ideas, then asking other people what they thought of the ideas. I'm pretty sure that the Piss Paintings idea came from friends telling him about what went on at the Toilet, reinforced perhaps by the punks peeing at his Paris opening. He was also aware of the scene in the 1968 Pasolini movie, *Teorema,* where an aspiring artist pisses on his paintings. ''It's a parody of Jackson Pollock,'' he told me, referring to rumors that Pollock would urinate on a canvas before delivering it to a dealer or client he didn't like. Andy liked his work to have art-historical references, though if you brought it up, he would pretend he didn't know what you were talking about. The Torso Series also had art-historical references, of course, and Andy was conscious of at least two that I know of: Picasso and Degas. In fact, he used Picasso's erotic works as a defense when I yelled at him for leaving his Polaroids on my desk. Nonetheless, the true muse of Andy's sexual works in 1977–78 was Victor Hugo.

Andy saw Victor as the perfect source for ideas: someone with a fertile imagination who didn't know what to do with it. (Not unlike Brigid Berlin in the sixties.) The Venezuelan's own art was going nowhere: He signed rat traps and handed them out at parties; he dipped chickens' feet in red paint and called their footprints drawings. In the summer of 1976, when Halston rented Peter Beard's mill in Montauk, Victor let red-legged chickens run amok all over the living room. Even the indulgent Halston found that ''piece'' a bit too conceptual, especially since he had to pay for the reupholstering of the furniture and the sanding of the floors. Andy found Victor's antics funny, though when Halston rented *his* house in Montauk two summers later, Andy was quick to tell Victor, ''No chickens, okay?''

Halston claimed, in an interview he and Victor gave me after Andy's death, that *he* told Victor to do ''sex paintings'' for himself, but that Victor turned around "and talked Andy into doing it." Victor claimed the idea as his own. He also said that he gave Andy the idea for the Piss Paintings. In both cases, Andy paid Victor to be his collaborator: He was Andy's casting agent and sometime model on the Torsos; Andy's ghost pisser on the Oxidations. He would come to the Factory to urinate on canvases that had already been primed with copper-based paint by Andy or Ronnie Cutrone, who was a second ghost pisser, much appreciated by Andy, who said that the vitamin B that Ronnie took made a "prettier" color when the acid in the urine turned the copper green. Victor told me that Andy gave him vitamins to take too. "He'd say, you take them at night and you come here every day."

Did Andy ever use his own urine? My diary shows that when he first began the series, in December 1977, he did—I didn't witness the act of creation, he referred to it in passing. But he soon turned to Victor and Ronnie, as usual preferring to have others do the repetitive technical work for him. And there were many others: boys who'd come to lunch and drink too much wine, and find it funny or even flattering to be asked to help Andy "paint." Andy always had a little extra bounce in his walk as he led them to his studio, which was fast becoming the back room in more than name only. Victor was showing up with ever larger numbers of "assistants," hired by the hour at the Everard and St. Marks Baths.

All the Factory girls, except Catherine Guinness, were afraid to venture back there for a back issue, or to deliver a message to Andy. Finally, Fred had had it, too, and decreed, "No more raunch here, Victor." After much argument, he persuaded Andy to let Victor take a long roll of prepainted canvas to his new loft, where he could work on it whenever inspiration struck. Andy was afraid that Victor would cut off a piece for himself. Andy was right: Victor did, and when I interviewed him, he told me that Fred wanted to buy it for the Andy Warhol Foundation.

Victor's loft was on lower Fifth Avenue at 19th Street, just three blocks from 860 Broadway. It was a long, narrow white space, which Victor left undivided, so that you could see the king-size mattress on the floor at the far end as soon as you stepped off the elevator. The only enclosed space was the bathroom, which featured a gym-style group shower. Victor's loft became the new venue for Andy's Polaroid sex sessions. He was bouncier when he toddled off to those too. "I'm just going to Victor's for a little while," he'd say, around three in the afternoon, his customary time to get working on his art. "Don't go uptown without me, Bob." That meant I would have to listen to his broken record, "Sex Is So Abstract," all the way up Park Avenue. "I'd better hide these someplace Jed won't see them," he said one afternoon, shuffling his deck of dirty pictures. "Jed's so grumpy lately," he went on, sounding hurt. "But he should *know* that I'm not doing anything with all these guys. It's all Victor. It's all work."

It was all very bewildering. If one topic was taboo at the Factory, it was Andy's sex life. He wanted—demanded—to know every detail of ours, but his was strictly off limits. But then we were the kids and he was Pop—that was *our* nickname for him in the seventies. And whoever heard of kids asking their parents about their sex lives? In a Catholic family? Now Pop was making a public display of it.

After ten years of being good, since the shooting, Andy was being bad—tinfoil-Factory style—again. And somehow it was sad. Victor described those Polaroid sessions to me, and Andy's role, or lack of it, in them. I can't say I was surprised. "I remember," Victor said, "that many times when the guys saw Andy they were suddenly so shy. I'd say, 'C'mon, I'm paying you.' And Andy saw them . . . and he'd escape. He disappeared suddenly. Then he'd come back and say, 'It's finished.' 'Andy, we've just begun.' "

Halston added, "Victor used to tell me, when they were doing all that posing, that Andy would break out in those terrible sweats and get nervous and shake and have to go to the bathroom. He was having an organza in there." Only Halston could come up with that code word. Victor agreed, recalling how Andy always dashed to the bathroom and locked himself in after taking a few rolls of Polaroids of his naked models performing oral and anal intercourse. The Big Shot camera, it should be noted, focused only at three feet from the subject. Victor said that Andy never touched a model. And when he emerged from the bathroom, pale and cool again, he showed much less interest in the work at hand. "So, I realize," said Victor, "like Halston say, Andy must have had the organza." At his own orgy, Andy was the outsider.

Andy was the outsider everywhere. Even at home, even within his Factory family. On August 6, 1977, we celebrated his forty-ninth birthday at Montauk. It was just Andy and the kids—Fred, Jed, Pat, Catherine, Vincent with his fiancée, Shelly Dunn, Jay Johnson with Tom Cashin, Susan Johnson with her beau, Billy Copley. We had a casual dinner around the big picnic table in the kitchen: barbecued chicken from the local deli, birthday cake from Andy's favorite Manhattan bakers, Les Délices de la Côte Basque, champagne and Negronis, the Montauk house drink, Campari and vodka, heavy on the vodka. We put some old rock 'n' roll records on the stereo in the living room. Fred grabbed Shelly, Vincent grabbed Catherine, I grabbed Pat—we were all dancing, in quickly shifting couples and groups. Except Andy. He stood on the edge of the room, snapping an occasional Minox, looking a little bored and very lonely. I tried to pull him into our sock hop, but he pulled back and whimpered, "You know I can't dance, Bob." I stood with him for a few minutes, so that he wouldn't be the only wallflower at his own birthday party. "Gee," he said, in that wistful tone he used when he was feeling sorry for himself, "you kids get along so well." Then he slipped away to bed, leaving us to twist and shout.

That Thanksgiving, after a big fight, Jed persuaded Andy to have a few of us to dinner at the 66th Street house. It was a scene as poignant as Andy's birthday party. There was a huge, half-carved turkey in the center of the kitchen table—Jed had lost the battle to serve dinner in the beautifully decorated dining room, which Andy insisted was "too fancy to really eat in"—and seated around it were Catherine, Barbara Allen, Susan Johnson, Billy Copley, and Jed, all chatting and laughing. Andy had his chair turned away from the table. He was dead drunk and watching TV. "Have some 1952 Rothschild, Bob," he said, slurring, turning the sound up. That, it seemed, was his idea of entertaining at home on a holiday.

But then, more and more frequently, when I'd refer to "your house" in passing, he'd snap back, "You mean Jed's house." He often complained that "everything's the way Jed wants it. I'd never have a house that looks like this." Another constant refrain: "All I do is pay the bills around here. That's what I call love, when someone pays the bill for you now and then." *Bad* had missed at the box office when it opened in early 1977, but the way Andy went on you'd think *he'd* lost a million dollars on it—instead of Peter Brant, Joe Allen, and Fred Hughes. Jed was now trying to launch an interior-decorating business. Andy kept saying that he hoped Jed "gets some jobs quick," but he made it more difficult by refusing to let anyone see the best job Jed had done: his house.

Christmas was no happier than Thanksgiving. Jed turned up at the office Christmas lunch with a bruise on his forehead where Andy had slammed a door in his face. Fred, Vincent, and I joined forces to persuade Andy to dole out Electric Chair prints, which we could barely sell for $200 to clients then, for the staff. We decided to include two bottles of Moët et Chandon with each gift, vintage 1971, the same year as the prints—one of those nice Fred Hughes touches—without telling Andy in advance. He didn't mind when he found out, though he did say we should have ordered nonvintage, which was a few dollars less per bottle. The day before Andy had gone to Tony's Florist and ordered expensive miniature Christmas trees to be sent to Rex Reed, Liz Smith, Aileen "Suzy" Mehle, Eugenia Sheppard, Earl Blackwell, Elaine of Elaine's, Pearl of Pearl's, Mr. and Mrs. Ballato, Lee Radziwill, Diana Vreeland, Kitty Miller, Carroll de Portago, C. Z. Guest, the Heinzes, the Hammonds, Mrs. Long, the Jacksons, the Hoveydas, the Carimatis, Eleanor Lambert, Carrie Donovan, Estée Lauder, Calvin Klein, Diane von Furstenberg, Elsa Peretti, Marina Schiano, Joe Eula, Jane Holzer, Halston, Anita Loos, and Paulette Goddard, among others. The next day he sent me back to send an additional twenty or so to more journalists, hostesses, and potential portrait clients—the list kept growing. "Send a tree to John Schumacher," he instructed me, referring to the recently dismissed chairman of Bonwit Teller. How sweet of Andy to be nice to someone when he was down, I thought, until Andy added: "He was the first department-store person to give us an ad, and he's bound to get a big new job somewhere, right?" Is it any wonder that we Factory kids rolled out another nickname for Andy every holiday season: Scrooge.

Jed, as usual, bought a big tree for the house and decorated it with antique ornaments he'd collected all year. But Andy, as usual, wouldn't let him have a Christmas party at home—just Fred, Barbara Allen, and me for a quick glass of champagne before Halston's Christmas Eve dinner. That was a strained affair too, though it wasn't Halston's fault. We all knew that Mick Jagger and Jerry Hall were holed up in a London hotel, but nobody dared mention it to Bianca, who was putting up a good front. Jed, still bruised, was trying to avoid Victor, whom he hated for getting Andy involved in the sex paintings. And Andy, who had the flu, drank the larger part of a bottle of cognac, claiming it would make him better.

Not long after that, Andy and I went to Adriana Jackson's to meet a Milanese couple who collected Pop Art. They went on about how their teenage children "loved" Andy. "I wish I was as loved at home," he sighed, "as I am here tonight."

The more unloved Andy felt at home, the more he made Halston's house his home away from home. "This is the way I wish my house looked," Andy told me almost every time I went with him to a dinner or a party there. "Really modern and really empty."

"Andy had a special love affair with this place," Victor Hugo said in our interview. "This was like his fun house. He'd take a couple of vodkas and loosen up a bit."

"Don't forget the Valium," added Halston. They both denied that Andy ever took cocaine there, but I recall one occasion when I gave him some there. Whatever he took and however much he relaxed on his nights at Halston's, he was still the nerd amidst the beauties, the groupie amongst the stars—Liza and Liz and Bianca and Marisa and Barbara. Drinking and drugs didn't make Andy forget himself, they made him more himself, more relentless, pushy, grabby, infantile, and troublesome. Even among his own In crowd, Andy was still the outsider.

To begin with, Andy was Victor's friend, not Halston's. And Victor, with his hairy pranks, was an outsider in this group too. Victor was selling more and more of Andy's art to Halston, an arrangement that was also advantageous to Halston, because it was a way for Victor to make money, in commissions, without stretching the payroll of Halston Enterprises. When Victor talked Halston into renting Montauk, starting in 1978, the designer became Andy's tenant, as well as client, making Andy even more the supplicant, waiting for the rent.

The truth of the matter is that Andy envied Halston his success, his glamour, his tall, smooth, handsome look. He carried the envy with him from the fifties, when Halston the hatmaker hobnobbed with Bunny Mellon and Babe Paley, and Raggedy Andy couldn't make it past the boys from Serendipity. It was the same envy that had come through when I called him in 1973 to say I'd heard Halston was being bought by Norton Simon for $20 million: Andy had insisted that it must be $2 million, and was all "just paper anyway." He wasn't jumping for joy when Halston took the entire twenty-first floor at the Olympic Tower, in 1977, for his couture operation and administrative offices, and expanded the 68th Street boutique up two more floors. "Halston's so grand now," he said, as if he hadn't been using that adjective to describe Halston to me ever since he first took me to that party at Joe Eula's in 1971. And he couldn't help being jealous that it was Halston who sat in the center of the circle of movie stars and glamour girls who flocked to his parties and his house, even though Andy wouldn't dream of letting them through his own front door. As Halston told me, "Andy came to my house maybe ten thousand times. I never went to his house." Never? "Only the entrance." Bianca and Liza never even made it that far.

"Gee," Andy said again and again and again, "Halston really does have all the greatest girls at his house." At the Factory, we jokingly called it "Halston's House for Wayward Women." Bianca moved in after she left Mick. Liza was divorcing Jack Haley, Jr., Marisa was divorcing James Randall, and Barbara Allen had broken up with Philip Niarchos, after a three-year courtship. They all came to Halston for a shoulder to cry on, and new dresses to wear in pursuit of new beaus. They weren't wildly promiscuous—just modern women playing the field, hoping to find a love that would last. They mostly dated one guy at a time—though sometimes it was the same guy. Ryan O'Neal certainly made the rounds.

Andy was almost obsessively fascinated by the romantic adventures of Liza, Bianca, Barbara, and Marisa. At Halston's little parties for six or eight close friends, the girls spun out their tales of marital woes and divorce-court complications, and Andy, playing the good Catholic to the hilt, always vociferously encouraged them to go back to their husbands. "Halston wants them to get divorced," he told me time and again, "so he can have them all around him, but I told them to stay married." Of course, in his priestly mode, he also tried to get them to confess their sins, and hung on every juicy detail he could coax out of their hearts and into his tape recorder. Sometimes they made things up, especially about each other—just as I sometimes did about the O'Briens and the Netters when I first met Andy—to get Sony off their cases, and to laugh at Andy as he went into paroxysms of "Whats!" and "Reallys?" Then he'd act hurt and tell them, "You never told me that when it happened! And I thought you were a friend." (There was a good reason why Andy was often the last person to find out the *real* gossip in our group: Everyone knew that the minute he was told he'd repeat it to the person it was about, usually revealing the source in the process.)

Halston told me, "I said some of the raunchiest, most horrible things just to get a rise out of Andy. Just made it up, you know, with Bianca, Liza, whomever. Gory things that Andy would have on tape. And I know someday someone is going to think it's real. And it wasn't. It was just playing games."

The constant taping and picture taking gave Andy a role to play at Halston's parties, but it was a role that put more distance between him and the other players. It made the stars feel more starlike to have Andy lurking on the edge of the action, stealing glances through his Minox, nudging his Sony closer to catch their every breath. But it also put them off, tired them out, made them weary of Andy and his presumptuous intrusiveness. It can be exciting to know that the fly on the wall is watching, but when the fly lands in a drink . . . There were many nights when Andy wasn't wanted, and wasn't invited, no matter how much Victor pressed Halston to have him. Andy's presence could ruin a bash, as much as it could make it. He was both an instigator and an inhibitor. Or, as I often wrote in my diary in those days, "Andy was the life and death of the party."

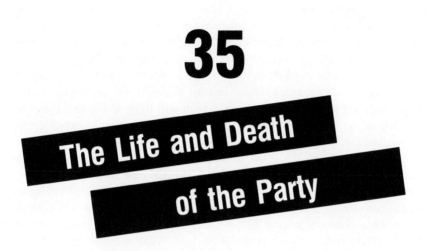

35

The Life and Death

of the Party

"It will be called Studio 54. It's in the old CBS studio where *The $64,000 Question* used to take place. Before that it was an opera house. You walk in under this big marquee. Then you walk into this enormous hall with very, very high ceilings and Art Deco mirrors and crystal chandeliers and then into this enormous, enormous room where there are like eighty-five-foot ceilings—it's like five stories. The dance floor is 11,000 square feet. Then upstairs is a balcony with a seating arrangement like a theater. I would say the opening night will be more like going to a premiere than going to a discotheque. I'm very excited about it because I think it could help change a little bit the lifestyle of New York."

That last line turned out to be the most prophetic understatement of the Disco Decade. It was from my interview with Carmen d'Alessio, a Peruvian-born party promoter who knew "everyone young, beautiful, and loaded" in the jet-set triangle formed by Rome, Rio, and Manhattan. She had been hired to launch Studio 54 by its owners, Steve Rubell and Ian Schrager, who were not yet familiar with the ins and outs of the international social scene, though they learned very, very fast. Carmen's interview ran in our April 1977 issue, just in time for Studio 54's opening—which was more like a riot than a premiere. It marked the beginning of an intense symbiotic relationship between the magazine and the club, each feeding the other's glamour, elitism, and cachet. It was as if *Pravda* had found its Kremlin, or the Vatican its *L'Osservatore Romano*.

Six months later, in our October 1977 issue, I interviewed Steve Rubell, who was already the undisputed king of the New York night. I told him that

I was continually amazed by the "Man in the Moon" prop that dropped from the ceiling over the dance floor several times a night and—in a blatant celebration of what many of the club's denizens were doing in the bathrooms and balcony—stuck a spoonful of twinkling lights up its nose, setting off electronic fireworks in its head. "Next we're doing a popper," said Steve, "with a cerebrum, a cerebellum, and all the parts of the brain. And the popper is going to shoot up the nose, which will light up the brain, and then the whole thing is going to explode. Every night it's going to explode—right on the dance floor."

I liked Steve. We hit it off immediately on the tour he gave me a few weeks before the West 54th Street club opened. He told me that he had started out with a steak restaurant in Rockville Centre, where my parents lived. From there, he and Ian Schrager, his roommate at Syracuse University, built a chain of twelve Steak Lofts in New York, Connecticut, and Florida. Then came a partnership with John Addison, the man behind Le Jardin, in a Boston disco, 15 Landsdowne Street. In 1975, Steve and Ian opened the Enchanted Garden in an abandoned country club on a city golf course in Queens. It became so popular that the traffic jams led local residents to get the city to close it down.

After I introduced Steve to Andy—who waited until the 54 bandwagon got rolling before he jumped on—a new element of friction entered our relationship, mainly because Andy repeated everything Steve said about me at four in the morning, and everything I said about Steve at four in the morning, and threw in some things neither of us said about each other just for the hell of it. It worked: Steve was soon closer to Andy than to me.

In some ways, Steve was a lot like Andy. He couldn't help playing both ends against the middle. He also couldn't help gossiping about the love lives of his star friends, though his scoops were usually accurate and he certainly wasn't the wallflower at the orgy or a lonely voyeur. Steve wasn't sneaky like Andy; he was almost too open. But like Andy he was always forgiven his indiscretions. It was simply impossible to resist his infectious enthusiasm for having fun and his almost innocent adoration of glamour and style. Like Andy, he made the stars feel more like stars. "After Bianca's birthday party," he told me in that interview, "we went back to her house and she and Halston made breakfast. Oh, it was fabulous. It was one of the most fabulous moments of my life."

Bianca's birthday bash, in May 1977, had been the first in a long line of ever more elaborate private parties at Studio 54. Steve controlled the guest lists and press coverage for these exclusive—and raucous—affairs, but it was Ian Schrager who created their dramatic and original themes, from the invitations to the busboys' brief uniforms. Ian had a theater designer's flair for whipping up a magical atmosphere overnight out of nothing more than lights and shadows, scrims and curtains, tinsel, confetti, and a few well-chosen props.

"Why can't we do a play like this?" Andy had said at Bianca's party, as a naked black couple, their bodies washed in gold stardust, led a gold-harnessed white pony through a curtain of gold Mylar streamers onto the dance floor. Bianca, who just happened to be wearing white and gold too, had hopped onto the pony, much to the delight of the paparazzi, who almost outnumbered the one hundred guests invited by the host, Halston. As the disco version of "Happy Birthday" blasted from a phalanx of speakers, Mick had started dancing with Baryshnikov at the other end of the dance floor, and the paparazzi whirled around. I always wondered where Mick was when Bianca cooked breakfast for Halston and Steve later that night, and always thought that the party and the publicity it got Bianca were what really sent him flying into the arms of tall Jerry Hall.

Andy went to most of the private parties that followed that fall and winter and the next spring, and always moaned the next day about how we should be making "Broadway musicals just like that."

By the time of Steve Rubell's birthday party, in December 1977, the mob trying to get into Studio 54 was so large and out of control that the police had to close the street to traffic and the invited swells had to leave their limos on edgy Eighth Avenue and walk the last half block. "Take me with you! Take me with you!" people screamed when those of us with invitations wedged our way through the crush and the velvet rope slipped down for a second to let us in. That was the night of the first party within the party: only some of us received white cards with our invitations that let us behind a white curtain that divided the dance floor into an Out zone in front and an In zone in back—where Swifty Lazar and his wife, Mary, were doing the disco version of the hora with Marion Javits, Marina Cicogna, and Florinda Bolkan. It was also the night Sly Stallone made his first appearance at 54, surrounded by four muscular bodyguards, who were immediately surrounded by fourteen not-so-muscular body worshipers—and Andy, who was desperately trying to squeeze his Minox between the pecs and abs for pix of Rocky.

Andy wore his ruby bracelet, hidden under the cuff of his Brooks Brothers shirt, to the Valentine's Day "I Love New York" party hosted by Gilda Radner, Carrie Fisher, and Margaux Hemingway, three clients of P.R. man Bobby Zarem. It was packed with secretaries and office boys from movie and record companies, so Andy and I hung out in the deejay booth with Halston and the design assistant he'd imported from Paris, Princess Diane de Beauvau-Craon. That was Michael Jackson's favorite perch when he turned up at 54. One night, Michael and Andy found themselves together in the booth—it was like the blind leading the blind, the shy meeting the shy, each waiting for the other to say something.

* * *

In March 1978, Elizabeth Taylor celebrated her birthday at Studio 54.
In deference to the presence of a United States Senator—the guest of honor's
husband—Steve and Ian had attendants in the restrooms for the first and only
time I can recall. I know because one of them held her hand up like a stop
sign and told me, "No men in the ladies' room," when Margaret Trudeau,
the un-first-lady-like Canadian First Lady, tried to take me in with her.
Otherwise it was monkey business as usual at Studio 54. The highlight of
the party came when the Rockettes—all forty-eight of them—wearing black
leotards and holding sparklers, formed a circle around the birthday cake, a
portrait in buttercream of the birthday girl. Halston led her to her cake and
she made a wish and cut the first slice—right out of her left bazoom. The
paparazzi flashed like lightning as she devoured her own frosted nipple, then
waltzed with Halston while the Rockettes did high kicks all around them.
Andy and Bianca were standing close by, smooching for the cameras. Margaret Trudeau was also smooching, a little more believably, with the handsome young mystery man she had stolen away from Catherine Guinness.
His real name, I think, was Tom Sullivan, but we all called him by the title
of the autobiographical documentary he was making, *Cocaine Cowboy*. Timothy Leary and Sylvia Miles, not smooching, were also pushing their ways
into the picture. Only Senator Warner (Republican of Virgina), for some odd
reason, seemed camera shy. It was the only time I can recall Diana Vreeland
at Studio 54. In fact, I was holding her up on a banquette overlooking the
dance floor, as she shimmied to the disco version of "Happy Birthday."

"It really becomes more like pagan Rome every day," I told her.

"I should hope so, Bob!" declared the Empress of Fashion, shaking
her booty to the throbbing disco beat.

Just then, an avalanche of plastic snow fell from the sky—one of those
well-timed Ian Schrager touches—and Lauren Bacall slipped on a flake and
fell to the floor. "There goes Betty," said Diana, as the paparazzi zoomed
in for the kill.

One year after the opening, Andy was completely identified with Studio
54. The tabloids had taken to referring to "Halston-Liza-Bianca-Andy." A
surburban matron in a *New Yorker* cartoon asked her husband if that was
one person. For the first anniversary party, Steve asked his favorite foursome
to do "a little act, like a toast sorta." (Pat suggested this might be the time
to rush a joke disco tune of Andy's onto vinyl. "Oh Gee, Oh Wow, Oh
Really/It's All Fred's Fault, It's All Bob's Fault.")

The night of the party, we literally had to fight our way to the front
door—pandemonium is too mild a word for what was going on on West 54th
Street. Barbara Allen and I headed straight for the basement, which was
reached through a door behind the bar, a room full of freezers, and an
unpainted cement staircase with an unpainted steel bannister. Steve and Ian

had dressed up one of the cyclone-fenced storage bins by throwing some gold lamé cushions on the cement floor. It looked like a chic holding cell at a detention camp where all the prisoners of war were rich and famous: Truman Capote, Lester Persky, D.D. Ryan, Peter Allen, Lorna Luft, and, of course, Halston-Liza-Bianca-Andy. There were several models to keep the prisoners amused, and several dealers with names like Johnny C., Tommy C., Tony C., and Sarah C.—C did not stand for Castelli—to keep the models amused. Torture came in the form of the steady thump-thump of the dancers overhead. The song they played over and over that night was "Miss You," by the Rolling Stones—Bianca believed it was written for her.

After a few rounds of Stolichnaya, served in plastic cups or straight from the passing bottle, H-L-B-A decided they had better rehearse their act. Andy insisted that Catherine Guinness and I go with him to the rehearsal hall, a nearby boiler room. It was as hopeless as trying to teach him his lines for *The Driver's Seat*—he could never get beyond "Oh, uh." As we emerged from the boiler room, we saw Jed coming toward us, but much to my surprise he turned around and scurried away in the opposite direction. Andy started wailing, "I don't know what to do. I don't know what to do. You've got to go get him, Bob."

He'd disappeared. And I got diverted until H-L-B-A's act, which got a pretty unresponsive reaction from the crowd. Then Steve jumped up and shouted, "Open bar," which got long and loud applause. Back in the basement with H-L-B-A, the models and dealers were still swigging and sniffing. Andy, of course, wouldn't drink from the passing bottle, for fear of germs, nor would he sniff from the other passing bottle, for fear that someone would say he really did get Edie Sedgwick on drugs—that was what all the sneakiness and denial were really about. Instead, he slipped another Valium from his pocket and licked it off his palm, hoping no one in the chic little cell would notice. He soon left, worried about Jed.

The next morning he was jealous when I told him that he had missed what *WWD* dubbed "The Fashion Summit." Around four in the morning, Yves Saint Laurent, looking glazed and dazed on the arm of Marina Schiano, walked through the cyclone-fence gate of our little cage, and gave Halston a really big kiss on each cheek, French-style. Marina had the same satisfied expression that Kissinger wore after getting Nixon together with Mao Tsetung. Throughout Studio 54, from the basement to the bathrooms to the balcony, and the next day throughout the city, from Bloomingdale's to Bergdorf's to Barney's, the message flashed like a telegram from the front: "YSL and H made up!"

Meanwhile, across town on Park Avenue and 59th Street, the Queen of the Night was not amused. Why weren't exciting things like that happening in her club, Regine wondered, and why wasn't the In crowd coming there anymore? She was at the height of her international expansion, with franchises from Rio to Deauville, but the formula was faltering in New York. First, she tried to go casual, by opening a bistro around the corner called Reginette, where ties were not required and dinner went for $30 instead of $100. She came to lunch at the Factory and asked for our help. Fred said we should do what we could, because she had always been so nice to us in Paris and Monte Carlo—and because she agreed to his suggestion to have her portrait done, in exchange for a $40,000 credit at her clubs. We gave a star-studded dinner at Reginette honoring our March 1978 covergirl, Margaret Trudeau, but after dessert the stars zoomed across town to 54, not around the corner to Regine's.

Soon, Regine had another bright idea: "gay Fridays." For the first "gay Friday" she flew in a planeload of samba-school transvestites from Rio. We all liked Regine personally, but she was simply in the wrong place at the wrong time. She didn't understand that everyone wanted to go to Studio 54 not because it was gay but because it broke down all the old-fashioned barriers between gay and straight, young and old, rich and poor. It was a place where you usually knew half the people and wanted to know the other half. "A tossed salad" is what Steve always said he wanted it to be and that's what it was.

On any given night Liza danced with Lorna, who danced with her dentist, Dr. Alan Lazare, who danced with his wife, Arlene, who looked like, but did not dance like, Liza. Imee Marcos boogied with her bodyguards. Diane von Furstenberg led "Little Eddie," who wasn't little at all, but one of the strapping pretty boys in loose white T-shirts and tight black jeans whom all the movie producers and fashion designers and magazine editors fought over—then threw over for the next hot number from south Jersey or South Dakota or South America. Sometimes in the heat and the half light it was impossible to tell who was really dancing with whom. Jackie Bisset, Jackie Rogers, Roger Moore, Melba Moore, Mary McFadden, Maria Smith, Aerosmith, Rod Gilbert, Ron Duguay, Roy Cohn, Zipkin, Zarem, Zoli, the Flicks, the chicks, the tricks, the whole city, the whole country, the whole world seemed to be dancing together at Studio 54.

Except Andy. He stood on the sidelines, or sat in the balcony, groping the fake du Pont twins. Robert and Richard "du Pont" weren't strapping or pretty or hot. They were pale and wispy blonds, fey, silly, creepy, a lot like Andy when he first came to New York. We knew they weren't really du Pont heirs because we'd checked them out with Joanne du Pont, a portrait client who was not only born into the Delaware chemical dynasty, but had married a cousin as well—we called her Joanne "double du Pont." Andy didn't care. On the contrary, their being fakes only made him like them more. They often got into 54 by using his name or waiting outside for him to take them in. Almost everyone in our group avoided them, but Andy said he felt sorry for them. "They're not really such bad kids, Bob," he often told me. "You would like them if you got to know them. They have the best gossip.'' It didn't matter to Andy that their gossip was as dubious as their name, so long as they let him tape record it. They also let him fondle their crotches through their jeans, something Andy seemed unable to resist. It's only now that I realize how lonely Andy would have been on the sidelines without the fake du Pont twins.

My favorite dancing partner was Truman Capote. Or, rather, I was his. It began at the Elizabeth Taylor birthday party, when D.D. Ryan asked him to dance and, much to my surprise, he replied, ''I'll only dance with Bob Colacello.'' So he and I jitterbugged for half an hour together, with the paparazzi all around us, a new—and not unpleasant—experience for me. ''You're such a good dancer,'' Truman told me, '' 'cause you can lead *and* follow.'' He was trying to kiss me and telling me how much he liked me, and that my column was ''on the verge of being really good writing,'' and that I ''could be the best writer, after little ol' me, of course.'' I assumed this sudden burst of affection had something to do with his lack of friends after the ''La Côte Basque'' debacle. He was wearing a brown felt fedora and drinking like a fish. ''Wouldn't it be great,'' I thought, ''if I could get Truman to write for *Interview?*''

Truman had been pursuing me, for some reason, for some time. Two months earlier, in January 1978, Andy and I had been interviewing Lucie Arnaz at Quo Vadis. Truman was lunching at a corner table with a man who looked like a lawyer. He was much slimmer than when we had last seen him, when the *Esquire* bombshell hit, in late 1975, having spent a large part of the two years in various hospitals and clinics, drying out. He was wearing a conservative gray suit with a black shirt and black tie, an outfit that made him look like a cross between an elegant country squire and a Mafioso. I always noted what Truman wore, because he obviously thought about it and it indicated his state of mind. As we walked by his table on our way out, he piped up, in that squeaky insinuating voice of his, ''Hi, Andy. And how are *you,* Mr. Colacello?''

Two nights later, I ran into Truman at Studio 54. He was wearing a black suit with a black knit shirt buttoned at the collar, and looked almost priestly. He was sitting near the bar, sipping Perrier. He motioned for me to sit beside him, and started in with the compliments. ''You really did an exceptional job editing the Scavullo book,'' he said, referring to *Scavullo's Men,* for which I'd taped and shaped most of the interviews. ''Mine wasn't that great when I did it,'' he said, ''but when I read it, it sounded really great, and that was thanks to *you.*'' *Interview* was ''getting better and better.'' ''OUT'' was his ''favorite thing.'' I should ''write a book real soon.'' The next day, when I repeated Truman's compliments to Andy, he asked me if Truman had started drinking again.

A month later, at the end of February, when I ran into him at Studio 54, Truman was drinking again. He was wearing a brown suit with a peach shirt and an orange tie, and trying to nurse a vodka and orange juice. "I can stop whenever I want," Truman said, ordering another screwdriver. "It's because of these marvelous downs the doctor gave me that control the terrifying floating anxiety I have that makes me drink too much." He took a bottle out of his pocket and announced, "I have twenty-eight left." Then he changed the subject: "And how are you, my precious? I'm still reading 'OUT' faithfully. I know everything you do and everyone you see. You should call me up and come over to see the way I'm redecorating my place at the UN Plaza. I have a feeling you'll really like it."

A week later, we were dancing together at the Elizabeth Taylor party, and a week after that we were dancing together at Halston's big ball for Liza's birthday at his new Olympic Tower headquarters. "Truman really likes you, Bob," said Andy. He made it sound like a death in the family. Perhaps it was just too hard for him to watch one of his kids being pursued by the idol he'd been pursuing since 1949.

When I went to see him about a week later, Truman was dancing in the hall outside his apartment and making little devil's horns behind his ears with his fingers. For a second, I thought that Andy had been right that he was going to pounce on me. We were meeting to discuss the Oscar-night party at Studio 54 that Polaroid wanted him to co-host with Andy. "You're going to have to pay the price now," Andy had insisted. "And you can't say no, because Polaroid's giving us a lot of ads to get Truman to do the party." I pointed out that Truman had introduced us to his new infatuation, Bob MacBride, at the Halston party. "That was just to make you jealous, Bob" was Andy's comeback. When I said that Truman only liked middle-aged men, Andy, of course, told me that I "could" look middle-aged, and perhaps, at the rate I was going, I did.

Truman's apartment was on the twenty-first floor facing the United Nations Park and the East River. "Great view, isn't it?" he said, before I could. There was an L-shaped living-room-dining-room, a small kitchen off the entrance, and two bedrooms, which he didn't show me. It looked like a grandmother's apartment, but emptier. That is, it lacked the clutter of a grandmother's apartment, but every piece of furniture and every object was like something a grandmother would have. There were Victorian settees and club chairs covered in old needlepoint rugs, and needlepoint pillows, and his famous collection of glass paperweights that "snow" when you turn them upside down. "Well, let's go right to lunch," he said. He took me to La Petite Marmite, in the Beekman Hotel, right across the street from the UN Plaza.

I was hoping we'd talk about literature, since he thought I was such a good writer, but he wanted to talk about love. "Now, tell me all about your love affair that just ended." I was stunned, and asked him how he knew about it. He said Andy had told him "with a certain degree of glee in his voice. But whatever you do, *don't listen to Andy.* He'll always give you bad advice, because he wants you all to himself." I said that my job required too much going out and traveling to keep up a steady relationship, and that love was too hard anyway.

"You're falling for Andy's line," he insisted, "and he's wrong. He's all wrong. Life isn't worth living without love. That's the reason I became an alcoholic and had to be institutionalized—because of an affair breaking up. If your affair is really over, it'll take at least two years to return to normal, take it from me." He brought up Bob MacBride and said he liked him because he was so intelligent "and not in my business. He does all the most advanced computer experiments for IBM and Westinghouse. I can't live with anyone who competes with me. That was the problem with this person who drove me crazy. He wanted to be a writer, and he started putting my work down. Well, first of all, nobody can compete with me. I know I'm the best at what I do."

He also told me about his long-term relationship with Jack Dunphy, though he didn't tell me his name that day. He was also a writer, he said, "but he's really sweet. He lives in my house in Water Mill in the summer and he lives in my house in Switzerland in the winter. He likes to ski, and I hate to ski, so I never go there. After five years of the mountains, they were just crowding in on me. I can't take it. But we've been together for years, even though we don't have sex anymore. I know Andy doesn't think that's possible—that you can still love someone you don't have sex with—but that's Andy's problem: He doesn't know the first thing about love. He can't even spell the word."

I thought it was the right moment to bring up the party. "Wouldn't you like to give a really big ball at Studio 54? The Polaroid corporation would finance the whole thing." Truman loved the idea, and said he'd invite the same people he invited to his Black and White Ball, "with a few crossed off, of course." But when I explained that it had to be on Oscar night, which was less than two weeks way, he said that he was on deadline for the next installment of *Answered Prayers* in Esquire, and that we should give the party and use his name on the invitation.

I said that Polaroid thought there should be a hostess as well, to complement Andy and him, perhaps Gloria Swanson. "I don't want my name on an invitation with an old bag like Gloria Swanson," he snapped. I clinched the deal by telling him that Polaroid would give him one of their new instant movie cameras. He said he wanted it *before* the party, to give to Bob Mac-Bride. Like every celebrity I've ever met, Truman couldn't resist a freebie. He chuckled as he hugged me goodbye and then admonished me in a very loud voice as I flagged down a taxi, and pedestrians did double-takes, "Don't listen to Andy! He doesn't know anything about love!"

The Polaroid party was not exactly a success. The invitations got messed up by the computer. All sorts of VIPs got upset about not getting invited. By the time our friends and clients got theirs, they had already accepted other Oscar-watching parties around town. And every nut and groupie in New York was heading for 54. "This is the worst party you ever gave, Bob," said Andy when I got there. "And all the people you hate are winning Oscars." Polaroid fought with Steve over his $30,000 bill for the party. Steve and I fought about it too. Jed, Jay, and Tom fought with Fred, Vincent, and me because we wouldn't let Andy do a party the following week at Hurrah (for which Jay and Tom were now doing P.R.). And we lost the previously agreed-on sale of yet another Farah Diba portrait to an Iranian oilman who had a contretemps with the 54 doorman.

The only one pleased by the party was Truman, who was now calling 54 "Cinquanta-Quattro," and who acted like it was his biggest social triumph since the Black and White Ball. But then he was drinking so much again, and taking so many pills and so much cocaine, that he lost all perspective. "New York is entering its greatest period since 1963," he announced. "I mean, I want to stay up every night all night because everything is so interesting. It's a whole new period of *love*. Everybody is getting together with everybody again. And I really do think that it all came together at *my* party at Cinquanta-Quattro. Haw haw haw haw."

36

Politics and Dinner Parties

"Kill the Shah! Kill the Shah! Kill the Shah!" screamed hundreds of demonstrators in ski masks as cops on horseback pushed them back across Fifth Avenue, away from the Pierre Hotel, where the Empress of Iran was receiving a human-rights award at a July 1977 luncheon given by the Appeal to Conscience Foundation. It was that Imelda Marcos scene all over again, but bigger, nastier, closer to real violence. Again, Andy was frightened, frazzled, and blaming it all on me. And again, he didn't turn back. There was money to be made, and this time the chase was not in vain. Andy had done Farah Diba's portrait the year before; now he was hot on the trail of her husband's.

It was quieter in the Grand Ballroom, where the Empress stood on a receiving line with Governor Carey, Mayor Koch, and Ambassadors Zahedi and Hoveyda, greeting guests with a soft hello. "Your portraits are so beautiful," she told Andy, "much more beautiful than I am in reality." As we headed to our table, he told me, "Now is the time to pop the question about the Shah's portrait to Hoveyda. I mean, his face really lit up when the Empress said that, because it was his idea, so now he'll want to help us with the next one. Then there's the three kids, Bob. You could be on easy street, but you better hurry. You heard them yelling out there." We were seated with Carroll de Portago, Jean Tailer, and Nedda Logan, who said about the demonstrators, "I think they want a little more democracy."

"But some of them have black hands," said Andy. "I mean, we were in Iran and they don't have any blacks there. Do they, Bob?" Andy never ceased to amaze me. We had dashed from the taxi to the door in haste and

fear, and yet he'd noticed a pair or two of black hands in the jostling masked
mob. After lunch, the Empress gave a speech on the advance of women's
rights in Iran, the reason why she was getting the award. As she spouted
statistics on the enormous increase in female high-school and college grad-
uates, a woman from the University of Wisconsin suddenly jumped up and
shouted, "Lies! Lies! You're a liar!" She was immediately pounced upon
by Iranian security men in dark suits and dragged from the ballroom with a
hand over her mouth. "This is too scary, Bob," said Andy. "What are we
doing here?" "You know what we're doing here, Andy." "Oh, I know, but
there's got to be an easier way."

The politicians, philanthropists, and socialites shifted and coughed; the
Empress stuck to her text as if nothing had happened. There was much
murmuring and shaking of heads—she was losing the room. But then she
surprised everyone with a spontaneous coda. "I would like to say a few
words about what happened before," she said, "because not to would be a
little bit ridiculous, I think. I am very sorry for the inconvenience and noise
and traffic my presence here today has caused you. Perhaps what I am talking
about doesn't mean much in America, where women have so much freedom.
But in my country just the fact that I am even able to be here and speak to
you would have been impossible ten years ago for any woman, even the
Empress." A ten-minute standing ovation followed. "Pop the question quick,
Bob," said Andy. "Do it tonight."

I couldn't push for the Shah's portrait at the embassy dinner that night.
Hoveyda was too busy introducing the Empress around, and the Empress
just smiled and murmured, "Fine," when I asked her how "His Majesty"
was. "You should have told her how handsome His Majesty is," Andy said.

That was all Andy cared about, selling more portraits. There had been
signs that our Iranian business could backfire ever since we returned from
Teheran the previous summer, and landed in the middle of a tiff between
Hoveyda and Bob Wilson, who had withdrawn from the Shiraz Arts Festival.
Hoveyda was sure that Wilson did it "under pressure from the liberal Ma-
fia." Andy thought it was because Wilson had a better invitation from the
Avignon Festival. "I mean, people say they do things for politics, but they
just use politics to do what they want," he said.

The Iranian connection was becoming controversial, and for better or
worse we were connected with the Iranians, and getting more connected
every day. But Andy didn't *want* to see it that way. He preferred to think
that we could go on taking their money, without taking the political heat that
came with it.

So when the Shah's twin sister invited him to a ball, not long after the
Bob Wilson contretemps, in November 1976, Andy accepted with alacrity.
Princess Ashraf had two townhouses, side by side, on Beekman Place—one
for herself and her daughter, Princess Nilufar, and one for the various royal
aunts, nieces, and cousins who served as their ladies-in-waiting. Andy and

I were among the handful of Americans at the ball, along with Congress-woman Bella Abzug, who was the American delegate to a UN commission on women's rights—Princess Ashraf was its head. All the Iranian women, perhaps fifty or so, were wearing enormous taffeta ballgowns from Saint Laurent's new "Jewel" collection, in emerald, ruby, sapphire, amethyst, and topaz. Andy was beside himself: "This is the most beautiful party I've ever been to," he said. "I mean, to see all these women in the same dress in different colors. It's actually more like a movie scene than a real party, and Yves is like the costume designer for the movie, right? Only Marion Javits doesn't match. And how can Bella wear that hat? She doesn't know anything, right? God, every one of Yves's dresses costs $10,000, Bob. Oh, it's such a glamorous party. I wish every party could look like this. It's like, uh, a, uh, a dream."

A dream that was coming to an end. Two days earlier, Jimmy Carter had been elected President and human rights had replaced *Realpolitik* as the major motif of American foreign policy. The switch did not bode well for our most prominent autocratic ally, the Shah of Iran. Andy had contributed prints to the Carter campaign that year. Was he really for Carter? It's a complicated question, and our relationship with the Iranians was part of the answer.

The Carter connection was made right after he won the Democratic nomination in August, when the *New York Times Magazine* commissioned Andy to do a portrait of the candidate for a cover story by Norman Mailer. "Carter's really quiet," Andy told me, after he and Fred got back from Plains, Georgia. "She's the tough one, Rosalynn. She wears the pantsuit. Polyester. And his mother's so nutty. I don't think she and Rosalynn get along. They live in the worst house I ever saw, I mean for someone who might be President. It's like a little ranch house on Long Island—your parents' house is a lot nicer, Bob. They have wall-to-wall carpeting. Not real wool. None of the furniture is real either. It was all that fake colonial stuff from the big companies in North Carolina. And when we got there, Amy was riding her bicycle around in circles in front of the house. She has that nutty look too. Actually, the one I like the best was the mother, Miz Lillian. She kept saying that she looked like me. She sort of does. It was too nutty."

After the Carter cover ran on Sunday, September 26, 1976, Tom Beard and Frank Fowler, two Carter fundraisers Andy and Fred had met in Plains, came to the Factory to ask for an edition of prints for the Carter campaign. Fred was all for it, just as he had been for the McGovern prints in 1972. He saw the Democratic party as the aristocratic party, the historic home of Jefferson and Roosevelt, Harriman and Kennedy, Jackie and Lee. Andy saw the Democrats as the party of the immigrants and the poor, the underdog and the outsider. "I know I should be for the Republicans," he said, "because I hate paying taxes. But I just can't be a Republican. It wouldn't be right. I mean, I grew up in the Depression and we were eating salt-and-pepper soup, Bob, and, uh . . . uh, artists just can't be Republican, can they?''

What were his real politics? Which was the real Andy? The immigrant's son, the Depression child, the alienated artist who identified with the down-trodden and the left-out? Or the rich Society portrait painter, the ambitious power worshiper who assiduously pursued presidents and potentates, Democrat and Republican, Windsor and Pahlavi? Perhaps the contradiction was so great it was why he avoided thinking about politics seriously. "Politics and dinner parties don't go together," he once told Fred when Katie Schlumberger's poet husband, Tom Jones, asked if Andy would write a letter to Imelda Marcos for Amnesty International. "I can't write a letter like that to Imelda Marcos," he went on. "She'll never see me again."

It can also be argued that Andy's rare political decisions were nothing more than shrewd public-relations moves. The Carter prints balanced the Farah Diba portraits—as Fred put it, "It'll get the art world intellectuals and the liberals in the press off our backs about this Iran thing." Andy contributed an edition of fifty Jimmy Carter prints to the Democratic National Committee during the election campaign, then a second edition of 125, plus a Miz Lillian edition of 50, to help pay off the campaign debt after the election. But he didn't vote for Jimmy Carter. He didn't vote for anyone. Ever. And he skipped Carter's inauguration on January 20, 1977, to be at the opening of the Cats and Dogs show in Kuwait. There was a chance, it seemed, of Andy getting the portrait of the Emir. So Andy sent me instead, with my little Minox, to record Andy Warhol's "Impression of the Inauguration," which along with those of Rauschenberg, Lichtenstein, and others would make for Carter's latest fund-raising portfolio.

Andy did see the new President in February. Ambassador Zahedi gave a Valentine's party, with Andy as guest of honor, and he invited our Carter contacts. Tom Beard said he was looking forward to "the big bash at the Eye-ranians. I've heard about the mountains of caviar." He arranged for us to have lunch that day at the White House mess, the private dining room for senior staff. Our party took up two of the eight tables in the wood-paneled room. Catherine ordered a Bloody Mary and was served a Virgin Mary—Southern Baptist style. "The food is like Schrafft's," Andy whispered.

After lunch, we were given a tour of the real power center: the West Wing. In the Cabinet Room, each place at the table was set with White House notepads, pencils, and matchbooks, which were handed out to Catherine, Fred, Shelly, Vincent, et al., and Andy wanted us to turn them all over to him. Then Andy got a surprise invitation to meet with Carter in the Oval Office. He looked panicky as he was led off—and sure enough, the special assistant was back a minute later, saying Andy wanted me along to take pictures. In the antechamber, the secretary was having lunch at her desk. "Gee," said Andy, "here we are in the President's office, Bob, and the secretary is eating the same smelly tunafish sandwich that they eat in every office, with the same smelly pickle.'' He was trying to be funny, but he was trembling like a leaf.

A man in a gray suit strode through the Rose Garden outside the window, and then suddenly he was standing before us, right hand outstretched. It was the President. Andy and I jumped up. ''Hi, Andy, good to see you again,'' said Carter, and ushered us into the Oval office. Conversation was stilted, and Andy stood there shaking, not knowing how to break the ice. The President thanked Andy for his prints. ''It was a big help,'' he said. ''Oh, gee, thanks,'' said Andy, making it sound like goodbye. In fairness to Andy, it must be said that Carter was almost as awkward as he was. ''He's no Nelson Rockefeller'' was the way Andy put it later.

There was no caviar at the Iranian embassy that night. Zahedi thought that would please our Carter friends. It didn't.

In New York, we continued going to Ambassador Hoveyda's dinners: for the new Swedish ambassador to the UN; for the new American ambassador to Italy; for the new president of the General Assembly. When Hoveyda saluted him as ''a symbol of freedom,'' in a toast at one dinner, Andy whispered to me, ''That's why I'm here, Bob. As a symbol of freedom.''

In November 1977, one year after her Beekman Place dream ball, Princess Ashraf sat for her portrait at an embassy dinner in her honor. ''Why not take the Polaroids now,'' suggested Hoveyda, ''before she changes her mind or goes back to Teheran?'' Andy, as always, had his Big Shot ready and loaded, with plenty of extra film in his bag. The guest list was very cultural, as usual: Milos Forman, Elia Kazan and Barbara Loden, Frank Perry and Barbara Goldsmith, Lester Persky, Elliot Kastner. Andy said, ''They're all hoping the Iranians will finance their movies, right?'' Later, Princess Ashraf's Women's Lib cell showed up—Bella Abzug, Shirley MacLaine, Margaret Trudeau—and they had a nice consciousness-raising session in the little mirrored salon. ''What a great party,'' Andy said when we left. ''Hoveyda was so great to get her to sit right there. He really is our friend. I wish all the portraits could happen like that.''

Three days later, Andy marched into my office and threw the *Village Voice* down on my desk. ''I knew this would happen someday,'' he announced, pointing at the cover. There was Andy with the Empress of Iran, standing together under his portrait of her at the Iranian Embassy. ''THE BEAUTIFUL BUTCHERS,'' said the headline, and the story began with the line ''Torture tastes better with caviar.'' There were more party pictures inside, of the Kissingers, Elizabeth Taylor, and Liza Minnelli, all with Ardeshir Zahedi. Diana Vreeland was caught kissing the ambassador at his Valentine's Day dance, and the caption under the photo noted the alleged number of political prisoners in Iranian jails. It was red yellow journalism, left-wing McCarthyism. I couldn't take it seriously, and told Andy so, when I saw that it was written by Alexander Cockburn, who, as the son of a well-known British Communist, should have known better than to indulge in guilt by association. Fred dismissed the article too, and didn't let it stop Andy and him from attending Jimmy Carter's state dinner for the Shah the following week.

A few nights later, I was defending their decision to Henry Geldzahler, who had just been named New York City's Commissioner of Culture by the newly elected Mayor Koch. "I warned Andy not to go to that dinner for the Shah," said Henry, amused by the fact that the President and the Shah had been accidentally tear-gassed during the welcoming ceremony on the South Lawn, as the police repelled eight thousand demonstrators trying to storm the White House grounds. "How could you let Andy get mixed up with the Iranians, Bob? I can see Fred allowing something like that to happen for money, but you should have known better, you *studied* foreign affairs." I said that was why I knew that the Shah's government was relatively progressive and open, given the history of his country and the politics of the region. "What's wrong with Andy anyway?" Henry wanted to know. "He only talks about diamonds now and how he has to make more money every year than the year before. I think he's very unhappy." I now realize that Andy's old friend had made a connection that was true—between Andy's greed and Andy's unhappiness—but then I gave him the standard, and equally true, company line: rising Factory overhead. Henry said that it didn't excuse Andy's dealing with the "murderous" Shah.

Several days after Commissioner Geldzahler's scolding, Andy threw another piece of paper down on my desk and looked at me as if to say, "What do I do now?" It was a Xerox of a petition that Allen Ginsberg had sent for him to sign. It alleged, among other things, that in 1962 Princess Ashraf supposedly had been caught smuggling several million dollars' worth of heroin into this country. "Can this be true?" asked Andy. "I mean, are we really going to get into trouble for doing her portrait?" He put the Xerox of the petition in that month's time capsule along with the fan mail, the hate mail, the nut mail, and the record-company press releases, saying only, "I hope Allen Ginsberg doesn't call me about it."

In February 1978, Ambassador Hoveyda told us that the Shah's portrait was definitely on, and I went up to his office to look through files of official photographs, as His Imperial Highness was not available for Big Shots by Andy. I took about twenty photographs back to the Factory and Andy said that the Shah looked "scary" in most of them and he wished he could take his own Polaroids. With Fred's help, he settled on a shot of the Shah in formal military dress, a white jacket with gold-braided epaulets. Fred said it was "the most elegant" shot, and Andy liked it because the Shah was smiling, very slightly. "I guess I can make him look good," Andy said, as he gave his choice to Rupert Smith to blow up, "but it's not going to be easy. Don't make the negative too dark, Rupert." Rupert Smith had replaced Alex Heinrici as Andy's silkscreen printer in 1977.

"I wouldn't be too free with the eye shadow and the lipstick," Gisela Hoveyda advised Andy over dinner at Ballato's. "I mean, it should be your style, but . . ." "Oh, no, no, I know," Andy quickly concurred, "no lipstick." "Keep it casual but conservative," the ambassador suggested. I said that Andy was "trying to project the image of a modern monarch" with the Shah's portrait. The Hoveydas loved that line, and so did Andy. "I've got to remember it," he told me. "We should use it all the time."

We used it to headline an imperial interview—"Farah Pahlavi: Modern Monarch"—in our March 1978 issue. But we put Margaret Trudeau, not the Empress, on the cover. Some of our Iranian friends thought we had slighted their country. "How could you put that Canadian bitch on the cover," said Naz Alam, the daughter of the Minister of Court and a portrait client, "and my queen on page two?" I told her that the Trudeau interview had been done by Andy, and his interviews were always the cover stories. The interview with Farah Diba had been done by Rita Christopher, a freelance Washington journalist. It had been arranged by Ambassador Zahedi on the condition that he had approval of the transcript. I hated giving anyone approval of the transcript, but this was one case where what was right for the magazine was not necessarily good for the portrait business—and Andy had made it perfectly clear which he considered more important.

Fortunately, the interview was not a total puff piece; the Empress specifically addressed the demonstrations that had plagued her recent American visits. She blamed them, accurately as it turned out, not only on Communists but also "ultra-rightist fanatics in Iran who disapprove of some of our reforms, like the emancipation of women." Still, I wasn't thrilled when Zahedi called from Washington on deadline day to ask me to delete "one little thing." There goes the good stuff, I thought, preparing myself to be, as Andy was always instructing, "really aggressive but really charming." But he only wanted one line removed from the introduction—"She drinks Coca-Cola and smokes cigarettes." Those were "not very nice things for an Empress to do," he said. What he didn't say, but perhaps was thinking, was that they were not things a Moslem Empress should do. But then, it was easy to forget that she, and all the Iranians we knew, were officially Moslems.

As the political situation in Iran grew increasingly tense and murky that spring—the streets of Teheran running with demonstrators carrying photographs of the exiled Ayatollah Khomeini—Ambassador Hoveyda tried to put a good face on things in New York by stepping up his cultural entertainments. At the Hoveydas' cocktail party for the Metropolitan Museum's proposed cinematheque, Andy was surprised to find his old mentor from the late fifties, Emile de Antonio. "What are you doing here?" he asked de Antonio, who was avidly left-wing (and had become known for his anti-Nixon and anti-McCarthy films in the sixties). "I came with Renata Adler," said Antonio. "I won't ask you what you're doing here, Andy." "Oh, I came with Bob," said Andy.

Though I'd heard about him and read about him, this was the first time I'd met de Antonio and I found it fascinating to watch how Andy and he slid back into their old collaborative relationship after so many years. "You've got to give me a title for my next book," Andy pleaded. *"My Life as a Fiction,"* de Antonio proposed off the top of his head. "What a great title!" gasped Andy, jotting it right down on a matchbook cover. "You can't have it," said de Antonio. "I'm keeping it for myself."

Later, Andy decided, that "Dee," as he called him, "was being mean to me because of the Iran thing. But he should know it's just business. I mean, he was there because if the Iranians give money for the cinematheque, he'll have another place to show his documentaries, right?"

It was and it wasn't just business. Over the years, we had developed personal bonds with our Iranian friends, particularly Fereydoun and Gisela Hoveyda, so that even if Andy had considered dropping the Iranian business—which he never did—it wouldn't have been so easy. In March, Ambassador Hoveyda gave a birthday party for Barbara Allen. That was the first night we noticed how skimpy the caviar portions had become. "It was such a small bowl," said Andy, "and they only passed it around once. Maybe things really are getting bad." Fred thought otherwise. "Fereydoun doesn't want to be loved for his caviar," he said. He had a point: In times of trouble one does tend to test friends. But it also seemed symbolic of something larger, especially as the year went on and the situation in Teheran worsened and the sturgeon eggs at the Caviar Club became rarer and rarer, smaller and smaller, blacker and blacker.

One day in May 1978, our involvement with the Iranians turned into something more than a topic for verbal jousting at Manhattan parties: A man with a Middle Eastern accent called the Factory and said, "Tell Andy to be careful tonight. There's a bomb at the party." Andy was going to four parties that night, including one he was hosting and another in his honor, all publicized in advance. The first was a promotional cocktail party for *Interview* at Fiorucci, which had sent out two thousand invitations using Andy's name. Second was Dr. Denton Cox's dinner for Andy at Barbetta, which Suzy's column had written up the day before, including Ambassador Hoveyda's name. The papers had also noted Andy's expected appearance at the two big bashes of the night: MoMA's annual Party in the Garden and the opening of the disco Xenon.

I was at home changing when Vincent called with the news. He said it was probably "just some nut"—threatening calls weren't exactly uncommon at the Factory—but perhaps we should alert Fiorucci and Barbetta just in case. Andy picked up on another line and wailed, "What are we going to do, Bob? Should I stay home? Should we call the police? I knew this was going to happen someday.'' And I knew he was going to say that when it did.

I called the manager of Fiorucci. He was reluctant to call the police, saying he'd have his own people search the place. Then I went to pick up Andy in the limousine that Fiorucci had sent for us. He was, of course, a nervous wreck. He said he didn't want to go, but he was going. He wasn't wailing or whining anymore, but frozen in silence. That was Andy in a crisis: not so much calm as quietly fatalistic.

A thousand kids, and three plainclothes cops, were waiting for us at Fiorucci. Andy hid behind tall Averil Meyer and short Whitney Tower, Jr., while I dealt with the police. They had searched the place but had found nothing and asked for Andy's schedule for the rest of the night. They advised me to alert the West Side precinct that policed Barbetta's neighborhood. Which I did. I found Andy in the crowd, talking to a strange-looking kid who he said was "São's son." I thought that was odd as São Schlumberger's son was fifteen years old and in boarding school in France. "Your mother told me you were still in school," I said. "What are you doing in New York?" He said that he was working at a bank "that prints up all the world's currency." That sounded even odder, so I asked him where his mother was at the moment. He said she was at Xenon, and when I pointed out that Xenon wasn't opening until much later that night, he accused me of being paranoid. I was beginning to think that *he* was the anonymous caller. The fact that he, of all the kids in the place, was the one Andy was talking to only heightened my suspicion.

There were five uniformed policemen outside Barbetta when we arrived, and five inside searching the place. Andy scurried to the private room where the dinner was being held, while Vincent and I talked to the police. Ambassador Hoveyda looked weary as he said that he was sure the threat was due to his presence. In any case, there was no bomb to be found.

After dinner, Andy, Catherine, and I went to the MoMA garden party. A minute after we arrived and Andy was photographed, he said, "I can go now. They know I came," and dashed off with Catherine to Halston's house, where they were meeting Steve Rubell. Although he said that he wasn't worried about competition from Xenon—which was owned by the well-connected Peppo Vanini and Howard Stein—Steve wasn't taking any chances. He wanted his mainstays, Andy and Halston, at *his* club that night.

At Xenon the mob was unbelievable and the only one who was up for fighting it was Sylvia Miles, who plunged into the crowd shouting, "Sylvia Miles coming through!" Brigid Berlin, Jed, and I decided to give up, and took a taxi to 54. It wasn't too crowded for a change and soon we were all dancing in a circle. Andy appeared on the edge of the dance floor—and Jed grabbed Brigid and ran out of the club. Andy just stood there, pretending not to notice. I went over to him and he said in a woozy voice, full of vodka,

Valium, and Quaalude, "Oh, I met the cutest busboy. You should put him in *Interview,* Bob. Tell him you'll make him a big star."

It was one of Andy's standard lines. I used to find it funny, but after nine years it was beginning to drive me bananas. Still, I couldn't get mad at Andy that night. I was just so happy that we were both among the living, not bombed to smithereens by some Iranian lunatic, or São Schlumberger's fake son. Down in the basement I ran into Halston. Back upstairs I danced with Lorna Luft. I spotted Andy, half-hidden behind a big speaker, feeling up the busboy. Everywhere there were people I knew, and people I didn't know, all of them, it seemed, thrusting poppers and coke at my bobbing nose. It was a crazy all-night night, like so many then.

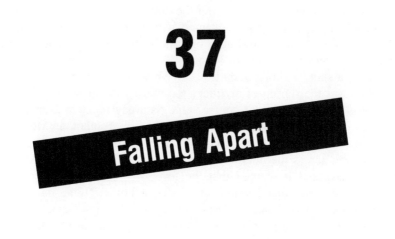

37

Falling Apart

I certainly wasn't the only person who was drinking a lot in the seventies (I drank eight or ten vodkas a day, starting at Factory lunches), just as I wasn't the only person who was making more and more trips to the bathroom for a "sniff," a "snort," a "hit," or a "blow" of "coca-cola," "vitamin C," "white magic," or "snow." By the middle of the decade, cocaine suddenly was everywhere, or at least everywhere we went, with the possible exception of the Iranian embassy. It went from something people tried to hide, except among close friends, to something people took for granted, and shared openly: from "I must go fix my face, see you in a minute," to "I must go powder my nose, want to come?"

In my diaries from early 1975, I always took coke with men in men's rooms; by the end of the year, I was in men's rooms with women and women's rooms with men—and there were lines to do lines outside both. What's amazing was that nobody cared about coming out the wrong door with the wrong sex: We were too high, too happy, too eager to get back to the table and pass the little bottle or the folded foil to the rest of our friends. None of us thought cocaine was really dangerous, or even addictive, back then. Heroin was off limits in our crowd, but coke was like liquor or pot or poppers, fuel for fun, not self-destruction.

I wasn't only being given cocaine, though for the editor of *Interview* there were always willing providers, hoping for a mention in "OUT." More and more I was also buying it. I liked having my own little bottle, so that I could sneak a snort when business dinners became boring, or when I had had one vodka too many and needed to counteract the down with an up. I liked having my own little bottle after the dinners too, at Studio 54, because then I could meet any beauty I wanted with that open sesame of the late seventies, "Want a hit?" And after one snort too many, I needed a shot of vodka to counteract the up with a down. The staircase to oblivion, I called it: a snort, a shot, a snort, a shot . . . "We were just so high we couldn't go home" was the refrain of my diary too many mornings.

It was taking its toll, of course. One Saturday night in January 1978, at an Iranian embassy dinner celebrating the engagement of Metromedia Chairman John Kluge to Patricia Gay, I started getting piercing pains in my right side and across the middle of my back. I had been home sick with flu for a few days and it seemed that the fever was coming back too. After dinner, I told Andy that I wanted to go right home. "Oh, shut up," he snapped back. "You're such a hypochondriac. Mrs. Lachman said something about having her portrait done. You better go talk to her, Bob, if you want to make a commission." I grabbed a cognac from the passing tray and made my way to Jacquine Lachman, the third wife of the man who owned a third of Revlon. As she chattered away about Christmas in Acapulco and February in Vail, I stood there stewing over Andy's callous hypocrisy. He had a double standard for sick employees, I decided, just as he did for everything else. When I wanted Jed to bring me some aspirin that night a few years back, Andy was worried about his bringing home my germs. But when he wanted me to work with him, he forgot about my germs as we taxied around town together. That night, for example, he insisted that I go on with him to Earl and Camilla McGraths', to meet producer Lucy Jarvis, who was talking about doing a Broadway play based on Andy's life. (Andy wanted Shaun Cassidy to play him and Kate Smith his mother.)

At Halston's after the McGraths', the pain in my side came back stronger than ever. Halston gave me a little blue pill and a glass of milk to wash it down. It was two in the morning when Bianca and Andy decided to go to 54. I said I was going home, as the pill hadn't helped. "Oh, c'mon, Bob," said Andy, "you're such a hypochondriac."

"I am *not* a hypochondriac, Andy!" I shouted. "I really have pains! I'm going home!"

Andy called bright and early on Sunday morning. He could barely contain himself. "Oh, God, we saw two famous people together who we weren't supposed to see together last night" was the way he began. "Oh, Bob, you're missing all the good stuff. I mean, you're not sick. Bob. You sound fine. You looked good last night. Oh, God, Liza really looked great. Oh, Bob, you don't know how exciting it is to see two famous people making it right in front of you."

It was Andy's usual way of telling a story, out of order, in breathless dribs and drabs, with lots of blanks where key details should be. He said he wasn't going to tell me who the other famous person was, but then he immediately added, "Oh, God, Baryshnikov really looked great too."

"Where was this?" I asked.

"At Halston's. We weren't supposed to be there but Bianca had to go back for something and there was Liza with Baryshnikov and Halston."

"And they were making it, Andy?"

"Well, they were necking. It was so great to see two big stars together like that. But they said he was moody. In the limousine. Halston said he never saw him moody like that before."

"You mean you went to 54 and left them there?"

"Yeah. Can you believe it? That's where they do it. You're missing everything, Bob."

I wasn't sure what I was missing. When Andy said "necking" it could mean a peck on the cheek. And "doing it" might be holding hands. I was more concerned with the next call—from Brigid Berlin, who was now working at the Factory full time. "You've got to get back to the office," she told me. "It's just going to hell. Catherine's running wild, giving all-day lunches, falling asleep on the couch in the dining room after lunch. And the other day, when I walked into the dining room to help her clean up, you know, she was making out with that boyfriend of hers who wears those gloves to cover up his burned hands. It was really disgusting." The Cocaine Cowboy's hands had been scorched in a light airplane crash. Andy always said that was the real reason Catherine kept trying to get him back from Margaret Trudeau.

By 1978, the Factory seemed to be slipping out of control, or turning into a daytime Studio 54. The phone never stopped ringing, and half the calls were from friends, and strangers, trying to get us to get them in 54 that night. The fake du Pont twins had become semipermanent Factory fixtures, sitting in the windowsills listening to everything that was said and repeating it all over town: "Andy and Bob want Peter Beard on the cover, but Fred wants Isabella Rossellini." If Brigid wasn't watching, they'd rifle through the big red book, jotting down the RSVP numbers from Andy's invitations and calling to say they'd be coming with him. Andy thought it was funny.

Victor Hugo was usually there, with prospective models for the sex paintings, and Chris Makos was usually there too, now, working on layouts for our photo book, *Exposures*. The two of them could be counted on to devour half the food before the lunch guests arrived. It drove Vincent and me crazy, but Andy didn't care. He floated through the lunches, saying how glamorous everything was, on his way to his studio to paint. Our swell guests didn't seem to care about the lack of food either, or the lack of Andy for that matter. It was as if they came to see each other over drinks, at some mad midday cocktail party. When we wanted them to leave we took them on a tour to get them out of the dining room, away from the bar and the bathroom.

For most of 1978, the walls of the main room were lined with Andy's hurriedly completed portraits of the Shah, in stately tones of blue and gray, and of Princess Ashraf, in more feminine, but equally restrained, shades of peach and lilac. We were waiting for the checks before shipping them to Teheran, and we waited for a long time. Leaning beside the Pahlavis were twenty-foot versions of the Piss Paintings.

One afternoon about this time, decorator Suzie Frankfurt sent an assistant down for the latest issue of *Interview*. He happened to to be a sixteen-year-old preppy from an old WASP family, handsome and shy. Somehow, Andy, abetted by Chris Makos, got him to strip down to his Jockey shorts and do jumping jacks in the middle of the Factory, while they photographed him. Suzie was furious and she told Fred off. "It's perverse," she said. "I stopped seeing Andy in the sixties because he was doing things like this, and I can't believe you'd let him do them now." There was "nothing wrong," Fred told her, "with a young person who has a beautiful body being proud of it. It's perfectly natural, and Andy was only doing the normal thing for an artist to do by photographing him."

That was Fred: always defending Andy outside the Factory, yet seething with resentment against him inside. It took a while for that resentment to surface, but it did—though Fred adamantly refused to see the reason for it. Instead, he drank more and more, and it started to show more and more. Fred was also taking cocaine in the late seventies and early eighties, though he was less open about it than the rest of us (and he has long since put it behind him). One night at Regine's, Fred coughed up his stash, and he and I ended up having a heart-to-heart about love. "It's hard for anybody to go out with you, Bob," he said, "because you're in this strange position of having a lot of power and no money. So it's all an illusion and not much reality."

I thought he was talking about himself, but then it's always easier to think about other people's problems than your own. Of course, we were both in the same position, and we didn't know how to get out of it, or perhaps didn't want to get out of it. I thought I was happy at the Factory, and, no doubt, Fred thought he was happy there too. It was hard to admit that we weren't. Meanwhile, at the other end of the table, Andy was "proposing" to Averil Meyer, Fred's "fiancée" that year. Sooner or later, Andy always proposed to the girls he said Fred was going to marry. He thought it was funny.

He also thought it was funny when Fred pulled his pants down at parties and wasn't wearing underwear, which Fred was doing more and more. He thought it was funny when Fred pulled the assistants' pants down or skirts up at the Factory after a drunken Factory lunch, which Fred was doing more and more. He thought it was funny when Fred fell down the stairs at night-clubs and in the Paris apartment, which Fred was doing more and more. "Oh, Fred's really drunk," he'd say, not so much concerned as amused.

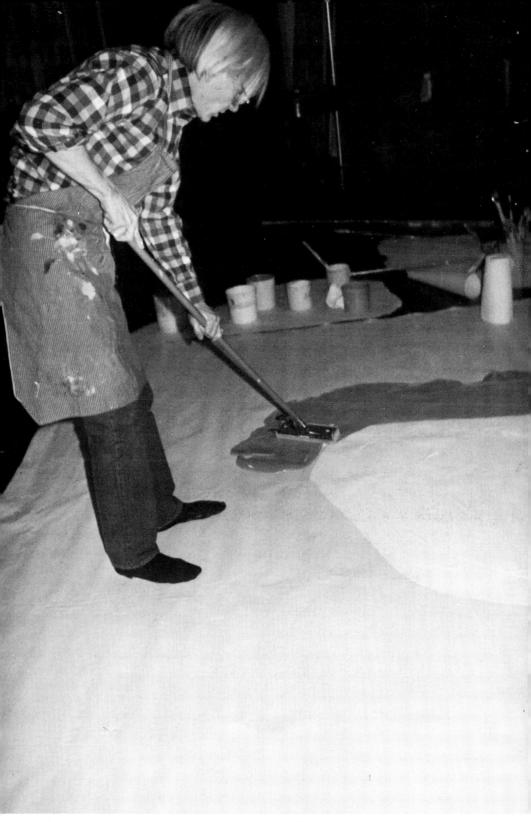

Mop art: Andy painting a very large canvas, circa 1975. (Photo Bob Colacello)

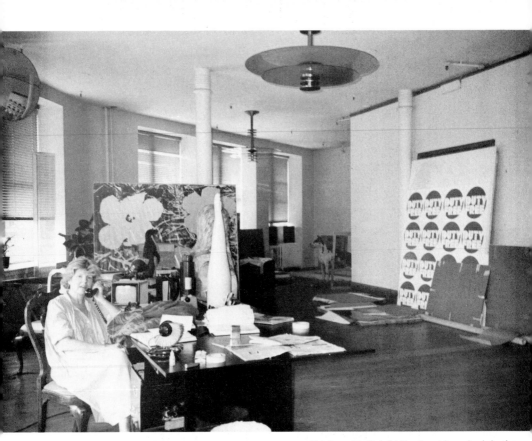

Factory III: Brigid Berlin at her desk in the front room at 860 Broadway, circa 1983. (Photo Paige Powell)

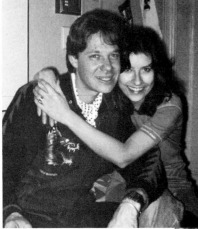

Interview ad director Barbara Colaciello with client Robert Lee Morris of Artwear. (Courtesy Barbara Colaciello)

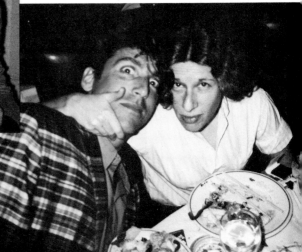

Interview art director Marc Balet with Fran Lebowitz, whose "I Cover the Waterfront" column was our most popular feature. (Photo Paige Powell)

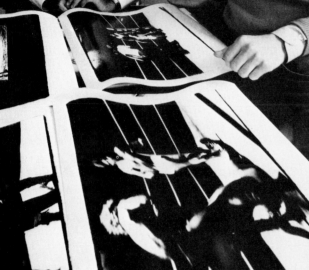

Interview editor Robert Hayes showing me a layout, 1980. (© *The Daily News*)

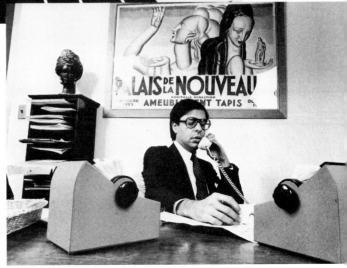

Me and my Rolodexes, one for America, one for Europe, 1980. (© *The Daily News*)

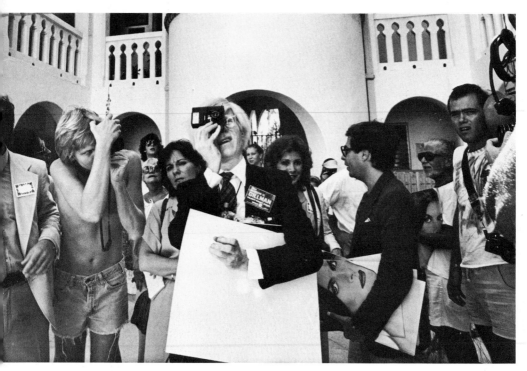

Miami Beach, 1980: Andy and me at an *Interview* promotion. (AP/Wide World Photos)

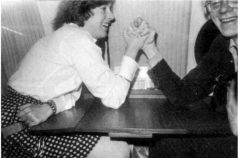

Jacksonville, 1976:
Catherine Guinness and
Andy armwrestling on
Chris and Sondra Gilman's
private plane. (Photo Bob
Colacello)

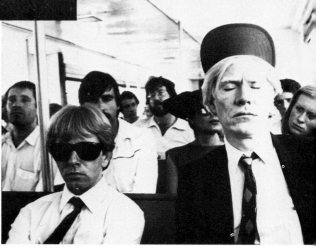

Fire Island Ferry, 1979:
Rupert Smith, Andy's silk-
screener, and Andy. (Photo
Bob Colacello)

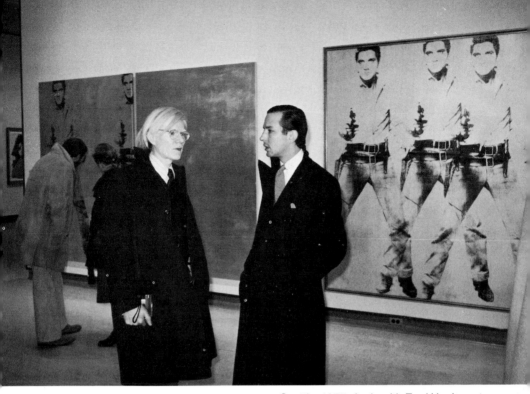

Seattle, 1977: Andy with Fred Hughes at
the Seattle Art Museum retrospective.
(Photo Bob Colacello)

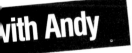
vith Andy

Naples, 1976: Andy, in his usual sleep
attire, eating a room-service breakfast.
(Photo Bob Colacello)

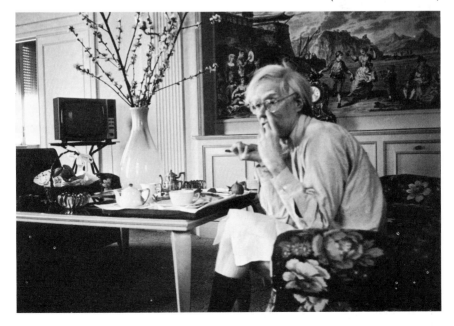

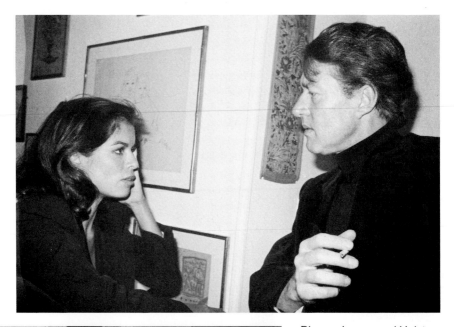

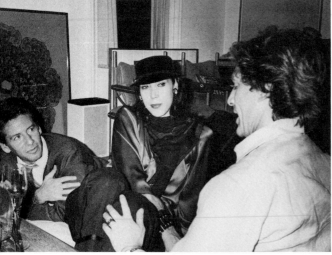

Bianca Jagger and Halston were at the center of Andy's seventies In crowd. (Photo Bob Colacello)

Marina Schiano, the YSL vice president who married Fred Hughes, with Calvin Klein *(left)* and Giorgio di Sant'Angelo, circa 1977. (Photo Bob Colacello)

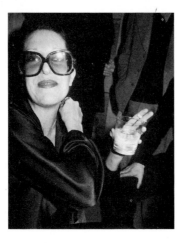

Elsa Peretti, famous for making jewelry—and scenes. (Photo Bob Colacello)

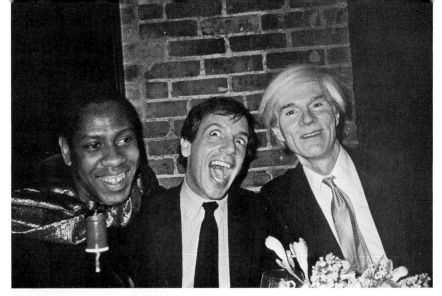

Interview fashion editor Andre Leon Talley, Studio 54's Steve Rubell, and Andy. (Photo Bob Colacello)

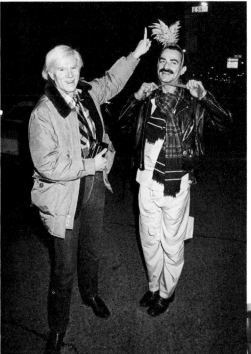

Andy and Victor Hugo, Halston's window-dresser and close friend. (© Ron Galella)

Andy, fully-dressed, with Victor Hugo, jock-strapped, at a Fire Island pool party, 1979. (Photo Bob Colacello)

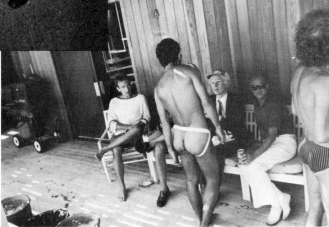

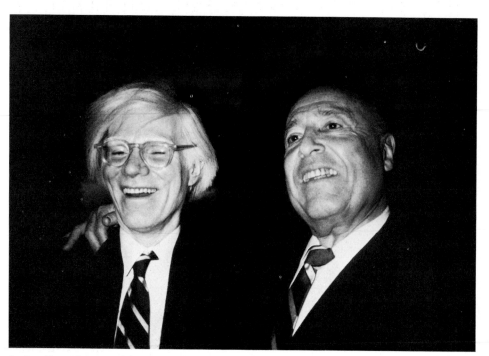

Andy with social powerhouse Jerry Zipkin, with whom he'd finally become friendly after two decades of trying. (Photo Bob Colacello)

Lynn Wyatt, a Warhol portrait client, and Truman Capote, another idol Andy had been chasing since the fifties, circa 1979. (Photo Bob Colacello)

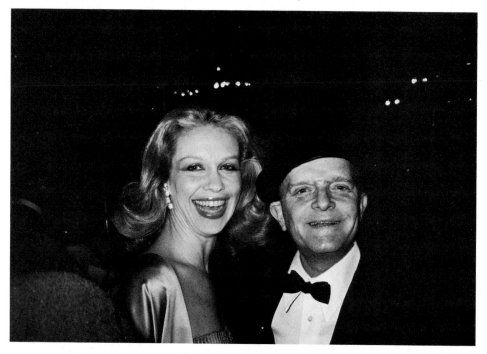

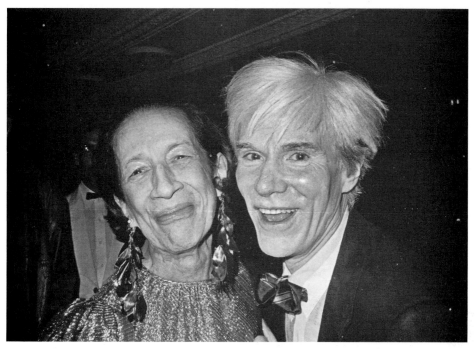

Diana Vreeland, Empress of Fashion, with Andy, circa 1981. (Photo Bob Colacello)

Fred Hughes *(right)* with Diana Vreeland and decorator John Stefanidis at Regine's, New York. (Photo Bob Colacello)

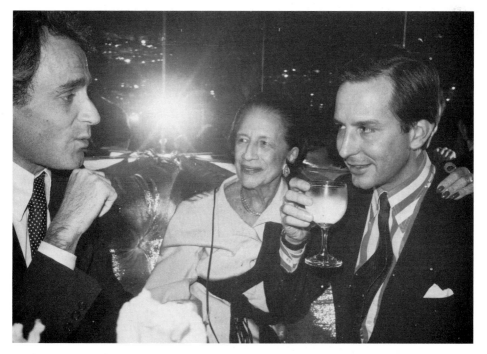

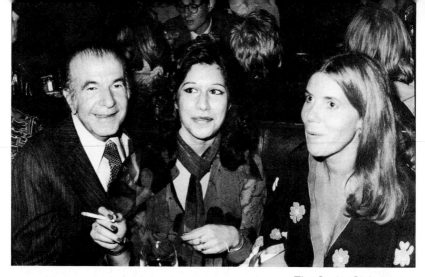

The Caviar Club: Iranian Ambassador to the UN Fereydoun Hoveyda, Nima Farmanfarmaian, and Gisela Hoveyda, before the Shah's fall. (Photo Robert Hayes)

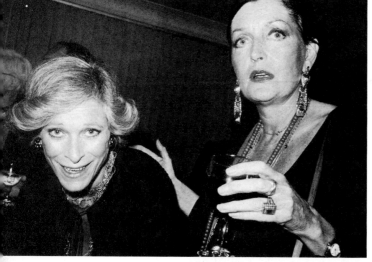

Nan Kempner, *(left)* a Warhol portrait client, and Maxime de la Falaise McKendry, who starred in *Andy Warhol's Dracula.* (Photo Bob Colacello)

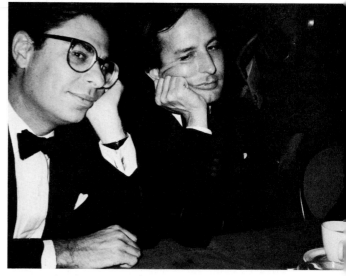

Social workers: me and Fred Hughes. (Archive BC)

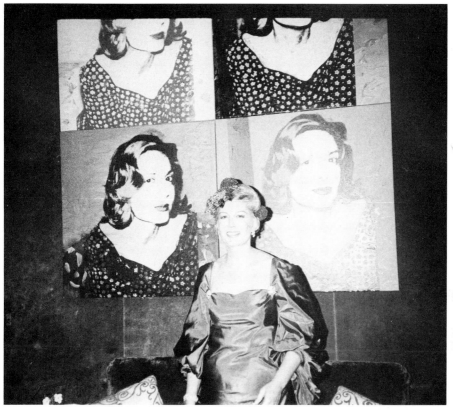

São Schlumberger and her Warhol portraits at home in Paris, 1981.
(Photo Bob Colacello)

Diane von Furstenberg, a Warhol portrait client and *Interview* advertiser, and me in her Fifth Avenue salon. (Archive BC)

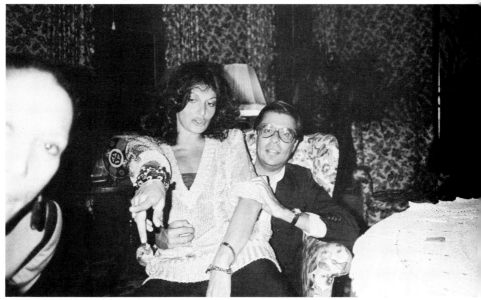

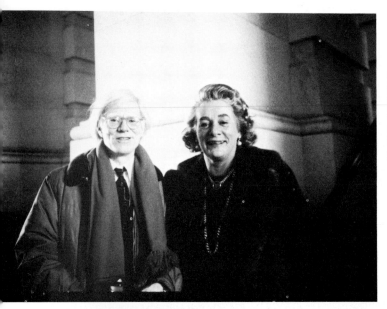

Andy with Happy Rockefeller, a portrait client, outside the United States Capitol after Reagan's 1981 inaugural ceremony. (Photo Bob Colacello)

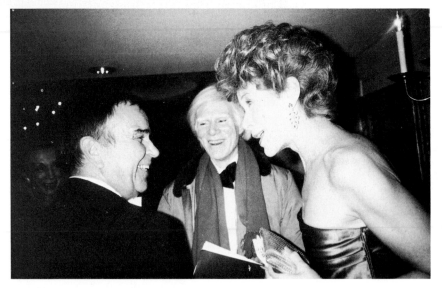

Former Carterite Andy with Reagan White House decorator Ted Graber and Betsy Bloomingdale at the inaugural bash. (Photo Bob Colacello)

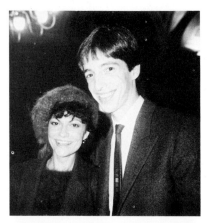

Ron and Doria Reagan, my secretary from 1981 to 1983, at the inauguration. (Photo Bob Colacello)

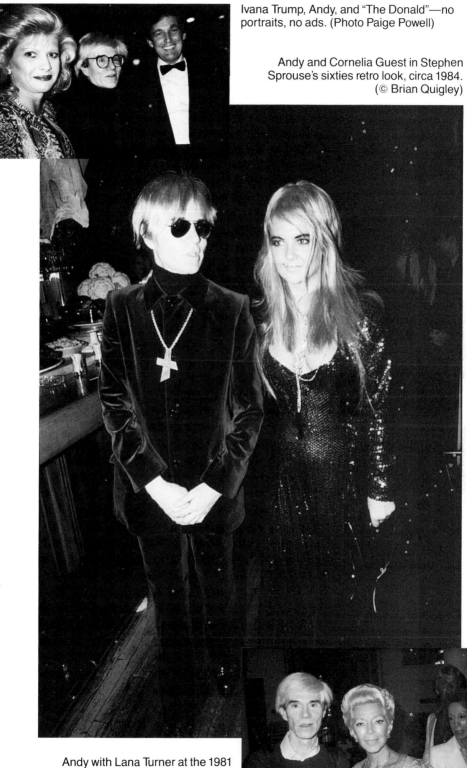

Ivana Trump, Andy, and "The Donald"—no portraits, no ads. (Photo Paige Powell)

Andy and Cornelia Guest in Stephen Sprouse's sixties retro look, circa 1984. (© Brian Quigley)

Andy with Lana Turner at the 1981 Deauville Film Festival. (Photo Bob Colacello)

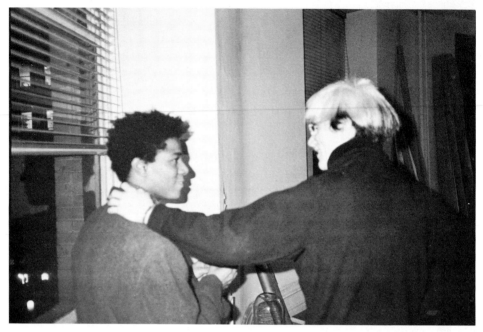

Andy making a rare gesture of affection, to artist Jean-Míchel Basquiat. (Photo Paige Powell)

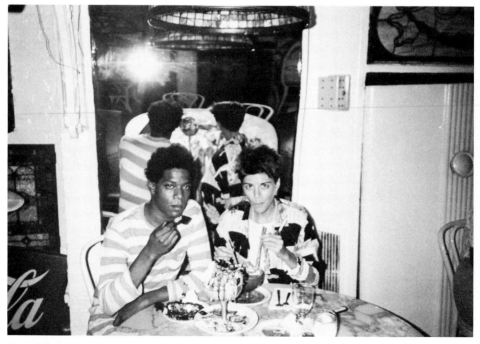

Jean-Michel Basquiat and his girlfriend Paige Powell, *Interview* ad director from 1983, at Serendipity. (Collection Paige Powell)

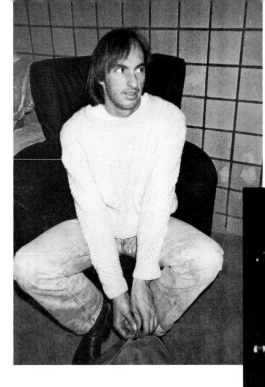

"These things just happen," said Andy of his obsessive relationship with Jon Gould, a Paramount Pictures vice president, here at the final Factory, circa 1983. (Photo Paige Powell)

Factory assistant Sam Bolton, Andy's last crush, 1986. (© Tony Guzewicz/Globe Photos)

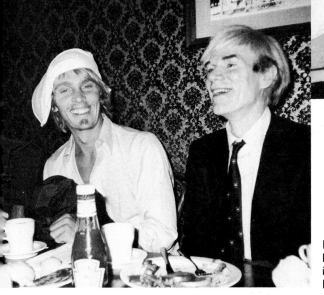

Photographer Christopher Makos played cupid for Andy in the eighties. (Photo Paige Powell)

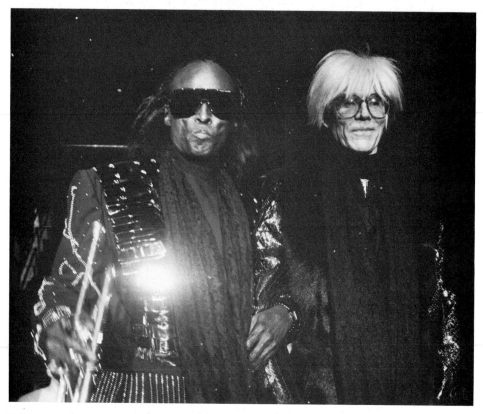

February 17, 1987: Despite severe gallbladder pains, Andy modeled in a celebrity fashion show at the Tunnel disco with Miles Davis. Five days later he was dead. These are the last photographs taken of him. (© Mark Cafferty)

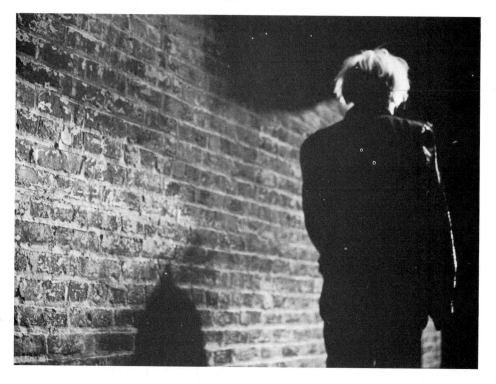

But he didn't think it was funny one Thursday in February 1978, when he arrived at the Factory carrying shopping bags full of "space toys," which he said was his "new collection"—and Fred screamed at him, really ranted and raved at the top of his lungs. "Why don't you start a pins collection? A needles collection? A scissors collection? A paper-bag collection?" This time *I* thought it was funny.

That was also the day that Andy unveiled his latest series of self-portraits. He returned to self-portraiture as regularly as Rembrandt, though I never thought he was trying to find himself. It was more like he was trying to leave an image for history of the way he wished he looked. It was another revision, another lie, though lies in their way tell other truths. These were stunning: double and triple exposure of Andy's profile in negative, white on black, red on black, black on black. He looked like a calm, neat, beautiful ghost. It wasn't easy working for a ghost, especially one who wanted to be calm, neat, and beautiful, and wasn't.

But there was something else in these self-portraits too, in the eyes especially, and you only saw it if you looked long enough: the fear, pain, and sadness that were always there, no matter how much Andy tried to silkscreen them out. And it was because I could see that, because I knew it was there, because I felt that whatever anguish I was going through, or Andy was putting me through, he was going through, and putting himself through, ten times more—that's why I stayed. I think that's why Fred stayed too. And maybe he stayed to the end, unlike me, because he understood it better than I did all along.

It wasn't easy. Fred paid a very high price for his devotion and loyalty to Andy. His health. His physical problems started around 1978. Sometimes it only took Fred a couple of glasses of champagne to fall down. He didn't pass out; he buckled at the knees and crashed to the floor. It was strange, but Fred dismissed it.

Diana Vreeland sensed our serious health problems long before Fred and I did. In late January 1978, after I'd been in bed three more days, she called and said she was worried about her boy around the corner. "You boys have too much on your shoulders," she told me. "My God, you boys *run* this city. Whatever Andy says, goes!"

Bernardo Bertolucci put the same idea another way: "A visit to New York wouldn't be New York without seeing Andy." The city would have gone on quite nicely without any of us, but Andy was the only artist in the middle of everything that counted in New York—fashion, media, money, politics—and Fred and I helped him get there and stay there. Andy was committed, driven even, to get to the top, get to the bottom, get it all down, and not only for himself, or fame, or wealth, or power, but for his art. He wanted to see everything and record everything, know everyone, and paint, photograph, and interview everyone. It was a daunting, endless task, and it took a lot out of him, and us.

Only those closest to him knew how determined and thorough this project was, because Andy deliberately made everything he did seem effort-less—and meaningless. He liked to turn everything, including himself, into a party joke, partially to hide his true intentions, partially because it was the only way he could deal with life. He expected us to get the joke and simultaneously to take it seriously. It was nothing more or less than he expected of himself. We were all walking a tightrope, and Andy's rope was thinnest and highest of all. "If I think about things too much," he told me many times, "I'll have a nervous breakdown."

Maybe that was one reason why Andy flirted with coke, though he was really sneaky about it. It's rarely pointed out, but cocaine is not only a stimulant, it's also a painkiller. The most immediate effect is numbness. And Andy wasn't taking anywhere near as much as the rest of us because he knew that he had the most addictive personality of all. It came out in his shopping, collecting, painting, pill taking—and in the way he'd throw back four or five straight vodkas in a row when he wanted to "get good and drunk." Of course, he always denied taking coke. I even heard him deny taking it as he was sticking it up his nose.

One night in April 1978, Andy and I had dinner at La Grenouille with Mick Jagger, Jerry Hall, and Barbara Allen. Then we all went back to Mick and Jerry's suite at the Pierre Hotel to listen to an advance tape of the new Rolling Stones album, the one with "Miss You," which Jerry said was written for her while she was away from Mick on a modeling assignment. Mick rolled some joints and poured some coke out on the coffee table. "Should I try it?" asked Andy. "Just this once to see what everybody's doing? Oh, I can't, I just can't." Then he quickly stuck his finger in it and rubbed some on his gums. "It's not really taking it," he said. "It doesn't get inside, does it? It's just making my mouth feel funny, like going to the dentist."

Andy had obviously done this before, and he had figured out a way in his mind to take it without taking it, just like sucking on chocolates and spitting them out and saying that wasn't "eating" them. Then, when he thought I wasn't looking, he stuck his finger in the pile and sniffed the coke up his nose. "You took it, Andy," I said. "I did not, Bob. You're making it up." Everyone laughed, including Andy, and when Mick went into the bedroom for a minute, he nudged me and said, "Do you think Mick will mind if we take some more?" He rubbed some more on his gums, saying again, "This isn't really taking it."

Later that same evening, we stopped off at a small party on our way to Studio 54, and another guest took out some cocaine. "Oh, I've never had it,'' Andy told him. "Can you teach me how to use it? Explain every step to me. It's so fascinating.'' So he showed Andy how you chopped it up, put it in lines . . . and then most of us dipped in, including Andy.

Finally, at three in the morning, we made it to 54, where Andy ended up in the basement, playing pinball with a press scion in a boiler room. Andy asked me to get more coke, and when I came back with a gram, he said, "Oh, let's take it here, so nobody sees us.'' I told him that everybody had seen him take it at the Pierre and the party, and he said, "But I didn't take any anywhere, Bob.'' Then he rubbed his white-tipped fingers across his gums. "I'm not taking it, Bob. I'm really not. You can't say I did.''

I started calling him a new nickname in my diary: The Great Denier. In February 1978, there was another scene he denied, or at least his raunchy role in it. Vincent and Shelly gave a party in their new apartment near Washington Square. The entire Factory was there, except Jed, mixing and mingling in the downstairs living room with Shelly's friends from Bonwit Teller, where she designed ads. Andy hung out in an upstairs bedroom with Victor Hugo, Chris Makos, and Ronnie Cutrone, who seemed to be having a gross-out contest for the boss's benefit. The boss loved it. They were bragging about how much their penises weighed, and Chris dared Andy to give him a blowjob. "C'mon, Andy,'' he said, "suck me off. You know that's what you really love.'' Andy tittered, and rubbed his tape recorder against Chris's crotch, as Chris necked with his new boyfriend, Peter Wise. Then Victor Hugo grabbed his latest discovery, and Andy held poor Sony between their grinding groins as he photographed the action with his free hand. I couldn't believe any of this was happening at Vincent and Shelly's joint office party. Even Catherine was disgusted. The three of us took a taxi uptown, and when Catherine and I called Andy on his tacky behavior, he said, "I didn't do anything bad, it was all Chris Makos.'' What about tape recording their crotches, I asked. "You're imagining things, Bob.''

Vincent and Shelly had married secretly in August 1977 in Montauk. He had wooed her away from Larry Rivers, and perhaps they were afraid the hot-tempered artist might show up. But then Vincent was secretive about everything, including how to change the paper on the Xerox machine. Needless to say, it was a quality that Andy appreciated. Vincent was privy to the contents of Andy's will. He kept the books, opened and closed the office, collected on Fred's art deals and Paul Morrissey's old movie-distribution deals, dealt with Montauk, the lawyers, the company pension plan, insurance coverage, bank accounts, and tax audits. In his spare time, he tried to produce Andy's TV show, which in 1978 was *still* in the experimental stage.

Andy was the best man at Vincent and Shelly's wedding. And he never made fun of their marriage, as he did of any romance the rest of us had. He wanted Vincent's life to be stable and homebound, to keep him doing all the dull tasks nobody else at the Factory would do. Andy was also the godfather to their first daughter, Austin Grey, born in 1982.

In many ways, Vincent was Andy's favorite "son." He was the one who started calling Andy "Dad" and "Pop." Vincent never yelled at Andy, like Fred and me, never mocked him in front of other people, like Brigid and Catherine. Sometimes Andy encouraged that behavior in his kids, to prove he could get our goats, but he also resented it. Vincent had great patience with Andy, and an enviable ability to shrug off his most childish pranks with a smile. He could even get Andy to pay the bills—which was like pulling teeth from a wild rhinoceros. He'd write out the checks in advance, so that all Andy had to do was sign them, and then sit there and quietly answer every one of Andy's penny-ante questions. He was Mr. Reliable, Vincent Straight-Arrow in his horn-rimmed glasses, company man to the core, hard-working, diligent, loyal, good.

Every so often, Vincent and I got high together on vodka. Invariably, we ended up talking about office problems for hour upon hour. He complained that our latest Park Avenue volunteer, Robyn Geddes, took too long to get the lunches from Balducci's. I complained that Chris Makos took too long to lay out the *Exposures* book. And we both wished Victor Hugo would go away for good. But whenever I pointed out that only Andy could do something about these problems and never would because he liked rivalries, confusion, and craziness, Vincent always stopped talking.

By spring 1978 we had all had it with the relentless antics of Victor Hugo, except Andy. He was more enthralled than ever. "Look at these greaaat photographs from Victor's party," he told me one day at the Factory. They were pictures of Edwige, "The Queen of Paris Punks," slitting her wrists. "Victor says it's punk jewelry," said Andy. "We're not running them in *Interview,*" I said, before he could suggest it.

Andy loved it when Victor showed up at 54 in a jockstrap or at a Halston party in a Halston dress, in both cases much to Halston's embarrassment. Victor later told me that Andy actually *paid* him to do these things. He said Andy would slip him some cash and tell him. "Okay, whore, go out there and do something." According to Victor, "Whenever I went to Studio in my jockstrap, the next day he'd give me a $20,000 painting. Andy must have given me a million dollars in artwork when he was alive." Perhaps Victor was exaggerating.

"I used to torture him," Victor went on. "He tortured me. But you know what it was—the Catholic thing. I come from Catholic background. But Andy have that guilt thing. I tell him, 'Andy, you better stop making money, because if not, you'll go to the other side from where your mother went.' He used to call me sometimes and say, 'Where did my mother went?

Where she went?' I never forgot that. 'Where did my mother went?' And I said, 'Well, your mother went to the right side and you know which side is the right side. And I'm not going to name it to you.' "

I only saw Andy get mad at Victor once. Victor "got a little crazy" late one night and painted over Andy's portrait of him (commissioned by Halston) with graffitilike swirls and squiggles, thinking this defacement was as important a moment in art history as Rauschenberg's rebellious erasure of a de Kooning drawing. Victor showed up at the Factory the next day with his handiwork. "You *ruined* them, Victor!" Andy railed, slipping out of his Pop persona for a second and revealing that he cared about his art. Then he slipped right back in and added, "It's forty thousand down the drain, Victor. Did you think of that?" Victor tried to tell Andy that they were "more interesting this way, more an idea now," and even had the nerve to suggest trading them for a pair of fresh portraits. "I'm not doing new ones for you, Victor," said Andy, stomping off.

But Victor was soon forgiven. Andy gave him a lunch at the Factory for his thirtieth birthday on April 4, 1978. He also came up with a present only he could find: a big box of antique burglar alarms. For the rest of the afternoon, sirens were ringing through the Factory.

Because of Victor, Halston had become a major client, right up there with the de Menils, the Brants, the Weismans, and the Iranians. But also because of Victor that relationship was increasingly at risk. Victor and Andy couldn't resist staging their Polaroid orgies at Halston's pristine house when Halston was out of town. Fred and I both warned Andy that he was getting carried away with Victor, and that sooner or later their capers would back-fire.

Halston was also encouraging his star friends to collect Warhols. That winter, for example, he helped me get Liza's portrait, and later she commissioned portraits of her mother and father, too. When I first discussed it with her, on the dance floor at Regine's, Liza wanted a full-length portrait. She said I should tell Andy that I envisioned her that way and not to tell him that she told me to say that. I told him, knowing that he would hate the idea whether it came from me or her, and he did.

Halston put in a good word for the standard head shot and Liza came down to the Factory to sit for her Polaroids, looking frazzled, an hour late. When it was time for her to leave, Brigid asked her to sign the guest book, Andy's latest idea for further IRS documentation. "Because/because/because/because," she wrote. "You're a great poet," gushed Andy. "We'll publish your poems in *Interview,* won't we, Bob?" Liza looked amazed. "It's from *The Wizard of Oz,"* she said. "Oh, you should put your poems to music," said Andy. Was he nervous? Playing dumb? Being funny? Saying anything to ingratiate himself with a star and client?

The portraits were ready six weeks later. It didn't really take that long, but Fred said clients wouldn't like it if they thought it only took a couple of weeks, so we always waited to deliver them. Liza wanted hers delivered to Halston's office, as she was in and out of town. There were four, in Liza's colors, red, white, and black. Andy was too nervous to be there when she first saw them, so I went up to the Olympic Tower. Liza arrived with her English secretary, Diana Wemble, carrying a little gray French poodle. She looked more frazzled than the day she had posed at the Factory, shakier, paler, down. But she came to life when she saw the portraits, which made her look happy, healthy, strong, and sexy. "I love them!" she screeched. She turned them sideways and upside down and said she loved them that way too. "Are you beautiful, or are you beautiful?" raved Halston. "Tell Andy," he told me, "I think they're his best since the Marilyns." Liza took all four.

That night, Andy and I had dinner with Lorna Luft. She was really worried about Liza, she said. Andy didn't say anything. He was afraid it might get back to Liza, or Halston, and as he always said, "We don't have the check yet, Bob." In this case the check was for $70,000, and Liza paid promptly.

Elsa Peretti was also falling apart. And taking too much coke. And having her portrait done by Andy, who made her look happy, healthy, strong, and sexy. But she wasn't buying Warhols on Halston's advice anymore. She was almost doing it to spite him, to show him that she could afford anything he could, and that his friend Andy was her friend too. She was also pulling Victor Hugo away from Halston, or maybe Victor was encouraging their feud for his own advantage. It's hard to say exactly why Elsa and Halston fell out in 1978, after so many years of being the closest friends and creative collaborators. He sometimes said that he had launched her as a jewelry designer, which was true, and that she dropped him now that her Tiffany line was such a huge hit, which wasn't quite as true. She sometimes said that she had loved him, which was true, and that he dropped her now that he was surrounded by bigger stars like Liza and Liz, which wasn't quite as true.

The big break, everyone agreed, had come the night she threw the sable coat he had given her for Christmas 1977 into his fireplace in front of his eyes. Whenever Elsa's name came up after that for years and years, Andy, who was at Halston's that night, never failed to mention the incident, always adding, "$35,000 up in flames, just like that." Then he'd snap his fingers, as if to say, How cool. But he was afraid of Elsa, and worried that her squabble with Halston would spill over into our business, which it did.

I always liked Elsa. She was earthy, soft-hearted, intelligent, sometimes even brilliant. But she was an extremely demanding friend, especially when the coke got out of control, which, by 1978, it had. It's hard to write a sentence like that about a friend whose coke I took, gladly, often, in quantity. But what happened to Elsa that spring sooner or later happened to many of us, including me that fall. The coke took over and damaged some vital human part, the brain, the heart, the liver. She was just the first, that's all, as she was in many other things. She was also one of the first to get better. Some never did.

In April 1978, a few days after Victor Hugo's birthday lunch at the Factory, Elsa asked me to be her date at a dinner Harry Platt, the old-guard chairman of Tiffany, was giving at Pearl's. As we left, Mr. Platt said he was counting on me to get Elsa home early, because he was expecting her at work first thing in the morning. Elsa didn't want to go home early. She wanted to go to 54. She gave me a snort in her limo and then I wanted to go to 54, too. We got there, went down to the basement, and ran right into Halston. He was with Steve Rubell and David Geffen, the young entertainment tycoon and art collector.

At first everything was okay, but then Steve said to Elsa, "Have another vodka, honeypie." "How dare you call me honeypie," Elsa snarled. "I'm not your girlfriend. You can't fuck me." David Geffen tried to explain that honeypie was a sweet American term, but Elsa told him to shut up, that she didn't even know him. Then she started screaming, "I am not American! I am European!" "Now listen here, Elsa," said Halston. "These are my friends, we were having a nice time, you came down here, Steve was nice enough to get you a bottle of vodka. I was happy to see you, but this is why I *don't* want to see you."

I took that as my cue to take Elsa upstairs, but when I suggested it, she only shouted louder at Halston, "I am not going to be thrown out of a *basement* by a *faggot queen* like you! You're nothing but a no-culture cheap faggot dressmaker!" "And you're nothing but a low-class cheap jewelry designer for Tiffany," Halston snapped back. "Get off your high horse." "Faggot, faggot, faggot!" Elsa kept screaming. "All right, Elsa," Halston said, "if you won't leave, I will." But before he could take a step, Elsa poured the bottle of vodka all over his shoes and then she threw it on the ground in front of him, where it shattered. At that, Halston, Steve, and David Geffen went running.

"I've done it!" Elsa bellowed in triumph. "I'm finished with them! I'm finally *free!*" Then she fell to the floor amidst the shards of glass and started crying. I tried to comfort her, but she hurled names at me and said I'd rather be with Halston than with her. She staggered over to a pile of pillows in a corner and passed out. There was no way I could move her, so I decided to let her be; she had a smile on her face and was snoring softly. I went upstairs and found Halston, who asked if Elsa was all right. I went back downstairs to check on her, and finally, at five in the morning, I was able to get her up. "I'm taking you home," I said. Just as I promised Henry Platt, I thought, real early.

When I woke up later that afternoon, I called Andy at the office to tell him what had happened. He had already heard, as had half the town. "Radio Rubell," we sometimes called it. "Oh, I just know Halston is going to blame this on you, Bob," Andy said. "And then he'll get mad at me. You should've never gone out with Elsa. Why did you?" To get Tiffany ads, I reminded him. "Oh, I know. It's just too hard. Everything's so mixed up now. And Jed's mad at me because of Victor. And Victor's fighting with Halston, because Halston says he's working for me more than he's working for him. And I just know Halston's going to use this Elsa thing to get mad at us, and then he'll send back all the paintings he, uh, hasn't paid for yet."

Four days later, Halston called me at the Factory. "That was some night with Miss Peretti, wasn't it?" Halston said. I said I had stayed in bed the whole next day to recover, and he said he wished he could have done that, but he had a collection to do. I wished the call would end, but Halston suddenly took on a severe tone and asked, "Who *really* does business for Andy down there?" I said Fred, but asked if I could help in any way. He said he'd call Fred. I immediately got Fred and Andy and told them I thought the shit was going to hit the fan. Victor was lurking nearby and he jumped on my line with glee. "The sheet ees going to heet the fan!" I wondered why he was clapping his fists together rapidly, like a kid expecting candy.

"Hi, H, what's up?" Fred said as cheerfully as he could when Halston called a minute later. We were all around the phone, Andy, Victor, Vincent, me. Halston told Fred that he was fed up with Victor's going around town saying that Andy was fed up with Halston's not paying his bills and that if Andy needed the money why didn't he ask Halston for it in the right way and if Victor was Andy's business agent then Halston didn't want to have anything to do with Andy anymore. Fred tried to interject a calming word, but Halston was obviously on a roll.

Fred said that Halston wanted to know exactly how much money he owed, and Vincent went to his files and came back with the figure $70,000. Halston said it was too much, he was sending the paintings back. Fred said he'd try to work something out, and get back to him. But before he could even discuss it with Andy, Halston called back and asked for Victor. That was the big mistake: to let Victor take the call, to let Halston know he was there and had heard it all.

Victor, of course, was only too happy to let Halston know, and was thrilled at the opportunity to shout at him in front of the entire Factory staff. Sounding a lot like Elsa, he called Halston a tacky dressmaker and said how dare he hold money over the heads of real artists like him and Andy. When he hung up, he proclaimed that Halston was finished and he didn't care, he was in the money now with Elsa, and he was going to take Elsa to 54 that night and get her to make another big scene. For good measure, he announced that he was taking an ad for himself on the back cover of next month's *Interview,* to reserve the space. It would just be his name, he said, under his defaced portrait by Andy.

Portraits and ads, ads and portraits.

Meanwhile, Fred was back on the phone with Halston, trying to calm him down. Andy was hiding out in Vincent's office, wailing, "I'm staying in for the rest of my life. I just don't want to see anybody anymore. People are too crazy. I'm never going out."

When Victor left, Andy came back into the front room and said to Fred and me, in a unusually contrite tone, "I have to get a divorce from Victor. But how am I going to do it?"

Fred screamed at him: "I told you all along not to get this involved with Victor!"

"But he was the one who really taught Halston about modern art, Fred," said Andy. "And I thought I was helping to get Victor out of Halston's hair by giving him work with us. Oh, what are we going to do? Halston's going to send all those paintings back."

Seventy thousand was a sizable loss, the equivalent, more or less, of *Interview*'s printing bills for three months, or a year's rent at the Factory. On the other hand, Andy probably spent that much in one month of daily shopping, and 1978 was the year of the $800,000 Portraits of Athletes commission from Richard Weisman, just for starters.

And, in the end, Halston's paintings didn't come back. Fred and I worked things out with him at our after-hours office, Studio 54.

Andy stayed in for two more nights. Then he couldn't take the reports from Radio Rubell about Ryan O'Neal bringing Tatum to 54 two nights in a row and everything else he was missing, and he gave up his self-imposed house arrest. His first night out, after a couple of Park Avenue dinners and a couple of hours at 54, Andy and I ended up with Halston, Liza, and Baryshnikov on the twenty-first floor of the Olympic Tower at three in the morning. I helped Halston serve drinks, Liza turned her portraits every which way for Misha, and Andy stood there beaming. "This is such a great night, Bob," he kept saying. "Gee, thanks for taking me out." At four we all went to Hurrah, and at five, when I saw Andy and Halston leave together, chatting and laughing, I finally felt that my work day was over. I remembered the name and address of an after-hours bar, the Cave, on East 22nd Street, where someone told me all the disco bartenders and waiters went when they got off work. It was seven in the morning when I got home, as blitzed as blitzed could be.

I didn't come to until I heard the doorbell ringing—it was Brigid. She said Andy and Fred had started worrying when I still hadn't shown up at two in the afternoon, especially since it was deadline day at *Interview.* I felt like an old man as she made me coffee, then took me down to the office in a taxi. Fred sent out for lunch for me, and when I told him that I couldn't remember anything I'd done at the Cave, but somehow had lost my glasses, he said, "Everybody's entitled to a nervous breakdown now and then." "Especially if you work at an insane asylum," I thought. I went back to Andy's studio and apologized for being so late on deadline day. "That's okay," he said. "You did such a good job making up with Halston." He paused to dip his brush into different-color paints, then said, "I just hope Bianca doesn't find out we're putting Jerry on the cover, Bob. Because if she gets mad at us, Halston will too."

"Blame it on me," I told Andy wearily. "Jerry Hall is a hot story right now, and I've got a magazine to run." I didn't *always* put the portrait business ahead of the magazine, even though Andy wanted it that way. But just in case, I instructed the *Interview* staff to keep quiet about Jerry's cover, at least until Bianca left for London after her birthday party on May 2.

Bianca cut her 54 cake between Ryan O'Neal and Baryshnikov that year. The year before it had been Mick and Baryshnikov. Andy kept whispering in my ear, "I hope she doesn't find out about the cover, Bob," and "Do you think Steve knows?" I finally snapped, "Not unless you told him!" and went off to dance with Truman, who was wearing a white hat, white scarf, white shirt, white sweater, white pants, and white shoes, and was extremely drunk on white vodka. A little while later, I was at the bar, trying to get a drink for Nan Kempner, when Truman tugged at my jacket and asked me to dance again. "Wait a second, Truman," I said, not thinking, "I'm getting Nan a drink."

"You mean that bitch Nan Kempner—Jerry Zipkin's best friend?" She heard what he said, and kept her back turned to him. "Come and dance," Truman ordered.

"C'mon, Truman," I said. "You're both my friends and I want you to make up. C'mon, Nan, turn around."

"Don't ask me to talk to that stupid bitch!" Truman screeched, slapping me across the face and knocking my glasses into my eye, which later turned black. I eventually put Truman in a taxi that night, and headed down to the Cave again, getting home sometime after ten in the morning.

Somehow I made it downstairs to Quo Vadis for lunch with an *Interview* advertiser, then I crawled back into bed. That night at a John Richardson party, Fred decided to have a "man-to-man talk" with me. "You can't keep going to crazy places like the Cave. You've got a great career ahead of you, Bob, and you're throwing it away." Then he suggested going to 54, where we ran into Little Eddie, who found some coke. We ended up at the Cave—talking about why I shouldn't go to the Cave, and other pressing office problems, like Brigid versus Catherine, Vincent versus Ronnie, Victor versus Halston, Bianca versus Jerry, and Jed versus Andy. Little Eddie tapped me on the shoulder. "I just wanted to ask you, Do they always have police in this place?'' I turned around, and sure enough, the place was being busted. The lights went on, the music went off, and I told Fred and Little Eddie to follow me quickly; I knew a secret exit.

The next birthday party that May was mine. It was at Diane von Furstenberg's big new apartment on Fifth Avenue. I was thirty-one years old, though Jerry Zipkin insisted that my sixty-one-year-old father looked more like my brother. My parents had the time of their lives, or so I like to think. Eleanor Lambert told my mother the Factory was actually the most fashionable place to have lunch in New York. Ambassador Hoveyda told my father that he was arranging an embassy for me in my old age. My mother told Halston that he put American fashion on the map. Halston walked me into a walk-in closet and gave me my (sparkling white) birthday present. Bianca told me she had put off her departure for London for me. I felt guilty about the Jerry Hall cover, until I heard that David Bowie was waiting in his limo downstairs for her. Little Eddie accidentally burned my sister Barbara with a joint. Tommy Kempner told me to tell Truman, who didn't show up, that if he bothered Nan again he'd send his six-foot-two son after him. Andy came late and left early, but I didn't care and I didn't take too much coke, or go to the Cave.

Two days later, I was rushing to get down to work, when Victor Hugo called and asked me why nobody wanted his ad in *Interview*. He had abandoned the idea of using Andy's portrait of him, but his new layout was almost worse: a Polaroid of Victor showing off his hairy armpit, with type exactly like Halston's ads. I tried an indirect response, saying that even Andy thought Victor was wasting his money advertising nothing in particular. "Eet's not Andy," he lashed out, "eet's you, you asshole licker. If you want to lick an asshole, lick mine—I have a bigger asshole than Halston! I am artist! You and your *Interview* lackeys are nothing, you're shit, you're assholes!" I knew Victor was calling from the Factory, and most of this was just another performance for his drinking buddy Ronnie Cutrone and the rest of the staff, just like his harangue at Halston. I had brought the phone into the bathroom with me and was actually sitting on the john as Victor hurled the scatological insults at me, so when he hung up mid-asshole, I just flushed the toilet and thought, that's the end of Victor Hugo for me, flushed, gone.

I was mad at Andy for starting up with Victor again, for not just telling him himself that we weren't running the ad because it was an insult to Halston and inappropriate for a magazine that was chasing after Bonwits and Bergdorfs, Bulgari and Carimati, and starting to get them. So when I got to the office I marched into the front room, where Andy was sitting on the windowsill reading Liz Smith and Suzy. "Listen, Andy," I said, "I'm sick and tired of Victor. He's not an artist, he's a window dresser who once read a book on Dadaism and I can't believe that you think he has good ideas. And if he thinks I'm going to go through another fight with Halston so he can do some stupid self-indulgent ad, he can just forget it. And you can forget it too.''

Andy finally put his paper down. ''Just because Victor yelled at you,'' he said, ''doesn't mean you have to yell at me.'' I said that *U.S. News & World Report* had just committed to four ads in the summer issues, and that I wanted to put those on the back covers. Fred said that was a good idea, but Andy huffed off. The next day he came into my office and said, ''Do you really want to ruin a person's life, Bob? I mean, Victor says we'll be ruining his life if we don't run this ad.'' I told Andy that if we did run it he'd be ruining my life, and he'd have to choose. Andy said that Fred would have to work it out. Fred took one look at Victor's hairy armpit photo and said there was no way that could be the back cover. Andy said that Fred would have to call Victor ''with the bad news. I'm staying out of it,'' he announced so Ronnie could hear. ''It's you and Bob who are doing this, Fred. Not me.''

That was on a Friday. On Monday, Victor called the Factory from San Francisco, where he had gone with Elsa for a Tiffany promotion. His message said he was going to get back at Halston and Andy, and he mentioned Valerie Solanis.

Fortunately, Victor stayed in San Francisco most of that summer. Halston rented a house in Fire Island with Steve Rubell. Andy rented Montauk to the Cocaine Cowboy. The whole gang, including Victor, got back together in August for the fiftieth birthday party Halston gave Andy at the 63rd Street townhouse. Steve Rubell gave Andy a silver garbage pail filled with one thousand brand-new dollar bills, and he and Victor dumped it over Andy's head. Andy scrambled to pick up every single single off Halston's floor.

Halston also gave a ''drag party'' that summer. The boys came as girls, and the girls came as boys. Fred and I weren't invited. Andy blamed it on Halston, but Halston later told me that Andy didn't want anyone from the Factory there, except Catherine—who went as a 54 busboy, in satin shorts and no shirt. Andy went as Dolly Parton.

The Factory summer was bracketed by two trips, during which all the pressures and tension of the office burst into the open. In June, we went to London for the opening of Andy's Athletes exhibition at the Institute of Contemporary Art, and Fred's drinking problem became undeniable. In September, we went to Los Angeles for the opening of Andy's Torso show at the Ace Gallery, and my liver problem became undeniable. Andy denied both.

The London trip got off to a bad start when Jed refused to go at the last moment. After the limo picked up a sullen, silent Andy, we headed uptown to Fred's, then took the Concorde to Paris—we always stopped in Paris whenever we went to Europe, and Andy always flew the Concorde now.

After the first time, in 1977, when the residents of Howard Beach, near JFK, were still trying to get supersonic flights banned because of the noise, he said, "It's the only way to fly. Everyone looks really beautiful and has great luggage. It's just like going to lunch in the best French restaurant, and just when you're finishing your cognac, you land. They should give all those people in Queens a free ride and then they wouldn't be against it." By the summer of 1978, five or six flights later, he was blasé about the Concorde—and stealing the streamlined silverware. He probably had service for forty-eight by the time he died. His only comment this trip was "Gee, every seat is full. Except Jed's."

The minute we got to the Rue du Cherche-Midi apartment, he said he wanted to go home. And he wouldn't go to Club Sept to check out the town, as he always did our first night in Paris. "You and Bob can do it for me," he said to Fred, handing him $200. "See where the money is and then I'll go with you tomorrow night."

Andy picked up as we got into our usual social swirl—lunch at São's, drinks at Yves's, dinner next door at André Oliver's, where a royal princess gave Fred a pill because she thought he looked depressed. Andy blamed that one pill for Fred's strange behavior during the rest of the trip, not too much champagne—or too much Andy.

The next night Florence Grinda, one of our best Paris friends, arranged for us to take Rod Stewart and Alana Hamilton to dinner at Maxim's. Rod and Andy had never met, and they were both obviously thrilled to be in each other's limelight. Rod was wearing a white suit with a black-and-white polka-dot bowtie and white opened-toed sandals, and all eyes were on us as we slipped into the number-one table. Fred ordered champagne and caviar to start. Then, out of the blue, Fred started kissing Andy. On his cheek. On his neck. On his shoulder. And telling him how much he loved him. "Stop it, Fred," said Andy, turning as red as borscht. "You don't believe me, do you?" persisted Fred, giving Andy another peck. The whole restaurant was watching. "Fred, stop it!" But Fred wouldn't stop, and he continued bussing Andy as we headed for Regine's in Rod's Rolls. Fred got crazier at the nightclub, throwing himself all over Andy and trying to kiss him on the lips. Andy turned his face away, but otherwise he just sat there, saying nothing, pretending this wasn't happening, as Fred giddily told him, "I really love you, Andy. I really, really love you."

The next day Fred was kissing Andy again at lunch at Yves Saint Laurent's. And the day after that, in London, he made a big scene on King's Road. It was hard to tell if he was being funny, or flipping out. We had lunch with Bianca, and then when we were windowshopping, Fred started pointing at Bianca and Andy and shouting like some circus barker, "You've read about them! You've heard about them! You've seen them on TV! Now meet them in the flesh! Andy Warhol and Bianca Jagger! Autographs only fifty pence!" Two punk kids actually stopped, but they told Fred they didn't want to pay. Meanwhile, Bianca was so embarrassed she was hiding out in a shop. And Andy just stood there, not knowing what to do.

Fred really flipped out the next night at a grand ball at the Turf Club. As we pulled up to the stately neo-Classical building, Andy said, "Gee, this is so much bigger than the White House." He and Bianca headed up the marble staircase to the Duchess of Marlborough's table. Fred and I hung back at the bar. Fred slipped into his high-toned tour-guide mode, going on about the club's history and architecture. Then, suddenly, he started crying, and saying that he couldn't take it anymore, all his great friends from the nineteenth century had died. Nick Scott, Jade Jagger's tutor, and I tried to get him back on track, but he started screeching, "You don't understand! You don't understand!" We steered him out to the garden and tried to calm him down. "All my friends are dead," he sobbed. I shook him and shouted, "Fred, this is the twentieth century! Forget all this crap about the past. We're living in the best time ever." I was trying to snap him back to reality, but I was also fed up with years of Fred's nostalgic poses and fantasies. "They're all dead," he kept sobbing, "everyone I ever loved."

I left him with Nick while I tried to find someone with coke, thinking that would sober him up—I know, I know, but I wasn't all that sane myself at that point. When I couldn't, I decided the best thing to do was tell Andy we had to take Fred back to the hotel. It was quite late anyway—this was our third party that night. Andy and Bianca were holding court for a bevy of young Guinnesses—Sabrina, Miranda, Hugo, and Erskine. I told them to meet me at the front door in about ten minutes. Then I went back downstairs and out to the garden to get Fred, who was in a daze, and Nick, who said he'd drive us back to the Dorchester. Finally, we were all in the car—Andy, Bianca, Fred, Nick, and I and an antique chair that Nick was delivering to his girlfriend—and about to take off, when Fred threw open the door and lurched out. "Fred," I shouted, as he literally *skipped* back into the Turf Club in his natty tuxedo. "Oh, you have to get him, Bob," said Andy. "I'm not getting him, Andy," I said. "I've had it."

Fred was very late for the lunch we were giving the next day at the Dorchester, and Andy was worried. Not about Fred, who was on the way down from his room, but about the message we had received from the manager that morning, asking us to check out right after lunch, two days early. "What could Fred have done to make them so mad at us?" Andy wondered. One of the girls at lunch said that she had been among the last to leave the Turf Club at five in the morning and she had seen Fred lying on the marble floor, raving at a servant who was asking him to leave, "I will not leave my house! This is my house! You don't understand!" She claimed that the servant swept Fred out the door with a broom, and that made Andy laugh.

Finally, Fred appeared, looking remarkably fit and elegant. He said that he had worked out everything with the manager and we wouldn't have to change hotels. "I reminded him of just who you were," he told Andy, "and just how much money we've spent in his hotel over the years." His accent was at its most clipped and English. "But why would they want us to leave early, Fred?" persisted Andy. "What did you do that was so bad?" Anyone else would have waited until he was alone with Fred, rather than ask in front of a table of twelve. But that was a Warhol specialty: public humiliation as entertainment.

Fred handled it as well as anyone could under the circumstances, casting his embarrassing confession as a perfectly normal night of fun and games. He said that he had "insulted a few more silly English debs at the Turf Club."

"We heard you were pushed out with a broom, Fred," Andy interrupted.

"I wasn't pushed out with a broom, Andy," said Fred, and continued his tale. He had decided to walk back to the hotel because it was such a nice night. On his way he passed an open café. That was his word for it. Café. At five in the morning. There he met five Scottish construction workers and invited them back to the hotel for a drink. When he arrived at the hotel, he checked his watch and wallet at the desk, a perfectly normal thing to do, though for some odd reason the stuffy staff seemed shocked. At that point his story skipped to its conclusion: He was missing his key and his shoes.

"You mean your handmade Lobb's shoes, Fred?" asked Andy mercilessly.

"Yes, my Lobb's shoes, Andy."

"You mean, your shoes fit some Scottish construction worker?"

At that, everybody laughed. Even Fred. What else could he do? He was crying out for help, in his own mixed-up way, and kept getting his pleas thrown back in his face as jokes.

A few nights later, back in Paris, he was screaming at the deejay at Castel's for playing a foxtrot when he had requested a waltz. "I deserve better treatment than this!" he shouted. "I've been coming to this dump since I was twelve years old!" Was Castel's even open, I wondered, in 1955?

Whenever I tried to say to Andy that I thought Fred had a problem, he either looked at me like I was nuts, or accused me of hating Fred. And it was difficult for me to talk to Fred about his behavior as he was supposed to be my boss. If I brought it up when he was sober, he became so embarrassed and dismissive I had to stop. If I brought it up when he was drunk, he became terrifyingly belligerent.

Plus I was having pretty serious problems of my own.

It was 98 degrees in Los Angeles when we arrived in September, but dry, as the Angelenos say, and the pain in my side was intense. We had to rush to lunch with Freddy and Marcia Weisman at the Hillcrest Country

Club, where the Athletes portraits commissioned by their son Richard were hanging in the Men's Grill. Various members told Andy, "They really are, what's the word I'm looking for, unique," and, "It's a highly unusual way of looking at sports." Andy whispered to me, "Nobody said they liked them, Bob."

Freddy Weisman offered to lend us a Rolls-Royce for me to drive while we were in town, as neither Andy nor Fred had a license, but I said I was in too much pain to drive, especially a borrowed Rolls. Freddy Weisman said it sounded like a liver problem, but Andy said, "Bob is a hypochondriac." He accused me of being lazy and spoiled as we rushed in a limo to the opening of Fiorucci's Beverly Hills branch. "This car costs a fortune," he said, "and we could be riding for free." I pointed out that I had arranged for Fiorucci to pay for the limo.

My pains didn't go away, as I sat beside Andy in a crush of five thousand kids, while he signed free copies of *Interview*. Before the end of the night, I still had to get through the Gianni Versace charity fashion show at Bullock's Wilshire and a "Kiddie Party" at Carole Mallory's, and there was no question of going back to the hotel early, no matter how bad I felt. Andy wanted me wherever he was, even though he also had Fred with him, and Joan Quinn, now *Interview*'s L.A. editor.

It was 101 degrees, but dry, the next day in L.A., and the pain was still there in my side, throbbing, sometimes dull, sometimes stronger. Wendy Stark played chauffeur in her Mercedes that day, saving Andy the dread limousine bill. We rushed from lunch in Venice with Andy's dealer, Doug Christmas, whom we called Doug Xmas, to drinks at Polly Bergen's (possible portrait), to dinner with Sue Mengers (possible portrait, or movie part for Andy), to more drinks at Claudia Ruspoli's (possible everything).

It was one in the morning when Wendy suggested going to see the former Bugsy Siegel house some friends of hers were trying to sell, and I told Andy I didn't want to go. I was feeling worse than ever and having a very hard time not drinking and not taking drugs when all around me people were partying the night away. "Go get a blow," Andy told me. "I can't have a blow!" I replied. "I'm sick." He told Wendy I was mad at her, and to convince her I wasn't, I went on until three.

It was 103 degrees, but dry, the third day, and the pain was still there in my side, sort of like Andy. Dagny Corcoran provided our free transportation, a long yellow limo, and we rushed from lunch at Tony and Kiki Kaiser's house in Santa Monica (possible portraits or movie deal), to the L'Ermitage Hotel to change, to Frederick Nicholas's house for dinner (possible portrait), to Andy's opening at the Ace Gallery out in Venice. Three thousand five hundred art addicts, kids, punks, bums, winos, weightlifters, and other assorted denizens of Venice Beach filled Market Street. Andy arrived in a cavalcade of limos and Mercedeses, because Fred and I had arranged for Tony Perkins and Berry Berenson, Marisa Berenson, Ursula

Andress, Polly Bergen, Sue Mengers, Wendy Stark, the Weismans, and the Quinns to follow us out to the beach. We had to fight our way into the gallery, which was so crowded we then had to fight our way into the back office, where we were barricaded to prevent Andy's wilder fans from knocking down the door.

There was a dinner for several hundred at Robert's a few blocks away, and getting Andy and his star-studded entourage to the restaurant was another feat of tactics and security. Somehow Pat Ast got left behind and it was quite a sight watching her, in red-and-white Halston elephant-print pants and cape, being pulled and squeezed through a slit in the door—it couldn't be opened wide or the mob would have surged in. By that time I was downing Stolichnaya at a rapid pace, and taking coke from all comers, and the pain in my side was going the way of my money, morals, and mind. Still it was hard to forget the sight of Andy autographing ''the biggest cock in L.A.,'' while Sue Mengers and Marisa Berenson looked on. Oh well, it was still the seventies, and this was Andy's Cocks, Cunts, and Assholes opening, his biggest so far.

38

Breaking Even

Interview's September 1976 issue with Diana Ross on the cover broke all previous sales records.

"Oh, really?" asked Andy, when the final count came in three months later. "Even though Richard Bernstein made her look so uh, uh, uhhh . . . dark?"

I said Diana Ross wasn't the only reason the issue had sold so well. September was always a very strong month, and by that time *Interview* circulation was on a steadily upward path that would continue all through the late seventies and on into the eighties.

"Oh, really?" asked Andy again, as if I were making it all up, then he toddled off to his studio without a word of approval, let alone praise.

But he was back in a couple of minutes, wearing that naughty-child look I'd come to dread. Then he uttered the words that always meant trouble: "Oh. I have a really good idea." I waited for the bombshell. "Let's put blacks on the next six covers."

"That's a terrible idea, Andy."

"No, it's not, Bob. You just said that Diana Ross was the biggest seller ever."

"Andy, I just told you that September was a big month anyway and we're going up anyway, so we don't really know that it was just Diana Ross. And for all we know it sold because the background was hot pink—I still think hot pink is what sells."

"So let's put a black with hot pink behind them every month."

"Andy." I was trying very hard not to yell.

"Listen, Bob, if something sells you should keep doing it, right? Let's put six blacks in a row on the cover. It would be great."

"It would be ridiculous. We're not *Ebony.*"

"*Ebony* makes a lot of money, Bob."

"Andy, the whole idea of *Interview* is to surprise people with something different every month—not to do the same thing over and over."

"This would be a surprise, Bob."

"*Andy.*" I still wasn't yelling, just gritting my teeth.

"Bob, blacks are big now. All the music is black, everybody dances like blacks. You dance like a black, Bob. I've seen you."

"*Andy.*" I just wanted him to stop and go away.

"All the models are black now. The blacks buy all the fashion now, and all the records. They go to all the movies, they have all the money. . . ."

"Andy, I can't believe you're saying what you're saying. It just doesn't make any sense."

"Yes, it does. Should we put Pat Cleveland on next? How about Cicely Tyson?"

"Andy, I'm not putting six blacks on the cover in a row."

"But Bob, it's the best idea."

"ANDY! I AM NOT PUTTING SIX BLACKS ON THE COVER IN A ROW! LEAVE ME ALONE!"

I was not opposed to Andy's idea because it involved blacks. Nor was he trying to advance the cause of civil rights. He was just thinking the way he always thought—repetitively—although even he painted his multiple portraits in different colors. I was opposed when Andy said we should put athletes on every month, Broadway stars on every month, big TV stars on every month, and young-beauties-whom-nobody-knows on every month.

It was his way of asserting control, of reminding us that *Interview* was his magazine, especially after March 1977, when his name was removed from the cover. Carole Rogers had been quietly lobbying for that for some time, passing on reports from newsdealers that potential readers often assumed that *Andy Warhol's Interview* was about Andy Warhol month after month and therefore didn't bother to pick it up. I had heard similar comments myself from first-time readers, advertising-agency types, or socialites sent subscriptions by Jerry Zipkin, who later told me they were surprised to find everything from fashion to politics inside, and not just the doings of Andy Warhol.

Prodded by Carole, I finally took the issue up with Fred, who said he was all for taking Andy's name off the cover. "He just let us put it on to please Peter Brant," Fred recalled. "I always thought it was tacky, and so did Andy." Andy agreed. "I never wanted it on, Bob," he told me in an annoyed, I-can't-be-bothered tone of voice. "Peter did. But he's not paying the bills anymore. I am. So go ahead and take it off. It probably will sell more without me."

Yet, every so often after that, when an ad lunch or portrait dinner was going well and everybody was laughing at our Abbott and Costello act, Andy would jokingly announce out of the blue, "Can you believe Bob took my name off my own magazine?" "You wanted it off," I'd counter. "Oh, I know," he'd say with a chuckle, and everyone else would chuckle too, no doubt thinking how wonderfully modest Andy was, and how jealous of Andy's fame Bob was. He even made me feel that way.

When we took Andy's name off the cover, we put the cover subject's name on, another Carole Rogers suggestion based on newsdealer input. Fred was vociferously opposed, saying it ruined the look, but Andy and I sided with Carole. To placate Fred the name had to be handwritten by Richard Bernstein to match the *Interview* logo. Soon enough, Carole was relaying newsdealers' complaints that it was too difficult to read the fancy script in the few seconds most people spent choosing a magazine from the jumble of the newsstand. Fred's solution was to order the name off altogether.

I sometimes went to Fred with contact sheets when I was unhappy with the choices made by Robert Hayes and Marc Balet—Fred's eagle eye for beauty invariably zeroed in on the most attractive shot. But more and more I avoided drawing Fred into magazine decisions, especially as he came in later and later, and always had so much art business waiting on his desk. I didn't value Fred's taste any less, but I had come to realize that for him taste was everything. News value, timing, impact were all secondary—he saw the magazine in an exclusively visual way, as if it were an object in an antique shop, a piece of decoration, the more special and exquisite the better.

Mostly we stuck to the trendy, glamorous, fast-track world we knew best, and mostly each cover outsold the same month from the year before by a substantial percentage. We had found a niche, or it had found us. We kept putting our friends on the cover: Jack Nicholson was our Christmas '76 cover, Mick Jagger done up as Santa was Christmas '77, and Bianca, set in a sapphire frame, was Christmas '78—to make up for Jerry Hall's cover earlier that year. We trotted out our glamour girls, some for the second time, month after month: Diane von Furstenberg, Berry Berenson, Jane Holzer, Margaret Trudeau, Barbara Allen, Andrea de Portago, Paloma Picasso with her new husband, Rafael Lopez Cambil, Diane de Beauvau-Craon, when she launched her own fashion line. We did Carroll Baker when *Bad* premiered, and Peter Beard when the International Center of Photography gave him a retrospective.

We also did many movie stars who appealed to us in a movie or two, before they were famous, mostly because we liked their looks and style. Sissy Spacek, Shelley Duvall, Isabella Rossellini, Mariel Hemingway, Ronee Blakley, Diahnne Abbott, and Carole Bouquet were all on the cover of *Interview* before any other magazine. We were particularly taken by the fourteen-year-old Jodie Foster, who turned up at the Factory dressed like her literary idol, Fran Lebowitz, in a tweed sports coat, Brooks Brothers button-down Oxford-cloth shirt, jeans, and Weejuns. Her mother, Brandy, had called first, asking if they could come to see some of Andy's prints, as Jodie was starting a contemporary art collection with the money she was making in the movies. When we met her, we all wanted her on the cover immediately—and not only because she was a potential client. This time the magazine and art businesses clicked instead of clashed, and Andy, Fred, and I all wanted the same person on the cover at the same time.

Usually, however, Andy and I fought about covers, and Fred only came into the process to mediate. The biggest problem was that Andy couldn't seem to get it through his head that there were only twelve months in a year. "Oh, you're going to get mad at me," he would tell me on many a morning, standing before my desk like a contrite kid, twisting his hands nervously, turning the pointy-tipped toes of his ostrich-skin cowboy boots inward. "I got really drunk last night at 54 and gave away at least ten covers. And I think I told them all they could be next month. I gave them all your number." Those were the good days. Usually I'd had no forewarning from Andy when the phone calls started coming in: from the major agent of the major star who had been on our cover just six months before, and the covers of *People* and *Newsweek* the previous week; from the aspiring actress sister of a 54 bartender; from the publicity-mad socialite who *might* have her portrait done; from the has-been soap-opera queen Andy was feeling sorry for; from the sixties Superstar he couldn't get off his back except by putting her on mine; even once from a cute cabdriver who had dropped him home at three in the morning—all calling to set up their promised photo session for next month's cover. "But Andy said," they always said when I informed them that our next several covers were already done. Or, if they were pushy, and they often were: "I thought this was Andy Warhol's magazine! Who are you?" Sometimes they demanded to speak to Andy, who usually told me to tell them he was out.

It was on days like those that I wished Andy would stick to counting ad pages. Ad pages were increasing dramatically—from 93 in 1976 to 162 in 1977, 225 in 1978, and almost 400 in 1979, the year *Interview* finally broke even. Though we still had under 100,000 circulation, our progress had been so noticeable that one night in April 1979, at a cocktail party at the Erteguns', Jann Wenner told me that he had "paid some big financial experts a lot of money to make a study of ways for *Rolling Stone* to expand and diversify. And one of their suggestions was to buy *Interview*."

Much of this progress was due to our new advertising salesperson, and later director of advertising, my sister Barbara. It was Andy's idea to hire her, not mine. He had been pursuing her ever since he first met her, in 1974, at the Rive Gauche boutique on Madison Avenue, where she was working after graduating from Rider College as a drama major. He came in, she recalls, and asked for a dress for his mother (who had already been dead for two years). She was helping several other customers at the same time, and Andy was so impressed by her carrying heavy coats from the Russian Peasant collection up from the basement stockroom that he told her, "Gee, you're really working hard. You should be working hard for me instead of Saint Laurent." The next day he told me the same thing, beginning a three-year nag. Every time Andy went into the boutique, or heard from Maria Schiano how great Barbara was doing, he would start in on how we should hire her to sell ads. And I would give him my mother's old line, Never hire a friend, or, God forbid, a relative. I didn't want my family mixed up in my business, and I didn't want Andy mixed up in my family. Some small part of my life, I felt, had to remain all mine.

One summer Saturday in 1976, Andy, Vincent, and I stopped at my parents' house in Rockville Centre on our way to Montauk. My parents weren't there, but Barbara was. Andy immediately asked her about the boutique and she launched into a series of hilarious anecdotes about some of the famous socialites who stopped there. "Oh, you have to come to work for us," said Andy. "Doesn't she, Bob?" I now was in the embarrassing position of saying no to my own sister. Fortunately, Barbara also had doubts about working with her brother.

But Andy was determined to hire Barbara. What really annoyed me was that he tried to present it as a favor to me, and cast me as an ingrate who was looking a gift horse in the mouth. Finally, when Sally Gilbert, who had replaced Sandy Brant, announced she was taking another job, Andy insisted that I call Barbara and offer her the job. "If you don't call her, I will," he said. So I called her, and Carole Rogers interviewed her, and she started in June.

Andy was right. She was great at selling. And we were a great team. We just had to look at each other to know what we meant, an advantage at the Factory, where everybody spoke in some kind of code, starting with Andy. And when I met potential advertisers at parties and told Barbara to follow up the next morning, they seemed to take a call from the sister of the editor much more seriously. Barbara rapidly increased our record and movie accounts and opened fashionable new accounts like Perry Ellis and Artwear. She also zeroed in on the most lucrative category: liquor and wine. By December 1977, she had her first big breakthrough, Wyrobowa vodka, the Polish challenger to Stolichnaya. Perrier-Jouet champagne soon followed. Her timing was perfect. The liquor companies were beginning to realize that *Interview* had a grip on the disco market, and that's where drinking trends started.

Shortly after Barbara started at *Interview,* we commissioned our first readership survey from Mark Clements Research, Inc., which does demographic studies for Condé Nast. The results defined our audience for advertisers, and I found it illuminating to know what kind of person read the magazine I was editing. For three or four years, I had instinctively been aiming to reach a young, educated, affluent, and stylish readership, but had had no real way of knowing whether it was working. Now I knew. And the results were as pleasing to me as they were to advertisers.

The basic figures: average age was twenty-seven, average income was $32,000, twice the American average, and very high for such a young group. Half our readers were male, half female, a unique mix, as most magazines attract one sex or the other. Over 80 percent had attended or graduated from college, and nearly a quarter of our readers had gone on to receive master's and/or doctor's degrees. Again, both figures were exceptionally high. We were definitely reaching the elite of the baby-boom generation.

Over 70 percent were single, and the average number of children per household was .03—"which means," Mark Clements explained, "they have nothing to spend their money on but themselves." And spend it they did. The statistics paint a telling picture of this young seventies elite: 96 percent went to the movies regularly, 84 percent visited museums and art galleries, 77 percent frequented discothèques and nightclubs, 66 percent went to rock concerts, 52 percent to the opera and ballet, 51 percent to Broadway shows, 34 percent to art and antiques auctions. They bought an incredible 84 record albums a year, and, for a generation that wasn't supposed to read, an incredible 38 books a year. And they certainly liked the high life: 56 percent drank champagne regularly, 14 percent hired limousines, and 10 percent of the car owners chose a Mercedes Benz. Fashion, travel, and decorating statistics were all extraordinarily high. In other words, *Interview*'s readers went everywhere and bought everything—except cribs, diapers, and toys. It was an advertiser's dream market.

As an editor, I was pleased by the numbers that measured reader loyalty: 65 percent responded to our readership survey, which Mark Clements said was very high; 92 percent read four out of four issues; and they turned to the magazine more than four times a month. We also had an exceptional "pass-along" rate of 4.1 readers per copy—our 82,000 average copies sold per month were reaching 336,000 readers. I was ecstatic. All the hard work suddenly seemed worth it: We were getting to people—the right people— and they liked what we were doing. Our hype was finally confirmed by fact.

I couldn't wait to tell Andy the great news. I should have known he would dismiss it. "You let Carole Rogers spend $4,000 on a bunch of numbers?" I told him that the entire magazine business was based on a bunch of numbers, and that our bunch was better than almost anybody else's. He looked at me as if I were nuts. Or was that withering stare the only way he could deal with somebody else's happiness, somebody else's success, even that of the editor of the magazine he owned? Why couldn't he see, I wondered, that my success was also his success?

He was nearly as unimpressed when Barbara succeeded in getting the all-powerful *New York Times* advertising columnist, Phil Dougherty, down to breakfast with Carole Rogers and me. It was probably the first time that we'd ever had a 9 A.M. meeting at the Factory, but we were rewarded with a full column cataloguing our recent advertising conquests and extolling the figures from our readership survey. When I showed it to Andy, he said, "Oh, great." And put his head back down into the *Daily News*.

A few minutes later he came into my office and said, "If Barbara really wants to sell ads, she's got to wear more makeup and lowcut dresses and chic high heels that she can get by trading for an ad. Then she should drop by the advertising agencies around five in the afternoon and invite the guys for a drink. You've got to tell your sister to do that, Bob." Just in case I neglected to tell my sister to turn herself into a tart for the greater glory of Andy Warhol, he constantly told her himself. Once, she foolishly told him about a client who had asked her out to dinner, which turned into a long cocktail party for two at his place. "Oh, did you go to bed with him?" Andy asked excitedly. "You *didn't?* Why not? Don't you want to sell more ads?"

Andy was obsessed with getting cigarette ads and frequently dropped by Barbara's desk to tell her to go after various brands he saw advertised in other magazines. She pointed out that they only advertised in high-circulation publications and that the absence of cigarette ads was a big selling point with the snobby fashion, jewelry, and fragrance advertisers who were the basis of our business. Andy came to me to complain that Barbara was "lazy." I tried to tell him that she was right; Calvin Klein and Halston didn't want their models opposite the Marlboro Man and the Virginia Slims girl. Cartier and Tiffany didn't want to follow Kool and True. "They call it ambience," I explained, "and it's one of the main reasons they advertise in *Interview,* because our ambience is so exclusive." It was all wasted on Andy, who insisted, "If we had cigarette ads, we'd be really big, Bob." Finally, he met an R. J. Reynolds vice president at a party and came in the next day with his card, telling Barbara that she should call him for an ad. Barbara followed orders and made an appointment with the tobacco executive. She gave him a half-hour spiel. "You'll get an ad," he told her, "when hell freezes over."

In 1979, *Interview* launched its own advertising campaign. It was designed by George Fertitta, of the Margeotes and Fertitta agency, which had been placing Kirin beer and Godiva chocolate ads in *Interview.* They came up with a great tagline: "*Interview*—We please some of the people all of the time." We took ads in the *New York Times Magazine, Town & Country, GQ, New West, Variety,* the *Hollywood Reporter,* and *W.* Andy was against it at first. "I can't believe you're actually giving money to John Fairchild's magazine."

Andy changed his tune about the ad campaign when the subscription coupons flowed in, particularly from *W.* And he was an enormous help, as always, with our stepped-up promotional efforts. Andy liked promotion for two reasons: It cost almost nothing, and it kept him in the public eye. On the first Saturday after each issue came out, Andy sat in the window of Fiorucci on East 59th Street and signed magazines. Fiorucci was style head- quarters for the disco kids, and we usually sold three or four hundred copies in an afternoon. Andy also trekked to Fiorucci in Boston, the Miracle Mile shopping center in Manhasset (with covergirl Debbie Harry in tow), the Southampton Bookshop in the Hamptons, the Hardware boutique in Fire Island Pines, wherever we thought he'd draw a crowd and sell some maga- zines. These day jaunts were rather exhausting, but Andy never said no when we asked him to do them. Barbara helped whip up a crowd by standing in the street shouting, "Meet Andy Warhol! Get a signed copy of Andy War- hol's *Interview!*" Andy always said it was "embarrassing" while she was doing it, but at the end of the day, when we toted up the sales, he always said, "Your sister really was great. We should bring her wherever we go." These promotions energized Andy—and the entire staff. It was fun for the *Interview* kids to have an outing with Andy, and it reminded them of just how famous and popular the man they usually saw as the office pest really was.

By 1979 we had a product worth promoting. Fran Lebowitz's *Interview* columns had been collected into a book called *Metropolitan Life,* which lingered on the bestseller list for most of 1978 and established our discovery as an internationally renowned author, "the natural successor to Dorothy Parker," as English *Vogue* dubbed her. Glenn O'Brien had returned to the *Interview* fold with a hot and quirky column called "Beat," which quickly became the tip sheet of the music industry, pointing the way to the latest trends in punk, reggae, and, later, rap, touting raw young talents like the B-52s long before the record companies signed them up. And in our Feb- ruary 1979 issue we boastfully announced a new regular monthly feature, "the world's greatest tale-teller on everything and *everyone*"—"Conversa- tions with Capote."

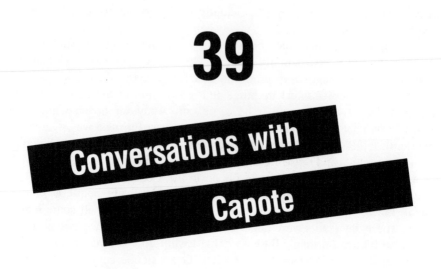

39

Conversations with Capote

It's hard to say who was really responsible for finally landing Truman as a contributor, Andy or me. The closer I had come to Truman, the more determined Andy became to make Truman his best friend instead of mine. After Andy's Athletes opened in London in July 1978, Fred and I decided to stay in Europe for Minnie de Beauvau-Craon's wedding to Duncan McLaren, a British art dealer, at the family château near Nancy. The European press was billing it as "the wedding of the year" and Minnie had agreed to give *Interview* the exclusive for America. Andy was also invited, of course, but he had reached his limit for a trip, two weeks, and was so mad at me for staying on—the first time I had done that since Mexico in 1972—that he refused to pay for my hotel room.

On my first day back at the Factory, Brigid told me, "Andy has really horned in on your affair with Truman while you were away." I reminded her that it wasn't an affair, and then called Truman to tell him I was back. "I'm having the best time with Andy," he said. "He just tape recorded one of the deepest moments in my psychoanalysis."

Andy—and Sony—followed Truman everywhere that summer and fall, from his psychiatrist to his masseur, from his barber to his dentist. "Oh, the greatest thing happened on First Avenue today," Andy told me after one of their dates. "This guy stopped in front of Truman and me and said, 'Two living legends! Wow!' Isn't that the greatest?" But there were also times when Andy arrived at the Factory with a disappointed look on his face. "Truman was boring," he invariably said. "He was trying not to drink."

I, too, was trying not to drink. After Andy's Torsos opening in Los

Angeles, in September 1978, I went to see Dr. Corcos, who had treated my anemia back in 1972, about those pains in my side, and he told me I had "toxic hepatitis," a self-induced condition that would lead to cirrhosis of the liver if I didn't stop drinking and taking cocaine immediately. "You're thirty-one," he told me, "but your liver's sixty-one. You've really got to take care of yourself for at least a year." When I told Andy, he said Dr. Corcos didn't know what he was talking about and that I should go to see Dr. Robert Giller, Halston's physician. I did run into Dr. Giller not long afterward at one of Halston's late-night bashes, and he told me he could cure me in a month with a megadose of vitamins. As he headed to 54 with the rest of the crowd, and I headed home, something told me to stick with my own doctor.

It was a struggle. Andy seemed to be waiting for me to slip, and when I did ten weeks after my diagnosis, he was finally satisfied. It meant he could spend the next day taunting me. "How come you got in so late today, Bob?" he wanted to know. I told him I had been up all night at Xenon and Crisco Disco. "How could you do that, Bob? What's your doctor going to say?"

That Halloween, I put on my black suit and a black witch's hat and headed for 54, determined to stay sober, just to prove to myself—and to Andy—that I could do it. Fortunately, one of the first people I ran into was Truman, who was proudly waving a bottle of Perrier. "I was talking to Liza and Steve," he told me, "and one was drunker than the other. They were both leaning on me." He took me by the hand, and all the while telling me not to drink, led me through the darkened tunnels and past the high piles of pumpkins that surrounded the dance floor. We stopped to chat with Lorna Luft, who was dressed as a lion tamer, and Dr. Lazare, D.D.S., who was dressed as an M.D., and his wife Arlene, dressed as a witch. We got caught up in a drag Miss Universe Contest, about two dozen men with broad shoulders and hairy chests posing as bathing-beauty contestants from outcast countries: Miss Uganda, Miss South Africa, Miss Paraguay, Miss Bulgaria. "There's that awful Gloria Vanderbilt," said Truman, "with that awful Sidney Lumet. I guess they're both so desperate they're getting back together. Heh-heh-heh." They were with Michael Jackson, who was then starring in Lumet's Ozoid remake, *The Wiz,* which got Truman cackling at the idea of starting a ménage-à-trois rumor. At two-thirty, thousands of black balloons cascaded from the rafters. Truman and I were still there, still sober, though for some reason I was sure he was on speed.

After that night, Truman started inviting me to swim with him in the pool at the UN Plaza Hotel. Whenever I arrived, Truman would say, "What took you so long? I've already done two hundred laps." Then, while I attempted ten, he'd dog paddle around me, chattering on about that day's Liz Smith and Suzy columns, spitting out chlorinated lines like "I just don't understand how that bright Aileen Mehle can go on writing about that dread-

ful Nedda Logan,'' which echoed around the pool, much to the delight of
the other swimmers.

After one of these swims, Truman asked me if I could get somebody
to roll one hundred joints as a present ''for Jack Dunphy'' on his birthday.
''He's out in Southampton,'' Truman explained, ''and he loves to smoke,
but he doesn't know how to roll the stuff.'' I asked a young friend to do it,
whom Truman rewarded with a one-joint tip and a pair of ancient formal
slippers, which he said were made especially for him by Lobb's on the
occasion of his famous Black and White Ball. The young friend wondered
why the faded stamp inside them said ''Brooks Brothers.'' I wondered why
Truman immediately started smoking the joints himself. Less than a week
later, he was on the phone asking for a hundred more. At least he wasn't
drinking, and at least I wasn't drinking with him.

The only time I saw Truman drink that fall was when Andy was with
us. It was as if he felt he had to perform for Andy's tape recorder, to tell
outrageous stories to keep Andy from being bored, to self-destruct in front
of Andy's needy eyes like so many lesser lights before him. A couple of
weeks before that Halloween party, Truman had invited Andy and me to a
Sunday brunch at his apartment. He'd said he wanted us to get to know his
new friend, Bob MacBride, better, and it would just be the four of us.
MacBride, a married man with six children, was a physicist and engineer
who wanted to be a sculptor. Truman had a history of falling in love with
married men, though in this case it was questionable whether the infatuation
was reciprocal. Andy was immediately convinced that was why Truman was
''being so friendly to us. He wants us to help Bob MacBride.'' Perhaps he
was partially right, though Andy always saw ulterior motives in everyone—
perhaps because those were the only kind he knew himself.

Bob MacBride greeted us at Truman's door and said that Truman didn't
want to be disturbed. He was in the kitchen, putting the finishing touches
on the meal he had been cooking for days. But Truman appeared soon
enough, waving his little hot-pink palms like a dancing doll, kissing and
hugging us and raving about the fantastic meal he was about to serve us. I
followed him back into the kitchen, which was suspiciously spotless, to help
with the drinks. He poured vodka into orange juice for Andy and himself,
and tried to persuade me to have a drink too. I told him I had already smoked
a joint at home, and as it turned out, thank God I had, because it certainly
helped make Truman's home cooking—cold black bean soup with globs of
sour cream; cold, slightly fried chicken, still pink; beefsteak tomatoes slath-
ered with Truman's secret-recipe ultra-creamy salad dressing—go down.
Andy and Truman were on their second or third screwdrivers, and Bob
MacBride and I were involved in a deep conversation about the relationship
between modern sculpture and nuclear physics, or something like that.

Truman kept interrupting, perhaps fortunately, to tell us how much he hated Halston, Liza, Steve, D.D. Ryan, Regine, Regine's, the Flamingo nightclub, sex with young boys, and YSL's perfume Opium. It was the liquor talking, and Sony listening, pushed ever closer by her husband. Then came the *pièce de résistance,* a homemade apple pie. "I baked it all by my little ol' self," said Truman. "Then why does it have that silver cardboard from a bakery under it?" Andy asked me when Truman went to the kitchen for another round of screwdrivers and Bob went to the living room for the plywood model of his proposed sculpture for a public square; it was based on esoteric mathematical formulas way beyond my grasp. "Wouldn't it make the best beachhouse?" said Truman of Bob's creation.

Brunch had started at two in the afternoon, and by five Andy and I were itching to leave. He murmured something about having to walk the dogs, but Truman was having none of it. It was time to go to *dinner,* he said, at his favorite Italian restaurant, which was just right around the corner, Antolotti's. "I'm not even going to change," he said. He was wearing custom-made denim overalls with a pink shirt, and topped off his outfit with a denim cap. Bob MacBride was wearing baggy store-bought jeans and an old flannel shirt. He put on a red nylon windbreaker that was hanging by the door, and Truman said, very sweetly and sincerely, "You really look good in that, Bob. I think I'm going to give you that." Bob MacBride beamed. "That was really nice," I said to Andy as we walked to Antolotti's. "Listen, Bob," he said, "when you have a wife and six kids and some famous star gives you a plastic jacket, it's like getting a diamond."

Andy made one more attempt to run home to Archie and Amos at Antolotti's door, but Truman just pushed him in. Truman ordered up more screwdrivers, an extra-large antipasto for four, and what he said was the best dish in the house, linguini with lobster sauce, then launched into my-night-at-the-Flamingo-with-Halston-Liza-Steve-and-D.D. for the fifth or sixth time. I noticed that Andy had let his tape run out, and then he managed an escape, leaving me to deal with a stuporific Truman and Bob MacBride's engineering equations.

"Andy's really a sweet boy," Truman said. "He cares about those dogs so much. I really have to find Andy a lover. I've always been a very good friend to Andy, you know. Well, I mean, after all, we were natural-born friends. But I always, oh, I don't know . . . kind of watched out for Andy. Andy used to go out with my mother. I mean, my mother was very elegant, and she *did* live on Park Avenue. She committed suicide. But Andy used to come over in the morning and take my mother out. Of course, she was just so happy to have someone to drink with in the morning, she didn't care who it was. Heh-heh-heh. But then one morning my mother said something really nasty to Andy. I never really found out just exactly what it was. But I got a pretty good idea, and then, I don't know, Andy told me about it seven or eight years later." (Andy had told me that

Truman's mother told him to leave her son alone, and called him a faggot.) Truman went on, rambling and gushing drunkenly, "I just love Andy and I love you and Fred's so nice . . .''

If Andy suspected Truman of using us to get Bob MacBride into the art world, a suspicion that seemed more likely when Truman started suggesting the four of us have dinner with Ivan Karp and Henry Geldzahler, I suspected him of using us to get himself back into Society. The *Answered Prayers* scandal of 1976 had died down, mainly because Truman hadn't published any new chapters in the following two years. Many people said he hadn't *written* any new chapters in the following two years. Diana Vreeland told us that even Truman's agent, Swifty Lazar, didn't think Truman would ever finish *Answered Prayers*. "Success hasn't agreed with Truman," she said.

Andy, of course, repeated Diana's comment to Truman and told Diana what Truman had said about the book she was working on with Chris Hemphill: "Diana's book is going to be really bad, because she wouldn't recognize the truth if it walked up to her and slapped her in the face.''

In November 1978, the Libermans gave a cocktail party for São Schlumberger. I was among the first to arrive, and Tatiana Liberman took me aside and asked if I was on good terms with Truman. She said she had invited him, but was afraid that it was a mistake, and asked me to help her take care of him. Truman and Bob MacBride arrived soon after this exchange, Truman in a brown-and-maroon plaid suit, a pink shirt, a maroon bowtie, maroon socks, and custom-made brown pumps with gold buckles. I tried to lead him into a far corner of the library, but he wanted to stand right at the top of the stairs so he could see everyone arrive.

Philanthropists Mary Lasker and Deeda Blair were the first to come up the stairs. They said hello to Truman. Then came man-about-town Bert Whitley, who didn't say hello to Truman. Joe and Estée Lauder did. Nan Kempner dashed right by into the living room, waving surreptitiously at me. Then Jerry Zipkin arrived, and followed Nan into the living room without so much as a nod. Truman said he thought it was time to circulate. I headed toward the library, but he wanted to follow Jerry into the living room. When Jerry saw Truman coming, he maneuvered his way toward the library, with Nan right behind him. Truman now wanted to go to the library, too, and I followed, just in time to see Jerry and Nan heading back into the living room. Finally, Billy Rayner approached Truman and me, and we had to stand still for a moment. "There's that dreadful Nan Kempner," Truman said provocatively. "Don't talk about my best friend that way," said Billy. "Better be careful," said Truman, "or I'll talk about you that way." I was beginning to be sorry that I had ever told our hostess that I'd take care of Truman.

A few weeks later, Reinaldo and Carolina Herrera gave "a little lunch," as they put it, for eighty at Doubles. It was a buffet, and when it came time to form tables, Countess Consuelo Crespi came to me and said in a low, nervous voice, "Do you speak to Truman?" I told her that I not only spoke to Truman, I swam with him. "Thank goodness," she said with a sigh of relief, "because Reinaldo asked me to put together a table of people who speak to Truman." She had chosen a table on the Vladivostok end of the room, and there sat Truman with Andy, Kenny Jay Lane, Denise Hale from San Francisco, and Elizinha Gonçalves from Rio de Janeiro. It seemed that the farther away from New York socialites lived, the less likely they were to be angry at Truman.

All was going well until Truman decided he was tired of Siberia, and wanted to tour the Continent. "I think I'll go circulate," he said. Consuelo, who has a nervous tic, Denise, who has a nervous stutter, and Andy, who was just plain nervous, started twitching, spluttering, and shaking. "You better go with him, Bob," said Andy. Only Kenny Lane kept his cool, as usual, saying, "Now this is going to be fun." We all watched as Truman stopped at every single table and said hello to every single person. When he came to Peter Glenville, who had been one of the anti-Capote captains in the Battle of La Côte Basque, we all held our breath. They seemed to be . . . talking! "Oh, Truman is really back in Society now," said Andy. Consuelo, Denise, and Elizinha nodded in agreement, delighted that they had accepted him at their table *first*. Only Jerry Zipkin kept his back turned when Truman approached. But then everybody said that Truman's next chapter was all about Jerry, though nobody will ever know for sure, because Jerry's prayers were answered: There never was a next chapter.

There was a next book, however, called *Music for Chameleons,* and ten of the fourteen short pieces in it were originally published in *Interview* in 1979. It all started one day in November 1978. Between swimming with Truman, smoking pot with Truman, dining with Truman, and dancing with Truman, it suddenly occurred to me that we should put Truman on the cover. Andy loved the idea: He already had entire days of Truman on tape. When I called Truman to say we wanted him on our January cover, he said he would only do it if Andy did the cover portrait himself. I explained that if Andy did Truman, he'd have to do every cover after that and we had to keep Andy's portrait business separate from the magazine's covers. "Well, if I'm not good enough for Andy," said Truman, "then his magazine isn't good enough for me."

I went to Andy with Truman's reply, and we came up with a counter offer: Andy would paint Truman's portrait, not for the cover, but as a personal gift, in exchange for Truman's contributing a piece to *Interview* every month for one year. "He really wouldn't have to do anything," Andy said. "Tell him that I'll just tape him with any person he wants every month and then Brigid will type it up and he can make something out of it. Tell him

it's a new way to write without writing. I'm sure he'll go for it.'' Truman
went for it. Then Andy started worrying that the first person Truman would
want to tape would be Bob MacBride. ''You did say any *famous* person,
didn't you, Bob?''

But Truman had been quite precise when we came to terms, and he
wasn't about to let Andy change them, or me forget them. ''Now remember,'' he had told me, ''you said I can do *anyone* I want. And my pieces
have to be the first feature in the magazine, right after the table of contents.
And there can be no advertising, photography, or illustrations on my pages,
unless I decide otherwise. The title 'Conversations with' will be in lower
case and handwritten in black: 'Capote' will be capitalized and set in *red*
type. Got that: red, not pink or orange. I can see it now. It'll look really
elegant. And the most important thing is that nobody, and I mean nobody,
including Andy, can change so much as a *comma,* without my permission.''

Yes, Truman. Yes, Truman. Yes, yes, yes, Truman. I said that a lot
during the following year, but it was worth it. ''Conversations with Capote''
made people take *Interview* much more seriously, especially people who
wouldn't deign to look at it before, like the heads of major advertising agencies, and the local literati. Even Jerry Zipkin said Truman's pieces were the
best things we had ever published, and sent out more gift subscriptions,
though he still avoided Truman when their paths crossed.

Truman's cover story ran that January, with a photograph of him in a
hot pink fedora by our regular cover photographer then, Barry McKinley,
and it sent up sales in what was traditionally a very slow month. Andy and
I taped Truman by the pool, over lunch at La Petite Marmite, up at Kron's
chocolate shop on Madison Avenue, and then over dinner at New York's first
nouvelle cuisine restaurant, Raphael on West 54th Street, where we were
joined by Ivan Karp, owner of the O.K. Harris gallery, his wife Marilynn—
and Bob MacBride, ''computer expert and sculptor.''

''Conversations with Capote'' debuted that February. Andy had taped
Truman at the apartment of Robert Livingston, a gay activist who was dying
of cancer, and at the office of Dr. Norman Orentreich, the highly publicized
dermatologist. The latter was more Andy's idea than Truman's—Andy was
still going to him for skin treatments and antibiotic pills after all these years.
Truman acquiesced, saying he liked ''the juxtaposition of life and death—
or vice versa.'' But it was the first and last time he based a piece on tapes
made by Andy.

The problem was that Andy overtaped and threw the conversations off
course, and then Brigid couldn't deal with typing up that much tape, and
Truman couldn't deal with cutting down that much material. They both
became quite hysterical over the fifty-page Orentreich manuscript, and finally Brigid exploded at Andy when he arrived at the Factory one afternoon.
''You just think the more the better,'' she told him. ''And you say the

stupidest things.'' Andy was used to Brigid's bluntness and hit back with a blunt line of his own, ''You look fat today, Brigid.''

I backed Brigid up, telling Andy that Truman's pieces shouldn't be like the interviews we did ourselves, but something only he could do. Brigid persuaded Andy to buy a tape recorder for Truman, so he could work on his own. ''Buy the cheapest one they have,'' he told her. When she brought it up to Truman's, Bob MacBride immediately noticed that it wasn't a Sony, and also gave Brigid a hard time about the interview he wanted her to set up for him with Buckminster Fuller. Then Andy accused Brigid of being in cahoots with Truman and Bob MacBride all along. ''So you made me buy that tape recorder for Bob MacBride, not Truman. Well, that's just great. I don't want him interviewing Buckminster Fuller. He's too sixties for us!''

After that, it was never clear how much of Truman's work was based on tapes and how much was based on his extraordinary recollection of dialogue. He never asked Brigid to transcribe another tape, and she never saw any tapes when she went up to his apartment to help him with his pieces. ''He would already have everything written out on a yellow pad,'' she told me later, ''in that small, neat, slightly flowery handwriting of his. And he'd go on about how he 'slaved over those goddamn tapes' and transformed them into 'little gems.' Basically, I was his audience. He'd try things out on me. And sometimes, just to make him feel that I was intelligent, I'd suggest a slight change and he'd say I was right and change it. But mostly I sat there and listened to him read from his yellow pad, because I thought everything was brilliant just the way it was.''

Brigid worked with Truman in his guest bedroom, which he had turned into an office and wallpapered with several hundred copies of his *Interview* cover. ''He *loved* that cover,'' Brigid said, ''with the pink hat and the yellow background. And it was funny to be sitting there with Truman with all these Truman heads everywhere. It was kind of like Andy's Cow wallpaper.''

Like Truman and me, Brigid was trying not to drink. It brought the three of us closer, and Truman liked to joke about our ''very exclusive A.A. cell,'' though only Brigid was a member of that organization. Andy, on the other hand, was no more supportive of Brigid's efforts than he was of mine, or Truman's. He'd often come into the office and say, ''It's so cold out, I can feel it in my bones. Wouldn't a nice hot Irish coffee be nice now, Brigid? You can have just one, can't you?'' Brigid would say she didn't want an Irish coffee, but Andy would give her a hundred-dollar bill and send her out to buy Irish whiskey and heavy cream. She'd whip up the drink for him and he'd take two sips and leave the remainder on the desk in front of her. Then, when she binged out, he'd walk around the office saying, ''I don't understand why Brigid just can't have one drink. What's wrong with her?'' In the warm weather, he'd come in and say how hot it was and suggest that Brigid whip up some piña coladas.

Of course, he was envious of Brigid's relationship with Truman. After one of her working visits to Truman's apartment, she made the mistake of telling Andy that Truman had read her "what he said was the rest of *Answered Prayers*. Stuff from old journals I think he's going to put in." Andy asked her if she had taped it. No. "You didn't tape it?" he said. "I can't believe it. What do you think you're doing? You're working for me, you know, not Truman. Do you realize what a great play that could be—Truman sitting there reading this great gossip. And you didn't tape it. I don't know what you're thinking sometimes." Brigid said that she thought it would be wrong to surreptitiously tape Truman working and then slip the tapes to Andy. "And then it would be part of your 'work,' right?" she told him. Andy gave her a filthy look, and walked away. She had hit the nail on the head.

Truman's next piece was on Bobby Beausoleil, the convicted killer who was, Truman wrote, "the key to the mystery of the homicidal escapades of the so-called Manson family." It was based on an interview he had done with Beausoleil a year earlier, when he and Peter Beard were working on a television documentary about San Quentin prison. Brigid was so impressed by it that she came straight to my apartment from Truman's and read it to me aloud. It was short, but amazingly concentrated. The character just leapt off the page at you, and just when you were starting to like him, he said something really murderous. Truman was pleased with it, too. He told me that he had "a much better grip on the form now, and it's going to get better and better and better." He said he thought Andy's interviews "meander around the personality without ever hitting it. But I'm going to show how, with just questions and answers, I can write a whole short story, or a perfect scene in a play."

And that's exactly what he did in the two best pieces he did for us, "A Day's Work," which we published in the June 1979 issue, and "A Beautiful Child," in the July issue. In the first, he followed a black cleaning lady named Mary from apartment to apartment, telling her story and the stories of the people whose homes she cleaned, in two hilarious and poignant pages. In the second, he re-created an afternoon he spent with Marilyn Monroe in 1955, and again in two pages brought her alive, as the ultimate actress, the sum total of all the insecurity, charm, and pain endemic to the breed, in a way that all the long and mighty books written about her never had.

Truman was in great form working on those pieces that spring. In February, he had had a facelift, and since then he hadn't been drinking at all, just smoking pot, lots of it. Still, he was slim and energetic, and his long-time friend C.Z. Guest told us that he hadn't been in such good shape or sounded so happy in years. "I'm glad he's getting back to his old self," she said, "and it's all because of the wonderful work he's doing for your magazine, Andy."

Andy, however, was getting worried about Truman's involvement with *Interview,* especially when Truman started calling it "our magazine." "Send him a little check every month," Andy advised me. "That way he won't really own anything. He likes getting checks. They're the only things he looks for in the mail." I explained that the copyright law didn't really work that way, and suggested that Andy get started on Truman's portrait, our agreed form of payment. "That's a terrible idea," said Andy. "If we give Truman his portrait now, he'll never finish a year's worth of work."

I began to share Andy's worries the day Truman called and said he wanted to have an "editorial meeting—first, just the two of us, and then with the rest of the staff." I suggested setting it up the following week and then let it slip by, but Truman was soon on the phone again. We had to have dinner *that* night, he told me, "to discuss all the fabulous ideas I have for our magazine." He ordered me to come up to his place directly from the office, and when I got there, handed me a cigar-sized joint of "Mauiwowee." As I took off for the Aloha state, he quickly proposed a letters-to-the-editor page, changing my "OUT" column from a diary into "something more like Liz and Suzy," and running ten pages in our next issue from Carl Van Vechten's book of photographs from the thirties, forties, and fifties. "Or do you think it's only worth eight?"

I wanted to say two, but took another puff instead and let him go on to his next idea: calling up "every major tastemaker in town" and asking his or her opinion of the latest movies, books, restaurants—"It's a very clever way of reviewing things without really reviewing them. Don't you love it?" Then he launched into his vision of our magazine, taking several more puffs himself along the way. "We're going to make *Interview* the magazine of the eighties and nineties," he said. "Just the way *Vanity Fair* was *the* magazine of the twenties and thirties, and *The New Yorker* was *the* magazine of the forties and fifties. There's no magazine that people can't wait to get; they just buy them like toilet paper now. But you just watch. When we get done with *Interview,* they're going to be fighting for it at the newsstands, hitting each other to get it first. But we have to give it a really big push and Andy's got to pull his weight. He's just not doing enough now. He's got to go on TV with me and push, push, push." I pointed out that Andy never did TV and with good reason: When we went on to promote his movies, the box office receipts always went down. "Well, I'll force him to go on," Truman said. "And I'll make him look good. I know how to do that. I'll do all the talking. Listen, honey, I'm getting paid seventy thousand bucks to give six lectures at all the University of California campuses and they're not paying me because I don't know what to do. You just leave everything to me. Should we have one more joint before we go to dinner?"

I grabbed my coat, but Truman insisted I leave it there. "We're just going across the street to Petite Marmite and you can get it when we come back here after dinner to look at the new ideas for layouts that I worked out."

I finally exited at 1 A.M., after seven solid hours of talking about *Interview* without letup. "It's like having *two* Andys now," I thought. And Andy I hated all of Andy II's ideas.

Fortunately, Truman soon left for California, and extended his tour to Utah and Illinois. Carole Rogers had two hundred copies of *Interview* shipped to each of his stops, and he signed them and gave them away at his appearances, just like Andy I. Unlike Andy I, he was also very effective at selling the magazine on the local talk shows, a fact he reminded me of after each and every appearance with a phone call to tell me "all the wonderful things I said about our magazine." He also called me the minute he landed in Manhattan that May. "C'mon over," he said. "I just got the best idea for our next cover! But I'm not going to tell you what it is until you get here." Truman's idea: Greta Garbo, painted by Andy, with fifteen of her closest friends talking about her inside. "Don't worry," he said, "I'll get them to talk." Then he handed me a large envelope bursting with "the best sinsemilla from San Francisco," and said, "Start rolling."

In July, Andy and Truman did an *Interview* promotion in Southampton. Although it was a huge success, it was also the beginning of the end. Barbara and a couple of other staffers went out Friday night and passed out flyers at the local discos. On Saturday morning they hit the beaches. We also had a skywriting plane flying from Westhampton to Montauk and back that day, spelling out "Andy Warhol's *Interview*" across the clear blue horizon—it cost remarkably little. Andy, Fred, and I limousined out with Andy's latest crush, James Curley, the dashing young son of Nixon's former ambassador to Ireland and Bush's current ambassador to France. Curley brought along Lisa Rantz, a perky fashion stylist who also had a crush on him. Andy told me I should give her a job.

We arrived in Southampton early and decided to take a walk on the beach, hoping to see Barbara or the skywriting plane. Andy turned skin-poison purple within five minutes, so we went to the bookstore. Truman was already there, signing away. "Where were you?" he said to Andy. "I've already autographed at least a hundred magazines." Truman's date was Jan Cushing, née Golding, now Amory. "So I hear," she said, "that Truman's going to do a real number on Lee Radziwill in next month's *Interview.*" Andy looked at me, and I looked at Fred, who said he was going to take another walk.

Truman had already done a real number on Lee a few weeks before on the Stanley Siegel show. He was furious at her for refusing to take his side in his lawsuit with Gore Vidal. Lee had serious problems of her own at the time, having just left San Francisco hotelier Newton Cope standing at the altar. Truman was unsympathetic. Lee had betrayed him, he said, and it was *her* fault that *he* was drinking again. Just a few days before our Southampton promotion, I was stunned to find him taking cocaine from a Princeton undergraduate in the back room at the Factory after a lunch for Gianni Versace. He had ranted and raved against Lee then too; there was no doubt that he was genuinely hurt. But this was the first any of us had heard about his upcoming attack on Lee in *our* magazine.

The line outside the Southampton bookstore grew longer and longer. Barbara was hawking her heart out, we had taken spots on the local radio and ads in the local papers, and as a further lure were serving Kirin beer and Godiva chocolates in the courtyard behind the shop. Truman was glowing, chatting up the fans and telling them to watch out for his next big piece, "It's going to be a killer-diller." Andy sat beside him, trying not to look too glum.

On Sunday, we took the *Interview* promotional tour to Fire Island Pines, with skywriting but without Truman, who said Fire Island was finished. It was actually at the height of its popularity, a nonstop orgy at the end of the Disco Decade. Rupert Smith, James Curley, and I picked up Andy in the limo. Jed was at the window, watching as we drove off. Andy said that Jed had asked him who Curley was the previous morning and he had said Rupert, and now he was worried because Jed had seen the real Rupert. "You really think people are dumb," I told him, "don't you, Andy?" He just laughed, and said, "Listen, Jed's no angel."

Marina Schiano had come with us too, and she and I attempted to hand out flyers on the beach, where most of the sunbathers were naked, on Quaaludes, and not in the mood to read, or move. The signing was at the Hardware boutique, adjacent to the Boatel, where the infamous afternoon "tea dance" was in full swing. Marina and I attempted to hand out flyers there too, but most of the dancers were in short-shorts and jockstraps, on poppers and coke, and not in the mood to read, or stop moving. "Who gives a shit about Andy Warhol" was a typical reaction. "I can see *her* any night at 54."

Monday, July 10, 1979, was the first time we asked Truman to change so much as a comma. His August piece had arrived that morning. It was titled "Nocturnal Turnings: or How Siamese Twins Have Sex," and it showed the effects of drinking on Truman's work. It was essentially Truman interviewing Truman—the Siamese twins—about everyone he didn't like, which is just what he did when he was drunk, make hate lists. This list read:

Billy Graham
Princess Margaret

Billy Graham
Princess Anne
The Reverend Ike
Ralph Nader
Supreme Court Justice Byron "Whizzer" White
Princess Lee
Werner Erhard
The Princess Royal
Billy Graham
Madame Gandhi
Masters and Johnson
Princess Lee
Billy Graham
CBSABCNBCNET
Sammy Davis, Jr.
Jerry Brown, Esq.
Billy Graham
Princess Lee
J. Edgar Hoover
Werner Erhard

He went on to write that everyone on his list was "full of horse manure" and Princess Lee most of all, because "she *is* a horse. . . . Don't you remember Princess Lee; that filly that ran in the fifth at Belmont? We bet on her, and lost a bundle, practically our last dollar."

While Andy, Fred, and Brigid stood by, I called Truman. I told him how brilliant his piece was and then started to say, "But, there's just one little thing that makes Andy nervous. Couldn't we just . . ."

"No," said Truman.

"But . . ."

"Either you publish the piece exactly the way it is or don't publish it at all."

I said that we were afraid of being sued, and he said that he would sign a piece of paper taking full responsibility; he'd call his lawyer right away. Then he asked to speak to Andy, who stuttered his way through a string of ohs, uhs, and buts, finally telling Truman that Fred had seen Lee, but then he was afraid to go any further and passed the phone back to me. Truman wanted to know what Lee had said to Fred about him, and I said that Lee was too smart to put Fred in that position, hoping he'd take a hint. I told him that Lee was not in the best shape after the Newton Cope debacle, and her children weren't exactly having an easy time of it either, and asked him to please, just this once, let us off the hook, just for me. He didn't answer. I said that *Interview* wasn't strong enough yet to get in trouble, and that Andy was so nervous about the whole thing he was thinking of canceling a trip to Europe. . . .

"Well, all right," Truman said. "I'll think it over."

As soon as Truman hung up, Bob MacBride called from the studio he had taken in 33 Union Square West, asking me to have his Bastille Day sculpture photographed for *Interview*. I told him we'd love to run a piece on it, hoping he'd report that right back to Truman. Something worked, because fifteen minutes later Truman called back and said, "Well, I've thought it over, and I'm doing this just for you, and I'm doing it just this one time, and don't ever ask me again. You can change Princess Lee to Princess X. And I hope Mr. Warhol calms his nerves."

I called Rhinelander florist's and asked them to send every orange lily—Truman's favorite—they had in the place to the UN Plaza. A few minutes after that, Truman called back and we all stopped in our tracks again. "I've been thinking it over some more," he said. "I don't like Princess X. Let's make it Princess Z. At least it rhymes. Heh-heh-heh."

Soon Truman had a new idea: He wanted the Christmas 1979 cover. "But he was already on this year," said Andy, against repetition for a change. He didn't want his own picture, I explained, but a black wreath surrounding the title of the novella-length piece he was working on: "Hand-Carved Coffins." Andy hated that idea. "A black wreath?" he said. "Oh, we can't have that on our cover, Bob. You better tell him before it's too late."

I did tell him, but he kept pushing. Finally, I decided the only way he'd accept the rejection was if we came up with someone so big for that cover that even Truman would realize it was best for our magazine. My idea: Henry Kissinger, whose memoirs were published that fall. I contacted his publisher about it, and while we waited to hear back, I kept Truman at bay.

Andy did his part too, deciding that now was the time to do Truman's portrait. We unveiled it at a birthday lunch for Truman at the Factory on September 28, 1979. It was one of Andy's best portraits: emblematic and personal, flattering but haunting. Andy did two panels and in both Truman's head and hand were floating on a white ground, as if he were lost in space, nowhere and everywhere at once. In one his fedora was bright yellow, in the other bright red, and in both his eyes were bright blue, as big and hard as marbles. Truman looked thin, smooth-skinned, and elegant, but he also looked shadowy, pulled, and plastic. I always thought that Andy's most effective portraits were of stars, because he captured the reality of their unreality, and vice versa. They were people who had become their images, and that's what so much of Andy's work was about: images, idols, icons.

Truman loved his portraits, and he loved his birthday lunch. He worked on the guest list with Brigid and me: Winston and C. Z. Guest, Lynn Wyatt, Halston, Victor Hugo, Steve Rubell, D.D. Ryan, Diane von Furstenberg, Barbara Allen. Bob MacBride was there, of course, and Truman's travel agents, Myron Clement and Joe Petrocik. Andy invited his new best friend,

Famous Amos, the cookie maker, and I came up with a surprise for Truman: President Truman's grandson, Clifton Daniels, Jr., whom I had met at Xenon a few nights before. Samantha Eggar had called that morning and said she had just arrived in town from L.A., so I asked her too. And Fred contributed two Kennedys—Kerry and Michael, the twin daughter and son of Ethel and Bobby. Then there was Mr. Ballato, who just happened to ring the bell with a panettone for Andy.

Brigid ordered a huge chocolate birthday cake, pounds and pounds of chocolate-covered strawberries and raspberries, and a singing telegram, working in the titles of all Truman's *Interview* pieces and ending with "Forget peyote, get Capote!" Brigid was so proud of herself for not drinking and she managed to keep Truman sober too. "I love you all," he kept saying. "I really, really do." He was fighting to keep back the tears.

But he wasn't about to drop the black wreath idea. He kept calling to find out if we'd heard from Kissinger yet. "*He* won't sell twenty-five copies," he said. He didn't issue any ultimatums, but he did say that he thought we'd be making "a big mistake." Meanwhile, Andy's attitude was hardening against Truman. "Who does he think he is?" was becoming a regular refrain. "His things for us aren't *that* good." I told Fred I was getting nervous about losing Truman. His advice was "Don't worry about it until there's a crisis. We function best in a crisis around here."

Kissinger turned us down at the last possible moment, thus joining the short list that included Richard Avedon, Candy Bergen, and later Meryl Streep. We decided to go with Andy's first choice all along: Priscilla Presley. She had given us an insipid interview completely dominated by her then boyfriend, model Michael Edwards—she couldn't answer the simplest question without looking at him first. She refused to discuss Elvis and only slipped once, when I jokingly suggested that she must have had lots of champagne and caviar in her Graceland days, and she blurted out, "No, never. Elvis hated fish!"

I would have fought for Truman's cover if he hadn't fixated on that depressing black wreath, or if I had liked "Hand-Carved Coffins" more. I thought it was too much like *In Cold Blood,* and that its ending was unbelievable. And Truman didn't help his case any by telling us about the December cover that *Esquire* was doing for his short story "Dazzle"—a necklace with his title and byline in the middle of it. "It's the same thing he wants us to do," said Andy. "Except he's giving them the color, and he wants us to take the black and white."

Truman never said anything to me about our decision, though he complained about it to Brigid. Just before Thanksgiving, he called her in a panic, sure he was having a heart attack. She hurried to his apartment and discovered the truth: He had been drinking and taking coke and pills for four days straight. "Nobody loves me," he kept moaning, "nobody loves me."

Though he agreed to go on contributing to *Interview* for another year, it was impossible to pin him down on the delivery of the pieces he said he was doing. He promised us a chapter of *Answered Prayers,* but then disappeared for weeks, boozing and blacking out. Lester Persky bought the movie rights to "Hand-Carved Coffins" for $500,000 and Random House accepted *Music for Chameleons* against the million-dollar advance they had already paid him for the undelivered *Answered Prayers.* It seemed that when the financial pressure was off, Truman was even less inclined to put pen to paper. And the downhill slide hastened.

When *Music for Chameleons* was published in September 1980, Truman invited Andy, Brigid, and me to a celebratory lunch at La Petite Marmite. He was half an hour late and wearing a brown shirt over a blue shirt in lieu of a jacket. A floppy brown cap hid his recent hair transplants. He got things off to a bad start by ordering Andy to turn off his tape recorder. "What we're going to discuss today," he said, "is too important to be tape-recorded." Then he launched into a fifteen-minute explanation of why *Music for Chameleons* wasn't number one on the *New York Times* bestseller list, even though it was number one on the *Time* magazine list. "But it's the first book of *belles lettres* to make it to number four on the *New York Times* list!" he said at least four times.

Then he railed against Diana Vreeland's book, which had just been published; railed against Earl Blackwell and Eugenia Sheppard, who were waving at us from across the room; railed against Cecil Beaton, for putting down *Answered Prayers* in a letter to C.Z. Guest; railed against Dick Cavett for giving him a hard time about his husband chasing on Cavett's TV show. "Why is it," he said, "that you always think of the real good line when it's too late? I mean, Dick Cavett was so rude to bring up that poor-wife bit, as if *he* just stepped out of the wheat fields of Kansas. But what I *should* have said to him was, 'And when did you suck *your* first cock, Dick Cavett!' "

Andy said he liked Diana Vreeland, Earl Blackwell, Eugenia Sheppard, Cecil Beaton, and Dick Cavett, who everyone knew was straight.

"Isn't there *anybody* you don't like, Andy?" said Truman. "I mean, I'm going to start calling you Pollyanna Warhol. There must be somebody you hate."

Andy turned an angry red and told Truman that a certain movie producer *he* liked so much was seen leaving a pickup bar with eight hustlers.

"That's nothing," said Truman. "Everybody we know does things like that these days, including some of *your* best friends, Andy. Now *I'll* tell *you* something really interesting. I have this friend who's having an affair with a father *and* a son. The father fucks him up the ass while he sucks the son's cock. Now *that's* fascinating."

"Oh, really," said Andy. It was the kind of "really" he usually reserved for weather reports.

"Is that all you can say, Andy?" said Truman. " 'Oh, really?' I don't know what's wrong with you sometimes."

"Oh, really," said Andy again, even flatter.

Brigid asked Truman when he was going to get his next piece to *Interview*. "Well, I can't give you the chapter from *Answered Prayers* I was going to give you," he said, "because it's two chapters now and I couldn't get them both done in time, but one wouldn't make sense without the other. You see? And I'm so busy anyway, because I'm doing one-hundred-seventy public appearances to promote *Music for Chameleons*—Random House says they never have had such a demand for interviews and TV appearances. And then every night in December I'm going to be reading from my work at Lincoln Center. It's going to be a real theatrical experience and Lester Persky is producing it. And did I tell you that we've got Hal Ashby to direct "Hand-Carved Coffins"? Steve McQueen wants the lead, but I don't want Steve McQueen. Heh-heh-heh."

Andy said he liked Steve McQueen.

Truman said there was *one* thing he could do for *Interview* before he rushed off on his massive publicity tour: Let Brigid interview him. "Oh, and I almost forgot the presents I have for the three of you," he said, reaching under the table into a paper bag. "This is the limited edition of *Music for Chameleons* and we only published fifty for my closest friends." He handed each of us what appeared to be the regular edition stuck in beige cardboard slipcases that could have been glued together by Truman himself. Inside Andy's he had written, "Andy! Affection! Admiration!" Brigid's inscription was "Without whom etc." And mine, "Bob, you rascal."

Andy could barely contain his disdain, but I was touched. "Well, one of these days I have to write a book of my own," I said. "You should," said Truman, adding the line he had been feeding me for the past three years, "and I'm going to show you how to do it." And then I finally received the long-awaited advice from my literary mentor: "You should have lots of pictures."

"Gee, Bob," said Andy, on the way downtown. "I thought Truman always said you were a great writer." He held his "special edition" up for closer inspection. "Who does he think he's trying to kid?" he said. "He's just a big phony, right?"

There was no mention of *Interview* in Truman's preface to *Music for Chameleons;* nor did Truman call from his book tour with a daily report of how much publicity he was getting us. In fact, he seemed to have completely forgotten that the bulk of what turned out to be his last book was published first in our magazine. Andy, however, never forgot how much money Lester Persky had paid for "Hand-Carved Coffins," which was never made into a film, and he was even more perturbed when Persky also bought the rights to "A Day's Work" for another handsome sum. "Shouldn't we be getting part of that?" he asked, more than once.

I last saw Truman in Los Angeles in 1982. He was with Lester Persky and we met at the El Padrino Bar in the Beverly Wilshire Hotel. He was already soused when I arrived, at about four in the afternoon, and berated me bitterly for going to a dinner at Betsy Bloomingdale's with Jerry Zipkin. When he died two years later, I went to his memorial at Town Hall in New York. Aside from C. Z. Guest, Lynn Wyatt, and Jan Cushing, the social set was conspicuously absent. So was Andy.

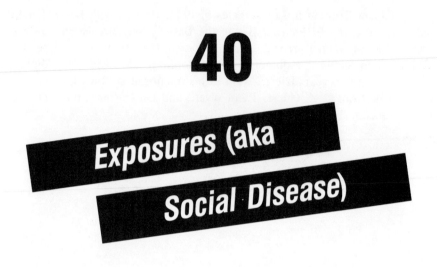

40

Exposures (aka Social Disease)

Sometimes Andy tried to be nice. And the way he did it was characteristic. He took you to a party to which you hadn't been invited. A really good party, of course, which made tagging along with Andy both more exciting and more embarrassing.

As Christmas 1978 approached, I was having a hard time keeping up with the social frenzy without vodka and coke. One afternoon when I was feeling particularly sorry for myself, Andy snapped me out of my blue funk with one of his golden invitations. "Would you like to come to Jackie's Christmas party with me?" he asked. He didn't mean Jackie Curtis, or Jackie Rogers. "Jed doesn't want to go," he added, lest I think he really was being nice, or I really was deserving.

Of course I *wanted* to go. Who wouldn't? But I was also wary of just showing up at Mrs. Onassis's, even with Andy. It was a very private party, I was a working journalist, and though we could hardly be called friends, she knew me well enough to have invited me if she'd wanted to. "Don't you think you should call and ask if it's all right?" I asked Andy. "I'm not going to do that, Bob," he said. "I'm sure it's okay. It's just a cocktail party. You can always bring a date to a cocktail party. I brought Jed last year and that was okay." I reminded him that Jed didn't write a gossip column. "Oh, c'mon, Bob," he pressed. "Just come. It'll get you out of your bad mood."

Mrs. Onassis greeted Andy at the door with a big smile, and when he introduced me, she said, "Oh, yes, I know Bob Colacello. I'm so happy you're here, Bob." She asked me what I'd like to drink, and when I said Perrier, she said they'd just run out, but someone was on his way with more.

"In the meantime, share mine," she said. "It's ours." She led me around the room, introducing me to Arthur and Alexandra Schlesinger, Peter and Cheray Duchin, and a couple who, she said, "were responsible for saving Grand Central Station." They quickly added that she was. She left me with them, saying she was going to check on the Perrier. Andy sidled up with Caroline Kennedy and told me, "Oh, uh, Bob, Caroline wants to tell you something." Caroline said, "I hope you're not writing this up in your column, with everybody's name listed or anything." I assured her I wouldn't, and Andy assured her I wouldn't too.

Lee Radziwill was there, of course, wearing purple evening pajamas by Valentino. Jackie's Valentino pajamas were red, and their good friend Karen Lerner's were black. "I guess Valentino's really the one," said Andy, who was very good at recognizing designer labels. "God, isn't this glamorous? Aren't you glad you came, Bob?" he went on. "God, there's Warren Beatty." Among the other guests were Pete Hamill, Jean Stein, Lally Weymouth with the dread Alexander Cockburn, and John Warnecke, the architect who designed the JFK memorial grave at Arlington National Cemetery. John Kennedy, Jr., who was still in his teens, sat in one corner with his school buddies, too shy to mingle. It wasn't a typical Society cocktail party by any means: Intellectuals vastly outnumbered socialites, there wasn't a bejeweled European title in sight, and I was probably the only person in the room who wouldn't vote for Teddy Kennedy. In fact, there was something in the air of Camelot Lost, something serious, sedate, hushed.

Andy was thrilled when Jackie asked us to stay on for "a little dinner." After most of the guests had left, the butler opened the doors to the dining room, where a buffet had been set out. It was very American: Virginia ham, creamed chicken, new-potato salad, Cape Cod lettuce in a very light vinaigrette. Andy and I sat on a sofa with Caroline, plates in laps—he was always more comfortable hanging out with the kids. When we left, Jackie said again how happy she was that he had brought me. "Gee," said Andy when we hit the street, "she really loved you, Bob. She even let you drink from the same glass. I wouldn't do that." He laughed. "Aren't you glad you came?" Well, I certainly wasn't feeling blue anymore.

The next day, Andy came into my office and said. "You're not going to believe what just happened. Jackie just called and told me off! She said, 'How dare you bring Bob Colacello to my house, Andy. He writes a column!' I told her that we told Caroline you wouldn't write anything and she said, 'Well, he better not, Andy. I'm holding you responsible.' Can you believe it? I mean, it was like a whole different person."

I was stunned, but I couldn't help but admire the brilliance of both her strategy and her manners. She had done nothing to make me feel uncomfortable. On the contrary, she'd won me over. And then she'd put her foot down with my boss the next day. I told Andy that I thought it was a clever and effective way to deal with the situation.

"How can you say that, Bob?" he said. "She was being so mean on the phone. You should've heard her. I told her how nice you were, but she didn't care. Oh, she's really terrible. Who does she think she is. I hate her now."

Andy simply couldn't understand why Jackie Onassis would be miffed at him for bringing an uninvited gossip columnist to her home. Invasion of privacy was an alien concept to him. Unless, of course, he thought *his* privacy was being invaded. Not long after the Onassis Christmas party, Jed invited Paloma Picasso and Rafael Lopez Cambil for drinks at Andy's house. Andy, as usual, was furious. "When I get home from a hard day's work," he told me, "seeing all these people all day long, I don't want to see any more people." But Paloma, I protested, was an old friend. Andy cut me off. "If Jed came to the office more," he said, "he would see people there and he wouldn't have to see them at home."

Thank God I don't live with him, I thought. He was impossible, so demanding and so ungiving, so needy of the loyalty and love he was incapable of returning. I often forgot that, and took Andy's insecurity as insensitivity, his emotional anguish as meanness. Sometimes, when things were going badly between us, Andy would startle me into remembering that he was feeling hurt, too. One night in March 1979, Andy and I went to Cartier's seventy-fifth anniversary party. In exchange for ads, I helped their chairman, Ralph Destino, line up celebrity recipients for their revived Santos watch, including Nureyev (who demanded the all-gold version), Paulette (who was peeved when she saw his and realized that hers was half stainless steel), Truman, and Andy. Somehow I lost Andy in the crush and he left without me. I called him when I got home to see what had happened. He was already half asleep, full of Valium and Grand Marnier. "You told Paulette you loved her tonight," he said groggily. "You never told me that you loved me, Bob." Was he serious? I told him that I had just said it to calm her down. "You never say it to calm me down, Bob."

Andy gave me a tiny painting of a heart for my birthday that May. The heart was mint green, but the background was shiny black. He had done a bunch of small heart paintings for Valentine's Day, "for all my 54 friends," he said. Some were black and gray, others were candy-colored. I liked mine the best, because it was both hard and sweet—just like Andy, I thought. Andy had left it on my desk, wrapped in an *Interview* cover, which is what he usually used for gift wrapping. When I thanked him for it, he said, "Those are your favorite colors, aren't they, Bob?" They were.

Still, my resentment, anger, and unhappiness grew. A big part of the problem was *Exposures*. I hated the fact that I was ghostwriting again, that every time I typed "I" it was Andy, not me. When I'd worked on the *Philosophy* book that had seemed liberating, but now it felt humiliating, especially since the stories "I" was telling were mine, not Andy's. In some cases, I put Andy at scenes where only I had been. It was a form of lying, of course, but there was no other way to write an Andy Warhol book, no more Warhol way.

When we began the process as usual, by taping, he contributed a line or two for every ten or twelve of mine. "Just make it up" was his literary motto, and when I gave him completed chapters, he counted pages the way he counted ads, just as he had with the *Philosophy* book. His only concern regarding content was that we not offend anyone who might take an ad or have a portrait painted, which meant almost everyone we were writing about.

In the end, *Andy Warhol's Exposures,* like every book by Andy from the *Philosophy* to the posthumous *Diaries,* was as much about denial as revelation. At the same time I was dealing with the seventies, Pat Hackett was struggling with Andy's version of the sixties. The most credible portions of that book, *Popism,* were based on her interviews with Henry Geldzahler, Emile de Antonio, and other sixties players, not Andy. He emitted a long litany of lines about drugs and sex at the Factory like "I never knew what was going on," and "I never knew what was really happening."

Andy was as passive about the visual aspect of *Exposures* as he was about the text, even though it was meant to be a book of Andy Warhol photographs. (Many were mine, another lie.) We hired Chris Makos as art director, a good decision creatively, but a financial disaster. I had offered him the standard $3,000 fee, but he insisted on being paid $10 an hour, and then took two years to lay out the book. This was costing Andy and me money, not the publisher, Grosset & Dunlap, because *Exposures* was to be the first book in a co-publishing company we had formed with them. It was called Andy Warhol Books and I was editorial director. That meant we received 50 percent of the profits, instead of a 15 percent royalty, but it also meant that we paid production costs.

When Grosset informed us that Chris's sizing was off by several inches on every page and all the mechanicals had to be redone by their art director, we paid for that too. Our $35,000 advance, of which I was to receive half, went almost entirely on such expenses. Chris also printed our photographs, another creative plus and money minus. Andy and I liked the way he brought out the contrasts between the blacks and whites, and the unfinished rough edges that were his trademark. We were not as pleased, however, when we found out that he had trained a young Italian immigrant how to print in his style, and paid him a dollar of the ten dollars we were paying him per print. "Chris is such a hustler," Andy often said, disparagingly when he was being hustled, admiringly when Chris was taking advantage of somebody else.

Chris also hooked us up briefly with his friend Victor Bockris, who offered to help with the taping and transcribing of *Exposures.* Andy thought he was "nutty"—a word he used as both a compliment and a putdown, depending on his mood—because of an article Bockris had written for *Screw* magazine, entitled, "Who Does Andy Warhol Remind You of Most? Muhammad Ali." Chris and he made one tape of Andy without me, and then Bockris gave me a transcript in which it took four pages to establish that Andy had met Mick Jagger at Baby Jane Holzer's house and several more to decide whether the party there had been "great" or "bad." As much as I hated to admit it, I was going to have to write the text myself.

When I showed a first draft to Bob Markel and Jane Wesman at Grosset, their favorite chapter was "Marisa Berenson's Wedding"—which came straight from my "OUT" column. They suggested that I be credited as co-author of the text, not only out of fairness but because that way I could do the TV shows Andy wouldn't. When I told Andy, his reaction was surprisingly muted, as if he didn't really care. "If they think it's a good idea," he said, "then I guess it is."

That was April 1978, and I didn't sit down to churn out the final draft until January 1979, mainly because I dreaded it so much. I finally finished the Bianca Jagger and Paulette Goddard chapters on my own, but then I drafted Brigid to help me. Almost every night that winter, she came to my place, or I went to hers, and after I smoked two or three joints, I dictated to her, turning myself into Andy, imitating the way he talked and, as best I could, the way he thought. Every so often, Brigid would snap, "That's you, not Andy. He'd never say that." I'd take another puff and get back into character. In some ways, it was more like acting than writing. But it worked. Some nights we turned out entire chapters, on Halston, for example. Or stretched a page of Andy on tape into six pages of me telling stories in Andy's voice, on Diana Vreeland, for example.

One night in February 1979, Brigid arrived completely drunk. She said she hadn't been able to find a taxi, "and this bar was just there, so I popped in and had four vodkas in five minutes." In Brigid's drinking tales, bars walked up to her and dragged her in. She asked me for another vodka, but after months on the wagon, my bar was down to one bottle of Rumanian red wine. Brigid insisted I open it. The cork broke, and when I pushed it in with a knife, Transylvanian vinegar splashed all over my face. I started to scream about trying not to drink, and then Brigid remembered that she had brought a present for me from Kron's chocolate shop. "They were closing," she said, "but I made them stay open and I forced them to write something on the chocolate. You're going to love it." The chocolate slab was indeed embellished in curly pink letters. "Social Disease," it said, and under that, "BB-BC-AW."

Social Disease was what we wanted the book to be called. It perfectly captured the tongue-in-cheek tone of the text and photographs, and made fun of Andy's obsessive partying and the world of discos and society in general. We had been through *My 879 Best Friends, Name Dropping,* and *Andy Warhol's Rolodex,* but none fit as well as *Social Disease.* Andy loved it, Fred loved it, Chris, Brigid, and I loved it—and for a while, Grosset loved it. Then someone at B. Dalton, the all-powerful bookstore chain, said they'd have to order fewer copies for their suburban and small-town stores if that was the title, and we settled on *Exposures* for lack of anything snappier. We also threw out our first cover: a black-and-white snapshot of Jackie Onassis and Bianca visiting Liza backstage with *Social Disease* stamped across it in bright red.

That night at my apartment, Brigid and I managed to write the Monique and Sylvia chapter—it actually wrote itself, as Mesdames Miles and van Vooren were "walking anecdotes," as Brigid put it. She consumed the Rumanian red as if it were Château Margaux, and I picked at the chocolate slab, even though my doctor said chocolate was bad for the liver. "Did you notice," Brigid asked, "how I had them put Andy's initials last, since he has the least to do with this book?" I noticed hers were first.

Brigid and Andy had the strangest relationship. They were like a long-married couple who had nothing left in common but their fights. And neither could give the other the slightest sense of satisfaction; theirs was a relentless contest to show each other they could care less. Once, when Andy had tried to give her a painting, she'd told him she'd rather have a washer and dryer instead. Yet she flew into a rage every time Andy spelled her name "Brigitte." Andy, of course, kept his feelings in check, and in doing so kept her in check too. Always check, never checkmate. That was the Andy Warhol technique: total tension, no resolution. He wanted the game to go on and on and on . . .

Brigid and I finished the text at the end of February. Andy said it was "boring. But I guess that's because I've heard all those stories a million times." Thanks a lot, I thought. "And it sounds so *bland*," he continued. "Can't you make it more . . . ?" More what, I asked. "Uhhh, well, just a little more . . ." Intelligent? Clever? Funny? Should we use bigger words and longer sentences? "Well, yeah, but . . ." His only specific suggestion was to delete "The Best Family" chapter, on Jackie, Lee, and assorted other Bouviers and Kennedys. That was the chapter Grosset wanted in the most. I agreed to show it to Fred, who said it was amusing. Andy acquiesced.

He wouldn't give in on paying Brigid, however, saying that she didn't really do anything. "But she worked at night," I told him, "and edited me as I went along."

"Then *you* pay her," he said. As our advance had been eaten up by our expensive art director, I promised Brigid 20 percent of my future royalties. It was Brigid he was being cheap with, not me this time. He readily agreed to split ownership of the limited-edition portfolios of *Exposures* photographs that Bruno Bischofberger published: The deal was 50 percent to Bruno, 25 percent each to Andy and me. Chris Makos printed those too and, as of this writing, profits have not yet covered expenses.

Chris finished the layouts in May 1979, and we went through the book with Andy and Fred. Andy's only request was to take out some photographs of Mick, Bianca, Arnold Schwarzenegger, and Muhammad Ali, and replace them with "the office kids." Chris was in a hurry to get the meeting over with and annoyed by Andy's meager comments. In the course of the project, I had watched his relationship with Andy go from idolatry to antagonism. At the Factory, that meant they grew closer.

Andy was even more blasé about the new cover design. Rupert Smith and Chris worked on it together, supervised by me. It was a collage of the book's stars—Truman, Margaret Trudeau, Steve Rubell, et al.—with patches of bright, flat color. Andy said he "hated" it, but never made any effort to get us to change it, or to change it himself. Another "Andy Warhol" book was done.

Well, at least, I thought then, my name was on it this time. When a magazine editor who was interested in the first serial rights said the text was "the most witty, observant and evil social commentary since Noel Coward," I was 50 percent pleased. But there was also a tug of embarrassment. We weren't writing *songs* after all. Yes, good journalism can be entertaining—I think it should be. But the most essential element in any nonfiction work is honesty. And I knew that so much of *Exposures* exposed nothing at all.

In December 1978, for example, Studio 54 had been busted, making headlines around the world. Federal agents grabbed Ian Schrager at the disco one morning and found almost a million dollars hidden everywhere, from behind the pipes in the basement to up in the cupola. Steve was stopped in his Mercedes, with another hundred thousand dollars stashed in the trunk. It was the story of the decade, and we were in the middle of it, but the only reference Andy allowed in *Exposures* was: "All the scandals help business because there's no publicity like bad publicity." What Andy really said and really thought about one of his best friends' arrest, indictment, and imprisonment was very different and totally typical.

My first reaction was to put Steve on the cover of *Interview:* He was our friend, and he was news. When I suggested it to Andy, he said, "Well, maybe, let's think about it." Despite Andy's sudden nervousness, we rushed Steve into a tux and onto the February 1979 cover, with a red background for Valentine's Day.

Steve returned the favor with a huge party for the tenth anniversary of *Interview* in June 1979. Ian created a scrim of covers, which hung from the ceiling to the dance floor, and I spent days rounding up our cover stars to arrive with Andy, including Debbie Harry, Jerry Hall, Diane von Furstenberg, Paloma Picasso, Lorna Luft, Barbara Allen, C. Z. Guest, Peter Beard, and Truman. At the height of the night, Steve made a toast. "I just want my good, good friend Andy to have a great time," he said. The deejay spun into Blondie's "Heart of Glass" and everybody danced. Except Andy, who spent most of the party in the balcony, "hiding out from the photographers." "But this is supposed to be a publicity party, Andy," I said when I finally found him three hours after we arrived. "I don't want any publicity," he said.

The Studio 54 scandal hit the front pages again soon afterward, when Steve accused White House chief of staff Hamilton Jordan of asking for cocaine at the disco. On the way uptown that afternoon, Andy told me, "I don't think Steve's a nice person. Because he probably offered it to Hamilton Jordan in the first place, right?" I told him I thought Steve had performed a great public service, and also reminded him of Carter administration officials and advisers we saw taking coke, and not only in discos. I also reminded him how worried he had been about the pressure Steve was under to name names in exchange for a deal from the prosecutor. "Why should I be worried, Bob?" he said. "I never took anything at 54." Right, Andy, I thought.

Three days later, the FBI called the Factory and asked for Andy. He made Fred take the call and say he was out. And he instantly came up with his alibi in case he was subpoenaed: "I never saw anyone take anything because I never went to the men's room, because I only go at home." I was half hoping the G-men did come by, just so I could see the expression on their faces when Andy told them that.

To show his support of a friend in trouble, he also avoided going to 54 after the FBI call. But as summer turned to fall, and the feared subpoena never materialized, he couldn't resist the occasional big bash.

Then, *New York* magazine hit the stands with a cover story exposing "Studio 54's List of Party Favors: Poppers for Bianca, Cocaine for—and—, $800 for Andy Warhol's Garbage Pail on his Birthday." Andy's first reaction was, "You mean they told me there was a thousand dollars in there and it was only eight hundred? Oh, I knew I should've counted it." Then the radio ads started: "Find out why Steve Rubell gave Andy Warhol $800 in this week's *New York* magazine!" And Andy said, "I'm never speaking to Steve again. How could he put me on a list like that? And give it to the IRS?"

Did Andy think he was the only one who took tax deductions? Steve called and explained that that was exactly what the list actually was, tax deductions for public-relations purposes, even the poppers were legitimate as they weren't illegal, and the so-called cocaine references were really cash payments for the political fund-raisers of people like Andrew Stein and Jerry Brown. Steve's lawyer, Roy Cohn, suggested that Andy and Bianca sue, but Andy couldn't sue—because the author of the article was Henry Post, Jed's constant companion that year. And Andy was busy trying to make Henry a better friend of his than he was of Jed's. The plot, as always, thickened.

In December 1979, Steve and Ian settled their case with the federal prosecutor's office, pleading guilty to tax evasion, and awaited sentencing.

They were hoping to do some sort of community service in lieu of a prison term. Building discos on naval bases was one suggestion, though I'm not sure whose. Steve called and asked if Andy could write a letter to the U.S. district judge, asking for leniency on the grounds that Studio 54 had revitalized New York nightlife and that his presence was essential to the continued success of an attraction that drew as many tourists as Lincoln Center or the Statue of Liberty. Steve said that Liz Smith, Ahmet Ertegun, Henry Geldzahler, and other civic worthies were penning appeals along those lines. Andy wouldn't do it, so Steve asked me to instead, and I did. Andy said I was "crazy" to go on record. "Steve was never that nice to you," he added.

In January 1980, Steve and Ian were sentenced to three and a half years in prison, a long time for tax evasion, especially since they were paying back everything they owed—some $2.6 million. The moral of the story seemed to be, You can fight city hall, but not the White House. To make matters worse, they were held at Manhattan County Jail, instead of one of the low-security federal "country clubs" to which white-collar felons were usually sent. Their presence in New York was necessary, the prosecutor argued, as witnesses in an ongoing criminal investigation, i.e., the Hamilton Jordan cocaine case.

Carmen d'Alessio went to see them once a week. "The visiting room is very nice," she told me. "They have a pay telephone, a Coca-Cola machine, everything. And all the other prisoners seem very nice too, except for this one with tattoos all over his arms who they told me was 'the bowling ball murderer.' " Steve and Ian took their medicine like real men, it seemed to me. Sometimes, Steve called me from the pay phone—he traded his cigarette allowance, he told me, for other inmates' phone time. "Talking on the phone keeps me going," he said. "I don't feel like I'm missing out on everything so much that way." He actually seemed to be better informed about the latest gossip than we were at *Interview:* Diana Ross had stolen "the guy from Kiss" from Cher; Count and Countess Crespi were having dinner at Halston's the other night; David Geffen had given him the address of "the hot new place in L.A." in case I was heading out that way; he was talking to Calvin about stepping up his *Interview* advertising; tell Andy not to worry. "I have to hang up now," he said suddenly. "I'm all out of dimes."

Steve called Andy once that winter and Andy was upset. "He wants me to send him *Popism,*" Andy said. "I can't do that." I asked him why. "Because the guards check everything and then they tell the IRS. That's how it works, Bob."

Another drama was unfolding as we were writing *Exposures,* though not a word of it was mentioned in our pages either: the fall of the Shah. In September 1978, Andy, Fred, and I were scheduled to attend the Shiraz Arts

Festival, along with Paloma Picasso, Rafael Lopez Cambil, Javier Arro-
yuelo, and São Schlumberger. There was going to be a show of Andy's
portraits of the Shah, the Empress, and Princess Ashraf. Then we were
going to spend a few days in Teheran, during which time, we hoped, Andy
would get to Polaroid the Crown Prince. That was the plan. Then rioting
resumed in Teheran and a movie theater with several hundred people in it
was burned down in Shiraz, some said by the Shah's secret police, others
by Communist agitators. Ambassador Hoveyda assured me that everything
was under control, and I assured Andy, Fred, Paloma, Rafael, Javier, and
São. We were all packing our bags when the telegrams arrived from the
Minister of Culture: "We regret to inform you that the Shiraz Arts Festival
has been canceled due to illegal manifestations by extreme xenophobic
groups. We look forward to inviting you to next year's festival."

"What are we going to do with all these portraits of the Shah and his
sister we haven't been paid for yet?" asked Andy. "You better call Hoveyda
and get a check quick." In October, *Time* magazine reported that the Shah's
family had been forbidden to do business with the government, and some
of our Iranian friends whispered that some royal relations had been stripped
of their titles, asked to leave the country, and told not to come back. "When
they strip you of your title," Andy asked, "do they strip you of your money
too?"

Nima Farmanfarmaian told us that her mother had called their house in
Teheran and asked how things were there. "Great!" said the maid. "We're
going to have a revolution any day." Nima also told me that Princess Ashraf
was secretly in New York, so I called a friend of the Shah's sister, Eric
Nezhad, and as delicately as possible suggested that she might like to come
down to the Factory to see her portrait. "Andy thought it might cheer her
up," I said. Eric called back a week later and said that Princess Ashraf
would like to come the following day, but we shouldn't tell anyone and there
shouldn't be anyone around except our staff. We canceled all appointments
and put off all deliveries until the following day. "Do we still call her 'Your
Highness'?" Andy wondered. "I would if I were you," said Fred.

Princess Ashraf arrived with Eric and an American Secret Service man.
She was wearing a beige silk suit, which Andy said looked like Dior couture,
and some simple diamond jewelry, which Andy said looked like recent Harry
Winston. He also said she looked better than when he had photographed her
the year before; "She must have had a facelift, right?" In any case, she
didn't look like a woman who had lost anything. She sat on a chair in the
front room, while Andy and I tried to make conversation and waited for
Ronnie to bring her portraits from the back. She let Eric do the talking for
her, while she silently sipped a cup of coffee. She said her portraits were
"nice" and asked if she could see some other things that Andy was working
on. He ran to the back himself this time and returned with his triple portrait
of the Shah. Those seemed to excite her more than her own. After twenty

minutes, she left. On their way out, Eric told me that they were going away for a week of sun, and after that they would call us for dinner at the Princess's house.

It was several months before we heard from Princess Ashraf again. In the meantime, everything we heard from Iran or about Iran was unpromising. In November, Ina Ginsburg called from Washington to report that Ambassador Zahedi had sent out letters announcing that he wouldn't be entertaining for the rest of the year because of the government crisis. This followed a *New York* magazine article claiming that his embassy was staffed by spies and was the scene of orgies. Ina also reported that her new best friend was the wife of the Moroccan ambassador and that everyone was saying that they would have the hot new embassy now that the Iranians were closing down. "Maybe Ina can get us some portraits from Morocco," said Andy. "What kind of government do they have there, Bob? Did you call Hoveyda for the check yet?"

Two days later, Nima called with fresh news from her mother, who had joined her father back in Teheran. The burning, she said, was limited to the downtown area; the northern hills where the rich lived were still calm. In the red-light district, the whores had put up large banners declaring, "The Shah lives for us and his sister is one of us!" The inside gossip was that in the next few days the Shah was going to have to leave, or start killing large numbers of people. "You better call Hoveyda right this minute, Bob," said Andy. "We're having dinner with him tomorrow night," I replied. "Great!"

We took the Hoveydas to Quo Vadis, where we were joined by Lily Auchincloss, Joanne du Pont, and Paul Jenkins. As soon as we sat down, the captain came to say there was a call for Fereydoun. While he took it, Gisela told us that he had been very worried lately because his mother and his brother, who had stepped down as prime minister as a sop to the mob, were still in Iran, and there had been a call in parliament to arrest his brother for crimes he had allegedly committed while in office. Gisela said Fereydoun had been trying to get through to Teheran all day and that this was probably his secretary calling with news. It was: All connections between the New York mission and Teheran had been cut off, Fereydoun told us, and when his secretary called the embassies in Washington, London, and Paris, they said their connections had been cut too. He suggested a drink, noting that when the Ayatollah took over that wouldn't be allowed. The Ayatollah Khomeini had recently been installed in a house outside Paris, and Gisela said she heard that his supporters had covered all the walls in sheets, because the wallpaper was a flower print and flowers weren't permissible Islamic images. "Oh really," said Andy. I didn't ask Hoveyda about the check.

Ten nights later, at the end of November 1978, we went to our last dinner at the Iranian embassy on Fifth Avenue. It was for Barbaralee Diamonstein, who had just published a book on the importance of preserving and restoring old buildings. Louise Nevelson was there, Leonore Hershey, the editor of *Ladies' Home Journal,* and Barbaralee's future husband, Carl Spielvogel, the chairman of what was then the largest advertising agency in the world. Present also was Fereydoun's cousin, the Iranian ambassador to Morocco. When he introduced us, Fereydoun said that he could help us arrange the King of Morocco's portrait. Andy lit up and told me later, "Gee, Fereydoun really is a friend." He didn't even ask me if I had asked about the check.

There were dollops of caviar on cream-cheese hors d'oeuvres, and Andy noticed that the peaches at dessert were canned. Then, as always, Ambassador Hoveyda stood to speak, even though, he said, "after so many years at the UN, I know that speeches mean nothing." He said that despite "my country having so many problems," he had decided to go ahead with this party for Barbaralee Diamonstein because her book was about something very important: keeping culture alive, finding in the past inspiration for the future, renewing history and life.

When he finished, Fred stood up and lifted his glass. "To you, sir!" he said. It was a simple, kind, and elegant gesture, Fred at his best. Everyone joined in his toast, and then Barbaralee made a speech of her own. "No matter how many problems the ambassador's country is having," she said, "we are all here because we are all artists. And art transcends everything. Art is eternal." I couldn't help but notice a gift from Andy to the Hoveydas that was propped up on the mantelpiece behind her: a small Torso painting of a twelve-inch cock.

As always, we all ascended the grand staircase to the grand salon, with its diplomatic blue furnishings and exotic Parisian mirrorwork, for coffee, cognac, and cigars. Andy and Fred sat on a sofa and, much to my chagrin, fell into an amazingly melodramatic fight. It began almost accidentally, when Fred mentioned that he had caught Brigid slipping Scotch into her coffee that morning. Andy said that he had caught Averil Meyer swigging tequila from a bottle that afternoon. "We shouldn't have any more liquor at the office," he declared.

"And then what do we do when somebody grand comes down for lunch and asks for a drink?" Fred countered.

"Listen, Fred," said Andy. "Bob can't drink, Brigid's in A.A., and now Ronnie's going too. And if the liquor's there, they'll drink it."

I couldn't believe what I was hearing. Was he putting on an act for the embassy audience? Whatever it was, Fred wasn't falling for it. He accused Andy of being more concerned with the Factory liquor bills than the Factory drinking problems.

"I am not, Fred! How dare you say that. I just don't want the kids turning into alcoholics. How can you say I'm just being cheap? I'm not cheap."

"What about the constant complaining about the phone bills?"

"I never complain about the phone bill!"

"You never shut up about it as a matter of fact, Andy. I'm the one who has to listen to you go on and on and on and . . . You drive *me* crazy about every single cent *Jed* spends!"

"I do not!"

"You're always telling me his bills are twice as much as they really are! How many times have you done that? HOW MANY TIMES, ANDY!" Fred was screaming now.

"I don't have to listen to this," Andy huffed, getting up and going into the other room.

Fred broke down. "Andy and Jed are driving me crazy," he told me. "And what thanks do I get? They *both* hate me now, just because I try to mediate." He stood up. "I just can't stand it anymore!" And walked out of the room too. We were exiting from the Caviar Club in style.

The next day, Andy completely forgot about banning booze at the Factory, Ayatollah-style.

In early December, Nima Farmanfarmaian said her parents were moving to New York and didn't know what to do with their house in Teheran, as nobody was buying anything anymore. There went Andy's fantasy of installing a Shah print in every rich Iranian's foyer. That week, Marion Javits told us that she had visited Princess Ashraf at her Beekman Place townhouse. "She can't think about anything," Marion said, "except getting her brother out alive." There went Andy's dream of Ashraf buying her portraits to cheer herself up.

On January 3, his hopes were momentarily revived when he saw a message for me from Ashraf's secretary. "They must have a fortune in Switzerland," he told me. "Tell her she can pay us anywhere she wants and we won't tell anybody. But don't say it on the phone, try to get to see her. I bet she has lots of those gold coins with the Shah's picture on them. Tell her we can trade. I want to start buying those, Bob. The price is really going down, and it's still gold, right?" Princess Ashraf's secretary wanted to know if I could get a couple of Her Highness's house guests into Studio 54 that night.

The Shah flew into exile on January 16, 1979. On February 1, the Ayatollah Khomeini made his triumphal entrance into Teheran. That night, Andy and I watched the seven o'clock news over the phone together. What looked like millions of people—the men with shaved scalps, the women in black chadors—struggled to get close to his helicopter. Then the camera cut to a close-up of the Supreme Leader, shaking his fists. His harangue was translated as he delivered it: "I pray to God that the hands of all foreigners are cut off."

"Why don't you call up São in Paris," said Andy on the other end of the line, "and see if she'd like some portraits of the Shah? Tell her we have them in every color."

Though the potential loss can only be surmised, Andy's actual loss on the Iranian deal—for three portraits of the Shah and two of Princess Ashraf, which were never paid for—was $95,000. He still owned the undelivered paintings, but the market for them was suddenly limited. Still it was an inconsequential sum for Andy's booming art business by 1979. Ten days after the Shah's exit, Andy's Shadow paintings were shown at the Heiner Friedrich Gallery in SoHo. There were 102 six-foot paintings in the exhibition, eighty of which had been bought by the Dia Art Foundation, which was run by the youngest de Menil daughter, Philippa. The price: $20,000 each, $1.6 million total.

Andy had got the Shadow idea from Ronnie Cutrone and started painting them in 1978. "Andy always wanted to be an Abstract Expressionist," Ronnie says, "because he thought he would be taken more seriously. And he would tell this to Fred and Fred would say, 'But you're Andy Warhol. You have to paint *things.*' And Andy would sulk. So I told him to paint things *and* be abstract. And he asked me what I meant and I said, 'Paint shadows.' "

When seen as a group, hanging side by side in an uninterrupted line across the four walls of a large room, the Shadows are among Andy's most beautiful paintings: spare, brooding, mysterious. Ironically, they were actually Shadows of hard-ons. Nonetheless, the Warhol formula of repeated image and varied color achieves a kind of classicism with this series. But the Shadows exhibition didn't convert any art-world intellectuals to Andy's cause.

Maybe that's why Andy swung to the other extreme with his next big series of paintings: the Retrospectives and Reversals of 1979. Like the aging Giorgio de Chirico, he plundered his own past, cynically dragging out his old silkscreens from the sixties—a nightmare every Warhol collector had always feared. Then he inked the Soupcans, Marilyns, Electric Chairs, and so on across the canvasses prepainted by mop, some in combinations of various famous images (Retrospectives), others in negative of their famous originals (Reversals). Some were shown the following year at the Bruno Bischofberger Gallery in Zürich and the Daniel Templon Gallery in Paris. The two dealers, as usual, paid Andy in advance, probably splitting the $800,000 that Fred had set as the minimum for an Andy Warhol series. That was the amount the Michael Zivian Gallery, in New York, paid for the Space Fruits Series it commissioned and exhibited in May 1979.

Andy stepped up his print production greatly in 1979, putting out no fewer than eleven separate editions, including Space Fruits and five different sets on the Shadows theme. Those were small editions, of three to fifteen portfolios each, but the After the Party edition, which was to be sold with a limited edition of the *Exposures* book, numbered one thousand. There were also two editions of Grapes (of fifty and forty portfolios) and Gems (twenty portfolios), which I always thought were a gimmick allowing Andy to tax deduct some of his ever-growing collection of loose stones, precious and semi-precious. The Grapes I and II and Gems portfolios were published by Andy Warhol Enterprises, not commissioned. Andy obviously needed some expenses to offset the huge income his art business was generating. And he was encouraged to come up with more and more editions by his printer, Rupert Smith—who was paid by the piece.

Andy's creative directions to Rupert were sometimes direct: no red, lighter, darker. But often they were as vague as those he gave me on *Exposures:* He wanted the prints to be more something or less something, but he couldn't say what that something was. Andy always refused Rupert's invitations to supervise the work in progress at his studio in Tribeca. "I don't want to see your doors and sinks and ashtrays," he told Rupert, "because then I'll start imagining how robberies and floods and fires could happen there too."

Andy liked to take Rupert to swank parties at Regine's or Halston's, where Rupert, who looked like a cross between a Beach Boy and a Hummel figurine, often felt out of place, and then ask him, "Should we get really drunk?" When Rupert did, Andy complained to Fred or me, "You've got to get Rupert out of here. He's telling everyone that he does all my work."

In November 1979, Andy's last major exhibition of the decade, "Portraits of the 70s," opened at the Whitney Museum. This time the art world had to pay attention, though, for the most part, they didn't like what they saw. Robert Hughes delivered what he thought was a mortal blow in *Time* magazine. It exemplifies the almost visceral loathing of Andy by the American intellectual establishment:

> It is sometimes said that Andy Warhol . . . is the [John Singer] Sargent of our times. Certainly no painter with an equivalent reputation—deserved or not— has spent so much time on celebrity portraiture: Warhol's show is an anthology of famous faces from show biz, art and fashion, an album of discoland and the Concorde set. Whether these images will look as interesting after 50 years as Sargent's do is another question. Certainly they do not today. What they lack is Sargent's ability to realize and construct a painting. Warhol's admirers, who include David Whitney, the show's organizer, are given to claiming that Warhol has "revived" the social portrait as a form. It would be nearer the truth to say that he zipped it into a Halston, painted its eyelids and propped it up in the back of a limo, where it moves but cannot speak. . . .

The Whitney Museum has something to gain from the promotional effort it is making with this show: it needs money, and Warhol is so well known that any exhibition of his work can be relied on to bring crowds. But though Whitney Director Tom Armstrong announces in the catalogue that "I have never wavered from the mark with Monsieur Warhola . . . when the last lifeboat is launched I want old Blondie at the oars," there are others who may not want to join him in the shallows on this particular raft of the Medusa, crowded as it is with the glittery, the raucous, the beady-eyed and the badly painted.

Andy's reaction: "They gave me two whole pages. With three photographs. In color."

A day or two later, he came into my office and said, "Oh, I figured out why Bob Hughes hates us. You must have written something mean about him in 'OUT.' " I recalled a reference, from a couple of years back, to the critic's tie not matching his shirt. "That's it, Bob," said Andy. "People really care about those things. They really do. Especially intellectuals."

Andy's opening at the Whitney was a high point of the fall social season. Nan Kempner gave a dinner for ninety at Mortimer's first and then the limos drove around the corner to the museum. Andy insisted on walking and I walked with him. "It's too embarrassing," he said, as we turned onto Madison Avenue and saw the waiting photographers and TV crews. He spent most of the party with Carolina Herrera on one arm and Florinda Bolkan on the other.

There was no wallpaper this time, just the portraits, over fifty of them, hung in pairs. It was a decade's work, ten years of popping questions and popping Polaroids, of business dinners and art business, an impressive array of powerful images that probably will look as interesting in fifty years as Sargent's do—maybe even Goya's. Though it represented only part of Andy's seventies subjects, only the Iranian royals seemed to have been left out. Not because Andy was ashamed; the museum was worried about violence—only two weeks earlier hostages had been taken in the American embassy in Teheran. Also left out were clients who had had only one portrait done, because Tom Armstrong, David Whitney, and Fred decided that repetition was the key to Andy's style. "That's what they deserve for being cheap," said Andy.

The only exception to the diptych format hung in a smaller room off the main gallery: eight 1974 portraits of Julia Warhola, in all their haunting, nervous, almost abstract splendor, unexpected icons from another world. Several guests told me that they found these portraits more interesting than anything else in the show, though whenever anyone asked Andy about them, he gave them the same old line, murmured like a prayer, "She's fine. She's fine."

Many of the famous people on the walls were also at the party—Leo Castelli, Ileana Sonnabend, Ivan Karp, Henry Geldzahler, Jane Holzer, Joe

MacDonald, Halston, and Victor Hugo, wearing half a dress. The top half. Over black mesh tights. There were also plenty of potential portraits roaming the room, waiting to be popped: Sly Stallone, Doris Duke, Lord Snowdon, Averil Meyer's rich mother, Sandra Payson. I was in hot pursuit of the young Countess Sylvia Serra di Cassano, determined to present Andy with a fresh trophy to go with those I had already helped put on his Whitney walls: Liza, Truman, Paul Jenkins, Gale Smith, Countess Cristina Carimati—I was good with countesses. And Italians. My date that night was Countess Marina Cicogna.

But the night, I felt, belonged to Fred. More than anyone else, he had made Andy the era's social portraitist. And the evidence was there on the walls too; all his hard-won conquests, all the glamorous Parisians Andy always said Fred had slept with rather than give him real credit, all the tough tycoons and their wives Fred had wined and dined into multiple commissions: Yves Saint Laurent, Hélène Rochas, São Schlumberger, Diane von Furstenberg, Gianni and Marella Agnelli, Sidney and Frances Lewis, Freddy and Marcia Weisman, Kay Fortson, Marion Block, Kimiko Powers, Tofu Teshigahara (the number-one flower arranger in Japan), Mick Jagger—a tough tycoon if there ever was one.

It *should* have been Fred's night. It wasn't. He had too much to drink at Nan Kempner's dinner and got into a very public fight with Diana Vreeland at the museum. Diana made the mistake of telling Fred he was drunk. "So are you!" he snapped. Diana no doubt had consumed her usual string of straight vodkas. "Now listen here, Fred," she snapped back, "don't try to pass the buck. It isn't like you. And it isn't very attractive." Fred screamed that he was "sick and tired" of being told what was attractive by Diana. It was almost like slapstick, Fred and Diana going at each other—in the same voice and with the same gestures. But it was also pathetic to see Fred turn on the woman he loved to the point of imitation.

"What's wrong with Fred lately?" Florence Grinda asked me, as we stood there watching the spat. She told me that Fred had recently "made a big scene with Maria Niarchos in London. It was quite funny actually. He was telling her how much he'd loved her since she was two and he was four. But then he got really heavy, insisting she should get divorced for him. Maria was quite upset. It's a shame really, because everybody likes Fred."

Other friends were beginning to express similar feelings of concern, but Diana Vreeland was really worried about Fred. She and I had had several talks about his behavior; in fact, it was hard to get her off the subject when we were alone. One night, she went on about the beard that Fred had just shaved off. She hated his beard. It was "slovenly" she said. But she was disappointed after it came off, "because Fred *still* doesn't have that look I loved him for: well-proportioned, simple, good clothes, worn perfectly, everything just so. No accessory other than *neatness*. You know exactly what I mean, Bob. Well, I'm afraid he's lost it."

Style was more than surface for Diana; it expressed the very essence
of a person. And Fred's style had changed. He had been so impeccable in
his Savile Row suits, so quietly proud of being elected to the Best Dressed
List in 1974. Now he liked to show off the shredded linings of the same
suits and announce, "Those idiots who vote for the Best Dressed List should
see this!" They had, and stopped voting for him. Diana saw the decline in
Fred's appearance as a sign of an inner collapse. "His *spirit* is broken,
Bob," she said. "He used to have such spirit, such enthusiasm." She blamed
it on drink *and* drugs. "You can't tell me he isn't taking cocaine, Bob,"
she said. "Everybody else is. Why should Fred be any different?"

She also blamed it on Andy, and wanted me to talk to him. "It probably
won't do the least bit of good," she said. "Andy doesn't *really* listen to
anyone, does he? But you can't just stand there and do nothing, Bob! It's
too big a problem to be ignored." Not too big for Andy to ignore. He told
me that Fred didn't have a drinking problem. Then he told Fred that I had
been putting him down to Diana behind his back. And Fred told me how
hurt he was.

"DAVID LLOYD KREEGER'S HOUSE IS THE MOST VULGAR, HIDEOUS MON-
STROSITY I HAVE EVER SEEN IN MY ENTIRE LIFE!" Four nights after the
Whitney bash, Fred was at it again. We were in Washington, D.C., the first
stop on our three-week *Exposures* tour, at a dinner for a dozen capital grandees, including Senator and Mrs. John Heinz, given by John Coleman in the
Jockey Club of his Ritz-Carlton Hotel. Fred was screaming at the top of his
lungs, lambasting the taste of the most important art collector in Washington, whose house we had visited earlier in the day. "Oh, Fred," said Andy.
"It's a really nice house, Fred. Be quiet, Fred." He was practically begging.
Fred ostentatiously dragged his chair to the next table, where some preppies
sat laughing at his antics. "He needs a cold shower," said my dinner partner, Anne Kinney, who had been telling me about their latest purchase, a
three-million dollar Jackson Pollock. Thank God, I thought, Karen Lerner—
who was producing a "20/20" segment on our tour—had decided not to
videotape the dinner.

Ina Ginsburg, *Interview*'s Washington editor, and I had been working
on Andy's Washington visit for weeks. She had arranged for Andy to sit in
the presidential box at the Kennedy Center, with National Security Adviser
Zbigniew Brzezinski and his wife, for Liza Minnelli's opening the previous
evening. I had persuaded my friend Elizinha Gonçalves to come along as
Andy's date. She was well known in Washington because her ex-husband
had been the Brazilian ambassador during the Kennedy administration, and
she dazzled the local socialites and gossip columnists with her ruby-and-
diamond necklace. "Oh, God," said Andy, "I've never had such a glamorous date. It was just so hard to watch Liza doing the same old stuff instead

of staring at those rocks. I mean, Elizinha's rubies are even bigger than Paulette's. Gee, thanks, Bob.''

Ina had also lured one-tenth of the Senate to Coleman's big book party—Javits, Percy, Pell, Metzenbaum, Pressler, Sasser, Pryor, Zorinsky, and Heinz—much to the delight of "20/20" and the *Washington Post* art critic, Paul Richards, who was also tracking our every move for a day-in-the-life-of-Andy-Warhol piece. The cocktail party was such a hit that nobody wanted to leave, so we decided to retreat to Andy's suite, taking several senators with us.

That's when Fred's behavior first crossed the line. "I'm so grateful to you," he told me with a loud slur, "for bringing Elizinha into our lives. She's really FABULOUS! If it's okay with you, buddy, I'd like to FUCK ELIZINHA!" I told him to please lower his voice, everyone could hear, as Elizinha slipped between the senators to the other side of the small, crowded room. "I WANT TO FUCK ELIZINHA!" Fred shouted again, in case anyone hadn't heard him the first time. Then, at dinner, he insisted on changing places, so he could be beside her. He tried to pull her legs apart under the table, but she found the perfect way to put him off. "I can't think of you in those terms, Fred," she said, "because I know your true love is Diana Vreeland." He had, of course, been propositioning her in his D. V. voice.

After dinner, Elizinha made me see her to her room and push a chest of drawers against her door. Meanwhile, Karen Lerner had persuaded Senator Heinz to come back up to our suite to interview Andy for "20/20." As he was from Pittsburgh too, she wanted him to ask Andy why he hadn't popularized Heinz ketchup instead of Campbell's soup. When I returned to the room, the senator and his wife, Teresa, were gone, and Ina Ginsburg looked distinctly displeased. "Something has to be done about Fred," she said. Thomas Ammann, who was traveling with us, confirmed Ina's story: While I was out of the room, and Andy was being videotaped by "20/20," Fred had apparently taken Teresa Heinz into the bedroom and offered her cocaine. "What does he think he's doing? I'm a senator's wife," she had told both Ina and Thomas. "And there's a TV crew in the next room!"

"Oh, I can't believe Fred would really do that," said Andy, after they told us the story. Then we heard a crash from the bathroom. Fred was in there with Paul Richards and somehow a towel rack had gotten ripped out of the wall. I let Fred have it as soon as the *Post* reporter left. "Fred, you've really got to stop drinking," I said. "I'm not drunk," he said. "Fred, you are drunk and you offered cocaine to Mrs. Heinz." He denied it. "And how could you be putting down Kreeger's house so loud, Fred?" Andy chimed in. "I work for a genius," was Fred's reply, "and I'm not going to stand for a lowering of standards. And I'm not going to live the kind of life where I can't say what I believe at all times."

"But you don't have to scream it," said Andy. "You just have to stop drinking."

He had finally said it to Fred. But Fred was too far gone to listen and slammed the door on the way out. Thomas, Ina, and I stayed up for another hour with Andy, trying to persuade him to tell Fred he couldn't continue on the tour with us, to shock him into doing something about his drinking problem. "I just can't tell him that," Andy whimpered. "Fred's not that bad, is he?"

The *Exposures* tour, which went on for three more weeks, was almost as depressing as writing the book had been, and the entire process made me think about my future for the first time since I'd come back to the Factory, after my Mexico and Bridgehampton sojourns in 1972. In August 1979, I had told Pat Hackett for the first time that "I felt like quitting." A month later, Andy had told me for the first time that I should. It was a Sunday morning and I called him at home to say that our lunch date had been confirmed; it was with Louise Danelian, a Los Angeles lady who owned several Courrèges boutiques, and she was commissioning an $8,000 drawing of her teenage son. "You can take the Polaroids in their suite at the Regency after lunch," I told Andy.

"Oh, okay," he said, quickly adding so I couldn't sign off, "Why don't we have a Calvin Klein ad in the new issue?" It was a touchy subject with me and Andy knew it. I had asked Calvin to lunch three times that month and each time he had canceled at the last minute. And it wasn't the first time that Andy had asked me the same question since the issue came out. "I don't know why Calvin isn't advertising," I snapped. "It's Sunday, I'm taking you to do a portrait, and you're still asking me about some stupid ad! It's no use, you're just never satisfied."

"Who do you think you are, Bob?" Andy said, dripping icicles of sarcasm. "Go look for another job, *darling*. You have half the book."

"I know I have half the book, *Andy*. But half the photos are mine, the entire text is mine, and I'm doing all the promotion!"

Andy hung up.

I called him back and apologized. And I made a promise to myself. I was going to get this portrait today and Calvin's ad tomorrow. I was going to sell so many ads and make *Interview* so successful that we would never have to take a single cent from Andy Warhol Enterprises again. I was going to sell so many portraits and make so much money in commissions that I would never have to ask Andy for a raise again. Because I knew that was what the fight was really about—money. Andy had given me a raise at the beginning of the yea.—from $450 to $600 a week, or $31,200 a year. I hadn't had a raise in two years, but it had still been the usual struggle to get it.

A few days after our fight, Andy was on my case again. After a 1978 trip to Brazil to deal with a rogue edition of *Interview,* I had convinced Andy and Fred that it was about time to trademark our name. It was expensive and time-consuming, but it had to be done. My reward was a new notion of Andy's: He wanted to trademark the "OUT" title and use it on an eight-page *daily*. He expected the *Interview* staff to work on it, at no extra pay. When I told him that I thought the trademark should be shared between him and me, he gave me his coldest glare and asked, "Why?"

"Because it's my column and my word."

"Oh, then we'll just use photos."

"Well, I'm not working on it, unless I own part of it."

"Oh, well, maybe Chris Makos can do it then."

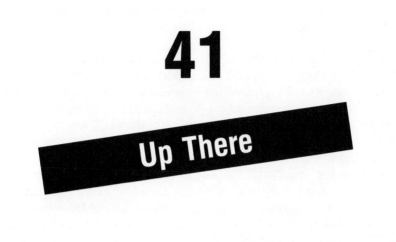

41

Up There

From an unpublished interview with Andy Warhol by Scott Cohen, October 1980:

> SC: You're fifty-two and still a virgin?
> AW: Yeah, I'm still a virgin.
> SC: With all these beautiful people hanging around, don't you ever get turned on?
> AW: Well, I think only kids who are very young should have sex, and people who aren't young should never get excited. After twenty-five, you should look, but never touch.

Was he still a virgin? I think that technically he was. Whatever little sex he may have had in his fifty-two years was probably a mixture of masturbation and voyeurism—to use his word, *abstract.* Andy chose his words carefully and he knew that the opposite of abstract was figurative, concrete, real. By the late seventies, Andy was desperately trying to have *real* sex—that's what all the groping and grabbing in discos and limos was all about—but the sad truth was that the Society boys and male models he chased didn't want to go home with Andy, they wanted to go out with Andy Warhol. And so *he said,* again and again, until he convinced the press, his kids, and most of all himself: I don't want to have sex, because I don't want to be involved. The fear of involvement covered the pain of rejection. And what began as a psychological defense mechanism became the curse of his existence, poisoning every relationship he had, cutting him off from all emotional intimacy. Where did that leave Andy at the beginning of the eighties? I sat in on that Scott Cohen interview and the line that rang truest was: "I think it's horrible to live."

On December 21, 1980, Jed left Andy. It was a Sunday morning, and as the car that would take him to the airport waited outside their door, Jed told Andy that, when he returned from his skiing trip to Vail, he was moving into the West 67th Street apartment he had bought a few months earlier as an office for his growing decorating business. He was going to share it, he said, with his new partner, Alan Wanzenberg, a good-looking young architect who had recently left I. M. Pei's office.

At first Andy handled it the way he did his mother's death and didn't tell anyone anything. But try as he might, he couldn't hide Jed's departure, or his own stifled anguish, for long. On Monday, Chris Makos told me that Andy had called him at eight in the morning and "was saying strange things like, 'There's no Christmas spirit at my house.' " I assumed it was his usual Scrooge mood. On Tuesday, Andy didn't turn up at the office Christmas lunch until four in the afternoon, when everybody was back at their desks. "I'm not giving any art this year," he announced. That was an annual line, too, but this year Vincent and I didn't try to change his mind. We already knew what had happened. Jed's friend from *New York* magazine, Henry Post, had whispered the news to Brigid at lunch, and she had whispered it to Vincent and me. None of us dared mention anything to Andy.

That night, Marina Schiano called and said that she had begged Jed to put off telling Andy he was leaving until after Christmas. "Don't get me wrong," she said. "I understand completely why Jed had to do what he did. But my heart goes out to Andy. It's no joke, thirteen years with someone and then one day he gets up and walks out. And *four days before Christmas.*"

Jed called Andy on Christmas Day, but Andy wouldn't come to the phone. Still, Andy pretended to all of us at the office that it was no big deal. But he wasn't acting right, I felt. For one thing, he decided to go on a diet— and he was already so thin. The day after New Year's, I called him from Brooks and Adriana Jackson's house in Key West, and asked him if everything was okay. "Oh, yeaaaahhh," he said in his fakest tone. "Everything's greaaattt. Couldn't be better."

"Well, Marina's worried about you," I said, trying to convey my own concern.

"Listen, Bob," he snapped, "tell Marina it's none of her business. I'm very happy and I'm so lucky to finally have that problem out of my life."

And yet the man who swore he would never get involved again started getting involved with someone new the very day after Jed left.

Jon Gould was vice president for corporate communications at Paramount Pictures. Andy had Brigid send him a dozen red roses at his office in the Gulf & Western building on Columbus Circle, with the excuse that he might get us ads. Andy had met Jon a month earlier through Chris Makos. Chris had met Jon at the baths, though he kept that fact secret until much later, when Jon was firmly ensconced in Andy's life and threatening to push Chris out.

Jon seemed to have two personalities, two styles, two lives: straight and gay, preppy and flamboyant, on his own in Los Angeles and with Andy in New York. He was twenty-seven when he met Andy, very tall, almost handsome from some angles, almost ugly from others, with thinning hair and a muscular build, awkward when he walked into a room, agile on the ski slopes and the dance floor. He was extremely proud of his old New England roots and counted Nathaniel Currier, of Currier & Ives the printmakers, as a great-great uncle. His family lived on a nine-hundred-acre estate in Amesbury, Massachusetts, that had been founded by their direct ancestors circa 1620. They also owned a summer house in New Hampshire, a big classic gray clapboard facing the Atlantic, filled with wicker furniture, snapshots of family clambakes, and a collection of framed *New Yorker* "summer issue" covers going back to the twenties. Jon had graduated from New England College, where he'd concentrated both on business and the arts, including drama and dance, in June 1977. He'd spent that summer at Harvard in the highly selective Radcliffe Publishing Program, making many of the friends that would form the nucleus of his New York clique, including Gary Fisketjohn, Morgan Entrekin, Jonathan Roberts, who later was involved with *The Preppy Handbook,* and Katy Dobbs, whose first New York job was at *Glamour* magazine. Jon landed a job in the advertising department of *Rolling Stone,* where he caught Jann Wenner's eye by increasing movie ads by 400 percent in one year. A pitch letter he wrote to Barry Diller got him the job at Paramount in 1978. "He couldn't believe it," says Katy Dobbs. "I mean, Jon was this kid from New Hampshire, really *green.* It all happened so fast for him, maybe too fast. And then along came Andy."

Old money, Harvard, Hollywood—it was a résumé that Andy couldn't resist. And there was something else about Jon Gould that drew Andy toward him: like Jed, he had a twin brother named Jay. "Isn't it weird?" Andy told me. When Jon called to thank him for the roses, Andy ordered Brigid to send him a dozen every day, still using the ads alibi. After two weeks, Jon asked Chris to get Andy to stop; the roses were embarrassing him at work.

Andy had cast Chris in the Cupid role, and he advised Andy "to go for it. Even if it's unrequited, it's good for you to let your feelings out."

"I had to convince Jon that it was worthwhile to be with Andy," Chris says. And Andy started convincing him in the way he knew best, by taking him along to glamorous parties: C.Z. Guest's dinner for the Herreras at Doubles; Bianca's birthday dinner at Mortimer's. We all went to 54 after that dinner and I could hardly believe my eyes when I saw Andy being thrown around the dance floor like a scarecrow by André Leon Talley. His wig looked as if it were about to fall off, but Andy was oblivious of everything and everyone but Jon, who stood watching from the bar. "I wanted to show Jon I could dance," Andy told me the next day, "because he's the best dancer. But he just said I embarrassed him by dancing with a boy. Oh, what am I going to do, Bob? You have to get to know him and tell me what to do."

On Jon's birthday, Andy invited him to the opening of *The Little Foxes* and took him backstage to meet the star, Elizabeth Taylor. Then he asked Thomas Ammann and me to join the two of them for dinner at Le Cirque. I liked Jon. He was bright, articulate, polite, and he complimented *Interview* a lot. The only thing that worried me was the way Andy hung on his every word and laughed loudly at all his jokes, even when they weren't meant to be jokes.

A few nights later, after another Society dinner at Doubles, I dropped Andy off at Jon's loft about fifty blocks out of my way. I could see that Andy was crazed with anxiety and needed to talk to someone. "Jon said I could come over to watch TV," he said. "Maybe tonight will be the night. Oh, Bob, I don't know what to do. You're a Taurus, give me some tips on how to handle Tauruses."

The next day Andy told Chris that he would buy him a gold watch if he could get Jon to fall for him, or better yet, move in with him. Chris persuaded Jon to spend the following weekend with Andy at his friend Peter Wise's family house on Cape Cod. Andy was so excited that he ran out and bought Jon a double strand of pearls. Chris showed me the Polaroids he took of Jon wearing them on the beach. They were big and baroque and Jon looked uncomfortable in some shots and self-satisfied in others. "He wondered what was going on," Katy Dobbs says. He was worried, she says, about a seemingly offhand remark Andy had made in a recent *Interview* cover story: "I sleep with a sock." The sock, Jon had told her, was his. Andy had stolen it from his gym bag. "There was tremendous ambivalence," she says, "on Jon's part."

And a giddy determination on Andy's. He desperately tried to make himself more attractive. He never wore his glasses anymore, only his bright blue contacts. He tried mascara to look prettier. He wore Cub Scout pants to look younger. He replaced his plastic shopping bag with a backpack to look more macho. He grabbed Sabrina Guinness's lipstick in an elevator one night and smudged it across his cheeks. "Who do you think you are? Diana Vreeland?" I teased. "It works, Bob, it works!" he shouted in joy. He was lifting weights and losing weight. And showering Jon with gifts: lizard boots from Susan Bennis/Warren Edwards, a Barry Kieselstein-Cord sterling silver belt, a gold Rolex, a Bulgari signature watch, a drawing of the Bulgari watch. It sometimes made me mad to watch this sudden spurt of extravagance, especially when I thought about the time Fred got him to do Jed's portrait and Andy did it in miniature. But that was the point of what he was doing: If he had lost Jed because he was stingy, then he was going to win

Jon with his generosity. Jed complained of his coldness and neglect. Well, he was going to show Jon just how warm and attentive he could be. He was going to show all of us. And show Jed too.

At the end of May, when Jon flew to L.A. for his monthly Paramount meetings, Andy had Brigid send him one hundred "love letters" a day. These missives consisted of misprinted "Earhole Productions" labels gummed onto blank envelopes containing blank sheets of hotel stationery. "That way there's no writing, no evidence, no palimony, right?" said Brigid. Perhaps. But Andy had also come up with a way to respect Jon's intense desire to keep his gay life private and still to let him know that Andy was back in New York, pining away.

He was also wasting away. He seemed to live on shreds of salad, sips of fruit juice, and vitamin pills. "You're too thin," I told him one day in June. "No, I'm not," he said, angry at me for bringing the subject up. I had gone to his house to pick up some drawings he had to sign for a client and he was frantic because Archie, who had just had an operation on his stomach, was trampling all over them. Then Jed called to check on the dogs and Andy turned stiff and sour. "Uh-huh," I heard him saying. "Oh, really. Uh-huh. Yeah. No. Well, you're not here, so how would you know?" His cheekbones pressed against his skin, his wrists looked as if they were about to snap, and for the first time I thought of Andy as an old man. A couple of days later, Dr. Cox told him that he couldn't go on a trip to the West Coast because he had walking pneumonia.

Within a week, he insisted on getting out of bed to fly to Atlanta for an *Interview* promotion at the Limelight disco. They flew down ten *Interview* staffers and contributors and a pack of paparazzi for a big party, but Andy refused to come out of the manager's office for an hour and a half—he was talking long distance to Jon. On the Fourth of July weekend, Andy was down in the dumps because Jon went to see his family in New Hampshire and didn't invite Andy along. We went to a screening of *Raiders of the Lost Ark,* at Paramount.

As we walked home on Central Park South, Andy opened up. "I guess it's kind of great to have a family," he said. "Jon really cares about his so much. But I don't have a family. I never wanted to, so I guess now I'm happy. I never had a grandmother. Isn't that strange?"

"Why don't you ever see your brothers?" I asked.

"Oh, I'm mean to them. I always say I'm out of town." He didn't say anything for half a block and then he went back to Jon. "I have to be in love with Jon," he said, "or I'll go crazy."

"Try not to think about it so much, Andy."

"If I don't think about it, I'll go crazy."

After I dropped Andy, I went to a party full of fashion models and rich kids. A new arrival from California approached me and asked, "Do you know Andy Warhol?" He's my boss, I said. "Do you know Jed Johnson?"

Pretty well, I said. "His new friend Alan?" Not so well. "Alan's old friend Steve?" Barely. "Well," said the Californian, puffing out his pecs, "I just broke up with Steve." That was what fame came down to: some kid getting off on being the ex of the ex of the ex of the ex of a star, while the star went home alone.

At the end of July, Andy and I went to Newport, Rhode Island, with Ina Ginsburg for an anti-suicide benefit chaired by Nuala Pell, the senator's wife. Despite Ina's sidelong glances and nervous titters, Andy told everyone we met that he was *for* suicide. The only problem was that he wasn't joking. Whenever he and I were alone, he started in on Jon. He was upset because Jon had turned down his invitation to come to Newport with us. "I mean, this is just what he likes, right?" he asked, as he stared out the window of the Bellevue Avenue mansion where we were staying at the roaring waves hitting the rocks of Cliff Walk. "Oh, what should I do, Bob? I can't *not* see him. We finally slept in the same bed, but . . . How do you do it? I mean, he really likes me. Rupert's so aggressive. I wonder how he does it?"

I told Andy that I had always considered myself a bit of a romantic retard, but next to him I felt like I had a doctoral degree from Errol Flynn University. It worked—he laughed. Still laughing, he said, "I guess the reason nothing happens with me and Jon is . . . we're both girls, right?"

"Can't we talk about something else?" I finally pleaded. "Why do you have to be so obsessed with Jon?"

"These things just happen, Bob." That became his line after that whenever we discussed "the Jon problem." On the way to the Newport airport, where our chartered Cessna was waiting, Andy startled Ina again by saying, several times, "Oh, I hope it crashes. That would be a good ending."

That summer Andy decided to become a male model. Chris Makos took test shots for his head sheet and Andy asked Zoli down to lunch. Zoli agreed to represent Andy for special assignments, which is agency lingo for celebrity endorsements. "Oh, I want to be a regular model," said Andy. "I think it would be so much fun to go around with my portfolio like all the other kids."

"You mean you're willing to do *go-sees?*" Zoli asked—models' auditions.

"Oh, yeah," Andy said. "And runway. And catalogue. And editorial. Can't you get me in those great jean ads, jumping up and down with a bunch of other cute guys?"

Zoli said he'd try. After that, Andy's first question every day when he arrived at the Factory was "Did Zoli call?"

Zoli did get him a couple of runway jobs and Daniela Morera put him in a *L'Uomo Vogue* spread jumping up and down with some other cute guys, but it was obvious that he was being used for his joke value. That October,

Halston asked him to model in a Martha Graham charity fashion show at Bloomingdale's. He didn't appear until the end of the show, accompanied by Victor Hugo. His face was caked with makeup and he wore a voluminous royal blue taffeta smock with a big red bow around his neck. He looked like a cross between a clown and a Christmas present. Victor wore the same outfit in emerald green. As Andy minced down the runway, I could hear the ladies around me buzz. The words they used were *weirdo, creep,* and *sissy.*

The next day, I told Andy Halston and Victor had made a fool of him. "They did not!" he yelled. "I looked great! You're just jealous, Bob, because you're too short to model."

Two weeks later, we had another fight over the latest Chris Makos photos of Andy, drag pictures of Andy looking like the corpse of Candy Darling. "But Andy looks like a beautiful young girl in these photos," said Chris. "Yeah, Bob," said Andy, lifting one of them to his eyes to admire his flawless white skin and long blond locks. "What's wrong with these photos? I look really good."

That Thanksgiving, we were in a box at Madison Square Garden for Rod Stewart's concert. Andy was sitting in front of me, jerking his head violently up and down and side to side, not in time to the music. His wig was teased out into a wild punk pouf and I could tell that he thought he looked real cool. I thought he looked like a three-year-old having a temper tantrum or a fifty-three-year-old having a nervous breakdown. When he turned around and saw the expression on my face, he gave me a sick little smile and said, "Oh, I know I'm going crazy, Bob. But you don't really care, do you?"

The emotional turbulence of the past two years had taken its toll and Andy's work showed it. I wasn't sure if he cared about that either. After the 1979 Retrospectives and Reversals, he'd got stuck in a rut, recycling old ideas, as if he were too tired or too distracted to come up with anything new.

For his first big series of paintings and prints of the eighties, Andy reached back to his fifties staple: shoes. The Diamond Dust Shoes of 1980 actually started out as an advertising assignment from another staple: Halston. Victor Hugo sent down a big box of various styles to be photographed for the ad campaign of Halston's shoe licensee, Garolini. Ronnie turned the box upside down and dumped the shoes out. Andy liked the way they looked spilled all over the floor. So he took a few Polaroids and had Ronnie take a lot more. The diamond-dust idea was stolen from Rupert Smith, who had been using the industrial-grade ground-up stones on some prints of his own. He was foolish enough to tell Andy where to buy it and foolish enough to be surprised when it turned up as Andy's art. "Oh, it fell on my painting and stuck," said Andy. It was the first time since I had started working for Andy that I was totally turned off by his work. He said I didn't know what I was talking about, adding just to be sure to get Mrs. Garolini to buy a big one for their showroom. I did, but it was one of the few sales—none of Andy's dealers in Europe or America wanted to do a Diamond Dust Shoe show.

Andy had more success with another big series in 1980: Ten Portraits of Jews of the Twentieth Century. The prints, which were done first, marked the beginning of a long line of formulaic editions, and the paintings were practically copies of the prints. The idea came from New York dealer Ronald Feldman. Around the office, the working title was "Jewish Geniuses," because Feldman had sent down a list of over one hundred candidates and every one of them was an indisputable master in his or her field. "Why are they all so smart, Bob?" Andy asked. "Could it be something in their diet? Don't you wish you were Jewish sometimes?"

Andy thought about Jews a lot. He was fascinated by them, afraid of them, dying to be accepted by them—but he never mentioned that his mother's grandmother was Jewish. Often, he seemed to think that almost everyone he met was Jewish and hiding it. He regularly said things like: "Can you be Jewish and named Cathy?" "She had that plain, good, pretty look, so she must be Jewish." "She was putting down kids and dogs, trying to make me think she's not Jewish." Part of it came out of his feeling of rejection by the Jewish intellectuals of the art world. When Helen Frankenthaler suggested Kenneth Noland for the series one night at Elaine's, Andy's comment to me was "I never knew Kenneth Noland was Jewish! So that's why he gets such good reviews."

The final choices were more Feldman's than Andy's: Einstein, Freud, Kafka, Martin Buber, Gertrude Stein, George Gershwin, Louis Brandeis, Golda Meir, Sarah Bernhardt, and the Marx Brothers. Andy wasn't sure who Buber and Brandeis were. He liked Golda Meir, "because we already have a screen of her." And he showed some mild enthusiasm for the Hollywood contingent, Groucho, Harpo, and Chico, and for Sarah Bernhardt, who he couldn't believe was Jewish. He let Rupert and Ronnie do almost all the work on this series, as if he were afraid to get close to it, for fear that his real feelings might come out. It's a pity, because the finished products were mechanical and dull.

He seemed embarrassed and annoyed at the first showing of Ten Portraits of Jews of the Twentieth Century, at the Jewish Center of Washington, in Bethesda, Maryland, in March 1980. "Everybody's Jewish here, Bob," he said. "It's a Jewish center, Andy. What do you expect?" "They're all asking me 'why' and 'how,' Bob. What do I say?" "Tell them you admire the intelligence and creativity of the Jewish people, because you do." "I do?" A man came up to Andy and asked, "Did you use all these different patches of color to show all the different facets of Gertrude Stein's personality?" Andy said, "Yes."

Then Ronald Feldman came over and told us that he had sold so many portfolios of prints that he was raising the price from $6,000 each to $9,000 each. "You mean the price just went up while we were standing here?" asked Andy, suddenly less embarrassed and annoyed. Feldman explained his brilliant marketing strategy: He had divided the edition of 250 portfolios into 10 groups of 25, each priced in increments of $3,000. The first group had been sold at $3,000 before the opening, sight unseen, to cover his costs. By the time we left the Jewish Center, Feldman had hit the $12,000 level, and some of those who had paid a lower price a few hours earlier were reselling their portfolios at a profit on an instant secondary market. "Oh, this is so great," said Andy. "We've got to get Ron to give us some more Jewish ideas, Bob."

Andy also did a big German series in 1980—portraits of Josef Beuys, whom many saw as the most important figure of postwar German art. The Beuys by Warhol series was jointly commissioned by the Hans Meyer Gallery of Düsseldorf and the Lucio Amelio Gallery of Naples. Beuys was everything Andy was not: intellectual, political, anti-fashionable. At the press conference after the Naples opening, Beuys went on and on about art and history and philosophy, while Andy sat there staring at São Schlumberger's big emerald ring.

Beuys was very involved with the new Green Party and let it be known that he would like Andy to contribute a poster for their 1980 election campaign. Andy agreed—the Beuys deal was too big to say no. When the then Factory receptionist, Princess Ingeborg ("Pingle") of Schleswig-Holstein, a sweet-hearted, plain-dressing young German aristocrat, heard about it, she had a fit. The Green Party was an East German front, she said. Fred told her that Andy had to do it for business. "You care more about money than my country!" Princess Pingle screamed. Later, in tears, she told me she was considering quitting her job. "I just can't go on working for a person," she sobbed, "who would make a political statement without even knowing what it means."

Andy had a talk with Princess Pingle. He told her that Beuys couldn't possibly be a Communist. "His daughter wants to be a model," he said. (Actually, Andy wanted to make her a model.) Princess Pingle calmed down, but still Andy worried. What if his rich German portrait clients thought like her? What if the Greens really were Communist and he got in trouble with the IRS when Reagan came in? What if he didn't do the poster and Beuys got mad? "Oh, I know what to do," Andy told me. "*You* write my name and my line on the poster for me, Bob. That way I can always say I didn't know what was going on, right?" So, in my best fake Warhol script, I wrote, "ANDY WARHOL DÜR FÜR GRÜN."

"This is so ridiculous," I told Andy. "*You* endorsing an *environmental* party."

"Oh, I know," said Andy. "And I can't even go to the country, right, Bob?"

We laughed our way through the litany of Andy's complaints against nature.

"I can't go to the beach . . ."

". . . because you turn purple."

"I can't go to the mountains . . ."

". . . because you can't breathe."

"I can't go to the, uh, woods . . ."

". . . because it's so itchy."

For a moment, it was like the days of our Abbott and Costello act.

The only person Andy really wanted to paint in 1980 was the Pope. He had been wanting to paint the Pope, any pope, since at least the early sixties. At the Naples opening of his Beuys show, word came from one of the vast network of Italian socialites he had competing to land the Holy Father that the holy moment was at hand. Andy and Fred got up at five the next morning and rushed to Rome in a limo, but the supposedly private audience turned out to be an audience for five thousand. "At least we were in the front row," Andy said, "but the Pope thought Fred was me."

In 1981, Andy's big series were the Dollar Signs, which harked back to the Dollar Bills of the early sixties, and the Myths, which brought him full circle to the cartoon idols that launched his Pop Art career. Recycled or not, Andy's art was bringing in more and more money. By 1980, the art business was probably grossing about $5 million a year. Each of the big series was at least an $800,000 deal, and there were many smaller deals and sales of earlier works too. After the 1979 Whitney show, the private-portrait business hit new heights. I estimate that in the early eighties Andy was painting about fifty clients a year. At $40,000 for a two-panel portrait—and many clients commissioned four or more—that added another $2 million to the annual total.

On one afternoon in Miami alone, three local socialites sat for their Polaroids in rapid succession, though we had to make sure that they didn't see each other going and coming from Andy's suite, because they were bitter rivals. On another day in Zürich, Bruno Bischofberger took us to a client in the morning, Thomas took us to a client in the afternoon, and an Argentine man stopped us on the street and asked, "Are you Andy Warhol? Can you paint my wife's portrait?" We took the man and his wife back to the hotel, and while Andy popped the Polaroids, Fred checked out the check.

Between 1980 and 1982, I sold almost a million dollars in art myself, most of it commissioned portraits. My clients included Lynn Wyatt, Florinda Bolkan, and Diana Ross, who stunned us by paying her $95,000 bill—for four portraits of herself and each of her three daughters—on the spot.

Consuelo Crespi helped me get the Krizia designer, Mariuccia Mandelli; Ina Ginsburg introduced me to the Hyatt Hotels tycoon, Jay Pritzker; Ina's friend Gaetana Enders, the wife of the American ambassador to Canada, led me to Conrad Black, the financial whiz kid of Toronto. After her husband was transferred to Brussels, Gaetana arranged for Andy to do the portrait of the old Belgian Surrealist, Paul Delvaux, which grew into a $120,000 deal and an exhibition sponsored by Baron Léon Lambert at his elegant art-filled bank. Adriana Jackson, who had helped me snare my first "victim," Maria Luisa de Romans, back in 1972, now sent me her younger sister, Loleta Marinotti, as well as the Bertis, who were the leading manufacturers of industrial dishwashers in Italy. She also talked Iolas into commissioning the Alexander the Great paintings and prints, another substantial deal. I split my commission with some of these helpful ladies; Andy rewarded others with their own portraits.

Then there was Lily Auchincloss. Andy had a thing about getting her portrait. She was one of those people he'd been pursuing since the fifties, when he was making the magazine rounds and she was a stylish young heiress working in the features department of *Bazaar.* "She's a van Ameringen, Bob," he reminded me every time her name came up. "That's International Flavors and Fragrances, Bob. They sell the perfume to all the big perfume companies. Do you know how much money that is, Bob?" Andy wanted Lily's portrait so badly he even made a donation to her pet cause, the Cathedral of St. John the Divine. No doubt his desire was fueled by the fact that Lily was also a trustee of the Museum of Modern Art, another obsession of his since the fifties. So when she invited me to spend a weekend at her house in Bermuda, Andy was beside himself. "Tell her she doesn't have that much time to have her portrait done," were his farewell words. "I mean, while she still looks good."

Something told me that sales pitch would not work. And I never made sales pitches in any case. People knew that Andy painted portraits. They also knew that I worked for Andy. I waited for them to put two and two together, although I wasn't above dropping a hint at an appropriate moment. When our conversation quite naturally came around to Andy, I told Lily about his latest portraits. "I'm not the portrait type," she said. "I don't want to wake up every morning and look at *me.* " She added that she would like to buy something by Andy, "so long as *you* get the commission." I recommended a Mick Jagger portfolio, as we only had two left and I was sure they would increase in value. (Shortly before Andy died, Lily sold hers for the same price she paid for it, $16,000. It's now worth ten times that.)

My social life was paying off, for me and Andy. But the people I was selling to were also becoming my friends, and that made Andy nervous. I was making more and more trips on my own. I found it easier to sell Andy without Andy there, pushing me to pop the question and blow the deal. On weekends, I often went to Washington and stayed at Ina Ginsburg's house, editing the interviews she was doing with increasingly high-level politicians and officials, Republican and Democratic, going out to cocktails and dinners looking for new stories and new clients. I went to the Amazon with São Schlumberger and ten art collectors from the Museum of Modern Art's International Council. I went to Colombia with Diane von Furstenberg and came back with a twelve-month advertising contract.

In February 1980, Andy, Fred and I were in Zürich, and scheduled to depart for Düsseldorf in the morning. I decided not to go with them after all and drove to Gstaad with Thomas Ammann instead. It was a turning point of sorts, that road not taken, and afterward they seemed increasingly envious of my social life. In Gstaad I ended up staying with Bill and Pat Buckley. They asked me back every winter and also to Connecticut for summer weekends. In the spring and fall of 1980, their Park Avenue lunch parties usually included Jerry Zipkin, Estée Lauder, Nan Kempner, Fran Stark, and Betsy Bloomingdale, all of whom had either just spoken to Nancy Reagan that morning or were going to speak to her that afternoon. Except Bill Buckley, of course: He had just spoken to or was about to speak to Ronnie.

In July 1980, Denise and Prentis Hale invited me to their 10,000-acre ranch north of San Francisco. "You can't say no to Denise," Andy told me. "If we can get her portrait, we'll get that whole crowd." Andy liked Denise for two reasons. He said she was "the smartest of all those ladies because she puts her jewelry on and off in the limo where the hotel safe people can't see how big it is." And she was the ex-wife of Vincente Minnelli, which meant she was the ex-stepmother of Liza, which meant Andy had something to talk to her about.

Prentis Hale was the semiretired chairman of Carter Hawley Hale, which owned Neiman-Marcus, Bergdorf Goodman, a few hundred other department stores, and the Waldenbooks chain. He had become like a second father to me and Andy wasn't happy to hear the advice he had given when I told him about my liver problems: "Anybody who doesn't treat you right, who puts you down, drives you to drink and drugs, get rid of 'em. Cut 'em right out of your life." Nor was Andy thrilled to hear about Prentis Hale's collection of Renoirs and Bonnards. "If they like Impressionists," he always said, "they don't like my art." Prentis didn't. But Denise wanted her portrait in the worst way and Andy was waiting, Polaroid packed, for the call from the Coast when I went to stay with them for the second time. "Tell her we can trade for jewelry," he said. I thought that would work as well as telling Lily Auchincloss she was running out of time.

After a long weekend by the heated pool in the ninety-degree heat, I flew to Los Angeles with the Hales in their corporate jet. That night, Denise and Prentis gave a small dinner in a private room at Le Restaurant for William French Smith and his wife, Jean, and William Wilson and his wife, Betty. "They're the inner-inner," Denise explained. "They're the ones Reagan really listens to.'' As it turned out, Smith became Attorney General, and Wilson, after convincing Reagan he should establish diplomatic relations with the Holy See, was the first ever American ambassador to the Vatican.

At the Hales' dinner, the conversation moved to a discussion of the way the press was covering the Reagan presidential campaign. Bill Smith and Bill Wilson seemed more worried about the media than about Jimmy Carter. Wilson seemed to blame me personally for the press's not reporting Carter's alleged transfer of two jet fighters to Libya. ''I didn't know about that,'' I said. But before I could explain that I was probably interviewing Diana Ross when it happened, he shouted, ''I'm telling you it's true!''

Janet de Cordova, the wife of the producer of ''The Tonight Show,'' stepped in and told Wilson that while I wasn't a Washington correspondent, I had some pretty good ideas about how to help Reagan's image with young voters. Wilson glared, Smith nodded, and Denise beamed. When I finished, Prentis said, ''Young man, you could do a great thing for your country if you got Andy to switch.'' Everyone agreed, as Prentis went on to say that he didn't know why young people would admire ''an artist who can't paint, but they do, so we have to get him on our side.'' Then he paused and added, ''And if Andy did switch, I'd know for sure that he's a big whore.''

When I got back to New York two days later, I broached the idea of doing a portrait for the Reagan campaign to Andy and Fred. To make it more palatable, I said I was almost certain that I could sell several more to his rich supporters after the election. Andy had already done a portrait for the Kennedy campaign, but it was obvious that Carter was going to win the nomination at the Democratic Convention in New York the following week. Fred immediately vetoed the idea, saying it would look ridiculous to switch from Kennedy to Reagan. ''Why?'' I said. ''It just shows that you think Carter's doing a bad job.''

The ensuing argument was not really about politics, though it had a lot to do with power. That became all too apparent when Andy announced that it was his birthday and he was taking Fred, Thomas Ammann, Richard Weisman, and a Texan friend of his to lunch. ''Fred says you can't come,'' Andy told me, ''because you'll just get into a fight with Richard.''—Weisman was a big Carter booster. After the lunch, I found out the real reason why Fred didn't want me there. Thomas told me that the Texan offered to buy 25 percent of *Interview* for $2 million. Of course, neither Fred nor Andy mentioned a word of that to me.

In October, *New York* magazine asked Andy to do a portrait of Reagan for their cover and Andy wavered, as it wouldn't be an endorsement and it was becoming more apparent every day that Reagan was going to win. Fred vetoed that out of hand too, saying, ''Andy's not an illustrator.'' It was the same week that Andy's Beatles cover for *Rolling Stone* hit the stands— approved by Fred.

The day after the election, Andy called from Düsseldorf and asked to speak to me. "Oh, Bob, I'll do Reagan's portrait now," he said. I said he should have done it when Prentis Hale asked, or *New York* asked. I didn't think they would want it now. "Oh, Bob, you've got to get me in with the Republicans. You've got to."

Two days later, he called from Paris. "Are you going to the Inauguration?" he asked. I said my Republican friends could probably arrange for me to cover it for *Interview.* "Oh, can I come as your photographer, Bob?" asked the instant Reaganite convert.

Andy and I did cover the inauguration together. Or rather, he said, "Oh, this is too glamorous, Bob," for four days and four nights, and I took notes and photographs for my "OUT" column, knowing my photographer would never part with his. Andy also stole my idea for a Christmas present for Jerry Zipkin that year: the last Carter White House Christmas card, signed by Jimmy and Rosalynn. Then he also stole *my* card, saying he'd lost his. "To Zip, love Andy," he wrote—in his own hand—across it, not even "Andy and Bob." Jerry roared with laughter when Andy gave it to him and said he was taking it with him to Palm Springs to show the Reagans at the Annenbergs' New Year's Eve party.

Meanwhile, I had arranged interviews with two of the Reagan children, Patty Davis and Ron, Jr., for our November issue, which turned out to be perfect timing, when their father won the election, and led to a tremendous amount of national and international pickup for *Interview.* We didn't see Patty again, but Ron and his new wife, Doria Palmieri, were living in New York and Andy and I began to go out to dinner and the movies with them, just the four of us, and four Secret Service agents.

After the election and Ron and Doria's hush-hush City Hall marriage, Andy and I took them to Nippon for a celebratory dinner. They seemed like two simple, normal kids, thrust into a complicated, abnormal situation. They said they got married so quickly and quietly to avoid going through tense events like all their parents meeting for the first time in front of TV cameras at the White House. Ron was about to tour with the Joffrey II ballet company and Doria said that meant she had to give up her job at a small publishing company in the Village. She wondered if she could do interviews for us. Maybe she could get us Frank Sinatra, I said. She said she'd try, if we could get her David Bowie. "Do you think you'd be interested in my father?" Ron asked.

In March 1981, when the Joffrey II tour was over, Doria started looking for a job, as Ron's ballet salary was a pittance and the Reagans believed in making their kids stand on their own two feet. I hired her as my secretary. And while her presidential name certainly didn't keep her from getting the job, as it might have elsewhere, she was more than qualified. I was impressed by the way she had handled a difficult transition with spunk, tact, humor, and intelligence. I had watched her keep the press hounds and political hangers-on at bay, bring Ron back down to earth, and win over her formidable mother-in-law as well as her mother-in-law's formidable friends, including Pat Buckley and Jerry Zipkin. If she could handle that, I thought, she could handle working at the Factory. And, unlike the well-meaning heiresses that Fred usually hired for me, Doria Reagan could type, file, take dictation, and answer the phone properly. After twelve years, it was about time I had a real secretary.

Nancy Reagan posed for the December 1981 *Interview* cover but not, as many assumed, because her daughter-in-law worked for us. Jerry Zipkin, not Doria or Ron, got us the First Lady. And Mike Deaver approved it because he believed it would be helpful to have the President's wife on the cover of a young, hip magazine after the White House china crisis, not because Doria worked there. Andy was indifferent, and sure it would never happen.

I thought she would be the perfect Christmas cover: Red was her color and she had the right combination of glamour, substance, and shock value— Nancy Reagan by Andy Warhol! It would also be a scoop; she hadn't given any in-depth print interviews yet, only a television one to Barbara Walters. And it would make the rest of the press look at *Interview* with new respect. I wrote a short note to Jerry, asking him to ask her, with a postscript saying that we'd always count him among our close friends whether he did or not. Jerry showed the note to Mrs. Reagan and she said yes just like that—she liked the postscript, Jerry said.

Then Mike Deaver called and pressed for a list of questions to be approved in advance. I explained that wasn't our style. Jerry convinced him that prepackaged questions would produce stiff answers and that our casual approach would work out just fine. Finally, Mrs. Reagan's press secretary, Sheila Tate, called to set the time and date. "So, it's just you and Doria, right?" she said. Doria was coming to relax everybody, not to participate in the interview. But it was also key to have Andy there—that was the whole point! I could almost *see* the distasteful expression on Sheila Tate's face as she said, "*Andy Warhol*. Well, I'll have to ask Mrs. Reagan about that."

"Oh, no," I told Doria. "I'm really in a fix. Andy's acting like he could care less, but if I have to tell him he can't come, he'll take it out on me." Doria said she'd call Sheila Tate and explain the situation, and was back in a few minutes with the good news: Mrs. Reagan "didn't blink an eyelash" when Sheila Tate told her about Andy. Everything was set. I couldn't believe it was actually happening: an exclusive interview with the First Lady, before *Vogue* or *W* or *Ladies' Home Journal*, before *Time* and *Newsweek*. I ran to the Factory side of the office to tell Andy, barely stopping at my sister's desk to tell her to call every advertiser we ever had or hoped to have. Andy's reaction was: "Oh, really. Do I have to go too?"

The day before our trip to Washington, Jerry called. He was in a state. "I just had this horrifying vision," he said, "of Andy starting off the interview with one of those crazy questions of his, like 'How big is the President's cock?' So *please,* for my sake, be sure to drive it through that head of his—*no sex questions.*"

Andy was livid. "Does Jerry think I would do something like that? He doesn't really know me, but you do, Bob. How can you even *think* that I would do something like that?"

The first thing Andy said to Nancy Reagan when we arrived at the White House was: "I have a bet with Doria that Ron will never get into Joffrey I." She didn't laugh. Then he went off onto a long, fragmented riff about "how weird Hollywood people are," including his standard line, "they talk behind your back instead of to your face." I think she thought he was talking about her. "I'm sorry, Andy," she said several times, "I just don't get what you're saying."

Mrs. Reagan wanted to talk about her newly chosen cause, the anti-drug program. I think he thought that she was talking about him. "I never saw anyone take drugs," he said several times. "Have you, Bob?" I sat there, frozen in a cold fury, my mind emptying of all the serious questions I had planned to ask her. The next day, I went back to the White House for the photo session, with Robert Hayes and our photographer, Chris Alexander, but without Andy. I was much more relaxed, and so was Nancy Reagan. She became teary-eyed when Chris Alexander brought up their recently deceased mutual friend, Rosalind Russell. But she was all smiles for the camera. It was obvious that she liked it a lot more than the tape recorder.

A few days after the interview, Paul Morrissey stopped by the Factory and Andy couldn't wait to tell him that Nancy Reagan was Jewish. "She told us that Nazimova was her grandmother," he said, "and I remember reading somewhere that Nazimova was Jewish. So that means *she's* Jewish, right?"

"Andy," I corrected him, "Nazimova was Nancy Reagan's *god*mother, not *grand*mother."

"You can have a Jewish godmother?" said Andy. Then, making sure that Doria wasn't within earshot, he added, "Well, Nazimova was a lesbian. Did you know that, Bob?"

Later, Mrs. Reagan told Doria that she had been stunned when Andy went off on his long tangents, because she had been under the impression that he barely talked and that I usually asked most of the questions. She had felt sorry for me during the interview, Doria said, because Andy seemed to be deliberately throwing me off track. All that showed in the transcript. Brigid and I labored over it for hours, trying to make Andy sound as if he knew what he was talking about. We only made minor adjustments to Mrs. Reagan's short, tentative sentences—she often used "where" when it should have been "which" or "that." One major adjustment: In her anti-drug remarks, Mrs. Reagan put pot in the same category as heroin and cocaine. I not only disagreed with that but also thought it would destroy her credibility with the very audience she was trying to reach. After some discussion with Deaver and Tate, it was agreed to delete her references to marijuana. (And I went home that night and smoked a guilt-free joint.)

Mrs. Reagan called me at home when the Christmas issue came out. "Hold a minute for Mrs. Nixon," the obviously ancient White House operator announced. When I repeated the line to Mrs. Reagan, it really broke the ice. She said that she liked the interview, especially the preface, in which we taped Ron reminiscing about her. She *loved* the photographs and wanted to order one as a Christmas present for the President. She kept me on the phone for twenty minutes. She wondered what Doria would like for Christmas. She asked my opinion of her problems with the press. She giggled girlishly as I described the frantic social life of Gstaad. And she returned again and again to what was obviously the real purpose of her call: She was worried to death that her children might be kidnapped by Libyan agents and pleaded with me to tell Ron and Doria that they must keep their Secret Service protection. "Just don't say it comes from me," she said, like a real mother.

The Nancy Reagan cover was a home run: talked about, written about, praised, and pilloried. It so infuriated Alexander Cockburn that he did a four-page *Village Voice* parody, with Andy and me asking the same questions of Hitler. Even I had to admit it was funny—hysterically funny.

The entire issue had a great mix of subjects, from Diana Trilling to Buzzy Kerbox, Hawaii's World Cup surfer, great photographs by Bruce Weber and Robert Mapplethorpe, and the greatest lineup of bylines yet: from Liz Smith and Rex Reed to Debbie Harry interviewing the Swiss artist who won an Oscar for the *Alien* sets. There was also an excerpt from Fran Lebowitz's second book of collected columns, *Social Studies,* which had just hit the *New York Times* bestseller list, making Andy dislike her all the more: "I finally talked to Fran," he told me. "I tried to give her a lot of bad advice and ruin her life."

And we had seventy-six pages of advertising, just under our biggest ever September issue (which had included eighteen pages from Calvin Klein). And the ads ranged from Martha of Park Avenue and Palm Beach to a hot new rock star called Prince posed in a bikini in a shower with a crucifix. December capped another record-breaking year for advertising sales: Total pages were up 20 percent, revenues were up 30 percent to $628,000. I decided to give everyone on the *Interview* staff a raise.

Andy and Fred wouldn't give me a raise though, for the third year in a row. All this good news should have made them happy, but for some reason it didn't. Maybe they were both too racked by personal problems by then.

Andy's problem was loneliness, and Jon Gould.

Fred's problem was drinking, and Andy.

All through 1980 and 1981, Fred's drinking continued to rage out of control. Night after night there were ugly, aggressive scenes. Sometimes his aggression was directed at me. In June 1981, when Andy came down with walking pneumonia, Fred and I went on the planned West Coast trip without him. At the *Interview* promotion party in Seattle, whenever anyone complimented me on the magazine, Fred told them that it wasn't a money maker, as if he were a competitor instead of its president. In Los Angeles, at the dinner my friend Marina Cicogna gave to unveil the portrait of my client Florinda Bolkan, Fred attempted to stand on his head in the middle of Marina's Venetian-style salon and screamed, "I WILL NOT BE A GOOD BOY! I WILL NOT BECOME A BORING GROWN-UP LIKE THESE PEOPLE!—all the while glaring upside down at me.

I wasn't the only object of Fred's scorn. In fact, the more he liked or admired a person, the bigger a scene he made, and the more flowers he sent the following day with an abjectly apologetic note. There was a scorcher at the Metropolitan Museum involving two of Fred's idols, Jackie Onassis and the would-be king of Italy, Vittorio Emmanuel II. He was asked to be an usher at the New York memorial of another long-time idol, Cecil Beaton, but was so hung over that he arrived after everyone had been seated. He lashed out at his friend Pilar Crespi at Mortimer's over a nine-year-old perceived slight. He shouted, "MIDDLE CLASS! MIDDLE CLASS!" at the Herreras and the Erteguns at Elaine's and then threw glasses against the wall. He railed against the Catholic Church at Courtney Kennedy's prewedding dinner and was asked to leave by her mother, Ethel. Diana Vreeland had me on the phone for two hours after that incident. "I never thought that Fred would end up as a bum," she said.

His fantasy life was out of control too. One night at Mr. Chow's he got going on his tiresome tale about his family having owned Houston. When I heard him add that they had also owned Manhattan, I couldn't help laughing. Andy told me that I shouldn't make fun of Fred. "He's probably telling the truth," he said. That was the night that Andy started introducing *me* as "Fred Hughes."

Of course, Fred was under a lot of business pressure, especially since his entire social life, like mine, was expected to be one long business dinner. And there were other reasons for Fred to drink in 1981. Both his father and his grandfather died that year. Andy said no one was allowed to mention the deaths to Fred or to anyone else; that was the way Fred wanted it. And Fred yelled at Barbara Allen because she had told Cornelia Guest about his father's death and Cornelia had sent him a note.

Nonetheless, the big problem was Andy. It was all too obvious that Fred drank to get his attention and all too obvious that Andy didn't want to give it to him. Fred's drinking problem guaranteed Andy the upper hand. Once a year he had a very public "man-to-man talk" with Fred and told him in front of all of us that his drinking was "bad for business." And then, Fred wouldn't drink for a week or two. But when he started in again, Andy said nothing, or made excuses for his behavior, and Fred's behavior went from bad to worse.

Jerry Zipkin took me aside a few nights after Fred somehow managed to expose Pat Buckley's breast at a dance at the Carlyle. Things had gone far enough, said Jerry. It reflected very badly on Andy and me; it was time to do something. "You know how much I like the *three* of you. But I can't go on defending you forever."

Fred's most explosive scene that year was aimed directly at Andy. We had gone to Paris in March 1981 for Nelson Seabra's Red Ball. Fred was already feeling slighted because Seabra, a Brazilian grandee, had asked Andy and me for dinner, and him for after dinner. That same week, Birgitte de Ganay was giving a dinner at La Fleury, the family château at Fontainebleau, and Florence Grinda asked her to invite the three of us. We drove out in a chauffeured Mercedes with Florence, Fred in new salmon suede evening slippers from Hermès. Andy teased him about them. And then started moaning, "This is so glamorous," the moment he saw the moat.

"Gee, thanks, Florence," Andy said on the way back in the car, with Fred in the front seat next to the driver, zooming up the autoroute toward Paris. Then Andy suggested that Florence do some work for *Interview*. For some reason, that set Fred off. "I'M SICK AND TIRED OF YOU ACTING LIKE YOU HAVE ANYTHING TO DO WITH *INTERVIEW*, ANDY!" he shouted. "WHEN I'M THE ONE WHO DOES ALL THE WORK! AND WHAT THANKS DO I GET? YOU AND BOB TAKE ALL THE CREDIT. THAT'S ALL I EVER HEAR. ANDY AND BOB. BOB AND ANDY. ANDY AND BOB. BOB AND ANDY!" He was standing up in his seat now, turned around toward us, shaking his arms in the air, his fists clutched so tightly that his knuckles had turned white. Florence was sobbing, pleading with him to calm down, saying what a great team the three of us were. "Everyone in Paris says it," she said. "Everyone loves the three of you together."

"ANDY AND BOB! THAT'S WHO EVERYBODY LOVES. THEY TREAT ME LIKE A PIECE OF SHIT!" He suddenly lurched across the back of his seat at Andy, as if he wanted to hit him. Andy didn't flinch, but the driver swerved to the side of the road and stopped the car. He said he wouldn't be able to continue unless Monsieur Hughes controlled himself. Poor Fred soon passed out.

Florence said it was sad to see Fred destroying himself, he was such a special person, something should be done to help him. I suggested a drying-out clinic. "Fred doesn't have a problem," Andy insisted. "You just get too uptight, Bob. You should have a drink."

42

Down There

In September 1981, I was invited to the Deauville Film Festival, and when I told Andy, he wanted to go too. Then he wanted to get Jon Gould invited too. "It's the kind of thing he might do," he said, "because he'll think it's good for business." After Jon was invited, Andy said Fred had to come too. Ina Ginsburg came with us, as a director of the American Film Institute.

Fred was drunk almost every night. Ina couldn't understand how the knowledgeable, sensitive, and charming man who took her on architectural walking tours by day turned into a madman by night. "We call him Dr. Jekyll and Mrs. Vreeland," said Andy, making Betty Boop eyes at Jon Gould, who still laughed at everything Andy said, just as Andy still laughed at everything Jon said. They shared a double room with a double bed, but Andy kept whispering that nothing was happening and wondering why. Ina, Fred, and I did a lot of waiting in the Hotel Royal lobby for what we called "the honeymooners." Andy said Jon couldn't decide what to wear and "it was so much fun just watching him change clothes three times. He looks good in everything."

Jon seemed so different since that first dinner at Le Cirque a year and a half earlier. I had really liked him then, but now I wasn't so sure. He seemed arrogant, nervous, silly, pushy, and fashion-crazed, and Andy seemed to be spoiling him and driving him crazy at the same time. With Andy nodding in total and constant agreement, Jon turned every meal into a discussion of what I should be doing with *Interview*. I was beginning to wonder if he wanted my job. Chris Makos later told me that he did—"That was what he really wanted out of Andy all along,'' Chris said, "not jewelry. The jewelry was Andy's trip.''

Something else was adding to the tension between me and Jon and Andy at Deauville: Jon's boss, Barry Diller, had given me a job. It was a very small job: a one-minute "IN and OUT'' spot on Paramount's new TV show, "Entertainment Tonight.'' But I think Jon was envious that I was a social friend of Barry Diller's (mainly through his girlfriend Diane von Furstenberg), and Andy—well, Andy was jealous on principle.

When the producer of the show, Andy Friendly, first called that July and said that Barry Diller had suggested testing me, I asked whether I could be identified on screen as "Editor of Andy Warhol's *Interview* magazine.'' He said he thought that would be a good idea, because they wanted my spot to be like my column. I ran to tell Andy. "Oh, we were trying to get Tinkerbelle that job,'' he said. "Jon introduced her to all the bigwigs. I wonder why they don't want her. I think she's the greatest.'' Tinkerbelle was an Andy Warhol Superstarlet who never quite made it. Then Andy told me that he had been offered the job and turned it down. "You'll never get it,'' he added for good measure.

When Friendly called two months later and said that they had liked my tests and I had the job, Andy said, "Oh, I bet they don't pay anything.''

"They're paying me for one minute,'' I told him, "what you pay me for a week.''

"Oh, really,'' he said. "Well, tell them if it doesn't work out with you, I'm still available.''

After my first two or three segments ran, I brought a tape of them to the office to show the *Interview* staff, all of whom had been rooting for me from the start. Andy chose that moment, in front of them, to tell me, "Oh, you're going to be mad at me, Bob—I'm competing with you now. I'm going to do an In and Out thing on 'Saturday Night Live.' ''

Andy lasted three weeks; I made it through six. But I was almost relieved when Barry brought in a new producer, Jim Bellows, who found my ideas "too sophisticated.'' I couldn't take Andy's jealousy anymore. "Look at the positive side,'' Diane von Furstenberg told me. "Andy and Fred are jealous of you because they know you have the power.'' I tried to see it that way, but it was already too late.

In December 1981, I took what turned out to be my last trip to Europe with Andy and Fred. We flew to Brussels for the Delvaux show, and back four days later, without stopping in Paris either way. None of us could stand to spend more time than that together. Even so, Andy and I had a nasty fight at a portrait-pushing lunch Gaetana Enders had set up for us in Antwerp. "Bob's in the Mafia,'' Andy told the table out of the blue. It was a line he liked to use every so often. I decided it was going to be the last time he did. "If I were in the Mafia, Andy,'' I said calmly, "I wouldn't be sitting at this boring lunch trying to sell your boring portraits.''

In the car on the way back to Brussels, Andy told me I should leave my job if I was so unhappy. I said I was leaving Brussels on the first plane out. A few minutes after I got to my room at the Hotel Amigo, a bellboy appeared with a big box of Belgian chocolates. The note said, "XX Andy."

Leaving a job of twelve years is never easy. Leaving a job that you think is your life is harder. It took me another year, but I think I had started preparing to go months before that fight in Brussels. Marina and Michael of Greece had introduced me to Morton Janklow, the lawyer and literary agent, and when I needed someone to work out my "Entertainment Tonight" contract in 1981, I turned to him. It was my first step toward liberation, though I didn't see it that way then. Mort gave me a late-afternoon appointment, and as the dinner hour approached, we were still talking. The story of my years at *Interview* and the Factory had come pouring out, and Mort was fascinated. "It's amazing," he said, "how this seemingly weak, passive guy has completely taken control of all these bright, strong people. It would make a great book."

I didn't want to write a book, I said, I just wanted a fair deal from Andy. I loved my *Interview* job, but I wanted to share in the success I had largely created, not to have to hustle portrait commissions to pay my bills. Mort agreed to take care of my "Entertainment Tonight" papers and to act as my behind-the-scenes adviser in negotiations with Andy. I knew if Mort called him directly, Andy would freak out. Agents, lawyers, and contracts were forbidden for Factory workers.

Mort and I met to work out a negotiating position: I was basically asking for an increase in salary from $600 to $1,000 a week, after three years without a raise, and some equity in *Interview,* perhaps in 5 percent annual increments building to somewhere between 15 percent and 25 percent, in any form of shares or options most advantageous to Andy's tax structure. I didn't think these were unreasonable requests, especially since Carole Rogers had resigned in April 1981, and I had assumed her responsibilities as associate publisher, though I was denied her title.

I asked Fred to lunch to discuss my proposals, telling him that I thought he should have some shares in the magazine too. He said he'd talk things over and get back to me. He never got back to me. (And he never told me that he already owned 10 percent of *Interview* as a commission for working out the 1976 buyback from Peter Brant and Joe Allen. Instead, he let it drop in *Manhattan Inc.* magazine, a few months after I had left.) Meanwhile, *Interview* advertising and circulation continued on a steep upward trajectory all through 1982. And I was selling twice as much art as before.

Andy continued constantly complaining about his expenses to me, especially after the landlord informed us that he was tripling the rent when the 860 Broadway lease was up at the end of 1983. He had Chris Makos looking for "bargain" buildings to buy in out-of-the-way neighborhoods like the far West Village and the Lower East Side. Then Fred stepped in and found an old Con Edison factory on Madison Avenue between 32nd and 33rd streets. The space was enormous, with three separate wings, each with its own entrance: One would be for the Factory, one for *Interview,* and the third would be rented out. The price wasn't bad for midtown real estate: $1.5 million. Andy was in a state. He was taking a mortgage for the first time in his life, even though at that point he already owned five substantial properties: the houses on East 66th Street and 89th and Lexington, another on the Bowery at Great Jones Street, the Montauk compound, and forty empty acres in Carbondale, Colorado.

The prospect of moving into spacious new offices cheered me. *Interview*'s side of 860 Broadway had gotten severely cramped. The advertising department had grown to three full-time salespeople, my sister and her deputies, Paige Powell and Robert Becker. They could no longer fit in the main editorial room, where the staff had also grown, and had moved into my old office. Just behind it, a new office had been carved for me out of part of the painting studio. Like the old one, it had two doors, so I still felt as if I were working in a passageway rather than a room. And the partition between it and the studio stopped far short of the ceiling. I could hear Andy and Chris Makos lifting weights and doing calisthenics to punk music, as well as discussing that night's plan for the seduction of Jon Gould. And Andy could hear every word I said. "Why are you saying that, Bob?" he often shouted over the wall.

Fred was more excited than anyone else about the new building. He curtailed his drinking significantly and got up early every morning to supervise the demolition and construction work at the site. Everyone noticed the change in him, especially Diana Vreeland. "He's a new man," she told me. "He finally has something to *do.*" It *was* good to have the old Fred back, and he and I spent many pleasant hours together going over the architect's plans, deciding how best to use *Interview*'s wing, envisioning the great parties we'd throw for Andy in the top-floor ballroom. Andy, predictably, remained indifferent. His standard line about the new building was: "Put me in the basement. I don't need a lot of space."

The implication was that we wanted the new building, not Andy, and that the hundreds of time capsules and ever-expanding collection of fifties school desks had nothing to do with the fact that you could barely cut a path from the freight elevator to the front of our present quarters.

Andy had something else to worry about in 1982. The big beach book that summer was *Edie: An American Biography,* by Jean Stein, edited by George Plimpton. It presented Andy as a craven manipulator and an amoral voyeur, who had the other Superstars keeping tabs on Edie Sedgwick's drug taking so that he could be there with his movie camera when she overdosed. Andy had been putting down Jean Stein for years, saying she'd never finish her book, and now she had turned his own tape-recording technique on him, to devastating effect. *Edie* revived all the old perceptions about Andy's degeneracy and evilness, all the old tales that we had spent a decade eradicating. Like everyone else at the Factory, I rose to his defense and spread the party line at lunches and dinners: Jean Stein had wanted to be a Superstar herself in the sixties and couldn't cut it with the other girls; the book was an act of resentment and revenge. What really bothered me, however, was that I knew my heart wasn't in it this time. In fact, I had to work very hard to convince myself that Jean Stein wasn't right about Andy.

Andy's reaction showed that a raw nerve had been touched. It was the first time I had ever seen him let bad publicity make him that mad. He was particularly infuriated by a birth certificate reproduced in the book, for an Andrew Warhola, born in Forest City, Pennsylvania, on October 28, 1930. The mother's name had been blacked out, presumably because it wasn't Julia Warhola and that would imply something very strange about Andy's birth, like illegitimacy, for example. "This is not my birth certificate," Andy wailed. "This is not my birth certificate. Oh, I hate Jean Stein. I really, really hate her." Really, really meant really, really. (It wasn't Andy's birth certificate: Forest City High School records show that *that* Andrew Warhola graduated in 1947 and applied to a pre-dental program at the University of Scranton. His photograph on file bears no resemblance to Andy.)

Pat Buckley, and her friend Shirley Clurman of "20/20," took me to lunch after *Edie* came out. "It's about time you got yourself out of that unspeakable place," Pat bellowed. "You're too good for that pack of creeps and sickos!" I told them that I wasn't *that* good myself and that the place where I worked was nothing like the sixties Factory described in *Edie*. Then I went back to the office and found Andy taking Polaroids of a German boy giving Victor Hugo a blowjob.

Andy spent many weekends that summer visiting his Montauk tenants, Halston and Victor Hugo. He still hated the beach, but Jon Gould loved it— so he went to the beach. But even Halston and Victor were mystified by the couple's behavior. "They'd come out of their cottage," Halston told me, "and they'd be all in pearls. And, you know, it's really odd to see a man dressed in pearls, especially Andy, because he would always be wearing blue jeans. And Jon would have the biggest pearls, with emeralds and diamonds and everything else in between. But, I mean, big booming stuff. And then the next day, they'd have all these Cartier diamond bracelets on and Andy would have them under my leftover sweaters with holes in them, which Victor would sell him for like fifty dollars. He would have these diamond bracelets up to his elbows practically, on both arms. But if you mentioned it, they disappeared. They'd go back to their little cottage.''

Andy changed his will in 1982, and we all wondered if he was leaving everything to Jon Gould. Anything seemed possible where Jon was concerned. But only Fred and Vincent were included in the locked-door meetings with the lawyers in the dining room, and they weren't saying. Was Jed in Andy's original will? I remember asking Vincent. He ran his index finger across his throat and said, ''Not anymore.''

At the end of the summer, Andy and I were on the Eastern Shuttle, on our way to the Reagans' state dinner for Ferdinand and Imelda Marcos. My invitation had arrived without one for Andy, and after a few days, I had called Muffie Brandon, the White House social secretary, and told her that my life would be hell if Andy wasn't invited too. Now, on the shuttle, I had him where I wanted him. He was coming with me, not the other way around, and he knew it. ''Did Fred ever talk to you?'' I asked. ''About what?'' Andy asked. ''About my raise?'' I answered, thinking I'd take one step at a time. ''I asked him months ago.''

''No, he never did,'' said Andy. ''But you can't have a raise, Bob. I have too many bills with the new building.''

''Andy, I think you better get yourself to the White House tonight. I'm going to go with Jerry Zipkin and a couple of ladies from California.''

''How can you say that to me, Bob?''

''Andy, I haven't had a raise in almost four years now and I'm doing so much more work. I should be making a thousand dollars a week, at least.''

''Okay, you can have eight hundred.'' He paused. ''Oh, what should I do? Jon is fighting with his cousin and they have to sell the loft, and then he wants me to help him buy an apartment, but I said he should move in with me and he said that he needs just a, uh, small place, uh, to show his parents when they come to town. What should I do, Bob? Jon makes me so mixed up, Bob. But he's a really good person. He really is. And he knows a lot about magazines. Jann Wenner loved him.''

At the White House, Andy's major concern was finding a phone he could use to call Jon. He made me ask a Marine Guard as soon as we got there, and he spent a large part of the cocktail hour, and the entertainment period after dinner, sequestered in some office chatting with his heart throb. Well, at least he didn't blurt out the inside gossip one of my Reaganite friends had told me that afternoon: Mrs. Marcos had offered herself, backed up by a chorus of Filipino dancing girls, as the after-dinner entertainment, but Nancy had nixed it, saying they already had booked the Fifth Dimension.

The next day, Vincent came into my office and said, ''So the boss told me he upped your salary to seven hundred.'' It was eight hundred, I pointed out.

In October, Ambassador Francis Kellogg and his wife, Mercedes, invited me to Thailand for the two hundredth anniversary celebration of the royal family. The Kelloggs put together a very glamorous group for the Thailand trip: São, Elizinha, Thomas, Franco Rossellini, and Doris Duke (who floored me with her passion for rhythm and blues greats like B. B. King and Muddy Waters—and confirmed Truman Capote's story about her closeness to Elvis). In Bangkok, we were joined by a young Venezuelan couple, Patty and Gustavo Cisneros, who had flown from Caracas on their private jet.

Andy went around town telling friends like Steve Rubell and Bianca Jagger, ''Bob thinks these rich people really *like* him. Doesn't he know they're just using him to get publicity?'' Doris Duke, Patty Cisneros, and Elizinha asked me not to run their pictures in *Interview,* but I did anyway. Andy asked me when Patty was coming to town to have her portrait done. ''Gotta bring home the bacon,'' he said for the one billionth time since I'd met him.

Fred brought me the worst news. ''You have to start traveling with Andy and me again,'' he said with a slim smile. ''We need you in Madrid at the end of January, for Andy's Guns, Knives and Crosses show at Fernando Vijande's gallery. You have to help out with all those Spanish ladies. Just what you love.''

Guns, Knives and Crosses was Andy's big series for 1982. He had been collecting antique guns and daggers over the past year and photographing them so he could tax-deduct them as props. Then Fernando Vijande, a sleepy Spanish dealer we called ''Fernando Hideaway,'' proposed a show in Spain. ''What should I do, Bob?'' Andy asked. ''You went to school in Madrid.'' (I had taken my junior year abroad there.) The first things that came to mind were the Inquisition and the Civil War. ''Oh, I can do the guns and knives for the war, right?'' said Andy. ''But what should I do for the Catholic thing.'' ''Crosses,'' said Fred.

Fred also gave me the latest update on the new building. The architects, he said, had *forgotten* to allow space for the central air-conditioning ducts and the only place to put them at this late stage was through the second floor of the *Interview* wing, where my office was going to be. ''Its not so bad,'' Fred told me. ''Only *half* your ceiling will drop to six feet.'' Fred's office would keep its fourteen-foot ceilings and be painted Diana Vreeland red.

The 1982 Factory Christmas lunch—the last at 860 Broadway—was miserable. No crashing Superstars, no rising real stars, no ladies with limos, no disco kids. ''And no Balducci's,'' Andy ordered. ''We can't afford it.'' Instead, he littered the Ruhlmann table with open boxes of Whitman Samplers, the used models for the Candy Box paintings he was giving his celebrity friends and a very few Factory workers. Meanwhile, the office was ablaze with angry whispers: Andy *was* helping Jon Gould buy an apartment. It cost $460,000 and was in the Hotel des Artistes on West 67th Street, right next door to the building where Jed lived.

"Oh, Bob," he said on his way to the back room, loud enough for the empty-handed *Interview* staff to hear, "you can have anything you want for Christmas."

"I'd take something big," Vincent advised me a little later, "because you're not getting a bonus this year." Andy had given me $5,000 for the past three years. "The boss has cash-flow problems."

I put off choosing my Christmas painting, because I was too busy closing the February 1983 issue. The covergirl was Nastassja Kinski, photographed by Jean Pagliuso and interviewed by Jodie Foster. I had an interview with Prime Minister Seaga of Jamaica. It had been arranged by Gustavo Cisneros, who promised me Felipe González of Spain next. It was my first interview with a head of state—though I didn't know, when we put that issue to bed, that it would be my last interview in my last issue of *Interview*.

For New Year's, I flew to La Romana, the Dominican Republic resort that Oscar and Françoise de la Renta had put on the map, on Patty and Gustavo's Gulfstream II. Also aboard were John Gutfreund, the cigar-chomping chairman of Salomon Brothers, and his quirky, generous second wife, Susan, who was just beginning to make her mark on New York Society with her extravagant dinners in their lavish River House apartment. I liked the Gutfreunds and I wasn't one of those who turned up my nose at Susan's caviar, chili, and floating island menus—those were all my favorite dishes.

Of course, I thought Susan Gutfreund was a likely candidate for an Andy Warhol portrait. I was subtly, or not so subtly, dropping my hints all weekend in La Romana, but Susan wasn't picking up on them. Instead, I was stunned to land Patty. She didn't want her own portrait, she said, that was too much of an ego trip. She wondered if I could arrange for Andy to do a portrait of Simón Bolívar, Gustavo's historical idol, as a surprise birthday present for him. I didn't tell her that his first reaction would probably be "Who's Simón Bolívar?"

At breakfast on our last morning, John Gutfreund asked me about Andy's business. I told him about the new building and how worried Andy was about the $1.5 million mortgage. "Tell Andy," John said, "that I'll give him a mortgage. With *Interview* as collateral. No, I take that back. With *you* as collateral."

It was just a sociable compliment, but it got me thinking as we flew back to New York. Why was I dreading going back to work on Monday morning? Why was I dreading moving into my new office with its six-foot ceilings in a couple of months? How much longer was I going to let Andy and Fred slap me down, as if I were a child with nowhere else to go? I was almost thirty-five years old—did I really want to spend the rest of my life as Andy Warhol's lackey? By the time we landed, I had an answer to all those questions: I was going to get shares in *Interview,* Andy and Fred were going to treat me like a partner, or I would quit.

That night, I came up with a better approach: I wasn't going to ask him to *give* me shares, I would offer to *buy* them, with the commissions I made from selling art. Vincent had already asked me to defer some of last year's commissions, which had almost hit the $100,000 mark, and I was sure I could double that amount in 1983. It was the perfect solution! It would save Andy money now when he needed it, reassure him that I would continue selling art and lots of it, and keep me very happy for a very long time.

On Monday morning, I headed downtown thinking everything might just work out. After lunch, I found Andy sitting in the dining room, in his exercise outfit, waiting for his coach. "How was your trip?" he asked. "Did you sell anything?" I told him about the Cisneros commission. "Who's Simón Bolívar?" he asked. Then I told him that I had decided on my Christmas present: a big Hammer & Sickle painting. "Oh, can't you take something else?" he said. "We only have two of those left, because I traded two with Julian Schnabel the other day, and I could sell those. We might need the money. The new building costs so much. Don't you want a big Shoe?"

He didn't say we had sixty of those left, and we couldn't sell them. He didn't complain about how much his boyfriend's new apartment cost. He didn't even bother to look up at me, as he slowly turned and studied the pages of Christie's catalogue for "A Very Important Jewelry Sale."

I walked back to my office. After a minute or two, I walked back to the dining room. Andy had the jewelry catalogue pressed to his eyeball now. "Andy, I was thinking," I said. "Since you have cash-flow problems and want me to defer my commissions, what if we took those commissions, plus all the commissions I'd be getting in the next few years, plus some money I have in the bank from last year's commissions—and we put all this toward me buying part of *Interview,* just a small part."

"I can't. I can't," Andy whined like a terrified child. "You can't ask me that, Bob."

At least he was looking up at me now, with a cold, hard, defiant look. It was an I-dare-you look, but his voice grew whinier and whinier, more and more helpless, as if someone were forcing him to repeat again and again, "I can't. I can't. I can't."

"But Andy, why can't you even *consider* it?"

"You know why. I can't. I can't."

I walked back to my office for the last time.

There was a call from Thomas Ammann when I got home at the end of the day. Andy had called him, he said, and told him about our confrontation. Thomas knew that Andy wanted him to deliver a message. "Who does Bob think he is?" my boss had told my best friend. "Every time he comes back from one of these rich trips with these rich people, he's so unhappy and he thinks who he is. He's such a problem. Why doesn't he go freelance so he can just travel around with these rich people and sell more portraits? Doesn't he know that these rich people just see him because he puts their names in *my* magazine?''

That did it. I was going to show him once and for all who my real friends were. I was sick of seeing the world the way Warhol saw it. Sick of assuming that all marriages were for money and that all friendships were based on business. Sick of my boss pushing me into a rich social life and then mocking me for it. Sick of him putting down my Republican connections and then expecting me to get him invited to the White House. Sick of being made to feel guilty because the success of *Interview* led to my own success. Sick of selling paintings for an artist who didn't even care what he painted anymore. Sick of the Fred problem, the Jed problem, the Jon problem. Sick of the jealousy, resentment, cynicism, hypocrisy, and denial. Sick of the sickness.

On Wednesday morning, I called Mort Janklow, to check my emotions, to make sure that quitting immediately was the right decision. ''Go ahead and do it,'' he said. ''I don't usually advise people to leave a job until they have something else, but I think in your case you should. For the first time since we began discussing your situation well over a year ago, I think you're ready to do it. And that's the most important consideration.''

That night I had dinner with Bianca, Barbara Allen, and Thomas. He knew what was going on, but Barbara and Bianca wondered why I was so quiet. I couldn't talk, for fear I'd cry. It had finally hit me. I wasn't just leaving a job; I was leaving my baby, the child I'd watched grow month by month, year by year, for thirteen years.

I quit the next morning.

After he read my letter of resignation, Fred instructed everyone at the office to say that I was taking a leave of absence.

Andy went to my sister Barbara and told her, ''Tell Bob, if he can't find a new job after a couple of months, he can always come back.''

43

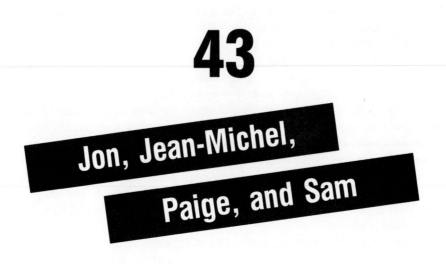

Jon, Jean-Michel, Paige, and Sam

"Oh, hi, Bob." It was Andy. We hadn't seen each other since I quit two months before. I was standing in line at my bank when he spotted me through the window and decided to come in. He was with his new assistant, Benjamin Liu, a sweet-faced Victor Hugo discovery, whose nighttime name was Ming Vauze. I had just returned from another long weekend in La Romana at Patty and Gustavo's with Elizinha, Jerry Zipkin, and the Kel-loggs—they were still my friends, even though I could no longer put their names in Andy Warhol's magazine. Diana Ross had rounded out the house party.

"Hi, Andy," I said. "Hi, Benjamin."

"Oh, we saw Diana Ross last night," Andy said. "She said she had a really good time with you. And, uh, I thought that it would be great if she could interview Frank Sinatra for the magazine and she said she would if we set it up. Do you think you can help us get him? Maybe you could call up Nancy Reagan and ask her to help?"

I couldn't believe what I was hearing. Frank Sinatra never gave inter-views and Doria Reagan had quit *Interview* when I did. Was this Andy's idea of reconciliation? He had been going around town telling people I had quit because I was crazy. I gritted my teeth and said, "I don't work for you anymore, Andy."

I wasn't working for anyone. I wasn't sure I wanted to work *for* anyone ever again. After I'd quit, I'd had offers or feelers from the New York *Post*'s Page Six and the Washington *Post*'s style section, *House & Garden* and *Town & Country,* Paramount Pictures, and the Vatican Foundation, among others.

I was tempted by the last, if only to make sure Andy never got the Pope's portrait.

I avoided Andy all through the spring of 1983. Then, in May, Bianca invited me to her birthday dinner at Mr. Chow's and I accepted, knowing Andy would be there, thinking I was strong enough to face him again. He was at one end of a long table, with Jon. "Hi, Andy," I said. "Oh, hi, Bob," he replied as I headed for the other end, where Diane von Furstenberg and Barry Diller were sitting. Halston invited everyone back to his house for a nightcap. Andy and Jon left early, making a point of saying goodbye to me. Halston signaled me to stay. "Andy was hurt and shocked when you left," he told me. "Now he's starting in on Vincent, saying he doesn't sell as much as you, he isn't very creative. . . . I told him to be careful. Vincent's all he's got."

Oh, well, I thought, I'm glad I'm out of there.

The next morning, Mort Janklow called. "You'll never guess what I have on my desk. A proposal for a book by Andy Warhol: *How to Be an Artist*. He wants me to represent it." Mort said he would turn it down if it made me uncomfortable. I said it made me uncomfortable. And avoided Andy for the rest of the year.

When I did run into Andy, he bombarded me with backhanded compliments on the cover stories I was writing for *Parade,* where I had signed on as contributing editor. "Your Twiggy story was great, Bob. But she doesn't look good anymore." "I loved your story on Clare Boothe Luce. You should marry her, Bob." "We were going to do Jodie Foster, but then we decided she had too much publicity." I smiled and said nothing when he invariably asked, "So who are you doing next?"—knowing full well he'd be doing that person next too.

In early 1984, Fred called and asked if I would consider consulting for *Interview*. I told him that the contract I had just signed with *Vanity Fair* ruled that out. But I decided it was time to bury the hatchet and asked São to invite Fred and Andy to the birthday party she was giving me in May. Fred was our first acceptance. Andy never responded. Finally, the night before the party, as São and I worked on the seating plan in her Carlyle suite, Fred called. He sounded tired and beleaguered. Andy wanted to come, he said, with Jon Gould and four other friends. "Fine," São said, and moved Andy from her table to the one nearest the kitchen.

My dinner partners were Doris Duke and Marina of Greece. My new boss, Tina Brown, was opposite me. "What a party!" she said, beaming. "This is what I want the magazine to be like—Bill Buckley on my right and Steve Rubell on my left."

My mother was also at my table. Andy had come over and told her, "We really miss Bob." "I think he was being sincere," she said, "but I'm still lighting a candle to the Blessed Virgin every Sunday to make sure you never have to go back to that place."

I thought he was being sincere too. I also thought that he just couldn't accept that one of his kids had gone off on his own, without jumping out a window to do it, or disappearing back into the woodwork. It meant he was losing control.

1984 was not a good year for Andy. And his tortured affair with Jon Gould had a lot to do with it. Jon had mostly been staying at Andy's house since late 1982, but he also had his apartment on the West Side, the one that Andy helped him buy. The gnawing question in Andy's mind was "What does Jon do there?" He wanted Jon at his house all the time. And the more possessive Andy became, the more elusive Jon became.

"Sometimes I thought my job was to take care of Jon for Andy," Benjamin Liu later told me. "Andy wanted to show him that he could do things for him because he couldn't give him youth and beauty." Andy had Benjamin do everything from pick up Jon's dry cleaning to help decorate his apartment. "Andy would say, 'I'm moving my current wife next door to my old wife.' "

Jon was steadily acquiring contemporary art, according to Benjamin, and Andy was giving him fifties furniture, according to Chris Makos. Chris's job was to organize "fun, young things" for Andy to do with Jon at night. "Jon was so stingy with the time he gave Andy," Chris said. "If we didn't do what he wanted to do, he would sit there and complain. He was a real nag."

"Jon was a whiner," Benjamin agreed. "Not a seducer. That's how he got Andy to do everything for him. And he could get Andy to do things no one else could. Jon got Andy *to take the subway* to the Bronx Zoo and they had to change lines and it took forever for the train to come. Andy was so nervous!"

Other sources, less caught up in the competitiveness of the Factory, portrayed Jon Gould differently, not so much selfish and mercenary as mixed-up and torn, especially about his relationship with Andy. "I would see them together on Sundays on Columbus Avenue," Susan Blond said. "You could tell he really wanted to be with Andy. But there was another side of Jon. He wasn't sure if Andy was good for his career at Paramount. He wanted to be taken seriously and he knew that you weren't once you were Andy's date. And he talked about having a family. He talked about that a lot."

Thomas Ammann told me he was touched and embarrassed when Jon showed him the collection of dolls he kept at Andy's house. "He called them 'our children,' " Thomas said, "sort of joking, but sort of not. Andy and Jon had this strange fantasy of having children together."

Jon's friends saw a completely different picture. "Jon described his relationship with Andy as a father-and-son thing," Katy Dobbs said. "They were great buddies, and great fun to be with. It was sort of fun to see them in their bedroom slippers, with the Fiesta Ware and the dogs, eating in the kitchen.'' Jon's friends were allowed in Andy's house? Was that another way of getting back at Jed?

Jon had his own room at Andy's house, directly above Andy's on the fourth floor in the front. But Andy's housekeepers, Nena and Aurora, told their brother Agusto, the Factory bodyguard, that Jon slept with Andy in his bed—and that was whispered around the Factory.

It's always invasive to speculate about another person's sex life, but it seems unavoidable in Andy's case. Sex was a major subject of some of his art and most of his movies. Sex, or the lack of it, might be the key to understanding his insecurity, cynicism, jealousy, and coldness. And whether he had sex with Jon, in particular, has direct bearing on Andy's physical and mental condition during the last four years of his life.

Jon Gould told Katy Dobbs that his relationship with Andy was "asexual,'' explaining that "the shooting had affected Andy's sex life, because he was embarrassed by his body, with all the scars, and was uncomfortable a lot and in pain.'' Halston said he thought that the most that ever happened in Montauk "was while Jon was taking a shower, Andy probably looked at him and got, you know, some satisfaction.'' Chris Makos didn't think it even went that far. "I spent weekends with Andy and Jon in hotel suites and houses that Andy rented,'' he said, "and I just don't think that they ever did anything. That was what Andy was moaning and groaning about.'' Chris never did get that gold watch.

When asked if Jon went out with other people while he lived at Andy's, Katy Dobbs said, "At first Andy didn't want him to, but eventually Jon said to Andy, 'Look, this is what I need; I'm thirty years old.' And Andy went along with it.'' Went along with it and suffered. He was down for weeks after Victor Hugo told him that he had encountered Jon Gould at the baths, in March 1983. Victor said he felt obligated to tell Andy, "because of the AIDS thing.''

AIDS hit the Factory early, when it was still known as "gay cancer.'' The first of our friends to go, in 1981, was Joe MacDonald, the star model whose portrait Andy had painted in 1975. Then Jed and Andy's friend from *New York* magazine, Henry Post, came down with it. In the fall of 1982 it came closer: Robert Hayes's roommate developed Kaposi's sarcoma—and everyone started checking himself for purple spots. Eighteen months later, in April 1984, Hayes himself was rushed to Lenox Hill Hospital with a severe case of pneumonia. He remained there for three months, until his family flew him home to Canada to die. I visited him just before he left. I'd never seen death's presence so evident, so mockingly obvious, in someone

so young. "I'm just trying to get better," he said, "but I can't seem to."
Every word was an agony. "Did you see the flowers," he asked, nodding
faintly at a basket of wild lavender and daisies, "that Andy sent?"

I knew all about the flowers and the note that Brigid had to badger
Andy to copy out in his own hand, after she composed it on the typewriter.
No one expected him to visit Robert and no one expected him to attend the
memorial that summer. But Fred told him, "You better go or else." And
he went, slipping into the last row late and slipping out the second the
service ended. Most people never knew he was there, but my sister Barbara
saw him.

I ran into Andy the night I first heard about Robert Hayes's pneumonia,
at a book party for Taki at Mortimer's. Andy was wearing what he always
wore from 1982 to 1985—black turtleneck, black jeans, black sneakers, black
backpack—and chewing bubble gum, a habit he had revived from the sixties
in a further effort to look trendy and young. I asked if he had any news of
Robert Hayes and, cracking gum, he said, "He's in Lenox Hill," making it
sound like Paris, or Disneyland. What I didn't know then was that Andy
had spent a long stretch of that winter visiting Jon Gould in the hospital.

Actually, Andy took Jon to New York Hospital on February 4, 1984.
He too was suffering from pneumonia and he was hospitalized for eighteen
days. Andy visited every night, staying until eleven-thirty some nights. A
hospital employee who grew fond of Jon said that he had introduced Andy
as a friend. She had no idea what their real relationship was, but she "sensed
that they were very close but couldn't picture them together." One day after
Jon was released, Andy brought him back, and he stayed another twelve
days. Jon told his hospital pal that he wanted to go to California, because
he heard there were better facilities there and other kinds of treatment. It's
not clear whether his pneumonia had been diagnosed as AIDS-related at this
point, or how much Andy knew, though Jon was treated by Dr. Denton Cox,
Andy's long-time physician and friend.

The crisis brought Andy and Jon closer together at first. Jon invited
Andy to his family's house in New Hampshire that Easter, along with Katy
Dobbs. "Andy loved going up there," she said. "He loved being part of
that real Americana—Jon's family lived in a storybook town. He was charmed
by Jon's normal family life, and you could see how much he enjoyed the
family gatherings and the closeness." Katy said that early Sunday morning,
while everyone slept, Andy put bags of presents outside their bedroom
doors—"Like the Easter Bunny."

But the way Jon chose to deal with his illness eventually led him away
from New York and Andy—who tried his best to follow every step of the
way. When Jon gave up drinking, Andy gave up drinking. "He wouldn't
have one vodka," Benjamin said. When Jon took up crystals, Andy took up
crystals. When Jon joined a New Age movement called DMA, Andy joined
too. Still, Jon accused him of persisting in his worship of fame and fortune

and faking his sudden interest in "inner peace." As Jon made longer and longer trips to Los Angeles, where he pursued his movie career and signed up for est weekends, it was becoming apparent that he wasn't taking Andy with him.

I ran into Jon in December 1984, at E.A.T., the Madison Avenue gourmet shop. He was buying dried fruits and looked fine. He said things were going great for him at Paramount, now that his friend Frank Mancuso had been named president, but that he might have to "bite the bullet" and move to the Coast. He didn't mention what I had already heard, that he was dating Mancuso's teenage daughter and telling friends he wanted to have a family.

The day after Christmas 1984, Brigid called me from the Factory. Andy had rented a house in Aspen, she said, and taken Jon, Chris Makos, and Peter Wise. There were rumors going around that Andy was now buying a townhouse for Jon, to keep him from moving to Los Angeles, she added. She told me, "No one calls Andy anymore, except Jean-Michel Basquiat, Keith Haring, and Kenny Scharf—he's another one of those dumb graffiti artists. But I don't think a single socialite has called since you left. And Andy hasn't taped in two years. When he has to do an interview, he's running around looking for a tape recorder."

What? Had he stopped taping because I was no longer at his side telling him stories? Or had Jon, with his obsession for privacy, made him stop? What happened to his wife Sony, I asked?

"Oh, he's been divorced from Sony for a long time," Brigid said. She also told me that Si Newhouse had met with Andy and Fred about buying *Interview,* but they turned him down, "so he bought a sixties painting instead. Andy will never sell *Interview.* It's the only thing he's got left." She signed off with a description of Andy's Christmas present for the staff that year, scarves silkscreened with the New Age message "The only way in is out."

Andy didn't buy Jon a townhouse, but he gave him something else in a last-ditch effort to keep him in New York: *Interview*'s March 1985 special "Health" issue. Jon did the cover story on Shirley MacLaine, who went on about the "God-force" that emerged from whole grains if you cracked them the right way. And his influence pervaded half the issue, with stories on the gurus of crystal healing, holistic medicine, and positive thinking. Andy, however, interviewed his Park Avenue dermatologist, Janet Sartin, and there were a few other stories on *his* traditional medical interests, such as plastic surgery and collagen injections. The dichotomy was glaring—and widening.

That winter, Steve Rubell was readying his comeback disco, Palladium, and one night he took Andy to see it, "to get ideas for the art I wanted to use." Andy didn't volunteer his own work, Steve said, but he offered to help get Basquiat, Haring, and Scharf involved. "Andy was with Jon Gould that night," Steve told me. "And I put on the sound system for them and Jon just started dancing, all by himself, in the middle of the dance floor. He was the first person to dance there, actually. Jon loved to dance. And Andy loved to watch Jon dance. I'll never forget him standing in the corner, just watching and watching, like nothing else mattered, he was so happy. I got this feeling, I mean, it's terrible to say it, but I thought *this* must be how they do it—if they do it—Jon dances and Andy watches.

"I'll tell you one thing for sure," Steve added, "Andy wasn't the same after Jon moved to L.A. He didn't care who he went out with anymore, and he had a lot less energy."

In March 1985, Jon Gould bought the Beverly Hills house of actress Joan Hackett, who had died of cancer. He told Andy that it was a real bargain, only $100,000. The Factory whisper was that Jon had sold some of Andy's gifts and Andy was hurt when the jewelers told him. Susan Blond's realtor husband, Roger Erickson, told me that Andy was upset when he mentioned that Jon had sold the Hotel des Artistes apartment for $450,000— apparently Andy didn't know.

In any case, a week after Jon moved to L.A., Andy flew out with Pat Hackett, to work on *The Party Book,* which they were co-authoring. Andy told Joan Quinn that he wanted to open an *Interview* office out there and he started looking at buildings in the million-dollar range. "Whenever we passed a phone booth," Pat told me, "Andy would jump out to make a call. Then he'd come back and be quiet for a while. I knew he was calling Jon, but Jon wasn't taking his calls. I think Jon was embarrassed to be associated with Andy in front of his young movie-biz friends. He was really popular with that crowd. They saw him as cool and smart and ahead of the pack." A few days after Andy arrived in town, Jon flew to New York.

Benjamin Liu said that Jon went to India with "an important person in the crystal movement" and came back with an intestinal virus. Andy worried about Jon, Benjamin said, and sometimes sent him small amounts of cash in the mail, "like your mother would do." And when Jon came to New York on Paramount business, he stayed at Andy's house, which made Andy very happy for a week or two.

But in September 1985, on Labor Day weekend, Jon told his friend Katy, "This is the first time I'm not staying at Andy's."

It was all over, the affair that never really was.

Katy Dobbs put the split into perspective, from Jon's point of view. "For self-preservation reasons," she said, "Jon had to make his world very small and really focus on staying well. He went to California for his career and his health, because there were a lot of things out there, and because he needed to be on his own, without Andy. They were both very hurt and depressed. It was just like a divorce. But Jon had no choice. He was trying to save his life."

"Never twins again" was all Andy said to Benjamin Liu. When anyone asked about Jon, several Factory sources said, Andy always answered, "Jon who?" And changed the subject. One month after Jon dropped him, Andy crossed Los Angeles off the tour itinerary for *Andy Warhol's America,* a photo book he did with Chris Makos. "Andy was never more cynical and bitter," Chris said, "than after he and Jon broke up."

Andy pulled away from Chris Makos in the following year, perhaps because there were no more young fun evenings to organize, perhaps because having him around reminded Andy of Jon. The official Factory line was that Andy was tired of Chris's habit of ordering several of the most expensive items in restaurants and then taking them home in doggie bags.

On the other hand, Pat Hackett said that "after Jon dumped Andy, he became nicer to those of us who had stuck it out. Like me. I really didn't get along with Andy sometimes. But in the last two years we became much closer. He was a nicer person to be with."

There was a noticeable decline in both the quality and quantity of Andy's art during the Jon years. It was as if Andy couldn't deal with love and work at the same time. 1983, when Jon lived with him almost continuously, was Andy's least-prolific year since 1971 (when he was producing three movies). He seemed too distracted to paint a big series, as he had almost every year since the 1972 Maos, and Rupert did most of the work on the latest Ronald Feldman print edition, Endangered Species. The Day-Glo elephants, pandas, zebras, and butterflies looked as if they had been whipped up with the children's-bedroom market in mind. A smaller edition of prints that year, done for a Japanese company, was called Love. The models were Andy's art assistant, Jay Shriver, and his exercise coach, Lydia, and their nude bodies grazed one another but didn't connect.

In 1984, during Jon's hospitalization and the period of closeness between them that followed, there was another edition of prints, for a German company this time, called Details of Renaissance Paintings—Day-Glo rip-offs of bits of Botticelli's *Birth of Venus,* Leonardo's *Annunciation,* and Uccello's *St. George and the Dragon* (the last perhaps the ugliest piece of work in the entire Warhol oeuvre). And that was pretty much it.

Ronnie Cutrone's late-1982 exit from Andy's employ was no doubt the other major factor behind this artistic drought. But it's interesting to note that Andy started painting a lot in late 1984, when Jon started spending more time in California. And when Andy had a fresh brain to pick, a new talent to compete with and steal from, to manipulate and dominate—Jean-Michel Basquiat.

Glenn O'Brien had brought Basquiat to the Factory for the first time in 1981. He was barely twenty, a half-Haitian, half-Puerto Rican kid from Brooklyn, with a headful of dreadlocks and pocketfuls of pot. Glenn had met him back in 1977, when he was still doing his art in the subways and signing it "Samo," and he had been begging Glenn to introduce him to Andy, his idol, ever since. "Are you sure it's all right for him to be up

here?'' was Andy's first reaction the first time he saw him. Then, Henry
Geldzahler started buying his canvases, with their stick figures and handwriting, for a couple of thousand dollars, and the Annina Nosei Gallery in
SoHo signed him up, and raised his price toward the ten thousand mark. In
1982, Bruno Bischofberger suggested that Andy trade portraits with Basquiat. Andy no longer saw Basquiat as a rough-looking black boy who might
mug him, but as a rising star of the art world, whose paintings were going
for $20,000 in Düsseldorf and Zürich.

I was still working at the Factory when Basquiat came by to sit for his
Polaroids. He took a few shots of Andy too—and was back in a couple of
hours with his finished portrait of Andy, this twisted stick figure with shards
of hair framing his head, like a voodoo halo. Primitive and stylized, it
captured Andy's frantic strangeness, his sadness, and his sweetness. "Oh,
I'm so jealous,'' moaned Andy. "I haven't even picked out a Polaroid yet,
and you're all done. I mean, you're even faster than Picasso. God, that's
greaaaat.''

Basquiat smiled shyly.

Two years later, in May 1984, Basquiat had his first show at the Mary
Boone Gallery, and his prices hit $50,000. The centerpiece of that show
was an homage to Andy: a painting of a big peeled banana on a silver
ground. Then Bruno Bischofberger asked Andy and Basquiat to do a series
of paintings together. Basquiat loved the idea. And so did Andy. It was the
way to start painting again. For one year, from the fall of 1984 through the
summer of 1985, Basquiat went to the 33rd Street Factory almost every
afternoon to work with Andy. Then, like every new favorite, he went out
with Andy at night. Andy even provided him with a girlfriend, Paige Powell,
who had become director of advertising at *Interview* when my sister left
three months after me.

Paige Powell was a kind, bright, slightly naive girl from Portland, Or-
egon, who was swept off her feet by Andy's sudden attention, just as we all
had been. Of course, she told Andy everything he wanted to know about
Basquiat, from the size of his cock to what he was painting when he wasn't
working with Andy. As Basquiat's pot problem grew into a coke problem
and then a heroin problem, Andy told her she had to get him off drugs, but
he never told her to stop seeing him. He was too addicted to the inside dope
he was getting on the protégé he had turned into an assistant.

Paige Powell, Bruno Bischofberger, and Thomas Ammann believe Andy
tried to get Basquiat off drugs himself. He certainly *talked* about Basquiat's
problem a lot with all of them, in a conscious effort, I suspect, to counteract
the underlying message of *Edie:* that Andy liked to watch people self-
destruct. Whenever I saw Basquiat with Andy in 1984 and 1985—at Café
Luxembourg, Mr. Chow's, the Palladium—Jean-Michel was going to the
bathroom a lot and coming back with a fine white mustache, and Andy didn't
seem to mind. One night at the Palladium, Andy told Basquiat, "Bob likes

to smoke, give him a joint''—and out of the pocket came a giant bud of sinsemilla. Basquiat chain-smoked pot openly, everywhere, and Andy didn't seem to mind. Joan Quinn also recalled Andy asking her to try to get pot for Basquiat, when they were in L.A. together in 1984.

Andy always seemed his happiest when he was with Basquiat. He liked having an artist in his entourage for the first time. Andy had been snubbed by the New York art world for so long and now suddenly the new generation was clinging to his coattails. Or was he clinging to theirs? Haring and Scharf were also constantly coming by the Factory and going to parties with Andy. Francesco Clemente and Julian Schnabel maintained more distance, but were equally admiring in interviews and over dinner tables. ''There are three great American artists in this century,'' Schnabel once told me, ''Pollock, Andy, and me. And Andy would agree.''

''I really don't know,'' Andy once told me about Schnabel's work. ''I just don't understand it. Maybe it's good. But maybe it's not.'' Andy's standard, private line about his graffiti groupies was ''They just copied all Ronnie Cutrone's bad ideas. Didn't they? But they're such sweet kids.''

At the Tony Shafrazi Gallery opening of the Warhol-Basquiat show in September 1985, Andy was signing autographs on catalogues, magazines, arms, legs, and bellybuttons. Basquiat was floating around in a beaming daze. At first glance their shared paintings looked like Basquiats. Andy had sprinkled the canvases with corporate logos and slogans, hand done to look as if they were silkscreened, and then Basquiat had splashed on his urban voodoo dolls. But the longer I studied these colorful hybrids, the more it was apparent that, although Basquiat had won the battle of each and every painting, Andy had won the war. It might look like a Jean-Michel Basquiat show, but the idea behind it was pure Andy Warhol. Two artists signing one painting—what could be more Warholian?

The reviewers said as much when they wrote that Andy could be expected to play such conceptual games, but Basquiat had forsaken the thing that made him interesting in the first place: his one-of-a-kindness, his integrity. ''Jean-Michel took his reviews very seriously,'' Paige Powell told me. ''When his show with Andy was criticized, he dropped Andy, and Andy was very hurt.''

In one month, September 1985, Andy lost his fantasy lover, Jon—and the best art assistant he ever had, Jean-Michel.

Basquiat had already left Paige for Jennifer Goode, the sister of Area owner Eric Goode. Paige was upset, and worried that she might be pregnant by Basquiat. When she told Andy, he surprised her by saying that it would be great if she were pregnant, she could bring the baby to the office, he would help her a lot. Paige wasn't pregnant, but Andy and Paige grew closer—and closer.

* * *

"The thing is, I fell in love with him," Paige later said. "I always played my relationship with Andy down in the office. But Andy would spend all his time in my office. I mean, it was so obvious. And I did everything with him. Almost every night we went out together. And he called me in the morning and when we got home from being out. I would go to the studio on weekends and do work while he painted. Whenever we went out, we always left together and that's what he wanted. He did the same thing with me that he did with Jon Gould. He didn't want me to go out with anybody else. He told me, 'Well, I guess I should buy you an engagement ring.' "

All through 1985 and 1986 I saw Andy and Paige together everywhere, or at least everywhere there were ads to be sold: designer parties at Bergdorf's, Saks, and Macy's, Calvin Klein and Carolina Herrera fashion shows, and Le Cirque at night when it turned into Seventh Avenue East. Andy was always wearing his newer, younger, look: neon Nehru jackets by Stephen Sprouse, black jeans, white running shoes, giant red or yellow glasses, and his whitest, wildest wig yet. Paige was always carrying a big stack of *Interviews* and often snapping pictures with her free hand. These were used on the party pages of the magazine, to stimulate more ads. Paige was also learning, she said, how to turn advertising contacts into corporate art clients. Ads and portraits. Portraits and ads. Was Andy really falling in love with his director of advertising—and rising art saleswoman—or just making her think that?

"Paige married a magazine," Andy told John O'Connor, another *Interview* staffer, when he asked about her.

Meanwhile, Andy had a new Factory crush. Sam Bolton started working at the Factory as Fred's assistant, in September 1985, shortly after Jon Gould stopped staying at his house and Jean-Michel Basquiat stopped calling. Typically, for a Fred hire, he was from a distinguished old New York and Newport family, good-looking, a little mixed-up, not too ambitious, and only nineteen years old. Andy didn't pay any attention to him during his first two weeks on the job. Then, out of the blue, Andy surprised Sam with an invitation to a cocktail party at artist Hedy Kleinman's loft. When they were left standing together in a corner at one point, Andy surprised Sam again. "Are you going to be my favorite now?" he asked. "Oh sure," Sam answered, blushing. In the taxi uptown, Andy told Sam that he had to go to a business dinner and tried to give him a fifty-dollar bill "to go out with a friend." Sam told him he had money. "I'm sure Andy was testing me," he said later.

Apparently Sam passed the test, because Andy was soon taking him to all kinds of parties. One of the first was at Yoko Ono's apartment in the Dakota, and among the other guests were Bob Dylan, Madonna, Iggy Pop, and David Bowie. Later, Andy told him that Yoko "drove him crazy," Sam said, "because she always got him to do things for her. Andy liked Sean [Lennon] a lot and he did his portrait for free, which he never did. And then he got carried away and said he would do one a year for the rest of his life, and when Yoko brought Sean down the next year, Andy said to me, 'Oh, you've got to get me out of this.' But he took the Polaroids anyway.''

Andy also took Sam to dinner with Cheryl Tiegs, who was wearing a leather jacket with a hand-painted portrait of Basquiat on the back. ''Andy was stabbing the jacket,'' Sam recalled, ''and saying 'Do you think he can feel this?' He told me that he was down on Basquiat because he was on heroin.''

Sometimes Andy took Sam to the little dinners at Odeon, Mr. Chow's, and Nippon that Paige organized to woo advertisers. Needless to say, Paige and Sam were not overly fond of each other. The other regulars at these dinners were Stephen Sprouse, who had traded Andy his complete 1985 line of clothes for his portrait, and Tama Janowitz, who had first met Andy when she was living with Ronnie Cutrone. Andy disliked her intensely then, but he grew much fonder of her when her first novel, *Slaves of New York,* made her famous. Andy loved the opening pages of Tama's downtown roman à clef, which were essentially a graphically descriptive list of numerous penises, and he bought the movie rights from her. Ronnie, who was no longer on speaking terms with Tama, told me later, ''I was sure Andy did that to annoy me.''

After these dinners, when Andy got home, he called Sam, to make sure he got home too. Did he call Sam before he called Paige, or vice versa? I wondered. ''Andy called me every night at eleven,'' Sam said, ''even when we didn't go out together. And he'd say things like 'Do you still love me?' ''

Was Sam ever ''in love'' with Andy?

''After he died, I realized I never loved anyone as much,'' Sam said, ''but it was more like the love for a father, or a best friend.'' He hesitated, then added, ''and it was like romantic love, I guess, a little bit.''

Did they ever go to bed?

''Andy wanted to, he tried, believe me. He was not asexual. He would have had sex with me, if I had let him. He was too possessive. He drove me crazy if I went out for a night with the boys. He'd say, 'You don't love me anymore.' He'd accuse me of having sex, having affairs. He would say, 'You wore tight pants that night, so you want to go to bed with him or her or whoever.' And I wasn't sleeping with anyone. Because I knew it would hurt Andy. I knew he considered me his boyfriend even though I wasn't.

''He wanted me to move into his house, but he never let me see anything but the front hall. He would say, 'I need someone at home.' And he'd say that some night we'd make popcorn and get in bed and watch TV. But then somehow he always got out of it. And he'd always say about my grandmother, 'Get the money. We can go off together and you can support me.' ''

Of course, a week after Andy first asked him to be his ''favorite,'' Sam started coming in on Saturdays, just like Paige. Andy drew and Sam taped and then they both painted. ''He would always say, 'Can't you paint faster?

Faster. Faster.' '' Sam said he mostly helped with portraits, and also sorted
out and dated time capsules. ''The portraits were like Liza-style, that glossy
look. Fred didn't bring in the portraits. Bruno Bischofberger did. Iolas a
few. And Andy was constantly asking everyone for suggestions for what to
do.''

And the suggestions came faster than ever in 1985 and 1986. Ronald
Feldman commissioned a big series of Ads paintings and prints. An Amsterdam gallery commissioned a big series of Reigning Queens paintings
and prints. One German dealer wanted Frederick the Greats. Another German dealer wanted Lenins. The Martin Lawrence Gallery in Los Angeles
ordered up ninety-nine paintings of Campbell's Soup Boxes. The North
American Watch Company asked Andy to immortalize their Movado watches
and the Daimler-Benz Corporation had him do the same for their Mercedes
cars. ''Andy finally stopped worrying about money in 1986,'' Rupert Smith
said. ''He had so much work that even Agusto [the security man] was doing
the painting. We were so busy, Andy and I did everything over the phone.
We called it 'Art by Telephone.' ''

That's what a lot of it looked like. But one 1986 series stood out: the
Camouflage Self Portraits, which Andy started doing on his own, without
any commission. One could barely see his face through the forest green and
olive drab splotches, but in a way these hidden faces were much more honest
than the glamorized masks he had presented in his sixties and seventies self-
portraits. Maybe Andy was beginning to comprehend what he had been
doing all along—splotching up the truth, altering the record, protecting himself in the jungle, hiding.

''Also, Andy finally had a real studio,'' Rupert continued, referring to
the hundred-foot-long open space on the top floor of the fourth Factory.
''Even though it had terrible lighting. He had to fight to get it, because Fred
wanted it to be the ballroom originally and Andy was supposed to paint in
the basement.'' Andy had said he wanted to paint in the basement. And
then he refused to move his studio from 860 Broadway until the lease was
finished at the end of 1983, nine months after everyone else was ensconced
in the new building. By that time, the basement was already full, with time
capsules, back issues, and Andy's assorted collection of finds, fakes, and
junk. And there wasn't any need for a ballroom, because there wasn't anyone
to organize the balls.

Far from being a host with the most, Fred seemed to exist in an increasingly isolated and lonely shell, struggling with his drinking, falling
down even when he wasn't drinking, cut off from the friends he had when
he was. Some friends who still cared, like Mick Jagger and Jerry Hall,
blamed his decline on his boss. ''Andy *represses* everyone around him,''
Jerry Hall told me during the July 1984 Paris couture collections. She said

that Mick wanted to help set Fred up as a private art and antiques dealer, but Fred couldn't conceive of leaving Andy. And yet it was Andy from whom he was most estranged.

"Andy and Fred weren't getting along at all," Sam Bolton said. "They started every day with a fight. Andy was always pushing Fred to do more and Fred was always telling him to get off his back. Andy said Fred was too grand, he had to get a younger attitude."

Paige Powell said, "Andy hardly spent any time with Fred in the last two and a half years. At dinners, Fred would be seated opposite Andy and Andy wouldn't even talk to him. I would feel uncomfortable and Andy would say to me, 'He's drinking.' But then the next day, or soon after, he would tell me, 'You should try to work with Fred. You could learn from Fred.' Andy never wanted to fire Fred, but he never wanted to be with Fred."

"In the end, it was like an old marriage," Daniela Morera told me. "Andy was treated very badly by Fred. Right in front of Andy, he would say, 'Don't believe him. He's vicious. He wants to get something out of you.' I had the feeling that Fred hated Andy—actually, that they couldn't stand each other. But Fred expressed it, and Andy did not."

Andy and Brigid fought too. And Brigid and Fred. "Fred would scream at her from that little balcony outside his office," Sam said, "but Brigid would just sit there, knitting or something, with her dogs, Fame and Fortune." Brigid was long out of her rebellious-heiress phase and deeply into two of her mother's passions: pugs and needlepoint. She brought her dogs to the office every day and spent much of her time there stitching evening slippers, which she sold for $2,000 a pair to visiting art dealers—Fred had been one of her first customers, back at 860 Broadway. Now they barely spoke. "And the last straw with Andy," Brigid told me, "was when my mother was dying and he never once asked me how she was, just how much jewelry she was leaving and when he was going to get to see it."

Apparently, the fourth Factory wasn't the most pleasant place to work. "The building was a real lemon," Brigid said. "A day didn't go by without four workmen coming to fix the heat, the pipes, the plumbing, the leaks in the roof, the phones going down, or sewage seeping into the basement—it drove Vincent crazy. And Andy's office! He couldn't even get into his office. It was filled to the ceiling with boxes and bags. But I don't think Andy cared."

"The door only opened a crack," Sam said. "Andy would just stick his arm in and throw things into these boxes that were already full of stuff. Once he put some important papers in there by mistake and I had to look for them. And all these mice came running out."

Mice weren't the only problem at the fourth Factory, according to inside sources. Small paintings were being stolen, some by a member of the staff who had a drug problem. It was easy, because of the maze of halls and staircases and the three exits. A part-time assistant was selling coke on the premises, sometimes in exchange for the stolen paintings. Andy either didn't know about these things, or thought he was powerless to stop them. "He seemed to be withdrawing," *Interview* managing editor Glenn Albin said, "even from the new young kids who came to work at the magazine. He hardly spoke to anyone." Paige said he couldn't deal with the fact that there were now forty-five employees on payroll, and Benjamin Liu told me that Andy started saying, "I really miss Bob pulling in all the Society people."

At a party at the Palladium, on a Saturday night in December 1985, Andy went on about my *Vanity Fair* profile of Amalita Fortabat, the Argentine billionairess whose portrait he had painted—thanks to Gaetana Enders. Sunday morning Fred called. "Andy and I were wondering," he said, "if you wouldn't like to get commissions for us again." I told him I would think it over, and for half a day I did. That night, at the Met's annual Costume Institute ball, Andy was at Halston's table in his red glasses and fright wig. He waved half-heartedly, like a sad little kid. I can't sell portraits for him, I thought; I can't give him an excuse to call me every morning, every night, forever. Three months later, when Fred asked if I wouldn't like to have lunch to discuss the idea, I told him I was going to Europe and would call when I got back. I didn't. I didn't want to end up like him, battered and bitter.

But Andy didn't give up. He gushed again when we crossed paths at a Saks fashion show in September 1986. He was with Paige and they were clicking away with their matching hot pink Le Clique cameras at me and my date, Estée Lauder. "C'mon, Bob," the cosmetics queen commanded. "I don't want to lose my front-row seat."

"Oh, God," Andy whined in my ear. "I can't believe you're with *Estée,* Bob. Can't you ask her for some ads?"

On September 17, Jon Gould died in Los Angeles. He fought and denied his illness to the end. Joan Quinn had seen him at a screening a month earlier, "clutching the seats to get up the aisle." As word of his rapid deterioration spread, Fred took Andy aside at the Factory and told him that Jon was dying of AIDS. "Andy was very, very upset," said Sam, who witnessed the scene. When Paige asked Andy what hospital Jon was in, because some friends wanted to send flowers, Andy said, "Well, I know he's in California. And I think he works for Paramount." Paige almost started laughing. "I couldn't believe him." Like Sam, she didn't think that Andy was worried about having contracted AIDS. "If he was worried," Paige said, "he would have been a wreck."

Katy Dobbs called Andy to offer her condolences. "I guess we have a lot of great memories of Jon," she said. "That's what it all comes down to," Andy replied. "It's just the memories." Katy told me, "I could tell that he had already distanced himself from it all. And had already mourned Jon's disappearance.''

Had he? Or was he avoiding mourning as usual? And hiding his hurt and fear as usual?

Within days of Jon's death, Andy started painting what would turn out to be his final big series of paintings: The Last Suppers. ''Andy wanted to paint condoms next,'' Paige said, ''but Fred thought it was a terrible idea.'' The Last Suppers idea and commission came from Iolas. Iolas planned to show the paintings in a bank in Milan, across the street from the church where the Leonardo da Vinci original is. ''Andy really got excited about the Last Suppers,'' Sam said. And they led to several other religious paintings, based on garish Catholic images that Jay Shriver found for him in the Hispanic shops on 14th Street.

''Andy wasn't depressed,'' Paige said, when he worked on the Last Suppers that last fall. ''It was just a coincidence. I mean, when he painted the Guns, Knives and Crosses, did that mean he was going to die too? He wanted to live. He went to the nutritionist all the time and exercised for an hour every day. That's really hard to do, unless you're really motivated.''

''Andy would take a big bag of vitamins every day,'' Sam said. ''And drink all kinds of teas. But then he would break down and eat chocolates. We would go to Serendipity and get *half* a chocolate fudge sundae. And every day, I would get him two scrambled eggs on an English muffin. With ketchup, not butter. Then he read in the *New York Times* that the place I was going to was condemned by the Board of Health and he wanted me to go to this other coffee shop that was further away. And he was always nervous that I was going to the closer one.''

44

The End

Andy started a new collection in 1986: pedestals. Wood pedestals, marble pedestals, alabaster pedestals, wood pedestals painted to look like marble and alabaster. They were to be used for the new sculptures he wanted to make: portrait busts. "The whole point," said Stuart Pivar, a collector who often accompanied Andy on his shopping forays in the mid-eighties, "was to go back to the portrait clients and sell them busts of themselves. He was always debating, Should it be life size? Should it be larger than life?"

Andy was not going to sculpt these busts by hand. "There was this place on Madison Avenue and 57th Street," Pivar explained, "that had a machine which took your picture and made a portrait bust from it." When the instant-bust shop went out of business, Andy sent Pivar searching for the machine. He tracked it down to an L.A. garage, where its inventor had stored it in an advanced state of disrepair. "Andy was willing to put it together," Pivar said, "and just before he died, I worked out a deal for him to buy it for $250,000. He was very excited about it."

In the first week of November 1986, Andy enjoyed two successful openings at two important New York galleries. At the Dia Art Foundation, Hand-Painted Images, 1960–62—the breakthrough half-Expressionist, half-Pop paintings of cartoons and advertisements—reminded everyone of just how far ahead of the times Andy had been from the start. At the Larry Gagosian Gallery, Oxidation Paintings—the titillating but beautiful piss paintings shown for the first time since their creation ten years earlier—reminded everyone of just how far ahead of the times Andy still could be. Amusingly, after more than a decade of bad reviews or no reviews, the so-called serious American critics were as gushy about these urinary canvases as their European counterparts had been about Andy's work all along.

The Dia opening was the first time I had gone to a Warhol show since I'd quit the Factory nearly four years earlier. Andy beckoned me to the corner where he was signing autographs, and when the photographers crowded in on us, we instinctively leaned toward each other, finally friends again, smiling for the cameras. As it turned out, these were the last pictures taken of us together.

"Bob and I have a good relationship now," Andy had told Thomas Ammann a few weeks before. When Thomas told me, he added, "You know, even when Andy was mad at you for leaving, he always asked me, 'How's Bob?' But he has never *once* asked me, 'How's Jed?' "

After he moved out, in 1980, Jed came for the dogs every Sunday, but Andy either hid upstairs, or refused to talk to him. And yet he once showed Sam Bolton the photograph of Jed that he was still carrying in his wallet.

In the same month as his double hit at Gagosian and Dia, Andy's fleeting relationship with Sam Bolton came to an abrupt end. His crush, as always with Andy, was unrequited, frustrating, possessive, and unhappy. In late November, they had a "big fight," as Sam put it, after Andy discovered that he had stayed up into the wee hours with Halston and Victor Hugo. "We just watched TV and talked, about Andy actually," Bolton told me, "but when Andy found out, he got really mad, especially since I didn't tell him."

Sam continued going to work every day, but the favorite was suddenly the outcast. Andy and he barely spoke, and he taunted Sam by drawing even closer to Paige. That Thanksgiving, following her lead, Andy ladled out soup to the homeless at the Church of the Heavenly Rest on East 90th Street. And his new line to Paige after advertising dinners was "maybe you should come home with me." He also asked her to look into adopting a baby for them to raise. Had he finally had it with boys? Was he seriously considering changing his life and settling down with a woman and child? Or was it all part of some convoluted subconscious ploy, so twisted and automatic that even Andy couldn't figure out what he was really doing?

In early December, some of the old gang—including Andy, Halston, Bianca, Steve Rubell, and me—were reunited at a small dinner given by Liza Minnelli for her new husband, sculptor Mark Gero, after his Madison Avenue gallery opening. The long white walls of Liza's East Side apartment were lined with Andy's multiple portraits of her mother, her father, and herself. But despite the decor, it wasn't like the old days. The hostess had recently graduated from the Betty Ford Center, which meant drugs were out, and on the dot of midnight, she yelped, "Okay, guys! I've got to get up at four in the morning to fly to Rome to start a movie. I hate to break up the party, but everybody out!"

"Well, shall we go someplace for a nightcap?" Calvin Klein asked Halston.

"Your place or mine?" asked Halston.

We went to Halston's. When we arrived, Halston took Calvin and his new wife, Kelly, on a tour of the upper level, Bianca and Dick Cavett sat at one end of the huge living room discussing the Nicaraguan situation, Steve darted from group to group, and Andy, Paige, and I sat at the other end, not knowing what to talk about.

"Do you still keep your diary?" Andy asked me at last, as if he had been waiting for the right moment all along. I said yes, and he told me that I should "make it into a novel." I tried to change the subject, but Andy persisted. "It's a greaaaat idea, Bob," he said again and again and again. "Make it into a novel." The more he said it, the more I wondered if he knew my secret: After four years of turning down offers, I had finally asked Mort Janklow to get me a deal for a book about Andy.

Vincent and Shelly invited me to their office Christmas party two weeks later, marking my official return into the Factory fold. It was good to see "the kids," as Andy still called them—Pat Hackett, Chris Makos, Glenn O'Brien, Ronnie Cutrone, Fran Lebowitz—most of whom were edging forty, like me. Fred, who had passed that turning point two years earlier, cornered me with a sad story, half complaint, half confession. It had been a hard year for him, he said. He had had an operation on his knee. "The boss" was driving him crazy. He had been "really bad" at Nell's—the hot new night-spot—a few nights before and had to write them an apology. He looked more beaten down than ever, weary and frail. Andy arrived rather late, just as I was leaving. "Gee, why are you going, Bob?" he asked. Those were the last words Andy said to me.

On Christmas Day, Andy and Paige served dinner to the homeless again. "I didn't go home to Portland," Paige said, "so I could spend the holidays with Andy." He called her a few minutes after she had dropped him off that night and told her that he was upset. "He said he was thinking about his mother," Paige recalled, "and how he sent her back to Pittsburgh when she got really sick at the very end and he wished he had kept her with him. He was all choked up talking about it."

1987 began with another artistic triumph for Andy: an exhibition of his photographs at the Robert Miller Gallery. Everyone from Jean-Michel Basquiat to Jerry Zipkin—neither of whom had paid much attention to Andy in the last few years—turned out for the opening, which was so crowded that Andy had to retreat behind a desk, where he sat signing catalogues. It was more like one of his shows in Düsseldorf or Paris than New York. "People came up to Andy," said John Cheim, the co-director of the gallery, "as if they were paying obeisance to the Pope."

The 35mm black-and-white photographs, taken between 1982 and 1986, covered almost the entire range of Warholian iconography. There were close-ups of flowered wallpaper and five-and-dime window displays, still-lifes of Fiesta Ware and silverware, portraits of Lana Turner, Brooke Shields, and Truman Capote, a bare-chested weight lifter, another chest in a James Dean T-shirt with a crucifix grazing the neckline, dolls dressed as priests and nuns, the Washington Monument and the Statue of Liberty, the World Trade Center and the Empire State Building, a Mao photo pinned to a Chinese wall. It was as if Andy had stripped the paint and silkscreening ink from his art and for the first time offered up his naked, original images.

But, typically, there was a twist, an old-fashioned human touch that both undercut and emphasized the modernity of the medium. The images were repeated, in groups of four, six, nine, and twelve, and each group was stitched together, by sewing machine, with the leftover thread hanging from the seams of the completed piece. Even more typically, the clever idea was stolen, this time from Chris Makos, who had been experimenting with stitching his own photographs for some time. Most typically, Andy—through his time-tested technique of flattery combined with bribery—was able to make Makos complicit in the theft. Chris arranged for Lance Loud's younger sister, Michelle, who desperately needed work, to do the sewing for Andy. Chris also printed Andy's photographs, or had his assistant do them, for a stiff fee, of course. Indeed, after studying the catalogue, I wouldn't be surprised to learn that some of the photographs were taken by Chris, or at least set up by Chris—that weight lifter, those Venetian blinds, that hotel lamp all look more Makos than Warhol to my eye. When Chris saw the results of this uncredited collaboration hanging on the gallery walls, he reacted like a man waking from a dream to find that his roommate had run off with the rent money. "What a greaaaat idea," he taunted Andy at the opening. "Where did you get such a greaaaat idea, Andy? Huh, *Andy? Huh?*"

A few days later there was a rave review in the *New York Times*—Andy's first since the sixties—which hailed the stitching in particular as a brilliant visual and conceptual stroke.

I saw Andy for the last time on January 14, 1987, at Nell's. He was with Paige and Fred at a long table that also included Bob Dylan and Sting. The dinner was being given by Nell for the English actor Ian McKellen. We waved at each other across the crowded room.

Four days later, Andy, Fred, and Chris Makos boarded the Concorde for Paris on their way to Milan for *The Last Supper* opening. Andy had wanted to take Paige and had told her to tell Fred that she was going. When she'd told Fred, he'd snapped, "Absolutely not." When she told Andy, "he didn't do anything," Paige said. "I was mad—well, I didn't get mad—but he should have stuck up for me." So at the last minute, Andy had asked Chris along, even though they weren't on the best of terms. Apparently, his presence was less threatening to Fred, and there was no thought of Andy's traveling alone with Fred.

They arrived in Milan the morning before the January 22 opening and checked into the deluxe Hotel Principe di Savoia, where Andy and Chris shared a two-bedroom suite and Fred had a room on another floor. That afternoon, Daniela Morera, *Interview*'s Italian editor, who had organized their Milan press and social schedules, came to the suite. Andy informed her that he didn't want to do any interviews, not even the one she had worked weeks to get with *La Repubblica,* one of Italy's most prestigious newspapers. He told her that he wasn't feeling well, that he had pains in his side. Daniela thought it might be his kidneys, but Andy said it was the flu. Nonetheless, he agreed to go to the dinner for two hundred that Mariuccia Mandelli and Aldo Pinto were giving that night to unveil the private theater they had installed in their Krizia fashion house. "But he wouldn't check his coat," Daniela recalled. "He said, 'No, no. I have to keep myself warm.' He had on a sweatshirt, a sports jacket, and a quilted coat—*inside!*"

After dinner, Fred went back to the hotel, but Andy and Chris followed Daniela to the penthouse apartment of a potential portrait client, Laura Cerlosoni, the niece of jeweler Marina B. "She has a swimming pool on the terrace," Daniela elaborated, "and several Breughels. She talked the whole time with Andy about jewelry and portrait prices."

Andy had pains the next day too, which he still insisted were flu symptoms, especially when he heard that Daniela was recovering from a virus. Still, Daniela said, "he was charming and nice," all through a long and grueling schedule. In the morning there was a press conference with over two hundred journalists, TV reporters, and photographers. At lunch, designer Gianni Versace asked Andy to paint a pair of heads of Christ for his library. The opening itself, from four in the afternoon until nine in the evening, was followed by a big dinner party given by interior decorator Dino Franzin.

Daniela Morera says the opening was "the biggest event that ever happened in Milano. They were expecting five or six hundred people, but there were five or six *thousand.* One paper said ten thousand. The police had to close off the street, and all the socialites arriving in their limousines couldn't get in. Every designer was there. Versace. Krizia. Moschino. The whole Missoni family. Every big artist. Every art director. All the graphic artists. And the public, the kids. People came on trains from the suburbs. People sent flowers. Andy was surrounded by white lilies, sitting behind a white Formica table, getting exhausted. He was signing catalogues, posters, magazines, glasses, scarves, gloves. People were pressing, screaming to get things signed, waiting for hours. I was screaming to bring bodyguards. Chris was helping Andy. But Fred wasn't around. Even that morning, at the press conference, when I asked him if he was coming upstairs, he said, 'I have nothing to do with *that.* ' ''

Hanging serenely above this mob scene were two of Andy's paintings of *The Last Supper,* each nine feet by twenty-one feet, divided into five panels. One was simple and severe, reminiscent in style of the sixties Disasters series. The other was superimposed with price tags and corporate logos—fifty-nine cents, Dove, GE—not unlike the 1984 collaborations with Basquiat. The setting for these paintings, that mob scene, Andy's last opening, was eerily appropriate: Palazzo delle Stellini—the Palace of the Stars—an eighteenth-century convent converted into an ultramodern bank. Across the street, in the Church of Santa Maria della Grazie, was Leonardo's *The Last Supper.*

"Iolas worked out the deal with the bank," Daniela said. "Andy told me the whole thing was Iolas's idea." It was Alexander the Greek's last show too. The sacred-monster art dealer died within months of the sacred-monster artist. "In Italy," Princess Maria Gabriella di Savoia, the would-be king's sister, told me later, "we believe that Leonardo da Vinci carries a curse."

The day after his opening, Andy was feeling so bad that he didn't leave his hotel suite, though to make Daniela happy he did go through with the interview for *La Repubblica,* reclining on a couch in a gray sweatsuit. Daniela brought him "homeopathic medicine for pain, because he wouldn't take chemical medicine. And he said he wanted chocolates, but then he didn't eat them." That was a sure sign that Andy knew the pain was from his gallbladder, not the flu, though he kept this to himself. The following morning, cutting his trip short, he flew back to New York with Chris, leaving Fred in Europe.

He was feeling better when he got back to New York, and he plunged into his latest commissions: portraits of Beethoven for Herman "the German" Wunsche and a big series of paintings and prints, titled *The History of TV,* for Ronald Feldman. But on February 5 the pain came back. Andy was having dinner at Nippon with his good friend John Reinhold and, for the first time since their break, Sam Bolton. They were supposed to go on to a movie, but in the middle of dinner Andy suddenly said he had to go home. Reinhold asked him what was wrong and Andy said, "Nothing."

"C'mon," said Reinhold.

"Oh, it's just a little pain," said Andy, dashing out of the restaurant. Later, Reinhold recalled, "You could tell he was really in a lot of pain. Andy just didn't like to complain about being uncomfortable."

Reinhold had replaced Fred and me as Andy's closest confidant. He was a precious-gems dealer in his late thirties, but his friendship with Andy went much deeper than diamonds. Andy would turn down swell dinner parties to go to the movies with Reinhold—and this wasn't a romance. They had been introduced in 1978 by Reinhold's cousin, Andy's sixties confidant Henry Geldzahler. "It was just magic" was the way Reinhold explained their instant rapport, sounding just like Andy. They were alike in many ways. Both were shy, insecure, secretive, lonely worrywarts. And weird. John Reinhold was married, but it was mutually agreed that his wife and Andy would never meet, and in ten years they never did.

Reinhold and Andy often talked two or three times a day, chitchatting for hours, even long distance when Andy was on a trip. Andy often called Reinhold from a pay phone on his way downtown and asked him to meet for what they called "nervous coffee." They would usually go to a Brew 'n' Burger near Reinhold's office and talk about whatever was bothering Andy lately: work problems, love problems, Fred problems, Sam problems.

Had Reinhold noticed a change in Andy in the last year or two of his life?

"Yes," he said, "first of all, he went out much less in the last few years. It would be dinner and a movie and maybe stop for ice cream. He'd be home by eleven, eleven-thirty. And there was a strong sense of loneliness. I would drop him off at that big house and then we'd speak five minutes later."

John Reinhold noted one other important change in Andy's behavior in the last few years: "He started going to doctors like Dr. Li."

Dr. Linda Li was a chiropractor-nutritionist who treated Andy several times in January and February 1987, at the Li Chiropractic Healing Arts Center on upper Broadway. Andy had first met her in 1984, with Jon Gould. Jon's death had done nothing to diminish Andy's belief in the healing power of crystals. He continued seeing another chiropractor recommended by Dr. Li, Dr. Andrew Bernsohn, whom he called "the crystal doctor." Bernsohn's therapy consisted of passing pieces of amethyst and quartz over his patients' bodies, to increase their energy. When Pat Hackett expressed some skepticism about Bernsohn, Andy replied, "I know he believes in crystals himself, because he's afraid of what happens if you don't do it right."

Andy used to laugh when Paulette Goddard went on about the physical effects of wearing emeralds or rubies; now he was placing his life in the hands of semiprecious shamans. The first thing one saw at the last Factory was a giant rock crystal, perhaps two feet wide and almost as high. "Andy had tons of crystals," Sam Bolton said. "And he wore a lot of crystal necklaces. This one big one was always falling off his neck."

On Thursday, February 12, Andy was feeling well enough to give a Valentine dinner with Paige at Texarkana. One of their thirty guests was Andy's long-time physician, Dr. Denton Cox. Though Andy saw Dr. Cox fairly often socially, he had stopped visiting his office for annual physicals in 1984. Cox, talking after Andy's death, told me Andy didn't make any mention that night of his latest gallbladder problems. He just said, "I've been bad. I've been eating chocolate and butter."

The next day, Friday, February 13, the pains came back. Andy was exercising with his trainer, Keith Peterson, when he complained of pains in his side. Thinking it might be a muscle spasm, Peterson told him to stop exercising and said he'd see him on Monday. A little later, Andy buzzed Brigid on the intercom and asked her to come up to his studio. "I have the best chocolates from Sweden," he said, leading her into temptation. Brigid was leaving for a fat farm near London the next day—she hadn't told Andy because she knew he'd say she couldn't have a vacation—and was in the mood for one last binge anyway. So she tossed down a bunch of bonbons and passed the box back to Andy. "I want some soooo bad," he said, "but I've got a bad pain." He pointed to his right side.

Brigid, who'd had her gallbladder removed in 1979, had encouraged Andy to do the same ever since. "I must have shown him my scar a million times," she said, "so that he could see it was just a hairline. 'Just get it out and get it over with,' I always told him. 'It's no big deal.' But he just wouldn't listen. You know how stubborn he could be. So when I started in again that day, he told me, 'Oh, shut up. It'll be okay. Want another piece of candy?' Anything to change the subject, as usual."

And anything to avoid hospitalization. "Whenever he would pass a hospital," Benjamin Liu said, "he would cover his eyes or block his view. And he'd get mad at me if we passed the Columbus–Mother Cabrini Hospital."

"I don't know how Andy could stand the pain," Brigid continued. "It's like having a heart attack. He did carry Demerol around with him ever since that time he collapsed at Elsie Woodward's in the seventies." Sam said that Andy had started taking painkillers after their dinner at Nippon the previous week.

Andy stayed in bed most of that weekend, watching TV—including "Andy Warhol's Fifteen Minutes," which had recently premiered on MTV—his own TV show at last. On Saturday, February 14, he went to see his dermatologist, Dr. Karen Burke, who had been giving him collagen injections to fill in his wrinkles, and told her about his gallbladder pain—only Andy would consult a skin doctor about a gallbladder problem. Burke told him to go see Dr. Cox as soon as possible. Andy told her he would call him Monday. On Monday, February 16, he canceled his exercise classes for the entire week, but he didn't call Dr. Cox. Instead, he went to see Dr. Li, who massaged his side vigorously.

Andy was feeling much worse on Tuesday, February 17, but after work—the last day he came to the Factory—he rushed off to the Tunnel, where he was booked to model the avant-garde menswear of Japanese designer Koshin Satoh in a celebrity fashion show. Despite how bad he felt, there was no way Andy was going to miss a modeling job. Andy had switched agencies to Ford after Zoli died of AIDS. "Andy loved being a Ford model," says Sam. "I think he loved it more than anything else."

"Andy stood in a cold dressing room for hours," said Stuart Pivar, who had taken him to the Tunnel in his limo, "waiting to model. He was in terrible pain." In the last photograph of Andy ever taken, coming down the runway with Miles Davis, his eyes were alight with the thrill of stardom, but his lips were tense and taut, as if he were holding on for dear life. "Get me out of here, Stuart," he gasped backstage. "I feel like I'm going to die." Although Pivar says Andy's pockets were filled with crystals, they couldn't stop the pain. That night, Andy told Pat Hackett the next morning, dictating his last diary entry, he took Seconal, Valium, and aspirin to knock himself out.

Andy finally called Dr. Cox Wednesday morning, February 18. He arrived at his office just as Mrs. Nicholas Ruwe, the wife of the American ambassador to Iceland, was leaving. "She was thrilled to meet Andy," Dr. Cox said. "And Andy asked her about a show he had in Reykjavik and she told him how great it was and Andy was charming. Here he was in so much pain and he was, well, working." The moment he was alone with Dr. Cox, however, Andy dropped the charm. "I'm not afraid of death," he told Cox straight off, "but I don't want to go into the hospital. You have to help me stay out of the hospital."

Dr. Cox gave Andy a complete examination. According to Cox, "everything was fine," except his gallbladder, of course. Dr. Cox told him "the sonogram showed that it was so acutely infected that it was in danger of becoming gangrenous." He recommended immediate surgery, but Andy wouldn't hear of it. Because of the severity of his condition, Dr. Cox had Andy see Dr. Bjorn Thorbjarnavson, who had operated on the Shah's gallbladder, that afternoon. He also recommended immediate surgery.

John Reinhold called him later: "I knew something was wrong, because he was rambling on. He must have been on something." But Andy told his closest friend nothing about his desperate condition.

Brigid also spoke to Andy that day. She had called the Factory from London, and when they said that Andy wasn't coming in, she called him at home and asked if anything was wrong. "Oh, nothing," Andy said, "just a little flu." Then, to throw her off, he joked, "and you're fired and so are your dogs." She was more surprised when he asked for her sister Chrissie's number, because she and Andy weren't really friends. But she didn't make the connection: Chrissie's gallbladder had burst a few years before and she had miraculously survived. Andy called Chrissie and stunned her by asking her to come over—even Brigid had never been in Andy's house. Chrissie told him that she was dashing out to an ice-skating party, but Andy kept her on the phone for almost an hour, bringing up a new subject every time she thought the conversation was finished, never mentioning anything about his gallbladder, just murmuring vaguely about "not feeling well."

On Thursday, February 19, in more pain than ever, Andy went to see Dr. Cox again, who repeated the sonogram which showed his gallbladder getting worse. Andy insisted on seeing a "nonsurgical" physician, so Dr. Cox sent him to Dr. Michael Schmerin. He also told Andy that he had to be operated on as soon as possible, that his gallbladder might burst at any moment, causing peritonitis and almost certain death. All three doctors urged Andy to check into New York Hospital that afternoon, so that Andy could have the operation first thing Friday morning. Andy insisted on putting it off for another day. Moving the operation to Saturday might have been a fatal error—many medical professionals say hospitals, especially Manhattan hospitals, are not as well staffed on weekends.

Andy told Pat Hackett that he was going to "the place" to have "it" done—he couldn't bring himself to say the words "hospital" and "operation." He also told her, "Don't tell anyone. I'll give you the story after," which made her laugh, because he made it sound like an exclusive scoop she had to protect. "Andy didn't want anyone to know he was in the hospital," Vincent later told me, and, in fact, on Thursday only Pat, Vincent, and Fred knew that Andy was going into the hospital the next day. "The worst thing," Paige Powell said right after Andy's death, "is that Andy didn't tell me he was going into the hospital. And I'm so mad at Vincent and Fred for not telling me. Because I would have gone to the hospital and stayed with him."

On Friday, February 20, Sam Bolton somehow found out and called Andy around eleven to wish him luck. "Andy was really rushed," he said. "He was running around hiding things." A little later, Ken Leland, a young friend of Chris Makos who had recently taken Benjamin Liu's job of picking Andy up in the morning and accompanying him on his shopping route to work, arrived in Stuart Pivar's limousine—Andy had refused to go in an ambulance because it reminded him of when he was shot. Leland found Andy "rummaging through his stuff" in the dining room, a mounting stack of bags and boxes filled with gems and junk. It seemed that was one of the reasons why Andy hadn't wanted to go into the hospital immediately: He needed time to stash his vast and scattered collection of jewelry and other valuables in the safe he kept in his bedroom and other hiding places.

At New York Hospital, Andy, dressed all in black with a gray scarf around his neck, checked in as "Bob Robert." He was greeted by the staffer who had gotten friendly with him when Jon Gould was there and he gave her the latest *Interview,* an *Interview* T-shirt, and an *Interview* silk scarf. He told her several times that he didn't want any visitors or any calls. "He looked good," she said, "and he was in good spirits."

"We just took the elevator up to his room," Ken Leland later told *Details,* "and turned on the TV. I got him flowers for his room and he said, 'What did you do that for?' I also got him an assortment of his favorite things, like the *National Enquirer, TV Guide,* the *Post,* and the *News* . . . also *Dreamgirl* by Mary Wilson and *His Way* by Kitty Kelley. We sat and watched *Divorce Court* and he was rooting for the guy who actually lost."

It sounds like traveling with Andy: He moaned and groaned for days before the trip and all the way to the airport, but once he was on the plane, he opened a movie-star bio and accepted his fate without complaint. "He saw it wasn't so horrible," said Dr. Cox, who visited him that afternoon. "He liked his room and the nurses and wasn't terrified at all."

After Dr. Cox left, however, Andy called Dr. Burke and told her, "Well, Dr. Cox has got to save me now." According to Burke, he said it like a dare, and that sounds familiar too. He was always saying to Fred or me, "Well, you got me into this, now you have to get me out of it."

Before he fell asleep that night, at one in the morning, Andy called Paige and asked her to run some errands for him the next day. He still didn't tell her where he was.

The next morning, Saturday, February 21, John Reinhold called Andy's house and was told by either Nena or Aurora that Andy was "on a trip." He knew that couldn't be true, so he called Vincent, who told him not to worry, Andy was all right. But Vincent, following orders, wouldn't say where Andy was.

Andy *was* all right. The three-hour operation, which had begun at 8:45 A.M., was a success. Andy's gallbladder—it was gangrenous—was removed without complications. After another three hours in recovery, Andy was brought back to his room and he called Vincent to say he was fine. Then he called Fred. They visited him later that afternoon, as did Dr. Cox, who told them that Andy was doing so well he would probably be able to go home sooner than expected.

About the same time that Fred and Vincent were secretly visiting Andy in the hospital, I left New York for Zürich, to meet São Schlumberger and go to Thomas Ammann's châlet in Gstaad. I couldn't wait to tell my news: Mort Janklow had sealed the deal on my book, this book.

"The timing is perfect," Thomas said. "Andy is having a kind of revival lately. Important people in the art world in America who never liked him are changing their minds, and in Europe Andy just gets bigger and bigger." He said that Andy had major museum shows coming up in Germany and Austria, and that now Mary Boone, the hottest art dealer in New York, wanted to give him a show, of the 1984 Rorschachs paintings.

"In Paris too," São agreed, "people who know about art speak about Andy differently in the past year or so. They accept his real importance. Finally."

"And you're getting along with Andy again," Thomas added, "which is good. Because you don't want to write just a putdown."

I didn't. That's why I had let some time pass. But I was mad at Andy again, I told them, because the same day Mort had called to say my deal was done, Fred had called Mort and asked him to represent Andy's diaries.

Thomas and São were incredulous. Andy could never publish his diaries while he was still alive, they both said, looking ever so slightly worried. He was just playing with me, as usual, they said. I wasn't so sure. I knew how competitive and cutthroat Andy could be. "Andy will end up loving your book," Thomas tried to reassure me, "because it will make him more famous. I think it's great that you do it now, while he's on top. Why wait until Andy dies, twenty, thirty years from now?"

Two hours after I slid into a deep jet-lagged nap, Thomas woke me. "Bob, I have something to tell you."

I opened my eyes.

"Andy died."

I closed my eyes.

A call from New York, a gallbladder operation, heart failure . . . I couldn't believe what I was hearing. I just wanted to go back to sleep. I felt guilty, angry, and lost.

The phone started ringing and it didn't stop for the rest of the night: art dealers wanting Warhol paintings from Thomas, newspaper reporters wanting Warhol quotes from me. William Norwich of the *Daily News* told me that Andy's New York friends were all "devastated," especially Paige. She had laughed out loud when Tama Janowitz called with the shocking news, but when she called Andy's house and Fred answered it she knew it was true.

Fred had got the news first, shortly after Andy was pronounced dead at 6:31 A.M. on Sunday, February 22. Andy had listed him as "next of kin" on the hospital registration form. Fred immediately called Ed Hayes, the dapper criminal lawyer he had recently met through Reinaldo Herrera, and asked him to represent the Warhol estate, of which Fred was executor. Then Fred, Vincent, and Ed Hayes went directly to Andy's house. Andy's brothers learned of the death when John Warhola made his usual Sunday call to Andy and, like Paige, got Fred instead.

When Thomas called Andy's house, Fred told him that the funeral would be in Pittsburgh and the family wanted it to be small and private; there would be a memorial service in New York later. Thomas said that Fred sounded "in control, very businesslike." But later that night, a source told me, Fred went home and drank an entire bottle of vodka with Sam Bolton. "He was half in shock," Sam confirmed, "and half giddy."

I could understand why. As much as I mourned Andy's death, there was an element of relief in my feelings too—and, unlike Fred, I hadn't worked for him in some time. That night, however, as we watched the Swiss TV coverage, studded with the English words that Andy had added to the international lexicon, "Factory," "Superstars," "Underground Films," and "Business Art," we remembered Andy's good side, his gentleness, his humor, his humility. Thomas said that Andy was the only artist he knew who didn't hang his own work—there wasn't a single Warhol hanging at Andy's house. And I laughed a little when I realized that Andy had died on George Washington's birthday.

* * *

"POP ART KING DIES" ran the banner on Monday morning's *Daily News*. Andy's death was front-page news from Los Angeles to West Berlin, but even in death there was still a difference in the way he was perceived on the opposite sides of the Atlantic. In Europe, the press treated Andy's death like Picasso's, saying that the art world would never be the same without him. In America, they treated it more like Elsa Maxwell's, saying nightlife would never be the same without him.

Inevitably, rumors about the cause of his death crisscrossed the ocean too. One West German paper, *Bild Zeitung,* quoted unnamed New York Hospital sources who said that Andy had had AIDS. Thomas's sister Doris had a friend who knew a doctor at the hospital who said that Andy hadn't taken his prescribed medication after the operation. Suzie Frankfurt said she had a friend who knew the technician who did the tests on Andy before the operation and nothing was wrong with his heart. Paul Warhola came to suspect that "one of the Factory kids" visited Andy in the hospital late Saturday night and gave him some unspecified pills.

Over the following weeks and months, the controversy would grow, leading to investigations by both New York City and New York State, and a lawsuit by the Warhol estate against New York Hospital, alleging negligence and inadequate care. Ed Hayes claimed Andy's intravenous liquid intake and outtake weren't properly monitored, leading to overhydration, respiratory arrest, and cardiac arrest. "Drowning is the simplest way to put it," Hayes said. The lawsuit is still pending, but it is perhaps worth noting, as M. A. Farber and Lawrence K. Altman said in a major *New York Times Magazine* piece, that Andy "was among the two-tenths of 1 percent of patients under age 60 who die while hospitalized after routine gallbladder surgery in New York State."

Drs. Cox and Burke lashed out publicly at Dr. Li for "mashing" Andy's gallbladder, and New York Hospital barred the private nurse they recommended to Andy in the first place. Everyone wanted to know why she waited until 5:45 A.M., when she said she noticed that Andy had turned blue, to call for help. Had she dozed off? Or left the room? "On Warhol's chart," the *Times* story said, "there are entries at 4:30 A.M. that he looked 'pale' and, 45 minutes later, that he looked 'paler'—as well as an entry that he 'slept most of the night.' But state investigators say they suspect these notes by Ms. [Min] Cho, who told the hospital that she was reading her Bible in Warhol's room, were actually written after the artist died."

Min Cho's lawyer accused the hospital of making her the scapegoat. And even if she had been asleep or away when Andy died, the question still remains: Why did his heart stop? "There's something called 'voodoo death,' " a doctor associated with New York Hospital told me. "When witch doctors have people so scared, they say, 'You will die!'—and you do, on the spot.'' He speculated that Andy could have awoken in the middle of the night and, finding himself alone in a strange place, died of fright. I can't help thinking that this theory, laughable in most cases, might have applied to Andy. Maybe it was fear that got him in the end.

Back in Gstaad, the phone kept ringing all day Monday. Liza Minnelli wanted to know what to say about Andy's art on the "Today" show. Marina Schiano railed against the hospital and told me that Jed was "really cracked up at first, but he's a little better now.'' Steve Rubell said that the night Andy died "Francesco Clemente walked into Odeon and started crying.'' He also said that Elizabeth Taylor had called him and wanted to know who had Andy's tapes. "She was worried,'' Steve said, "because Andy used to get her to tell him everything when she was drinking, like how big all her husbands' cocks were and how they were in bed.''

I called Paulette Goddard at her Locarno house, which she rarely left anymore, except for the occasional visit to Zürich to switch her money from one bank to another. "Isn't it wonderful the way the world loves Andy?'' she said. "The *whole* world. He's page one in Milano, Zürich, Paris, New York, *everywhere*. They got the message. Isn't that nice? I'm so happy for Andy. And for you too, because you had a lot to do with that. Aren't you proud? Andy's on the list of ten. The all-time greats. There's Jesus and Charlie and Andy.'' She never told me the other seven.

Perhaps the most touching reaction to Andy's death was Stephen Sprouse's: "Who will we do things for now?''

At the Factory, it was their first Monday without Andy. Ronnie Cutrone stopped by and later he said that "everyone was acting like nothing happened. Agusto was painting and drying paintings with a hair dryer, because there was work that was unfinished when Andy died. It was strange. Andy's studio hadn't been touched yet and I noticed a little painting on the side that said, 'Heaven and Hell are just one breath away.' I think it was the last thing Andy had painted.''

In Zürich, on that same day, *Parkett,* the Swiss art journal, received a package from the Factory that they thought contained Andy's last work. They were planning a special Warhol issue for April, and for months there had been discussions with Andy about a limited-edition print that would be inserted in 120 deluxe copies. He wanted to do something Swiss, he said, and Thomas's office had been sending him materials for ideas: pictures of cuckoo clocks, postcards of the Matterhorn, packages of Toblerone chocolate. So everyone was surprised when they opened the package sent just before Andy went into the hospital: It contained four stitched-together photographs of skeletons.

"Death was very much on his mind," Thomas told me after the *Parkett* people called him. "He was so sensitive, Andy, so instinctive. He must have known."

I called the Factory that Wednesday, and got Brigid. "We're all okay," she said, sounding shaky. "It'll go on, it'll go on. Fred's been wonderful." I asked to speak to him, but she said he was locked up with Ed Hayes, deciding what to do about the hospital. "It's too abstract," she told me, "just like Andy always said, 'It's too abstract. It's like shopping at Bloomingdale's.' "

She said that Vincent had taken her to Andy's house, because she had wanted to see it, "just once, right? It was unbelievable. I wanted to puke. You couldn't *get in* the dining room, there were so many shopping bags and boxes and statues. It was disgusting. Sad. The only thing I could think was 'Has Jed seen this?' And then I went upstairs to Jon Gould's room and when Jon left Andy didn't move one thing. Andy's Valentine's Day cards to Jon were still in the drawer. And the *whole house* was filled with shopping bags filled with Andy's collections. It was so sick. I mean, you could really see from looking at the house just how fucked up Andy was, how sick and unhappy. Because it was all consumption and possession and just that, just having things to have them, not to make the house look good or anything."

I asked Brigid when the funeral was and who was going, but she was vague and said I should talk to Vincent. I thought there might still be time to fly back for it, because the autopsy that the Warhol estate had demanded would delay it a day or two. Vincent was vague too. He said he "thought" the funeral was on the following day, Thursday, but the family wanted it very private and he wasn't sure whether even Fred and he would go.

The entire Factory, most of the *Interview* staff, and Ed Hayes, who had never met Andy, flew to Pittsburgh the next day. Andy's brothers later denied that they ever wanted to keep the funeral small or private—that decision was Fred's, and Fred's alone, with Vincent still following orders. In fact, Andy's relatives couldn't understand why his glamorous friends had snubbed him in the end. They were thrilled by the flowers sent by Mick Jagger and Jerry Hall, but wondered why they were the only ones, not knowing that Fred hadn't allowed the name and address of the funeral parlor to be given to anyone else. Fred was furious when Joan Quinn turned up from Los Angeles, having been slipped the location of the funeral by an *Interview* staffer, saying that her "crazy red hair" might upset the pious Warholas.

"It seems at times he wandered far away from the church," Monsignor Peter Tay told the one hundred mourners assembled in the onion-domed Holy Ghost Byzantine Rite Catholic Church on Pittsburgh's working-class North Side, "but we do not judge him, we do not condemn him." The monsignor went on to quote Luke 23: 39–43, "Jesus forgave the thief on his right. He did not forgive the thief on his left."

The burial followed in the tiny, snow-covered St. John the Baptist Cemetery, overlooking a highway junction in suburban Bethel Park. Andy was laid to rest a few feet downhill from the double gravesite of his mother and father. His housekeepers, Nena and Aurora, wept. His silkscreener, Rupert Smith, stood off to one side, "looking really forlorn," according to Joan Quinn. "And Paige really went crazy. She wanted them to open the big bronze coffin, but they wouldn't, so she flung a copy of *Interview,* an *Interview* T-shirt, and a bottle of Estée Lauder's Beautiful perfume into the grave." The last was a touching choice: When Lauder launched her new product the year before with a promotion lunch for "the one hundred most beautiful men in New York," Andy was thrilled to be on the list, a beauty in someone's eyes at last.

Then everyone went to the $7.95-per-head chicken-and-dumpling lunch arranged by Andy's sister-in-law Margaret Warhola at a nearby restaurant called the Mona Lisa Lounge. And the Factory contingent flew back to New York and got to work on the memorial service, which was set for April 1, April Fool's Day.

The memorial service at Manhattan's St. Patrick's Cathedral was stirring and stately, festive and sad, lovely and grand. A legion of fellow artists came out to pay him homage: Oldenburg, Lichtenstein, Hockney, Serra, Sonnier, Arman, Christo, Marisol, Schnabel, Clemente, Chia, Basquiat, Haring, Scharf, and Jamie Wyeth—though Andy would have noted the absence of the two he would have wanted most, Rauschenberg and Johns. Still, as everyone said, he would have loved it. Don Johnson of "Miami Vice" (and an early *Interview* cover) and Patti D'Arbanville, the mother of his child (and star of *Andy Warhol's Flesh*), received communion. So did Claus von Bülow. Jerry Zipkin and Regine seized front-pew seats. "How could D.D. Ryan wear a *red* coat?" muttered São Schlumberger. "How could Bianca wear a hat so big it blocks everyone's view?" groused D.D. Ryan. Halston and Liza sat in the right nave, Calvin and Kelly Klein sat in the left nave, and Steve Rubell darted from one to the other. Fran Lebowitz complained about the pack of journalists on the cathedral steps asking her for a comment. "I told you what to say," rock writer Lisa Robinson, another Max's Kansas City veteran, told Fran. "I'm too grieved to talk today." From ex-Baby Jane Holzer to ex-Ambassador Fereydoun Hoveyda, they were all there, three generations of Superstars, covergirls, portraits, advertisers, dealers, collaborators, friends.

Brigid, looking like a lady in the pearls she inherited from her mother, who had died three weeks after Andy, read from the Scriptures. John Richardson compared Andy to "that Russian phenomenon, the holy fool: the simpleton whose quasi-divine naiveté protects him from an inimical world." Yoko Ono gave a eulogy—someone had suggested Liza Minnelli but Fred said no. And Nicholas Love, a young friend of Fred's whom Andy hadn't known but would surely have pronounced "a real beauty," read from *THE Philosophy of Andy Warhol*—Pat had wanted to, but Fred said no; Brigid had proposed me, but Fred said no. But none of that mattered at St. Patrick's. We were all there to praise and to pray for Andy, together: "Our Father who art in Heaven . . ."

This rare camaraderie carried on to the lunch that followed in what was once Billy Rose's Diamond Horseshoe nightclub below the Century Plaza Hotel, Steve Rubell and Ian Schrager's newest hotel acquisition. Fred and Gerard Malanga walked arm in arm around the room, which had been painted silver for the occasion. Viva proposed marriage to Paul Morrissey. Sylvia Miles kissed Monique van Vooren. Jed was there with Jay and Susan, and for a moment I remembered how great it felt to be young and carefree and spending the summer in Rome. And Philip Johnson, Andy's long-time champion, in his owl frames, beamed with the word that the Museum of Modern Art was going to give Andy a retrospective, finally.

Andy's estate was first estimated at $15 million, but as the paintings were counted, the real estate tallied, and the shopping bags emptied, it was revised upward toward the $100 million mark. His will named Fred Hughes as sole executor and as president of the Andy Warhol Foundation for the Visual Arts, the beneficiary of practically his entire fortune. There was a $250,000 bequest to Fred. Andy's brothers were to be given an amount no larger than $250,000, at the discretion of the executor. Fred could have given them nothing, but each of them ultimately received about $600,000, including $334,000 each from pension plans said to have been found in Andy's home safe, and they signed waivers agreeing not to contest the will. John Warhola was named vice-president of the foundation and Vincent Fremont was named alternate executor of the estate and director of the foundation. Unlike Fred, Vincent wasn't left any money. Some insiders think that the money Fred was left was repayment for his *Bad* investment. If true, that means that Andy didn't leave anybody anything.

A few weeks after the memorial, Lana Jokel showed her 1972 Warhol documentary for a few of Andy's friends. I arrived shortly after Sylvia Miles, who was wearing layers of shiny black satin and Spandex, and fake ponyskin boots. "Guess who I ran into on 57th Street today. Peter Frampton!" was how she greeted me. "You remember Peter Frampton?" I remembered a very long, very late night in a Studio 54 sideroom with the seventies rock star and eleven of his groupies.

Then came Dr. Denton Cox with Charles Rydell, one of the original *Interview* investors and, along with the late Jerome Hill, host of so many Algonquin dinners and Bridgehampton weekends at Windy Hill. Sylvia immediately pounced on Dr. Cox about Andy's death, saying, "We're all going to grill you separately so you may as well just tell us now what really happened and then you can enjoy the rest of the evening."

Before Dr. Cox could say anything, there were two more arrivals: David Bourdon, the former *Life* magazine art critic, who was writing a book on Andy's art; and Taylor Mead, the former Superstar, who was writing a book titled *Son of Warhol*. They sat down beside me, and there we were, three biographers on a couch, facing poor Dr. Cox, who asked for "a big Scotch." He took a deep breath and said that he had loved Andy, as we all had, and had gone over and over what he could have done to treat Andy better, and that he was resolved in his own mind that he had done everything right. He said Andy had ignored his advice to have his gallbladder out for years and that on the day Andy had finally come to see him, he had examined him thoroughly, including a rectal examination. "Well, I shouldn't say something about the rectal examination that isn't really relevant."

"Yes, you should," Charles commanded forcefully. "Tell them what Andy said, because it proves you did the goddamn rectal examination."

"Well, Andy said when I performed the rectal examination, 'Nobody's been there for a long time.'"

Just then Jed arrived, now one of New York's four or five top decorators. Then came Paul Morrissey.

Dr. Cox continued, saying he had run through every scenario of how it could have been different. "Intensive care," he claimed, "the hospital would never have gone for in Andy's case, even though he was a celebrity. I could have put Andy in a ward, where there's more supervision, but you just don't do that with people who can afford a private room. I even offered to move Andy to a corner room when it opened up, but Andy said no. And the private nurse was Korean, just like all the staff nurses. She had been on staff herself, so they all knew her; she was part of the group."

Cox was careful to note that the hospital recommended the private nurse, not he. He attacked the New York State report slapping the hospital as "slipshod." And he seemed particularly upset that the *New York Times* printed his name when the state report came out, saying it was the only newspaper to do so. "That's why I call it the *Kremlin Times*," said Paul, laughing.

Lana showed her documentary. As Andy demolished Barbara Rose on the VCR, I watched Jed watching Andy. I noticed how much his hands looked like Andy's, and how he was twisting his long fingers as Andy always did when he was nervous. When the film was over, Jed left.

The rest of us stayed for dinner, and eventually Paul and I left together and walked up Madison Avenue, talking about Andy. Or rather, Paul talked and I listened.

"Andy always wanted to do what everybody else wasn't," he said. "That was his basic impulse: 'Movies have plots, so I'll make movies without plots.' He'd get that far. But then he didn't know what to do next. He could make that first leap, but he couldn't take the second step. He had to find someone to do that for him.

"Andy was the strongest-willed person I knew. He willed himself an artist, a famous celebrity, a society figure, a rich man. But Andy wasn't happy with all his money. Fred says he was, but I didn't think Andy looked like he was enjoying life when I saw him.

"You know what Andy really was: a primitive in a sophisticated world. That's why people were attracted to him. John Richardson was onto something about Andy being a Russian village idiot/saint type. Andy was a holy fool."

And a holy terror.

Epilogue:

Andy Is Everywhere

When I began this book three years ago, I saw it as an act of liberation from my former boss. I know now that there is no escaping the holy terror. As Brigid Berlin shouted hysterically in Lana Jokel's 1972 documentary, "Once you're connected to Andy, you're *always* connected to Andy." Even in death, Andy is everywhere—and this book is one more offering to his omnipresence.

My file of Warhol clippings since he died in February 1987 is now over six inches thick. And that's not counting the pile of magazines that have put him on their covers, publications as diverse as *Newsweek* and *Details, Art in America* and *The Advocate.* "Everyone will be famous for fifteen minutes" has become the media motto of our time, as likely to turn up on the sports pages—or on a Don Henley hit single—as in the art sections. *Those* have been packed with ads for Warhol exhibitions. In New York City, in May 1987, for example, there were Warhol shows at the Robert Miller, Larry Gagosian, and Martin Lawrence galleries, a Warhol film retrospective at the Whitney Museum, *and* a Warhol symposium at the Dia Art Foundation. The news has been full of reports of his ever-rising auction prices—in May 1988, an early sixties work, *210 Coca-Cola Bottles,* went for a record $1.43 million. In Pittsburgh, a fan has erected a fourteen-foot by forty-eight-foot billboard plastered with the same photo of Andy repeated four times, and an Andy Warhol Museum will open in 1992. At the Brooklyn Academy of Music, *Songs for Drella,* a memorial concert by Lou Reed and John Cale, sold out a four-night run, and has been recorded for an album. One feature-length Warhol documentary has already aired on American and British TV; another, titled *Superstar*, is on its way. There are Andy Warhol watches, Andy Warhol stamps, and a whole line of Andy Warhol calendars, date-books, and stationery from the same company that marketed the Cabbage Patch Doll. Somewhere in the San Fernando Valley lurks an Andy Warhol robot waiting for producer Lewis Allen to bring it to Broadway in *A No-Man Show.*

Why the relentless fascination? Part of it, I think, has to do with the way Andy died. In a sense, it represented one of everyone's worst night-mares: going into the hospital for a routine operation and never coming out again. And then it was followed by one of everyone's favorite fantasies: selling all your junk for a fortune. In April 1988, it took Sotheby's ten days to auction off ten thousand lots of Andy's hoard—jewelry, watches, Art Deco, fifties furniture, American Indian blankets and baskets, American Empire consoles and settees, primitive portraits, contemporary paintings, even his cookie jar collection, which went for over $250,000. The total sale exceeded $25 million.

The continuing Warholmania also stems from the art world's serious reappraisal of Andy's work and reputation since his death. The extent of this was shown by the February 1989 Warhol retrospective at the Museum of Modern Art, a museum that, to Andy's constant despair, never gave him a show while he was alive. The lines were almost as long as those for the museum's 1980 Picasso blockbuster, and the museum gift shop could barely keep up with the demand for mass-produced Marilyn buttons, Elvis posters, and Cow shopping bags. It also traveled to Chicago, London, Cologne, Venice, and Paris.

The success of both the MoMA retrospective and Sotheby's auction can largely be attributed to the astute management of the Warhol estate by its executor, Fred Hughes. Andy's death, and the enormous responsibility it placed on him, seemed to sober Fred and focus his energies on the important job to be done. But at Sotheby's Fred was sporting an elegant walking stick. At MoMA, he was leaning on it hard to hold himself up. Nine months later, at Diana Vreeland's memorial service, he was in a wheelchair. Fred now thinks that the falls he suffered in the late seventies, which we all attributed to too much champagne, were actually the first symptoms of his multiple sclerosis.

Nonetheless, he continues to head the Andy Warhol Foundation for the Visual Arts, based at the fourth and last Factory on East 33rd Street. In 1989, the foundation issued its first list of stipends to a Warholian range of organizations, from the Museum of the Moving Image to the art department of the Convent of the Sacred Heart School. And Fred also pulled off a financial coup in the summer of 1989, when he sold *Interview*, which was losing money, to its old owners, Peter and Sandy Brant, for $12 million.

Vincent Fremont has abandoned his TV projects to avoid conflict of interest with his duties as executive manager of the estate and co-director of the foundation. The third director, John Warhola, a taciturn retired Sears salesman, makes periodic visits to New York for board meetings, and is active in the Pittsburgh Children's Museum, which now offers silkscreening classes for a generation of future Warholites. Andy's older brother, Paul Warhola, a loquacious retired junk dealer, has announced his debut as an artist with his Heinz Baked Bean canvases.

The estate's suit against New York Hospital drags on, and Ed Hayes has also been kept busy by Bianca Jagger's pending libel suit against *The Andy Warhol Diaries,* edited by Pat Hackett, and published by Warner Books in May 1989. Halston was also thinking of suing, but fell ill with AIDS shortly after they came out, and in late 1989 moved to San Francisco, where he spent the last months of his life with his family. By that time, Steve Rubell, who had told me several times, ''I come across great in the diaries,'' had already died of liver disease.

I deliberately didn't read the 807-page *Diaries* when they were published; I didn't want my reaction to them to influence my writing. Now that I have read them, I tend to agree with the only other person I know who has read them from beginning to end, São Schlumberger, who sees them as a contemporary *Remembrance of Things Past.* They are extremely novelistic, though they also remind me of one of my favorite works of nonfiction, the memoirs of Mrs. Mussolini, for their fishwife tone. But whether or not the snide descriptions and the mean gossip are strictly accurate, the *Diaries* have a larger truth buried inside them—how alienated and desperate Andy really was.

Ultra Violet beat the diaries, and everyone else, with her memoir, *Famous for Fifteen Minutes,* and Viva gave it a killing review in the *New York Times Book Review.* Taylor Mead's *Son of Andy Warhol* has yet to appear, but David Bourdon's hefty art tome, *Andy Warhol,* is now on better coffee tables from Düsseldorf to Tokyo, alongside Rainer Crone's *Andy Warhol: The Early Works 1942–1962,* Jesse Kornbluth's *Pre-Pop Warhol,* Nat Finkelstein's *Andy Warhol: The Factory Years 1964–1967,* and *Warhol by Makos.* And Victor Bockris, a short-time *Interview* contributing editor, has come out with *The Life and Death of Andy Warhol.* Though he bills himself as an insider, and his take on the early years of Andy's life is sensible and thorough, his picture of the seventies Factory is often unrecognizable.

If my book has any value, it is to set the record straight about the time I worked at the Factory. And the story of my working with Andy parallels the story of every close collaborator Andy ever had—and he was never without collaborators. Starting with Nathan Gluck, in the early fifties, the list also includes Gerard Malanga, Henry Geldzahler, Brigid Berlin, Paul Morrissey, Fred Hughes, Jed Johnson, Pat Hackett, Vincent Fremont, Ronnie

Cutrone, Rupert Smith, and Christopher Makos. In almost every case there was the same creative tension and competitiveness that sooner or later turned into love/hate.

And, in the end, what do I feel about Andy Warhol, the artist and the man? I admire the work as much as ever, but more than anything, I feel sorry for him. Not long after he died, Fred gave Thomas Ammann permission to invite a few of Andy's friends, most of whom had never seen his house, to dinner there before Sotheby's carted off its contents. At one point, I went to the bathroom, Andy's bathroom, off his bedroom on the second floor. It obviously had been left untouched since the day he went to the hospital. Two baskets filled with squeaky toys for Archie and Amos were still sitting under the old-fashioned white porcelain sink, along with four pots of potpourri. The shelves above and beside the sink were lined with bottle after bottle and package after package of fragrances and beauty products, mostly opened and partially used, and often four or five of the same brand. I started to make a list:

Halston Cologne for Men, Geoffrey Beene's Grey Flannel, Guerlain's Habit Rouge, St. John's Old Gold, Dans un Jardin Rose Geranium, Shelly Marks Mignonette, Shelly Marks Jasmine, Shelly Marks Damask Rose, Shelly Marks Lemon Verbena, Shelly Marks Amber, Shelly Marks Potpouri, Xerac BP/10 "for treatment of Acne," Exsel Selenium Sulfide Lotion "for scalp," Interface Herbal Rub Scrub, Cetaphil Lotion Lipid-Free Skin Cleanser, Noxema Antiseptic Skin Cleanser Pads, Clinique Dramatically Different Moisturizing Lotion, Roy Collagen Cream by Linda Silver, Glycel GSL Anti-Ageing Cream, Glycel Cellular Cleanser, Glycel Cellular Toner, Glycel GSL Cellular Clay Mask, Pure Bio-Chelated Extract of Barberry, Imu-Stim 1 Whole Fresh Plant (Echinacea Species) by Wildwood Botanics, E-Plus Natural Roll-on Deodorant, Lavoris Mouthwash, Astring-o-sol Breath Sweetener . . .

This was as much as I could write down on the backs of some business cards I'd found in my pocket, and only about a quarter of what was on those shelves. It was just the beginning of what Andy Warhol thought he needed to face the world.

Index